SLAVERY

In The

STATES

Selected Essays

NEGRO UNIVERSITIES PRESS
NEW YORK

Originally published in 1893-1914

Reprinted 1969 by
Negro Universities Press
A DIVISION OF GREENWOOD PUBLISHING CORP.
NEW YORK

Library of Congress Catalogue Card Number 68-55929

SBN 8371-2085-3

PRINTED IN UNITED STATES OF AMERICA

CONTENTS

SLAVERY IN THE STATE OF NORTH CAROLINA

SERIES XVII   NO. 7–8

JOHNS HOPKINS UNIVERSITY STUDIES
IN
HISTORICAL AND POLITICAL SCIENCE
HERBERT B. ADAMS, Editor

History is past Politics and Politics are present History.—*Freeman*

SLAVERY IN THE STATE OF

NORTH CAROLINA

BY

JOHN SPENCER BASSETT, Ph.D. (J. H. U.)
Professor of History and Political Science, Trinity College (North Carolina).

THE JOHNS HOPKINS PRESS, BALTIMORE
PUBLISHED MONTHLY
JULY-AUGUST, 1899

PREFATORY NOTE.

The author desires to express here his sense of obligation to the many friends who have so kindly made suggestions and furnished him with facts bearing on this monograph. Their cheerful compliance with his requests has made the work easier than it might have been. Among those to whom he is especially indebted are, Dr. B. F. Arrington, Dr. Thomas Hill, and Maj. D. W. Hurt, of Goldsboro, N. C.; Dr. K. P. Battle, of the University of North Carolina; Dr. J. D. Huffham, of Henderson, N. C.; Rev. J. B. Richardson, of High Point, N. C., and Col. John D. Whitford, of Newbern, N. C. To each of these gentlemen he returns his sincere thanks.

DURHAM, N. C., July 7, 1899.

CONTENTS.

Slavery in the State of North Carolina.

INTRODUCTION: GENERAL CHARACTERISTICS.

The story of slavery in the State of North Carolina may be considered in two parts, the dividing point of which is the year 1831. Before this year the general conditions of the slave were more humane than after it. Public feeling on the question was then unimpassioned. Some people opposed it; some favored it. It seems to have been discussed in a sane way, as a matter of public policy and without any extraordinary excitement or recrimination. After 1831, or about that year—for no fine and distinct dividing point can properly be made—the conditions of slavery became more severe. One law after another was passed which bore hardly on the slave, until at last he was bound hand, foot, and brain in the power of his master. Moreover, public feeling became inflamed. Slavery could no longer be discussed as a public policy, and there arose with most people in the State a fervent intolerance of all views advanced against the system.

The causes of this remarkable development have often been enumerated. Later on in this work I propose to explain the matter with some degree of fulness in a chapter on the development of the pro-slavery sentiment. Here it cannot be necessary to do more than point out the general facts of the process.

In this sense the chief cause of this change was the invention of the cotton gin and the consequent opening up of the cotton industry, not only in many parts of North Carolina,

7

but in the entire Gulf region. This gave a strong impetus to the settling of large plantations which hitherto had been limited for the most part to the rice producing regions. A wide extension of slavery could never have been made on the basis of the small farm, where there was necessarily much white labor. In North Carolina, and elsewhere, no doubt, it was noticeable that slavery, even in the days of the greatest excitement over the slave question, was of a milder type in the western counties. Here the farms were small. Slave-owners had but few slaves. With these they mingled freely. They worked with them in the fields, ploughing side by side. The slave cabins were in the same yard with the master's humble home. Slave children and, indeed, slave families were directly under the eye of the master, and better still, of the mistress. On such farms from five to twenty slaves was a usual quota, although their number often went to fifty and even higher. Could this type of bondage have predominated in the South, it is likely that slavery would sooner or later have softened itself, as in the disintegrating Roman Empire, into some less austere forms of servile labor, until at last it came by successive stages to the light of freedom. That it did not happen was due to the aristocracy of cotton.

The triumph of the cotton aristocracy did not come in a day. In 1800 North Carolina was, except certain sections in the far East, in the grasp of the small farm system. There were then many people in the State who opposed slavery. Some of them were statesmen who, like Jefferson and Washington, looked to the day of freedom. They were strong enough to offset and keep down a certain thorough-going tendency to deal with slaves in a summary manner, which from the first was not wanting with some legislators. But as the large estate prevailed, the pro-slavery influence became stronger. The arguments on this side were naturally aggressive; and those on the other side were conservative. The former caught the support of the younger men in politics. As time passed the older party was weakened

by the death of its leaders, and the new party gained
strength.	It was in 1831 that the latter was able definitely
to triumph over the former.

There are two well-known facts that secured this decisive
victory; that is to say, the Nat Turner rebellion and the
beginning of the more vigorous anti-slavery agitation in the
North. The former won the victory; the latter undoubtedly made it forever sure.

Looking behind these two facts, however, it is worth
while to ask how much the newer development of slavery,
due to cotton cultivation, had to do with these two occurrences. To attempt to answer this question here would be to
anticipate the task of the historian of slavery in general. I
shall only venture to suggest that it may be probable that
the growing harshness of slavery, either in Virginia or in
the far South, led Nat Turner to make his futile attempt
at freedom. With more confidence I might assert that the
certain extension of slavery in the Gulf States, as well as
in the older slave States, nerved the anti-slavery associates
of Garrison to a fiercer battle. They saw, they must have
seen, that the enemy against whom they contended was
every day growing stronger. This aroused their efforts
in the first instance, and made the fight more bitter throughout its course. This increased strength of slavery was due
to cotton. But for this the famous contest in the Virginia
Legislature of 1831 might have had another end. Mr.
D. R. Goodloe[1] is authority for the view that such a triumph
of anti-slavery in Virginia would have carried North Carolina against slavery. Such a victory in either State, or in
both, would have broken the sectional balance in the United
States Senate and secession would have been blighted ere it
had sprouted.

---

[1] See a manuscript sketch by Mr. Goodloe himself, which is preserved among the papers of the Trinity College Historical Society.

CHAPTER I.

THE LEGAL STATUS OF THE SLAVE.

The spirit of the slavery legislation in the State of North Carolina conforms to the development that has been indicated. Before, and immediately after, 1800 many of the laws passed indicated a milder spirit. After that they became more austere till they finally partook of the spirit of harshness to which allusion has been made. But this development did not come because of deliberate cruelty on the part of the slave-owners. There are throughout the period of greatest restriction enough humane laws and more than enough humane custom to show the contrary. It came as a logical consequence of the conviction that the future development of Southern society as well as the safety of the Southern people demanded that slavery should be perpetuated. Before this iron necessity every impulse to humanity, every suggestion for a better elevated negro race, was made to fall. Now and again some sharp-eyed pro-slavery advocate would discover some way by which it was thought that the slave could lift himself out of slavery, and the way would be as promptly closed up. At one time it was teaching slaves to read, again it was allowing negroes to preach to their race, again it was allowing free negroes to attend muster, and sometimes it was allowing a slave to hire his own time. In every case the Legislature was prompt with its veto. And yet it is certain that the feeling of the community was not so harsh as these laws indicate. Severe laws were often not obeyed. Besides some other provisions of the law, the single case of the State *vs.* Will is sufficient evidence of this humaner feeling. This case is remarkable because it settled, in 1834, just at the time when the

10

pro-slavery sentiment was in the flush of victory over the conservatives, the question that a slave had a right to defend himself against the apparently murderous attack of his master or overseer. Such a decision granted the slave all the rights of a moral conscience and gave the lie direct to the notion that the slave is not a person, the notion which underlay the Dred Scott decision.

These two opposite tendencies of greater austerity and of greater sympathy within the bounds of slavery existed conjointly throughout the period we have under consideration. In considering the legal status of slavery as well as the general social conditions of slaves, the reader will often remark the outcropping of one or both of them.

The Slave in Court.—During the period of statehood the slave law of 1741 continued the basis of the law of slavery, although it was frequently modified. By this law two or more justices of the peace and four freeholders were constituted a court to hold the trial of a slave.[1] But in 1793 (chap. 5) the slave received the additional security of being tried for offenses involving life, limb, or member before a jury of twelve slaveholders in open County Court, but "in a summary way." If, however, the County Court were not to meet in regular order in fifteen days after the arrest of the slave, the sheriff was to call a special court of three justices of the peace and twelve disinterested slaveholding jurymen, as before provided, and these were to have the powers of the County Court for the case at issue. The owner was to have notice and might defend his slave, and if the case went against the slave he paid the costs; but if the master were unknown the slave was allowed counsel. What was meant by the expression "in a summary way" was defined in an explanatory act a year later (Laws of 1794, chap. 11). It was at first intended doubtless that the court should not be bound by the ordinary rules of pleading. Now it was declared with more explicitness that the jury should

[1] See the author's "Slavery and Servitude in the Colony of North Carolina," pp. 28–29.

return a verdict on the evidence submitted by the Court, and
that the Court should give judgment "agreeable to the verdict of the jury and the laws of the country." By this it
seems that the penalties inflicted on white men for the crimes
in question were extended to slaves convicted of the same
crimes.

Further guarantees of security were given in 1816 (chap.
14) when it was provided that slaves charged with capital
offenses should be tried in the Superior Courts; and that
the trial was to be conducted as the trial of a freeman,
unless the charge were conspiracy. It was expressly stated
that there must be a presentment by the grand jury; that the
owner must be notified; that the hearing might be removed to
another county on affidavit of owner; that an offense clergyable for freemen was to be clergyable for slaves; and that
the slave with the advice of his master might challenge the
jury for cause. Otherwise the trial was to follow the law of
1777 (chap. 2) and that of 1779 (chap. 6). If the charge
were conspiracy the trial was to be by special commission of
Oyer and Terminer issued by the Governor to a Superior
Court on the petition of five freeholders in the county in
which the conspiracy was alleged to have occurred. Conspiracy was an exceptional affair in reference to the slave; but
for ordinary cases the status of the slaves improved steadily.
In 1818 a slave on trial for his life was given the full right of
a freeman to challenge jurors.[1] Thus in the matter of his life
the standing of the slave approached nearly to that of the
freeman.

In 1820 a further distinction between the trial of a freeman and a slave was obviated when it was provided that
when a slave was convicted of a capital offense the costs
should be paid by the county.[2]

Minor offenses were tried differently. By the law of 1741
they were tried in the same way as capital offenses. But in
1783 (chap. 14) it was enacted that a justice of the peace

---

[1] Revision of 1821, chap. 972.   [2] *Ibid.*, chap. 1073.

before whom the case of a slave was brought should try the case at once, if it were less than a capital crime and if, in his judgment, the penalty ought not to be heavier than forty lashes. Such trial was to be "in a summary way." Cases between these minor cases and capital cases gradually came to be tried in the County Courts, as capital cases were to be tried in the Superior Court. Here also the trial was to be conducted "under the same rules, regulations and restrictions as the trials of freemen;" and the slave was entitled to a jury of slaveholders.[1]

The law as just stated remained in force till the war, with the difference that the cases hitherto left to the County Courts went now to one or more justices of the peace, if they chose to sit on the case, and the penalty was to be whipping not to exceed thirty-nine lashes on the bare back. Appeal was, by law of 1842 (chap. 3), to be allowed to the County or the Superior Court. Such offenses were what were called "inferior offenses" and crimes which if done by free persons would be cognizable in the County Court. Some of the "inferior offenses" ought to be mentioned. Among them were insolence to a free white person; slandering a free white person, or trespassing on the property of such a person; intermarrying or cohabiting with a free negro; having sexual intercourse or indulging in grossly indecent familiarity with a white female; trying to teach a slave to read or to write—the use of figures excepted; exhorting or preaching or holding any other public religious service where slaves of different families were assembled; playing cards, dice or nine-pins, or gambling for money, liquor or other property; raising cattle, hogs, horses, etc.; producing a forged pass or certificate of freedom, and some other offenses. Felonies and other offenses of slaves not given for trial to a justice of the peace were to be tried before the Superior Court in the manner of the trials of freemen and before juries of slave-owners.[2] Conspiracy to rebel was

---

[1] Revised Statutes, 1837, p. 582.   [2] Revised Code, pp. 510-11.

also construed a felony and punishment was to be death or transportation.

The payment of the owners for slaves executed by law was a hard matter to settle. At the beginning of statehood the State paid the owner for the slave, and in 1779[1] the Assembly fixed the maximum value of such a slave at £700, continental money, then much depreciated. In 1786 (chap. 17) the Assembly repealed all acts allowing payment for executed slaves, since, as it declared, "many persons by cruel treatment of their slaves cause them to commit crimes for which many of the said slaves are executed." Masters now for financial reasons protected their slaves from prosecution, and there was a demand for a return to the old system. Formerly the burden had been borne by the whole State, and this was considered unfair to the counties which had few slaves. The final solution lay in local action. In 1796 (chap. 27) seven eastern counties were authorized to lay a tax to pay for slaves executed within their respective borders, the owner to receive two-thirds of the value of the slave, as estimated by the jury that pronounced him guilty. This amount, however, was not to be paid unless the jury was convinced that the owner had properly fed and clothed the delinquent slave. A tax for such a purpose was to be levied on the black polls of the county. This law seems to have worked well for within a few years several other counties had been granted the same privileges.

Runaways.—In the above section the development was in favor of a more humane treatment of a slave. There had been an honest desire to secure justice to the slave, and the graver offenses were put on the same basis as in the graver cases of freemen. It could be done because in no way was the perpetuity of slavery concerned. This was not true in regard to runaways. Such slaves threatened the very life of slavery. The law of colonial days on this subject had been stringent; and that was slightly modified after the

---

[1] Laws of 1779, 3d session, chap. 12.

Revolution. Such enactments as were made had to do chiefly with persons who aided runaways. Thus in 1779 (1st session, chap. 11) it was made a capital felony to steal or seduce away a slave and this law remained in force till the war.[1] This probably referred to persons who stole slaves as property; but in the same act it was further provided that whoever aided a runaway to escape should on conviction pay £100 to the owner of the fugitive and, in addition, whatever damages might be incurred. In 1793 (chap. 5) it was made a capital felony for a ship captain to take, or knowingly allow others to take, a slave out of the State without the written consent of the slave's master.

In the days of exasperation against the anti-slavery party in the North more stringent rules were made. From 1825 till 1833 there were three laws passed, the substance of which was to make the stealing of a slave with the purpose of sending him out of the State, or the aiding of one to escape out of the State, a felony punishable by death.[2] This law remained in effect till 1860.[3] This was no doubt aimed at Northern men bent on working the Underground Railway. For ordinary cases of persuading slaves to run away or for harboring runaways one should on conviction pay the owner of the slave a fine of $100 and damages and be liable to fine of $100 more, and might furthermore be indicted and fined another $100 and imprisoned not more than six months.[4] The latter amendments were passed in 1821 and 1830.

The Slave's Right to Hunt.—Here, too, the question of the perpetuity of slavery was involved. For slaves to hunt with a gun jeopardized the masters' lives. Throughout the period of statehood there was no disposition to relax the strict prohibition of this practice. Anyone who found a slave so hunting might take the gun for his own use and carry the

---

[1] Revised Statutes, chap. 34, sec. 10, and Revised Code, chap. 34, sec. 10.   [2] Revised Statutes, chap. 34, sec. 11.

[3] Revised Code, chap. 34, sec. 11.

[4] Revised Statutes, chap. 34, sec. 73, and Revised Code, chap. 34, sec. 81.

slave to the nearest constable who should at once give the slave twenty lashes on his bare back and the owner should pay the same reward as was paid for taking up a runaway.[1]

The Slave's Right to Travel and Trade.—The patrol, which had been established in 1753,[2] became steadily a more permanent institution as the people became more convinced of the necessity of keeping slavery unassailed. In 1779 (3d session, chap. 8) it was required to make a general search once a month and to report to the County Court. Slaves off their masters' plantations on Sunday were to be arrested, unless they had passes or were in the company of a white man. In 1794 (chap. 4) it was provided that the patrol should be appointed by the County Court whenever it should think necessary. No more than six men should be appointed to the district of each militia captain. The patrol was to be in office one year, was to have stipulated fees and one-half of the money from fines under this act of 1794, and was to be exempt from road and jury duty. Two patrolmen going together were to cover a district at least once a fortnight. They might whip—not to exceed fifteen lashes— slaves found off their master's land without permission.

In 1802 there was an alarm over a reported slave insurrection in Bertie and adjoining counties. This induced the Assembly to provide a still more efficient patrol.[3] The County Court was now authorized to appoint patrolers in such numbers and under such rules as it might think necessary, the patrolers retaining the powers and privileges conferred by the act of 1794. To support the patrol the County Court was given the authority to levy a special tax of one shilling on each black poll. In the same year (1802, chap. 68) the militia of Gates, Pasquotank, and Camden Counties were constituted a patrol. The captains were directed to divide their companies into squads of four or five men who

---

[1] Revised Statutes, chap. 111, sec. 23, and Revised Code, chap. 107, sec. 26.

[2] See author's "Slavery and Servitude," p. 38.

[3] Laws of 1802, chap. 15.

were to search their respective neighborhoods once in three weeks and to whip slaves found at large.

No further change was made in the patrol till 1830 (chap. 16, secs. 1 and 14) when the County Court was given authority to appoint, if it saw fit, a Patrol Committee of three persons in each captain's district who might appoint as many patrolers as they thought necessary, provided that this should not prevent the County Court from appointing patrols as they saw fit. The patrol was now given large powers of arrest. The patrolers were enjoined to visit suspected places, to disperse assemblages of slaves, to be diligent in arresting runaways, to detect thefts, and to report persons who traded with slaves. The patrol, or any two of them, should "have such powers as may be necessary to a proper discharge of the duties herein enjoined," ran the law. If a negro who was being whipped was insolent to them he might be further punished not to exceed thirty-nine lashes in all. The Patrol Committee was given power to discharge patrolers and to appoint others in the vacancies. To refuse to serve on the patrol was punished by a fine of $20, to go to the support of the patrol, and in 1835 (chap. 22) it was enacted that persons who refused or neglected to perform the duties of this office should be fined $25.[1]

There was more than one reason why masters did not want their slaves to meet at slave-meetings about the neighborhood. It afforded opportunity for concocting mischief; and it demoralized the slaves by bringing them into contact with the worst negroes of the community, by keeping them up till late at night, and by giving them a desire for idleness. Accordingly the laws were always against such slave-meetings. In 1779 (2d session, chap. 10) it was enacted that an ordinary keeper who entertained slaves against their master's will should forfeit his license. In 1794 (chap. 4) it was declared that no person should permit any negroes, bond

---

[1] See Revised Statutes, chap. 86; also Tate *vs.* Neale, 1 Hawks, 418, and Revised Code, chap. 83.

or free, to meet on his property for drinking or dancing on penalty of fine of £ 10.

The commonest crime of slaves in all ages is no doubt theft. The negro has been called thievish by nature. Certainly in American slavery he showed a decided tendency to petty thievishness, so that it was necessary to throw a great deal of legal restraint around his petty business relations with others. Various laws were passed on this subject. A slave must not trade with any other person without the written consent of his master, the article for which permission to trade was given being expressly specified.[1] Between 1826 and 1833 a series of laws enumerated the articles which slaves might not sell without the consent of their masters. These were articles raised on the farm, tools, food supplies, and articles prepared for sale, as staves, cloth, and gold and silver bullion. Other persons were forbidden to sell anything at all to slaves; provided, however, that this should not hold when slaves traded with the written permission of their masters between sunrise and sunset, Sunday excepted; but this proviso was not to apply to the sale of spirituous liquors, arms, and ammunition, unless they were for the master's own use.[2] How rigidly this law was enforced may be seen from the fact that in 1846 (chap. 42) it was enacted that this section should not be construed to mean that the master of a slave was not to give him these prohibited articles to carry from one place to another.[3] Further indication of the rigidness of the law is seen in the statement of what should be considered presumptive evidence in such a case. It was enacted in 1826 (chap. 13, sec. 6) that if a slave should be found in a place used for trade between nine o'clock and daybreak, or at any time unless his master sent him; or, if a slave should stay in such a place, unless sent thither by his master, for fifteen minutes with the door shut; or if he should come out of such a place with articles which

---

[1] Laws of 1779, 1st session, chap. 11, and 1788, chap. 6.
[2] Revised Statutes, chap. 34, secs. 75–78.
[3] Revised Code, chap. 34, secs. 83–92.

might have been purchased therein; it should be presumptive evidence against him.[1] Shipmasters, many of whom were from the North, were forbidden to entertain negroes or mulattoes, slaves or freemen, on their ships between sunset and sunrise or on Sunday, unless the said negroes had permission from their masters or from a justice of the peace, or unless they were employed on board.[2] Negroes who violated this law were presumed to be disposing of stolen goods.

Of a somewhat similar nature was the custom of allowing a slave to hire his own time. This was a practice by which a slave paid his owner a certain sum of money for his own time and then followed some line of work in which he was proficient. The more industrious negroes who had trades, as blacksmiths, carpenters and bricklayers, often did this. From one hundred to one hundred and fifty dollars a year was the amount usually paid by a slave for his own time. Most slaves who hired their time did it with the intention of buying their freedom, and many of them accomplished their purpose. The practice gave the slave more liberty of action and it was considered undesirable both because it increased the number of free negroes and because it removed the slave so hiring from the strict control of the whites. Accordingly it was enacted as early as 1794 (chap. 4) that no slave should hire his time on penalty of being hired out for a year by the sheriff at the direction of the County Court, the proceeds to go to the poor. There is good reason to believe that this law was not generally executed, but it remained on the statute book throughout the period of slavery.[3] Neither should a slave be allowed to go about as a freeman, using his own discretion as to his employ-

---

[1] Revised Statutes, chap. 34, sec. 78, and Revised Code, chap. 34, sec. 88.

[2] Revised Statutes, chap. 34, sec. 76, and Revised Code, chap. 34, sec. 93.

[3] Revised Statutes, chap. 111, sec. 31, and Revised Code, chap. 107, sec. 28.

ment or living in a house to himself and remote from other slaves, as a freeman, even though his master should consent.[1]

The Slave's Right to Life.—In 1774 it was enacted that a person who willfully killed a slave should be imprisoned a year for the first offense and suffer death for the second.[2] In 1791 it was further enacted that if a person should be convicted of maliciously killing a slave he should on the first conviction be held guilty of murder and should "suffer the same punishment as if he had killed a freeman." But in 1801, in the case of the State *vs.* Boon, this law was declared inoperative on the ground that the clause which fixed the penalty was ambiguous. There were, it was said, various ways of punishing freemen for murder. Since the law left a shade of uncertainty in the penalty the prisoner was entitled to the doubt and in this case was released.[3] Two of the five judges of the court gave it as their opinion that the malicious killing of a slave was murder at common law, and the three others did not contradict the opinion. It is possible that it was under this influence that such a principle began to be held by the courts, since Chief Justice Taylor declared in 1820 that if a white person killed a slave under such circumstances as constituted murder he might have been punished for that offense.[4] A difficulty arose, however, if the case could be extenuated to manslaughter. No punishment was provided for that offense, and the prisoner was uniformly discharged. The Assembly, accordingly, in 1817 enacted that "the killing of a slave shall partake of the same degree of guilt, when accompanied with like circumstances, that homicide now does." This, the Court held in 1820,[5] was designed "to make the homicide of a slave, extenuated by a legal provocation, man-

---

[1] Revised Statutes, chap. 111, sec. 32, and Revised Code, chap. 107, sec. 29.

[2] See the author's " Slavery and Servitude," p. 43.

[3] North Carolina Reports, vol. 1, p. 103 (edition of 1896).

[4] Hawks's Law, p. 217.   [5] *Ibid.*, p. 210, State *vs.* Tackett.

slaughter." After stating the common law in regard to
manslaughter the Court added that in the very nature of
slavery "many acts will extenuate the homicide of a slave,
which would not constitute a legal provocation if done by a
white person." The defining of these acts was not
attempted, but it was presumed that the Court and jury
would estimate them seriously in individual cases, with due
regard to the rights of slaves and white men—"to the just
claims of humanity, and to the supreme law, the safety of
the citizens."

In 1823 the Supreme Court in the case of the State *vs.*
Reed, declared directly that the killing of a slave might be
tried as murder at common law, Chief Justice Taylor and
Justice Henderson acquiescing and Justice Hall dissenting.
The grounds of the decision were the law of Nature and
Christianity. Justice Henderson made the very substantial
statement that the law of slavery gave the master the control of the services of the slave and that it would be not
too scrupulous in adjusting the means of enforcing these
services. "But the life of a slave being in no ways necessary
to be placed in the powers of the owner for the full enjoyment of his services the law takes care of that; and with me
it has no weight to show that, by the laws of ancient Rome
or modern Turkey, an absolute power is given to the master over the life of his slave. I answer, these are not the
laws of our country, nor the mode from which they were
taken. It is abhorrent to the hearts of all those who have
felt the influence of the mild precepts of Christianity." The
argument of Justice Hall was on the basis that the slave
is a chattel. Now if a slave be killed the law provides that
the owner has an action for trespass against the slayer. But
if killing a slave be murder at common law the offender
would be answerable both *civiliter* and *criminaliter*. The
Legislature could not have intended to create such a condition. Besides, the Legislature in 1774 (chap. 31) passed a
law to punish the killing of a slave. If such an offense had

been cognizable at common law the Legislature need not have made a statute on the subject.[1]

The effect of this decision was modified shortly afterwards in the case of the State *vs.* Hoover, where it was held that if a slave died from moderate chastisement of his master every circumstance which in the general course of slavery might have hurried the master to excess would be tenderly regarded by the law. But where the punishment was barbarously immoderate and accompanied by painful privation of food, clothing, and rest, it is not correction *in foro domestico*, indicates deliberate killing, and is therefore murder.[2]

The next question to be taken up in this connection was that of the culpability of a white man who cruelly beat a slave. In 1823, in the case of the State *vs.* Hale,[3] it was held that a battery committed on a slave, no justifying circumstances being shown, was an indictable offense. But it was explicitly stated that circumstances which would not justify a battery on a free person might in the nature of slavery justify an assault on a slave. "The offenses," said the Chief Justice in a sentence which casts a clear light on one phase of slavery in the South, "are usually committed by men of dissolute habits, hanging loose upon society, who, being repelled from association with well-disposed citizens, take refuge in the company of colored persons and slaves whom they deprave by their example, embolden by their familiarity, and then beat, under the expectation that a slave dare not resent a blow from a white man." This principle did not apply, however, to the assault of a master on his slave. This latter case was taken up in 1829 in the case of the State *vs.* Mann,[4] when it was decided that a master was not to be indicted for battery on his slave, that he who has

---

[1] North Carolina Reports (new edition), vol. 9, p. 454.
[2] See 4 Devereaux and Battle, p. 365.
[3] *Ibid.*, p. 582. Here the defendant is called Hale. Later cases cite this case as State *vs.* Hall.
[4] North Carolina Reports (new edition), 13, p. 263.

a right to the services of a slave has a right to all the means of controlling his conduct that belong to the owner, and that this rule would apply to the hirer of a slave. The decision was given by Justice Ruffin. Although, as he affirmed, there was no question about a master's right to inflict any kind of corporal punishment short of death on his slave, he still stated the general grounds for such a principle. There had been no prosecutions of masters for such an offense. Against this general opinion of the community the Court ought not to hold. It was erroneously said that the relation of master and slave was like that of parent and child, and it was held that a parent could not commit a cruel battery on his own son. The object of the training of a son was the life of a freeman, and the means to be used was moral and intellectual instruction. With slavery it was otherwise. "The end," ran the decision, "is the profit of the master, his security and the public safety; the subject, one doomed in his own person and his posterity, to live without knowledge and without the capacity to make anything his own, and to toil that another may reap the fruits. What moral considerations shall be addressed to such a being to convince him what it is impossible but that the most stupid must feel and know can never be true— that he is thus to labor upon a principle of natural duty, or for the sake of his own personal happiness. Such services can only be expected from one who has no will of his own, who surrenders his will in implicit obedience to that of another. Such obedience is the consequence only of uncontrolled authority over the body. There is nothing else which can operate to produce the effect. The power of the master must be absolute to render the submission of the slave perfect. I most freely confess my sense of the harshness of this proposition. I feel it as deeply as any man can; and as a principle of moral right every person in his retirement must repudiate it. But in the actual conditions of things it must be so. There is no remedy. This discipline belongs to the state of slavery. They [the discipline and slavery] cannot be disunited without abrogating at once the rights of the master and absolving the slave from his subjection. It constitutes the curse of slavery to both the bond and free portion of our population. * * * The slave, to remain a slave, must be made sensible that there is no appeal from his master; that his power is in no instance usurped; but is conferred by the laws of man at least, if not by the laws of God." The Courts could not fix the punishment due to the violations of duty by the slave. "No man can anticipate the many and aggravated provocations of the master to which the slave would be constantly stimulated by his own passions or the instigations of others to give, or the consequent wrath of the master prompting him to bloody vengeance upon the turbulent traitor—a vengeance generally practiced with impunity because of its privacy." I do not think that one can find anywhere in the annals of modern justice a decision more brutally logical, and more void of that genial spirit of progressive amelioration which should run through a legal development. Justice Ruffin announced his own horror of the decision he was giving and consoled himself with the thought that the softening feeling of the masters in general for the slaves was increasing and with the decreasing numbers of the slaves, would eventually enable the relations of slavery to be more humane—a result more likely to come in this way "than from any rash expositions of abstract truths by a judiciary tainted with a false and fanatical philanthropy." Was it not the duty of the Court to give such a decision that would help on the humanizing process by giving the Courts the right to restrain excessive cruelty of masters towards slaves rather than by crystallizing into a judicial opinion the brutal theory of the harshest days of slavery to scotch the wheels of the progress that it was desired to see abroad?

It was fortunate for the slave, it was fortunate for the State, that this spirit was not permanent in the Supreme

Court decisions. In 1834 the case of the State *vs.* Will,[1] established the distinctly milder principle that a slave who was barbarously attacked by his master might defend himself with physical force. The facts of the case were these: Will was a slave who became angry because another slave was allowed to use a hoe which Will used and had helved in his own time. In his rage he broke the helve and went to his work. When the overseer knew of it he took his gun and rode to the place at which Will was at work. He called the slave to him, who approached humbly with his hat off. Some words were exchanged when Will began to run. Then the overseer fired, making a wound in the back of the fugitive which might have proved fatal. The terrified slave was pursued and caught by the overseer and two slaves, but in the struggle of arrest he cut the overseer with a pocket knife so that the overseer bled to death. All the circumstances showed that Will had acted in supposed self-defense. His plea was manslaughter—one of his counsel was B. F. Moore,[2] then young and unknown, but afterwards one of the leading lawyers of the State. At the outset Mr. Moore was confronted by Judge Ruffin's opinion in the case of the State *vs.* Mann. These sentiments he distinctly challenged. "It is humbly submitted," said he, "that they are not only abhorrent and startling to humanity, but at variance with statute and decided cases." Judge Henderson's opinion in the State *vs.* Reed was quoted to show that the master's power extends only to the services of his slave. Point by point Judge Ruffin's opinion so far as it related to the general relation of master and slave was combated. One eloquent passage will indicate the nature of the attack. Judge Ruffin had said that the slave must be made to realize that in no one instance was the master's power usurped. This, exclaimed Mr. Moore, repressed thought

---

[1] See "The Trinity College Historical Society Papers," series II, p. 12; also 1 Devereaux and Battle, p. 121.

[2] Mr. G. W. Mordecai was also associated with the defense, but Mr. Moore's argument won the case.

and "reduced into perfect tameness the instinct of self-preservation," a result difficult to accomplish and lamentable if accomplished. But if the relation of slavery required "that the slave shall be disrobed of the essential features that distinguish him from the brute, the relation must adapt itself to the consequences and leave its subjects the instinctive privileges of a brute. I am arguing no question of abstract right, but am endeavoring to prove that the natural incidents of slavery must be borne with because they are inherent to the condition itself; and that any attempt to punish the slave for the exercise of a right which even absolute power cannot destroy is inhuman and without the slightest benefit to the security of the master or to that of society at large. The doctrine may be advanced from the bench, enacted by the Legislature, and enforced with all the varied agony of torture and still the slave cannot believe and will not believe that there is no instance in which the master's power is usurped. Nature, stronger than all, will discover many instances and vindicate her rights at any and at every price. When such a stimulant as this urges the forbidden deed punishment will be powerless to proclaim or to warn by example. It can serve no purpose but to gratify the revengeful feelings of one class of people and to influence the hidden animosities of the other."

The opinion was written by Justice Gaston, who two years earlier had said in a public address: "Disguise the truth as we may, and throw the blame where we will, it is slavery which, more than any other cause, keeps us back in the career of improvement."[1] Now he showed himself a humane judge: He said: "Unconditional submission is, in general, the duty of the slave; unquestioned legal power is, in general, the right of the master. Unquestionably there are exceptions to this rule. It is certain that the master has not the right to slay his slave, and I hold it to be equally certain that the slave has the right to defend himself against the unlawful attempt of his master to deprive

---

[1] Address at Chapel Hill, June 20, 1832, p. 24.

him of life. There may be other exceptions, but in a matter so full of difficulties, where reason and humanity plead with almost irresistible force on one side, and a necessary policy, rigorous indeed, but inseparable from slavery, urges on the other, I fear to err should I undertake to define them." Neither would he define legal provocation, but he did say that a slave's unlawful violence excited by his master's inhumanity ought not to be construed as malice. "The prisoner," said the Court, "is a human being, degraded by slavery, but yet having organs, senses, dimensions, passions like our own." No malice was shown in the evidence and the killing was pronounced manslaughter. It was a notable case and it fixed a humaner spirit in the law of slavery in North Carolina until the end of that institution.

But one more case before the Supreme Court will be mentioned, that of the State *vs.* Jarrot,[1] in 1840. It was declared, that the difference between homicide through malice and homicide through passion was to hold as much in the trial of a slave as in that of a white man; but the same matters which would be sufficient provocation for a freeman would not be sufficient when a slave had killed a white man. Some words of a slave might be so aggravating as to arouse the temporary fury which negatives the charge of malice, "and this rule holds without regard to personal merit or demerit of the white man." The insolence of a slave would justify a white man in giving him moderate chastisement at the moment, but would not authorize an excessive battery, or moderate correction after the insolence was past. The rule that where two parties become angry and fight on equal terms till one kills the other the crime is manslaughter is not to apply to slaves, but to equals only, it being the slave's business to avoid such a contest. But if the battery endangers the slave's life it will reduce homicide by him to manslaughter.[2]

---

[1] North Carolina Reports, 23, p. 75.
[2] This decision also was written by Judge Gaston.

In regard to the slave's legal status a curious case has
come under my notice. The late Dr. John Manning, widely
known as Professor of Law at the State University, told
me that Judge Ruffin, the senior, told him that a case was
once decided in the North Carolina Supreme Court in which
it was held that a white man could not be convicted of fornication and adultery with a slave woman, because such a
woman had no standing in the courts. The case, said Judge
Ruffin, was decided early in this century, but it was agreed
that in the interest of public morality it should not be published.[1]

---

[1] Inquiry of the Clerk of the Supreme Court fails to discover the
papers in reference to the case ; but since there is no other index to
the Supreme Court cases than the printed reports it is quite possible
that the papers are preserved, but so lost among a vast number of
documents that only a long and careful search would bring them to light.

CHAPTER II.

FREE NEGROES AND EMANCIPATION.

Emancipation.—During the colonial period emancipation was forbidden except for meritorious conduct to be adjudged by the County Court,[1] and this law was confirmed by the Assembly in 1777 (chap. 6) and further explained in 1796 (chap. 5).[2] At the beginning of the Revolution "some evil-minded persons intending to disturb the public peace" liberated their slaves and left them at large in the community. The authorities in Perquimons and Pasquotank counties took up the negroes and resold them into slavery. The Legislature confirmed these sales and provided that other such slaves at large might be sold in the same way; provided, however, that this law did not extend to such of these negroes as had enlisted in the patriot army.[3]

These slaves had been freed by the Quakers, who were at that time very active in favor of emancipation. Their liberated slaves were going about, said the Assembly, "to the terror of the people of the State." The law which forbade their liberation was a failure, because it left the duty of informing of its violation to freeholders only and made their action optional. To remedy this condition the Assembly in 1788 (chap. 20) gave the duty of informing on such liberated slaves to any freeman, and thus secured the co-operation of the landless whites who were usually strangely willing to have a fling at the slaves and who, no

---

[1] See the author's "Slavery and Servitude," pp. 64–66.

[2] When the Superior Courts were created the judging of meritorious conduct was left to them. Revisal of 1821, chap. 971.

[3] Laws of 1779, 2d session, chap. 12.

29

doubt, were anxious to get the reward offered for such information.

After the San Domingo revolt in 1791 much concern was felt in the Southern States lest the success of the slaves there should inspire attempts at insurrection in the United States. Several new features of the slave law were added, one of which provided that no slave should be liberated unless he could give bond in the sum of £200 that he would remain quiet and orderly.[1]

In 1830 (chap. 9) it was made more difficult to emancipate. Now, the petitioner must notify his intention at the court house and in the *State Gazette* six weeks before the hearing of the petition; he must give bond with two sureties for $1000 that the said slave should conduct himself well as long as he or she remained in the State, that the slave would leave the State within ninety days after liberation, and the said liberation should invalidate the rights of no creditor. Executors of wills by which slaves were directed to be liberated must secure consent of the courts and take steps to send the negroes out of the State and guard against the loss of creditors. A slave more than fifty years old might be liberated for meritorious conduct to be approved by the Court without subsequently leaving the State, provided that the master swore that the emancipation was not for money and that he gave bond that the negro would conduct himself well and not become a charge on the county. No slave was to be liberated except by this law.[2] This law remained in force till the war.[3] Within the strict conditions herein embraced, ruled the Supreme Court in 1841, it was the policy to facilitate emancipation.[4] Besides this method, slaves were occasionally freed by special Act of the Assembly.

[1] Laws of 1795, chap. 16.
[2] Revised Statutes, chap. 111, secs. 57–64.
[3] Revised Code, chap. 107, secs. 45–53.
[4] Cameron *vs.* Commissioners of Raleigh (the Rex Will Case), 1 Iredell's Eq., p. 436.

Among the various cases reported from the Supreme
Court in regard to emancipation there are several from
which the point is obtained that the freedom of slaves could
be acquired through prescription. For instance, it was held
that when a woman who had once been a slave, but who for
thirty years or more, had been treated as a free person, and
her daughter with her, then a granddaughter must be free;
for it would be proper to infer that so long an enjoyment
of freedom must have followed legal emancipation. It was
not attempted to fix the time necessary to constitute such
liberation by prescription; but in the cases cited thirty and
forty years are the periods mentioned.[1]

In Sampson *vs.* Burgwin[2] a decided tenderness for the
slave is observed in the Court. Here suit was brought to
invalidate the emancipation of a slave, because, being but two
years old when liberated and being freed along with her
mother, she could not have performed meritorious services. The Court held that the act of liberation was that
of "a court of conclusive jurisdiction, and could not be
impeached by evidence that she had not and could not perform such services." It also decided that a petition of an
owner to free slaves need not be in writing, and that "in
an action by a negro to try his right to freedom if evidence
of his being reputed to be a freeman is offered it is admissible to show in reply acts of ownership inconsistent with
reputation." The opinion was by Ruffin, Chief Justice.

Granting permission to liberate was not liberation, as was
held in the case of Bryan *vs.* Wadsworth.[3] Here Elizabeth
Bryan, of Craven County, had in 1808 received permission from the County Court to liberate her slave Abram
for meritorious services and gave the bond required for
the same; but further she did not go. She kept Abram
as a slave till 1820, when she sold him. He then sued for

---

[1] Brookfield *vs.* Stuart, 6 Jones, p. 156; Cully *vs.* Jones, 9 Iredell,
p. 168; Strange *vs.* Burnham, 12 Iredell, p. 41.

[2] 3 Devereaux and Battle's Law, p. 28.

[3] 1 Devereaux and Battle's Law, p. 384.

his freedom. He lost the case. It was held that only the master could emancipate and that the Court only gave permission to emancipate.

The harshness of the law led to various subterfuges in regard to emancipation. It was attempted to hold slaves in nominal servitude, but in real freedom. This was opposed for the general reason that it increased the free negro class and whenever a case involving such a trick came before the Supreme Court it was severely handled. A case in point was that of the Quakers, which arose as follows: In 1817 William Dickinson conveyed a slave to the trustees of the Quaker society of Contentnea, to be held in a kind of guardianship, to be kept at work but to receive the profits of his labor, and ultimately to be free when his freedom could be effected by the laws of the State. In 1827 the matter was before the Supreme Court. It was in evidence that nothing was said about sending the slave out of the State when he should be freed. On the contrary it seemed to be the purpose of the parties to keep him in the State till free, and then to let him go where he would. The opinion was by Taylor, Chief Justice. He declared that the practice of the Quakers was emancipation in everything but name. By statute a religious society could hold property for its use only, and in a conveyance to it for a purpose forbidden by the policy of the laws nothing was passed. That the Quakers did not hold this slave, or other slaves, for their own use was shown by the fact that slaveholding was against their well-known principles. Justice Hall dissented. He thought a religious society might hold personal property unlimitedly and seems not to have approved of the law which fixed such stringent measures against emancipation.[1] Regardless of this decision, as will be seen later on, the Quakers, as a society, continued to hold slaves for purposes of emancipation.

A case not unlike this occurred in 1822, when Collier Hill left slaves to four trustees, one of whom was "Richard

---

[1] Contentnea Society *vs.* Dickinson, 1 Devereaux, p. 189.

Graves, of the Methodist Church," with the injunction to
keep the said slaves for such purposes as "they [the trus-
tees] shall judge most for the glory of God and the good of
the said slaves." The case came before the Supreme Court,
and the opinion declared that such a bequest, "when it could
be fairly collected from other parts of the will that the testator did not mean by the bequest any personal benefit to
the legatees, was held to constitute them trustees for the
purpose of emancipation," and as such purpose was illegal
it was held that the trustees take the property in trust for
the legal heirs.[1]

In all these cases the cast-iron necessity of keeping
slavery unbendingly confined to its present condition, cutting off the least tendency to amelioration, is clearly seen.
Slavery absolute—nothing short of it—and as few free
negroes as possible; that was the idea.

As time passed this feature of the law became harder.
Most severe was a case before the Court in 1849. The facts
were these. William Quarry, of Mecklenberg, conveyed by
deed absolute to Peoples and others a slave woman Linney,
who was married to a freeman. Desiring that she might continue to live with her husband he conveyed to the same
parties twelve acres of land with a house on it, presumably
for her use. No consideration was paid, although it
was duly acknowledged. The defendants claimed that they
were absolute owners, that the donor conveyed the woman
and her family to provide for her comfort and to prevent
the division of the family. They allowed the husband to
occupy the house with his wife for a certain rent. They
took her and her children under their personal care and
agreed to control their conduct. Yet the arrangement
would not do at all. It was, said the Court, qualified
slavery, and the conveyance was void. Linney and her
children were given to the heirs of the donor, and, moreover,

[1] Huckaby *vs.* Jones, 2 Hawks, p. 720. See also Stephens *vs.* Ely,
1 Devereaux's Equity, p. 497.

the donees were held liable, "with just deductions," for the profits due from her services while in their hands, and because the defendants had attempted to defraud the law they were to pay the costs.[1]

Severe as these cases seem the Court showed that within the range of the fact that the free negro class must not be extended they were disposed to be as humane as possible. In the case of Redding *vs.* Long,[2] a grantor had given slaves in trust during his lifetime and directed the trustee to send them to Liberia after the grantor's death, if they wanted to go. The Court declared that this will was not against the spirit of the laws. "Though slaves have no capacity to make contracts," said the Court, "yet they have both mental and moral capacity to make election between remaining here and being slaves, and leaving the State and being free."

Free Negroes.—Slaveholders disliked and feared free negroes because they demoralized the quiet conduct of the slaves. These negroes were under no direct control of the white man. They might aid the slaves in planning a revolt, in disposing of stolen property, in running away, and in any other act of defiance. Privilege after privilege was withdrawn from them. At first they had most of the rights and duties of the poor white man; they fought in the Revolutionary armies, mustered in the militia, voted in the elections, and had the liberty to go where they chose. At length they lost their right to vote; their service in the militia was restricted to that of musicians; and the patrol came more and more to limit their freedom of travel. Taxes and road duty alone of all their functions of citizenship were at last preserved. The story of the appearance of these progressive limitations is not a pleasant one.

It was in 1787 (chap. 6) that the Assembly enacted that no free negro should entertain a slave at his house at night or on Sunday, on penalty of fine. If the fine was not paid the culprit was to be hired out long enough to pay it. The

[1] Lemmond *vs.* Peoples, 6 Iredell's Equity, p. 137.
[2] 4 Jones' Equity, p. 216.

same law forbade a free negro to marry or to cohabit with
a slave without the written consent of the master, and in
1830 (chap. 4, sec. 3) such relations were forbidden even
though the master gave his written consent, and the penalty
for violation was thirty-nine lashes.[1] In 1795 (chap. 16)
free negroes who settled in the State were required to give
bond of £200 for their good behavior, in default of which
they were sold by the sheriff for the benefit of the public.
In 1826 (chap. 13) a free negro was forbidden to be on a
ship at night, or on Sunday, without a pass from a justice
of the peace, unless, indeed, he were employed there; but
the punishment for a violation of this law fell on the captain
of the ship. Neither must a free negro trade with a slave,
and a free negro must have a license from the County Court
to hawk or peddle.[2]

The collection of fines from free negroes was often difficult, and in 1831 (chap. 13) the Legislature enacted that
when the Court had reason to believe that a free negro
could not pay the fine imposed upon him it might direct that
he be hired out to the highest bidder for a time long enough
to pay the fine. The bidder who bid the shortest time took
the negro. The relation between hirer and hired was to be
the same as that between master and apprentice. A free
negro was not to be hired out in this way for a longer term
than five years. If a longer term was the lowest bid the fine
was to be reduced to an amount which five years' service
would satisfy.[3] Later it was thought necessary to provide
that such a free negro should be well supplied with food,
clothing, medicine and lodging; that he should be kept
employed in some useful and industrious occupation, that
he should not be taken from the county during service, and

---

[1] State *vs.* Fore, 1 Iredell, p. 378.

[2] Laws of 1830, chap. 7, and 1831, chap. 28.

[3] The constitutionality of this law was questioned but it was upheld
by the Supreme Court. See State *vs.* Oxendine, 1 Devereaux and
Battle, p. 435, and State *vs.* Manuel, 4 Devereaux and Battle,
p. 20.

that he should be produced in Court at the end of his service or oftener, if so ordered by the Court.[1]

In 1826 (chap. 21) the relation of the free negro to the State was pretty thoroughly restated by law. With free negroes were now to be included all persons of negro blood to the fourth generation inclusive, though one ancestor in each generation may have been white.[2] It was declared that no free negro should move into the State; and if one did so and did not leave within twenty days after being notified of the provisions of this law he should be fined $500, or held to labor for ten years or less. After paying such a penalty he must leave within thirty days or suffer a repetition of the punishment. He who brought in a free negro to settle in the State should pay a fine of $500.[3] Any able-bodied free negro "found spending his or her time in idleness and dissipation, or having no regular or honest employment," was to be arrested and made to give bond for good behavior, in default of which he or she was to be hired out for such a term as the court might think "reasonable and just and calculated to reform him or her to habits of industry or morality, not exceeding three years for any one offense." Furthermore the Courts might bind out the children of such free negroes who were not industriously and honestly employed. Persons hiring free negroes under this act were required to furnish them with proper food and clothing, to treat them humanely, and to teach them some trade or other useful employment. In the later days of slavery[4] the hirer was to give bond to perform this duty, and on failure he was to pay the negro the amount of the bond, and also to lose his services and be liable for a misdemeanor. A further check was placed on the number of free negroes in 1830

---

[1] Revised Code, chap. 107, sec. 77.

[2] See State *vs.* Dempsy, 9 Iredell, p. 384.

[3] It was under the operation of this law that Lunsford Lane was driven from the State. See the author's ''Anti-Slavery Leaders of North Carolina,'' p. 60.

[4] Revised Code, chap. 107, sec. 77.

(chap. 14) when it was provided that those who were willingly absent from the State for more than ninety days together should not be allowed to return to it. It was a capital offense without benefit of clergy for any person of color to rape a white female.[1] By law of 1830 (chap. 10, sec. 2) a free negro was forbidden to gamble with a slave, or to allow a slave to gamble in his house. A further restraint came in 1840 (chap. 30) when a free negro was forbidden to carry a gun or other deadly weapon without license from the County Court.[2] A free negro was not allowed to sell or to give spirituous liquor to any person whatever,[3] and if a free negro were charged with the support of a bastard child, the Court might order him bound out for such a sum as would maintain the child.[4] Thus it will be seen that in regard to his rights of conduct the free negro was reduced more and more to the position of the slave.

The legal status of the free negro was peculiar. Was he a freeman, or was he less than a freeman? The former he was by logical intent; yet he was undoubtedly denied, as has just been stated, many rights which mark the estate of freemen. At any time in the eighteenth century, I suppose, there would have been no question about the free negro being equally a freeman with the whites. After the severe laws of the third and fourth decades of the nineteenth century opinion changed. It was thus that it was as late as 1844 that the Supreme Court undertook to fix the status of free negroes. It then declared that "free persons of color in this State are not to be considered as citizens in the largest sense of the term, or if they are, they occupy such a position as justifies the Legislature in adopting a course of policy in its acts peculiar to them, so that they do not violate the great principles of justice which lie at the foundation of all law."[5] This position is further illustrated by the opinion of the Court in regard to the free negro's right to

---

[1] Laws of 1823, chap. 1229.   [2] State *vs.* Lane, 8 Iredell, p. 256.
[3] Laws of 1844, chap. 86.   [4] Revised Code, chap. 107, sec. 76.
[5] State *vs.* Newsom, 5 Iredell, p. 250.

defend himself against physical force. It was held in 1850 that insolence from a free negro to a white man would excuse a battery in the same manner and to the same extent as insolence from a slave.[1] In 1859 the Court became more explicit. It declared that a free negro was in the peace of the State, and added at length: "So while the law will not allow a free negro to return blow for blow and engage in a fight with a white man under ordinary circumstances, as one white man may do with another or one free negro with another, he is not deprived absolutely of the right of self-defense, but a middle course is adopted" by which he must prove "that it became necessary for him to strike in order to protect himself from great bodily harm or grievous oppression."[2]

More important still is the history of free negroes and suffrage.[3] The first State Constitution provided that free-holders should vote for members of the State Senate and freemen for members of the House of Commons. By statute a freeholder was one who owned in fee or for life fifty acres of land. When the Constitution began to operate it was a day of strenuous danger. Free negroes were enlisted in the patriot armies, and discharged the other burdens of government. They were admitted also to the privileges of citizenship. Negro freemen voted for members of the Commons and when they were freeholders they voted for members of the Senate. Having formed political alliances they found protectors in their party allies, and, eventually, foes in their party opponents. As they became more and more the object of suspicion there was a stronger demand for their disfranchisement. In some localities they ceased to vote at all. This was probably where the political party with which they affiliated was in the minority. In many communities they voted and were protected by their friends.

---

[1] State *vs.* Jowers, 11 Iredell, p. 535.

[2] State *vs.* Davis, 7 Jones, p. 52.

[3] See the author's paper on "Suffrage in North Carolina," Report of the American Historical Association, 1895, pp. 272–3.

Of course, where they did not vote it was through their own will—whether it was influenced by choice or by fear of the whites. Unquestionably, they were not a desirable class of voters. In Granville County, it is said, they lost the favor of the people because they persistently voted for one Potter, a demagogue of plausible speech, who had not the respect of the best whites. At length it came to be regarded as a blot on a man's political record to have the support of the free negroes. It was not unusual for candidates to twit one another with such support and for the one to reply that he would give up the negro vote if the other would do the same.[1]

In the triumph of the pro-slavery views, about 1830, the free negro was destined to lose the franchise. The matter came to a head in the Constitutional Convention of 1835. Already a law had been passed to forbid the free negro to hold office in the State. I do not know just how the act which called the Constitutional Convention came to include in the objects of the convention the consideration of the disfranchisement of free negroes. Perhaps it was a compromise wrung from the men of the West by those of the East in order to get popular representation. Its consideration was made optional. There were many friends of the black man in the convention, but the majority was against him. Realizing their position they tried to secure a law which would save the franchise to the more industrious and intelligent of the free negroes. It was therefore proposed to limit the right to vote to such of this class as had a freehold estate worth $250. The debate on this proposition was long. It was argued by the affirmative that this would be an incentive to the thrift and good conduct of the free negroes; that it would make the better men in that class friends of the whites in case of slave riot; that many free negroes had fought in the Revolution; that they usually

---

[1] See David Dodge: "The Free Negroes of North Carolina," *The Atlantic*, Jan., 1886. David Dodge is O. W. Blacknall, Esq., Kittrels, N. C.

voted for good men when they voted, and that if they were
taxed they ought to vote. It was admitted that the bill of
rights was intended to apply to white men only; but, it was
said, expediency demanded the present concession. It was
not denied that the prejudice against these people was justified by the unworthiness of many of them; but the whites
were largely responsible; for, it was added, "the whites are
the principal corrupters of the morals of these people." Mr.
Shober, of Surry, an extremely western county, was more
outspoken. He said that it was sufficient for him that a
free negro was a human being, that he had a will and was
a free agent. If held liable for taxes and other burdens he
ought to have some privileges. Said Mr. Giles: "It was
charged that the vote of the free negro could be purchased—
purchased by whom? Undoubtedly by white men. The
Legislature had been remiss in its duty to the free negroes.
Instead of improving their situation they appear to have
acted on a principle of hostility toward them." The convention ought to do something to raise them from their
degradation. Judge Gaston also spoke for the negro.
After Macon he was the most distingished man in the convention. The question, said he, was not the giving of a
right but the taking of one away. He was willing to
restrict the right of suffrage; but those free negroes who
possessed freeholds were honest men and perhaps Christians
and they should not be politically excommunicated on
account of their color. "Let them know that they are part
of the body politic, and they will feel an attachment to the
form of government, and have a fixed interest in the prosperity of the community, and will exercise an important
influence over the slaves."

On the other hand, it was argued that a free negro was
not a citizen, and that if he had ever voted it was illegally.
Being called freemen in the abstract did not confer on them
the dignity of citizenship. Fighting in the Revolution did
not make them citizens any more than it made citizens of
the slaves, many of whom fought in the Revolution. The

lot of the free negro was not a hard one. "It far surpassed
the nondescript situation of the ancient Helots and villeins,
or the ignoble condition of the oppressed peasants of
Poland." A slave was not a citizen. When was a freed
slave naturalized? And until naturalized could he be a
citizen? Citizens of one State have privileges of citizens in the other States, and yet North Carolina severely
restricted their coming to its borders, thus implying that
they were not citizens. It was granted that the better class
would suffer hardship in losing the right of suffrage, yet
the interest of a few must yield to the general good.
Although, it was said, free negroes voted elsewhere in the
State, yet the privilege was not allowed to those in the eastern counties, and they had accepted the restriction "with
cheerfulness and contentment." The cold logic of the
views of the majority was stated by Mr. Bryan, of Carteret,
as follows:

"This is, to my mind, a nation of white people, and the
enjoyment of all civil and social rights by a distinctive class
of individuals is purely permissive, and unless there be a
perfect equality in every respect it cannot be demanded as a
right. * * * It may be urged that this is a harsh and
cruel doctrine, and unjust, and by no means reciprocal in
its operation. I do not acknowledge any equality between
the white man and the free negro in the enjoyment of political rights. The free negro is a citizen of necessity and
must, as long as he abides among us, submit to the laws
which necessity and the peculiarity of his position compel us
to adopt."

Mr. McQueen, of Chatham, continued the argument: The
Government of North Carolina did not make the negro a
slave, said he. It gave the boon of freedom, but did that
carry the further boon of citizenship? "Is there any solid
ground for the belief that a free mulatto can have any permanent interest with, and attachment to, this country? He
finds the door of office closed against him by the bars and
bolts of public sentiment; he finds the circle of every

respectable society closed against him; let him conduct
himself with as much propriety as he may, he finds himself
suspended between two classes of society—the whites and
the blacks—condemned by the one and despised by the
other; and when his favorite candidate in the election prevails, it communicates no gratification in his breast, for the
candidate will be a white man, and he knows full well that
the white man eyes him with contempt." More relentless still
was Mr. Wilson, of Perquimons. He said: "A white man
may go to the house of a free black, maltreat and abuse him,
and commit any outrage upon his family, for all of which the
law cannot reach him, unless some white person saw the act
committed—some fifty years of experience having satisfied
the Legislature that the black man does not possess sufficient
intelligence and integrity to be intrusted with the important
privilege of giving evidence against a white man. And after
all this shall we invest him with the more important rights of
a freeman?"

After the discussion had continued two days, the matter
was carried against the free negro by a vote of 65 to 62.
It was the strongly slaveholding East that carried the vote;
for, of the majority, 47 votes were eastern and 18 were western, while of the minority 40 were western and 22 eastern.
The amendment to the Constitution as finally adopted read:
"No free negro, free mulatto, or free person of mixed blood,
descended from negro ancestors to the fourth generation
inclusive (though one ancestor of each generation may have
been a white person) shall vote for members of the Senate
or House of Commons."

There were more free negroes in North Carolina in 1860
than in any other State except Virginia. Rigorous as they
were the North Carolina laws against these people were
more lenient than the laws of Virginia or of any other State.
Consequently many free negroes quietly crossed into the
former State and settled there undisturbed in the northern
or southern counties. They took the poorest land. Usually they rented a few acres; often they bought a small

"patch," and on it dwelt in log huts of the rudest construction. In either case they supplemented their resources by
following some simple trade. They were well-diggers,
shoemakers, blacksmiths, fiddlers, hucksters, pedlers, and
so forth. Besides, they were easily called in to help the
whites on occasions of need. There were a very few who
accumulated money and some of these became slave-owners.
Although it was against the law for them to come into the
State, their arrival was tolerated both because the law was
recognized as severe and because their services were wanted
in the community. Many of them had Indian blood in
their veins, and when such was the case they were a little
distant towards the slaves. Unambitious, often immoral,
they were of the least value to society, which, indeed, offered
them no inducement to be better than they were. They
usually were on terms of friendship with that other class
of incompetents, the "poor whites." Sometimes these two
classes lived on terms of sexual intimacy. In Granville
County there was a pretty well authenticated story of a white
woman who had her colored lover bled and drank some of
the blood so that she might swear she had negro blood in
her and thus be enabled to marry the object of her affection.
She succeeded in her purpose and the couple lived to rear
a family of children.[1] I have been speaking of free negroes
who lived in the country districts. In towns they fared
better and accumulated wealth.

Regardless of the severe laws there were not a few free
negroes who acquired wealth and consideration. Of th s
class were notably Rev. John Chavis, Lunsford Lane and
John C. Stanley. The first of these will be noticed in
another chapter, the second has been treated by the author
with much fulness elsewhere,[2] and here I shall speak of the
third only.

---

[1] David Dodge [O. W. Blacknall] in *The Atlantic Monthly*, Jan.,
1886.
[2] "Anti-slavery Leaders of North Carolina," p. 60.

John C. Stanley was a mulatto, the son of an African born slave woman, who was brought to Newbern, N. C. (from the West Indies), before the Revolutionary War. He was a barber by trade and throughout his days of manhood was known as "Barber Jack." He was a faithful servant, and in 1808 he was liberated by the General Assembly on petition of Mrs. Lydia Stewart, into whose possession he had come. He soon began to acquire negro slaves and land till at length he had sixty-four slaves and as many more bound free negroes working his several plantations. Says Col. John D. Whitford: "He was popular, too, with both slave and free negroes generally, notwithstanding he was a hard taskmaster. Yes, he worked all well and fed and clothed indifferently."[1] He married a moor, a copper colored woman who was not a slave. He got his start in the barber business—although he made much of his money by discounting notes. Certain white men of means who did not care to go openly into the business of sharp discounting, took him for a partner and furnished the means. He had three sons, John, Alexander and Charles. John became an expert bookkeeper and was employed in that capacity by a prominent firm. John C. Stanley amassed a fortune supposed to be worth more than $40,000; but in his old age he lost much of it by bad management. His family held themselves aloof from the other negroes of the community. They were members of the Presbyterian Church, to which Mrs. Stewart, his former mistress, had belonged. This lady lived till 1822, and when old and feeble could be seen on the streets in fine weather supported on the arm of her faithful old servant—now fourteen years a freeman. Thus she took the air and thus she went to church on Sunday. When the couple had arrived at the church, John would conduct her to

---

[1] See Raleigh, N. C., *Morning Post*, Dec. 5, 1897. Other facts not mentioned by Col. Whitford are from statements made to the writer by Maj. D. W. Hurt, Goldsboro, N. C.

her pew and then leave her to take his seat with his own
family in the place assigned to colored people.

Many of the free negroes were in circumstances of independent thrift, and from many parts of the State I have had
evidence that some negroes were slaveholders. In Newbern especially there were a number of such thrifty colored
men. Notable among these was John Good. He was a son
of his master and for a long time a slave. When the master
died, his two surviving children, who were daughters, had
but little property besides this boy, John, who was a barber.
John took up the task of supporting them. He boarded them
in good houses and otherwise provided for them well. His
faithfulness won him many friends among the best citizens,
and when both of his mistresses were married these friends
united to persuade the owners to liberate him as a reward
for his services. Unfortunately, freedom proved no boon.
He fell into bad habits, took to drink and soon died. There
were other thrifty and notable free negroes in the same
place, as, for example, John Y. Green, a carpenter and con-
tractor; Richard Hazel, a blacksmith of means; Albert and
Freeman Morris, described as two "nice young men," and
thoroughly respected, tailors by trade; and Scipio, slave of
Dr. Hughes, who was a blacksmith and owner of a livery
stable. Another was Fellow Bragg, a tailor who was thoroughly conscientious and so good a workman that prominent people were known to move their custom to the shops
at which he was employed in order that he might work on
it. Most of these men moved to Cincinnati sooner or later.
What became of them after that I do not know.[1] The conditions here recorded for Newbern were not unusual for
North Carolina towns in general. Everywhere there were
usually a number of prosperous free negroes. Most of them
were mulattoes, not a few of them were set free by their
fathers and thus they fell easily into the life around them.

---

[1] The facts in this paragraph are from Maj. D. W. Hurt, formerly
of Newbern, but now of Goldsboro, N. C.

This mulatto class was partly due to the easy sexual relations between the races. A white man who kept a negro mistress ordinarily lost no standing in society on account of it. The habit, though not common, was not unusual. Often the mistress was a slave, and thus there were frequent emancipations either by gift or by purchase of liberty, till the stricter spirit of the laws after 1831 checked it.

CHAPTER III.

RELIGIOUS LIFE.

I have already said that the central idea of slavery in North Carolina was a determination to perpetuate the institution, whatever the price, and at the same time a disposition to make it as gentle as possible for the slave, provided that doing so did not tend to loosen his bonds. This same idea is found in the master's regulation of the religious life of the slave. Without question he was willing to make the slave a Christian. He was anxious to do it. He spent money with more or less bountifulness to do it. This was sometimes done by men who were not Christians themselves, but who wanted their slaves to be Christians for the purposes of discipline; but oftener it was done out of pure benevolence, and with a devout purpose to accomplish the spiritual welfare of the negro. Persons who have formed their opinions of Southern society from the popular works of certain novelists are apt to think of the slave-owner as a fine-bred gentleman of cavalier instincts and patriarchal feelings. Such an estimate is but half true. There was in the South—in North Carolina it was very strong—a large class of slave-owners who approached more nearly to the English farmer type than to the English gentleman type. They were usually self-made men, of fair intelligence, and of some education. They were generally thrifty and often wealthy. _The majority of them were Christians, mostly of the Methodist, Baptist and Presbyterian Churches. This class of men has received but little attention from those who have written of Southern society, and yet it was the backbone of that society. There was little that was ideal about such men. They were humdrum, but they were honest, pious and substantial, and they were numerous. Such people are to be compared, not only in wealth, but in general social development as well, with the upper farmer class in the North and West. I do not mean to say that they were all of the South. The planter class, in the ordinary use of the term, was there, and it was the governing class and the class that touched the outside world. It went to summer resorts, and to Congress, and to political conventions, and it got into novels, and sometimes into history, and it was usually benignly patriarchal, but the farmer class as a class came closer into touch with the slave and in a hundred ways softened the harshness of an institution which no one knew how to modify in law.

It was, indeed, in a harsh spirit that the law came at last to regulate the religious relations of the slave. In the beginning, when the slaves were just from barbarism and freedom, it was thought best to forbid them to have churches of their own. But as they became more manageable, this restriction was omitted from the law[1] and the churches went on with their work among the slaves. A large number of negroes were converted and taken into church membership, some of the more intelligent negroes were taught to read and were licensed to preach. Some churches made a specialty of work among the slaves. Often negro preachers held services with their own race and sometimes established separate congregations, though the latter was not the rule. The advantage of this system was that it was developing the negro into self-dependence religiously, but doing it under the intimate oversight of the whites among whom he was interspersed. Never before or since was the relation between the negro and his white neighbors so auspicious. The change came openly in 1830, when a law was passed by the General Assembly which destroyed the hopes of all those who were favorable to this movement. It was enacted that no free person or slave should teach a slave

[1] See the author's "Slavery and Servitude," p. 50.

to read or write, the use of figures excepted, or give to a
slave any book or pamphlet.[1] This law was no doubt
intended to meet the danger from the circulation of incendiary literature, which was believed to be imminent; yet
it is no less true that it bore directly on the slave's religious
life. It cut him off from the reading of the Bible—a point
much insisted on by the agitators of the North—and it forestalled that mental development which was necessary to
him in comprehending the Christian life. The only argument made for this law was that if a slave could read he
would soon become acquainted with his rights. Caruthers
thought it a shame that a Christian people would make such
arguments. "How dare you," he exclaims, "by your
impious enactments doom millions of your fellow-beings to
such a gross and perpetual ignorance!"[2] A year later a
severer blow fell. The Legislature then forbade any slave
or free person of color to preach, exhort, or teach "in any
prayer-meeting or other association for worship where
slaves of different families are collected together" on penalty
of receiving not more than thirty-nine lashes.[3] The result
was to increase the responsibility of the churches of the
whites. They were compelled to abandon the hope of seeing the negro made his own evangel and to take on themselves the task of handing down to the slaves religious
instruction in such a way that it should be comprehended
by their immature minds and should not be too strongly
flavored with the bitterness of bondage. With the mandate
of the Legislature the churches acquiesced.

As to the preaching of the dominant class to the slaves
it always had one element of disadvantage. It seemed to
the negro to be given with a view to upholding slavery. As
an illustration of this I may introduce the testimony of

---

[1] Revised Statutes, pp. 209, 578, and Revised Code, p. 218.

[2] See the unpublished manuscript of E. W. Caruthers's book on
"Slavery," p. 396. It is preserved in the library of Greensboro
Female College, Greensboro, N. C.

[3] Revised Statutes, p. 580, and Revised Code, p. 576.

Lunsford Lane.   This slave was the property of a prominent
and highly esteemed citizen of Raleigh, N. C.   He hired
his own time and with his father manufactured smoking
tobacco by a secret process.   His business grew and at
length he bought his own freedom.   Later, he opened a
wood yard, a grocery store and kept teams for hauling.
He at last bought his own home, and had bargained to buy
his wife and children for $2500, when the rigors of the law
were applied and he was driven from the State.   He was
intelligent enough to get a clear view of slavery from the
slave's standpoint.   He was later a minister, and undoubtedly had the confidence and esteem of some of the leading
people of Raleigh, among whom was Governor Morehead.
He is a competent witness for the negro.   In speaking of
the sermons from white preachers he said that the favorite
texts were "Servants, be obedient to your masters," and
"he that knoweth his master's will and doth it not shall
be beaten with many stripes."   He adds, "Similar passages
with but few exceptions formed the basis of most of the
public instruction.   The first commandment was to obey
our masters, and the second was like unto it; to labor as
faithfully when they or the overseers were not watching
as when they were.   I will not do them the injustice to say
that connected with this instruction there was not mingled
much that was excellent."   All this was natural.   To be a
slave was the fundamental fact of the negro's life.   To be
a good slave was to obey and to labor.   Not to obey and not
to labor were, in the master's eye, the fundamental sins of a
slave.   Such a condition was inherent in slavery.   On the
other hand, many of the more independent negroes, those
who in their hearts never accepted the institution of slavery,
were repelled from the white man's religion, and thus the
support of a very valuable portion of the race was lost.
This condition of affairs was not to be entirely remedied
by having negro preachers; but it might have been amelior-
ated by it, and if, in the long course of time, the church
work among the slaves could have been done entirely by

negro preachers acting under white supervision the salvation of the slave would have been very near its accomplishment.

As it was, it is no doubt true that many slaves were
reached by religious influences. Through the teachings of
the church many were enabled to bend in meekness under
their bondage and be content with a hopeless lot. There
are whites to whom Christianity is still chiefly a burden-
bearing affair. Such quietism has a negative value. It
saves men from discontent and society from chaos. But
it has little positive and constructive value. The idea of
social reform which is also associated with the standard of
Christian duty was not for the slave. Those very few who,
like Lunsford Lane, did work themselves heroically to freedom were acting on principles not usually preached from
the pulpit in the latter part of our period.

How a slave looked at the religion that was brought to
him may be seen from the following words of Lunsford
Lane, who seems to have been a consistent Christian:

I was permitted to attend church, and this I esteem a great blessing. It was there I received much instruction, which I trust was a
great benefit to me. I trusted, too, that I had experienced the renew-
ing influences of divine grace. I looked upon myself as a great sin-
ner before God, and upon the doctrine of the great atonement,
through the suffering and death of the Saviour, as a source of continual
joy to my heart. After obtaining from my mistress a written permit,
a thing always required in such cases, I had been baptized and
received into fellowship with the Baptist denomination. Thus in
religious matters I had been indulged in the exercise of my own
conscience; this was a favor not always granted to slaves. There
was one hard doctrine to which we as slaves were compelled to listen,
which I found difficult to receive. We were often told by the minister how much we owed to God for bringing us over from the benighted
shores of Africa and permitting us to listen to the sound of the gospel. In ignorance of any special revelation that God had made to
master, or to his ancestors, that my ancestors should be stolen and
enslaved on the soil of America to accomplish their salvation, I was
slow to believe all my teachers enjoined on this subject. How surprising, then, this high moral end being accomplished, that no proclamation of emancipation had before this been made! Many of us

were as highly civilized as some of our masters, and, as to piety, in many instances their superiors. I was rather disposed to believe that God had originally granted me temporal freedom, which wicked men had forcibly taken from me—which now I had been compelled to purchase at great cost. * * * There was one very kind-hearted clergyman whom I used often to hear; he was very popular with the colored people. But after he had preached a sermon to us in which he urged from the Bible that it was the will of Heaven from all eternity that we should be slaves, and our masters be our owners, many of us left him, considering, like the doubting disciple of old, "This is a hard saying, who can hear it?"[1]

Dr. Caruthers, whose long pastorate in Guilford ought to have given him good grounds for speaking, said that slaves knew little of the Bible, except as they picked it up from others, "and that little," he adds, "they don't know half their time whether to believe or disbelieve. It is often said that many of them become very pious people, and although we can't know the heart, charity would lead us to believe or hope so; but no thanks to slavery or the slave laws." It was the Lord's work. The negroes who were spoken of as pious, said he, did not have "those enlarged views or that expansion of soul which is always imparted by scriptural and enlightened sentiments of immortality."[2]

All the churches of North Carolina, so far as I have been able to ascertain, received freely negro members. Every church had its space reserved for negroes. It was almost invariably in the gallery, if there was one, or in the back of the church, if there was no gallery. In the ceremony of the Lord's Supper, after the whites had partaken, the sacrament was administered to the negro members. In many churches, particularly of Methodist and Baptist denominations, which had often many colored communicants, there was a special service in the afternoon by the white preacher for the negroes. It was to these two churches that most of the negroes joined themselves, although there were some in each of the other leading bodies. There was much reason

[1] See Hawkins' "Memoir of Lunsford Lane," 64–66.
[2] See manuscript book on "Slavery," p. 294.

for this. These two churches in North Carolina were organized for the masses. Their doctrines were easily comprehended and emotional; and the negro is a creature of emotions. Moreover these bodies made special efforts to reach the negroes. They went among the large slave plantations as missionaries. Other denominations paid more attention to household slaves. In not a few cases Methodism began with negro congregations and in at least one place it was introduced by a negro preacher. But true as it was that the Methodists and Baptists attracted the negroes more strongly, it was perhaps equally true that the Quakers, in proportion to their own numbers, were more closely intimate with the negroes than any other religious body in the State. Of this more will be said later on. Let us now consider the Methodists and the slave.

In the eighteenth century the record of the Methodists was clearly against slavery. John Wesley himself said that the slave trade was the sum of all villainies, although Whitefield was not opposed to it. The anti-slavery sentiment was strongest in the Northern Conferences, although it was not unknown in the Southern. As early as 1780 the Conference of all the Church declared: "Slavery is contrary to the laws of God, man and nature and hurtful to society, contrary to the dictates of conscience and pure religion, and doing that which we would not that others should do to us and ours."[1] In 1784 the Conference resolved to expel from membership those who bought and sold slaves.[2] This step was calculated to arouse much opposition in the South among the laymen, even if the preachers had favored it. It occasioned much criticism and aroused much feeling in both Virginia and the two Carolinas. In the spring of 1875, Dr. Coke arrived in America. He preached strongly against slavery and got the Virginia Conference to petition the Legislature for gradual emancipation. This made him very unpopular, so much so that he barely escaped bodily violence. The slaveholders now withdrew their slaves from

---

[1] Conference Minutes, p. 25.   [2] *Ibid.*, pp. 47–48.

contact with Methodist preachers.[1] The Conference of
1785 thought it prudent to rescind its former action, but
was particular to add: "N. B.—We do hold in the deepest
abhorrence the practice of slavery, and shall not cease to
seek its destruction by all wise and prudent means."[2] So
far as an open declaration for emancipation is concerned,
the Conference was quiet for some time; but in 1795 it
showed its concern in the negro's welfare by setting apart a
fast day "to lament the deep-rooted vassalage that still
reigneth in many parts of this free and independent United
States," and it added: "We feel gratified that many thousands of these poor people are free and pious."[3]

As the Church became strong enough to organize Conferences, in the various sections the question of the existence
of slavery was referred to these bodies and thus localized to
an extent. But one particular question that concerned all
was the propriety of allowing a preacher to hold slaves. As
early as 1783 the Conference forbade a preacher to own
slaves in a State where it was legal to free them.[4] Much discussion grew up over this matter early in the present century.
Finally it was settled on the lines earlier adopted. It was
agreed in 1816 that no slaveholder should hold office in
States which allowed emancipation and subsequent residence of the liberated negro. Here was a distinct compromise fixed on the principle of sectional conditions, the principle which four years later the Missouri compromise
followed in the broader sphere of politics.[5] The Church
continued the former strong declaration against slavery in
the abstract, a declaration which, it was likely, was supported
by Southern preachers. It was on the compromise of 1816
that the fight which led to separation in 1844 was made.

[1] Drew: "Life of Dr. Coke," pp. 132–139.
[2] Conference Minutes, p. 55.
[3] *Ibid.*, pp. 163–164.
[4] *Ibid.*, p. 41, and the Discipline of 1821, p. 69.
[5] See the Discipline of 1817 and Redpath's "Organization of the
Methodist Episcopal Church South," p. 10.

The occasion was the censure voted against Bishop Andrew because he had married in Georgia a woman who owned slaves. The Southern organization which was now formed continued its protest against slavery. The first edition of its Discipline, 1846, said in the words of the older Discipline: "We declare that we are as much as ever convinced of the great evil of slavery. Therefore, no slave-holder shall be eligible to any official position in our Church hereafter where the Laws of the State in which he lives will admit of emancipation and permit the liberated slave to enjoy freedom. When any traveling preacher becomes an owner of a slave or slaves, by any means, he shall forfeit his ministerial character in our Church, unless he execute, if it be practicable, a legal emancipation of such slaves, conformable to the laws of the State in which he lives." Furthermore, preachers were to enforce prudently on their members the duty of teaching slaves to read the Bible and to attend church services. Colored preachers and officials were guaranteed the privileges of their official relation "where the usages of the country do not forbid it." Of all of these ameliorating conditions to the slave but one was applicable in North Carolina; for here he could not be legally emancipated and remain in the State, nor could he be allowed to preach or be taught to read the Bible. It only remained for him to aspire to be some church official lower than a preacher. The original strong desire to christianize the negro, which the Methodists never forsook, was clearly bound and held in restraint in conformity to the newer spirit of harshness that, as has already been said, seized the State Legislature about 1830.

The labors of the Methodists among the slaves began in the very first days of Methodism in the State. The General Conference in 1787[1] urged the preachers to labor among the slaves, to receive into full membership those that seemed

---

[1] See Minutes of Conference, p. 67. The Methodist Church in America dates from 1784.

worthy, and "to exercise the whole Methodist Discipline among them." How well these efforts prospered may be seen from the following figures: In 1787 there were in North Carolina[1] 5017 white and 492 colored members; in 1788 there were 5263 white and 775 black members; in 1789 there were 6644 whites and 1139 blacks; in 1790 there were 7518 whites to 1749 blacks; in 1795 there were 8414 whites to 1719 blacks; in 1800 there 6363 whites to 2108 blacks; in 1805 there were 9385 whites to 2394 blacks; in 1810 there were 13,535 whites to 4724 blacks; in 1815 there were 14,283 whites to 5165 blacks; in 1820 there were 13,179 whites to 5933 blacks; in 1825 there were 15,421 whites to 7292 blacks; in 1830 there were 19,228 whites to 10,182 blacks; in 1835 there were 27,539 whites to 8766 blacks, and in 1839, which is the last year for which I have been able to obtain the figures, there were 26,405 whites to 9302 blacks. Here was a rapid proportional gain of the blacks over the whites. In 1787 there were not 10 per cent. as many black as white members; in 1839 there were 35 per cent. as many. The membership for each race varied notably, but the variations were wider with the negro race. This indicates, it must be supposed, the more emotional nature of the negro. A wave of revival feeling which would sweep over the country would swell the roll of membership and a few years of coolness would contract it.

Although there were negro Methodists in most sections of the State, they were most numerous in the eastern counties. In this section the Methodists often began their work with an appeal to the slaves—"negro churches," their meeting houses were often called by the more aristocratic denominations. An illustration is Wilmington. Here William Meredith, a Methodist preacher, arrived at the beginning of this century. He began to work among the

---

[1] The estimates are based on reports in the Minutes. It is doubtful whether some charges near the State boundaries were in North Carolina or out of it. Therefore, the figures may not be absolutely correct, but for purposes of comparison they are adequate.

slaves. He bought a lot, and through the penny collection from the blacks and the scanty contributions of the few poorer whites who had joined with him, a building was completed. This was the beginning of Methodists in the town. Hither came Bishop Francis Asbury in 1807 and preached twice in one day. On the same day, John Charles, a colored preacher, preached at sunrise. The feeling of friendship for him seems to have been great and the good Bishop writes in his journal that it was "a high day on Mount Zion." The attitude of the community was not always tolerant of this "negro church." There were various disturbances, and once the building was wrecked by a mob.[1]

More striking, but not so typical, is the story of the planting of Methodism in Fayetteville. Late in the eighteenth century, Fayetteville had but one church organization, the Presbyterian, and that had no building. One day there arrived in town Henry Evans, a full-blooded free negro from Virginia, who was moving to Charleston, S. C., where he proposed to follow the trade of shoemaking. He was perhaps free born; he was a Methodist and a licensed local preacher. In Fayetteville he observed that the colored people "were wholly given to profanity and lewdness, never hearing preaching of any denomination." He felt it his duty to stop and work among them. He worked at his trade during the week and preached on Sunday. The whites became alarmed and the Town Council ordered him to stop preaching. He then met his flock in the "sand hills," desolate places outside of the jurisdiction of the Town Council. Fearing violence he made his meetings secret and changed the place of meeting from Sunday to Sunday. He was particular to violate no law, and to all the whites he showed the respect which their sense of caste superiority demanded. Public

---

[1] See "Early Methodism in Wilmington," by Dr. A. M. Chreitzberg, in the Annual Publication of the Historical Society of the N. C. Conference, 1897, p. 1; also Wightman: "Life of Bishop Capers," p. 136.

opinion began to change, especially when it was noticed that
slaves who had come under his influence were more docile
for it. Some prominent whites, most of whom were women,
became interested in his cause. They attended his meetings and through their influence public opinion was
reversed. Then a rude frame building was erected within
the town limits and a number of seats were reserved for the
whites, some of whom became regular attendants at his
services. The preacher's reputation spread. The white
portion of the congregation increased till the negroes were
crowded out of their seats. Then the boards were knocked
from the sides of the house and sheds were built on either
hand and in these the blacks were seated. By this time the
congregation, which had been unconnectional at first, had
been taken into the regular Methodist connection and a regular white preacher had been sent to it. But the heroic
founder was not displaced. A room was built for him in
the rear of the pulpit and there he lived till his death in
1810.

Of Henry Evans, Bishop Capers said: "I have known
not many preachers who appeared more conversant with
the Scriptures than Evans, or whose conversation was more
instructive as to the things of God. He seemed always deeply
impressed with the responsibility of his position * * *
nor would he allow any partiality of friends to induce him
to vary in the least degree from the lines of conduct or the
bearing which he had prescribed to himself in this respect;
never speaking to a white man but with his hat under his
arm, never allowing himself to be seated in their houses and
even confining himself to the kind and manner of dress
proper for slaves in general, except his plain black coat in
the pulpit. 'The whites are kind and come to hear me
preach,' he would say, 'but I belong to my own sort and
must not spoil them.' " Rare self-control before the most
wretched of castes! Henry Evans did much good, but he
would have done more good had his spirit been untram-
meled by this sense of inferiority.

His last speech to his people is noteworthy. Directly after the morning sermon for the whites it was customary to have a sermon for the blacks. On the Sunday before Evans' death, as the latter meeting was being held the door of his little shed room opened and he tottered forward. Leaning on the altar rail he said: "I have come to say my last word to you. It is this: None but Christ. Three times I have had my life in jeopardy for preaching the gospel to you. Three times I have broken the ice on the edge of the water and swam across the Cape Fear to preach the gospel to you, and if in my last hour I could trust to that, or anything but Christ crucified, for my salvation, all should be lost and my soul perish forever." Of these words Bishop Capers justly says that they were worthy of St. Paul.[1]

The opposition that was encountered in Fayetteville and in Wilmington had been due to the more active abolition turn of the Church in the North. In 1785 Dr. Coke arrived in America on a visit to the Church. He preached abolition and gave it an impetus among the Methodists which resulted in memorials and remonstrances to the Legislature. Before this the large slave-owners had encouraged preaching to their slaves.[2] They now became fearful that the slaves would be incited to violence, and generally in the South, Methodist ministers were forbidden access to the slaves. It took some time to live down this unfavorable impression and it was only when it was seen that the Southern preachers did not approve of the interference with the agitation against negro slavery that public sentiment came around. There was the most urgent need for such preaching. Of the negroes around Wilmington, Bishop Capers says: "A numerous population of this class in that town and vicinity were as destitute of any public instruction (or, probably, instruction of any kind as to spiritual things) as if they had not been believed to be men at all, and their

---

[1] Wightman: "Life of Bishop Capers," pp. 124–129.
[2] Drew: "Life of Dr. Coke," pp. 132–139.

morals were as depraved as, with such a destitution of the
gospel among them, might have been expected." To this
state of things the masters were indifferent; for, adds the
Bishop, "it seems not to have been considered that such a
state of things might furnish motives sufficient to induce
pure-minded men to engage, at great inconvenience or even
personal hazard, in the work of reforming them. Such
work, on the other hand, seems to have been regarded as
unnecessary, if not unreasonable. Conscience was not
believed to be concerned in it."[1] And yet when conveyed
the negroes made good Christians. Says the same authority: "I believe I have never served a more Christian-hearted
people." The preacher had a great influence over them.
Church trials were rare among them and the numbers
increased constantly. They were faithful in giving to the
church. The pastor's salary at Wilmington was derived
almost wholly from their scant resources; for the few white
members were very poor. They were attached to their
preacher, as many a pound cake or warm pair of knit socks
or gloves from their hands testified.

Sometimes a congregation outgrew in dignity the hum-
bler persons who had at first constituted its chief elements.
Such was the case at Raleigh. Here there were at first a
large number of colored members, and when the church
building was erected they contributed their part. They were
given seats in the gallery. At length there was an opportunity to buy a church which might be turned over solely
to the negroes. Both whites and blacks worked with their
might to get the necessary money. When it was at length
secured, there was a two-fold rejoicing; by the negroes
because they had a building of their own, by the whites
because the negroes were out of the white man's church.
This negro church now became a mission and a white
preacher was assigned to it by the Conference. Usually
an old preacher of kind disposition and good judgment was
sent to them. They were still under the oversight of the white

---

[1] Wightman: "Life of Bishop Capers," p. 163.

congregation from which they drew for Sunday school teachers and other church workers.

The Baptists were early in North Carolina, but until the establishment of the Missionary Baptist Church in 1830 they were hardly as zealous for converting the unsaved as later. I have not found evidence that they began by working up congregations among the slaves as did the Methodists in some places, but from the first they took great care to bring under religious influence the slaves of their own members and through these the negroes generally came to be reached at length. The records of Sandy Run Church, in Bertie County, as early as 1773, show that there were negro preachers for the negro members, and that these were instructed not to hold services at the time of the regular meeting of the whole church, at which it was designed that the slaves might also be present. Both colored preachers and colored members were under the control of the white congregation. They had no voice in general church affairs, but would be heard in church meeting in cases which related to their own race. There were in some eastern sections colored deacons who were given charge of the colored members and who made report from time to time to the church meeting.[1]

It has been found impossible to get an estimate of the number of negroes in the Baptist Church in North Carolina. Here the congregational idea was strong, the reports to the associations were not very full and do not always show the number of members. In 1830 the Baptist State Convention was formed, and from that time the minutes are published for the Missionary Baptist Church in North Carolina, but in the few years for which the number of members are reported, there is no distinction made between blacks and whites. It is only in the Chowan Association that I have had a glimpse of numbers. Here there were in 1843, 4575 white to 1228 black members; in 1844, 3241 whites to

[1] For many of the facts here presented I am indebted to Dr. J. D. Huffham, of Henderson, N. C.

1160 blacks; in 1848, 4619 whites to 1541 blacks; in 1850, 4668 whites to 1476 blacks; in 1855, 6960 whites to 2545 blacks, and in 1860, 7539 whites to 3043 blacks.   This proportion was strong, but it must be remembered that the Chowan Association lay in the East, and that it was in a region which was strong in Baptist faith.   It was not representative of the denomination on this question.

The care of the Church over the life of the slave was commendably faithful, especially over the relation of master and slave.   As early as 1778 it was decided that a marriage between slaves ought to be respected, even though it was against the law of the land, and that any member who broke the marriage vows of servants ought to be denied fellowship.[1]   In 1783 it was declared by a meeting in the Sandy Creek Association that a master should give his servants liberty to attend family prayers in his house, that he should exhort them to attend, but not use force.[2]   How this duty was fulfilled may be seen from the memoir of Capt. John Freeman, a prominent Baptist of Chowan County, who died in 1794.   It is said of him that although he had many slaves "his lenity towards them was very remarkable.   If any of them transgressed, his general method to chastise them was to expose their faults before the rest of the servants and the whole family when they were at family worship in the morning, who, when assembled at morning prayer, would talk to them, exhort and rebuke them so sharply for their faults that he made others fear.   *   *   *   He was so very affected for the spiritual welfare of his family that often he seemed almost convulsed, and this extraordinary zeal was not the impulse of a moment, but his constant practice for seventeen years."[3]

The above statements apply to the Baptist body before the separation of the Missionary Baptists from it.   For a view of the attitude of the latter toward slavery, the best

---

[1] Biggs: "History of Kehuckee Association," p. 47.
[2] Purefoy: "History of Sandy Creek Association," p. 60.
[3] Biggs: "History of the Kehuckee Association," pp. 95–96.

source at hand is Purefoy's "History of the Sandy Creek Association." Here it is seen that the question of a valid marriage between blacks was still unsettled. The Association was asked in 1805 to settle it.[1] After three years' postponement it was answered that such a marriage should be valid, "when they come together in their former and general custom, having no [other] companion." Rev. Purefoy, commenting on this, says[2] owners should endeavor to keep married slaves from being separated, even if they put themselves to some inconvenience in buying, selling, or exchanging them.

To the buying and selling of slaves for profit Baptists in both East and West were opposed. In 1818 the Chowan Association was asked if a Christian could consistently buy slaves in order to sell them to speculators. The answer was clear: "We believe that such practice is at war with the spirit of the gospel and shocking to all the tender feelings of our nature. We answer No."[3] In 1835 Sandy Creek Association spoke still more emphatically. It said: "WHEREAS, We believe it inconsistent with the spirit of the gospel of Christ for a Christian to buy or sell negroes for the purpose of speculation or merchandise for gain. *Resolved, therefore,* that this association advise the churches of which it is composed to exclude members who will not abandon the practice after the first and second admonition."[4] When in 1847 the Association was asked if it was agreeable to the gospel for Baptists to buy and sell human beings or to keep them in bondage for life, the only answer vouchsafed was to refer the interrogators to the minutes of 1835. The slavery dispute was then well-nigh in its stage of highest passion, and it is not unlikely that the Church authorities did not like to take a more definite position on either the first or second part of the query.

[1] Purefoy: "History of Sandy Creek Association," p. 76.
[2] *Ibid.*, pp. 93–94.
[3] "Minutes of the Chowan Baptist Association," 1818, p. 7.
[4] Purefoy: "Sandy Creek Association," pp. 163–164.

The Baptists, like the Methodists, early in the century had negro preachers, most notable of whom was Ralph Freeman. Ralph was a slave in Anson County in the neighborhood of Rock River Church. Soon after his conversion he felt an impulse to preach, and early in this century he was licensed by his church for that purpose. Soon afterwards he was ordained to the regular ministry. He did not have specific charges, but traveled and preached through his own and the adjoining counties. Says Rev. Purefoy: "He became a good reader and was well versed in the Scripture. He was considered an able preacher and was frequently called upon to preach on funeral occasions, and was appointed to preach on Sabbath at Association, and frequently administered the ordinance of baptism and the Lord's Supper. He was of common size, was perfectly black, with a smiling countenance, especially in the pulpit while speaking. He was very humble in his appearance at all times, and especially when conducting religious services. Great personal respect was also shown him by the brethren whom he visited in his preaching excursions." Rev. Joseph Magee, a white Baptist minister, became much attached to Ralph. They used to travel and preach together and after the fashion of the times it was agreed between them that the survivor should preach the funeral sermon of the one who died first. This task fell to Ralph. Although his friend had moved to the West, the colored preacher was sent for all the way from North Carolina to come and fulfil the promise made years earlier. Ralph complied with great success and before a large audience. When the Baptists divided on the question of missions, Ralph sided with the anti-mission party, and so fell into disfavor with the others. This he regretted, but a greater blow, which also fell about the same time, was the statute which forbade negroes to preach. He was greatly mortified, but submitted, and with that passes from our notice.

In proportion to their strength the Quakers did more for the negroes than any other religious body in North Carolina. They did not have very many colored members, but before the Revolution they set themselves to free those they did have; and they did not stop until the process was accomplished. The Yearly Meeting of the very first year of the war, 1776, appointed a committee to go about and aid Friends to free their slaves. This committee was expected to act in co-operation with the various monthly meetings. Thus a considerable number were liberated in the following year. The committee reported that they found among the Friends a great willingness to forward the work. But they had acted contrary to the law of emancipation which required that slaves should be freed for meritorious conduct only. Forty of those thus emancipated were taken up and sold into slavery again. The Quakers complained that this was done under a law passed in 1777, after the slaves were liberated. At considerable expense they fought the matter through County and Superior Courts and won the verdict; but the Assembly was then appealed to and in 1779 it passed a law confirming the sales of these negroes and directing that all other negroes similarly freed should be sold into slavery in the same manner as if they had been freed after the passage of the law of 1777. The reason for this extraordinary procedure was no doubt the law of 1741, which was held to be still in force. The Friends, however, were not satisfied. They appealed to the Assembly. They based their theory on the principle "that no law, moral or divine, has given us a right to, or property in, any of our fellow creatures any longer than they are in a state of minority." They appealed to the statement of the rights of man in the Declaration of Independence, and showed that the sale of the negroes in question was in opposition to the spirit of the North Carolina Bill of Rights, which forbade the passage of *ex post facto* laws. This petition was signed by the eleven men who had owned the slaves in question and was sent to the Assembly, but on the advice of persons friendly

to the Quakers it was not presented.[1] This did not deter
the Friends from further petitions. One was sent in 1787,
another in 1788, and another in 1789. The petitions were
about various matters, but none of them amounted to anything. In 1792 they petitioned again, asking the repeal of
the law restricting emancipation, and demanding that it
"never again disgrace the annals of a Christian people." The
petition failed, but they did not cease to send others in the
years following. In 1817 they asked the Legislature to
take joint action with Congress for the colonization of the
free negroes. The petition failed, and the next year they
voted $1000 to the American Colonization Society. For
some time there seems to have been no further connection
with this society.

The instruction of the slaves in religious and educational
matters aroused the energies of the Quakers. They became
awakened in this matter in 1780, when it seems that but little
had been done. In 1787 it was asserted that one of the two
leading objects of their activities toward the negro was to
care for, protect, and instruct the freed negroes. The
immediate result of this interest does not appear; but in
1815 Friends were exhorted by the Yearly Meeting to prepare schools for the literary and religious instruction of
the negroes,[2] and in 1816 a school for negroes was opened
for two days in each week. Some progress was made, as
may be seen by the reports. Most of the negroes in the Western Quarter who were minors had been put in a way to get "a
portion of school learning." The Quarter recommended that
males be taught to "read, write and cipher as far as the Rule
of Three," and that females be taught to read and write
merely.[3] In 1821, Levi Coffin and his cousin, Vestal, opened

[1] A chief source of facts relating to the Quakers and Slavery has
been "A Narrative of Some of the Proceedings of the North Carolina
Yearly Meeting on the subject of Slavery within its Limits." (See
"Slavery and Servitude," p. 50, note 1.)

[2] Quaker pamphlet cited above, p. 24.

[3] *Ibid.*, p. 24. See also Weeks: "Southern Quakers and Slavery,"
p. 231.

a Sunday school for the blacks at New Garden and began to teach some slaves to spell; but when they could spell words of two or three letters they were withdrawn by their masters. The former attempt must have been as unsatisfactory as that of the Coffins, since the standing committee of the Quakers reported in 1821 that they could find no way to educate colored children except in the families of Friends. Either in this way or otherwise some progress was undoubtedly made, as appears from the reports sent in to the Yearly Meeting. When the Assembly passed the law forbidding slaves to be taught to read and write the Quakers petitioned for its repeal, and they also asked for the repeal of the law forbidding colored persons to preach. They said: "We consider these laws unrighteous and contrary to the spirit of Christianity, offensive to God; and your memorialists believe, if not repealed, they will increase the difficulties and dangers they are intended to prevent."[1] Furthermore, they asked for the enactment of a law to instruct slaves in religion and in reading, so that they could read the Bible.

To accomplish the liberation of slaves in the face of the laws they had recourse to corporate ownership. In 1808 a committee was appointed on the state of the people of color, and its recommendation, which was adopted, was that certain trustees should be appointed to whom should be conveyed the slaves whom it was desired to emancipate. These slaves were to be held in nominal bondage, but the trustees were to retain only so much power over them as should be for the good of the slaves' conduct. Thus an idle negro might be coerced moderately. The Friends took this step on the advice of Judge William Gaston, who was always a friend of freedom and of the slave. At first some Friends opposed the project, but they gradually changed their views and the custom continued in force until the Civil War. As soon as this plan was in operation, slaves began to disappear from among the Quakers. Many of them

---

[1] See Quaker pamphlet cited, p. 34.

were sent out of the State—either to free territory in the
United States or to Africa or to the West Indies. A few
could be freed by the consent of the County Courts. A
considerable number, especially those who were connected
by family bonds with the slaves of persons not Quakers, as
well as old persons who were not fit to begin a new life in
a new place, were retained in the hands of the trustees.
The general result of this relation, however, was to move
the negroes out of the State; and this was no doubt due
partly to the legal aspects of the case as seen in the decision
in the Contentnea Society *vs.* Dickinson, to which reference
has already been made.[1]   This decision might well convince
the Quakers that they could not hope to make society ownership a permanent feature and they used more and more
the practice of sending the slaves away.   Another inducement to send the slaves away, and an earlier one, was the
liability of having them become a charge on the society.
It is with evident feelings of relief that the agents of the
Eastern Quarter in 1820 reported that the four hundred
slaves who were owned by the Yearly Meeting had been
managed so as to avoid expense, except for sending some
away.   In 1822 the number in hand was four hundred and
fifty and the Yearly Meeting ordered that the trustees
should receive no slaves except from Quakers.   It was for
this reason that a committee was appointed to examine the
laws of the free States to see if negroes might be sent
thither.   In 1823 this committee made its report in favor of
Ohio, Indiana and Illinois, and steps were taken to remove
the slaves as rapidly as possible, and $200 was voted to
defray the expenses.   They were sent to Pennsylvania, to
the Northwest, to Hayti, and, perhaps, to Liberia.   Six hundred and fifty-two had gone by 1830 and four hundred and
two were still under care.   The expense of moving so many
had reached $12,769.50, not all of which had been borne
by the North Carolina Friends, for in 1829 the Rhode

---

[1] See Quaker pamphlet cited, p. 32.   Although this decision was
not given till 1827, the case was begun earlier than 1822.

Island Yearly Meeting had contributed to the work $1351.50. Sometimes the negroes themselves paid part of the expense of removal by being hired out for wages, the surplus earnings being saved for this purpose. But the Friends were not ungenerous in this matter. On one occasion four women had promised to go and leave their husbands in slavery. At the last moment they refused to go, and the Friends bought the husbands at an expense of $1400 and sent them along with the faithful wives. The owners of the husbands were here equally benevolent, for they sold them at half their value. The last important removal was in 1836, when fifty-seven persons were sent to the Northwest and two hundred were left in the possession of the society. Many of these were old people and children. Death rapidly thinned the one class, and the members of the other were sent away as they became grown. In 1848 the number was about twelve, and it was said by the Committee on Sufferings: "It is believed that there is no instance of any [slaves] being held among us so as to deprive them of the benefit of their labor."[1]   In 1856 there were eighteen still under care.

The work of the Quakers was not easy. "Such," says the narrative of the Committee on Sufferings, from which I have already taken so much, "it would appear was the prejudice against freeing the slaves, the danger of their being carried off and sold in distant parts, the ignominy of their situation; that there was no way but to remove them to the free governments as fast as their circumstances would permit." Many Quakers and other persons moved from North Carolina to the Northwest, and the Friends often sent slaves whom they desired to free along with these emigrants. Sometimes a large number would be sent, and trusted Quakers would go along with them with authority to effect emancipation. Sometimes a ship would be chartered, as when the negroes wanted to go to the West Indies.

---

[1] Quaker pamphlet cited, p. 40.

To the Quakers must be given, also, much of the credit
for the organization of the North Carolina Manumission
Society. This society existed in the region around Greensboro, where the non-slaveholding element was strong. It
had members who were not Quakers, but it had many, perhaps a majority, who were of that faith. This society had
many branches and its inception was doubtless due to the
efforts of Charles Osborn, a Quaker minister, who organized various branches in Guilford County in 1816. In the
same year these branches were organized into a general
society, and in the following year this society agreed to
act in connection with the American Colonization Society.
To this move there was, however, much opposition, mostly
from the Quaker members. These were largely abolitionists and they looked upon colonization as an aid to slavery.
The minority seceded and continued to meet at New Garden
till most of them had moved to the West. The society,
however, continued to grow. In 1821, Benjamin Lundy
appeared in North Carolina and made anti-slavery speeches
in Guilford and Randolph Counties. He came from Tennessee, where Elihu Embree had already inaugurated a
promising anti-slavery movement.[1] In 1824 the term
"Colonization" was dropped from the name of the society.
In 1825 there were thirty-three local societies[2] with a total
of more than 1000 members. In 1827 there were forty
branches; but this was the flood-tide of the movement.
Public sentiment was turning against the cause of the abolitionists, as has been already seen. In 1834 the society had
its last meeting. Of those who had been leaders many had
emigrated. Many of the rank and file had either gone
away or been frightened by the greater vehemence of the
pro-slavery advocates. Whatever of vitality it had left
seems to have been thrown into support of the Under-

[1] Hoss: "Sketch of Elihu Embree." Publication of Vanderbilt
Southern History Association, No. 2, 1897.
[2] Weeks says thirty-six, but names only thirty-three. "Southern
Quakers," p. 240.

ground Railway. It became in its later days emphatically abolitionist. It advised its members to subscribe for Lundy's paper, and in 1830 it passed resolutions in support of William Lloyd Garrison.[1]

The Presbyterian Church of North Carolina had never so large a proportion of negro members as the Methodist or Baptist Churches, but it opened its doors as freely to the slaves. These were given special seats and admitted to the sacrament of the communion after the whites. That many of them became faithful and obedient Christians there can be no doubt. Rev. J. D. Mitchell, a Presbyterian pastor of Lynchburg, Va., said in 1858, after twenty-seven years in the pastorate: "Our colored members have exhibited a uniform consistency of moral and religious character. In my long pastorate I remember only three cases of discipline among the servants. * * * Instances of high-toned piety are frequent among them."[2] The *Southern Presbyterian* bore evidence that the Bible was often read in the churches where there were negroes, especially the parts dealing with the duties of master and slaves. The reading of the Bible, it thought, was not necessary to getting to heaven, and if slaves were taught to read they would read incendiary literature more than the Bible. "There are more pious persons among the blacks," it added, "than among any similar class of people in the world."[3] It is likely that the attitude of this Church in North Carolina did not differ materially from the spirit of these utterances.

At first the Church was not hostile to emancipation in the abstract, but it was not inclined to wholesale abolition in actual practice. In 1787 the Synod of New York and Philadelphia declared that it highly approved of universal liberty and of "the interest which many States had taken in promoting the abolition of slavery;" but since indolent and

[1] See "North Carolina Manumission Society," by C. C. Weaver, Trinity College (N. C.) Historical Papers, series 1, p. 71.
[2] Quoted in De Bow's *Review*, vol. 24, pp. 277 and 279.
[3] *Ibid.*, vol. 18, p. 52.

ignorant persons would be a disadvantage in a community, it urged that slaves be educated, that they be encouraged to buy themselves, and that members use all efforts to secure abolition of slavery.[1]   In 1795 the question of fellowship with slaveholders was up, but elicited nothing but an injunction to brotherly love and charity. The same body in 1815 urged members to give religious education to the slaves, so that they might be fit for freedom when God might "open the door for their emancipation." At the same time it declared that trading in slaves and cruelty toward them were contrary to the spirit of Christ. The split between the Northern and Southern wings of the Church was already in sight, although it did not proceed so rapidly as among the Methodists. In 1818 the General Assembly endorsed abolition in the abstract and expressed sympathy for the South where most of the virtuous people were thought to be for emancipation. It urged such people to continue their efforts and exhorted others not to make "uncharitable reflection on their brethren, who unhappily live among slaves whom they cannot immediately set free." It also spoke decidedly against the separation of slave families by sale. Any church member who would do this ought to be suspended from fellowship, "unless there be such peculiar circumstances attending the case as can but seldom happen."[2] For some time after this the question was not brought up; but in 1835 it would be ignored no longer. A committee was appointed on the matter, and the next year it reported that slavery was a civil question and ought not to be considered by the Assembly. After some debate the matter was indefinitely postponed. But it was up again in 1845, when it was resolved that "since Christ and his inspired Apostles did not make the holding of slaves a bar to communion, we, as a Court of Christ, have no authority to do so; since they did not attempt to remove

---

[1] See "Presbyterianism and Slavery," an official document published for the use of the General Assembly in 1836.
[2] *Ibid.*, pp. 6–8.

it from the Church by legislation, we have no authority to legislate on that subject." The progress of the slaves could not be obtained by ecclesiastical legislation or by "indiscriminate denunciations against slaveholders, without regard to their character or circumstances." The resolution passed by 168 to 13 votes.[1] By such action this conservative Church put off its division till the war was actually at hand. This relation of the general Church to slavery must have influenced the attitude of the local Church. It no doubt kept up a conservative and abiding interest in the welfare of the slave on the part of the Church authorities.

What Henry Evans was in the Methodist Church and Ralph Freeman in the Baptist, John Chavis was in the Presbyterian Church. In native ability he was no doubt equal to either of the other two, but in education he was superior to them. He was, probably, born in Granville County, near Oxford, about 1763. He was a full-blooded negro of dark brown color. He was born free. In early life he attracted the attention of the whites, and he was sent to Princeton College to see if a negro would take a collegiate education. He was a private pupil under the famous Dr. Witherspoon, and his ready acquisition of knowledge soon convinced his friends that the experiment would issue favorably. After leaving Princeton he went to Virginia, sent thither, no doubt, to preach to the negroes. In 1801 he was at the Hanover (Virginia) Presbytery, "riding as a missionary under the direction of the General Assembly." In 1805, at the suggestion of Rev. Henry Patillo, of North Carolina, he returned to his native State. For some cause, I know not what, it was not till 1809 that he was received as a licentiate by the Orange Presbytery. Although he preached frequently to the regular congregations at Nutbush, Shiloh, Island Creek, and other churches in the neighborhood, I do not find that he was called to a church as pastor. Mr. George Wortham, a lawyer of Gran-

[1] See "American Slavery as Viewed and Acted on by the Presbyterian Church in America," by Rev. A. T. McGill, 1865.

ville County, said in 1883: "I have heard him read and explain the Scriptures to my father's family repeatedly. His English was remarkably pure, containing no 'negroisms;' his manner was impressive; his explanations clear and concise, and his views, as I then thought and still think, entirely orthodox. He was said to have been an acceptable preacher, his sermons abounding in strong common sense views and happy illustrations, without any efforts at oratory or sensational appeals to the passions of his hearers. He had certainly read God's Word much and meditated deeply on it. He had a small but select library of theological works, in which were to be found the works of Flavel, Buxton, Boston, and others. I have now two volumes of "Dwight's Theology," which were formerly in his possession. He was said by his old pupils to have been a good Latin and a fair Greek scholar. He was a man of intelligence on general subjects and conversed well." He continued to preach till in 1831 the Legislature forbade negroes to preach. It was a trial to him and he appealed to the Presbytery. That body could do nothing more than recommend him "to acquiesce in the decision of the Legislature referred to, until God in his providence shall open to him a path of duty in regard to the exercise of his ministry." Acquiesce he did. He died in 1838 and the Presbytery continued to his widow the pension which it had formerly allowed to him.

Mr. Chavis' most important work was educational. Shortly after his return to North Carolina he opened a classical school, teaching in Granville, Wake, and Chatham Counties. His school was for the patronage of the whites. Among his patrons were the best people of the neighborhood. Among his pupils were Willie P. Mangum, afterwards United States Senator, and Priestley H. Mangum, his brother, Archibald and John Henderson, sons of Chief Justice Henderson, Charles Manly, afterwards Governor of the State, Dr. James L. Wortham of Oxford, N. C., and many more excellent men who did not become so distinguished in their communities. Rev. James H. Horner, one of the best teachers of high schools the State has produced, said of John Clavis: "My father not only went to school to him but boarded in his family * * * The school was the best at that time to be found in the State."

All accounts agree that John Chavis was a gentleman. Mr. Paul C. Cameron, a son of Judge Duncan Cameron, and a prominent man in Orange County, said: "In my boyhood life at my father's home I often saw John Chavis, a venerable old negro man, recognized as a freeman and as a preacher or clergyman of the Presbyterian Church. As such he was received by my father and treated with kindness and consideration, and respected as a man of education, good sense, and most estimable character. * * * He seemed familiar with the proprieties of social life, yet modest and unassuming, and sober in his language and opinions. He was polite—yes, courtly; but it was from his heart and not affected. I remember him as a man without guile. His conversation indicated that he lived free from all evil or suspicion, seeking the good opinion of the public by the simplicity of his life and the integrity of his conduct. If he had any vanity he most successfully concealed it. * * * I write of him as I remember him and as he was appreciated by my superiors, whose respect he enjoyed." The same gentleman adds that the slaves were amazed to see a negro receive so much respect from the whites. Others have confirmed Mr. Cameron's statement.[1] From a source of the greatest respectability I have learned that this negro was received as an equal socially and asked to table by the most respectable people of the neighborhood. Such was the position of the best specimen of the negro race in North Carolina in the days before race prejudices were aroused. It goes without saying that such a negro would not receive the same

---

[1] The facts here given were collected by Dr. Charles Phillips, of the University of North Carolina, and used by Dr. C. L. Smith for the short sketch of John Chavis, which he included in his "History of Education in North Carolina," Washington, D. C., 1888, pp. 138-140.

treatment to-day. That such is true is due to that strenuous state of feeling which preceded and followed forcible emancipation. So much the cause of humanity would have gained could slavery have been removed by reason!

In 1830 John Clavis, described as an educated colored Presbyterian preacher, was teaching a school for free colored children in Raleigh. Joseph Gales attended a public examination at this school in April, 1830, and said in his paper: "It was an example, both in behavior and scholarship which their white superiors might take pride in imitating." He complimented a speech in which Chavis told his pupils that they possessed but an humble station in life; but that even they could make themselves useful.[1]

The Protestant Episcopal Church was not indifferent to the spiritual welfare of the slaves, although it had not so many slave members as some other churches. The proportion is indicated for 1857, as follows: Communicants, white 2341, colored 345; and catechumens (Sunday School pupils), white 1105 and colored 488. In 1858 it was: Communicants, white 2364 and colored 353; and catechumens, white 943 and colored 351. I have been unable to find full statistics for the whole time, but the above figures show the proportions for the years when this church probably had its largest number of members.

Here the members must have been mostly house servants, since the Episcopalians were largely slaveholders, and the 2364 communicants must have owned many thousands of slaves. Usually the colored people occupied the seats reserved for the slaves, as in other churches. Sometimes there were special missions for the slaves. Capt. T. W. Battle, of Edgcombe County, had one, but discontinued it after a year because the slaves took no interest in it. Mr. Josiah Collins and Rev. W. S. Pettigrew had similar enterprises in Washington County, and there seems to have been one in connection with the church at Tarborough.[2]

---

[1] Raleigh *Register*, April 19, 1830.
[2] For facts here mentioned I am indebted to Dr. K. P. Battle of the University of North Carolina.

CHAPTER IV.

INDUSTRIAL AND SOCIAL RELATIONS OF SLAVERY.

Population.—At the outbreak of the Revolution there were by the most probable estimate 36,000 colored people in North Carolina.[1] From then till 1790 no facts for an estimate have come under my observation. From the latter date till 1860 the numbers of whites, free negroes and slaves, as included in the census tables, were as follows:

Year.	Whites.	Increase. Per Cent.	Free Colored.	Increase. Per Cent.	Slaves.	Increase. Per Cent.	Total.
1790	288,204	. .	4,975	. .	100,572	. .	393,751
1800	337,764	17.19	7,043	41.56	133,296	32.53	478,103
1810	376,410	11.44	10,266	45.76	168,824	26.65	555,500
1820	419,200	11.36	14,612	42.33	205,017	21.43	638,829
1830	472,823	12.79	19,534	33.74	245,601	19.79	737,987
1840	484,870	2.54	22,732	16.31	245,817	.08	753,419
1850	553,028	14.05	27,463	20.81	288,548	17.38	869,039
1860	629,942	14.42	30,463	10.92	331,059	14.73	992,622

From this table it is seen that the increase of the whites was slow, being normal at about 13½ per cent., a rate decidedly slower than that maintaining since the war. This slow increase is no doubt due largely to emigration which took off many of the non-slaveholding farmers to the Northwest and many of the slaveholders to the far South. The latter movement was strongest from 1800 to 1840; the former from 1830 to 1860. Where the two overlapped, from 1830 to 1840, the population was well-nigh stationary.

---

[1] See "Slavery and Servitude in North Carolina," p. 22.

The number of free negroes depended on the number of emancipations plus the natural increase in the free negro families. Emancipation was considerably practiced till 1820. After that the laws grew harder on free negroes. Many of them left the State, and thus the increase was reduced. During the last decade of slavery this increase was smaller than ever before, and had slavery endured till 1870 it would, no doubt, have been well-nigh nothing.

Of the slave population the greatest increase was from 1790 to 1800, when the slave trade was still allowed, but after this source of increase had been destroyed there is a decided falling off. The remarkable drop from 1830 to 1840 has sometimes been attributed to an erroneous census. If the claim be true then it is still true that the increase was very small, since from 1830 to 1850 it was only 17.48 per cent. In the days when many whites moved to Georgia and Alabama, and other cotton States, there must have been a considerable drain on the numbers of the slave population. But later on when the great demand for slaves in these States had raised the price paid for them a great many more were sent. This probably accounts for the slow increase in the census tables after 1830.

There were 34,658 slaveholders in North Carolina in 1860, and these owned in all 331,059 slaves, or an average of 9.6 to each owner. In Virginia there were 9.4 slaves to each owner, and in South Carolina there were 15. For North Carolina there had been from 1850 till 1860 a lessening of the number of slaves to an owner, since it was in 1850 10.1 slaves to each owner.

Distribution.—In the colonial period the eastern counties had most of the slaves; but throughout the period of statehood the West acquired continually more of them. It never had as many as the East, but along the upland rivers, and wherever in the West there was fertile land, there the large slave-tended farm was found. This was true of the upper Roanoke section of the Yadkin, and of other river sections. In 1790 there were in the western counties 30,068 slaves

and in the East 70,504. In 1860 the same western counties
had 146,463 slaves and the eastern 184,596. In the West
the ratio of increase in seventy years was 387 per cent.,
while in the East it was 161 per cent. In 1790 there were in
the same western counties 136,655 whites, and in 1860 the
number was 385,724. In 1790 the same eastern counties
had 151,549 whites, and in 1860 they had 244,218. Thus it
will be seen that for these seven decades the ratio for the
increase of the whites in the West was 182 per cent., and for
those in the East it was 61 per cent.[1] Plainly enough the
West was gaining rapidly on the East in regard to slave
population. This was partly due to the extension of the
area of cotton cultivation. Counties like Mecklenberg,
Anson and Union were properly under the influence of the
western ideas and life in 1790; but in 1860 they were great
cotton counties and largely slaveholding. Moreover, in
other western counties, which by 1800 were past the pioneer
stage, there grew up continually numerous wealthy families.
They owned slaves. The slaves competed with the small
white farmers. Thus there began slowly that process by
which slavery always eats out all the life of a free yeomanry.
The small farmers sold their farms and moved to the
Northwest, the slaveholders bought the farms and consoli-
dated landholding. Had slavery continued till the present
time some wonderful changes would have taken place in this
part of the State. There is every reason to believe that
besides the tobacco industry, which might profitably have
been conducted here, this would have become, along with
parts of Virginia, a notable breeding ground for slaves to be
sent southward.

The progress of the slave population in the State could
not have been due in any considerable extent to importa-

---

[1] Of course the selection of a dividing line between the East and the
West is a matter more or less arbitrary, but the change of a dozen
counties along this line, where white and black populations remained
relatively constant, would make no appreciable difference in the
proportions given in the text.

tion.   Before the final prohibition of the foreign slave trade
by Congress in 1808, there was a strong feeling against it
in North Carolina.   In 1774 the Provincial Congress of the
colony resolved that they would not import or purchase
any slaves brought into the colony after November, 1774.[1]
This was part of the body of resolutions by the first Provincial Congress, and was due as much to the desire to
retaliate on Great Britain as to opposition to the slave
trade.   How well this resolution was executed I am not
able to say; but it was, no doubt, often violated; for, in 1786
(chap. 5), the Assembly passed a law the preamble of which
ran: "WHEREAS, The importation of slaves into this State
is productive of evil consequences and highly impolitic."
In accordance with this patriotic sentiment 40 shillings was
to be levied on each imported slave under seven years old and
over forty, and £5 on those from seven to twelve and from
thirty to forty years, and £10 on those from twelve
to thirty years.   This duty was to be levied whether
the slaves were imported by land or by sea.   This was
aimed avowedly at the slave trade, and exception was made
in favor of incoming settlers who brought slaves, and persons who received foreign slaves by gift, marriage or inheritance.   Besides, a tax of £5 was to be collected on all
slaves imported directly from Africa.   A further section prohibited the introduction into the State of slaves from the
States which had then recently liberated their slaves, and
directed that those already so imported should be sent to
the places whence they came.   The motives for making this
law I can know only inferentially.   There seems to have
been behind it an honest desire to restrict the number of
slaves in North Carolina, and a purpose to protect domestic
slavery from the disquieting influence of the more unman-
ageable slaves from Africa and the West Indies.

The public opinion, however, soon changed, and the act

---

[1] "Colonial Records of North Carolina," IX, p. 1046.   Also
" American Archives," 4th series, I, p. 735.

was repealed in 1790. But almost immediately there
occurred an incident which secured the enactment of still
severer laws against the slave trade. I refer to the Haytien
outbreak, which occurred in 1791. These outrages, bad as
they were, were exaggerated in American minds and filled
Southern hearts with terror.[1] In 1794 (chap. 2) a strict law
was passed forbidding the importation of slaves or indented
colored persons under a penalty of £100 fine. This law
did not forbid a person who came into the State to settle
to bring his slaves with him. A year later (Laws of 1795,
chap. 16) it was provided that this privilege should not
apply to persons coming from the West Indies, the Bahamas
and the "southern coast of America," if the imported
negroes were over fifteen years old.

The foreign slave trade was prohibited by Congress from
1808, and in the same year the North Carolina Assembly
repealed its law of 1794.[2] The National Statute left the
disposition of the illegally imported slaves to the States in
which they should be taken up. The North Carolina
Assembly took up the matter in 1816 (chap. 12), and enacted
that such slaves should be sold by the sheriff for the use of
the State, one-fifth to go to the informer. This law
remained in force till the war.[3] This National Statute could
not have been enforced very well, if at all, before 1816, for
the law of that year provided that slaves imported into the
State from abroad before 1816 and the descendants of the
same should not be sold according to this law, but that the
owners thereof should have legal titles made out and certified by the sheriffs. In view of this law and of the general
loose administration of the National Statute in the South,
it is safe to say that it was not always enforced in North
Carolina after 1816.

---

[1] See Du Bois: "Suppression of the Slave Trade," pp. 72 and 73.
[2] Laws of 1808, chap. 16.
[3] Revised Statutes, chap. 111, secs. 1–6, and Revised Code, chap.
107, secs. 1–6.

As to the prices of slaves it has been impossible to procure any trustworthy evidence. It is enough to call attention to the fact that the opening of the cotton industry with the greater demand for slaves in the Gulf States continued to advance the prices. Slavery became more profitable, and North Carolina found it fixed in her life more than was formerly expected. It has already been pointed out how slavery extended itself at this period into the western counties with the probable reason that this region raised slaves for the Southern markets. It was the ever acting law of economic rent applied to slaveholding. As the price of the product increased, territory that was formerly below the point of diminishing returns was now taken within the area of cultivation.

The Regulation of the Slave's Life.—Next to the loss of liberty the worst evil connected with slavery was the fact that it left the welfare of the slave to the accidental temper of the master. If the latter were humane and intelligent the slave fared well. If he were otherwise the slave fared poorly. A correspondent has called to my attention the fact that a master's treatment of his slaves corresponded relatively to his treatment of his children: good father, good master; careless or cruel father, careless or cruel master. There were all kinds of masters as there are all kinds of fathers. Some undoubtedly were cruel; some undoubtedly were wisely humane; many were neither the one nor the other, but gave their slaves such care as custom demanded, just as many men clothe and train their children without really having any opinions of their own about the matter.

Of the slave-owners there were the holders of large slave herds and the holders of few slaves. Of the former there was the cultured class of planters and the more ordinary class of wealthy farmers about which I have already spoken. The gentleman planter type was not so numerous in North Carolina as elsewhere in the South. Such masters were often absentee landlords, though this was not general in

the State.   Here their relation to the slaves was patriarchal.
As a class they were careful of the slaves' health and morals,
and philanthropic students of the theories of good master-
ship.   The wealthy farmers rarely lived away from their
estates.   They were usually religious.   They were thrifty and
honest.   Their sons worked in the fields along with the
slaves, sometimes leading the plow gang, and sometimes
swinging a cradle in the harvest.   Their wives superintended
the making of the slave clothing, the cooking of the slave
dinners, and the nursing of the slave patients.   Here the
slave fared best, and this class was strong in North Carolina.
It extended all over the State, and was extensively found
in the West.   The lot of the slave who belonged to the owner
of few slaves might be bad—and was usually not good.   He
was frequently overworked or underfed.   The straitened
condition of his master, often not an enlightened man, was
responsible for this.

Next to the master the overseer was the most important
personage.   If the master were absent his powers were
great.   He was usually a white man, but rarely a slave.
Often a man owned several plantations, on each of which
he would place an overseer, and over all of which he would
keep continual oversight.   Overseers were of two classes.
Those on large plantations must be men of intelligence and
men who could take care of slaves as property.   They commanded good salaries, often getting $100 a month.   On the
smaller plantations inferior men were employed, and the
slaves there were not so well cared for.   Here an overseer
was well paid at from $200 to $400 a year.   What an overseer should do properly to fulfill his office may be seen in
the statement of a master in *De Bow's Magazine* in 1856.[1]
In managing negroes, says the writer, the first aim of the
overseer should be to obey the instructions of the master
in respect to them; the second to satisfy them that he is
doing so.   He should always allow the slave easy appeal to

---

[1] Vol. 21, p. 277.

the master, and not to do so must be due to bad temper, false dignity, or the notion that the slave has no rights. If a slave makes a false complaint he should be punished for it, and the privilege of complaining should not extend to matters affecting the overseer's character, for a negro may not testify against a white man. Some overseers declared that no negroes should complain of them, and that if they did, they (the overseers) would whip them in spite of the masters. "This," exclaimed the writer, "is simply brutal and no man of spirit will permit it." Still it is bad policy not to punish a slave without the consent of the master. An overseer should be kind to the slaves, speaking in a low tone, but firmly. Negroes should not be fretted at, for it injured their capacity for work, and when practiced on the young had been known to lessen their value. Fretting also injured the overseer. "The habit of swearing at or before negroes an overseer should never indulge in. If the negro is not allowed to swear because it is disrespectful to the overseer, the latter should not swear because it is disrespectful to his Maker. Besides, it shocks some pious negroes and sets a bad example to them all." The overseer should visit the cabins and promote cleanliness there, see that clothes and shoes are repaired, and on Sunday he should require all the slaves to appear in clean clothes. He should rather encourage their taste for finery than ridicule it. He should consult with the old men about the work—some of them were very intelligent. He should be disposed to share their labor. "Nothing more reconciles a negro to his work than the overseer sharing it with him. Let him go with them in heat, rain and cold. If they shuck corn at night let him be with them." Another writer in the same magazine[1] declared that no one should try to manage slaves who had not firmness, fearlessness and self-control. Punishment should not be cruel. "If ever any of my negroes are cruelly and inhumanely treated, bruised, maimed, or otherwise

---

[1] Vol. 21, pp. 617–620.

injured," the overseer was dismissed. Each place was to keep enough milch cows to furnish milk for the slaves. The overseer must care for the sick, especially for the pregnant women. Nurses should be provided for the sick, and mothers of young children should not be assigned full tasks. These regulations were prepared by two successful farmers who did not live in North Carolina yet they are standards for slavery as a whole, and bring to us vividly the office of the overseer. Possibly they were never enforced entirely. Certainly they could not have been always enforced, but there is no doubt that the spirit of them was present on many plantations. It was this spirit and its practical realization in many ways which gave some foundation to the claim that the master provided better for the physical wants of the slaves than the freed negro provides for himself in the days since the war. The claim is to-day debatable, but it is necessary to remember that physical wants are not the chief thing in life.

I have been able to get the following account of slave life on a rice plantation near Wilmington, N. C. My informant is a son of the gentleman who owned the place for some years before the war, and in his young manhood he was overseer on the farm. He is now a prosperous physician, and I have every reason to believe that his information is trustworthy. He says: "There were about one hundred slaves on the plantation. They were called at dawn and went to the fields under the care of drivers at sunrise. Two meals were served each day, one at 9 a. m. and one at 1 or 2 p. m. The daily allowance of food was one quart of meal, which was given from March 1 till October 1, one-half a pound of meat, and one pint of molasses a week for each adult. Sweet potatoes were given from October to March instead of meal, and peas were allowed in planting time. There was a regular allowance of tobacco. The meals were prepared by the cooks and sent to the field ready cooked. Milk was furnished at the cook's place. The tasks were light, and most of them were finished by 2 p. m.

After they were done the slaves might do what they liked. They usually slept or went fishing. Among themselves the slaves were immoral, but, generally speaking, there were no illicit relations between them and the white men. The white boys were sometimes intimate with the housemaids. The slaves went to Sunday School, and the owners of this and the adjoining farms paid a Methodist preacher to preach to them once a month." But my informant saw but small results in the field hands. The negroes were contented and happy among themselves, if let alone by outside influences. The owner always counted on their stealing and took no notice of small offenses. They were not allowed to go off the plantation, except by special permission. They were not allowed to buy whiskey, but occasionally the master would give it to them, and it was a race trait that all of them, men, women and children, liked it. Under the care of his owner the slave's health was good, much better than it is now. Slave mothers frequently neglected their children, while for the children of the whites they manifested great affection. This last point is often corroborated. Said another gentleman: "I have often seen the slave women come from the fields to the house of the old woman who took care of the small children during the day, take their babies in their arms, nurse them, and put them down without the least show of affection."

"Negro slavery," continued the gentleman whose statements I was just quoting, "was profitable in producing rice, cotton and turpentine. One good hand could thus make in rice from $300 to $400 a year above his expenses, and in turpentine he could make as much as $1000 a year. On the farm in question $10,000 a year was cleared in bank from the rice crop. When masters made no profit it was because the negroes were not properly cared for. Few of the old slaveholders had runaway negroes. These negroes usually afflicted people who had recently begun to have slaves, particularly Northern men who had married and settled in the South. These people did not understand the negro, and expected too much from him. A man who was cruel to his negroes was not highly respected in the community by the best people. An evidence of the solicitude of the good masters for their slaves was the difficulty which the authorities experienced in getting slaves hired to them to construct fortifications at the outbreak of the war. Masters would not trust their slaves in the hands of the officers. Among the prominent characteristics of the negro," concludes my informant, "were no gratitude, no resentment and a deep love of home."

By the side of this statement I am fortunately able to place the account of slave life on the plantation of a well-to-do farmer of the central part of the State. The farmer was a well-known Baptist preacher, and the account is from his son, who is now a respected minister in the same church. The locality was in the area of cotton production, and on the farm were from forty to fifty slaves. The narrator says:

I never saw or knew [my father] to whip [a slave] save sometime to correct a child for some evil, and then the whipping was light. He never overworked them, for I was for a number of years foreman of eight or ten plows. They started to work when I started; when I rested they rested; when I stopped at evening they stopped; when I got a holiday they got one. They ate what I ate, though at different tables. Never a day's ration was issued to any of them. They were well housed and were allowed to use all the firewood they needed from the same yard from which the white family got its own supply. They were well shod and clothed, wearing the same kind of goods I used on the farm—all home-made. In winter all the slaves, from the youngest to the oldest, wore woollens. My father retained two of the best physicians in the county to give them any needed attention, the same as his family had. He gave each year to each slave large enough to work a "patch of ground" and the time to work it, in order that each might have some money of his own to spend as he chose. The breeding women he was always careful should never be worked too hard or in any way strained. When any of the slave children were very sick they were brought into the house of the white family and there attended as one of the white children. He always provided for them to go to church on Sunday, allowing them to use the farm teams when necessary. They were invited to family prayers in the room of my parents. He often urged his children to read the Bible to them in their own houses, for each slave family had a separate home, which, in the main, was more comfortable than three-fourths of the colored people now have, or perhaps nine-tenths of them. One of his old slaves told me recently[1] that he has never been as happy or well provided for since he has been free as he was while a slave. Much more I could say, but this is perhaps enough. I state the above on my honor as a Christian minister. P. S.—He never allowed his sons to whip any of the field hands.

In a further communication the same gentleman says of slavery as an institution:

It never paid my father, only by the increase of his slaves. His land was poor and this may have been the reason why he never made any money by it only as above stated. He never kept any account of debtor and creditor in running his farm. I was very well acquainted over the county in *ante bellum* days and knew of but one or two parties who failed to clothe well and treat well their slaves. Those parties, like some of this day, never had a good set of harness, or good stock or farm tools. In all my section of the county I knew of no whites who did not own some land and have their own homes. I knew but one free negro, a woman, and she lived with my father. She was a housemaid and worked for her victuals and clothes.

The difference between the conditions of slaves in North and South Carolina is illustrated graphically in the following statement of a negro whom Mr. Olmsted met in South Carolina about 1855.[2] The negro was free, and with his son had come from Rockingham County, N. C., to peddle out two wagon loads of tobacco in eastern South Carolina. Said the old man in the course of the conversation:

"Fac' is, master, 'pears like wite folks doan ginerally like niggers in dis country; dey doan ginerally talk so to niggers like as do in my country; de niggers ain't so happy heah; 'pears like the wite folks is kind o' different, somehow."

"Well, I've been thinking myself the niggers did not look so well here as they did in North Carolina and Virginia; they are not so well clothed, and they don't appear so bright as they do there."

"Well, massa," was the answer, "Sundays dey is mighty well clothed, dis country; 'pears like dere ain't nobody looks better Sundays dan dey do. But, Lord! working days, seems like dey had no

---

[1] This narrative was sent me in 1896.
[2] "Journey to the Seaboard Slave States," pp. 389-393.

close dey could keep on 'em at all, master. Dey is almost naked
wen dey's at work, some un 'em. Why, master, up in our country
de wite folks, why some un 'em has ten or twelve; dey doan hev no
real big plantations like dey has heah, but some un 'em has ten or
twelve niggars, maybe, and dey juss lives and talks along wid 'em.
If dey gits a niggar and he doan behave himself, dey won't keep him;
dey juss tell him, sar, he must look up anudder master, and if he doan
find himself one, I tell 'ou, wen the trader cum along, dey sell him
and he totes him away. Dey always sell off all de bad niggars out
of our country; dat's de way all de bad niggar and all dem no-account
niggar keep a comin' down heah; dat's de way on't, master.''

To this, which is offered only for what it is worth, add the
statement of Mr. Olmsted himself: "So far as I have
observed," he says, "slaves show themselves worthy of trust
most where their masters are most considerate and liberal
to them. Far more so, for instance, on the small farms in
North Carolina than on the plantations of Virginia and
South Carolina."[1]

Here we have three pictures, more or less complete, of
slave life (1) on a fertile farm in the East, under conditions
of extensive farming, (2) on a large farm in the central part
of the State, and (3) on the small farms of the western part
of the State. I must believe that each picture is given fairly,
so far as it goes. All show that slavery in North Carolina
was not so harsh as elsewhere. To this conclusion I may
add the positive evidence of Mr. Olmsted. He says: "The
aspect of North Carolina with regard to slavery is, in some
respects, less lamentable than that of Virginia. There is not
only less bigotry upon the subject and more freedom of
conversation, but I saw here, in the institution more of the
patriarchal than in any other State. The slave more
frequently appears as a family servant—a member of his
master's family, interested with him in the fortune, good or
bad. This is the result of less concentration of wealth in
families or individuals * * * Slavery thus loses much
of its inhumanity. It is still questionable, however, if, as

---

[1] "Journey to the Seaboard Slave States," p. 447.

the subject race approaches civilization, the dominant race is not proportionately detained in its progress."[1]

I am able also to publish the following from a gentleman of great intelligence and humanity, who was intimately connected by birth and association with the most prominent people of the State. He says:

I did not like the institution of slavery, but I wish you to know: (1) That while the laws were severe the natural amiability of the people tempered the administration of them. I never whipped a grown up slave in my life, nor did my father, nor brothers; and such families were the rule and not the exception. Nor did I ever witness any of the scenes of barbarity so much spoken of. Although a large slaveholder, and raised among slaveholders, I never saw a grown person punished in my life. By grown person I mean fifteen and sixteen years old and upwards. The separation of husband and wife, parent and young child, were not common. My family never did it, nor did any of the families known to me, and I am sure that the great majority of families in North Carolina would not allow it. (2) To balance the cases of barbarity I wish you to remember that the wives and other dependents of slaves were protected by the owners from brutality on the part of their slave-husbands, etc. The awful, horrible brutality of drunken husbands and fathers as seen in England, and the cities of the North was not allowed in the South. (3) You should not attribute to slaves the fine feelings of whites. They had recently been savages. Separation of children from parents, etc., was not to them what it is to whites. But there was in practice no more separation than in New England families, whose children as a rule scatter over the whole face of the earth. (4) The sum of misery was no greater among them *practically* than among the laboring classes in free countries. You may not believe all this, but I hope that it will be within your plan to mention that slave-owners claim this.

On the subject of mulattoes the same correspondent writes:

The number of mulattoes must not be held to prove corresponding licentiousness on the part of the whites. Many of them were descended from Indians and many were descended from mulattoes lawfully married. * * * The mulattoes were employed in towns and were hence more observed. I have seen great plantations with not one of them—all black.

If I were defending a side in the never ended controversy about the treatment of slaves by their masters, it would only

[1] "Journey to the Seaboard Slave States," p. 367.

be necessary to point out here that the essence of the misery
of slavery in the South and elsewhere was not physical
suffering, however frequently or infrequently that may have
occurred, but the mental and spiritual wretchedness that
follow a loss of liberty.   If you deny the rights of man to
the negro slaves you cut the heart out of the anti-slavery
argument.   By the side of the above testimony I shall place
some statements from an unpublished book[1] of Dr. Eli W.
Caruthers, of Greensboro, N. C., well known as the author of
some valuable volumes relating to the history of the State.
For events he claimed to know about he was the best kind of
authority.   Speaking of beating slaves cruelly, he said: "I
have known a number [of instances] myself in which
nobody in the neighborhood had any doubt that the death
of the slave was caused by the severity of his treatment, but
no attempt was made to punish the cruel perpetrators of the
deeds."[2]   The conjugal and parental instincts in the slaves
were lessened on account of the frequent breaking of family
ties by masters.   "I have known some instances," said he,
"in which [the slave family] have been permitted to live on
in great harmony and affection to an advanced age, but
such instances, so far as my observations have gone, have
been 'like angels' visits, few and far between.'   Generally, in
a few weeks at most, they have been separated, sold off
under the hammer like other stock and borne away to a
returnless distance."[3]   An evil result of this condition of
affairs was that the negroes did not regard marriage as
strictly as they ought.   They married carelessly and
separated easily.   The result was much licentiousness.   A
few Christian owners did what they could to prevent the
separation of their married slaves, but after their death, if
not before, the slaves were sold for debt or to satisfy less
scrupulous heirs.[4]   In his own congregation was an excel-

[1] "American Slavery and the Immediate Duty of Slaveholders."
See the author's "Anti-Slavery Leaders," p. 56.
[2] *Ibid.*, p. 282.   [3] *Ibid.*, p. 299.   [4] *Ibid.*, p. 307.

lent man and wife, both slaves, who were very fond of one another and of their children. Their master died in debt. Their eldest daughter was sold to a speculator, and other children were also sold. The honest parents were heart-broken and succumbed under their sorrow. "I could fill a volume with similar instances," exclaimed the indignant writer.[1]

From an intelligent gentleman, who was a large planter in the eastern part of the State, I have the following:

Slaves were generally fed three times a day; but I knew several men who fed only twice a day. I practised medicine on many plantations and never found negroes that were so badly fed that it interfered with my treatment. A few people stinted their children and their slaves also. Usually the slave fared as well as the child, relatively speaking. If any difference was made it was in favor of the slave, who was property. I knew a few people who treated slaves badly. Such masters were brutal by nature. The morality of the negro was greater then than now. One fault, however, was the putting of more than one family into one room. This was not unusual on plantations. The profit to the employer of the labor of the slave was perhaps greater than that of the negro freeman to-day. The negro pays in a region where the ground has to be stirred steadily; but he does not pay in a grass or grain country. He has not enough of the faculty of direction for the latter. The negro does not want or need free circulation of air in his living quarters. As a rule he sleeps in badly ventilated apartments and seems to suffer no ill effects. This is a conclusion from my experience as a physician. They always sleep with their heads covered up. Nearly all like the taste of whiskey.

From the same source I am able to give an incident, piteous as it is, but which from the trustworthy and direct source from which it comes to me I am not able to doubt. It illustrates most touchingly the hardships which came from breaking the Africans into slavery. About the beginning of this century when the large Collins plantation on Lake Phelps, Washington County, was being cleared a number of negroes just from Africa were put on the work. One

---

[1] "American Slavery and the Immediate Duty of Slaveholders." See the author's "Anti-Slavery Leaders," pp. 308 and 310.

of the features of the improvement was the digging of a canal. Many of the Africans succumbed under this work. When they were disabled they would be left by the bank of the canal, and the next morning the returning gang would find them dead. They were kept at night in cabins on the shore of the lake. At night they would begin to sing their native songs, and in a short while would become so wrought up that, utterly oblivious to the danger involved, they would grasp their bundles of personal effects, swing them on their shoulders, and setting their faces towards Africa, would march down into the water singing as they marched till recalled to their senses only by the drowning of some of the party. The owners lost a number of them in this way, and finally had to stop the evening singing. This incident was related to my informant by the gentleman who was overseer on this plantation when the incident occurred.

CHAPTER V.

THE TRIUMPH OF THE PRO-SLAVERY
SENTIMENT.

Slave Conspiracies.—The possibility of slave insurrections
was a source of the greatest solicitude to the Southern
whites. This was heightened about the close of the last
century by the Haytien outbreak and by the Nat Turner
attempt in 1831. Probably the slaves as a body were more
rebellious a century ago, when many of them were fresh
from African freedom, and probably the whites as time
passed knew better how to keep the slave from rebellion.
Certain it is that after the early decades of the nineteenth
century there were no attempts at conspiracy among the
North Carolina negroes.

After the reported conspiracy in Beaufort County, just
before the Revolution, no further trouble is reported till
1802. In that year the extreme northeastern part of the
State was thrown into paroxysms of terror by reports of a
slave insurrection. It is difficult to say just what was the
extent of the danger there. The insurrection was at first
reported to have gone through the counties of Camden,
Currituck, Pasquotank, Perquimons, Chowan, Hertford,
Martin, Bertie, Beaufort and Washington. At some places
the slaves were reported to have done great havoc, though
no definite acts of outrage were mentioned. Eighteen
negroes were reported to have been executed and a large
number to have been arrested. After awhile it was realized
that "various extravagant and unfounded reports," as the
Raleigh Register[1] put it, had been circulated. On July 27,

---

[1] June 1, 22 and 29, 1802.

1802, this paper published a full story of the affair by a reliable witness. It appears that in May of this year a report came to be circulated that the negroes were about to revolt. All those who were strongly suspected were arrested. Excitement ran high, and mob violence was averted with difficulty. The negroes were at length frightened into confession. They admitted that June 10 had been set for the beginning of a general insurrection, and that they were threatened with death if they revealed it, or if they did not join it. On the night of the tenth they were to form into groups of seven or eight, fire the houses of the whites, kill the white males over six years old, kill the women, black and white, except the young and handsome white women, who were to be kept for wives, and the young negro women, who were to be kept for waitresses. After finishing in the country they were to go to Plymouth, N. C., where they expected reinforcements, and where the work of destruction was to be continued. A few arms were deposited in the swamps, and they expected to get others. They had been told by their leaders that the rising would cover the whole country. The leaders were obstinate, but after much whipping they confessed to the conspiracy. Two of them were executed, and the others were whipped and sent to their homes. How a whole State might be terrified by such reports as were then in the air is seen by the fact that false alarms were given in Halifax and Franklin Counties, and in the former a negro was tried and convicted, but the community soon recovered from its shock, and both whites and blacks joined to petition the Governor to pardon him.[1]

In 1805 an outbreak of a similar kind was reported in Wayne County, about which a correspondent wrote to the *Register*[2] as follows: "We have been engaged in this county in the trying of negroes for poisoning the whites ever since Monday last. One suffered death at the stake (was burnt

---

[1] Raleigh *Register*, August 10, 17 and 24, 1802.
[2] *Ibid.*, July 23 and August 13, 1805.

alive) on Saturday last, for poisoning her master, mistress
and two others. Two more are under sentence of death, and
are to be hanged on next Wednesday." Thirteen, it was
said, were in prison, but some of them had been brought
from Sampson and Johnston Counties. The accused confessed that the plan was to kill the chief white men, and to
keep the others in slavery. Later advices stated that one
more negro was executed besides the two mentioned, and
others had lesser punishments, as whipping, pillorying,
transporting and cropping the ears. In neither of these
outbreaks, it will be noticed, is there mention of Northern
emissaries. Whatever plan there was among the negroes
was probably due either to their own suggestion or to some
negro who came in from the West Indies. Either source
was not improbable. There must have been then, and perhaps always, a large number of stronger minded slaves who
resented their situation. Of this class was one, "Yellow
Jack," who was advertised in 1812 as a runaway, who had
been overheard to say that "all should be free, and that he
saw no reason why the sweat of his brow should be
expended in supporting the extravagance and idleness of
any man," or words to that effect.[1]

In 1822 there was a slave rising in Charleston, S. C., in
which Denmark Vesey figured as leader. It had no effect
on the slaves of North Carolina, much to the relief of the
whites there.[2] But in 1821 there had been trouble of some
kind in Jones County. The militia was called out, and in
1823 the Assembly allowed its claim for services. The
Nat Turner insurrection of 1831 aroused great feeling in the
State, and this was chiefly responsible for the state of terror
that possessed the adjacent counties immediately thereafter,
when news was circulated of a similar conspiracy in Sampson and Duplin. The terror spread as far as Wake, and
even Raleigh was put into a state of defense, even the old

[1] Raleigh *Register*, June 5, 1812.
[2] *Ibid.*, August 20, and September 6, 13 and 1822.

men past the militia age volunteering for service. Johnston County called on Raleigh for ammunition and received a supply. The report stated that seventeen families had been murdered by the slaves. When it was reported in Hillsborough that Raleigh was in imminent danger the former place at once raised a military company and sent it to the latter. On careful investigation the reports were found to have been much exaggerated. It seems that a free negro had revealed a concerted plan in Duplin, Sampson, New Hanover, Wayne and Lenoir Counties for the negroes to rise on October 4, 1831, march to Wilmington, where they expected to get arms and recruits. Whatever plan there was, no whites were harmed. Twelve alleged leaders were taken and shot, and three others were hanged in Duplin, and the people were restored to confidence. In Wilmington the excitement had been painful. At one time it was reported that the infuriated blacks had reached a point two miles from the city. The whole available population was put under arms.[1] When men were so carried away by the prevailing fear as to credit such reports as the latter it was not unlikely that some of their judgments were wrong. I have it on the authority of the son of the man who was at that time sheriff of Sampson County that the negroes executed for this crime there were innocent, and that he had often heard his father say as much. This was the last attempted slave insurrection, so far as I have been able to learn, in North Carolina. It is singular that we find no more periods of terror from reported slave insurrections after the triumph of the pro-slavery element. It would be interesting to know whether or not these frights were of political origin.

The Growth of the Pro-Slavery Sentiment.—Intimately connected with the reported slave conspiracies was the growth of a stronger pro-slavery sentiment. Each period of excitement tended to weaken the arms of those who hoped

---

[1] Raleigh *Register*, October 15 and 21, 1831.

for final emancipation. It has been said that the Nat Turner insurrection and the active campaigns of Garrison and his associates turned the South into pro-slavery advocates. The statement is but partly true. The process of change in sentiment had begun some time before, and these events only hastened its culmination.

There was for some years before 1831 a considerable pro-slavery sentiment which made its presence felt in the Legislature. It was strongest in the East where there were more slaves. Opposed to it were the western counties. As they became more and more slaveholding, the non-slaveholding element leaving largely for the Western States, the pro-slavery faction was strengthened. They were, moreover, a party of action and they drew young men. Those who hoped for emancipation had no plan of action. They only awaited for some door to be opened to effect their hopes. They could not approve of the procedure of the abolitionists in the North. They realized that latent public opinion in the South was such that it would be folly to argue against slavery on the grounds of the rights of man. The half-hearted opposition they could make had no chance against the fervid arguments of the convinced and enthusiastic supporters of slavery.

The steps by which the pro-slavery minority was converted into a majority are obvious. In 1818 Mr. Mears, of New Hanover, introduced a bill to prohibit the teaching of slaves to read and write. It was lost on the second reading.[1] A year later a similar bill was unanimously rejected.[2] In 1825 a bill to prevent the escape of slaves by assuming the privileges of free negroes was indefinitely postponed. In 1825 free negroes were required to have license from the county justices to live in Raleigh. Licenses were given to those only who could prove good character.[3] In the same year the Governor in his annual message referred sarcasti-

[1] Raleigh *Register*, December 18, 1818.
[2] *Ibid.*, December 10, 1819.   [3] *Ibid.*, February 18, 1825.

cally to resolutions of the Ohio Legislature in regard to
abolition in the Southern States. He appreciated the interest of the non-slaveholders, but hoped they would "shortly
learn and practice what has familiarly been termed the
Eleventh Commandment, 'Let every one attend to his own
concerns.' "[1]   In the same year a bill to restrain improper
conversation between mulattoes and free negroes on the
subject of freedom was lost in committee.[2]   Another bill to
prevent the education of slaves, a bill to prevent free negroes
from migrating to North Carolina and a bill to forbid
emancipation societies were introduced but lost, the second
by a vote as close as 56 to 47.[3]   Evidently the pro-slavery
men were in earnest.[4]

The matter became graver in 1826.   In his message the
Governor referred to a petition from the Vermont Legislature
to the North Carolina government praying for the abolition
of slavery. The Northern agitation, he thought, "demanded
from us a sleepless vigilance." He recommended revision
of the laws relating to the militia, to the patrol, and to the
immigration of free negroes.[5]   A warm debate followed in
the Senate. Mr. Speight, of Greene, was particularly bel-
ligerent. "As a North Carolinian he felt that he was being
imposed upon, and that there was an improper attempt to
dictate to the Southern States in what manner they should
govern their own property; and before he would tamely
acquiesce in any infringements of his rights in this par-

---

[1] Raleigh *Register*, November 29, 1825.

[2] *Ibid.*, December 6, 1825.

[3] *Ibid.*, December 30, 1825, and January 3, 1826.

[4] It is curious to read the estimate of the North Carolina Manumission
Society in 1825, as to the sentiment of the people of the State on the question of emancipation. They said that $\frac{2}{60}$ of the people wanted immediate
emancipation, $\frac{8}{60}$ wanted gradual emancipation, $\frac{4}{60}$ wanted emigration, $\frac{6}{60}$ were totally indifferent, $\frac{18}{60}$ were ready to support schemes of
emancipation, $\frac{8}{60}$ opposed emancipation because impracticable, and
$\frac{3}{60}$ were bitterly against it. See Weeks: "Southern Quakers and
Slavery," p. 241.

[5] Raleigh *Register*, December 29, 1826.

ticular he would destroy the constitution, law and everything most dear to him." He favored referring the matter
to a committee. Mr. Forney, of Lincoln, counseled moderation. "There was," he said, "a good deal of sensibility
excited whenever this subject was mentioned, and a disposition was felt to take umbrage when no offense was
intended." The Senate referred the matter to a committee,
but with what result does not appear.[1] In the Assembly of
1827-28 there were several bills in regard to minor features
of the slave controversy, but none passed. In 1828-29 a
bill was introduced to prohibit the education of slaves and
on the recommendation of the Judiciary Committee it was
rejected. Both here and in the following year other bills
were introduced to restrict the activity of slaves, but they
failed to pass. It was only when the Governor sent in to
the Assembly a copy of an inflammatory circular found in
North Carolina and in other States, that passion rose to
summer heat again. Slavery, said the Governor in his
message, was a fixity, and "it would be criminal in the
Legislature to attempt to avoid any responsibility growing
out of this relation." It was known that free negroes had
helped to circulate such literature as this, and it was recommended that they be required to give bond not to do so in the
future. The Governor's note of warning was heard. The
first bill introduced was to regulate the patrol. A committee
of the House of Commons was instructed to inquire into
the expediency of preventing the education of slaves, and a
number of other restrictive bills and resolutions followed
quickly.[2]

The incendiary publication referred to was by one Walker,
of Boston.[3] I presume this was David Walker, the third
edition of whose "Appeal in Four Articles" had just been
issued. This appeal, said he, was made to rescue the negro
from wretchedness in consequence of slavery, ignorance, reli-

---

[1] Raleigh *Register*, January 2, 1827.
[2] *Ibid.*, November 18 and 25, and December 2, 1830.
[3] *Ibid.*, December 9, 1830.

gious teachers and the colonization plan. It was written by a negro and was intended to incite negroes to progress. They were urged not to be content with the position of menials, but to educate their children. The habit of the whites of teaching negro children in Sunday Schools was denounced, evidently because it tended to make the negroes contented with slavery. Garrison reprinted much of this pamphlet in one of the early numbers of the *Liberator*.[1] It was not openly and violently incendiary, to be sure, but it aimed to make the negro discontented with his lot, and falling into the hands of slaves might well be construed to lead to any kind of a stroke against their shackles. To the North Carolina Legislaure it was a most serious matter. The Senate went into secret session on it, the second secret session in the history of the State. The bill to prevent slaves being taught to read and write was taken up and went through the Senate on its second reading without a division. Mr. Robert P. Dick, of Guilford, protested in the name of many of his constituents who conceived that it was their duty to teach the slaves to read the Bible.[2] The bill was finally enacted. The tide had turned. The pro-slavery minority that had often tried to pass this bill had at last been able to get it through. This faction was not only supreme in the Assembly, but it soon became supreme in society at large. It took its case into the realm of literature. Arguments sociological, arguments ethnological, arguments psychological, arguments biblical, and goodness knows how many others were hurled at the slave. The very nature of the controversy engendered passion. The abolitionist considered slavery a crime against the slaves. His saying so reflected on the moral integrity of the masters. Specifications of the criminality were enumerated. The masters became angrier. The passions once kindled might be relied on to keep themselves burning. It would have

---

[1] *The Liberator*, April 23, 1831.
[2] Raleigh *Register*, December 9, 1830.

taken admirable self-control for either side to have stopped
or to have turned aside the flood. Said Mr. Julius Rock-
well: "It is no credit to the civilization of the nineteenth
century that slavery could not have been abolished without
that horrid war." It was slavery itself that defeated the
humaner forces of civilization. Had slavery not been
slavery the minds of men might have been calmer in its
presence, but then there had been no need of abolition.

After the triumph of 1830 the dominant faction was more
determined than ever to protect slavery. The Governor in
his message in 1831 referred to the discontent among the
slaves, and recommended the organization at the expense
of the State of a reliable county militia to be held ready to
march at a moment's notice. His recommendation was not
adopted. Neither were a number of bills brought in to
restrict the action of slaves.

In 1835 a joint committee on incendiary literature, of
which Thomas G. Polk was chairman, reported in favor of
a permanent policy in regard to such literature. This the
State could undoubtedly do and "no other State, and no
other portion of a people of any other State can claim to
interfere in the matter, either by authority, advice, or persua-
sion; and such an attempt, from whatever quarter it may
come, must ever be met by us with distrust and repelled with
indignation. * * * Whatever institution or state of
society we think proper to establish or to permit is by no
other State to be disturbed or questioned. We enter not
into the inquiry whether such institution be deemed by
another State just or expedient. It is sufficient that we think
proper to allow it. * * * We do full justice to the
general sentiments and feelings of our fellow-citizens in
other States, and are fully aware that the attempts to injure
us are made by a small minority—composed probably of
many misguided and some wicked men, and that these
attempts meet with no favor, but on the other hand with
marked disapprobation from a large majority of the communities in which they are made. Still it must be recollected

that from the nature of the means employed the danger to us is the same." "We asked not assistance," continued the committee, "to put down insurrectionary movements among our slaves, for should such occur we are fully able to put them down ourselves. But we ask that our slaves and ourselves may be relieved from external interference. Left to themselves, we believe our slaves, as a laboring class, are as little dangerous to society as any in the world. But we do ask, and think we have a right to demand, that others do not teach them evil of which they do not think themselves." The report closed as follows: "Though we feel the greatest attachment for the Union, and would do all in our power to strengthen and perpetuate it, yet we are not ready to surrender those very rights and blessings which that Union was formed to protect; and should the means now adopted prove ineffectual in stopping the progress of these attacks on our peace and happiness, we would invoke the aid of the other slaveholding States that there may be concert of action in taking such steps as the occasion may demand."[1] With this report were some resolutions in the same spirit, and these were passed by a large majority.

By the side of this I should like to place a resolution which the *Raleigh Register*, June 4, 1836, said had just been adopted by the New England Anti-Slavery Society. It read:

Resolved, That regarding a surrender of the right of free discussion upon the altar of Southern slavery as involving on our part the commission of moral suicide, treachery to the cause of civil liberty, of humility and guilt before high Heaven, we hereby pledge ourselves to one another—to the oppressor and the oppressed—to our country and our God—that, undeterred by threats or persecution at common law, whether in the messages of the governors, the pages of our theological reviews, or the reports of legislative committees—come what may, gag law or lynch law, we will never cease to work for its exercise—full, free, and undiminished—until the last fetter shall be broken and slavery and prejudice shall be buried in one common grave.

---

[1] Raleigh *Register*, January 5, 1836.

Alas! that was a good way to bury slavery, but neither the resolutions of the North Carolina Assembly nor those of the New England Society were calculated to diminish prejudice.

The change in public opinion is well illustrated by the course of the *Raleigh Register.* Its editor, Joseph Gales, had left England in 1794 on account of a certain connection with a violent pamphlet of a French republican flavor. His love of liberty made him steadily opposed to slavery. He was a follower of Jefferson and later on a Whig. He certainly did not represent the general sentiment on the slavery question, but even the opinions of his paper were not proof against the pro-slavery impulse of public thought. In 1818 the *Register* described slavery as "a Upas tree of most frightful dimensions and most poisonous qualities." In 1825, when another paper declared that the *Register* was "very little in unison" with the opinions of the great body of slaveholders, Mr. Gales replied:

We consider slavery an evil, a great evil, but one imposed on us without our consent, and therefore necessary, though we cannot believe irremediable, hopeless and perpetual. On the simple question: "Ought slavery to exist" we presume but few persons would answer in the affirmative, and still fewer would be found bold enough to advocate the practice as being right in itself or to justify it, except on the broad plea of necessity. That it would conduce equally to the interest and happiness of the slaveholding States to get rid of this part of our population few will deny. It is a dead weight which mars all enterprise and clogs the wheels of the political machine. None can doubt that if North Carolina could give the whole of her colored population for one-half the number of whites she would be among the foremost in the race of active improvements now running by most of the free States. We hope the time will come, though it is probably far distant, when a better order of things will prevail in this respect.[1]

In 1830 the *Register* had begun to change its tone. It pronounced "highly seditious" the anti-slavery articles then

[1] Raleigh *Register*, September 20, 1825.

appearing in the *Greensboro Patriot,* of which William Swaim was the editor.   In 1835 the *Register* declared itself as follows:

Until recently we were disposed to regard the movements of the abolitionists with indifference and contempt ; but it is folly to shut our eyes to the fact that they are rapidly augmenting in numbers, and that their zeal and exertion are increasing in even greater ratio.   By a late circular, signed by Arthur Tappan, Lewis Tappan, the Rev. Dr. Cox, etc., it seems that they are determined to raise $30,000 during the present year to be devoted to printing and circulating *gratuitously* inflammatory papers calculated to do extensive mischief.[1]

Four weeks later the same paper, on the authority of Lewis Tappan, said that the abolitionists had printed 175,000 abolition circulars, of which 1000 had been destroyed in Charleston. "The rest," said Tappan, "are accomplishing the designs intended throughout the United States. We will persevere, come life or death. If any fall by the hand of violence, others will continue the blessed work." By this time the *Register* was out and out a pro-slavery organ. This change in sentiment in a most conservative paper—the editorial management of which remained continually in the same family—father and son—during this entire period, must have been indicative of a much stronger popular change.[2]

Co-existent with the facts just mentioned there was a strong political side to this change. The Whigs were, for most of the period before the Civil War, more opposed to slavery than the Democrats. They now found themselves uncomfortably placed between two fires. Abolitionists charged them with favoring slaveholders. Pro-slavery people charged them with a leaning towards Northern abolition doctrines. Each charge was denied. In each there was some

---

[1] Raleigh *Register*, October 1, 1835.
[2] Sometime before his death in 1842 Joseph Gales went to live in Washington City, leaving the editorial management of the paper in the hands of his son. I can find no date for this, but it was hardly so early as 1835. At that time the paper announced at its head that it was published by "Gales and Son."

show of truth. Whiggery was already being dragged into the maelstrom of sectionalism, which was destined to destroy it. In North Carolina it did not dare to oppose slavery. At the time about which I have been speaking, another issue overshadowed all others. It was the question of apportionment of seats in the Assembly. The Constitution provided that each county should have equal representation. The western counties were larger than many eastern counties and demanded an apportionment of seats according to population. The struggle was won by the West, and the desired reform was accomplished by the constitutional convention of 1835.[1] This put a new complexion on State politics for a few years; but as soon as this issue was forgotten—and it was not long in doing so—the two parties were drawn into discussion of the slavery question. It was in the campaign of 1840 that the matter first became prominent. The *Standard,* a Democratic paper at Raleigh, called the Whigs "abolitionists." The *Register,* which was the leading Whig organ, charged Van Buren with favoring negro equality. The controversy became warm. The Democrats attacked Mr. Morehead, Whig candidate for Governor, because he had prepared a report against the bill to prevent the instruction of slaves. The Whigs replied that Mr. Haywood, the Democratic candidate, had done the same thing. The Whig candidate was looked upon with suspicion, because he was from Guilford County, where anti-slavery ideas were abundant. The Whigs replied by charging that Mr. Saunders, a Democratic ex-Congressman, had presented to Congress a petition from the Manumission Society of Guilford County. When the Whigs finally won in 1840 the *Register* announced the victory under the headlines: WHIGGERY VICTORIOUS! THE BLACK FLAG OF ABOLITION LAID LOW!

After 1840 the controversy slept till 1846, when the Wilmot Proviso was introduced. It now became violent.

[1] See the author's "Suffrage in North Carolina," Report of the American Historical Association, 1895.

The Democrats had the Whigs on the defensive. The latter were forced to repudiate the action of the New England Whigs, who had just endorsed the proviso in a convention at Springfield, Mass. The result was satisfactory. The Whigs were still strong, and carried the State by what was then a substantial majority of 7000. In 1848 the controversy for equal suffrage began, the Democrats favoring it and the Whigs opposing. It ran strong, but the feeling on the slavery question was not allayed. The two parties vied with one another in denouncing abolition.

In the storm of feeling which preceded the compromise measures of 1850, North Carolina was not untouched. The strongly conservative feeling of the State was brought into play, and the resolutions which were introduced into the Legislature were milder than they would have been in some other Southern States. On January 16, 1849, the Assembly resolved all but unanimously, that to forbid slavery in the District of Columbia or in the territories would be a "grave injustice and wrong" and contrary to the spirit of the Constitution, and that they were willing to stand by the Missouri Compromise. An amendment to these resolutions was offered by the House of Commons and concurred in by the Senate, pledging the State more strongly than ever to the Union and repudiating "whatever may suggest even a suspicion that it can in any event be abandoned. This amendment was introduced into the House by Edward Stanley, of Beaufort County,[1] who was a Union man of the strongest sort.

In the session of 1850-51 the same matter came up again. A joint committee was appointed to act for the two Houses. A report was prepared and submitted. It was in favor of accepting the Compromise of 1850, but sounded a note of warning in regard to the Fugitive Slave Law. There were many resolutions on this subject before the Assembly. One of them expressed, perhaps, pretty thoroughly the feeling

---

[1] Journal of the Assembly of 1848-49, pp. 717 and 725.

of most of the members. It ran: *"Resolved,* That we will have the Fugitive Slave Law or fight." Many amendments were offered to the resolutions of the committee, and an intricate debate was just beginning when the matter suddenly dropped out of the journal of the Assembly, leaving us to guess the cause. Perhaps it was because the Assembly was brought to realize the futility of bringing on a discussion which would create feeling and endanger the Union, all to accomplish no definite end. The compromise laws had then been passed in Congress, and as yet the Fugitive Slave Law had not been tried. It was evidently in the interest of good sense to say nothing about the slavery question.

The last decade before the war was quiet enough so far as the political relation of slavery was concerned. There was, as the crisis approached, a considerable amount of sectional recrimination, but it does not belong to the history of slavery, but rather to the larger history of the great sectional struggle. In the meantime, and, indeed, for a decade and a half previously, there had been no legislation of importance which bore on slavery. The status of the slaves had been fixed to the satisfaction of the masters by the legislation which came closely before or after 1830. This intermediate period was marked by profound quiet on the part of the slaves. The negroes were prostrate, restrained at every point by law. So completely were they subjected that they gave no trouble during the war that followed. During this war it was not found necessary to amend the law controlling the conduct of slaves at any vital point. This quietude of the slaves has been attributed to their good nature. It ought to be attributed to their lack of *esprit du corps,* their lack of organization, and their fear of the whites. They did not remain quiet because they loved slavery. They had small opportunity for rebellion. The counties were closely defended by home guards, embodied from the old men and the youths and in each State till the end of the war there were easily accessible bodies of troops which would have crushed with fearful promptitude an attempt at insurrection. No revolt that the negro could have made would have stood a week. That the negroes were willing enough to have their liberty, even at the expense of the lives of their masters, is shown by the readiness with which they enlisted into regiments in the Union Army, and by the desperate courage with which, raw as they were, they frequently bore themselves in battle when under the leadership of competent white officers.

AUTHORITIES.

With few exceptions, I have been thrown back on *Quellen,* and of this class of material the pieces have been varied and multitudinous. Slavery is unannalled so far as the slaves themselves are concerned. I have been forced to pick up information here and there as it is found in the documents and other literature of the white man. At best I can hope for but little more than that this, and other works of mine on slavery in North Carolina, may serve for a point around which many more facts not now in the range of my knowledge may be gathered, till at last the subject is known through and through.

My chief sources of information have been laws and legal opinions. Of these are:

Laws of North Carolina, 1790.

Laws of North Carolina, 1821.

Revised Statutes of North Carolina, 1837.

Revised Code of North Carolina, 1835.

Journals of the North Carolina Assembly.

Reports of the cases in the North Carolina Supreme Courts.

I have found much information in the newspapers of the day, particularly the Raleigh *Register,* and the North Carolina *Standard.*

Other materials of a more miscellaneous nature are:

Caruthers, E. W.: American Slavery and the Immediate Duty of Slaveholders, an unpublished manuscript now in possession of the library of Greensboro Female College (N. C.)

Wightman: Life of Bishop Capers.

Drew: Life of Dr. Thomas Coke.

Hawkins: Memoir of Lunsford Lane.

Biggs: History of the Kehuckee Association.

Purefoy: History of the Sandy Creek Association.

Weeks: Southern Quakers and Slavery.

Hoss: Sketch of the Life of Elihu Embree. Publications of Vanderbilt Historical Society, No. 2, 1897.

Smith: History of Education in North Carolina.

Olmsted: Journey in the Seaboard Slave States.

Du Bois: The Suppression of the Slave Trade.

North Carolina Colonial Records, Vol. IX.

De Bow's Review.

Weaver: The North Carolina Manumission Society. The Historical Papers of the Trinity College (N. C.) Historical Society.

Chreitzberger: Early Methodism in Wilmington, N. C. The first annual publication of the Historical Society of the North Carolina Conference of the M. E. Church South, 1897.

Gaston, Wm.: Address at Commencement at the University of North Carolina, 1832.

David Dodge [O. W. Blacknall]: Free Negoes of North Carolina. *The Atlantic Monthly,* January, 1886.

Minutes of the Conference of the Methodist Episcopal Church.

Disciplines of the Methodist Episcopal Church.

Minutes of the Chowan Baptist Association.

Minutes of the North Carolina Baptist Convention.

McGill: American Slavery as Viewed and Acted on by the Presbyterian Church in America.

"Presbyterianism and Slavery." Official document published for the use of the General Assembly of the Presbyterian Church at Pittsburg, 1836.

Journal of the North Carolina Episcopal Convention—not complete.

Bassett, J. S.: Slavery and Servitude in the Colony of North Carolina. Hopkins Studies in History and Politics, 1896. Anti-Slavery Leaders of North Carolina, *Ibid.,* 1897. Suffrage in the State of North Carolina. Publication of the American Historical Association, 1895.

A STUDY OF SLAVERY IN NEW JERSEY

JOHNS HOPKINS UNIVERSITY STUDIES

IN

HISTORICAL AND POLITICAL SCIENCE

HERBERT B. ADAMS, Editor

History is past Politics and Politics are present History—*Freeman*

FOURTEENTH SERIES

IX-X

A STUDY OF SLAVERY IN NEW JERSEY

By HENRY SCOFIELD COOLEY

BALTIMORE

THE JOHNS HOPKINS PRESS

PUBLISHED MONTHLY

September and October, 1896

CONTENTS.

INTRODUCTION.

An accurate and thorough knowledge of slavery as it developed in the United States can best be gained by a comparative study of the institution as it has existed in the various States. Preparatory to such a study, the experience of each. of these commonwealths needs to be investigated separately. This has been done in several instances very satisfactorily. The writer has aimed to follow lines of investigation already opened, and has pursued the history of slavery in New Jersey, his native State.

New Jersey history is conveniently studied in three periods : the period of the Proprietary Colony, 1664–1702; the period of the Province of the Crown, 1702–1776 ; and the period of the State. These divisions have not been adopted in the plan of this monograph, an arrangement by subject appearing more desirable ; but it is hoped that they have been sufficiently recognized throughout the paper. In general, in the Proprietary Colony we find the early beginnings of slavery ; in the royal Colony, a steady increase in the number of slaves, and special forms of trial and punishment for slaves prescribed in the criminal law. This was also the period of a strong abolition movement among the Friends, ending in 1776 with the denial by Friends of the right of membership in their Society to slaveholders. In the State the anti-slavery movement, largely under the leadership of the abolition societies, grew to greater and greater strength. Its influence showed itself in practical ways in the support given to negroes before the courts, in the extinction of the slave trade, and in the passage of the gradual abolition law of 1804.

The writer takes this opportunity to express his thanks for many courtesies received in the use of the New Jersey State Library at

7

Trenton, the New York Historical Society Library and the Lenox
Library at New York, the Bergen County Records at Hackensack,
and particularly to F.W. Ricord, Esq., Librarian of the New Jersey
Historical Society, for full and free access to its collections. The
writer wishes also to recognize most gratefully his obligation, to
Dr. Bernard C. Steiner for many valuable suggestions. as to the
method of investigation, and to Dr. Jeffrey R. Brackett for very
helpful criticism of the manuscript.

A STUDY OF SLAVERY IN NEW JERSEY.

CHAPTER I.

THE INCREASE AND DECLINE OF SLAVERY.

In nearly all of the English Colonies in America the institution of slavery was recognized and accepted by both government and colonists from the earliest period of settlement. In New Jersey the relation of master and slave had legal recognition at the very beginning of the Colony's political existence. The earliest constitution, the "Concessions"[1] from Lord Berkeley and Sir George Carteret in 1664, specifies slaves as possible members of the settler's family.

By the "Concessions" the Lords Proprietors granted to every colonist that should go out with the first governor seventy-five acres of land for every slave, to every settler before January 1, 1665, sixty acres for every slave, to every settler in the year following forty-five acres for every slave, and to every settler in the third year thirty acres for every slave. For the colonist's own person and for every able-bodied servant other portions of land were given, and all, according to the text of the instrument, "that the planting of

---

[1] "The concessions and agreement of the Lords Proprietors of the province of New-Caesarea or New Jersey, to and with all and every of the adventurers, and all such as shall plant there." Leaming and Spicer, *Grants, Concessions,* etc., pp. 20–23.

the said province may be more speedily promoted." Some
have thought to see in these grants an unworthy readiness to
serve the interest of the Duke of York, President of the Royal
African Company.[1] That the desire of the Lords Proprietors
was anything different from that stated, namely, the rapid
development of the Province, I have found no evidence to
prove. To what extent slaves were actually imported even is
uncertain.

The earliest legislation in New Jersey bearing on the
subject of slavery is a provision in 1668 that, if " any man
shall wilfully or forcibly steal away any mankind, he shall be
put to death."[2] This provision constituted the sixth of the
" Capital Laws " passed by the General Assembly at Elizabeth-Town.[3] It, therefore, merely formed a part of the general criminal code and was intended for the protection of
persons of white race only. Another reference to slavery of
a similar character is found in the " Fundamental Laws "
agreed upon by the Proprietors and settlers of West Jersey in
1676. A chapter designed to secure publicity in judicial proceedings concludes with the declaration " that all and every
person and persons inhabiting the said Province, shall, as far
as in us lies, be free from oppression and slavery."[4]

---

[1] Bancroft, *History of U. S.*, 9th ed., Vol. II, p. 316, refers to the Proprietors as, in this action "more true to the prince than to humanity."
Whitehead, *East Jersey Under the Proprietary Governments*, maintains
strongly that Bancroft's expression is not warranted by the evidence.

[2] Leaming and Spicer, p. 79.

[3] The provision when reënacted seven years later has the same position,
L. and S., p. 105.

[4] Leaming and Spicer, p. 398.

That slavery was an institution which the dwellers about the Hudson
and Delaware recognized and had some acquaintance with, is shown by the
action of a Council at New York in 1669. A certain Coningsmarke, a
Swede, popularly known as "the long Finne," having been convicted of
stirring up an insurrection in Delaware, as part of his punishment was
sentenced to be sent to "Barbadoes or some other remote plantation to be
sold." After having been kept prisoner in the "Stadt-house at York"
for a year, the long Finne was duly transported for sale to Barbadoes.
Smith, S., *History of New Jersey*, pp. 53, 54.

The earliest legislation implying the actual presence of slaves in the Province is an enactment in 1675 against transporting, harboring, or entertaining apprentices, servants or slaves.[1] From that time on laws having reference to slavery become more and more frequent.

In general, in the Proprietary Colony (1664–1702) slaves were regarded by the law very much as were apprentices and servants. In the "Concessions" and in the earlier legislation either slaves are treated in the same way as "weaker servants,"[2] or slaves, apprentices and servants are treated as forming one class.[3] Gradually there were established special regulations for the government of slaves, until toward the end of this period we find special punishments and a special form of trial.

To what extent slave labor was employed at this time it is difficult to estimate. That slaves were an important element in the economic life of the Colony seems probable in view of the amount of legislation relating to slavery. Mr. Snell says that the earliest recorded instance of the holding of negro slaves in New Jersey is that of " Col. Richard Morris of Shrewsbury, who as early as 1680 had sixty or more slaves about his mill and plantation." Mr. Snell thinks that by 1690 nearly all the inhabitants of northern New Jersey had slaves.[4]

Indian Slavery.

In New Jersey, as in many of the other Colonies, Indians were held as slaves from a very early period. I have found no evidence from which to determine in what year Indian slavery first existed, or what proportions it ever actually attained. That there were Indian slaves in the Province as

---

[1] Leaming and Spicer, p. 109.
[2] L. and S., pp. 20–23, *Concessions of the Lords Proprietors.*
[3] *Laws of* 1675 and 1682. L. and S., pp. 105 and 238.
[4] Snell, J. P., *History of Sussex and Warren Counties, N. J.*, p. 76.

early as 1682 there is sufficient proof. The preamble to an
"Act against trading with negro slaves" passed at Elizabeth-
Town in that year reads: "Whereas, it is found by daily
experience that negro and Indian slaves, or servants under
pretence of trade, or liberty to traffic, do frequently steal from
their masters," etc.[1] Throughout the Act in the several places
where slaves are spoken of, the designation is "negro or Indian
slave" or a similar term. In many of the Colonial laws
Indian slavery is recognized by the use of the enumerating
phrase "negro, Indian and mulatto slaves" where slaves are
referred to.[2] The advertisements for fugitives, found in the
newspapers of the early part of the eighteenth century,
show pretty clearly the actual presence of Indian slaves.[3]
Slaves of mixed race, half negro and half Indian, are also
mentioned.[4]

That Indians might be slaves under the laws of New Jersey
was established judicially by a decision of the State Supreme
Court in 1797.[5] The case was one of *habeas corpus* to bring
up the body of Rose, an Indian woman, claimed by the defendant as a slave. It was proved that Rose's mother, an
Indian woman, had been purchased as a slave and had always
been considered as such. The Chief Justice, delivering the

---

[1] L. and S., p. 254.

[2] Allinson, pp. 5, 31, 307, 315; Nevill, I, pp. 18, 242; *N. J. Archives*, III,
473; XII, 516–520; XV, 30, 351. Also in the *State Laws of* 1798 and 1820.
Paterson, p. 307, and *N. J. Statutes*, 44 ses., *Statutes*, 74. The expressions
"negro slaves or others," "negroes or other slaves" are found in *Acts of*
1682, 1695 and 1710. L. and S., pp. 237, 257; *N. J. Archives*, XIII, p. 439.

[3] Fugitive Indian men, apparently slaves, are advertised 1716 and 1720.
Boston *News-Letter*, July 23, 1716; *American Weekly Mercury*, Sept. 28,
1721; in *N. J. A.*, XI, pp. 41 and 58.

[4] In 1734, 1741 and 1747. *Am. Wk. Mer.*, Oct. 31, 1734; N. Y. *Wk.
Journal*, May 11, 1741; Penn. *Gaz.*, Oct. 1, 1747; in *N. J. A.*, XI, 393;
XII, 91, 403. One of these half-breed slaves is mentioned as the child of
an Indian woman. *N. J. A.*, XII, 403.

[5] *N. J. Law Reports*, VI, 455–459 (1st. Halsted). The State *vs.* Van-
Waggoner.

opinion of the court, said: "They [the Indians] have been so long recognized as slaves in our law, that it would be as great a violation of the rights of property to establish a contrary doctrine at the present day, as it would be in the case of Africans; and as useless to investigate the manner in which they originally lost their freedom."[1]

The Royal Governors.

The plan for the administration of New Jersey outlined in the Instructions from Queen Anne to the first royal governor, Lord Cornbury, included the regulation of slavery as existing in the Province and the development of an import trade in slaves from Africa. Lord Cornbury was directed to encourage particularly the Royal African Company of England, along with other enterprisers that might bring trade, or otherwise "contribute to the advantage" of the Colony. The Queen was "willing to recommend" to the Royal African Company that the Province "may have a constant and sufficient supply of merchantable negroes, at moderate rates," and the Governor, on his part, was instructed to "take especial care" to secure prompt payment for the same. He was to guard against encroachments on the trading privileges of the Royal African Company by inhabitants of New Jersey. 'He was to report annually to the Commissioners for Trade and Plantations the number of negroes imported, and the prices that they brought. The "conversion of negroes and Indians to the Christian religion" was even treated of. The consideration of the best means to encourage this pious movement was commended to the attention of the Governor, assisted by his Council and the Assembly.[2]

---

[1] It was decided that the slavery of this Indian woman had been sufficiently proved, and she was remanded to the custody of her master.

[2] L. and S., pp. 640, 642. Instructions from Queen Anne to Lord Cornbury.

The Slave Trade.

In the action of the Colony on the subject of the expediency of restricting the importation of slaves, we find some indication of the position which slavery attained among the institutions of the Province, and of the popular feeling as to the desirability of the use of slave labor. The question of an import duty was one upon which at times the views of Assembly, Council, and the Lords of Trade did not agree. Queen Anne's instructions to Lord Cornbury show clearly a desire to encourage the importation of slaves. The Governor was specifically directed to report annually to the home government the number and value of the slaves that the Province "was yearly supplied with." The earliest statute on the subject was in 1714, when a duty of ten pounds was laid on every slave imported for sale.[1] The legislation was called forth by the desire to stimulate the introduction of white servants that the Colony might become better populated.[2]

To what extent slaves were actually imported at this period is largely a matter of conjecture. A report from the custom house at Perth Amboy in 1726 gives "an account of what negroes appears by the custom house books to be imported into the eastern division of this Province" since 1698.[3] The report states that, from 1698 to 1717 none were imported, and from 1718 to 1726 only 115. It is hardly probably that this testimony gives an accurate indication of the real amount of slave importation. Many negroes must have been brought into the Province in such a manner as not to appear on the books of the custom house at Perth Amboy. It certainly would seem strange that it should be thought desirable in

---

[1] Allinson, S., *Acts of Gen. Assembly* (1702–1776), p. 31; *N. J. A.*, XIII, pp. 516–520; *Journal of Gov. and Council.*

This law remained in force for seven years from June 1, 1714.

[2] A similar law in Pennsylvania had been observed to have the desired effect.

[3] *N. J. A.*, V, p. 152.

1714 to pass an act laying a duty upon slaves imported, if actually, there had been little or no importation for fifteen years previously.[1]

The law of 1714 was permitted to expire in 1721, and for nearly fifty years there was no duty upon the importation of negroes, although during that period bills to establish such a duty were at several times before the governing houses.[2] In 1744, a bill plainly intending an entire prohibition of the importation of slaves from abroad was rejected by the Provincial Council.[3] That body declared that even the mere discouragement of importation was undesirable. The Council maintained that the Colony at that time had great need of laborers. An expedition to the West Indies had drawn off from the Province many inhabitants. The privateering profession had attracted many others. For these causes, wages had risen so high that "farmers, trading-men, and tradesmen" only with great difficulty were able to carry on their business. The Council expected little relief from Ireland ; for, since the establishment of the linen manufacture on that island, there had been little emigration. The Silesian war in Europe allowed slender hope of help from Germany or England. Under the existing conditions, encouragement of slave importation rather

---

[1] A similar inference may be drawn from information afforded by an extract from the minutes of the Friends' Yearly Meeting held at Burlington in 1716, given by Mr. J. W. Dally. From this extract we learn that certain Friends at a Quarterly Meeting at Shrewsbury had shown great solicitude for the discouragement of the importation of slaves, although the question had received consideration at the previous Yearly Meeting. Dally, *Woodbridge and Vicinity*, p. 73.

[2] In 1739, a bill was passed by the Assembly, but rejected by the Council. The Assembly and Council were just then at odds on the subject of governmental appropriations. Possibly the strained relations may have influenced the action on this bill. See *Assem. Jour.*, Dec. 5, 1738, Feb. 16, 1739, and *N. J. A.*, XV, 30, 31, 45, 50 (*Jour. of Gov. and Council*).

[3] The bill imposed a duty of ten pounds upon all slaves imported from the West Indies, and five pounds upon all from Africa. *N. J. A.*, VI, 219, 232, and XV, 351, 384, 385 (*Jour. of Provin. Council*) ; *Assem. Jour.*, Oct. 9 to Nov. 7, 1744.

than prohibition of it, was needed, in the opinion of the
Council. Again, in 1761, the question of a duty was under
discussion. The free importation of negroes had then become
a source of inconvenience. A large number of slaves were
"landed in this Province every year in order to be run into
New York and Pennsylvania" where duties had been established. Furthermore, New Jersey had become overstocked
with negroes. In response to two petitions from a large number of the inhabitants of the Colony, praying for a duty on
all negro slaves imported, a bill for that purpose was introduced
into the Assembly.[1] Governor Hardy, however, informed the
House that his instructions would not permit him to assent to
the bill,[2] and it was abandoned. At the request of the Assembly, the Governor laid the matter before the Lords of Trade,
and besought them for some relief.[3] Less than a year later
Governor Hardy assented to a bill[4] imposing import duties;
but insisted upon a suspending clause that the act should not
~~not~~ take effect until approved by the King. The Lords of
Trade, because of technical faults in the bill, did not lay it
before the King; but, at the same time, they disclaimed any
opposition to the policy of an import duty.[5]

---

[1] The Assembly voted that the duties to be provided for in this bill
should not be so high as to amount to a prohibition (*Assem. Jour.*, Dec. 3,
1761).

[2] He was forbidden to give his "assent to any act imposing duties upon
negroes imported into this Province, payable by the importer; or upon any
slaves exported, that have not been sold in the Province, and continued
there for the space of twelve months" (*Assem. Jour.*, Dec. 4, 1761).

[3] *N. J. A.*, IX, 345. Letter from Gov. Hardy to the Lords of Trade.
Assem. Jour., Nov. 30 to Dec. 8, 1761.

[4] Sept. 25, 1762. The act laid a duty of forty shillings in the Eastern
and six pounds in the Western division of the Province. The reason for
the discrimination was that Pennsylvania had a duty of ten pounds, while
New York charged only two pounds. Allinson, p. 253; *N. J. A.*, IX, 383
(Letter from Gov. Hardy to the Lords of Trade). XVII, 333, 338–385,
(*Jour. of Council*); *Assem. Jour.*, Sept. 23–25, 1762.

[5] *N. J. A.*, IX, 447 (Letter from Lords of Trade to Gov. Franklin).
XVII, 385; see also IX, 444.

Finally, in 1767, an act limited to two years was passed ;[1] and at its expiration a more comprehensive law followed which was in force during the remainder of the Colonial period.[2] The preamble to the law of 1769 states that the act was passed because several of the neighboring Colonies had found duties upon the importation of negroes to be beneficial in the introduction of sober, industrious foreigners as settlers and in promoting a spirit of industry among the inhabitants in general, and in order that those persons who chose to purchase slaves might " contribute some equitable proportion of the public burdens." It was enacted that the purchaser of a slave which had not been in the Colony a year, or for which the duty had not yet been paid, should pay to the county collector the sum of fifteen pounds.[3]

In 1773, several petitions were presented to the Assembly praying that the further importation of slaves might be prohibited and that manumission might be made more easy. In response, two bills were introduced for the above purposes, respectively. The bill regarding manumission, however, seems to have aroused such interest as to have overshadowed entirely the bill for laying a further duty on the purchasers of slaves ; for nothing is heard of the latter beyond its second reading .and recommitment.[4]

In the early years of the royal Colony, the home government is inclined to encourage the importation of slaves. The Assembly favors restriction of importation, apparently on purely economic grounds, and succeeds in passing a law to that end. For nearly fifty years the attempts of the Assembly to carry out its policy are defeated, at first by the Council,

[1] This law abandoned the awkward discrimination between East and West Jersey of the bill of 1762, and imposed a uniform duty for the whole Colony. Allinson, pp. 300 and 353. Whitehead, *Perth Amboy*, p. 320.

[2] This act was to be in force for ten years.

[3] Any purchase made upon the waters surrounding the Province was considered a purchase within the Province (Allinson, p. 315).

[4] *Assem. Jour.*, Nov. 30 to Dec. 13, 1773.

then by the opposition of the Governor in accordance with his official instructions, then by legal technicality. Finally, the resistance is overcome, and a law laying a duty is passed. Economic motives are again given as the cause of the legislation; but it is probable that the persistence of the Assembly was due to the influence of the Friends,[1] among whom a strong abolition movement had been going on.

Late in the year 1785, a petition from a great number of the inhabitants of the State was presented to the Assembly, praying for legislation to secure the gradual abolition of slavery and to prevent the importation of slaves. In response to this petition, an act was passed early in 1786[2] inflicting a penalty of fifty pounds for bringing slaves into New Jersey that had been imported from Africa since 1776, and a penalty of twenty pounds for all others imported.[3] Foreigners, and others having only a temporary residence, might bring in their slaves without duty; but might not dispose of them in the State. The legislation against the slave trade met with in the Colonial period was entered upon from considerations of economic expediency, if we are to judge from the explanations of the legislators. In the act of 1786 we find legal recognition of the ethical side of the question. The preamble declares that the "principles of justice and humanity require that the barbarous custom of bringing the unoffending Africans from their native country and connections into a state of slavery" be discountenanced.[4] Further petitions[5] for the suppression of the negro trade and the gradual abolition of

---

[1] See *N. J. A.,* IX, 346. Note by W. Nelson (editor).

Mr. Nelson thinks that the law of 1769 was caused by the anti-slavery movement among the Friends.

[2] *Assem. Jour.,* Nov. 1, 1785, to March 2, 1786. *Acts of Assem.*

[3] Persons coming to settle in New Jersey must pay duty on such of their slaves as had been imported from Africa since 1776; but were not charged for the others.

[4] Even this act continues, "and sound policy also requires," that importation be prohibited, in order that white labor may be protected.

[5] *Assem. Jour.,* Nov. 6–10, 1788.

slavery, one from the Society of Friends and another from
certain inhabitants of the town of Princeton, led the legislature in 1788 to pass a supplement to the law of 1786.   This
supplement[1] carried the non-importation principle still farther
and inflicted a forfeiture of vessels, appurtenances and cargo
upon those who fitted out ships for the slave trade.   Masters
of vessels who resisted the persons attempting to seize were
fined fifty pounds.   Not only was the import trade in slaves
forbidden, but the export trade also.   No slave that had
resided within the State for the year past could be removed
out of the State with the intention of changing his legal residence, without his consent, or that of his parents.   The prohibition did not apply to persons emigrating to settle in a
neighboring State and taking their slaves with them.[2]

The abolition law of 1804 and the increasing strength of
the public sentiment against slavery inclined masters to send
their negroes out of the State, and a further law forbidding
exportation was passed in 1812.[3]   Again, in 1818,[4] in answer
to a memorial from a number of the inhabitants of Middlesex
County, praying for a more efficient law to prevent the kidnapping of blacks and carrying them out of the State, an act
was passed inflicting heavy penalties, both of fine and imprisonment for exporting, contrary to law, slaves or servants of

[1] Acts of 13th Gen. Assem., *Assem. Jour.*, Nov. 6–25, 1788.

[2] These several provisions were virtually re-enacted ten years later in the
comprehensive slave law of 1798, excepting that the money penalties inflicted were, on the whole, made lighter.   Paterson, W., *Laws of N. J.*,
revised 1800, p. 307.

The law was not so construed by the courts as to prevent an immigrant,
bringing in slaves among his dependents, from ever and under all circumstances disposing of such slaves.   An instance in 1807 is recorded, when a
slave imported conformably to law was sold from prison after two years
residence within the State.   The State *vs.* Quick, 1st Pennington, p. 393.

[3] 36 Ses., 2 sit., *Statutes*, 15.   *Assem. Jour.*, Jan. 10–29, 1812; also Nov. 8,
1809.

[4] *Assem. Jour.*, Oct. 28 to Nov. 4, 1818.   43 Ses., *Statutes*, 3; also *Assem.
Jour.*, Jan. 19–30, 1818.

color for life or years.[1] Any person who had resided within
the State for five years, desiring to remove from it permanently might take with him any slave that had been his property for the five years preceding the time of removal, providing that the slave was of full age and had consented to the
removal. These facts must be proven before the Court of
Common Pleas, and a license to carry the slave out of the
State be given by the court. Any master of a vessel receiving
and carrying out of the State any slave for whose exportation
a license had not been obtained was liable to a heavy fine
and imprisonment. An inhabitant of New Jersey going on
a journey to any part of the United States might take his
slave with him; but if the slave was not brought back the
master became liable to a heavy penalty unless he could prove
that it had been impossible for the slave to return. These
provisions mark the final suppression of the slave trade in
New Jersey.

The Anti-Slavery Movement.

We find during the latter part of the Colonial period growing recognition of the iniquity of human slavery. It is among
the Quaker inhabitants that this moral development is observed.
As early as 1696,[2] the Quakers of New Jersey and Pennsylvania voted in their Yearly Meeting to recommend to Friends
to cease from further importation of slaves. A cautious dis-
approval of slavery is again seen in the action of the Yearly
Meeting in 1716. Out of consideration for those Friends
whose consciences made them opposed to slavery, " it is desired," the minutes read, " that Friends generally do as much
as may be to avoid buying such negroes as shall be hereafter
brought in, rather than offend any Friends who are against

---

[1] All the legislation on this subject reached its final and permanent form
in the compiled Statute of 1820 (44 Ses., *Statutes*, 74).

[2] Gordon, *History of N. J.*, p. 57.

it," . . . "yet, this is only caution, not censure."[1] These suggestions seem to have been received favorably and to have been put into practice. At a monthly meeting held at Woodbridge in 1738, it was stated that, not for several years had any slaves been imported by a Friend, or had any Friend bought negroes that had been imported.[2]

This is the period of the life and work of John Woolman (1720–1772), one of the earliest and noblest of those who in this country labored for the abolition of human slavery. But a poor, unlearned tailor of West-Jersey, his simplicity and pure, universal charity gave him far-reaching influence among the Friends. These qualities, as shown in his "Journal," together with the exquisite style of his writing, have called forth the admiration of literary circles. He travelled about as a minister among the Friends North and South, preaching and urging his associates to do away with slavery. In 1754, he published "Some Considerations on the Keeping of Negroes," in which he contends that slaveholding is contrary to Scripture.[3]

In 1758, the Philadelphia Yearly Meeting, largely as the result of a moving appeal by Woolman, voted that the Christian injunction to do to others as we would that others should do to us, "should induce Friends who held slaves 'to set them at liberty, making a Christian provision for them.'"[4] In succeeding years this Meeting expressed itself more and more resolutely as opposed to slavery. At one stage in the movement, New Jersey Friends who inclined to free their slaves, were deterred from so doing because of the law requiring masters manumitting slaves to enter into security to maintain the negroes in case they have need of relief. These masters compromised the matter by retaining in their possession young

[1] Extract given by Mr. J. W. Dally in his *Woodbridge and Vicinity*, p. 73.
[2] *Ibid.*

[3] Whittier, J. G., John Woolman's *Journal, Introduction;* also *N. J. Ar.*, IX, 346. Note by W. Nelson (ed.).

[4] Whittier's Introduction to Woolman's *Journal*, p. 19.

negroes and forcing them to work without wages until they reached the age of thirty, while at the same time declining to hold any slaves for life.[1] The movement proceeded by moderate advances. Mr. Dally states that a report was made to the Monthly Meeting at Plainfield in August, 1774, showing "that at this time only one negro, 'fit for freedom' within the jurisdiction of the Society, remained a slave."[2] Finally, in 1776, the Philadelphia Yearly Meeting directed the subordinate meetings to "deny the right of membership to such as persisted in holding their fellowmen as property."[3]

The persistent effort for the restriction of slave importation culminating in the law of 1769 was, no doubt, largely due to the growing anti-slavery sentiment among the Friends.[4] Again, in the fall of 1773, no less than eight petitions were presented to the Assembly from inhabitants of six different counties,[5] all setting forth the evils arising from human slavery, and praying for an alteration of the laws on the subject. The reforms desired were chiefly the prohibition of importation and increased freedom of manumission. Of the two bills introduced for these purposes, the one regulating manumission alone excited much interest; the other was soon dropped. A counter-petition against the manumission bill was presented, and, in view of the attention called forth, it was decided to have the bill printed for the information of the public and defer action until the next session; after which nothing further was done.[6]

A petition of strong anti-slavery character, praying the Legislature to "pass an act to set free all the slaves now in the Colony," was presented to the House in 1775 by fifty-two

---

[1] Woolman's *Journal*, p. 224.   [2] Dally, *Woodbridge*, p. 218.
[3] Whittier's *Introduction*, p. 23.   [4] *Supra*, p. 20.
[5] The counties were Burlington, Monmouth, Cumberland, Essex, Middlesex and Hunterdon.
[6] *Assem. Jour.*, Nov. 19, 1773, to Feb. 16, 1774; also Jan. 28 to Feb. 7, 1775.

inhabitants of Chesterfield in Burlington County.[1] In 1778, Governor Livingston asked the Assembly to make provision for the manumision of the slaves. The House thought that the times were too critical for the discussion of such a measure, and requested that the message be withdrawn. The Governor reluctantly consented, yet at the same time stating that he was determined, as far as his influence extended, "to push the matter till it is effected, being convinced that the practice is utterly inconsistent with the principles of Christianity and humanity; and in Americans who have almost idolized liberty, peculiarly odious and disgraceful." [2]

The New Jersey State Constitution, adopted in 1776,[3] contained no Bill of Rights. There was no provision ascribing natural rights to all persons. Although there is little doubt that the New Jersey courts would have been wholly opposed to construing such a provision as abolishing slavery; yet even if the courts had been so inclined, as happened in Massachusetts,[4] there was no opportunity for such a decision. The common law of England and the former statute law of the Colony were declared in force.

A society for promoting the abolition of slavery was formed in New Jersey as early as 1786.[5] A constitution adopted at Burlington in 1793 [6] provides for an annual meeting of members from the whole State and for county meetings half-yearly. The preamble, after mentioning "life, liberty and the pursuit of happiness" as "universal rights of men," concludes with the statement, "we abhor that inconsiderate, illiberal, and

---

[1] *Assem. Jour.*, Nov. 20, 1775.
[2] Bancroft, *Hist. of U. S.*, Vol. V., p. 411.
[3] Wilson, *Acts of State of N. J.* (1776–1783); also Poore's *Collection*.
[4] Winchendon *vs.* Hatfield, 4th Mass. Rep., 123.
[5] Williams, *Hist. of Negro Race in America*, p. 20.
[6] *N. J. Hist. Soc. Pamphlets*, Vol. VI.
The constitution adopted at Trenton in 1786 was frequently amended in succeeding years. The one agreed upon at Burlington in 1793 must have had some permanence, as it was printed and is now accessible.

interested policy which withholds those rights from an unfortunate and degraded class of our fellow creatures." The society was active and contained many able men. It was influential in obtaining the passage of laws for the gradual abolition of slavery,[1] and in securing before the courts the protection to slaves provided for in the statutes.[2] Its membership, however, in the early part of the present century, was not large. The president stated in 1804 that probably not more than 150 persons throughout the State were in active association with the society. The aims of the society at this period were moderate. The president, in an address in 1804, declared that it was not " to be wished, much less expected, that sudden and general emancipation should take place." He thought that the true policy was to " steadily pursue the best means of lessening, and by temperate steps, of finally extinguishing the evil." [3]

---

[1] *Assem. Jour.*, Jan. 28, 1794, records a " Petition from Joseph Bloomfield, styling himself President of a Society for promoting the Abolition of Slavery," praying that some measures may be established by law to promote the abolition of slavery." See also Nov. 22, 1802.

[2] The supreme court would not require persons acting with this end, to pay costs. In The State *vs.* Frees, the court refused to compel the Salem Abolition Society, the prosecutor of the writ of *habeas corpus* for the negroes in the case, to pay costs. The Chief Justice said that in no case would such prosecutors be compelled to pay costs; that "it was a laudable and humane thing in any man or set of men to bring up the claims of these unfortunate people before the court for consideration." *N. J. Law Rep.*, I, 299 (Coxe).

[3] There were local societies also. In 1802 the "Trenton Association for promoting the Abolition of Slavery" published its constitution, in order to evince to the public "that no improper or impertinent motives produced our association; and that no illegal, unjust or dishonorable means will be employed to accomplish our objects."

The members, convinced of the iniquity of personal slavery, had associated themselves together to endeavor by all constitutional and lawful means to ameliorate, as far as lay within their power, the situation of slaves, "to encourage and promote the gradual abolition of slavery," "and to improve the condition of and afford all reasonable protection and assistance to the blacks, and other people of color, who may be among us."

A petition in 1785, praying for the gradual abolition of slavery and the suppression of further importation of slaves, from a great number of the inhabitants of the State, resulted in the law of 1786 against importation and providing for manumission without security. This law is the first that recognizes that any question of ethics is involved in the holding of slaves.[1] Similar petitions to the above, from the Society of Friends and from citizens of Princeton, led two years later to the supplementary law of 1788 enacting very stringent measures for the overthrow of the slave trade.[2] A petition praying for the abolition of slavery, from certain inhabitants of Essex and Morris counties, was received in the Assembly in 1790, and referred to a committee. The committee reported to the effect that the position of the slaves under the existing laws was very satisfactory ; that, although it might be thought desirable to pass a law making slaves born in the future free at a certain age, for example, twenty-eight years, yet that, " from the state of society among us, the prevalence and progress of the principles of universal liberty, there is little reason to think there will be any slaves at all among us twenty-eight years hence, and that experience seems to show that precipitation in the matter may do more hurt than good, not only to the citizens of the State in general, but the slaves themselves."[3]

It was the "duty of the Acting Committee to carry into effect the resolves of the Association," " to give attention to all objects entitled to relief by the laws of the land," " to state their cases, by themselves or counsel, before the proper judicatures," etc.

Further, a Standing Committee of the Association had the following duties:

1. To superintend the morals and general conduct of the free blacks, and to give advice, instruction, protection and other friendly offices.

2. To superintend the instruction of children, and encourage them to good morals and habits of temperance and industry.

3. To place out children as apprentices.

4. To procure employment for men and women who are able to work, and to encourage them to bind themselves out to a trade. (*"True American,"* March 2, 1802.)

[1] *Supra*, p. 18.   [2] *Supra*, pp. 18 and 19.
[3] *Assem. Jour.*, May 24 and 26, 1790.

Notwithstanding the alluring optimism of the Assembly's committee anti-slavery petitions [1] continued to be presented to the House, and provisions to establish a system of gradual abolition were frequently before that body in the following years.[2] In the passage of the general slave law of 1798, a provision ordaining that all children born to slaves in the future should be free on attaining the age of twenty-eight years failed only by a very narrow majority.

In the year 1804, an act for the gradual abolition of slavery within the State was passed after the bill had run through two sessions of the legislature.[3] Every child born of a slave after the fourth of July of that year was to be free, but should remain the servant of the owner of the mother, as if bound out by the overseers of the poor, until the age of twenty-five years, if a male, and twenty-one years, if a female. The right to the services of such negro child was perfectly clear and free. It was assignable or transferable.[4] One person might be the owner of the mother and another have gained the right to the services of the child. Masters were compelled to file with the county clerk a certificate of the birth of every child of a slave.[5] This certificate was kept for future evidence of the age of the child. The owner of the mother must maintain the child for one year; after that period he might, by giving due notice,

---

[1] *Assem. Jour.*, Oct. 24, Nov. 21, 1792; Jan. 28, Nov. 10, 1794.

[2] *Assem. Jour.*, Oct. 25, 1792; May 21, 1793; Feb. 4, 1794; Feb. 14, 1797; Jan. 19, March 8, 1798.

[3] 28 Ses., 2 sit., *Statutes* 251. Here, again, the bill was introduced in answer to a memorial from the New Jersey Abolition Society. The bill was published for the general information of the people before it was finally acted upon. *Assem. Jour.*, Nov. 22, 1802 to Feb. 15, 1804.

[4] This point was established by the Supreme Court in 1827. The Chief Justice declared that services of this character were a "species of property," and were "transferred from one citizen to another like other personal property." Ogden *vs.* Price, *N. J. Law Rep.*, IX, 211–217 (4th Halsted).

[5] The book *Black Births* of Bergen County, contains the certificates for that county. The descriptions are generally very brief, frequently giving nothing more than the name of the child. It seems remarkable that such records should have been sufficient to prove a man's freedom.

abandon it. Every negro child thus abandoned, like other poor children, was to be regarded as a pauper of the township or county, and be bound out to service by the overseers of the poor. This provision, allowing masters to refuse to maintain children born to their slaves, was the source of considerable fraud upon the treasury, and was the cause of many supplements and amendments [1] to the law of 1804 in succeeding years. Finally, seven years later the provision was repealed,[2] the reason given being "it appears that large sums of money have been drawn from the treasury by citizens of the State for maintaining abandoned black children, and that in some instances the money drawn for their maintenance amounts to more than they would have brought if sold for life."[3]

In 1844, a new constitution was adopted in New Jersey.[4] The first article was in the nature of a Bill of Rights, and the first section read as follows: "All men are by nature free and independent, and have certain natural and inalienable rights, among which are those of enjoying and defending life and liberty, acquiring, possessing, and protecting property, and of pursuing and obtaining safety and happiness." Some believed that this section abolished both slavery and that form of involuntary servitude in which children of slaves were held by the

---

[1] 1806, 1808, 1809. 30 Ses., 2 sit., *Statutes*, 668; 33 Ses., 1 sit., *Statutes*, 112; 34 Ses., 1 sit., *Statutes*, 200.

[2] 1811. 35 Ses., 2 sit., *Statutes*, 313. This legislation also reaches its final form in the compiled law of 1820. 44 Ses., *Statutes*, 74.

[3] In 1806, the State Treasurer requested the "orders of the legislature with respect to payments demanded of him for supporting black children." His report the next year shows disbursements "for abandoned blacks" amounting to half as much as all other disbursements whatever. In 1809, the expenditure for abandoned blacks amounted to two-thirds of all other expenditure; the drafts upon the treasury for the support of blacks from the County of Bergen alone amounting to $7,033, out of a total State expenditure for blacks of $12,570. The Treasurer called the attention of the Assembly to these latter facts, and the House directed him "to suspend all further payments in all doubtful cases for the support of abandoned blacks." *Assem. Jour.*, Nov. 5, 1806; Nov. 2–21, 1809; also *Treas. Rep., Assem Jour.*, Nov. 13, 1807; Nov. 14, 1808; Nov. 8, 1809.

[4] Poore's *Collection*, p. 1314.

law of 1820. The ground for this belief was, doubtless, that remarkably liberal interpretation of a similar provision in the Massachusetts constitution of 1780, by which the Massachusetts courts decided slavery to have been abolished by that constitution.[1] The matter came up for adjudication before the New Jersey supreme court in 1845;[2] but that court did not follow the Massachusetts precedent. The court declared the section in question was a "general proposition, that men in their social state are free to adopt their own form of government and enact their own laws," "that in framing their laws, they have a right to consult their safety and happiness, whether in the protection of life and liberty, or the acquisition of property." The provision was not designed, the Justice said, to apply to "man in his private, individual or domestic capacity; or to define his individual rights or interfere with his domestic relations, or his individual condition." The court then held that the constitution of 1844 had not abolished slavery or affected the slave laws existing at the time of its adoption.[3]

Slavery was abolished by statute in New Jersey in the year 1846.[4] This action did not result in complete emancipation of the slaves. The abolition law simply substituted apprenticeship in place of slavery. By virtue of the act, and without the execution of any instrument of manumission, every slave became an apprentice, bound to service to his present owner, executors, or administrators, until discharged therefrom. How similar were the two conditions[5] is shown when we find many

[1] Mr. Moore says that this provision of the constitution of 1780 was "only a new edition of the 'glittering and sounding generalities' which prefaced the Body of Liberties in 1641;" yet the earlier instrument was never held to have abolished slavery. Moore, G. H., *Notes on the History and Slavery in Massachusetts*, p. 12.

[2] The State *vs.* Post. The State *vs.* Van Buren. *N. J. Law Rep.*, XX. 368-386 (Spencer).

[3] The case was carried up into the Court of Errors and Appeals, and the decision of the Supreme Court was confirmed. *N. J. Law Rep.*, XXI, 699.

[4] *Revised Statutes*, 382.

[5] The U. S. Census of 1850 reports 236 slaves in New Jersey, and the Census of 1860 reports 18 slaves. Evidently these must have been legally apprentices for life.

old provisions regarding slaves reproduced and reënacted for the government of the new apprentices created by the statute. Forms are established according to which apprentices may be legally discharged.[1] Penalties for enticing apprentices away or harboring them, or for misusing them, are provided. Apprentices are not to be carried out of the State, or sold to a non-resident. Yet this change of status represented a real improvement in the condition of the negro servant for life or years. The sale of an apprentice must be in writing and with the consent of the apprentice, expressed by his signature. An apprentice having a complaint against his master was granted the same remedy as that previously provided by law for apprentices and servants. Children born to negro apprentices were to be absolutely free from birth, and not subject to any manner of service whatsoever. They must be supported by the master until they attained the age of six years, after which they were to be bound out to service by the overseers of the poor.

New Jersey, as a State, showed also at times considerable interest in slavery in its larger aspect, as it affected general conditions in the United States. In January, 1820, the legislature passed resolutions against the admission of Missouri as a slave state.[2] Four years later resolutions were passed affirming, first, that in the opinion of the legislature, "a system of foreign colonization" represented a feasible plan by which might be effected "the entire emancipation of the slaves in our country;" second, that such an arrangement made convenient provision for the free blacks; third, that the evil of slavery being a national one "the duties and burdens of removing it" ought to be borne by the people and States of the Union. Copies of these resolutions were forwarded to the Governors of the several States, with the request that they lay the same before their respective legislatures, and to the New Jersey Senators and Representatives in Congress

---

[1] A new and interesting provision is that the apprentice shall not be discharged unless he desires to be.

[2] *Assem. Jour.*, Jan. 13 to 19, 1820.

asking their coöperation.[1]   In 1847, the legislature resolved[2] that the Senators and Representatives in Congress from New Jersey be requested to use their best efforts to secure the exclusion forever of slavery or involuntary servitude from any territory thereafter to be annexed to the United States, except as a punishment for crime. Two years later similar resolutions[3] were passed condemning the further extension of slavery, and urging the speedy abolition of the slave trade within the District of Columbia.

The Extent of Slavery.

The use of slave labor was quite general in New Jersey during the period of the royal governors. From quotations from the census reports, given by Mr. Gordon,[4] we learn that there were 3,981 slaves in the Province in 1737, 4,606 slaves in 1745, and 11,423 in 1790.[5] Though the number of slaves was increasing constantly during this period, that increase did not keep pace with the growth of population. Slaves constituted 8.4 per cent. of the population in 1737, 7.5 per cent. in 1745, and 6.2 per cent. in 1790. In Perth Amboy, the port of entry for the eastern division of the Province, slaves were especially numerous. According to Mr. Whitehead, it

---

[1] *Assem. Jour.*, Nov. 23 to Dec. 29, 1824, and 49 Ses., *Statutes*, 191.

[2] 71 Leg., 3 Ses., *Statutes*, 188.   [3] 73 Leg., 5 Ses., *Statutes*, 334.

[4] Gordon, T. F., *Gazetteer of N. J.*, p. 29.

[5] Blake, *Ancient and Modern Slavery*, p. 388, says that in 1776 New Jersey contained 7,600 slaves. No authority for the statement is given. As the U. S. Census of 1790 reports 11,423 slaves in New Jersey, if Mr. Blake's figures are correct, there must have been an increase of 3,823 slaves between 1776 and 1790. That there was such a large increase seems to me very improbable, when we consider, first, that such an increase would be at a rate double that observed in the next decade; second, that the years of the war presumably were not years when the number of slaves increased rapidly. If the slave population increased at a uniform rate from 1745 to 1790 there would have been more than nine thousand slaves in the Colony in 1776.

was reported that in 1776 there was in the town only one house whose inmates were "served by hired free white domestics."[1] In other places the labor of families was also very commonly performed by slaves.

The maximum slave population in New Jersey given by the U. S. Census Reports is 12,422 in the year 1800. The next census shows a decrease to 10,851, in consequence of the abolition law of 1804. The number of slaves reported rapidly diminishes with each succeeding census until the last record in 1860 shows but eighteen slaves[2] in the State. At the beginning of the present century New Jersey had a larger slave population than any other State north of Maryland, except New York.[3] The coast counties from Sandy Hook to the northern boundary, and the Raritan Valley, were the regions containing the great majority of the slaves. The three great Quaker counties of Burlington, Gloucester, and Salem, containing 23 per cent. of the total State population, contained less than 3 per cent. of the slave population. The effect of the eighteenth century abolition agitation among the Friends is here clearly shown.[4]

---

[1] Whitehead, *Perth Amboy*, p. 318.

[2] These must have been legally " apprentices."

[3] U. S. Census, 1800. Mr. Mellick notices this fact, and thinks that it was due to the large Dutch and German population. He says that the greatest number of slaves were to be found in the counties where the Dutch and Germans predominated. *Story of an Old Farm*, pp. 220–228.

[4] Population of New Jersey :

Year.	Total Population.	Slaves.	Per Cent. of Slaves.	
1737	47,402	3,981	8.4	(Gordon.)
1745	61,383	4,606	7.5	"
1790	184,139	11,423	6.2	(U. S. Census.)
1800	211,949	12,422	5.8	"
1810	245,555	10,851	4.4	"
1820	277,575	7,557	2.7	"
1830	320,823	2,254	.7	"
1840	373,306	674	.18	"
1850	489,555	236*	.048	"
1860	672,035	18*	.0026	"

* Legally " apprentices " for life.

CHAPTER II.

THE GOVERNMENT OF SLAVES.

Regulations bearing upon the faults and misdemeanors to which slaves are peculiarly liable first appear in New Jersey legislation in laws for the correction of truancy on the part of slaves and servants. As early as 1675,[1] under the Proprietary government, it was enacted that persons who assist in the transportation of a slave shall be liable to a penalty of five pounds and must make good to the owner any costs that he may have sustained. Those who entertain or harbor any slave known to be absent from his master without permission must pay to the owner "ten shillings for every day's entertainment and concealment."[2] The Indians by their reception of negroes appear to have caused the settlers some annoyance. We read in the Journal of the Governor and Council that, in 1682, it was "agreed and ordered that a message be sent to the Indian sachems to confer with them about their entertainment of negro servants."[3] Again, in 1694, the "countenance, harboring and entertaining of slaves by many of the inhabitants"

---

[1] Leaming and Spicer, p. 109.

[2] These provisions were virtually reënacted in a law for East Jersey, "against fugitive servants and entertainers of them," in 1682, just after that Province came under the government of the twenty-four Proprietors. L. and S., p. 238; N. J. Ar., XIII, 31, 33 and 157. In 1683, in West Jersey, in order to prevent servants from running away from their masters, magistrates and other inhabitants were directed to require from all suspicious travellers, a certificate showing that they were not fugitives. L. and S., p. 477.

[3] N. J. Ar., XIII, 22.

calls for heavier penalties. By a law of that year such entertainment, if it extends to as much as two hours, renders the
offender liable to a penalty of twenty shillings, and a proportional sum for a longer time.[1] Furthermore, any person may
apprehend as a runaway any slave found " five miles from his
owner's habitation" without a certificate of his owner's permission; and for this service the master must give recompense
in money at a prescribed rate.[2]

During the period of the royal governors there were two
new regulations bearing on the recovery of fugitives. Any
slave from another Province travelling without a license, or
not known to be on his master's business, was to be taken up
and whipped; and should remain in prison until the costs of
apprehending him had been paid by his owner.[3] Persons from
a neighboring Colony suspected of being fugitives must produce
a pass from a justice, " signifying that they are free persons,"
otherwise to be imprisoned until demanded.[4]

Under the State laws more stringent regulations referring
to fugitives are found. By the law of 1786 the freedom of
movement of negroes was very closely restricted. Negroes
manumitted in other States were not allowed to travel in
New Jersey. Any person who employed them, concealed
them, or suffered them to reside or land within the State was
liable to a penalty of five pounds per week. Free negroes of
New Jersey were not to travel beyond their township or county
without an official certificate of their freedom.[5] This severity
was modified somewhat by the law of 1798. A free negro
from another State might now travel in New Jersey provided
that he produced a certificate signed by two Justices of the

---

[1] That this entertainment of negroes was a real evil in the later Colonial
period is shown by an advertisement for a fugitive slave in 1750, which
reads: "and whereas he has been harboured once before, whoever informs
who harbours him shall have ten pounds reward." *N. J. Ar.*, XII, 644.

[2] L. and S., p. 340; *N. J. Ar.*, XIII, 205.

[3] Act for regulating of slaves, 1714; Nevill, I, 18.

[4] 1714. Nevill, I, 24.   [5] Acts of General Assembly.

Peace of his State showing his freedom.[1]   That all black men should be regarded as slaves until evidence appeared to the contrary, was ·held by the Supreme Court even as late as 1826.[2] Yet by the U. S. Census of 1820, New Jersey contained nearly twice as many free negroes as slaves.   The court receded from this position ten years later, the injustice of the ruling having become very obvious owing to the small proportion which slaves bore to the colored population.[3]

The ferries from New Jersey to New York constituted routes by which fugitive slaves occasionally escaped.   On July 4, 1818, a slave mingling in the holiday crowd gained a passage on the ferry-boat running from Elizabeth-Town to New York, and, after reaching the latter place, escaped.   The master of the slave sued the owner of the ferry-boat and obtained damages for the loss of the slave.[4]   Seven years later there is recorded a similar escape on a steamboat running from Perth Amboy to New York.[5]

The apprehension of fugitive slaves from other States was provided for with great care by a law of 1826.[6]   On the proper application[7] by the master, a fugitive might be arrested by the sheriff and brought before a judge of the inferior Court of Common Pleas.   If the judge deemed that there was enough proof he was to give the claimant a certificate, which should be sufficient warrant for the removal of the fugitive from the

---

[1] Any person harboring, concealing or employing any negro without such a certificate was liable to a fine of $12 for every week of such action. Paterson, p. 307.

[2] Fox *vs.* Lambson, *N. J. Law Rep.*, VIII, 339–349 (3rd Halsted).   This principle was authoritatively established, in 1821, by the case of Gibbons *vs.* Morse carried up to the court of errors and appeals, *N. J. Law Rep.*, VII, 305–327 (2nd Halsted); and reaffirmed in Fox *vs.* Lambson.

[3] Stoutenborough *vs.* Haviland, *N. J. Law Rep.*, XV, 266–269 (3rd Green).

[4] Gibbons *vs.* Morse.

[5] Cutter *vs.* Moore, *N. J. Law Rep.*, VIII, 270–278 (3rd Halsted).

[6] 51 Ses., *Statutes*, 90.

[7] Application by the master, personally or by attorney, to any judge of any inferior Court of Common Pleas or Justice of the Peace.

State. A case falling under this law, and carried up to the
Supreme Court in 1826, led to a debate in that court which
called in question the justice of the law. The judges concurred in discharging the prisoner, a negro claimed as a
runaway slave from Maryland; but showed great disagreement in the discussion of the merits of the case. Chief
Justice Hornblower held that questions of fact were involved,
such as, was the negro lawfully held to service in the State
from which he came? has he fled into this State? has the
claimant any right to his services? Here were facts which
must be judicially determined, "facts which involve the
dearest rights of a human being." These facts the Justice
believed should not "be tried and definitely sealed in a summary manner, and without the verdict of a jury."[1] The next
year, probably as the result of the discussion in the Supreme
Court, the fugitive slave law was amended.[2] A judge having
a fugitive brought before him must appoint a certain time
and place for the trial of the case, and associate with him two
other judges. Either party might demand trial by jury.[3]

Other Police Regulations.

Besides the provisions for the correction of truancy, various
other police regulations were established from time to time.
The early inhabitants of East Jersey appear to have been
much troubled by the thievishness of their slaves. The complaint was that slaves stole from their masters and others and
then sold the stolen goods at some distance away. In the
belief that a market was necessary to make pilfering worth
while, all traffic whatever with slaves was forbidden in 1682,

[1] The State *vs.* Sheriff of Burlington. Hurd, *Law of Freedom and Bondage*,
II, 64–67. Owing to disagreement among the judges as to the proper extent
of the discussion, the case was not given in the *State Reports*.

[2] 61 Ses., 2 sit., *Statutes*, 134.

[3] In the revision of 1847 virtually the same law was approved and so
stood as the fugitive slave act of the State. *Revision of 1847*, p. 567.

under heavy penalties.[1] If any slave were found offering goods for sale without the permission of his master it was the duty of the person to whom the article was offered to take up and whip the slave, for which service the master must pay a reward of half a crown.[2] Later, in the same Province, we read that slaves allowed to hunt with dog and gun killed swine under pretence of hunting. In 1694, slaves were prohibited from carrying any "gun or pistol," and from taking any dog with them into the "woods or plantations," unless accompanied by the master or his representative.[3] If any person "lend, give or hire out" a pistol or gun to a slave, that person must forfeit the gun or twenty shillings to the owner of the slave.[4] In West Jersey, in the Proprietary period, the selling of rum to negroes was found to be productive of disorder. Any person "convicted of selling or giving of rum, or any manner of strong liquor, either to negro or Indian," except the stimulant be given in relief of real physical distress, becomes liable to a penalty of five pounds by a law of 1685. As the offense was one difficult of detection, "one creditable witness or a probable circumstance" was accounted "sufficient evidence," unless the accused gave his "oath or solemn declaration that he has not transgressed the law."[5]

Regulations against harboring, trading with, or selling rum to slaves were reënacted during the period of the royal Governors, and in the State legislation.[6] Others were added, such as: the prohibition of large or disorderly meetings of slaves,[7]

---

[1] Similar penalties are found in the slave law of 1714, and thus held throughout the Colonial period.

[2] L. and S., 254; *N. J. Ar.*, XIII, 82. Law passed at Elizabeth-Town.

[3] Act passed at Perth Amboy. L. and S., 340; *N. J. Ar.*, XIII, 205.

[4] By the same law, no inhabitant should allow his slave to keep swine marked with another brand than the owner's. This provision was probably intended to prevent dishonesty on the part of masters.

[5] Act passed at Burlington. L. and S., 512.

[6] Laws of 1714, 1738, 1751 and 1798. Nevill, I, 242; Allison, 191; Paterson, 307.

[7] Laws of 1751 and 1798.

the rule that all slaves must be at home after a certain hour at night,[1] that slaves shall not go hunting or carry a gun on Sunday,[2] that slaves shall not set a steel trap above a specified weight,[3] that slaves shall not be permitted to beg.[4] For the correction of the smaller faults and misdeeds there was the workhouse. A law of 1754 provided that in the borough of Elizabeth, servants and slaves accused of "any misdemeanor or rude or disorderly behavior," being brought before the Mayor, may be "committed to the workhouse to hard labor" and receive corporal punishment not exceeding thirty stripes.[5] In 1799 the system was established throughout the State. "Any stubborn, disobedient, rude or intemperate slave or male servant" might be committed to the workhouse to endure confinement and labor at the discretion of a Justice of the Peace. The master paid the cost of maintenance of the slave while so confined.[6]

The Criminal Law for Slaves.

During nearly the whole period of the Proprietary Colony the same general criminal laws governed both slaves and freemen. The bond as well as the free were tried in the ordinary courts, for crimes and misdemeanors. In 1695 a change was made. Special courts were provided for the trial of slaves

---

[1] Nine o'clock by law of 1751, ten o'clock by law of 1798.

[2] Laws of 1751 and 1798. These laws, however, did not prevent a negro or slave from going to any place of worship, or from burying the dead, or from doing any other reasonable act, with his master's consent.

[3] In 1760 an "Act to regulate the size of traps to be hereafter set in this Colony" directed that any slave setting a steel trap above a specified weight "shall be whipped with thirty lashes and committed until the cost is paid." *N. J. Statutes*, p. 61.

[4] The law of 1798 imposed a penalty of $8 for permitting slaves to beg, one-half to be paid to the overseers of the poor and one-half to the person who prosecuted.

[5] Nevill, II, 25, 29.

[6] An act for the establishment of workhouses in the several counties of this State. Paterson, 379.

and an exceptional form of punishment was prescribed for slave offenders.[1] Slaves accused of a felony or murder were to have trial by jury before three Justices [2] of the Peace of the county, and on conviction were to receive, in general, the punishments "appointed for such crimes." [3] Under the royal governors, the law of 1714 adhered to the principle of special courts for slaves. Ordinarily the trials of slaves for capital offences were to be before three or more Justices of the Peace and five principal freeholders of the county; but the master might demand trial by jury.[4] In 1768 the use of special courts was discontinued, and slaves accused of capital offences were once more tried in the ordinary courts [5] as freemen were. The reason given for this return to earlier practice was that the method by special courts had "on experience been found inconvenient." [6] Throughout the period of the royal governors special forms of punishment were provided for slaves. Not until 1788, under the State government, was it enacted that all criminal offences of negroes should be punished in the same manner as the criminal offences of other inhabitants of the State were.[7] Even under the State legislation the provisions allowing corporal punishment or transportation to be substituted in some cases for the usual punishment, at the discretion of the court, violated somewhat the principle of uniformity of procedure.

As might be expected from the grade of civilization developed in the various Colonies and the accompanying stringent

---

[1] Act passed at Perth Amboy, 1695. L. and S., 357.

[2] One being of the quorum.

[3] The special punishment provided was, that slaves convicted of stealing should receive corporal punishment, not exceeding forty stripes, the master making good the amount stolen.

[4] Allinson, 18.

[5] The courts mentioned were the Supreme Court, Court of Oyer and Terminer and General Gaol Delivery, and Court of General Quarter Sessions of the Peace.

[6] Allinson, 307.   [7] Acts of 13th General Assembly.

criminal code, the punishments provided for slaves in New Jersey throughout the Colonial period were severe and often cruel.[1] As early as 1704 the Lords of Trade recommended to the Queen the repeal of an act lately passed by the Assembly because one clause inflicted inhuman penalties upon negroes.[2] By the slave law of 1714[3] any "negro, Indian or mulatto slave" murdering or attempting the death of any freeman, wilfully murdering any slave, committing arson, "rape on any free subject," or mutilation of any free person, is to suffer the penalty of death.[4] The manner of death, however, is not specified, but is to be such as the "aggravation or enormity of their crimes" (in the judgment of the justices and freeholders trying the case) "shall merit and require." The testimony of slaves was admitted in the trials.[5] When a slave was executed, the owner received for a negro man thirty pounds and for a

---

[1] That in the rough, frontier conditions of the Proprietary Colony the punishments were sometimes cruel, although slaves were tried in the ordinary courts, is evident from an instance given by Mr. Mellick. He says that in 1694 a Justice presiding at the Monmouth court of sessions, sentenced a negro convicted of murder to suffer as follows: "Thy hand shall be cut off and burned before thine eyes. Then thou shalt be hanged up by the neck until thou art dead, dead, dead; then thy body shall be cut down and burned to ashes in a fire, and so the Lord have mercy on thy soul, Cæsar" (*Story of an Old Farm*, p. 225).

[2] *N. J. Ar.*, III, 473, Representation of Lords of Trade to the Queen. Allinson, p. 5.

[3] Nevill, I, 18; Allinson, 18.

In the Journal of the Governor and Council, *N. J. Ar.*, XIII, 439, 440, 448, we find record that the Council in 1710 passed "An Act for deterring negroes and other slaves from committing murder and other notorious offenses within this Colony." The provisions are not given.

[4] Poisoning was sometimes practiced by slaves in the Colonial period. In 1738 two negroes, found guilty of destroying sundry persons by poison, were executed at Burlington. At Hackensack, in 1744, a negro was executed for poisoning three negro women and a horse. *N. J. Ar.*, XI, 523, 537; XII, 223.

[5] At the trial of the negro man "Harry" in Bergen County, 1731, who was hung for threatening the life of his master and poisoning the slave "Sepio," many negroes were summoned as witnesses. Bergen Co., "Liber A," p. 24.

woman twenty pounds, the money being raised by a poll tax
upon all the slaves in the county above fourteen years of age
and under fifty.[1] This payment made good to the master a
loss of property due to no fault of his.   Further, it left him
no inducement to transport the slave out of the Province and
thus encourage other negroes to crime by allowing the hope
that punishment might be escaped.   In the case of slaves
attempting rape, or assaulting a free Christian, any two justices of the peace were authorized to inflict such corporal
punishment, not extending to life or limb, as they might see
fit.   Slaves stealing under the value of five shillings were to
be whipped with thirty stripes; if above five shillings, with
forty stripes.[2]

A form of execution frequently chosen was burning at the
stake.   At Perth Amboy, in 1730, a negro was burnt for the
murder of an itinerant tailor.[3]   In Bergen County, in 1735,
the slave "Jack" was burnt.   He had beaten his master,
several times had threatened to murder his master and the
son of his master and to burn down his master's house, and
when arrested tried to kill himself.[4]   In Somerset County, in
1739, a negro was burnt for brutally murdering a child,
attempting to murder the wife of his overseer, and setting fire
to his master's barn.[5]   In 1741 two negroes were burnt for

---

[1] Bergen County Quarter Sessions in 1768 ordered that Hendrieck Christian Zabriskie should have thirty pounds for his negro named Harry, lately
executed for the murder of Claas Toers. The money was collected from the
slave-owners of the county, upon the basis of an assessment of ten pence per
head upon all slaves in the county. Bergen Co. Quar. Sess., January 27, 1768.

[2] In Hackensack in 1769, a slave pleading guilty to the charge of stealing, was whipped at the public whipping-post and before the houses of two
prominent citizens, with thirty-nine lashes on each of three days, being
taken from place to place tied to a cart's tail. Bergen Co. Quar. Sess.,
October 24, 1769.

[3] *Am. Wk. Mercury,* Jan. 14–20, 1729 (1730); (*N. J. Ar.,* XI, 201).

[4] Bergen County, "Liber A," p. 36.

[5] *Boston Wk. News-Letter,* Jan. 18–25, 1739 (*N. J. Ar.,* XI, 558). In the
same county, five years later, a negro was burnt for ravishing a white child.
Pa. Gazette, Dec. 14, 1744 (*N. J. Ar.,* XII, 244).

setting on fire several barns in the neighborhood of Hackensack.[1] Mr. Whitehead says that the New York " Negro Plot "
of 1741 caused many executions by burning as well as by
hanging in New Jersey. He describes a case ten years later,
near Perth Amboy, when all the negroes of the neighborhood
were compelled to witness the execution.[2]

The criminal law of 1768, which supplanted the provisions
relating to capital offences in the act of 1714, represents an
increase of severity. It appointed the penalty of death for
the crimes made capital under the earlier law, and for others
as well. A slave convicted of manslaughter, or of stealing
any sum of money above the value of five pounds, or of committing any other felony or burglary, was to suffer death or
such other pains and penalties as the justices might think
proper to inflict. In this law, as before, there was no specifi-
cation as to the manner in which death might be inflicted.[3]

Under the early State legislation the severe and peculiar
forms of punishment provided for slaves by the Colonial laws
disappeared. In 1788, it was enacted that all criminal offences
of negroes, whether slaves or freemen, should be " enquired
of, adjudged, corrected and punished in like manner as the
criminal offences of the other inhabitants of this State are." [4]
This principle was firmly established by the passage in 1796
of " An Act for the punishment of Crimes," a comprehensive
and fundamental criminal law, which, in general, prescribed
one punishment for all persons guilty of a particular crime,
mentioning no distinction between bond and free.[5] Slaves
continued, however, to be to some extent the subject of special
criminal legislation. By the law of 1796 a court might
impose upon any slave, in place of the usual punishment,

---

[1] Bergen County, " Liber A," p. 44.
[2] Whitehead, W. A., *Contributions to the Early History of Perth Amboy*, pp.
318–320; also *Wk. Post Boy*, July 2, 1750 (*N. J. Ar.*, XII, 652).
[3] Allinson, 307; *N. J. Ar.*, XVII, 483, 485, 486 (Jour. of Prov. Council).
[4] Acts of 13th Gen. Assem., Nov. 26, 1788.   [5] Paterson, 220.

corporal punishment at its discretion and not extending to
life or limb, for any offence not punishable with death. By
the act of 1801, when slaves were convicted of arson, burglary,
rape, highway robbery, or assault with intent to commit
murder, the court might choose to order them to be sent out
of the United States.[1] In this case the owner was compelled
to give bond that he would faithfully execute the court's
decree, and finally file a certificate that the sentence has been
complied with.

Negro Plots.

We have seen that by the police regulations enacted for the
government of slaves, negroes were forbidden to assemble
together in companies, except with their master's consent for
some reasonable purpose, such as to attend public worship or
to bury their dead. Furthermore, slaves must be at home
after nine o'clock at night.[2] These provisions were probably
called forth by fear of slave insurrections; but it is difficult
to determine to what extent the legislation was connected with
actual experience of negro plots.

In 1734, a rising in East Jersey,[3] near Somerville,[4] was
feared. Certain negro quarters some miles remote from the
master's dwelling-house had become a rendezvous for the
negroes of the neighborhood. The slaves round about stole
from their masters provisions of various sorts which they carried to their place of meeting and feasted upon, sometimes in
large companies. It was claimed that at one of these meetings some hundreds had entered into a plot to gain their
freedom by a massacre of the whites. A belief on the part
of the negroes that they were held in slavery contrary to the

[1] 25 Ses., 2 sit., *Statutes*, 77. See also on this subject, *Revision of* 1821, pp.
736, 793, and 44 Ses., *Statutes*, 74, sec. 20.

[2] *Supra*, p. 37.

[3] *N. Y. Gazette*, March 18–25, 1734, gives a detailed account of the conspiracy.

[4] Mellick, p. 226, says that the excitement was near Somerville.

positive orders of King George appears to have been an element contributing to the excitement. According to the plan of the conspirators, as soon as the weather became mild enough so that living in the woods might be possible, at some midnight agreed upon, all the slaves were to rise and slay their masters. The buildings were to be set on fire and the draught horses killed. Finally, the negroes, having secured the best saddle horses, were to fly to the Indians and join them in the French interest. Suspicion of a negro plot was first aroused by the impudent remarks of a drunken slave. He and another negro were arrested, and at their trial the above details were brought out. The insurrection believed to be threatening was suppressed with considerable severity.[1]

That delirium of the New York people in 1741, known as the "Negro Conspiracy," appears to have spread to some extent into neighboring New Jersey also. Mr. Whitehead thinks that this panic caused many executions in New Jersey.[2] In one day seven barns were burned at Hackensack; an eighth caught fire three times, but fortunately was saved. It was believed that these were set on fire by a combination of slaves, for one negro was taken in the act. The people of the neighborhood were greatly alarmed and kept under arms every night. Two negroes charged with committing the crime were burned.[3] Mr. Hatfield quotes from the Account Book of the Justices and Freeholders of Essex County the following items: "June 4, 1741, Daniel Harrison sent in his account of wood carted for burning two negroes." . . . "February 25, 174½, Joseph Heden acct. for wood to burn the negroes Mr. Farrand paid allowed 0. 7. 0. Allowed to Isaac Lyon 4/ Curr^y for a load of wood to burn the first negro, 0. 4. 0."[4] Mr. Whitehead

---

[1] About thirty negroes were apprehended; one of them was hanged, some had their ears cut off, and others were whipped. Poison was found on several of them. *N. J. Ar.*, XI, 333, 340.

[2] Whitehead, *Perth Amboy*, p. 318.   [3] *N. J. Ar.*, XII, 88, 91, 98.

[4] Hatfield, *History of Elizabeth, N. J.*, p. 364.

says that, in 1772, "an insurrection was anticipated, but was prevented by due precautionary measures."[1]

Mr. Hatfield tells of a panic regarding negroes at Elizabeth-Town during the Revolution.[2] In June, 1779, a conspiracy of the negroes to rise and murder the people of the town was discovered. The Tories, whose plundering expeditions had been very exasperating, were held responsible for this new danger also. The resentment aroused by these occurrences caused the Court of Common Pleas to enter severe judgments against many Tories. Mr. Atkinson states that in 1796 there was, among the whites, great fear of negro violence, and a feeling of bitterness toward the slaves was developed.[3] The agitation was caused by the attempts of certain blacks to set fire to buildings in New York, Newark and other places.

[1] Whitehead, *Perth Amboy*, pp. 318–320.   [2] Hatfield, p. 476.
[3] Atkinson, J., *History of Newark, N. J.*, pp. 170–172.

CHAPTER III.

The Legal and Social Position of the Negro.

The subject of manumission began to demand legislative action at the time of the royal governors. According to what forms manumission should be legal, what limitations it might be expedient to place on the power to manumit; these were considerations which then became of great consequence and retained their prominence even until after the disappearance of slavery from New Jersey life. Furthermore, the interpretation given by the courts to the existing law of manumission often decided for the colored man whether his position was that of freeman or slave.

Very early in the eighteenth century it is recorded that experience had shown "that free negroes are an idle, slothful people and prove very often a charge to the place where they are." [1] Therefore, the law of 1714 had a provision designed to prevent freedmen from ever coming upon the township as paupers. It enacted that any master manumitting a slave must enter into "sufficient security," "with two sureties in the sum of 200 pounds," to pay to the negro an annuity of 20 pounds. In case of manumission by will the executors must give such security. Owners or their heirs were obliged to maintain all negroes not manumitted according to law. The desire to save townships the expense of supporting freedmen was not recognized to such an extent as to allow unfortunate negroes actually to suffer. An act of 1769 states

---

[1] Law of 1714. Nevill, I, 18.

definitely that if the " owner becomes insolvent and so incapable of providing for his slaves, who shall by sickness or otherwise be rendered incapable of maintaining themselves, they shall be relieved by the township the same as white servants."[1] In 1773, in response to several petitions, a bill providing for manumission without the giving of security was introduced in the Assembly. The bill stated that the manumission law of the Colony had on experience been found too indiscriminate, the requirement of equal security in all cases working, in some instances, to "prevent the exercise of humanity and tenderness in the emancipation of those who may deserve it." In view of the great opposition as well as favor with which the bill was received, the House ordered that the bill be printed and referred to the next session.[2] At the next session, in 1775, the various petitions presented for and against the bill led to another postponement to the following session;[3] by which time the greater interests of the Revolution crowded out the consideration of this matter.

Immediately after the Revolution we find a peculiar form of manumission, that by special act of the legislature. On three occasions previous to the year 1790, slaves that had become the property of the State, through the confiscation of Tory estates, were set free by act of the legislature.[4] The negroes were given their freedom in recognition of past services to the State or to the Federal cause.[5]

---

[1] Allinson, 315. The law of 1679 reënacted the requirements of the law of 1714.

[2] *Assem. Jour.*, Nov. 30, 1773, to Feb. 16, 1774.

[3] *Assem. Jour.*, Jan. 28 to Feb. 7, 1775.

[4] 1784, 1786 and 1789; 8 Ses., 2 sit., *Statutes*, 110; 11 Ses., 1 sit., *Statutes*, 368; 14 Ses., 1 sit., *Statutes*, 538.

[5] There is record of an interesting case of this form of manumission in 1840. Cæsar Jackson, a colored man of Hackensack, was a slave in law, having been born previously to the year 1804. His late master, Peter Bourdett, had inserted in his will a request that, at his death, the slave Cæsar Jackson should be set free. The heirs of Peter Bourdett desired to carry out his request, but had been unable to do so. They had given

In 1786, changes were made in the law of manumission. Slaves between the ages of twenty-one and thirty-five, sound in mind, and under no bodily incapacity of obtaining a support, might now be emancipated without security being given for their support. A master must first secure a certificate signed by two overseers of the poor of the township and two Justices of the Peace of the county, showing that the slave met the requirements as to age and health. He might then manumit the slave by executing a certificate under his hand and seal in the presence of two witnesses. A similar manumission by will was valid. In all other cases the master (or his executors) was compelled to give security that the negro should not come upon any township for support.[1] These provisions were virtually reënacted in the slave law of 1798.[2] A supplementary law in 1804 provides for registration of instruments of manumission by the county clerk.[3] Such record by the clerk was receivable as evidence in the courts.[4]

The New Jersey courts interpreted the law on manumission in a liberal spirit. They were ready to presume a manumission, if an actual, formal emancipation according to law could not be proven, whenever the circumstances seemed to warrant such a procedure. In 1789, a negro woman who had lived and worked in the neighborhood of Shrewsbury as a free woman for seventeen years, with no claim upon her as a slave,

---

Cæsar Jackson a lot of land in the township, and he had erected on it a dwelling-house for himself and his family; but he had been unable to obtain a deed for the land, as he was still a slave at law. In view of these circumstances Cæsar Jackson was emancipated by act of the legislature. 64 Ses., 2 sit.. *Statutes*, 19. See also *Assem. Jour.*, Jan. 29 to Feb. 17.

[1] Acts of Gen. Assem., 1786.   [2] Paterson, 307.

[3] 29 Ses., 1 sit., *Statutes*, 460. The registration book for Bergen County is entitled "Liber A. Manumition of Slavery." It records: (1) the certificate by two overseers of the poor and two Justices of the Peace; (2) the deed of manumission; (3) the Justice's certificate that the deed is executed voluntarily.

[4] The certificate of health and capacity need now be signed by only one overseer of the poor.

was declared free by the Supreme Court. The court held that
the above facts proven were *prima facie* evidence of freedom
and would compel the defendant to prove a strict legal property, which he had not done.[1] Similarly, six years later, the
court decided that a certain negro woman, who had been
promised her freedom by her mistress, and who had lived for
ten years as a free woman with the acquiescence of the person
claiming her, was entitled to her freedom.[2] Verbal declarations by a master that after his death his slave should be free,
as a reward for good behavior, entitled the slave to receive
his liberty. In the opinion of the court, these declarations
amounted to an actual manumission to take effect on the master's death ; or, if they were regarded as proving nothing
more than a promise, it was still a promise binding upon the
master's executors.[3] A case in 1794[4] shows the limit to which

---

[1] The State *vs.* Lyon, *N. J. Law Rep.*, I, 462. A slave woman named Flora
had been the property of a certain Dr. Eaton, of Shrewsbury. He had
frequently declared that he was "principled against slavery; that he never
intended Flora to belong to his estate ; nor should any of his children be
entitled to hold her as their property." After his death his wife had stated
that she had set Flora free. From that time Flora was considered in the
neighborhood as a free woman ; and lived and worked as such, with no
claim upon her as a slave, for seventeen years. During this time she had
married a free negro, with whom she had since lived. They had two
children whom they had supported by their industry and kept with them
until one, Margaret, was seized and forcibly carried away as a slave. The
court decided that this Margaret Reap must be set at liberty, as the above
facts were not opposed by proof of strict legal property.

[2] 1795. The State *vs.* M'Donald and Armstrong, *N. J. Law Rep.*, I,
382 (Coxe.) A slave had been promised her freedom upon the death of
her mistress. From the time this death occurred the negro had lived as a
free woman and had worked for herself in various places. She had married a free negro and had three children by him. For ten years the husband of her late mistress acquiesced in the arrangement, but at the end of
this period gave to a man a bill of sale for the negro. The court held that
these facts were sufficient evidence of the woman's right to her liberty.

[3] 1790. The State *vs.* Administrators of Prall, *N. J. Law Rep.*, I, 4
(Coxe) ; also Halsted, *N. J. Digest*, pp. 831, 832, sec. 23.

[4] The State *vs.* Frees. *N. J. L. R.*, I, 299 (Coxe.)

the Supreme Court was willing to go on this subject. It was held that mere general declarations of an intention to set negroes free, unaccompanied by any express promise or understanding, were insufficient authority for the court to declare the negroes free.[1]

In 1793, we find a very liberal interpretation of the law when the court ignores the legal requirement of security. A certain slave owner had, by will, manumitted all his slaves. One, a boy, could not be considered as manumitted until the administrators had given the security required by law. Instead of giving security they united with the heirs in selling the boy. The court decided that the boy was entitled to his freedom whether the administrators had given the security or not.[2]

Slaves left by will to be sold for a term of years and then be free, were held to be free from the time of sale. As soon as sold they were merely servants for a term of years and no longer slaves. Any children born to them during the period of service were free.[3]

The authority of the act of 1798 was judicially established in 1806. The supreme court declared that instruments of manumission must be executed conformably to that law.[4] Again in 1842, in a case to prove legal settlement,[5] it was

---

[1] If a master had made a contract with his slave for his freedom and the terms had been fully complied with, the negro was entitled to his freedom although afterwards sold by his master. Halsted, *N. J. Digest*, pp. 831, 832, sec. 26.

[2] The State *vs.* Pitney. *N. J. Law Rep.*, I, 192 (Coxe.)

[3] 1790. The State *vs.* Anderson. *N. J. Law Rep.*, I, 41.

[4] The State *vs.* Emmons. *N. J. Law Rep.* (1st Pennington, 3rd ed., pp. 6–16). The counsel for the State endeavored to establish a distinction between emancipation as it respects the owner, and emancipation as it respects the State. He argued that so far as the master was concerned any kind of manumission might be valid, but at the same time be void so far as it affected the government. The court held that "slavery was an entire thing;" that a negro could not be considered as at once slave and free.

[5] The Overseers of the Poor of Perth Amboy *vs.* The Overseers of the Poor of Piscataway. *N. J. Law Rep.*, XIX, 173–181 (4th Harrison).

held that "a deed of manumission although acknowledged and recorded, was not valid unless executed in the presence of at least two witnesses"[1] as the act of 1798 required.[2]

Rights and Privileges of Slaves and Free Negroes.

The protection of slaves from ill-treatment by their masters received some attention in New Jersey legislation. As early as 1682, in the Proprietary Colony, one section of a "Bill for the general laws of the Province of East New-Jersey" provides "that all masters and mistresses having negro slaves, or others, shall allow them sufficient accommodation of victuals and clothing."[3] Queen Anne's instructions to the first royal governor, Lord Cornbury, required him to endeavor to get a law passed protecting servants and slaves from "inhuman severity" on the part of their masters. The "Instructions" directed that this law should provide capital punishment for the "willful killing of Indians and negroes" and a suitable penalty for the "maiming of them."[4] Again, in the early legislation of the State, one of the reasons given for the enactment of the slave law of 1786 was "that such [slaves] as are under servitude in the State ought to be protected by law from those exercises of wanton cruelty too often practiced upon them." Any person "inhumanly treating and abusing" his slave might be indicted by the grand jury, and on conviction might be fined.[5]

---

[1] There had been many instances in which deeds of manumission had been executed conformably to law in every respect, excepting that there had been but one witness. These manumissions were made valid by a special act of the legislature in 1844 (68 Ses., 2 sit., *Statutes*, 138).

[2] In a case of postponement of a trial by *habeas corpus* the defendant was ordered to enter into recognizance to produce the negro at the future trial and, in case of adverse judgment, to pay for the services of the negro during the intervening time. Halsted's *Digest*, p. 831, sec. 21. In another case the defendant was ordered to enter into recognizance not to send the negro out of the State (Halsted's *Digest*, p. 831, sec. 22).

[3] L. and S., 237.   [4] *Ibid.*, 640–642.

[5] Laws of N. J., 1786. This provision was repeated in the law of 1798.

The owner[1] of a slave was held in law obliged to support the slave at all times, provided that the negro had not been legally manumitted. If the master became insolvent and so unable to provide for his slave, the negro, if unable to maintain himself, was treated as a pauper. Any person, " fraudulently selling an aged or decrepit slave to a poor person unable to support him," was liable to punishment by a fine of $40.[2] A master who had disclaimed all responsibility for the support of his slave could not be held liable to a third person for the negro's maintenance.[3] Yet, if the overseer of the poor had found the slave in actual want, it would have been his duty to give immediate relief, and then recover from the master.

The value and need of some amount of education for slaves was recognized soon after the establishment of the State government. The law of 1788 provided that all slaves and colored servants for life or years, born after the publication of the act, should be taught to read before they reached the age of twenty-one years. Any owner failing to supply this instruction was to forfeit the sum of five pounds.[4]

---

[1] After the master's death the heirs were held responsible for the slave's support. Chatham *vs.* Canfield, *N. J. Law Rep.*, VIII, 63–65, decided what circumstances were sufficient proof of a testator's ownership of a slave to make the executors liable for the negro's maintenance (1824.)

[2] Law of 1798. Paterson, 307.

[3] 1840. Force *vs.* Haines, *N. J. Law Rep.*, XVII, 385–414 (2nd Harrison.) Force had refused to support his slave, an infirm and helpless cripple. Elizabeth Haines, having maintained the negro for several years, finally sued Force for the cost of " board, clothing, and necessaries furnished for his slave."

[4] Acts of 13th. Gen. Assem. The provision was reënacted in the law of 1798.

At first sight this fine might seem trifling; but it was probably quite sufficient to be a severe penalty, considering the small charge made for teaching at the time. School bills given by Mr. Mellick show how low the charges were. Christopher Logan had a bill against the " Estate of Aaron Melick Dec'd," " To Schooling Negro boy Joe 61 days $1.39;" later " Wm. Hambly, teacher," charges " $4.16 for 159 days Schooling." (*Story of an old Farm*, p. 608.)

All black men were presumed to be slaves until the contrary appeared, as has been shown earlier in this paper.[1] The Supreme Court held to this position even as late as 1826, when the free negroes numbered twice as many as the slaves, and only receded from it ten years later when the injustice of the ruling had become very evident. Nevertheless, the court early decided that any person claiming a particular negro as a slave must prove a good title to him.[2] A negro thus claimed need not prove himself absolutely a freeman in order to obtain his liberty. If he disproved the right of the person who claimed him, that was sufficient. That the negro had been actually held as property and had acquiesced in the arrangement was no proof of a good title.

In most cases at law no slave might be a witness. He was allowed to testify in criminal cases when his evidence was for or against another slave.[3] The presumption of slavery arising from color must be overcome before a negro could be received as a witness. A slave might not be a witness even to show whether he were bond or free. His declarations on that point might not legally be accepted as evidence.[4] That a negro was reputed free from childhood, or had lived to all intents and purposes as a freeman for more than twenty years, the courts decided was sufficient proof to overcome the presumption arising from color, and permit the negro to be admitted as a witness.[5] Free negroes, therefore, were commonly received as witnesses.

In 1760 [6] the enlistment of slaves, without the express permission in writing of their masters, was forbidden. This provision evidently was caused, not by prejudice against the negro, but by unwillingness to deprive masters of the services

---

[1] *Supra,* p. 34.

[2] 1795. The State *vs.* Heddon. *N. J. Law Rep.*, I, 377.

[3] Acts of 1714 and 1798.

[4] 1826. Fox *vs.* Lambson, *N. J. Law Rep.*, VIII, 339–347.

[5] *Ibid.*, and Potts *vs.* Harper, *N. J. Law Rep.*, III, 583.

[6] Nevill, II, 267.

of their slaves. The occasion of the prohibition was the
raising of one thousand volunteers for a campaign against
Canada in the French and Indian War. To what extent
negroes in New Jersey took part or aided in the Revolution
it is difficult to determine. A law of 1780 for the recruiting
of the remainder of New Jersey's quota of troops for the
service of the United States forbids the enlistment of slaves.[1]
The following year a law for the same purpose repeats the
prohibition.[2] Yet slaves from New Jersey served, in various
capacities, both the State and the Federal Government during
the war. Two instances are recorded when a slave was manumitted by act of legislature as a reward for faithful service
of the Revolutionary cause. Peter Williams, a slave who
belonged to a Tory of Woodbridge, having been taken within
the British lines by his master, escaped through them in 1780.
He served for some time with the State troops and later
enlisted in the Continental army, serving there until the close
of the war. When his master's estate was confiscated he
became the property of the State, and, in 1784, was set free
by an act of the legislature.[3] Five years later a slave named
Cato, part of the confiscated estate of another Woodbridge
Tory, received his freedom in the same manner. The act
declared that Cato had " rendered essential service both to this
State and the United States in the time of the late war."[4]

In the Colonial period freedmen were denied the right to
hold real estate. The law of 1714 enacted that no negro,
Indian, or mulatto thereafter manumitted should hold real

---

[1] 5th Assembly, *N. J. Laws.*   [2] Wilson, 209.
[3] 8 Ses., 2 sit., *Statutes*, 110; *Assem. Jour.*, Aug. 30 to Sept. 1, 1784.
[4] 14 Ses , 1 sit., *Statutes*, 538; *Assem. Jour.*, Nov. 13–25, 1789. In 1786
another negro, named Prime, the property of the State, was emancipated by
special statute. He had formerly been the slave of a Tory of Princeton.
No specific reason was given for this action other than, that " the legislature
was desirous of extending the blessings of liberty and the said negro Prime
hath shown himself entitled to their favorable notice." 11 Ses., 1 sit.,
Statutes, 368.

estate "in his or her own right, in fee simple or fee tail" but the same should "escheat to her Majesty, her heirs and successors."[1] A free negro was entitled to vote in the State during the early years. The suffrage was not confined to whites by the constitution adopted in 1776.[2] Article IV states that "all inhabitants of this Colony, of full age, who are worth fifty pounds . . . and have resided within the county" for twelve months, are entitled to vote.[3] A new constitution in 1844 limited the elective franchise to whites.[4]

The provision for allowing free negroes to gain a legal settlement is of interest, because upon legal settlement depended the responsibility of a township for the support of its colored paupers. A manumitted slave had a legal settlement in the place where his master's legal settlement was.[5] The children of slaves born free were deemed settled in the township in which they were born; but might gain a new settlement in the same manner as whites, or in any township where they had served seven years.[6] No slave whose master had not become insolvent could gain a legal settlement in any township.[7] This inability of slaves to acquire a settlement was

---

[1] Nevill, I, 18.   [2] Poore's *Collection.* Wilson, *Acts* (1776–1783).

[3] In 1793, as proof of the illegality of an election for fixing on a site for the Middlesex County jail and court house, it was stated that "a negro man was admitted to vote, who had no legal residence, and his declaration that he had been manumitted in another State was received as sufficient proof of his being entitled to vote." The implication here is that a negro able to show clear proof of his freedom, and having a legal residence, was entitled to vote. The State *vs.* Justices, etc., of Middlesex, *N. J. Law Rep.*, I, 283, 284 (Coxe).

[4] Poore's *Collection,* 1315.   [5] *Law of* 1798. Paterson, 307.

[6] 1820. 44 Ses.; *Statutes,* 166.

[7] 1824. South Brunswick *vs.* East Windsor, *N. J. Law Rep.*, VIII, 78–83 (3rd Halsted).

As has been shown, *Supra,* pp. 45 and 51, a helpless slave was not allowed to suffer because his master was able to maintain him and yet refused to do so. It was the duty of the overseer of the poor of the township where such a slave happened to be, to give relief and then recover from the owner if possible.

established in several cases carried to the Supreme Court, where one township endeavored to prove the legal settlement of a destitute negro in another township, and then to shift the burden of his support.[1] It is the latest form in which I have found the influence of slavery traceable in New Jersey law.

Social Condition of Slaves.

The use of slave labor was, in the eighteenth century, very general in the eastern portion of New Jersey. Interesting information on the social condition of slaves is afforded by advertisements in newspapers[2] published during the Colonial period and in the early years of the State. Male slaves were employed as farm laborers of all sorts, stablemen, coachmen, stage drivers, sailors, boatmen, miners, iron workers, saw-mill hands, house and ship carpenters, wheel-wrights, coopers, tanners, shoemakers, millers, bakers, cooks, and for various kinds of service within the house or about the master's person. Slave women were employed at all kinds of household service, including cooking, sewing, spinning and knitting; and as dressing maid, barber, nurse, farm servants, etc. If a woman had children she was rendered less desirable as a slave. That the laxness of morals ordinarily found among African slaves was present in New Jersey is sufficiently evident.[3] Frequently slave women were offered for sale for no other reason than that they had children. They were, in some cases, sold without their child.

---

[1] 1824. South Brunswick *vs.* East Windsor.

1842. Overseers of the Poor of Perth Amboy *vs.* Overseers of the Poor of Piscataway, *N. J. Law Rep.*, XIX, 173–181 (4 Harrison).

1857. Overseers of Morris *vs.* Overseers of Warren, *N. J. Law Rep.* (2 Dutcher, 312).

[2] The Newark *Centinel of Freedom*, the Trenton *True American* and excerpts from the Colonial journals published in *N. J. Ar.*, XI and XII.

[3] See The State *vs.* Anderson, *N. J. Law Rep.*, I, 41, and The State *vs.* Mount, *N. J. Law Rep.*, I, 337.

The newspapers contained many notices of reward for the
return of fugitive slaves. In some cases the returned fugitive
seems to have been treated very leniently. One instance is
recorded in which he received no punishment whatever.[1] In
another case the advertisement promises that if he "shall
return voluntarily, he shall be forgiven, and have a new
master."[2] Slaves of both sexes and various ages were among
the fugitives. A man fled and left behind a wife and child.
A woman with a child of nine months ran away. Slaves
occasionally escaped by the ferries from Elizabeth-Town and
Perth Amboy to New York.[3] In 1734, three were thought
to have gone off in a canoe toward Connecticut and Rhode
Island. Others attempted to get on board some vessel, or
sought a chance to go privateering. A slave sometimes escaped
on the back of his master's horse.

Negroes were frequently sold for a term of years. Slaves
were at times hired out by their masters;[4] occasionally a plantation together with the negroes to cultivate it was rented, or a
mine with the slaves to work it.[5] A negro indented servant is
mentioned in 1802. In 1794, a slave was given as a donation
to the Newark Academy to be sold for as much as he would
bring.[6] The Rev. Moses Ogden bought him for fourteen
pounds. Mr. Atkinson states that this clergyman owned a
number of slaves whom he employed to work his farm lands.[7]
The slave's position as a chattel is brought out clearly in many
advertisements of sales where slaves are classed with horses,
cattle, farming utensils and household goods.[8]

---

[1] *Centinel of Freedom*, VI, No. 34.   [2] *Ibid.*, IV, 45.   [3] *Supra*, p. 34.
[4] *Centinel of Freedom*, VI, No. 14.   [5] *N. J. Ar.*, XII, 186, 251.
[6] Atkinson, *History of Newark, N. J.*, 170–172.
[7] Moses Newell Combs, another Newarker of the same period, was a representative of the anti-slavery sentiment. He was noted for the free school
which he established for his apprentices, but also advocated zealously the
emancipation of slaves. This latter principle he himself put into practice
by manumitting a negro that he owned (Atkinson, 148).
[8] For example, the notice of the sale of a farm at Elizabeth, in 1801,
reads: "On the above farm is also to be sold a negro man with four children,
a horse, chair, cows, and farming utensils" (*Centinel of Freedom*, VI, 11).

Slaves were, on the whole, well treated in New Jersey. In
most cases, they lived in close personal relations with the
master's family and were regarded by him as proper subjects
for his care and protection. As early as 1740 there is record
of a slave that could read and write.[1] Frequently slaves spoke
both English and Dutch.[2] Many slaves played the violin
with considerable proficiency. Under the Colonial laws, it is
true, slaves accused of crime received severe treatment; but
this severity must be viewed as part of the criminal law of an
eighteenth century Colonial society, stern both from its origin
and from its individual development.

Mr. Mellick, in his "Story of an old Farm," gives a very
entertaining description of slavery on a farm at Bedminster
in Somerset County. The first negro purchased was a pic-
turesque creature of somewhat eccentric habits. He was a
"master-hand at tanning, currying and finishing leather;"
and, indeed, these accomplishments were the attractions that
overcame the scruples of the family against slave-holding, at
a time when there was great need of help in the tannery. The
slaves of the farm were granted their holidays and enjoyments.
In the week following Christmas they generally gave a party
to which the respectable colored people of the neighborhood
were invited. The whole week was one of great festivity, and
but little work was expected of the blacks. Again, the day
of "general training" (usually in June), was another great
holiday for these slaves. This drill of the militia was regarded as a kind of fair and was a time of great sociability.
The family negroes all attended in a large wagon, taking with
them root beer and ginger cakes to offer for sale.

Mr. Mellick gives copies of bills for the schooling[3] of the
negro children, showing that in this family the law that slaves
should be taught to read was well observed. When the farmer
died, his will disposed of the negroes so that those who did

---

[1] *N. J. Ar.*, XII, 51.   [2] *N. J. Ar.*, XI, 209; XII, 102, 306.
[3] *Supra*, p. 51, note.

not remain on the old farm were comfortably placed with friends of his. The boys and girls were sold for terms of years merely. This shows a considerate interest in the happiness of slaves, together with a consistent regard for the welfare of his family.[1]

Slavery was very evidently an institution in New Jersey life. During the eighteenth century especially, the use of slave labor became very common in many sections. Yet, in other parts, during the same period, an anti-slavery sentiment was growing, the strength of which was shown when the Friends in 1776 denied the right of membership in their Society to slave holders. The anti-slavery movement progressed steadily, after the Revolution largely under the leadership of the abolition societies. Its influence toward practical ends is seen in the extinction of the slave trade; in the activity of various philanthropic men in securing to negroes their rights before the courts; and, later, in the gradual emancipation begun in 1804.

After the gradual abolition of slavery in New Jersey had been secured by law, the local anti-slavery movement merged into the larger agitation going on throughout the nation. The resolutions of the legislature in 1824, 1847, and 1849 show that the people of New Jersey early recognized the connection of the institution of slavery with national interests.

---

[1] Mellick, A. D., *Story of an Old Farm*, pp. 602–612.

BIBLIOGRAPHY.

The following is a list of the principal works used in the preparation of this monograph:

Allinson, Samuel. Acts of the General Assembly of the Province of New Jersey (1702–1776). Burlington, 1776.

Atkinson, Joseph. History of Newark, N. J. Newark, 1878.

Bancroft, George. History of the United States of America. 9th ed.

Bergen County Records. "B. C. Liber A," folio May 29, 1715 to 1790. "Black Births, 1804," folio July 28, 1804, to March 14, 1843. "Liber A of Manumition of Slavery," June 17, 1805, to July 26, 1841.

Blake, W. O. Ancient and Modern Slavery.

Brackett, J. R. Status of the Slave.

Census Reports of the United States.

"Centinel of Freedom." Newark, N. J.

Dally, J. W. Woodbridge and Vicinity. New Brunswick, 1873.

Gordon, Thomas. History of New Jersey. Gazetteer of New Jersey, 1834.

Hatfield, E. F. History of Elizabeth, N. J. New York, 1868.

Laws of New Jersey. Yearly edition. Revision of 1821; Revision of 1847.

Leaming and Spicer. The grants, concessions and original constitutions of the Province of New Jersey. The acts passed during the Proprietary governments, and other material transactions before the surrender thereof to Queen Anne. The instrument of surrender and her formal acceptance thereof. Lord Cornbury's commission and instructions consequent thereon. Philadelphia.

Mellick, A. D. The Story of an Old Farm or Life in New Jersey in the Eighteenth Century. Somerville, N. J., 1889.

Moore, G. H. Notes on the History of Slavery in Massachusetts.

Nevill, Samuel. Acts of the General Assembly of the Province of New Jersey (1703–1761). Woodbridge, 1761.

New Jersey Archives. Vols. I–X. Documents relating to the Colonial History of the State of New Jersey (1631–1776), Vols. XI–XII. Excerpts from various Colonial newspapers, treating of New Jersey History, Vols. XIII–XVIII. Journal of the Governor and Council (1682–1775). Trenton, 1890–1893.

New Jersey Law Reports. I–XXIX (1790–1863).

Paterson, William. Laws of the State of New Jersey, revised and published under the authority of the legislature. Newark, 1800.

Poore. Charters and Constitutions.

Proceedings of the General Assembly of New Jersey.

Smith, Samuel. The History of the Colony of Nova-Caesarea, or New Jersey. Burlington, 1765.

Snell, J. P. History of Sussex and Warren Counties, N. J. Philadelphia, 1881.

"True American." Trenton, N. J.

Whitehead, W. A. Contributions to the early History of Perth Amboy. New York, 1856. East Jersey under the Proprietary Governments. Newark, 1875.

Whittier, J. G. (editor), John Woolman's Journal.

Williams. History of the Negro Race in America.

Wilson, Peter. Acts of the Council and General Assembly of the State of New Jersey (1776–1783). Trenton, 1784.

SLAVERY IN RHODE ISLAND, 1755-1776.*

PART I.

INTRODUCTION: SLAVERY BEFORE 1755.

I. THE LAW AND THE SLAVE.

Introduction. The history of slavery in Rhode Island, from 1755 to 1776, is the history of the decay of the institution in that colony. Anti-slavery sentiment and agitation may be traced back to the time of Roger Williams, the founder of the colony. Moore speaks of "the humane efforts of Roger Williams and John Eliot to abate the severity of judgment against captives, and mitigate the horrors of slavery in Massachusetts." Beside these, several of the leading spirits of the seventeenth century had raised a protest against the institution of slavery, but it was not till 1717 that any organized effort against slaveholding was made, and it was not until the time of the approaching revolution that this feeling and this thought became at all general.

During these years many forces, economic and social, were active, undermining the institution of slavery, and modifying public opinion with regard to slavery and the slave trade. A consideration of these forces and their varied manifestations is necessary.

*The sources of this account of slavery in Rhode Island in the last generation preceding the Revolution are, besides the books and pamphlets referred to in foot-notes, the contemporary newspapers, the manuscript records of Providence (town meeting, town council and probate), those of the N. E. Yearly Meeting of Friends, those of certain churches in Rhode Island, and the Moses Brown Papers.

Legislation in the Seventeenth Century. May 18, 1652, the following act was passed by the representatives of Providence and Warwick:[1] "Whereas there is a common course practiced among Englishmen, to buy negroes to the end that they may have them for service or slaves forever, for the preventing of such practices among us, let it be ordered that no black mankind, or white, being forced to covenant bond or otherwise, serve any man or his assigns longer than ten years, or until they come to be twenty-four years of age if they be taken under fourteen, from the time of their coming within the liberties of the Colony, and at the end or term of ten years to set them free as the manner is with English servants, and that man that will not let them go free, or shall sell them away elsewhere, to that end that they may be enslaved to others for a longer time, he or they shall forfeit to the Colony forty pounds."

In March, 1675-6, another law of like nature was passed.[2] The New England colonies were in the habit of selling as slaves the Indian captives they took in their frequent wars. Rhode Island enslaved few, perhaps none; still there were Indian slaves carried into Rhode Island, and it was with reference to these that the act of March, 1675-6, was passed. This provided that "no Indian in this colony be a slave but only to pay their debts, or for their bringing up, or courtesy they have received, or to perform covenant, as if they had been countrymen not in war."

Results of This Legislation; Manumission. What Williams has said[3] of the law of 1652 is true both of that law and the law of 1675-6 just quoted. They were both admirable laws, but they were lacking the public sentiment to give them practical force in the colony. They were the expression of a part of the colony rather than the whole, and that part, it will be observed, was the northern. The principle, however, embodied in these laws, persisted; masters sometimes gave slaves their freedom, and slaves took advantage of

---

[1] "R. I. Colonial Records," I., 243.

[2] Wilkins Updike, "History of the Narragansett Church," p. 171.

[3] G. W. Williams, "History of the Negro Race in America," I., p. 263.

it where possible, to secure their freedom. The result was that at the beginning of the eighteenth century there was a considerable number of free negroes. Emancipation became more and more common, and the colony began to fear that it would have to support negroes whose years of usefulness had been spent in work for their masters, and who were manumitted by them when old and helpless. To prevent this abuse, an injustice to slave and to commonwealth, the Rhode Island legislature in 1728–9 passed a law,[1] providing that when aged or helpless slaves were manumitted, security in the sum of not less than one hundred pounds should be given to the town treasurer.

Yet, in spite of the seeming demand for a law, it must be said that these abuses were comparatively rare. Manumitted servants were usually given a small establishment with their freedom, and were generally able to care for themselves. "A negro man and woman, in 1735, by Ind'y & Frugality, scrap'd together £200, or £300. They sailed from Newport to their own country, Guinea, where their savings gave them an independent fortune."[2] With the growth of Providence, many emancipated slaves shared in the increase of general prosperity, and left behind them effects sufficient to attract the attention of the town council. Among many others was "Jack Harris, a negro man, so called," who died December 21, 1745, and left one hundred and forty-five pounds eleven shillings and five pence, much of it, unhappily, in colonial bills; also John Read, who died December 31, 1753, and left one hundred pounds; Andrew Frank,[3] who died intestate, October 6, 1755, and left to the town two hundred and twenty-nine pounds and six pence, besides an old Bible and farming implements. These facts indicate that the position of the slave in Rhode Island, partly because of public opinion as expressed in the two acts already quoted, and partly for economic reasons, was practically the same as that of the apprentice or indentured white servant. The position of the free negro or Indian was determined as among the colonists themselves by

[1] R. I. Laws, 1730, p. 162.
[2] "Boston Evening Post," 1735.
[3] "R. I. Historical Tracts," No. 15, p. 177.

family, wealth and social attainments.   It has been asserted, however, [1] that an examination of the legislation of this period will lead one to believe that there existed some jealousy of the negro, and a desire to infringe upon the acquired liberties of the free negro.   Let us consider the truth of this proposition.

Legislation from 1700 to 1755.   In 1704[2] on account of thefts committed after nightfall, negroes were forbidden to be abroad after nine o'clock, on penalty of whipping.   No housekeeper was to be allowed to entertain them after this time, on penalty of five shillings fine.   An act of 1708[3] increased this fine to ten shillings.   In 1714,[4] slaves having run away under pretense of being sent by their masters and having on this account been carried out of the colony and often lost to their masters, it was enacted that no person should transport any slave over a ferry or out of the colony without a certificate from the master, on penalty of twenty shillings fine ; that all ministers of justice and others should aid in arresting and returning all slaves seeking to escape in this manner.   An act of 1718[5] provided that all slaves who should be found purloining or stealing should be tried and punished by a court consisting of two or more justices of the peace or town officers of the town where the offence was committed, instead of in the general courts of trial and gaol delivery as before.   There was the right of appeal to the higher court only in case the owner of the slave should desire it and would give bond to prosecute the appeal.   In 1743,[6] there was an Act "for the more effectual punishment of negroes that shall attempt to commit rape on any white woman."   In March, 1750–1,[7] an Act was passed, supplementary to the acts of 1704 and 1708, "to prevent all persons Keeping house within this colony, from entertaining Indian, Negro or Mulatto servants or slaves : "

[1] Williams, "History of the Negro Race in America," I., 264.

[2] R. I. Laws, 1730, p. 50.

[3] "R. I. Colonial Records," IV., 50.

[4] R. I. Laws, 1730, p. 72.

[5] R. I. Laws, 1719, p. 101.

[6] R. I. Laws, 1745, p. 263.

[7] R. I. Laws, 1752, pp. 92-3.

" Whereas great disorders and Burglaries are oftentimes
raised and committed by Negroes, Indians and other impudent
Persons, entertaining such Indian, Negro and Mulatto servants and slaves, and selling them strong Liquors and receiving
and bargaining with them ; by Means whereof such servants
and slaves are induced and tempted to pilfer and steal from
their Masters and Mistresses, to the utter Ruin of such Servants, and to the great Injury of the Public," it is therefore
enacted, that no one shall sell liquor to any Indian, mulatto,
or negro servant or slave, under penalty of a fine of thirty
pounds, one-half to the informer ; no householder shall entertain any such without the owner's consent, nor furnish opportunities for dancing or gaming, under penalty of fine or
imprisonment ; transgressors (if not whites) shall have their
housekeeping broken up and be set to work for the town ;
colored servants or slaves abroad after nine o'clock shall be
apprehended and, in the morning, whipped, unless the owner
will pay ten pounds ; trading with slaves was also forbidden.

Character of this Legislation. None of these laws, I
think, indicate that the negro was treated with particular
severity.[1] The attempt was made to prevent the numerous
thefts which were committed by slaves, though seemingly with
little success. A law was also passed to prevent the escape
of slaves from their masters, but this, it must be remembered,
was as much in the interest of the public as of the master.
A poor stranger was always liable to become a charge upon
the town, and it was therefore by no means an uncommon
thing to return a poor white person to his or her place of legal residence. By this law for the return of fugitive slaves,
therefore, no peculiar discrimination was made against the
slave or against the negro. It is true these laws, unlike the
laws of 1652 and 1675-6, do not prohibit slavery but are permissive and regulative. The interests of the owner of land
and of slaves had become important since the opening of the

[1] Slaves were never subjected to severer punishments than whites for
the same offences, as has been the case in some states ; and they enjoyed
the protection of the laws for offences against their persons equally with
the whites. — *E. R. Potter, Report to R. I. Legislature, 1840.*

century, and were now deemed worthy of consideration. The laws of 1652 and 1675-6, as has been said, were the expression of the northern and democratic part of the colony ; the slave laws of the eighteenth century, on the other hand, were the expression of the wealthier southern counties, and were based not on grounds of principle but on grounds of interest and expediency. This change was occasioned by the growth of the Narragansett Plantations, and the increase in maritime trade, which centered in Newport. These laws, however, were not cruel ; they simply expressed what were commonly recognized as the rights of the master over the slave. As Williams says,[1] negro slaves were ratable at law as chattel property, and could be taken in execution to satisfy debts as other personal property. He cites this instance :—

"In October, 1743, Comfort Taylor of Bristol sued and obtained judgment against a negro named Cuff Borden for two hundred pounds and cost of suit for a grievous trespass. Cuff was a slave. An ordinary execution would have gone against his person ; he would have been imprisoned and nothing more. In view of this condition of affairs Mrs. Taylor petitioned the General Assembly praying that authority be granted the sheriff to sell Cuff as other property to satisfy the judgment. The Assembly granted her prayer as follows : 'upon consideration whereof, it is voted and resolved, that the sheriff of the said county of Newport, when he shall receive the execution against the said negro Cuff, be, and is hereby fully empowered to sell said negro Cuff as other personal estate ; and after the fine of twenty pounds be paid into the general treasury, and all other charges deducted out of the price of said negro, the remainder to be appropriated in satisfying said execution.' "[2]

This procedure was not, however, peculiar to the legal treatment of negroes. It was not a rare occurrence to sell poor white debtors in similar cases. For example, Julian Welford and Christina Renshen, two women convicted of theft in Newport, not having an estate, were sold to pay the costs,

[1] "History of the Negro Race in America," II., 278.

[2] "R. I. Colonial Records," V., 72-3.

"but they scarcely sold for enough to pay the person who whipped them."[1]

White Slave and Black Slave.   This was the legal status of the servant or slave, black or white, in 1755, as nearly as we can determine.   The essential difference between the white slave and the black was that there was usually a limit to the white man's servitude, and his children were not subject to the same condition of servitude.   The reason for this lies in the cause of the servitude in each case.   In the case of the white, this was debt or crime for which the penalty was transportation with service.   In the case of the negro and Indian, this cause was a one-sided war, with ensuing captivity and servitude for the weaker race.   With none of the same race or family to care for his interests, there would necessarily not result in the condition of the negro or Indian slave, the same modifications as in the condition of the white slave. Accordingly while we find the treatment of all classes of slaves to be practically the same, public opinion among the colonists, and first of all among Englishmen in the old country, did not go so far as to allow condemnation of their fellow-countrymen to life-long servitude save rarely, and so far as I know rarely allowed the enslavement of children on account of the enslavement of a parent, at least when one parent was left to support the children.

II.   THE CHURCH AND THE SLAVE.

The Activity and Teaching of the Church of England..   We will now examine into the relations of the slave with the church, for these even more than his legal status determined his future social position, and a clear understanding of these relations is necessary to a complete comprehension of the social position of the slave in 1755, and the movement of the following years which ended in the abolition of the slave trade and the emancipation of the slave.

In 1730 Mr. Usher, missionary at Bristol, wrote the Society for the Propagation of the Gospel in Foreign Parts: "I have

[1] "Newport Mercury," 1761.

had sundry negroes make application for baptism that were able to render a very good account of the hope that was in them, and their practices were generally agreeable to the principles of the Christian religion. But I am not permitted to comply with their request, and my own duty, being forbid by their masters."[1] In 1740 one negro is reported as baptised. In 1746 thirty negroes and Indians are reported as belonging to the congregation, but complaint is still made of opposition from masters to the baptism of their slaves.[2] Masters felt that baptism was inconsistent with a state of slavery, and therefore made strenuous opposition to the baptism of their slaves, not only here but elsewhere.

Dean Berkeley wrote in 1731 with reference to the negro slaves,[3] "The religion of these people, as is natural to suppose, takes after that of their masters; some few are baptised, several frequent the different assemblies, and far the greater part none at all."

Mr. McSparran, missionary in Narragansett, in 1741, reports that he has begun the catechetical lecture for the negroes, and spends one hour immediately preceding divine service in catechising and instructing these poor wretches, who for the most part are extremely ignorant; and whether from the novelty of the thing, or as he hopes from a better motive, more than fifty slaves give their attendance. His journal contains this entry under date of August 2, 1741: "Dr. McSparran catechised the negroes, and there were present on that occasion at church, near about or more than one hundred." In 1743 Mr. Honeyman at Newport reported "an hundred negroes who constantly attend the public worship of God."[4]

The Society for the Propagation of the Gospel in Foreign Parts, already referred to, though owning a plantation in the Barbadoes and being "under the necessity of purchasing fresh hands from time to time to keep up the stock," early began to take an interest in the religious instruction of the negroes,

[1] Updike, 454.
[2] Updike, 459, 463.
[3] Updike, 177.
[4] Updike, 460, 168, 461.

and when they could not send special catechists wrote to
their missionaries "to use their best endeavors at proper
times to instruct the negroes," and "to recommend it zealously to their masters to order their slaves at convenient
times to come to them that they might be instructed." [1]   In
"an address to masters and mistresses of families in the English Plantations abroad," issued by this society, we find the
following : " Let me beseech you to consider them not merely
as slaves, and upon the same level with laboring beasts, but
as men slaves and women slaves, who have the same frame
and faculties with yourselves, and have souls capable of being
made happy, and reason and understanding to receive instruction in order to it."

The influence of such publications was undoubtedly great
in mitigating the severity of slavery, especially among Church-
men in the colonies.   It was through such publications and
through its missionaries that the English church materially
modified the relations of master and slave.

The Attitude of the Quakers Toward Slavery.   The second ecclesiastical force operative at this time was the Society of Friends.   They were the first, so far as we can learn,
to put forth an organized effort against slavery.   In 1717 the
Friends' Yearly Meeting Record says : " The subject of slaves
considered and advice given that letters be written to the
Islands and elsewhere not to send any more slaves to be sold
by any Friend."   In 1727 the practice of importing negroes
was censured ; and by the middle of the eighteenth century
the emancipation of slaves had gradually become a matter of
action by the whole Quaker body.   " Similar attempts in
other sects were rather the acts of individuals." [2]   'Yet slavery
was still permitted by the Friends as by other religious
bodies, and by the State.   This marks the difference between
the middle and the end of the century.

Influence of the Church upon the Status of the Slave.
Slavery in 1755 was among many recognized as an evil,

[1] Humphrey's History of the Society.
[2] Von Holst, " History of the United States," I., 279.

yet it was permitted; toward the close of the century it was felt as an evil and was prohibited. In 1755 the slave in his relation with his master was treated under law as chattel property. He could be bought and sold, punished or emancipated at the will of his master so long as this did not interfere with the interests of the colony. Yet in his relations with the State, on the other hand, the slave was more than chattel property, for he could be arrested, tried and punished according to the ordinary procedure unless the master interfered, and the master could be prevented from manumitting a slave where the slave would be liable to become a charge upon the community. These relations to the State, and especially the relations to the master, were modified, we have seen, by the teaching and activity of the church. The church, perhaps more than any other one thing, determined the *status* of the slave in 1755, economic causes more than any other determined the *extent* of slavery at this time.

III.   THE SLAVE TRADE AND THE EXTENT OF SLAVERY.

The Growth of the Slave Trade. It is necessary for us next to ascertain the extent of slavery in Rhode Island in 1755, and first to consider the development of the slave trade, which determined largely the extent of slavery.

In the earlier history of the colony there was a demand for labor which could be met only by the immigration of free labor, or the importation of slave labor. England encouraged it because it was more profitable to her commerce, and expressed herself as anxious "for the well supplying of the plantations and colonies with sufficient numbers of negroes at reasonable prices."[1] The colony engaged in it, on the other hand, because her merchants also found it profitable for them. They could get molasses in the West Indies, convert it into rum in their Rhode Island distilleries, exchange the rum in

[1] "The assiento, a contract with the old French Guinea Company for furnishing Spanish America with negro slaves, was conveyed to the English by the treaty of Utrecht (1713) and assigned to the South Sea Company, who thereby agreed to land 4,800 slaves annually for thirty years in the new world." *Arnold, History of Rhode Island, II., 48.*

Guinea for slaves and gold-dust, trade some of their slaves for more molasses again, and make after all a very handsome profit. For these reasons the slave trade in Rhode Island grew rapidly during the early years of the eighteenth century.

Previous to this "Barbadoes was the source whence Rhode Island received most of her slaves. From twenty to thirty was the average annual supply, and from thirty to forty pounds each the usual price. No more than these could be disposed of, owing to the general dislike our planters have for them, by reason of their turbulent and unruly tempers, to the natural increase of those already here, and to the inclination of our people in general to employ white servants before negroes."[1] In 1708 Governor Cranston said that from 1698 to December 25, 1707, no negroes were imported into Rhode Island from Africa. That same year, however, the colony laid an import tax of three pounds on each negro imported,[2] and other acts followed which showed that the trade with Africa direct, or by way of the West Indies, was by this time well established. February 27, 1712, because the tax imposed in 1708 had been evaded, "for preventing clandestine importations and exportations of passengers, or negroes, or Indian slaves into or out of this colony," an act was passed providing that masters of vessels should specify the number, sex and names of the slaves in their cargo, and the persons to whom they were consigned.[3] July, 1715, an act was passed to prohibit the importation of Indian slaves, because "divers conspiracies, insurrections, rapes, thefts, and other execrable crimes have been lately perpetrated in this and the adjoining governments by Indian slaves, and the increase of them in this colony daily discourages the importing of white servants from Great Britain."[4] Another act similar to the act of 1712 was also passed, regulating further the importation of negro slaves. This provided that persons importing slaves "shall enter their number, names and sex in the naval office," and

[1] Arnold, "History of the State of Rhode Island," II., 32, quoting "R. I. Colonial Records," IV., 54.
[2] "R. I. Colonial Records," IV., 34.
[3] R. I. Laws, 1730, p. 64.
[4] R. I. Laws, 1730, p. 82.

shall pay to the naval officer a tax of three pounds per head. This act applied to persons also, bringing negroes from adjoining provinces, excepting travelers who did not remain in the colony more than six months, and excepting slaves imported directly from Africa. It directed a portion of the income from this tax to be expended for repairs on the streets of Newport. An act of 1717[1] ordered one hundred pounds more to be paid out of the impost duty fund for paving Newport streets. An act of June, 1729,[2] ordered that half of the income from this duty be applied to street improvements in Newport, and half to the building and repair of "great bridges on the main." The impost law of 1712 was repealed in May, 1732, by order of the king.[3] It had been an important source of revenue to the colony, but its effect had been to restrict the slave trade to some extent, and so to injure the English interests. It was for this reason that it was repealed. The result of the repeal seems to have been favorable. Governor Hopkins stated[4] "that for more than thirty years prior to 1764 Rhode Island sent to the coast annually eighteen vessels carrying 1,800 hhds. of rum. The commerce in rum and slaves afforded about £40,000 per annum for remittance from Rhode Island to Great Britain." As the trade grew Newport became more and more the central market. Captain Isaac Freeman, with a coasting sloop, in 1752, wanted a cargo of men and molasses from Newport within five weeks. His correspondent wrote that the quantity could not be had in three months. "There are so many vessels lading for Guinea we can't get one hogshead of rum for the cash."[5] It is probable that the trade in Rhode Island was much more extensive than in the other New England colonies. Dr. John Eliot says: "The African trade was carried on in Massachusetts and commenced at an early period, but to a small extent compared with Rhode Island." Samuel Dexter says: "Vessels from Rhode Island have brought slaves into Boston. Whether

[1] "R. I. Colonial Records," IV., 225.

[2] R. I. Laws, 1730, p. 183.

[3] "R. I. Colonial Records," IV., 471.

[4] "R. I. Colonial Records," VI., 380.

[5] "American Historical Record," I., 316; Geo. C. Mason.

any have been imported into that town by its own merchants I am unable to say." In the latter half of the century Rhode Island still maintained this pre-eminence, and its chief mart, Newport. During this period Bristol also became noted as a slave port, and Captain Simeon Potter, one of her famous slave traders, flourished about 1764; but before this, by 1755, the trade to Rhode Island had begun to fail.

Reasons for the Decline of the Slave Trade. The decline of the slave trade and of slavery as an institution in Rhode Island in consequence, is due to both moral and economic causes. Some historians assert that slavery was wrong and therefore fell; others that it fell because it was unprofitable. In Rhode Island it fell both because it was wrong and because it was unprofitable; public sentiment, usually expressed in religious terms among the colonists, pronounced it wrong; public, and often individual action in this matter, was based on grounds of expediency, profit and loss. The motive of their procedure was moral, the method of their procedure was calculative and utilitarian.

The strongest moral force antagonistic to slavery was that presented by the faith and conduct of the Quakers, who for half a century dominated in the politics of the colony, and exerted a stronger influence upon the thought and activity of the colony than any other sect. It may, indeed, be questioned whether the high moral spirit and endeavor of Roger Williams would not have been without conspicuous results had he not been followed by this Quaker succession. Another strong moral force at work against slavery was that of the Society for the Propagation of the Gospel in Foreign Parts. The activity of this society in the colony, already described, and the reading of the annual sermons delivered before the society, a kind of literature at that time most influential, did much to modify the relations of master and slave, and finally to do away with the system of slavery altogether.

The physical and economic reasons for the decay of slavery in Rhode Island are more important. "The climate was too harsh, the social system too simple to engender a good economic employment of black labor. The simple industrial

methods of each New England homestead   *   *   *   made
a natural barrier against an alien social system including
either black or copper-colored dependents.   The blacks soon
dwindled in numbers, or dropped out from a life too severe
for any but the hardiest and firmest-fibred races." [1]   Added
to these were two other, distinctly economic, causes : first,
the diminished demand because of the multiplication of laboring white people, and second, the diminished supply and the
increasing difficulty in getting slaves, especially good ones.
Captain David Lindsay writes from Anamaboe in 1753 :
"The Traid is so dull it is actuly a noof to make a man
Creasy.   *   *   *   I never had so much Trouble in all
my Voiges." [2] Increased competition also acted with the
diminished supply and demand to make the risks in the trade
greater and the profits consequently less.

Extent and Distribution of Slavery.   These changes in the
slave market determined the extent of slavery in Rhode
Island from time to time.

The following is a table of the population of Rhode Island
at different dates :

	White population.	Negroes, slave and free.
1708	7,181	425
1730	17,935	1,648
1749	32,773	3,077
1756	35,939	4,697
1774	59,707	3,668

Two explanations of this table are necessary.   The census
of 1730 did not include the towns east of the Bay, which were
not added to the colony until 1746.   This will account for a
part of the increase of negroes appearing in 1748.   Beside
this, about 1730–48 Rhode Island merchants had traded
largely to the West Indies, bringing back negroes as a part
of their cargoes, and in 1732 the impost tax had been repealed.   The falling off in the increase of negro population

[1] Wm. B. Weeden, "Economic and Social History of New England,"
p. 451.

[2] "American Historical Record," I., 339.

in the period between 1748 and 1756 is due to the fact that negroes, who made excellent seamen, were often induced by the masters of vessels to run away and go to sea. Allowing for these facts, an examination of the table shows that the negro population increased somewhat more rapidly than the white population during the first half of the eighteenth century.

How then was this negro population distributed? "Of the negroes and slaves in Rhode Island," says Potter,[1] "the greater part were in a very few towns, Newport, North and South Kingstown, Warwick, Bristol, Portsmouth and James-town. By the census of 1748–9 the town of South Kingstown had more negroes in it than any other town except New-port. This is also true of the census of 1774 and 1783." In 1774, out of a population of 3,668 negroes, Newport had 1,246, South Kingstown 440, Providence 303, North Kings-town 211, Jamestown 131, Portsmouth 122, and Bristol 114. Earlier than this "King's county (now Washington), which contained one-third of the population of the State, numbered more than a thousand slaves. The census of 1730 gives a less number, but it was popular to conceal numbers from the observation of the home government. Families would aver-age from five to forty slaves each. They owned slaves in proportion to their means of support. The slaves and horses were about equal in number; the latter were raised for ex-portation. Newport was the great slave market of New England. There were some importers of slaves in Narra-gansett; among them were Rowland Robinson and Colonel Thomas Hazard."[2] In Newport there were twenty-two still-houses. "The large exportation of New England rum to Africa, which in return brought slaves, increased the wealth of the place to an astonishing degree. There were but few of her merchants that were not directly or indirectly inter-ested in the traffic. Some forty or fifty sail of vessels were in this employment, and it was thought a necessary append-age to have one or more slaves to act as domestics in their

---

[1] Report to R. I. Legislature, Jan., 1840.

[2] E. R. Potter, Report to R. I. Legislature, Jan., 1840.

families." [1]   Newport was then the centre of the trade, while the Narragansett Plantations were the stronghold of the institution of slavery.

We have now given the nature and extent of slavery in Rhode Island in 1755, as determined by preceding thought and legislation, by existing institutions, and by the development of the slave trade.   This discussion has been necessary to a clear understanding of the subsequent history of slavery in the colony.   In fact, because of the paucity of material, this is not only a wise but the only possible presentation of the conditions of slavery in Rhode Island in 1755, for of legal records, public documents, literary remains, or private memoranda or correspondence for the year 1755, defining the nature and extent of slavery in the colony, there may be said to be nothing.   We have next to consider how these conditions were modified by the different forces and institutions in the few years preceding the Revolution.

[1] Peterson, " History of Rhode Island," p. 104.

PART II.

SLAVERY BETWEEN 1755 AND 1776.

I. SLAVE LEGISLATION.

Laws, 1755–1774. As has been said, negroes made excellent seamen, and were often induced to go to sea on privateers
and merchant vessels, without consent of their owners. To
prevent this an act was passed in 1757[1] which provided that
commanders of privateers or masters of any other vessels,
carrying slaves out of the Colony without consent of their
masters, should be fined twenty-six pounds; owners of slaves
carried off to recover double damages where the master of a
vessel shall be deemed to have knowledge of a slave's being
carried off; masters of vessels resisting search to be judged
knowing of such carrying off. In 1765 another act was passed
regulating the manumission and freeing of negro and mulatto
slaves. This act provided that the slave freed should procure sufficient security to indemnify the town from charge. [2]
In 1770 an act was passed " for breaking up disorderly Houses
Kept by free Negroes and Mulattoes, and for putting out
such Negroes and Mulattoes to Service." After repeating
the provisions of the act of 1751, for "breaking up from
housekeeping" any free negro or mulatto who shall keep a
disorderly house, "or entertain any Slave or Slaves at unreasonable Hours or in an extravagant Manner," the statute
proceeds:

"And if such free Negroes or Mulattoes have been Slaves,
and manumitted by their Masters, the respective Town-
Councils are hereby empowered (if they shall think proper) to
put out, and bind them as Servants for a Term of Time not
exceeding Four Years, upon such Conditions as they shall
think most for the Interest of the Town: And to commit

---

[1] " R. I. Colonial Records," VI., 64-5.
[2] R. I. Laws, 1767, p. 234.

them to the Work-House until suitable Places can be had for them," and "that the Wages of every free Negro or Mulatto, so bound out, which shall remain after the Expiration of his Servitude, and which shall not have been expended in maintaining him and his Family, be paid to such Servant, unless the Town-Council shall think it most for the Interest of the Town and of such Servant, to reserve the same for the Maintenance of himself and his Family." [1]

September 10, 1770, the laws for restraining Indian and colored servants, and regulating the manumission of slaves in Newport, were revised. Those found abroad after nine o'clock at night were to be confined in a cage, instead of the jail, till morning, and then to be whipped with ten stripes, unless redeemed for a small sum by their masters. In cases of manumission the owner was to give proper security that the subject would not become a public charge, and the free papers were to be recorded. Suitable penalties were imposed for violation of this law, and a failure to conform thereto invalidated an act of manumission. [2] The statute applied only to Newport, where, however, the greater portion of the slaves in the colony were held. A bill was also ordered to be prepared, to prevent the further importation of slaves into Rhode Island, but no action was had upon it at present. [3]

The Law of 1774; Origin. In June, 1774, the most important act [4] yet proposed was introduced into the Rhode Island legislature and passed. It read as follows :

" Whereas the inhabitants of America are generally engaged in the preservation of their own rights and liberties, among which that of personal freedom must be considered as the greatest, and as those who are desirous of enjoying all the advantages of liberty themselves should be willing to extend personal liberty to others," etc., it is enacted that all slaves thereafter brought into the State shall be free, except slaves of persons traveling through the colony, or persons coming

[1] R. I. Laws, 1772, pp. 24, 25.
[2] Laws of 1772, pp. 34, 37.
[3] Arnold, II., 304.
[4] " R. I. Colonial Records," VII., 251-2.

from other colonies to reside, and that citizens of Rhode Island owning slaves shall be forbidden to bring any slaves into the colony, except they give bond to carry them out again in a year.

As we have seen, in 1770, a bill had been ordered to be prepared to prevent the further importation of slaves into Rhode Island, but nothing further had been done. Meanwhile, in 1772, the Sommersett decision had been given in England. [1] "The effect of this decision upon the colonies," says Arnold, [2] "was to confirm the views already expressed by many writers, to stimulate legislation against the system, and to hasten the emancipation of slaves in New England."

At the Providence town meeting, May 17, 1774, Jacob Schoemaker having died intestate, and having left six negroes upon the town, it was voted "that it is unbecoming the character of freemen to enslave the said negroes ; and they do hereby give up all claim of right or property in them, the said negroes, or either of them, and it is hereby recommended to the town council to take the said negroes under their protection, and to bind the small children to some proper masters or mistresses, and in case they should not be personal estate of the said Jacob Schoemaker, sufficient to pay his just debts, it is further recommended to said council to bind out either or both of the adult negroes for that purpose," and "Whereas, the inhabitants of America are engaged in the preservation of their rights and liberties ; and as personal liberty is an essential part of the rights of mankind, the deputies of the town are directed to use their endeavors to obtain an act of the General Assembly, prohibiting the importation of negro slaves

[1] In this case Lord Mansfield decided that the slave Sommersett must be discharged because there was no positive law sanctioning the institution of slavery in England.

" The importance of the case for the colonies lay not in the assertion of the principle that slavery depended on positive law, for the American statute books were full of positive law on slavery; the precedent thus established determined the future course of England against the delivery of fugitives, whether from her colonies or from other countries." *Marion McDougall, " Fugitive Slaves," p. 12.*

[2] History of Rhode Island," II., 321–2.

into this colony ; and that all negroes born in the colony
should be free, after attaining to a certain age."

Of the town deputies Stephen Hopkins was one, and to
him has been given the credit for the passage of the subsequent act in the legislature.   Mr. Sidney Rider says [1] on this
point, "There is nothing contained in the town records to
show that Mr. Hopkins was present at the meeting, nor can
we find anything to connect him with the passage of the preamble or with the law itself ; nevertheless the style is very
like his style, and the mode of reasoning is his favorite mode.
He may have written it."   Mr. Foster says [2] that "at the
direct instance of Stephen Hopkins (himself for many years
an owner of slaves, though a most humane master), the General Assembly ordained" that slaves thereafter brought into
the colony should be free ;   *   *   "The letter of Moses
Brown to Robert Waln distinctly states that 'Governor
Hopkins was a member of the Assembly from Providence,
and was the person who dictated to me the following preamble to the act.'"   It is probable that Hopkins was an active
factor in the formulation, the introduction and the passage of
the act.   The fact, however, that strong pressure had been
brought to bear upon him by the Society of Friends to set at
liberty one of his own slaves, that he did not accede to this
demand, that subsequent efforts, continued from month to
month, appear to have been equally unavailing, that he was
finally dropped from membership in the society, and that he
did not emancipate his slave until his will in 1781 ; these facts,
I say, together with our knowledge of the state of the public
mind at the time, and the restless activities of Moses Brown,
lead me to believe that Hopkins was not the most active
factor, but that the individual who did most for the passage of
the act was Moses Brown.   But while Moses Brown, with the
assistance of Stephen Hopkins, formulated the measure, the
immediate reason for its formulation and introduction was the
action of the Providence town meeting, and the reason for
the passage of the measure lay in the state of public opinion
at the time regarding slavery.   Now, as in 1652, we see that

[1] "R. I. Historical Tracts," No. 9, p. xix.
[2] "R. I. Historical Tracts," No. 19, pp. 99, 249.

it was in the northern and more democratic part of the colony
that the anti-slavery sentiment was most developed, and exercised the strongest influence upon legislation, first in regard to the slave trade, and afterwards in regard to the institution of slavery itself.   Neither to any one individual nor to
the colony as a whole is due this act against the importation
of slaves, but largely to the economic and moral conditions of
the northern half of the colony.

November, 1775, a bill for emancipation was introduced
into the legislature.   The abolition of the slave trade had
been accomplished more than a year before.   It was now proposed to terminate the system of chattel slavery by declaring
free "all negroes as well as other persons hereafter born
within this colony," and to provide for the liberation of existing slaves at the will of the owners by proper regulations.
This bill was referred to the next session of the legislature,
and it was voted "that in the meantime a copy thereof be
published in the Newport and Providence newspapers, and
that the deputies of each town in the colony lay the same before their constituents in town meeting, and obtain their
opinions thereon and present the same to the General Assembly, at their next session."   In accordance with these instructions the Smithfield deputies were ordered by their constituents to make the bill a law.   In this same year the amount
necessary as security in case of manumission was made one
thousand pounds.   This change was probably necessary on
account of the depreciation of currency.

Character of Slave Legislation.   Slave legislation in Rhode
Island may be divided into three classes.   The first was char-
acteristically in the interest of the master.   Laws were made
to prevent slaves escaping from masters, and to prevent their
being absconded by masters of vessels.   The second class
was in the interest of the colony.   Negroes were forbidden to
be abroad after nine o'clock at night, security was to be given
for negroes upon their being freed, strong liquors were not
to be sold to them, disorderly houses kept by negroes were to
be broken up, and a revenue was to be derived from the importation of slaves.   The third class of legislation was that

enacted in the interests of the slave himself. This consisted
of laws regulating and then abolishing the importation of
slaves, and laws restricting or prohibiting the holding of
slaves. Legislation of the first kind continued until active
legislation began against slaveholding. The first and third
forms of legislation are accordingly distinct in time, though
they are not as distinct in time as they are in form, for even
before it was thought necessary to legislate in the interest of
the master, two laws had been placed on the statute books in
the interests of the slave, namely the laws of 1652 and 1675–6.
This fact leads me to believe that the interests of the owner
of slaves were never considered of paramount importance except where they were one with the interests of the colony
itself. The number of owners of slaves was comparatively
so small, moreover, that, although their social influence was
great, it could not be expected that legislation would be directed by them, and in their interests alone. The interests
of the slave importer and those of the colony were, perhaps,
even less nearly allied. Slavery was the life of trade, but it
was not therefore necessary that slaves should be brought to
Rhode Island, it was argued. So the law of 1774 must be
considered not so much a blow at slave trade as a blow at the
ownership of slaves in Rhode Island. The slave trade carried
on by Rhode Island vessels flourished many years after this
date, and slavery itself flourished for a time, but such limitations were already placed upon it as insured its final extinction. There was no emancipation proclamation, there were
no distinct slavery and anti-slavery parties, but there were
other anti-slavery conditions, economic, social and moral,
which made the abolition of slavery in the course of events
an absolute necessity.

II. SOCIAL LIFE OF THE SLAVES.

The Sale of Slaves. The social life of the slave in Rhode
Island was similar to that of a servant in an old English
family of that period. Our knowledge of the slave's social
position and social attainments is derived largely from newspaper advertisements of the time, and from family records.

Upon the arrival of a cargo of slaves they were put up at auction by the master of the vessel, or by some merchant of the town. These auction sales were held at the old inns. October 14, 1766, a negro was advertised for sale by auction, at the Crown Coffee House opposite to the Court-House in Providence.[1] In the case of private sales of slaves the printer often acted as broker. For example, an advertisement in the Providence *Gazette*, March 4, 1775, reads, somewhat face- tiously, " to be sold, a young negro girl born in this town, about 16 years of age, very active, strong and healthy. Would do exceedingly well on a farm, is good natured, has other good qualities, and like the rest of the world has some bad ones, though none very criminal."

Social Attainments. Some of these advertisements indi- cate considerable ability in the slaves, especially the adver- tisements for runaway slaves. These advertisements were often headed by the rude cut of a black man, hatless and with frizzled head, running. One advertisement in the Newport *Mercury*, November 3, 1761, speaks of an escaped negro who speaks good English, and is " very artful and insinuating." Others may be mentioned : July 9, 1763, " ran away Sarah Hammet, a lusty mulatto slave, about thirty eight, wore a dark colored camblet short wrapper, old grey petticoat very much patched, brown camblet bonnet, is polite, ingenious at drawing, embroidering, and almost any kind of curious needle- work." October 16, 1773, " ran away Cæsar   *   *   plays well on the violin."

Newport Gardner was one of the most celebrated negro characters of this time. " In his person he was tall and straight and well formed ; in his manners he was dignified and unassuming." He was a man, too, of superior powers of mind. " He taught himself to read after receiving a few lessons on the elements of written language. He taught himself to sing, after receiving a very trivial initiation into the rudiments of music. He became so well acquainted with the science and art of music that he composed a large number of tunes, and was for a long time the teacher of a very numer-

[1] "R. I. Historical Tracts," No. 15, p. 207.

ously attended singing school in Newport." [1]   He could also write, cipher, and speak French.   His one failing in common with many other negroes was a love for drink.

Knowledge of Trades.   In the trades many acquired some proficiency.   The Newport *Mercury*, April 27, 1772, advertises a negro blacksmith who makes anchors ; May 13, 1775, a negro who has worked in a rope-walk and spins a good thread. The Providence *Gazette*, July 28, 1770, advertises as missing " Quam, aged thirty, by trade a cooper, strayed probably in a delirious condition, is of a serious thoughtful turn of mind, and inclined to talk but little."   November 7, 1775, "ran away, Guinea, a clothier by trade, sometimes pedlar of chocolat, gingerbread, Indico and sleve buttons."   Advertisements often recommend servants as capable of either town or country service.   Advertised wants indicate to some extent the demand.   *Mercury*, February 15, 1773, "wanted two negro boys from twelve to seventeen for gentlemen in towns ;" August 7, 1773, wantèd, negro from sixteen to twenty-five, " free from bad smell, strait limbed, active healthy, good tempered, honest, sober, quick at apprehension, and not used to run away."   These advertisements do not indicate a demand for slaves in any particular locality, or for any particular purpose other than general service.   The slaves received their industrial and social training in the home of their first master, and if they learned easily and were faithful, were seldom sold. This fact, together with the fact of the increasing competition of free labor, shows why there were apparently so few slaves acquainted with the trades, and why in reality this number became less and less as the population of the colony increased.

Occupations.   In the domestic work of the colonial household the slave boys were given the errands and the light service about the house.   Some of the families in Providence, for example, had rain-water cisterns for their chief supply of water, " but these were few, and it fell to the lot of the boys, some of whom were negroes, to go with two pails and a hoop

[1] Ferguson's " Memoir of Hopkins," p. 90.

across the bridge for a supply at the town pump." [1]   Another
common watering place was the Mooshassuc, which was the
only accessible fresh stream.   "The murmurs of ancient inhabitants against the brawls and disturbances of boys and
negroes, who, morning and evening, congregated near the
mill, with their masters' cattle, assure us that the early days
of Providence had a delightful experience of patriarchal manners.   *   *   The annoyance had become so great that an
act of the Assembly, 1681, was passed in order to give some
check to the disturbances.   By a communication in the
Gazette, March 30, 1765, however, it appears that the nuisance
was still unabated.   The boys and negroes still disturbed the
quiet of the Town street by 'riding in droves' to Mill River
(the Mooshassuc), every morning and evening, racing as they
went, without hindrance from the constables of those days." [2]

In the south country "every member of the family had his
particular horse and servant, and they rarely rode unattended
by their servant to open gates and to take charge of the
horse." [3]   In Narragansett we find that Robert Hazard had
twelve negro women as dairy women, each of whom had a
girl to assist her.   "Each dairy maid had the care of twelve
cows, and they were expected to make from one to two dozen
cheeses every day." [4]   Slaves were sometimes hired out when
there was nothing at home for them to do.   Hezekiah Coffin
writes to Moses Brown, October 29, 1763, "send us word
by the first opportunity what the negroes wages was, that we
may settle with his master."

Care for Slaves; Amusements.   The quarters of the slaves
were in the garrets of the large old mansion houses and in
the outhouses.   They were generally comfortable, if we can
judge anything from the scanty figures regarding mortality.[5]
The slaves were dressed very much as the circumstances

[1] Stone, "Life of Howland," p. 25.

[2] "R. I. Historical Tracts," No. 15, p. 57.

[3] Channing, "Early Recollections of Newport," p. 91.

[4] Higginson, "Larger History of the United States," p. 237.

[5] Newport "Mercury," December 28, 1772, gives the mortality for Newport, 1760, whites 175, blacks 52; 1772, whites 205, blacks 51.

of their masters and the nature of their occupations would permit. Advertisements of runaway slaves gave descriptions of the clothing worn at the time as a means of identification. The *Mercury*, February 23, 1773, advertises a runaway negro man "Jack, wore striped flannel shirt, buckskin breeches, dark striped waistcoat, butternut barkcolored lappelled jacket, grey homemade bearskin great coat, new with large metal buttons, one pair of blue yarn stockings, one pair black ribbed worsted stockings, calfskin turned pumps, pinchbeck buckles, felt hat." Another runaway negro is described as having taken with him several articles of apparel so as not to be described by that. This was probably true of many who ran away. For this reason the description of the clothing worn by runaways cannot be relied upon as an exact account of the clothing generally worn by slaves.

The amusements of the slaves were like those of the English servants. The old corn-huskings of Narragansett were greatly enjoyed by the negroes. For these, invitations were sent out to all the friends in the neighborhood, and in return the invited guests sent their slaves to aid the host by their services. "After the repast the recreations of dancing commenced, as every family was provided with a large hall in their spacious mansions, and with natural musicians among their slaves. These seasons of hilarity and festivity—sometimes continuing for days—were as gratifying to the slaves as to their masters, as bountiful preparations were made, and like amusements were enjoyed by them in the large kitchens and outhouses, the places of their residence."[1] Holidays were also observed by the negroes, often independently of master or mistress. "I remember," says Mr. Hazard, "when on the spacious kitchen being removed from the old John Robinson house, there were sixty ox-cart loads of beach sand taken from beneath the sleepers, which had been used to sand the floor, a large portion of which, no doubt, had been danced through the cracks by the jolly darkies of the olden time, who in some instances permitted their masters' families to be present at their Christmas and holiday pastimes as a matter of favor only." Often the distinctions between master and

[1] T. R. Hazard, " Recollections of Olden Times," p. 119.

slave disappeared altogether. "The children of the two," says Mason,[1] "grew up together. The ties thus formed were often stronger than life. The loss sustained by the master was felt by the slave, and the disappointment of the one was a matter of regret with the other. And frequently the slave, rather than see his master turned out of doors, placed at his disposal the little that he had saved of his earnings. The servant expected to work for his master as long as he was able, and when he grew old and infirm he relied on being cared for by some member of the family. In this he was rarely mistaken. Those persons who can call to mind the kitchens of a former generation will remember the old pensioners who gathered in them. * * The slaves took the names of their masters. When they were ill the family physician attended them. When the girl who first played with her young mistress and then became her maid, was about to be married, she had a becoming outfit, and the clergyman who united the daughter united the maid. And when at last death claimed a victim, black and white mingled their tears at the open grave." This care which masters had for their servants is indicated in a letter which Jabez Brown wrote to his brother Moses, September 21, 1770: "Your negro boy Pero was knocked down by a paving stone hitting him on the back part of the head. He was taken up for Dead. But by bleeding etc pretty soon came to. He seems very comfortable, this morning and am in Hopes he will get about in a few Days, the Affair was perpetrated by an Irish man a Hatter by Trade, he has Secreted himself for the Present. I shall endeavor to have him apprehended if possible."

Election Day. One of the most interesting social customs among the Rhode Island slaves was the observance of election day. "In imitation of the whites, the negroes held an annual election on the third Saturday in June, when they elected their governor. When the slaves were numerous each town held its own election. This annual festivity was looked for with great anxiety. Party was as violent and acrimonious with them as among the whites. The slaves assumed the

---

[1] "Reminiscences of Newport," p. 106.

power and pride, and took the relative rank of their masters, and it was degrading to the reputation of the owner if his slave appeared in inferior apparel, or with less money than the slave of another master of equal wealth. The horses of the wealthy land-owners were on this day all surrendered to the use of the slaves, and with cues real or false, head poma-tumed or powdered, cocked hat, mounted on the best Narra-gansett pacers, sometimes with their masters' sword, with their ladies on pillions, they pranced to election, which com-menced generally at ten o'clock. The canvass for votes soon commenced, the tables with refreshments were spread, and all friends of the respective candidates were solicited to par-take, and as much anxiety and interest would manifest itself, and as much family pride and influence was exercised and interest created, as in other elections, and preceded by weeks of *parmateering* (parliamenteering). About one o'clock the vote would be taken, by ranging the friends of the respective candidates in two lines under the direction of a chief marshal, with assistants. This was generally a tumultuous crisis until the count commenced, when silence was proclaimed, and after that no man could change sides or go from one rank to the other. The chief marshal announced the number of votes for each candidate and in an audible voice proclaimed the name of the Governor elected for the ensuing year. The election treat corresponded in extravagance in proportion to the wealth of his master. The defeated candidate was, accord-ing to custom, introduced by the chief marshal, and drank the first toast after the inauguration, and all animosities were forgotten. At dinner the Governor was seated at the head of the long table under trees or an arbor, with the unsuccess-ful candidate at his right, and his lady on the left. The after-noon was spent in dancing, games of quoits, athletic exercises, etc. As the slaves decreased in number these elections be-came more concentrated. In 1795 elections were held in North and South Kingstown, and in a few years, one was held in South Kingstown only, and they have for years ceased." [1]

[1] Updike, " History of the Narragansett Church," p. 177.

Free Negroes. We have already spoken of the condition of the free negro during the first half of the century. In the latter half of the century the manumission of slaves was a far more common occurrence, and the number of free negroes was consequently much greater. The most conspicuous among these, beside Newport Gardner, was Emanuel, an emancipated slave of Gabriel Bernon. " Turning to account the hereditary talent of his race, he established in Providence the first oyster house of which there is any record. It was in the Town street, near the site of the Old Custom House of a later day. To satisfy the craving of a thirsty generation he provided twenty-three drinking glasses, four 'juggs,' twenty-eight glass bottles, two bowls, with pewter plates, spoons, and cooking apparatus in proportion. The knowledge which he had acquired during his former service, ensured his prosperity. He was the first of a long line of such ministers to the public wants. Dying in 1769, he left a house and lot in Stampers street (where his wife carried on the trade of washing), and personal estate valued at £539, 10s. His gravestone in the North Burying ground is as substantial a memorial as those of most of the wealthier white men of his day." [1]

III. THE CHURCH AND THE SLAVE.

Changing Attitude Toward Slavery. During the years preceding the Revolution the attitude of the church toward slavery changed materially. Negro slaves came to be regarded less as heathen and subjects for missionary effort, and more as men, with rights to equal liberties with other men. On this point, the right of slavery, the position of the church became now more clearly defined. The Church of England, the Society of Friends, and Samuel Hopkins' church, were the ecclesiastical bodies most prominent in this movement. The position of the Church of England is best determined by an inspection of the annual sermons preached before the Society for the Propagation of the Gospel in Foreign Parts, and of the records of the same society.

[1] " R. I. Historical Tracts," No. 15, p. 177.

Church of England; Sermons. In 1755 Bishop Hayter preached the annual sermon. After showing that there could be no property in souls, he continued: "Let us administer to them the comfort of knowing, what good things God hath laid up in store for them if they act a right part, in that trying state of labor, in which God hath placed them under us. By thus alleviating their hard lot, and rendering it more easy and supportable to them we shall gain an advantage for ourselves, for it is the natural effect of such instruction to turn the eye-service of slaves into the conscientious diligence of servants. If we are not sufficiently actuated by the spirit of the gospel to be influenced by motives of humanity, let prudential reasons incline us to administer this Christian consolation to our fellow creatures, who are so strictly our property and so absolutely in our power that no one else can take upon him to help them without our leave and direction." In 1759 Bishop Ellis said: "The advantage of making good Christians even of the negro slaves, will also be very worthy of consideration. For in proportion as their obstinacy, sullenness, and eagerness for revenge shall come to be abated and altered by religion they will make better servants: And instead of needing to be always watched in order to prevent their doing mischief they may become guards and defenders of their masters, and there will be no longer any such revolts and insurrections among them as have sometimes been detrimental, if not even dangerous, to several of the colonies." In 1766 Bishop Warburton said in the course of his sermon, "The cruelty of certain planters, with respect to the temporal accommodations of these poor wretches, and the irreligious negligence with regard to their spiritual, is become a general scandal." In 1769 Bishop Newton said: "As it is now generally known and understood that Christianity maketh no alteration in men's civil rights and conditions, but every man is to abide in the same calling wherein he was called, whether to be bond or free, it is to be hoped that the proprietors and planters will be less jealous of their slaves being instructed in the true religion, which will soften and improve their manners, and make them subject not only for fear but for conscience sake, with good will doing service as to the

Lord and not to men;" still, he adds, slavery is to be much lamented.

Results. The results of this prudential reasoning upon the policy of the church in the colonies, and upon the attitude of masters toward their slaves are evident. The best illustration, perhaps, of the effect on the policy of the church, is the well known anecdote of the good elder whose ventures had uniformly turned out well, and who always returned thanks on the Sunday following the arrival of a slaver in the harbor of Newport, "that an overruling Providence had been pleased to bring to this land of freedom another cargo of benighted heathen to enjoy the blessing of a gospel dispensation."[1] In very much the same spirit Dr. Waterhouse said: "To see the negro women in their black hoods and blue aprons, walking at a respectful distance behind their master, to meeting, was not an unpleasant sight on those days." Its effect on the relations of master and slave was similar. In the earlier years of the century, as we have seen, masters were opposed to the baptism and to the education of their slaves. This opposition became less pronounced, in time, and less noticeable, and missionaries no longer made complaint of the masters. Still the number of slaves baptised did not increase perceptibly. The records of St. John's Church, Providence, then King's Church, show that three slaves were baptised in 1758, three in 1759, one in 1760, two in 1762, one in 1764, two in 1765, one in 1766, and two in 1775. The reports of Trinity Church, Newport, show in 1763 one baptism, in 1765 one. In the latter year the total number of communicants was 120, seven of whom were blacks, "who," the report says, "behave in a manner truly exemplary and praiseworthy."

Education. Efforts made to educate the slaves were not more successful. In 1731 there had been a bequest of land and four hundred pounds to build a school-house in Newport. January 9, 1763, the Reverend Marmaduke Browne, rector of Trinity Church, wrote the Society for the Propagation of the Gospel in Foreign Parts, and said that at the instance of the

[1] G. C. Mason, in "American Historical Record," I., 312.

associates of the late Dr. Bray, and with the hearty concurrence of the society he had opened a school for the instruction of negro children. This school, he said, was to consist of fifteen of each sex, was to be under his inspection, and would, he trusted, answer the intentions of the charitable persons concerned in it. August 3, 1772, the Newport *Mercury* gave notice of "a school opened by Mrs. Mary Brett, at her home, for the instruction of thirty negro children gratis, in reading, sewing, etc., agreeable to a benevolent institution of a company of gentlemen in London. N. B., satisfaction will be given to those who may send their young blacks." These three records are probably made respecting one institution, but whether they are or not, the fact that masters did little to encourage the education of their slaves cannot be doubted, especially in view of a subsequent item in the *Mercury*. This appeared March 29, 1773, and stated that on account of the difficulty in getting thirty negro children for the school, the project would be given up in six months if still unsuccessful.

Quakers. In contrast with the calculative philosophy which actuated the dominant thought, both economic and political and religious, of the time, stood the faith and activity of the Society of Friends. The Friends acted rather upon grounds of principle than for prudential reasons. They did not question so much as to whether slaves should be admitted to church membership and education, but fundamentally as to whether they should be free.

In 1729 the practice of importing negroes was censured. In 1758 a rule was adopted prohibiting Friends within the limits of the New England Yearly Meeting from engaging in or countenancing the foreign slave trade.[1] In 1760 John Woolman visited the yearly meeting held in Newport. "He saw the horrible traffic in human beings,—the slave ships lying at the wharves of the town,—the sellers and buyers of men and women and children thronging the market place. The same abhorrent scenes which a few years after stirred the spirit of the excellent Hopkins to denounce the slave trade and slavery as hateful in the sight of God to his con-

[1] Whittier's introduction to John Woolman's "Journal," p. 9.

gregation at Newport, were enacted in the full view and
hearing of the annual convocation of Friends, many of whom
were themselves partakers in the shame and wickedness." [1]
"The great number of slaves in these parts," says Woolman, "and the continuance of that trade from thence to
Guinea, made a deep impression on me, and my cries were
often put up to my Heavenly Father in secret, that he would
enable me to discharge my duty faithfully in such way as he
might be pleased to point out to me. * * * Understanding that a large number of slaves had been imported
from Africa into that town, and were then on sale by a member of our society, my appetite failed, and I grew outwardly
weak and had a feeling of the condition of Habakkuk, as thus
expressed : 'When I heard, my belly trembled, my lips quiv-
ered, I trembled in myself, that I might rest in the day of
trouble.' I had many cogitations and was sorely distressed.
I was desirous that Friends might petition the Legislature to
use their endeavors to discourage the future importation of
slaves, for I saw that this trade was a great evil, and tended
to multiply troubles, and to bring distresses on the people for
whose welfare my heart was deeply concerned. But I perceived several difficulties in regard to petitioning, and such
was the exercise of my mind that I thought of endeavoring to
get an opportunity to speak a few words in the House of
Assembly, then sitting in town. This exercise came upon me
in the afternoon on the second day of the Yearly Meeting,
and on going to bed I got no sleep till my mind was wholly
resigned thereto. In the morning I inquired of a Friend
how long the Assembly was likely to continue sitting, who
told me it was expected to be prorogued that day or the next.
As I was desirous to attend the business of the meeting, and
perceived the Assembly was likely to separate before the
business was over, after considerable exercise, humbly seeking
to the Lord for instruction, my mind settled to attend on the
business of the meeting ; on the last day of which I had prepared a short essay of a petition to be presented to the Legislature, if way opened. And being informed that there
were some appointed by that Yearly Meeting to speak with

[1] Whittier's introduction to John Woolman's " Journal," pp. 25, 26.

those in authority on cases relating to the Society, I opened
my mind to several of them, and showed them the essay I
had made, and afterwards I opened the case in the meeting
for business, in substance as follows :

" 'I have been under a concern for some time on account
of the great number of slaves which are imported into this
colony.   I am aware that it is a tender point to speak to, but
apprehend I am not clear in the sight of Heaven without
doing so.   I have prepared an essay of a petition to be presented to the Legislature, if way open ; and what I have to
propose to this meeting is that some Friends may be named
to withdraw and look over it, and report whether they believe
it suitable to be read in the meeting.   If they should think
well of reading it, it will remain for the meeting to consider
whether to take any further notice of it, as a meeting, or not.'
After a short conference some Friends went out, and looking
over it, expressed their willingness to have it read, which being
done, many expressed their unity with the proposal, and some
signified' that to have the subjects of the petition enlarged
upon, and signed out of meeting by such as were free, would
be more suitable than to do it there." [1]

Action by the Quakers ; Sentiment Against the Slave Trade.
As a result of the words of Woolman, the London Epistle for
1758, condemning the unrighteous traffic in men, was read,
and the substance of it embodied in the discipline of the
meeting as follows : " We fervently warn all in profession
with us that they be careful to avoid being any way concerned
in reaping the unrighteous profits of that unrighteous practice
of dealing in negroes and other slaves ; whereby in the original purchase one man selleth another as he does the beast
that perishes, without any better pretension to a property in
him than that of superior force, in direct violation of the
gospel rule, which teaches every one to do as he would be
done by, and to do good unto all ; being the reverse of that
covetous disposition which furnishes encouragement to those
poor, ignorant people to perpetuate their savage wars, in order
to supply the demands of this most unnatural traffic, whereby

[1] Woolman's " Journal," pp. 162-5.

great numbers of mankind, free by nature, are subjected to inextricable bondage, and which hath often been observed to fill their possessors with haughtiness and tyranny, luxury and barbarity, corrupting the minds and debasing the morals of their children, to the unspeakable prejudice of religion and virtue and the exclusion of that holy spirit of universal love, meekness, and charity, which is the unchangeable nature and the glory of true Christianity. We therefore can do no less than with the greatest earnestness impress it upon Friends everywhere that they endeavor to keep their hands clear of this unrighteous gain of oppression. * * It is also recommended to Friends who have slaves in possession to treat them with tenderness, impress God's fear on their minds, promote their attending places of religious worship and give those that are young at least so much learning that they may be capable of reading."

The following query was adopted in agreement with the foregoing, to be answered by the subordinate meetings : "Are Friends clear of importing negroes, or buying them when imported ; and do they use those well, where they are possessed by inheritance or otherwise, endeavoring to train them up in principles of religion?"

At the close of the yearly meeting John Woolman called together some of the leading members about Newport who held slaves. "About the eighth hour the next morning," says he, "we met in the meeting-house chamber, the last mentioned country Friend, my companion, and John Storer, [1] being with us. After a short time of retirement, I acquainted them with the steps I had taken in procuring that meeting, and opened the concern I was under, and we then proceeded to a free conference upon the subject. My exercise was heavy, and I was deeply bowed in spirit before the Lord, who was pleased to favor with the seasoning virtue of truth, which wrought a tenderness amongst us ; and the subject was mutually handled in a calm and peaceable spirit. At length, feeling my mind released from the burden which I had been under, I took my leave of them in a good degree of satisfac-

[1] John Storer was from England. It was probably through him that the London letter was introduced.

tion ; and by the tenderness they manifested in regard to the practice, and the concern several of them expressed in relation to the manner of disposing of their negroes after their decease, I believed that a good exercise was spreading amongst them." [1]

In 1769 the Rhode Island Quarterly Meeting proposed to the Yearly Meeting such an amendment of the query of 1760 as should not imply that the holding of slaves was allowed. This was an important step, for before this no one had gone farther than to censure the importing of slaves. The Yearly Meeting, accordingly, was not ready to do more than express its sense of the wrongfulness of holding slaves, and appoint a committee to visit those members who were concerned in keeping slaves, and endeavor to persuade them from the practice.

June 7, 1770, the committee appointed at the previous yearly' meeting announced that they had visited most of the members belonging to the Yearly Meeting who possessed slaves, "had labored with them respecting setting such at liberty that were suitable for freedom, and that their visits mostly seemed to be kindly accepted. Some Friends manifested a disposition to set such at liberty as were suitable, some others, not having so clear a light of such an unreasonable servitude as could be desired, were unwilling to comply with the advice given them at present, yet seemed willing to take it into consideration, a few others which we have with sorrow to remark were mostly of the Elder sort manifested a disposition to keep them still in continued state of bondage."

An example of the first class of men is to be found in the records of the South Kingstown monthly meeting for 1757, when "This meeting Received a paper of Richard Smith as his testimony against Keeping Slaves and his Intention to free his negro girl which paper he hath a mind to lay before the Quarterly meeting all which is Referred for further consideration." [2] These persons freed their slaves either of their own accord or at the first suggestion from Friends, but per-

[1] Woolman's "Journal," pp. 167-8.

[2] MS. Records of South Kingstown Monthly Meeting, I., 82, quoted by Miss Caroline Hazard, "College Tom," p. 169.

sons of the third class who were possessed with the ideas of
the previous century were very slow about manumitting their
slaves. "One of the Rodmans, a few years later, was in
trouble over a slave. He was condemned by his own meeting, but appealed to the quarterly meeting, which confirmed
the judgement of the monthly meeting given against him, 'on
account of his buying a negro slave,' and 'it is the mind of
friends that there ought to go out a publick Testimony &
Denial' of the purchaser, which was accordingly done, and a
solemn 'paper of frd^s Testimony of Disowning' was read at
the end of a First-day meeting." [1] Another famous slave case
was that of the Rathbuns, which was before the Kingstown
monthly meeting eight years. Joshua Rathbun, having
bought a slave, is brought to confess his error, as follows:

"WESTERLY the 27th of ye 12 mo 1765
To the monthly meeting of friends to be held at Richmond next

DEAR FRIENDS. I hereby acknowledge that I have acted Disorderly
in purchasing a Negro Slave which Disorder I was Ignorant of, at the
time of the purchase, but having conversed with several friends upon the
Subject of Slavery have gained a Knowledge that heretofore I was Ignorant of, both as to the Rules of our Society, as well as the nature & incon-
sistancy of making Slaves of our fellow Creatures, am therefore free to
condemn that Inconsiderate act and Desire Friends to pass it by, hoping
that I may be preserved from all conduct that may bring Uneasiness
Upon friends for the future am willing likewise to take the advice of
Friends both as to the bringing up and Discharging of the Afores^d negro.
JOSHUA RATHBUN." [2]

This, as Miss Hazard justly says, expressed very clearly
what must have been the general feeling of the day in regard to
slavery, and sounds like an honest change of heart. Yet half
a dozen years later it appears that Rathbun had assigned the
negro girl to his son, who had promised to free her at a suitable time, but had afterward sold her out of the colony. He
had done this without his father's consent; but the father
had not mentioned the matter to Friends. The son was read
out of the meeting, and the father advised to proceed against

[1] Miss Hazard, "College Tom," p. 170.
[2] Records of Meeting, quoted by Miss Hazard, p. 171.

him. As he did not, the meeting heretofore held at his house was discontinued, and finally he also was denied his membership.[1]

This incident shows the untiring effort of Friends toward the abolition of slavery in its very stronghold, nor did it cease with a few cases. John Knowles and Stephen Richmond in 1771 "Appears of a disposition to comply with friends rules in liberating their slaves." Three Friends "discovers something of a Disposition to comply," while four "Did Shew the Contrary Disposition." They were informed on the 29th of 7th mo., 1771, that all who did not free their slaves may 'expect to be Denied Membership.' Two months afterward a sturdy Friend appeared in meeting and 'saith that he shall not comply with the Rules of the Society, Respecting his Slaves to Liberate them,' and he and three others are therefore denied membership. On the "28th of 6th mo., 1773, Fr[ds] Appointed to Visit Slave Keepers made report that they don't find their is any held as Slaves by Fr[ds] and there are some y[t] are set at Liberty and no proper manuamission given therefore said committee are continued to see that they are manuamitted and make report thereof as soon as they conveniently can."[2]

Let us now turn again to the proceedings of the Yearly Meeting in 1770. We have seen that the committee appointed in 1769 to visit Friends who were owners of slaves reported at the meeting in 1770 the completion of their task. Another committee was accordingly appointed to consider the expediency of making the alteration in the tenth query proposed by the Rhode Island Quarterly Meeting the previous year. At an adjourned session the committee proposed the following: "Are Friends clear of importing, buying, or any ways disposing of negroes as slaves, and do they use those well that are under their care, not in circumstances through nonage or incapacity to be at liberty,—and do they give those that are young such an education as becomes Christians and are the others encouraged in a religious and virtuous life, and are all

[1] "College Tom," pp. 172–176.

[2] Miss Hazard, p. 176, quoting Records of South Kingstown Monthly Meeting.

set at liberty that are of age, capacity and abilities suitable for freedom?" The query as thus read, was approved and recommended to the several quarterly and monthly meetings with the exhortation "that they take care it be duly complied with."

The epistle from this meeting to the Friends in London reads as follows: "This meeting hath been under a weighty concern for some time on account of enslaving and keeping in bondage our fellow creatures, and after much exercise and deep travail of spirit on that account have come to this conclusion that Friends ought to be no ways concerned in importing, buying or any ways disposing of negroes as slaves, and that they set all at liberty that are of age, capacity and ability suitable for freedom."

Progress of the Movement; Sentiment Against Slaveholding. The next information we have as to the progress of this movement among the Friends in Rhode Island is found in their epistle to the London Meeting dated June 12, 1772. It reads as follows: "We also have to inform that the conclusion this meeting came to some time past respecting the enslaved negro, we are gradually endeavoring to affect, and have the satisfaction to inform that a few friends amongst us have freed them from their bondage, and with sorrow that some have been so reluctant hereto that they have been disowned for not complying with the advice of this meeting in that respect." In 1773 another epistle similar to that of 1769 was sent from the Rhode Island Quarterly Meeting to the Yearly Meeting proposing the freeing of all slaves. It read as follows: "It is our sense and judgment that truth not only requires the young of capacity and ability, but likewise the aged and impotent, and also all in a state of infancy and nonage among Friends, be discharged and set free from a state of slavery; that we do no more claim property in the human race, as we do in the brutes that perish, notwithstanding it is to be understood that the aged and impotent and also infants and those in their nonage be provided for, brought up and instructed as required by our 10th query."

In accordance with this recommendation the Yearly Meeting amended the tenth query as follows : " Are Friends clear of importing or in any ways purchasing, disposing of or holding mankind as slaves ; and are all those who have been held in a state of slavery discharged therefrom ; and do they use those well who are under.their care, that are in circumstances through nonage or incapacity to minister to their own necessities and not set fully at liberty, and do they give those that are young such an education as becomes Christians and are the others encouraged in a religious and virtuous life ? "

The epistle to the London meeting for this year reports the following progress : " We also inform that Friends' labor for the freedom of the enslaved negroes is still continued, and some Friends have manumitted them, others give encouragement of taking Friends' advice to free them, and when there hath appeared unrelenting obstinacy some such have been disowned since last year." The Epistle to the London meeting dated June 14, 1774, was written in very much the same spirit. It says : " By accounts brought into the meeting it appears that several among us have manumitted their slaves since last year, and some encouragement is given to expect the freedom of others, so that we are in hopes that those who have hitherto neglected it may be prevailed upon to let the oppressed go free." Their hopes were not without reason, for by 1782 no slaves were known to be held in the New England Yearly Meeting.[1]

These facts indicate that fourteen years before general colonial action was taken the importation of slaves was forbidden by the Society of Friends among its members, and fifteen years before a colonial law was made against the ownership of slaves, measures were taken by the Friends to abolish it, at once and altogether. The influence of such procedure can scarcely be over-estimated. The strong social influence of the Friends, and the high moral character of their faith and of their activity, both tended to produce a strong impression upon the thought and activity of the community.

Other Ecclesiastical Bodies ; Samuel Hopkins. There were no other ecclesiastical bodies so well organized in Rhode

[1] Whittier, introduction to Woolman's " Journal," p. 28.

Island as the English Church and the Society of Friends, accordingly other efforts toward the amelioration of the conditions of the slave or toward his emancipation were made by individual churches.

In Dr. Stiles' church at Newport there were, among eighty communicants in 1770, seven negroes. "These occasionally met by his direction in his study where," says his biographer,[1] "he discoursed to them on the great things of the divine life and eternal salvation ; counselling and encouraging them, and earnestly pressing them to make their calling and election sure, and to walk worthily of their holy profession. Then falling on their knees together, he poured out fervent supplication at the throne of grace, imploring the divine blessing upon them, and commending himself and them to the Most High."

The most prominent clergyman, however, connected with the movement inaugurated by the Friends, was Dr. Stiles' opponent in theology, Dr. Samuel Hopkins. Some time after the settlement of Dr. Hopkins in Newport he "became impressed with the state of the town in reference to the slave trade. There were some conscientious exceptions, but it was the general employment of men of business, so as to be the source of the support and prosperity of the people. There were more than thirty distilleries in operation, and more than an hundred and fifty vessels engaged in prosecuting the trade."[2] Newport was at this time the most important "mart for slaves offered for sale in the north, and the point from which they were shipped to southern parts if not taken directly there from the coast of Africa. If, too, a Dutchman in New York wanted a few slaves to work his land, he opened a correspondence with a Newport merchant, or if the market was dull in Newport, a portion of the cargo was sent to Boston."[3]

Cargoes of slaves were often landed near the church and home of Dr. Hopkins. His congregation was deeply involved in the guilt of slave trading and slave holding. "On

[1] Holmes, " Life of Ezra Stiles," p. 157.
[2] Patten, " Life of Hopkins," p. 80.
[3] Geo. C. Mason in " American Historical Record," I., 344.

the subject of emancipation, Dr. Hopkins was an advocate for slaves remaining quietly and peaceably in bondage, and diligently and faithfully performing as unto God the labors of their station, whether to masters who were kind and indulgent, or to those who were froward and severe ; till there might be an opportunity in divine Providence for them to become loyally and with the consent of their masters, free." [1] This opportunity Dr. Hopkins sought to bring about. He visited from house to house and urged masters to free their slaves ; he also preached several times against slavery, between 1770 and 1776. " His sermons offended a few, and made them permanently his enemies. One wealthy family left his congregation in disgust ; but the majority of his hearers were astonished that they of themselves had not long before seen and felt the truths which he disclosed to them," [2] and a few years later, as a church, passed this resolution, "that the slave trade and the slavery of Africans, as it has existed among us, is a gross violation of the righteousness and benevolence which are so much inculcated in the gospel, and therefore we will not tolerate it in this church."

Dr. Hopkins, further, took a deep religious interest in the slave as well as an interest in his emancipation. Soon after his installation at Newport in 1770, he formed a plan for sending the gospel to Africa. After he had matured it in his own mind, he communicated it to Dr. Stiles. About this, Dr. Stiles records in his diary, April 8, 1773, " Yesterday Mr. Hopkins came to see me and discourse with me on a design he is meditating, to make some negro ministers and send them to Guinea. * * * There are two negro men communicants in his church, that he is disposed to train up for this end. The one is Quamine, [3] a free negro, and the other Yamma, a servant. * * He wants, therefore, to contrive that these two negroes should be taken under tui-

[1] Patten, p. 82.

[2] Park, " Life of Hopkins," p. 116.

[3] Quamine had been delivered about 1750 by his father to a sea captain to bring him to Rhode Island for an education. After sending him to school a while the captain sold him for a slave. *Stiles' Literary Diary*, *April 13, 1773*, quoted by Park.

tion, perfected in reading the scriptures, and taught system-
atical divinity, and so ordained and sent forth.   *   *   Mr.
Hopkins desired me to talk with Quamine, and examine his
abilities, which I said I was ready to do." Another record,
dated April 13, contains the following: "Last evening
Quamine came to see me, to discourse upon the scheme of
his becoming a minister.   *   *   He reads but indifferently; not freely but slowly, yet distinctly, and pretty accur-
ately.   *   *   He has had but little time for reading;
seldom any but Lord's days.   I did not try him as to writing,
but he said he had begun to write last winter.   He is pretty
judicious but not communicative and I am doubtful whether
he would be apt to teach.   He certainly wants much improvement to qualify him for the gospel ministry, if indeed such a
thing were advisable."

The two men, though ill prepared in many respects, "still
retained a Knowledge of their native language, and were
intelligent, discreet and pious."   The two pastors, therefore,
finally decided to give them the necessary education, and to
this end issued a circular dated August 31, 1773, and signed
by them, and distributed it among the churches of Massachusetts and Connecticut.   This circular stated that Bristol
Yamma was fifty dollars in debt because he had not been able
to purchase his freedom under two hundred dollars, that he
must procure this by his own labor unless relieved by the
charity of others, and that for this reason, both to pay this
debt and to support the two men at school, money was desired.   To this appeal immediate and encouraging response
was made, and the next year the two negroes were sent to
Princeton for instruction.[1]

The Unorthodoxy of Reform.   Another plan formulated by
Dr. Hopkins a few years later, for the colonization of Africa,
shows the breadth of his intelligence and sympathies.   Yet
it is a curious fact that, respecting both him and the Friends,
it was the unorthodox party that did most for the slave.   The
utilitarian philosophy was everywhere prevalent.   In the

---

[1] This project was given up at the opening of the war because of the
removal of Dr. Hopkins and the lack of money.

church, it was, quite naturally, formulated in Biblical terms, so that it seemed truly to have a divine sanction. The philosophy of the church was the same as that of the time, it was only the expression of it that was different. With this philosophy, however, Hopkins and the Quakers seem to have broken as the Methodists did in England about the same time. It was, perhaps, their ability to think away the formulas of the dominant party that enabled them to discover what they thought to be a universal right to freedom, and further to believe in it, and act upon it. And, if it is agreed that it was the unorthodox party in Rhode Island that brought about the abolition of the slave trade and the emancipation of the slave, we may go farther and say that it was because Rhode Island was from the first quite unorthodox and independent, that she was the first among those prominently engaged in the slave trade, to abolish the trade and emancipate the slave.

Moral and Economic Reasons for the Decay of Slavery. That there were economic reasons for the decay of slavery in Rhode Island, is very true, but it is also true that before the Revolution these reasons, in part were not recognized, and in part did not exist. Slavery was still the life of trade, many of the most influential citizens and planters still owned slaves, and private individuals often engaged in small ventures in this profitable business. For example, in 1762 a hogshead of rum was sent to the coast and the following receipt was given for it : "Newport, April 24th, 1762. Received on Board the sloop Friendship, one Hogg^d Rum, marked W. H. No. 2 which on my arrival on the Coast of Africa, I promise to dispose of on the Best Terms & Invest the proceeds in Negro man slave and ship back the first convenient opportunity, on the proper account & risk of William Gifford, per me William Hudson."[1]

In spite then of the economic value of slavery up to the time of the Revolution, anti-slavery sentiment increased in force and was throughout the history of the colony so strong that Potter in his report to the legislature in 1840 dared

[1] Geo. C. Mason, in "American Historical Record," I., 344.

even to say that slavery was never countenanced by the legislature, perhaps never by public opinion.

But while it was for moral reasons that the slave trade and slavery were abolished in Rhode Island as early as they were, and in Rhode Island earlier than in the other colonies referred to, it was for economic and prudential reasons that the slave trade in Rhode Island was abolished before slavery, and the final abolition of slavery in the colony took the form it did. The law of 1774 against the importation of slaves into Rhode Island affected the slave trade but little. The only real difference was, that Rhode Island merchants sold their slave cargoes in other ports, especially the southern ports, where already the market was becoming much more valuable. The profit still continued to come largely to Rhode Island, if the slaves did not. For economic as well as for moral reasons, therefore, the law of 1774 was made possible. It did not affect so large a class of people as the later law against the ownership of slaves, nor did it affect even that class seriously. Its motive and spirit satisfied the moral demand, its form and letter satisfied the economic. But while this measure was not so important nor so far-reaching in its results, the law of 1784 against the ownership of slaves was quite important, and the forces which determined its enactment as a law were strong and numerous. We must now examine what was more distinctively the anti-slavery agitation which led up to the act of 1784.

IV. ANTI-SLAVERY AGITATION.

Anti-Slavery Literature. Much has already been said of the attitude of the church toward slavery, and the consequent abolition of the slave trade, in Rhode Island. The moral force thus aroused was also one of the strongest influences against the institution of slavery; but there was beside this and in addition to the organized effort of the church, an anti-slavery literature and the voluntary efforts of individuals.

Some of this anti-slavery pamphlet literature was made up of the sermons before the Society for the Propagation of the Gospel in Foreign Parts, which have already been mentioned.

Besides these there appeared in 1762, "Considerations on Keeping Negroes," by John Woolman. "Some of these pamphlets," he writes, "I sent to my acquaintance at Newport." In this paper he says: "When trade is carried on productive of much misery, and they who suffer by it are many thousand miles off, the danger is the greater of not laying their sufferings to heart. In procuring slaves on the coast of Africa, many children are stolen privately ; wars are encouraged among the negroes ; but all is at a great distance. Many groans arise from dying men which we hear not. Many cries are uttered by widows and fatherless children which reach not our ears. Many cheeks are wet with tears, and faces sad with unuttered grief, which we see not. Cruel tyranny is encouraged. The hands of robbers are strengthened. * * Were we for the term of one year only to be eyewitnesses of what passeth in getting these slaves ; were the blood that is there shed to be sprinkled on our garments ; were the poor captives, bound with thongs, and heavily laden with elephants' teeth to pass before our eyes on the way to the sea ; were their bitter lamentations, day after day, to ring in our ears, and their mournful cries in the night to hinder us from sleeping,—were we to behold and hear these things, what pious heart would not be deeply affected with sorrow?"[1]

May 14, 1768, the Newport *Mercury* contained an extract from the Boston *Evening Post*. The burden of this article was similar to that of Woolman's essay ; that while seeking liberty themselves, the colonists ought not to enslave others, and that masters ought to do to slaves as they would have slaves do to them. March 21, 1772, the Providence *Gazette* contained an advertisement for "proposals for printing by subscription a dissuasion to Great Britain and her colonies from the slave trade to Africa, shewing the Contradiction that the Trade bears to Laws divine and provincial ; the Disadvantage arising from it, and Advantage from abolishing it, both to Europe and America, particularly to Britain and her Plantations ; also shewing how to put the trade to Africa on a just and lawful Footing, By Jonas Swan, a Friend to the Welfare of the Continent." The Newport *Mercury*, Decem-

[1] Whittier's Woolman's "Journal," pp. 38–39.

ber 4, 1773, contained "Observations on slave Keeping, an extract from a pamphlet printed in Philadelphia," probably John Woolman's. September 24, 1774, the same paper contained "reflections on slave keeping," also from Woolman's pamphlet ; and on January 28, 1775, it printed a poem entitled, "To the dealers in slaves." March 4, 1775, the *Gazette* advertised a pamphlet by the editor, John Carter, for sale at the distill house. The title of this pamphlet was : "The potent enemies of America laid open, being some account of the baneful effects attending the use of distilled spirituous liquors and the slavery of the negroes." August 26, in the same year, the following communication was sent to the printer of the Providence *Gazette :* "Please to insert the following resolve of the Provincial convention for the large and populous county of Worcester in the Massachusetts bay, which may serve to show that while America is conflicting for the greatest of human blessings, liberty, the members of that benevolent body are not inattentive to the cause of the poor enslaved African." Then follow the Worcester resolves.

Object and Success of Agitation. Of these pamphlets and newspaper articles it is remarkable that only one treats of the slave trade. The real point of discussion was not the slave trade, but the principle involved in both the trade and the ownership in slaves. If the negro was a man and not a chattel, the only logical conclusion was that he must be treated as such. For years he had been, tacitly at least, recognized as a man, now he must be explicitly recognized and treated as such. A number of times, as we have seen, this feeling manifested itself and resulted in the manumission of slaves by their masters. These cases of manumission became much more numerous just before the war. The records of these are to be found in many town clerks' offices.

March 14, 1753, Obadiah Brown makes his will as follows : "My will is and I do hereby Order that my negro man Adam serve one whole year after my decease and after such one years servis to be free. I give him my said negro Adam 20 acres of land to be laid of on the North west corner of my farm in Gloucester." The will of John Field, dated June 26,

1754, was this : " As to my negro man Jeffery I do hereby order and my will is that he shall Chuse which of my Children or Grandchildren he shall think proper to live with, and so far give him his time as to chuse any of them, or any other Person as he thinks proper to take him—provided, that they he shall so chuse, give Bond to Keep my Heirs, Executors and Administrators from all Cost, Charge and Trouble that shall from thence accrue by reason of said negro, Jeffry's Maintainence, and in case none of my children shall see cause to accept of said Negroe, then he shall be kept and maintained by my executors hereafter named." A will of Casco ie Favor, free negro, dated November 9, 1762, reads as follows : " In the first place, I confirm and grant unto my Beloved wife, Judith, her Freedom, willing and requiring that she may enjoy the same without any Lett or Molestation." The will of Richard Browne, October 30, 1765, provides that his girl Phillis be freed after she is forty years old, his girl Sylvia at his decease, his girl Anna at forty, his old negro women not to be sold out of the family, his boy Peter to be freed at forty-five. The will of John Merrett, November 24, 1769, was : " I desire and direct my executors that if my Negro woman, Frank, be living at the time of my decease, a sum of money be given by them to some good honest person to take all kind care of her during her life, that she may be treated with all humanity and tenderness, she having been a very faithful servant, and if my negro man, Tom, may be thought by my executors, of ability sufficient to take care of himself, that they give him his freedom, if not that they dispose of him to a master to his own content, and touching the rest of my negroes that they may be disposed of so that there is good appearance of their passing the remainder of their days comfortable."

Will of Moses Brown. Our discussion would be incomplete without a notice of the will of Moses Brown. This was dated November 10, 1773, and read as follows : " Whereas I am clearly convinced that the Buying and Selling of Men of what Colour Soever as Slaves is Contrary to the Divine Mind Manifest in the Conscience of all Men, however some may

smother and neglect its Reproveings, and being also made
Sensible that the Holding Negroes in Slavery, however
Kindly Treated by their Masters, has a Great Tendency to
Incourage the Iniquitous Traffick and Practice of Importing
them from their Native Country, and is contrary to that
Justice, Mercy and Humility Injoined as the Duty of every
Christian ; I Do therefore by these presents for my Self my
Heirs etc Manumitt and set Free the following Negroes
being all I am Possessed of or am any ways Interested in Viz.
Bonno an african aged about 34 years, Cæsar aged 32 years,
Cudjo aged 27 years Born in this colony, Prince an African
aged about 25 years, Pero an African aged about 18 years,
Pegg born in this town aged 20 years. And One Quater
being the part I own of the three Following Africans viz.
Yarrow aged about 40 years, Tom aged about 30 years, and
Newport aged about 21 years. And a child Phillis aged about
Two Years born in my Family she having the same Natural
Right, I hereby give her the same power as my own children to take and use her Freedom, Injoining upon my Heirs
a careful watch over her for her Good and that they in case I
be taken hence give her suitable education or if she be bound
out that they take care in that and in all other respects as
much as to white children, hereby expressly prohibiting my
Self and my Heirs from Assuming any further power over a
property in her. And as all prudent men lay up in Times of
health and strength so much of their Honest earnings as is
over and above their needful expenses for Clothing etc so it is
my direction and advice to you that you deposit in my Hands
such a part of your Wages as is not from Time to Time
Wanted, taking my Receipt therefore, to put to Interest and
to apply it for your Support when through Sickness or otherwise you may be unable to Support Your Selves, or to be
applyd to the Use of your Children (if Free) and if not to the
purchasing their Freedom and if not wanted for these Useses
to be given in your Wills to such Persons or for such use as
you may think proper. And for your encouragement to such
Sober Prudence and Industry I hereby give to the first Six
Named (the other three having good Trades) the use of one
acre of Land as marked off on my Farm as long as you improve it to good purpose. I now no longer consider you as

slaves nor myself as your Master but your Friend and so long
as you behave well may you expect my further countenance,
support and assistance.   And as you will consider this as an
instrument of extending your Liberty so I hope you will
always remember and practice this my earnest desire and
advice that accompanys it, that you use not the liberty hereby
granted you to Licenciousness, nor take ocation or opportunity thereby to go into or practice the lusts of the flesh, the
lusts of the eye or pride on any ocation or Temptation, but
be more consious than heretofore and with love serve one
another and all men, not only to please Men but as fearing
and reverancing that Holy God who sees all the secret actions
of men And receive your liberty with a humble sense of its
being a Favor from the Great King of Heaven and Earth who
through his Light that shines upon the consciences of all
men, Black as well as white, and thereby sheweth us what is
Good, and that the Lord's requirings of each of us to do
Justice, to have Mercy and to walk humbly with our God is
the cause of this my duty to you, be therefore watchful and
attentive to that divine teaching in your own minds that
convinces you of sin and as you dutifully obey the enlighten-
ings and teachings it will not only cause you to avoid pro-
faneness and wickedness, as stealing, lying, swearing, drinking, lusting after women, frolicking and the like sinful courses
but will teach you and lead you into all that is necessary for
you to know, as your duty to the great master of all men, for
he has said respecting mankind—universally, I will put my
law into their inward parts, and write it in their hearts and
they shall All Know me from the least, to the greatest, and
therefore you can't plead ignorance that you don't know your
duty to the God that made you, because you can't all read his
mind and will in the scriptures, which is indeed a great Favor
and Blessing to them that can understand and obey.   But
there is a Book within you that is not confined to the English or any language, and as you silently and reverently wait
for its openings and instantly it will teach you and you will
be enabled to understand its language and as you are careful
to be obedient thereto and often silently read it, you will be
able to speak its language with African as well as English
tongues to your poor Fellow countrymen To the glory of

him who has wrought your deliverance from slavery to whose gracious care and protection I commit and fervently recommend you and bid you farewell." [1]

The occasion of this will of Moses Brown, as well as its nature, is curious. It was after "returning from the grave of his wife, and meditating upon the Lord's mercies and favors, and seeking to know what the Divine will was concerning him;" he says, "I saw my slaves with my spiritual eyes as plainly as I see you now, and it was given me as clearly to understand that the sacrifice that was called for of my hand was to give them their liberty." [2]

Another will, dated August 1, 1775, made by Eve Bernon, provides for the emancipation of her woman Amey, and the latter's son Marmy, and their keep in case they become disabled through sickness or otherwise.

The Movement in Narragansett. These manumissions we have recorded were mostly confined to Providence. There were also manumissions, as we have seen, in the cases of Friends in Newport and in the Narragansett country. Thomas Hazard, "perhaps the first man of much influence in New England," says his biographer, "who labored in behalf of the African race, when a young man on coming home from college was set by his father to oversee the negroes whilst they were engaged under a scorching sun in cultivating a field of corn. As he sat reading in the shade of a tree his mind went out in sympathy toward the poor slaves who were thus forced to labor for others in the heat of the sun, when he himself could scarcely keep comfortable while quietly sitting in the shade. This led to a train of thought that finally resulted in a conviction that it was wrong to hold slaves," and when he was being established by his father he refused the slaves that were offered him. [3]

A similar anecdote is told of another Narragansett magnate, Rowland Robinson : " Previous to establishing his house-

[1] Probate Records, VI., 73.

[2] Augustine Jones, " Moses Brown: a Sketch," p. 13.

[3] " Recollections of Olden Times," T. R. Hazard, p. 102. Miss Caroline Hazard, " College Tom," pp. 42–44, gives another story of the causes of his conversion.

hold Mr. Robinson engaged with others of his friends in
sending a vessel from Franklin Ferry to the Guinea coast for
slaves, out of his portion of which he proposed to select most
of his domestic servants and farming hands and dispose of
the remainder by sale as was the custom in those days. Up
to the time of the return of the vessel—such was the force
of education and habit—the cruelty and injustice involved in
the slave trade seemed never to have entered Mr. Robinson's
mind, but now when he saw the forlorn, woebegone looking
men and women disembarking, some of them too feeble to
stand alone, the enormity of his offence against humanity
presented itself so vividly to his susceptible mind that he
wept like a child, nor would he consent that a single slave
that fell to his share—twenty-eight in all—should be sold, but
took them all to his own house, where though held in servitude they were kindly cared for." [1]

Conclusion. These were the conditions and the modifications of slavery in Rhode Island during a part of the last century. We have seen that the church largely determined the
status of the slave, and that the economic conditions of the
colony determined the *extent* of slavery. We have seen the
growth of the sentiment against slavery, and its first result in
the abolition of the slave trade. In the next few years this
sentiment was strengthened by the anti-slavery agitation in
England and the other colonies, and by the revolutionary
spirit, and in 1784 an act was passed which provided that all
children born of slave mothers after the first of March should
be free, and that the introduction of slaves for sale upon any
pretext whatever should be forbidden. [2]

[1] "Recollections of Olden Times," T. R. Hazard, p. 121.

Higginson's version of this story is as follows: "Rowland Robinson,
said impulsively one day, 'I have not servants enough, fetch me some
from Guinea.' Upon this the master of a small packet of 20 tons belonging to Mr. Robinson, fitted her out at once, set sail for Guinea and brought
home eighteen slaves, one of whom was a King's son. His employer
burst into tears on their arrival, his order not having been seriously
given." *Larger History of the United States, pp. 237-8.*

[2] Rhode Island's legislation respecting slavery in the period from 1775
to 1785 has been treated in an essay by Dr. Jeffrey R. Brackett, entitled
"The Status of the Slave, 1775-1789," in a volume of "Essays in the
Constitutional History of the United States," edited by Professor J. F.
Jameson.

SLAVERY IN NEW YORK

SLAVERY IN NEW YORK,

WITH SPECIAL REFERENCE TO NEW YORK CITY.

By EDWIN VERNON MORGAN, A.M.

Establishment of Slavery.—In 1625 or 1626, the first negro slaves were brought to New Amsterdam, the settlement which later became the City of New York.   Among them were Paul d'Angola, Simon Congo, Anthony Portuguese, John Francisco, and seven other Africans, who were probably captured at sea.[1] Two years later three negro women arrived, closely followed by others who are spoken of as "Angola slaves, thievish, lazy, and useless trash."   These slaves, apparently, were the only ones introduced prior to the erection of patroonships and colonies in 1629, when the West India Company publicly promised to "use their endeavors to supply the colonists with as many Blacks as they conveniently can," a promise which, from several causes, was not fulfilled until the arrival in June, 1646,

First Slaves in New Amsterdam 1625

of the *Amandare*, the first slave ship to New Netherland whose name is recorded. At Barbadoes, where the vessel touched, "three negro wenches were spirited away," but the remainder of the cargo was sold in New Amsterdam for pork and peas. "Something wonderful was to be performed with them, but they just dropped through the fingers." What slaves were brought and whence they came is not stated.

On May 27, 1647, a committee of the States-General of Holland made a full report on the affairs of the West India Company, in the course of which it mentioned the fact that, in consequence of the unsettled condition of Brazil, "The Slave Trade hath long laid dormant to the great damage of the Company." In regard to New Netherland, it said: "That country is considered to be the most fruitful of all within your High Mightinesses' Jurisdiction. . . . The granting of Freedoms and Privileges hath indeed induced some Patroons and Colonists to undertake agriculture there ; but as the produce cannot be sold anywhere except in the adjacent places belonging to the English, who are themselves sufficiently supplied, those planters have not received a return for their labor and outlay. With a view, then, to give greater encouragement to agriculture, and consequently to population, we should consider it highly advantageous that a way be opened to allow them to export their produce even to Brazil, in their own vessels, under certain duties . . . ; and to trade it off there, and to carry slaves back in return. . . . By this means, not only would Brazil be supplied with provisions at a cheaper rate, but New Netherland would, by slave labor, be more extensively cultivated than it has hitherto been, because the agricultural laborers, who are conveyed thither at great expense to the Colonists, sooner or later apply themselves to trade and neglect agriculture altogether. Slaves, on the other hand, being brought and maintained there at a cheap rate, various other descriptions of produce would be raised."² In accordance with this report the States-General resolved upon February 10, 1648, that the people of New Netherland "be allowed to export their fish, flour, and produce, . . . to Brazil, in private or the Company's ships, . . . and in return to export, at certain duty from Brazil, to New Netherland and not elsewhere, as much merchandise, such as Slaves." Four years later the slave trade to Africa direct was also opened, but with results so meagre that Fiscal Van Dyck wrote on September 18, 1652, "No requests for Negroes has been presented from Patroons or Colonists here to my knowledge." The burghers of New Amsterdam petitioned Governor Stuyvesant in May, 1660, for "per-

mission to trade free and unobstructed in Ship
or Ships, along the whole of the west coast of
Africa," since those who would execute
"with Skipper or Merchant going to that
country a Draft of Partnership, which is beset
and pinched by such precise conditions" (as
those which at present exist) "would risk
their lives and goods, and at best gain nothing." Upon January 6, 1664, the Directors
sent word to Stuyvesant that they had entered into a contract with Symen Gilde, of the
ship *Gideon*, to take in a good cargo of slaves
at Loango, on the coast of Africa, and to fetch
them, by way of Curaçoa, to New Netherland,
and that Amsterdam was a partner for a fourth
of the cargo. Though the ship was due the
coming June or July, "with about 300 slaves
aboard," she did not arrive until a few days
before the Dutch surrendered to the English.ᵃ

During the war between Spain and the United Netherlands, the privateers which swarmed
among the Caribbean Islands and along the
Spanish Main occasionally brought prizes into
New Amsterdam. After the peace, hostilities
were carried on between Spain and France.
To privateers under the French flag, New
Amsterdam was a neutral port where captive
negroes and other prize goods were sold. In
1642 the *La Garce* brought in a few slaves,
and in 1652 a lot of forty-five negroes came in
on another privateer, which had captured them

from a Spaniard. A great part of the slaves who reached New Amsterdam, however, were imported either by private merchants in Holland, under a special permit from the Company, or by the West India Company itself. "We are resolved," wrote the Directors at Amsterdam in 1661, "not only that slaves shall be kept in New Netherland, as we have heretofore ordered, but that they shall moreover be exported to the English and other neighbours." In 1644, the Secretary of the Colony received from Governor Kieft, for four years, a young girl belonging to the Company, "daughter of great Peter, a black man," who, after the expiration of the specified time, "if yet alive," was to be returned. The Directors and Council resolved, in May, 1664, to pay a certain Captain Willet "in Negroes at such price as may be agreed on for a quantity of pork and beef equal to 600 lbs." Two months later they desired "to negotiate a loan of five or six thousand guilders in Wampum for the Honorable Company," to be paid "either in good negroes or other goods," although in November, 1661, they had been sufficiently prosperous to present New Amsterdam with three negro slaves.[4]

Civil Status of Negro and Indian Slaves. —The change of government which occurred in 1664 did not materially affect the status of negro slaves. The "Duke's Laws," published in March, 1664, declared: "No Christian shall be kept in Bond-Slavery, except such who shall be judged thereto by Authority, or such as willingly have sold or shall sell themselves." Fearful that this provision might be misunderstood, the framers added hastily: "Nothing in this law shall be to the prejudice of Master or Dame who have or shall by indenture take Servants for a term of years or for life."* In the amended laws, published about 1674, this provision appeared: "This law shall not set at liberty any Negro or Indian Slave, who shall have turned Christian after they had been bought by any person," a declaration which implied, but did not state, that inhabitants of New York might be born slaves. An act to encourage the baptism of negro, Indian, and mulatto slaves, passed October 24, 1706, established, however, the latter point. It provided that every negro, Indian, mulatto, and mustee should follow the state and condition of the mother and be adjudged a slave to all intents and purposes whatsoever. Slavery, therefore, might exist by reason of birth, voluntary sale, or by way of punishment for crime.*

The civil position of a slave before the law was determined by a number of acts, one of which, relating to minor offences and dated November 27, 1702, allowed masters to "punish their slaves for their crimes at discretion, not extending to life or member." An order of the corporation of New York, dated March, 1736, suggests the manner in which the right was used. It declared that citizens had free licence to send to the house of correction all servants and slaves, there to be kept at hard labor, and punished according to the direction of any one justice, with the consent of the master or mistress. Serious offences, such as murder, rape, or arson, were tried by a court peculiarly composed.'

By an act of December 10, 1712, three justices and five of the principal freeholders of the county constituted judge and jury, seven making a quorum. For this usual jury the jury of twelve might be substituted, provided the master so desired and paid the jury charges of nine shillings. The prosecution furnished the accusation, to which the offender was obliged to plead, apparently without the aid of counsel. How effectively an ignorant slave would conduct his defence one can imagine. In case of conviction the sentence was immediate death, "in such manner and with such circumstances as the aggravation or enormity of the crime," in the judgment of the judges, required. On March 11, 1684, a barn belonging to Jan Nagel, in Harlem, was burned with twelve head of cattle. It was fired by his negro slave, who ran away, and was found next day "hanging to a tree at the Little Hill by the common." The Mayor was asked what should be done with the body, and he ordered that it should be hanged on a gibbet. But the magistrates, fearing the effect of such a sight upon "their children, who were in the habit of going daily to the fields and woods, and who might be terrified thereby," cut it down and burned it.*

By the act of 1702, in a special class of criminal cases, the usual practice of English law was also strangely set aside. "Where slaves are the property of Christians and cannot, without great loss to their masters or mistresses, be subjected in all cases criminal to the strict rules of the laws of England," a slave guilty of larceny of not more than £5 suffered corporal punishment at the discretion of any one justice of the peace; his master, meantime, making good the stolen property. Another section of the same act declared that the evidence of a slave was not receivable in any case, civil or criminal, against a freeman. In cases of "plotting or confederacy among themselves, either to run away, or to kill or destroy their masters or mistresses," of arson, or the killing of their owner's cattle, the testimony of one against another was nevertheless admitted.

Turning from the civil disabilities to the civil privileges, we find that although even freedmen were forbidden to "hold any houses, lands, tenements, or hereditaments," and all persons were forbidden "to trade with any slave either in buying or selling, without leave of the Master or Mistress, on pain of forfeiting treble the value of the article traded for," the like restriction was not laid on the possession by a slave of other kinds of property. By the Game Law of November 10, 1702, a slave received £3 for killing a wolf and 30 s. for killing a whelp, in Suffolk, Queens, or Kings Counties, the bounty going apparently into his own pocket. On September 5, 1717, Sam, late a negro slave of George Norton, deceased, complained to the Governor that Ebenezer Wilson detained money and a negro willed him by Norton. The following is a copy of the petition:

"George Norton in his life time by his last Will and Testament in Writing gave to your poor Petitioner his Freedom from Slavery and thirty pounds in Money, as also one Negro Man named Robin; But Mr. Ebenezer Willson, the Executor of George Norton Deceased, will neither pay your poor Petitioner the Thirty Pound nor let him have said Negro Robin, although he has not (as your Excellency's Petitioner is inform'd) Inventary'd said Negro Robin as a part of said George Norton's Estate. And yet in the Winter when said Negro wants Cloaths he is forced to come to your poor Petitioner for a Supply. And so also when he is sick or lame he has come to your

said Petitioner several Times and lain upon
him for a month at a time. But so soon as he
is well and able to work Mr. Willson takes
him away and Imploys him in his own Service.

"Wherefore your Poor Petitioner humbly
pray that your Excellency wou'd be favourably
pleased to take his suffering Case into your
Consideration and find out some way (as in
your great Wisdom you shall see meet) to induce said Executor to do Right and Justice to
your Poor Petitioner in the case set forth." [9]

One case is recorded, if not more, where a
slave brought suit against his master. June
25, 1710, Joris Elsworth, of New York City,
complained to Governor Hunter, that his negro slave Will, claiming to be a freeman, had
brought suit against him for wages. The case
was tried before a jury at a session of the Supreme Court of the province, and a verdict
was given for the defendant, against whom it
is doubtful whether a slave could have brought
suit on any other plea than the one offered. [10]

Regulations Governing Slave Life.—
The main interest of the slave code turns on
the regulations to prevent conspiracy and sedition. The fear of servile risings was constantly in the minds of our ancestors. Their
savage legislation governing slave life is only
intelligible in the light of this fact. The corporation of New York passed an ordinance, as

early as March 15, 1684, that "No Negro or
Indian Slaves, above the number of four, shall
meet together on the Lord's day, or at any
other time, at any place, from their master's
service." They were not to go armed, moreover, "with guns, swords, clubs, staves, or
any other kind of weapon," on penalty of receiving ten lashes at the whipping-post. "An
Act for the Regulation of Slaves," passed November 27, 1702, which extended these regulations through the colony, reduced the number
allowed to meet from four to three. The desired end was not even then attained. Four
years later Governor Cornbury was obliged
to order the justices of the peace of Kings
County to take the proper methods for seizing
and apprehending all such negroes as had assembled themselves in a riotous manner or
had absconded from their masters; and six
years later, when William Hallet, Jr., of New-
town, in Queens County, his wife and five
children, were murdered by a negro and an
Indian slave, the Governor was obliged to
assent to another act for preventing the conspiracy of slaves."

The negro plot of 1712, the predecessor of
the famous plot of 1741, necessitated yet another,—"An Act for Preventing, Suppressing
and Punishing the Conspiracy and Insurrection
of Negroes and other Slaves," passed December 10, 1712,—which reiterated former provi-

sions and emphasized special points. By the
act of 1702, no person could employ, harbor,
conceal, or entertain at his house, outhouse,
or plantation, slaves other than his own
without their master's consent. By the latter
act, any one who knew of their entertainment
and did not report it must pay £2 or be imprisoned. The master who did not prosecute
the employer or host paid double the sum that
the employer or host should have forfeited.
On October 27, 1730, the Assembly passed
"An Act for the more effectual preventing
and punishing the Conspiracy and Insurrection of Negroes and other Slaves; for the better Regulating them, and for Repealing the
Acts therein mentioned, relating thereto."
This, the last and most comprehensive act
relating to slaves passed in New York before
the Revolution, announced, however, no new
principles, but contented itself with re-enact-
ing former statutes.[12]

The corporation of New York was not behind the Assembly in taking measures to
prevent conspiracies and passed several ordinances to reinforce the four acts last mentioned. As Sunday was the slaves' holiday,
and a favorite time for the hatching of plots,
the Sunday laws were intended to prevent
conspiracies quite as much as to enforce the
fourth commandment. "Servile labouring and
working," riding a horse through any street or

on the common, "rude and unlawful sports," and "fetching any water other than from the next well or pump to the place of his abode," and crossing from New York to Brooklyn without a permission were forbidden. On other days of the week no slave above fourteen years could appear an hour after sunset in the streets "within the fortifications, or in any other place on the south side of the fresh water," without a lantern and lighted candle, "so as the light thereof may be plainly seen." Slaves more advanced in years, since they were in the habit, when riding their masters' horses to water, to go prancing through the streets to the danger of passers-by, were forbidden "to ride in a disorderly fashion." They were also forbidden to clip household plate, to gamble with any sort of money, to assault or strike "any freeman or woman professing Christianity," to curse, swear, or "speak impudently to any Christian," to drive any sort of cart without a permit from the Mayor, except a brewer's drag, or to sell oysters, boiled Indian corn, or any kind of fruit."

Restraining measures, such as those embodied in the acts and ordinances just mentioned, were made necessary by the two servile conspiracies, to which reference has already been made as the Negro Plots. The earlier, that of 1712, broke out on a Sunday night in April, "about the going down of the moon," when a large body of slaves, who thought themselves ill-treated by their masters, armed with guns or rude weapons, met in an orchard, set fire to an outhouse, and assaulted those who came running up to quench the flames. In this way they killed nine men and wounded six others before the alarm was given by the firing of a great gun from the fort, and the soldiers dispatched by the Governor appeared and put them to flight. The militia, by beating the forests at the northern end of Manhattan, aided by sentries posted at the fords, succeeded next day in capturing all the conspirators but six, who, in their despair, killed themselves. Of the remainder, twenty-one were executed either by hanging, burning, or by being broken on the wheel. Many arrested for supposed complicity in the plot were afterwards released for want of evidence to prove their guilt.[14]

The second, or "Great Negro Plot," of March, 1741, though much more serious both in its nature and results, producing deeds "which almost parallel those done in the evil days of the Salem witchcraft," was yet, technically, scarcely a plot at all. Undoubtedly a considerable body of discontented blacks— especially those lately arrived from Africa— vaguely hoped and planned for the murder of their masters. But there is little reason to

suppose that the negroes who acted as domestic servants, and who constituted the mass
of the slave population, ever contemplated,
much less deliberately planned, a general servile insurrection.   In New York, as in Salem,
fear exaggerated the danger.

The first signs of the plot appeared during
the weeks between the twenty-eighth of February and the eleventh of April, when nine
fires followed in such quick succession that
they seemed certain to be of incendiary
origin.   Meantime the keeper of a low tavern,
his wife, two negroes, and Mary Barton, an
indentured servant of doubtful reputation,
were arrested on a charge of receiving stolen
goods.   A proclamation, offering a reward
of £100 and a full pardon to whoever
would give information concerning the supposed plot, was read to Mary, who, seeing
a loophole through which to effect her own
escape, suddenly remembered that the negroes
who were in the habit of meeting at her master's house had planned to destroy the city
and the fort, after which they would make her
master king, and one of themselves governor.
On the strength of her unsupported testimony
a veritable reign of terror began.   Citizens
removed their valuables from beyond the city
limits, and every black man not vouched for
by a master in good repute was lodged in jail.
The catalogue of victims included not only

one hundred and fifty-four negroes imprisoned, of whom fourteen were burned, eighteen hanged, two gibbeted, and seventy-one
transported, but twenty-four whites, four of
whom were executed. Among the latter was
a schoolmaster named Ury, suspected of being
either a non-juring Episcopalian or a Roman
Catholic priest. The magistrates, taking advantage of an old unrepealed law which forbade a priest to come into the province,
condemned Ury on the double count of being
implicated in the plot and of administering the
rites of his religion. When Mary became bold-
er and accused persons of quality and condition, men saw that the panic must be stopped.
But this was not done until a day for general
thanksgiving had been set apart.[16]

The Religious Status of Slaves.—In contrast to the cruel punishments of the negro
plots it is pleasant to find that, since negroes
and Indians were looked upon by our forefathers as children of the devil, efforts were
early made to Christianize them. But the
Dutch were not zealous in this work. Not
until December, 1660, does there appear
among the instructions given by the home
government to the Council for Foreign Plantations: "You are most especially to take an
especial care of the propogacôn of the Gospel
in the several Forraine Plantations. . . .
And you are to consider how each of the Na-

tives, or such as are purchased by you from other parts to be servants or Slaves, may be best invited to the Christian Faith, and be made capable of being baptized thereunto." [16]

Upon the occupation of New Netherland by the English the work went on with greater spirit. The "Duke's Laws" required all constables and overseers to urge the inhabitants to inform their children and servants in matters of religion. The instructions of James II., William III., and Queen Anne to the Royal Governors of New York, bade them, with the assistance of the Council, "to find out the best means to facilitate and encourage the conversion of Negroes and Indians to the Christian religion." Governor Dongan reported that the task was difficult. "It is the endeavor of all persons here to bring up their children and servants in that opinion which themselves profess ; but this I observe, that they take no care of the conversion of their Slaves." Twelve years later, in 1699, it was still found impracticable. Governor Bellomont wrote to the Lords of Trade : "A Bill for facilitating the conversion of Indians and Negroes (which the King's instructions require should be endeavored to be passed), would not go down with the Assembly ; they having a notion that the Negroes being converted to Christianity would emancipate them from their slavery, and loose them from their

service." [17]   On October 24, 1706, "An Act to
encourage the Baptizing of Negro, Indian and
Mulatto Slaves" finally passed the Assembly,
and later received the Royal assent.   It distinctly stated that the baptism of a slave
should not set him free.   The preamble and
the first section read: "Whereas divers of
Her Majesty's good Subjects, Inhabitants of
this Colony, now are, and have been willing
that such Negro, Indian and Mulatto Slaves,
who belong to them, and desire the same,
should be baptized, but are deterred and hindered thereof, by reason of a groundless opinion that hath spread itself in this Colony, that
by the baptizing of such Negro, Indian or
Mulatto Slaves, they would be free, and ought
to be set at liberty.   In order, therefore, to
put an end to all such doubts and scruples as
have, or hereafter at any time may arise, about
the same; Be it enacted by the Governor,
Council and Assembly, etc., that the Baptizing
of any Negro, Indian or Mulatto Slave, shall
not be any cause or Reason for the setting
them or any of them, at Liberty." [18]   This Act
soothed the fears of masters, and, as the church
registers attest, baptisms became frequent.
The Rev. Elias Neau, under the patronage of
the Society for the Propagation of the Gospel
in Foreign Parts, had established a school for
the religious instruction of slaves, three years
before, in New York City.   The slaves met on

the evenings of " Wednesday and Friday and
Sundays after Church," on the upper floor of
Mr. Neau's house.   None of the churches
could be used for a schoolroom, "because of
keeping them clean for the congregation," and
there was "no other public building convenient or capacious enuff."   The Rev. John
Sharp, seeing that the existing arrangements
were inconvenient, proposed, therefore, in
1713, that a catechizing chapel be erected,
"which would give a favorable turn to the
whole affair."   His plan seems to have been
adopted.

From Mr. Sharp, also, we learn something
in regard both to the marriage and to the
burial of slaves. The marriages were arranged,
he tells us, by mutual consent, without the
blessing of Church.   Husband and wife often
belonged to different families, and after marriage were sold many miles apart. Polygamy,
therefore, was frequent. After baptism a few
consented to break their "Negro marriages"
and "marry a Christian spouse."   However
highly colored these statements may be, it is
certainly true that the marriage of a slave was
not made legal before April 9, 1813. The law
enacted on that day reads: "All marriages
contracted or to be contracted hereafter,
wherein one or more of the parties were or
may be Slaves, shall be considered valid as
though the parties thereto were free ; The

Burial of
Slaves

children of such a marriage to be deemed legitimate." [10]

The burial of slaves was first made a subject of legislation on October 23, 1684. The text of the act is not accessible, and we are not able, therefore, to state its provisions. They probably forbade the private burial of slaves, for we find that Mees Hoogeboon, of Albany, was fined twelve shillings "for interring his negro in a private and suspicious manner." In October, 1722, the Corporation of New York ordered that all negro and Indian slaves dying within the city should be buried by daylight. In 1731, in 1748, and in 1763 this order was reissued, with the additional provision that not more than twelve slaves should attend any funeral under penalty of public whipping. On these occasions no pall, gloves, or favors were to be used. A slave who held a pall or wore gloves or favors was to be publicly whipped, at the discretion of the Mayor or of that one of the Corporation before whom he had been convicted. These regulations were probably made to prevent the conspiracy of slaves as much as for any other purpose. The fear of servile risings, as we have remarked elsewhere, is the key-note to the slave code of New York, as well as of the other colonies. Mr. Sharp suggests a second reason, when he remarks: "Slaves are buried in the Common by those of their country and complexion

without the office.   On the contrary, heathen-
ish rites are performed over them." [20]

Indian Slavery.—Both the beginning and
the end of Indian slavery are lost in obscurity,
although nearly all the laws enacted between
1664 and 1788 recognized its existence and
treated it as an integral portion of the slave
system. The first authoritative reference to
its existence appears in the statement of eight
citizens of New Amsterdam to the West India
Company, dated October 28, 1644, which declared that "The captured Indians, who might
have been of considerable use to us as guides,
have been given to the soldiers as presents,
and allowed to go to Holland; the others have
been sent off to the Bermudas as a present to
the English governor."   The second, which
refers to the emancipation of Indian slaves,
points to the conclusion that however desirable Indian slavery appeared to the people of
New York, it was not acceptable to the authorities.   In April, 1680, the Governor and
Council resolved " that all Indyans here, have
always been and are free, and not slaves—except such as have been formerly brought from
the Bay or Foreign Parts. If any shall be
brought hereafter into the government within
the space of six months, they are to be disposed of as soon as may be out of the government.   After the expiration of the said six
months, all that shall be brought here from

those parts and landed, to be as other free Indians." This resolve, if put in force at all, appears ere long to have become a dead letter. In July, 1703, Jacobus Kirstead, of New York, mariner, petitioned the Governor in regard to an Indian brought by him from Jamaica and sold as a slave. In the same month, twelve years later, Colonel Heathcote wrote home to Secretary Townsend: "The Indians complain that their children, who were many of them bound out for a limited time to be taught and instructed by the Christians, were, contrary to the intent of their agreement, transferred to other plantations and sold for slaves, and I don't know but there may be some truth in what they allege." As late as January 22, 1750, Colonel Johnson wrote to Governor Clinton: "I am very glad that your excellency has given orders to have the Indian children returned, who are kept by the traders as pawns or pledges as they call it, but rather stolen from them (as the parents came at the appointed time to redeem them, but they sent them away before-hand), and as they were children of our Friends and Allies, and if they are not returned next spring it will confirm what the French told the Six Nations (viz.): that we looked upon them as our slaves or negroes, which affair gave me a great deal of trouble at that time to reconcile. I cannot find that Mr. Abeel, who has a Seneca

child, or Vandrieson, who has got a Missisa-
gey, are to deliver theirs, which I am apprehensive will cause great disturbance." [21]

From the meagre data which these extracts
afford, the writer concludes first, that, compared to the body of negro and mulatto slaves,
Indian slaves were few in number ; and second, that the majority of them were either
captives or the descendants of captives taken
in war, or else West Indians who were con-
founded with mulattos, and imported as such.
That a considerable body of kidnapped red
Indians existed as slaves in New York at any
period he cannot believe.

Price of Slaves.—*I. Price of Slaves Newly
Imported.* In 1659, negroes purchased at
Curaçoa for $60 could not be sold at New
Amsterdam for the same price. In 1661, a
few sold there for $176 each, less the freight.
Three years later negroes brought $200 at a
certain sale, the highest price being $270.60,
and the lowest $134.20. On the same occa-
sion negresses brought about $129 each, al-
though in 1694, "good negresses" sold for
$240, and in 1723, anywhere from $225 to
$300. Negroes had risen in value, meantime,
to $250, and there remained, as long as the
importation of slaves continued.

*II. Price of Slaves whose Character and
Abilities were Known to their Masters.*

In 1705, a Bermuda merchant sold, in New

York City, a young negro woman, about eighteen, for $200, who had lived in his family some time. A negro wench, nineteen years old, "whom he brought up from infancy," was sold by Dr. Duprey, of New York City, in 1723, for $275. In the same year a negro wench and child, belonging to a former sheriff of Amboy, brought $375. In the inventory of an estate, in 1719, another negro wench and child stood for only $300. Able-bodied men were then selling for about $250.

During and just after the Revolution, the price of slaves appears to have varied exceedingly. The assessors in Ulster County in 1775, valued male slaves between fifteen and forty at $150, those between forty and fifty, ten and fifteen, and seven and ten, at $75, $90, and $50 respectively. Female slaves between the same ages brought $100, $50, $60, and $40. In 1783, the Council of Sequestration sold a negro boy for $56.25. Ten years later another (in Albany County) was bought for $100. Still a third was sold (in Richmond County) in 1798 ; $410 was his price, though by agreement he was to be manumitted in nine years. In the Oswego *Herald*, 1799, appears this advertisement : "A Young Wench—For Sale. She is a good cook and ready at all kinds of house-work. None can exceed her if she is kept from liquor.

She is 24 years of age—no husband nor children. Price $200 ; inquire of the printer." [22]

From the beginning of this century the price of slaves appears to have decreased. In 1801, Wm. Potter and Mary his wife purchased their freedom for $400. A negro nineteen years old brought in Rockland County, March, 1809, $250, and finally a negro woman, aged thirty-seven, with all the rights her present mistress had to the service of her children, was sold for $100.

From these facts we may draw the following conclusions : first, that while agricultural laborers were scarce, male slaves were more valuable than female, but when domestic servants, rather than farm hands, were in demand, the previous condition of things was reversed ; second, that in the years preceding the Revolution, slaves brought their highest price ; and third, that from 1790, when it became apparent that the legislature contemplated measures to bring about emancipation, the price of slaves gradually declined. A fourth and last conclusion is that, during the colonial period, the average price of both male and female slaves varied from $150 to $250.

CENSUS.

Until 1790 the censuses of New York were inaccurate, and it is well-nigh impossible to compute the number of slaves in the State before that date. The following figures are the best available * :

	WHITES.	SLAVES.	TOTAL POPULATION.
1664	7,000	" Very few."	
1678	2,000 " able to beare arms."	" Very few."	
1698		Kings Co., 293	18,067
1703	Five Counties about N. Y. City, 7,767	Five Counties about N. Y. City, 1,301	
1712	Five Counties about N. Y. City, 10,511	Five Counties about N. Y. City, 1,775	
1723		6,171	40,564
1731		7,231	50,291
1746		9,717	Without Albany Co., 61,584
1774		21,149	182,247
1790	314,142	21,324	340,121
1800	557,731	20,903	589,051
1810	918,699	15,017	959,049
1820	1,332,744	10,088	1,372,111
1830	1,873,663	75	1,918,608
1840	2,387,890	4	2,428,921

* Colonial Documents, F. B. Dexter's pamphlet, Censuses of the U. S. (since 1790).

IN NEW YORK CITY.

	WHITES.	SLAVES.	TOTAL.
1703	3,634	801	4,435
1712	4,880	960	5,840
1731	7,045	1,571	8,616
1737	8,945	1,719	10,664
1746	9,279	2,444	11,723

REFERENCES.

1. O'CALLAGHAN, *Voyages of the Slavers "St. John" and "Arms of Amsterdam,"* p. 13.
2. *New York Colonial Documents*, i., p. 246.
3. *Ibid.*, ii., pp. 222, 430.
4. *Ibid.*, ii., pp. 371, 474.
5. *Collections of New York Historical Society*, 1809, pp. 322, 323.
6. *Laws of New York*, 1752, p. 69.
7. DUNLAP, *History of the New Netherland*, ii., p. 165.
8. RIKER, *Harlem*, p. 438.
9. *New York Colonial MSS.*, lvi., p. 172.
10. *Ibid.*, lix., p. 21.
11. *New York Colonial Documents*, v., p. 39.
12. *Laws of New York*, 1752, p. 193.
13. DUNLAP, ii., pp. 129, 132, 159 ; VALENTINE, *Manual of the Common Council of New York*, i., pp. 571, 580.
14. *New York Colonial Documents*, v., pp. 341, 346, 356, 367, 371, 525 ; COFFIN, *Slave Insurrections*.
15. *New York Colonial Documents*, vi., pp, 186, 196, 199, 201-203 ; HORSMANDER, *Journal of Proceedings;* HORSMANDER, *The New York Conspiracy*.
16. *New York Colonial Documents*, iv., p. 36.
17. *Ibid.*, iv., p. 510.
18. *Laws of New York*, 1752, p. 69.
19. *Ibid.*, 1813, ii., pp. 201–202.
20. VALENTINE, i., pp. 566, 571.
21. *New York Colonial Documents*, v., p. 433 ; vi., p. 546.
22. LIVERMORE, *Cooperstown*, p. 171.

JOHNS HOPKINS UNIVERSITY STUDIES

Historical and Political Science

HERBERT B ADAMS, Editor

History is past Politics and Politics present History.—*Freeman*

ELEVENTH SERIES

IX–X

HISTORY OF SLAVERY IN CONNECTICUT

BY

BERNARD C. STEINER, Ph. D.

BALTIMORE
The Johns Hopkins Press
PUBLISHED MONTHLY
September-October, 1893

CONTENTS.

HISTORY OF SLAVERY IN CONNECTICUT.

INTRODUCTION.

Few questions have been more interesting to the American
people than slavery, and the number of works which have
appeared upon the subject has been proportional to the
interest aroused. The slavery of negroes has been discussed
from almost every point of view, and yet the influence of
slavery upon individual States of the Union and its different
history and characteristics in the several States have not
received the attention they deserve. There have been two
able works dealing with this branch of the subject, tracing
thoroughly the course of the institution of slavery in the two
States of Massachusetts and Maryland.[1] As Massachusetts
was the first State of the original number to free her slaves,
and as Maryland was a typical Border State, these mono-
graphs, apart from their accuracy and completeness, have
been valuable contributions to the study of slavery in the
separate States, but they stand almost alone.

It has been the intention of the writer to take up the history
of slavery in his native State—Connecticut. The development of slavery and the conditions surrounding it there were
not greatly different from those existing in the larger State
immediately to the north, yet there were certain phases of
the "peculiar institution" in Connecticut which yield a

---

[1] I allude to Dr. Geo. Moore's "Notes on Slavery in Massachu-
setts" and Dr. J. R. Brackett's "Negro in Maryland." Tremain's
"Slavery in the District of Columbia," in Univ. of Neb. Studies, and
Ingle's "Negro in the District of Columbia," in J. H. U. Studies, are
noteworthy. See also Morgan's brief account of "Slavery in New
York" in the Am. Hist. Ass. Papers. I might add Ed. Bettle,
"Notices of Negro Slavery as Connected with Pennsylvania," Vol.
I., p. 365 ff., Penn. Hist. Soc. Memoirs.

noteworthy return to the student.[1] Though the formal abolition of slavery in Connecticut did not take place until 1848,
there had been practically very few slaves in the State since
1800, and the treatment of the slave had been always comparatively mild and lenient. In the history of the opinion of the
people in regard to slavery, we shall find two fairly well
marked-off periods, under each of which we shall treat separately the legal, political, and social aspects of slavery. The
first of these periods extends from the settlement of the colony until the passage of the Non-importation Act of 1774,
and is characterized by a general acquiescence in the existence of slavery and a somewhat harsh slave code.

The second period, extending from 1774 to 1861, is marked
by the diminution and extinction of slavery. It might be
divided into two subdivisions. The first subdivision extends
from October, 1774, to the rise of the Abolitionists, about
1830, and is characterized by the gradual emancipation of the
slaves and amelioration of their condition.

In the second subdivision, lasting from about 1830 till the
Civil War, we find the formal abolition of slavery and the
rise of the slavery question as a political issue, culminating in
the resistance to the Fugitive Slave Act, and ending in the
Act of 1857. The period closes with the acceptance of the
Fifteenth Amendment in 1869.

---

[1] The author regrets that he was unable to consult Dr. Wm. C.
Fowler's "Historical Status of the Negro in Connecticut" until
these pages were passing through the press. Any new matter
therein contained has been embodied in foot-notes, as far as possible. The labor and research Dr. Fowler bestowed on his paper
make it very valuable. It appeared in Dawson's Historical Magazine for 1874, Vol. XXIII., pp. 12-18, 81-85, 148-153, 260-266.

PERIOD I.—1636-1774.

Indian Slavery.

In Connecticut, as in many other States, the first slaves were not of African race, but were aborigines, taken in battle and sold as slaves, in the same manner as the Anglo-Saxon forefathers of the early settlers had sold the captives of their spear, over a millennium before. After the fierce and bloody Pequod War, the colonists found on their hands a number of captive Indians, whose disposition formed a pressing question. It did not take long to decide it. To the shame of the conquerors, " Ye prisoners were devided, some to those of the River [Connecticut] and the rest to us " of Massachusetts.[1] Of those taken by the latter, they sent "the male children to Bermudas, by Mr. William Pierce, and the women and maid children are disposed about in the towns. There have now been slain and taken, in all, about 700." Connecticut's disposition of her share was, doubtless, much the same as that described above. In the same spirit, the Articles of Confederation of the United New England Colonies, in which both Connecticut and New Haven were included, when drawn up on May 19, 1643, provided that " the whole advantage of the warr (if it please God to bless their Endeavours), whether it be in lands, goods, or *persons*, shall be proportionally divided among the said Confederates."[2]

The Articles of Confederation also provided " that, if any servant run away from his master into any of these confederated jurisdictions, that, in such case, upon certificate of one magistrate in the jurisdiction of which the said servant fled, or upon other due proof, the said servant shall be delivered, either to his master or any other, that pursues and brings such certificate or proof." This was the first fugitive slave law in force in Connecticut.

---

[1] Mass. Hist. Soc. Coll., Series IV., Vol. III., p. 360.
[2] Plymouth Col. Rec., Vol. IX., p. 4.

Since it was found that certain Indian villages harbored fugitive Indians, the Confederation, on Sept. 5, 1646, decided that such villages might be raided and the inhabitants carried off, women and children being spared as much as possible, and added, to its eternal shame, that "because it will be chargeable keeping Indians in prison and, if they should escape, they are liable to prove more insolent and dangerous after, it was thought fit that upon such seizure...the magistrates of the jurisdiction deliver up the Indians seized to the party or parties endamaged, either to serve or to be shipped out and exchanged for negroes, as the cause will justly bear."[1] The Connecticut Code of 1646, following this resolve in its language, recognizes Indian and negro slavery.[2]

The Confederation, in 1646, took active part in endeavoring to make Gov. Kieft of New Netherlands return "an Indian captive liable to publicke punishment fled from her master at Hartford" and "entertained in your house at Hartford and, though required by the magistrate," she was "under the hands of your agent there denied, and was said to have been either marryed or abused by one of your men." "Such a servant," they say, "is parte of her master's estate and a more considerable part than a beast; our children will not longe be secure if this be suffered." This last sentence clearly shows the outcropping of the patriarchal idea. Kieft refused to give her up, and said, "as concerns the Barbarian handmade," it is "apprehended by some, that she is no slave, but a freewoman, because she was neither taken in war, nor bought with price, but was in former time placed with me by her parents for education."[3] By the Inter-Colonial Treaty of Sept. 19, 1650, the provision of the Articles of Confederation, in regard to fugitives, was extended to include the intercourse of the New Englanders and the Dutch.[4] King Philip's War again threw many Indian captives into the settlers' hands and,

[1] Hazard, II., p. 63.
[2] Title "Indians." Conn. Rec., I., 531. Not in Revision of 1715.
[3] Plymouth Records, IX., 6, 64, 190.
[4] Hurd, "Law of Freedom and Bondage in the U. S.," I., 269.

on May 10, 1677,[1] the General Court decreed, "for the prevention of those Indians running away, that are disposed in service by the Authority, that are of the enemie and have submitted to mercy, such Indians, if they be taken, shall be in the power of his master to dispose of him, as a captive by transportation out of the country." The syntax of the enactment is confused, its cruelty is clear.

The number of Indian slaves seems to have gradually decreased from death, intermarriage with negroes, and emancipation, though as late as May 1, 1690, Gov. Leisler of New York met with the Commissioners of Massachusetts, Plymouth, and Connecticut, and they all covenanted that in the contemplated Indian war, "all plunder and captives (if any happen) shall be divided to the officers and soldiers, according to the custom of War."[2]

Though the colonists entertained no doubt of their right to sell Indian captives, better Puritan nature revolted against the idea of perpetual hereditary slavery, and, as early as 1722, we find doubts expressed as to the status of the child of an Indian slave.[3]

Dr. Fowler states that Indian slaves were not considered as valuable as negroes.

Further remarks as to legislation in regard to Indian slaves will be found in a subsequent section.

Colonial Legislation on Slavery.

The earliest law on any of Connecticut's statute-books in regard to slavery is a quotation from Exodus xxi. 16, placed tenth among the Capital Laws of Connecticut, on Dec. 1, 1642, "If any man stealeth a man or mankind, he shall be put to death." This, however, was understood, of course, only to include in its protection persons of white race.

When or how negro slavery was introduced into Connecticut, we have no records to show. "It was never directly

---

[1] Conn. Col. Rec., II., 308.
[2] N. Y. Doc. Hist., II., pp. 134, 157.
[3] Trumbull's "Connecticut," Vol. I., p. 417.   Fowler, p. 152.

established by statute," says the editor of the Revision of the
State's Laws in 1821,[1] "but has been indirectly sanctioned
by various statutes and frequently recognized by courts, so
that it may be said to have been established by law."[2] Few
slaves were imported at first, and, on May 17, 1660, we find
the first reference to negroes in the Connecticut Records."[3]
Then the distrust of bondmen and the fear of treachery in
slaves, nearly always shown by masters, is revealed in the
General Court's order "that neither Indian nor negar servants
shall be required to train, watch, or ward in the Colony."[4]

The number of negroes was "few," not above thirty, only
two of whom were christened, in 1680,[5] and not until ten
years later had they sufficiently increased so as to call the attention of the legislators to their regulation.   Connecticut began
her black code in October, 1690,[6] by passing several measures, providing that a "negro, mulatto, or Indian servant"
found wandering out of the bounds of the town to which
he belonged, without a ticket or pass from an Assistant,
or Justice of the Peace, or his owner, shall be accounted
a runaway and may be seized by any one finding him,
brought before the next authority and returned to his master,
who must pay the charges.   Even a ferryman, transporting
a slave without a pass, was liable to a penalty of twenty shillings for each offense.[7]   A free negro without a pass must
pay the costs if stopped and brought before a magistrate.

The last two laws were repealed in October, 1797.[8]

The next statute, save one, referring to slaves was passed

---

[1] Probably Swift, author of the well-known "System."
[2] Revision of 1821, Title 93, Sec. 7, note.
[3] Dr. Fowler ("Hist. Status," p. 12) says negro slaves were in
New Haven Colony in 1644.
[4] Conn. Col. Rec., I., 349.
[5] They came sometimes three and four a year from Barbadoes.
Conn. Col. Rec., III., p. 298. Answer to Queries.
[6] Conn. Col. Rec., IV., p. 40.   Revision of 1808, Title CL., Ch. I.,
Secs. 1–4.
[7] This amount was later changed to $3.34.
[8] Hurd, II., p. 42.

in 1703.[1] This shows clearly the survival in colonial days of
the *potestas* of the *pater familias* coming down from the
absolute dominion of the house-father in ancient times. It
prohibits any "licensed innkeeper, victualler, taverner, or
retailer of strong drink" from "suffering any one's sons,
apprentices, servants, or negroes to sit drinking in his house,
or have any manner of drink there, without special order from
parents or masters."

Slaves seem now, for some time, to be repressed by laws
continually growing harsher. In May, 1708,[2] the General
Court, taking into consideration that "divers rude and evil-
minded persons, for the sake of filthy lucre, do receive property stolen by slaves," and desiring to prevent this and to better
govern the slaves, decreed that any one buying or receiving
from slaves property without an order from their masters, must
return the property and double its value in addition, or, if he
has disposed of the original property, treble its value, and,
if he will not do this, he is to be whipped with not over twenty
stripes. The slaves caught in theft were to be whipped with
not over thirty stripes, whether the receivers of the goods
from them were found or not. Further, "whereas negro and
mulatto servants or slaves[3] are become numerous in some
parts of this Colonie and are very apt to be turbulent and
often quarrelling with white people to the great disturbance
of the peace," it is enacted that a negro disturbing the
peace or offering to strike a white person, is to be subject
to a penalty of not over thirty stripes.

In spite of these harsher laws, emancipation was becoming
somewhat common, and the Colony feared that it would have
to support negroes whose years of usefulness had been spent
in work for their masters, and who were manumitted by them,

---

[1] Conn. Col. Rec., IV., 438. A penalty of 10 shillings was to be
imposed for a breach of this act. It does not seem to have been
included in any of the revisions of the statutes.

[2] Conn. Col. Rec., V., p. 52. This was in force in 1808. Title CL.,
Ch. I., Sec. 5.

[3] Revision of 1750, p. 229.

when old and helpless. To prevent this, in May, 1702,[1] the legislature provided that slaves, set free and coming to want, must be relieved by the owners, their heirs, executors, or administrators. To this act a second one was added in 1711, providing that if the owners or their representatives refused to maintain such emancipated slaves, it should be the duty of the selectmen of the various towns to do so, and then to sue the owners, or their representatives, for the expense[2] incurred.

The terrible war between the South Carolinians and the Tuscaroras, ending with the overthrow of the latter, left a large number of Indian prisoners in the hands of the Carolinians, who shipped them as slaves to the other colonies. This importation of vengeful, warlike savages alarmed the people of Connecticut and led to the first steps towards prohibition of the slave trade. The Governor and Council met on July 8, 1715, and considering the fact that several have brought into the colony Carolina Indians, "which have committed many cruel and bloody outrages" there, and may draw off " our Indians," if their importation be continued, and so "much mischief" may follow, they decided to prohibit importation of Indian slaves, until the meeting of the Assembly, and to require each ship entering port with Indians on board to give bond of £50 to transport them from the colony in twenty days. Further, Indians brought into the colony hereafter are to be "kept in strictest custody," confined and "prevented from communicating with other Indians," unless owner give the same bond as above to remove them from Connecticut in twenty days.[3]

The next October, the General Court, copying a Massachusetts Act of 1712, made the prohibition of bringing in Indian slaves permanent, since "divers conspiracies, outrages, barbarities, murders, burglaries, thefts, and other no-

[1] Conn. Col. Rec., IV., 375. A similar act to the same purpose was passed in May, 1703. Conn. Col. Rec., IV., 408. See p. 32.
[2] Conn. Col. Rec., V., 233. The whole was in the revision of 1808, Title CL., Ch. I., Sec. 11.
[3] Conn. Col. Rec., V., 516.

torious crimes at sundry times and, especially of late, have
been perpetrated by Indians and other slaves,...being of
a malicious and vengeful spirit, rude and insolent in their
behaviour, and very ungovernable, the overgreat number of
which, considering the different circumstances in this Colony
from the plantations in the islands and our having considerable numbers of Indians, natives of our country,...may
be of pernicious consequence."[1] The legislature decreed the
forfeiture of all Indians hereafter imported, and the payment
of a fine of £50 by shipmaster or other persons bringing
Indians.

The preamble quoted above shows that this measure was
not prompted by affection for the slaves, but by fear of them;
but it was the beginning of the end—the first law restricting
slaveholders' rights in Connecticut, to be followed by one and
another of the same restrictive kind, until all men who trod
the soil of the State were free.

The next law on the records was passed in May, 1723, and
provided that a slave out of doors after 9 P. M., without
order from master or mistress, might be secured and brought
before a Justice of the Peace by any citizen and, if found
guilty, should receive not over ten stripes, unless the master
were willing to pay a fine of ten shillings[2] to release him.
Any one who should receive such a slave must, on conviction,
pay a like fine, half to the town and half to the informer.

The black code was completed by the act of May, 1730,
declaring that a slave speaking such words as would be
actionable in a free person, should be whipped, on conviction,
with not over forty stripes and sold for the costs, unless the
master were willing to pay them. However, there was a ray
of justice in the provision of the law that the slave might
make the same pleas and offer the same evidence as a free
person.[3]

---

[1] Conn. Col. Rec., V., 534. Fee of 2s. 6d. for registering slave,
which must be done in twenty-four hours after arrival. The slave
must be taken away within a month.

[2] Amount to be paid later changed to $1.67. Conn. Col. Rec., VI.,
391. Repealed by Ch. IV., Oct. 1797.

[3] Conn. Col. Rec. VII., 290. In Revision of 1750, p. 40.

From this time on, the more engrossing subjects of the struggle between the French and the colonists, and the growth of material prosperity seem to have thrust aside the topic of slavery from the legislative halls. For forty-four years we find few more laws.[1] It is true, however, that at the General Assembly in 1738, "it was inquired—whether the infant slaves of Christian masters may be baptized in the right of their masters, they solemnly promising to train them in the knowledge and admonition of the Lord; and whether it is the duty of such masters to offer such children and thus religiously to promise." To the great credit of the colonists, both these questions were answered affirmatively, and thus the devout Christians of Connecticut, preserving the solidarity of the family, unconsciously went back to the early Aryan custom, that the God of the house-father should be worshiped by all under his sway. The growth of free ideas,[2] the coming of the Revolution, the increase of the slaves, "injurious," it was thought, to the poor and "inconvenient"—for the best motives are apt to be mixed of good and evil—led, in October, 1774, to the enactment of the law that "no Indian, negro, or mulatto slave shall at any time hereafter[3] be brought or imported into this State,[4] by sea or land, from any place or places whatsoever, to be disposed of, left, or sold within the State," and any offender against this law should pay £100.[5] So the State set herself as resolutely against the slave trade, as she was destined to do later against slavery itself.

---

[1] In 1727 it was enacted that masters and mistresses of Indian children were to use their utmost endeavors to teach them to read English, and to instruct them in the Christian faith. Reprint of 1737, p. 339. Hurd, I., p. 272.

[2] Conn. Col. Rec., XIV., 155. May, 1773, "Negro's memorial postponed to October." Nothing more of it.

[3] Conn. Col. Rec., XIV., 329.

[4] Note the early use of the word.

[5] Later the sum was fixed at $334. By act of October, 1798, such prosecutions must be begun in three years. Revision of 1808, Title CI., Ch. III. By Revision of 1821, Title 93, Sec. 5, fine put at $350.

A good review of the legal condition of the slave in these days is given by Judge Reeves,[1] who, "lest the slavery, which prevailed in this State, be forgotten," mentioned "some things that show that slavery here was very far from being of the absolute rigid kind. The master had no control over the life of his slave. If he killed him, he was liable to the same punishment, as if he killed a freeman. The master was as liable to be sued by the slave, in an action for beating, and wounding, or for immoderate chastisement, as he would be if he had thus treated an apprentice. A slave was capable of holding property in character of devisee or legatee. If the master should take away such property, his slave would be entitled to an action against him by his *prochein ami*. From the whole, we see that slaves had the same right of life and property as apprentices, and that the difference betwixt them was this, an apprentice is a servant for time and the slave is a servant for life."[2]

TRIALS CONCERNING SLAVES IN COLONIAL DAYS.

I have been able to obtain but few recorded cases in which the question of freedom or slavery came up in the courts

[1] Law of Baron and Femme, pp. 340-1. Reeves says, "If a slave married a free woman, with the consent of his master, he was emancipated; for his master had suffered him to contract a relation inconsistent with a state of slavery." Dane's Abridgment, II., p. 313, says, "In Connecticut the slave was, by statute, specially forbidden to contract." *Vide* Hurd, II., p. 42.

[2] In the Code of 1650, under the title, "Masters, Sojourners, Servants," the last named are forbidden, under penalty, to trade without permission of their masters, and provision is made for their recapture by public authority if they run away. Refractory servants are to be punished by extension of their time of service. The lawmakers, probably, had in mind the class known as indented servants, or redemptioners, in formulating this act. (Conn. Rec., I., 539.) In the Revision of 1715, title "Debts," it was provided that a debtor without estate "shall satisfy the debt by service, if the creditor shall require it, in which case he shall not be disposed in service to any but of the English nation," to prevent the sale of the debtor to the French in Canada. Delinquents under a penal law were, by an act of 1725, to be disposed of at service to any inhabitant of the Colony "to defray the Costs." (Reprint 1737, p. 314.)

during this first period. In the end of 1702 or beginning of 1703, a slave, Abda, belonging to Capt. Thomas Richards of Hartford, escaped from his master and was succored by Capt. Joseph Wadsworth of Hartford, who, on Feb. 12th, 1703, opposed the constable in executing a writ of arrest on Abda. This early fugitive slave case was brought before the Governor and Council on Feb. 25.[1] They recommended the County Court to examine the case. Apparently Abda brought an action on the case against Mr. Richards, as a counter suit, claiming damages of £20 from his master, "for his unjust holding and detaining the said Abda in his service as his bondsman, for the space of one year past." The verdict was for £12 damages, "thereby virtually establishing Abda's right to freedom," which he, a mulatto, seems to have claimed largely on account of his white blood.[2]

Mr. Richards pressed the case further and, in May, 1704, obtained from the General Court an order to have a hearing before it in October, on his petition concerning Abda.[3] At that time the case was brought up and the fugitive was returned to his master, as Gov. Saltonstall said, "according to the laws and constant practice of this Colony and all other plantations (as well as by the civil law) such persons as are born of negro bondwomen are themselves in like condition, *i. e.* born in servitude.[4] Nor can there be any precedent in this Government, or any of Her Majesty's plantations, produced to the contrary and, though the law of this Colony doth not say that such persons as are born of negro woman and supposed to be mulattoes shall be slaves (which was needless, because of the constant practice by which they are held as such), yet it saith expressly that no man shall put away or make free his negro or mulatto slave, etc., which

---

[1] Conn. Col. Rec., XV., 548.
[2] Moore's "Notes on Slavery," p. 112, quoting J. H. Trumbull in Conn. *Courant*, Nov. 9, 1850. Fowler, "Hist. Status," pp. 14-16.
[3] Conn. Col. Rec., IV., 478. Papers in Miscellaneous, II., pp. 10-21.
[4] This following as a precedent the Roman Law maxim, "Partus sequitur ventrem," at this early day in New England is noteworthy.

undeniably shows and declares an approbation of such servitude, and that mulattoes may be held as slaves within this government."[1]

A later fugitive slave[2] we find advertised for in the New York *Mercury* on July 28, 1760, and the advertisement has many little touches which go to show how slaves lived and were treated. "Run away from Abraham Davenport of Stamford in Conn., the 4th of June instant, a Mulatto Man Slave named Vanhall, aged 31 years, about 5 feet 4 or 5 inches high, very swarthy; has a small Head and Face, a large Mouth, and has an odd Action with his Head, when talking with any Person ; has very long Arms and large Hands for a Person of his size and has an old Countenance for one of his Age; his Hair, like others of his kind was but lately cut off; was brought up to the Farming business, is a lively active Fellow and pretends to understand the Violin. Had on, when he went away, a Felt Hat, a Grey Cut Wig, a light homespun Flannel lappelled Vest, which had been lined with fine old Cotton and Linnen Ticken, Doeskin Breeches, he took several pairs of Stockings and one or two pairs of Shoes, a Violin and a small Hatchet, &c., and 'tis probable he might change his Cloaths. Whoever takes up and secures said Mulatto, so that his Master may have him again, shall receive £5. Reward, and reasonable charges paid."

Late in Colonial times,[3] we find Hagar, a New London negress, appearing before the Governor and Council and pleading that she and her children were lawfully freed by her former master, James Rogers, and so her refusal to yield herself as a slave to James Rogers, Jr., his grandson, was justified. The decision was that she should give bond to prove her freedom at the next County Court and be secured from molestation in the meanwhile.

---

[1] Moore, Notes on Slavery, pp. 24-25, quoting J. H. Trumbull's "Hist. Notes," etc., No. VI.

[2] Am. Hist. Mag., XIII., p. 498. *Vide* Fowler, "Hist. Status," p. 148.

[3] Conn. Col. Rec., XV., p. 582.

SOCIAL CONDITION OF SLAVES IN COLONIAL TIMES.

On this topic comparatively little can be found. Each large[1] village had its negro corner in the Meeting House gallery and in the graveyard. In the larger towns, such as Norwich, New Haven, Hartford, and New London, there were several hundred negroes. They were for the most part indulgently treated and admitted, at least in many places, into the local churches as fellow-members with the white population.[2] They must, however, occupy their allotted gallery seats, which in Torrington were boarded up so that the negroes could see no one and be seen by none. If they attempted to sit elsewhere, or refused to go to church if made to sit there, excommunication was apt to follow.[3]

Among early negro slaves recorded in Connecticut are some belonging to John Pantry of Hartford in 1653, and one Cyrus, belonging to Henry Wolcott, Jr., of Windsor, and rated at £30 in his inventory.[4] Miss Caulkins states that early in the eighteenth century slaves were worth from 60 shillings to £30, and that later the best were valued as high as £100. She instances the purchase of a negro boy by Rev. William Hart of Saybrook in 1749 for £290, Old Tenor, about equal to £60 in coin.[5] In 1708, and probably the same state of things continued later, we learn the negroes mostly came from "neighboring governments, save some times half a dozen a year from the West Indies"; but "none ever imported by the Royal African Company or separate traders."[6]

---

[1] In 1726 Suffield voted Rev. Mr. Devotion £20 towards purchasing negroes. Trumbull's "Hartford County," II., p. 406.

[2] *E. g.* Phebe, colored servant of Joel Thrall, joined Torrington Church, 1756. Orcutt's "Torrington," p. 211.

[3] Jacob Prince, a free negro, was so excommunicated in Goshen. Orcutt's "Torrington," p. 218.

[4] 1680, slaves sold at £22. Conn. Col. Rec., III., 298.
Stiles, "Ancient Windsor," p. 489, notices an early deed of sale, dated 1694, from a Bostonian to a Windsor man, for a negro. Twenty-one negroes died in South Windsor from 1736 to 1768, of which number eleven belonged to the Wolcott family.

[5] Hist. of Norwich, p. 328. *Vide* Fowler, "Hist. Status," p. 148.

[6] Conn. Col. Rec., XV., 557.

391]   *History of Slavery in Connecticut.*   **21**

For the most part, only one or two negroes were owned by any person. In some parts of the State, as at Waterbury,[1] we find it customary for the clergymen to have two slaves, a man and a woman. Occasionally, however, more were owned by a wealthy man, as in the case of Capt. John Perkins of Hanover Society,[2] Norwich, who left fifteen slaves by his will in 1761. The slaves were generally kindly treated and were docile, though we hear of the death of a man in 1773 from lockjaw, caused by a bite in the thumb by a young slave he was chastising.[3] The majority, however, could show much more amicable relations. For example, Mingo,[4] in Waterbury, who, about 1730, when a boy, was hired out by his master to drive a plow, later to work with a team and, 1764, at his master's death, was allowed to choose which son he would live with. He chose to live with the one who kept the old homestead and remained there until he began keeping a tavern, when he left and went to another son's. He had a family, and left considerable property at his death in 1800. Indeed, as early as 1707, we have evidence of the possession of property by a negro, for, in October of that year, Lieut. John Hawley, administrator to the estate of John Negro, was granted power by the General Court to sell £10 worth of his land, it appearing from the Fairfield County Probate Records that he owed that amount more than his moveables would pay.[5]

Towards the close of this period, the reasonableness and justice of holding slaves began to be questioned and eman-

---

[1] Bronson's "Waterbury," 321. [2] Caulkins' "Norwich," p. 328.

[3] Caulkins' "Norwich," p. 329. Godfrey Malbone of Brooklyn owned 50 or 60 slaves. Fowler, p. 16.

[4] The first negro there. Bronson's "Waterbury," p. 321. He also refers to Parson Scovil's Dick, brought from Africa when a boy and sold several times, with the understanding he could return when he pleased. He left some property at his death in 1835, aged 90. Also to I. Woodruff of Westbury, who owned an Indian woman till her death in 1774. In Wintonbury (Bloomfield) there were probably not over a dozen slaves in all in colonial times. In Bristol a few of the farms were cultivated by slave labor, and one family owned three negroes. Trumbull's "Hartford County," II., pp. 35, 51.

[5] Conn. Col. Rec., VI., 35.

cipations, " from a conscientious regard to justice," begin to appear. One man in Norwich not only freed three slaves, but, " as a compensation for their services, leased them a very valuable farm on very moderate rate."[1] That section of the State seems to have been considerably stirred on this question, and in the Norwich *Packet*, July 7, 1774, we find an anti-slavery appeal of sufficient vigor to warrant quotation in full:

" To all you who call yourselves Sons of Liberty in America, Greeting:

" My Friends, We know in some good measure the inestimable value of liberty, But were we once deprived of her she would then appear much more valuable than she now appears. We also see her, standing as it were, tiptoe on the highest bough ready for flight. Why is she departing? What is it disturbs her repose? Surely, some foul monster of hideous shape and hateful kind, opposite in its nature to hers, with all its frightful appearances and properties, iron hands and leaden feet, formed to gripe and crush, hath intruded itself into her peaceful habitation and ejected her. Surely this must be the case, for we know oppositions can not dwell together. Is it not time, high time to search for this Achan? this disturber of Israel? High time, I say, to examine for the cause of those dark and gloomy appearances that cast a shade over our glory, and is not this it? Are we not guilty of the same crime we impute to others? Of the same facts, that we say are unjust, cruel, arbitrary, despotic, and without law in others? Paul argued in this manner—'Thou that teachest another, teachest thou not thyself? Thou that preachest a man should not steal, dost thou steal? Thou that makest thy boast of the law, through breaking the law dishonorest thou God?' And may we not use the same mode of argument and say—We that declare, and that with much warmth and zeal, it is unjust, cruel, barbarous, unconstitutional, and without law to enslave, *do we enslave?* Yes, verily we do! *A black cloud witnesseth*

---

[1] Caulkins' " Norwich," p. 329.

against us and our own mouths condemn us! How preposterous our conduct! How vain and hypocritical our pretences! Can we expect to be free, so long as we are determined to enslave? (Signed) Honesty."[1]

Before we turn from Colonial times,[2] the fact is worthy of note that, though "redemptioners" were not common in Connecticut, white men were often bound out to service for a term of years, as in other colonies. We find in 1670 a man sold to the Barbadoes for four years as a slave, for "notorious stealing," "breaking up and robbing of" two mills and living "in a renegade manner in the wilderness." In 1756, a town pauper in Waterbury,[3] for stealing, was whipped and bound out to the plaintiff, as a servant, till the sum stolen and the costs be paid by his work, and the law on the statute-books was that "all single persons, who lived an idle and riotous life," might be bound out to service to pay the costs of prosecution.

---

[1] The emancipation of slaves is not looked on by Dr. Fowler as greatly contributing to their welfare. He quotes an essay published in 1793 by Noah Webster, Jr.: "Nor does the restoration to freedom correct the depravity of their hearts. Born and bred beneath the frowns of power, neglected and despised in youth, they abandon themselves to ill company and low vicious pleasures, till their habits are formed; when manumission, instead of destroying their habits and repressing their corrupt inclinations, serves to afford the more numerous opportunities of indulging both. Thus an act of strict justice to the slave, very often, renders him a more worthless member of society." "Hist. Status of the Negro," p. 149.

[2] Dr. Fowler, "Hist. Status," pp. 12-18, calls attention to the fact that Louis Berbice, from Dutch Guiana, killed by his master, Gysbert Opdyck, commissary at the Dutch fort in Hartford, in Nov., 1639, was probably the first negro in Conn. He gives a list of the early owners of negroes and notes that in 1717, the Lower House passed a bill prohibiting negroes purchasing land, or living in families of their own, without liberty from the town.

[3] Bronson's Waterbury, p. 321.

PERIOD II.—1774-1869.

SLAVES IN THE REVOLUTION.[1]

The subject of using negroes in the army first came before the General Assembly in May, 1777, when a committee was appointed "to take[2] into consideration the state and condition of the negro and mulatto slaves in this State, and what may be done for their emancipation." I would hazard a guess that this committee was appointed in consequence of a resolution of the town of Enfield, on March 31, 1777, appointing a committee of three to prefer a memorial to the Assembly, to "pray[3] that the Negroes in this State be released from their Slavery and Bondage." The Assembly's committee, of which Hon. Matthew Griswold was chairman, reported a recommendation that the effective negro and mulatto slaves be allowed to enlist with the Continental bat-

---

[1] CONNECTICUT COMMITTEE OF SAFETY.

Monday, September 4, 1775.
At a meeting of the committee On information, by letter, from Major Latimer, "that one of the Vessels lately taken by Captain *Wallace*, of the *Rose*, man-of-war, &c., at *Stonington*, was by stress of weather drove back to *New-London*, with one white man, a petty officer, and three negroes on board, and were in his custody, and asking directions how to dispose of them, &c. And by other information it appears that two of the negroes belong to Deputy Governour *Cooke*, of *Rhode-Island*, and were lately seized and robbed from him, with and on board a vessel, by said *Wallace*, and that the other belonged to one Captain *Collins*. And, on consideration, *Voted and Ordered*, That the Major give information to the owner of the vessel, and, on his request, deliver her up to him, and send the white man to the jail at *Windham*, and the three negroes to the care of, and to be employed for the present by, Captain *Niles*, at *Norwich*, who is fixing out a small Armed Vessel, &c., until the Governour shall advise Deputy Governour *Cooke* of the matter, that they may, on proper notice, be returned to their owners."—Am. Arch., IV., III., p. 672.

[2] Livermore, "Historical Research," p. 113.
[3] Trumbull's "Hartford County," II., p. 151.

talions now raising in this State, under the following regulations and restrictions: viz., that all such negro and mulatto slaves as can procure, either by bounty, hire, or in any other way, such a sum to be paid to their masters, as such negro and mulatto shall be judged to be reasonably worth by the selectman of the town where such negro or mulatto belongs, shall be allowed to enlist into either of said battalions, and shall thereupon be, *de facto,* free and emancipated; and that the master of such negro or mulatto shall be exempted from the support and maintenance of such negro or mulatto, in case" he "shall hereafter become unable to support and maintain himself." Further, if a slave desire to enlist for the war, he may be appraised by the selectmen and his master may receive the bounty and half the slave's annual wages until the appraised sum be equaled. The Upper House rejected this report.

At that session, however, an act was passed that any two men, "who should procure an able bodied soldier," should be exempted from the draft, during the continuance of the substitute's enlistment. "Of recruits," writes Dr. J. H. Trumbull, "and draughted men thus furnished, neither the selectmen nor commanding officers questioned the color, or the civil status; white and black, bond and free, if able bodied, went on the roll together, accepted as the representatives or substitutes of their employers."

In October, 1777,[1] the Assembly passed an act similar to the one proposed in May. It authorized the selectmen, on application from a master of a slave, to inquire "into the age, abilities, circumstances, and character" of the slave, and, being satisfied "that it was likely to be consistent with his real advantage, and that it was probable that he would be able to support himself, and is of good and peaceable life and conversation," they could free the master from all liability for support of his freedman. This offered an additional inducement to masters to free slaves to make up the

---

[1] Revision of 1808, Title CL., Ch. I., Sec. 12. *Vide* Stiles' "Anc. Windsor," I., p. 491.

town's quota of men, and Dr. Trumbull says "some hundreds of black slaves and free men enlisted." The rolls of the companies show no distinction of color. The surnames Liberty, Freeman, Freedom are frequently found.[1] In Wethersfield, on the blank leaves of the book of town votes, among records of emancipation from motives of humanity, or for money, we find record of John Wright and Luke Fortune freeing their slave Abner Andrew, on May 20, 1777, to be their substitute in the army. Other certificates free slaves on condition of "enlisting in the Continental Army in Col. Wallis' Regiment" and "and after the customary three years service," and, as late as 1780, Caesar was manumitted by David Griswold there, on "condition of enlistment and faithfully serving out the time of enlistment," which was three years.[2]

David Humphreys commanded a company entirely composed of negroes, their roster showing fifty-six names,[3] first of which is Jack Arabas, of whom we shall hear again. It was said Humphreys nobly volunteered to command the company, when others refused, and continued its captain until peace was declared. The company was in Meigs' (later Butler's) regiment of the Connecticut Line.

At Fort Griswold, when Col. Ledyard was murdered, a negro soldier named Lambert avenged his death by thrusting a bayonet through the British officer who slew his superior, and then fell a martyr, pierced by thirty-three bayonet wounds.[4]

"As to the efficiency of the service they rendered," says Dr. J. H. Trumbull,[5] "I can say nothing from the records,

---

[1] Livermore's "Historical Research," p. 115.
[2] Am. Hist. Mag., XXI., 422. Trumbull's "Hartford County," II., 475.
[3] Williams' "Hist. of Negro Race in America," I., 361.
[4] Wilson, "Rise and Fall of the Slave Power," I., p. 19.
[5] Livermore's "Historical Research," p. 115. Lib Quy, native African, was a trusty Continental soldier from Norwich in 1780 and '81 (Caulkins' "Norwich," p. 331). Oliver Mitchell, a negro Revolutionary soldier, died of a fit in his boat, March, 1840, in which he had been to Hartford to draw his pension (Stiles' "Ancient Windsor," I., p. 489).

save what is to be gleaned from scattered files.... So far as my acquaintance extends, almost every family has its traditions of the good and faithful service of a black servant or slave, who was killed in battle or served through the war and came home to tell stories of hard fighting and draw his pension. In my own town—not a large one—I remember five such pensioners, three of whom I believe had been slaves, and were in fact slaves to the day of their death; for (and this explains the uniform action of the General Assembly on petitions for emancipation) neither the towns nor the State were inclined to exonerate the master, at a time when slavery was becoming unprofitable, from the obligation to provide for the old age of his slave."

An interesting Revolutionary case is that of the slaves of Col. William Browne of Salem, Mass., a Tory, whose large farm in Lyme was confiscated. It was leased for a term of years with nine slaves, who petitioned for liberty in 1779, through Benjamin Huntington, administrator on confiscated estates. The lessee offered to consent to their freedom without requiring a diminution in the rent. Mr. Huntington drew up their petition to the Assembly,[1] stating that they, " all friends to America, but slaves lately belonging to Col. Wm. Browne," who " fled from his native country to his master, King George, where he now lives like a poor slave," " though they have flat noses, crooked shins, and other queerness of make, peculiar to Africans, are yet of the human race, free-born in our country, taken from thence by man-stealers, and sold in this country, as cattle in the market, without the least act of our own to forfeit liberty; but we hope our good mistress, *the free State of Connecticut*, engaged in a war with tyranny, will not sell honest Whigs and friends of the freedom and independence of America, as we are, to raise cash to support the war: because the Whigs ought to be *free* and the *Tories* should be sold." They offer, if set free, to get security to indemnify the State

---

[1] Great Prince, Little Prince, Luke, Caesar, Prue and her three children. Livermore, " Historical Research," p. 116.

in case of their coming to want; but, though the Lower House was favorable, the Upper one refused to grant the petition.

OPINIONS OF THE FOREFATHERS ON SLAVERY.

One of the earliest in Connecticut to come out boldly against slavery was Rev. Levi Hart of Preston, who, on Sept. 20, 1774, at Farmington, preached a sermon at the meeting of "the Corporation of Freemen," in which he condemned the slave trade and severely criticized slave-holding.[1]

Dr. William Gordon of Roxbury, Mass., though living out of Connecticut, became interested in the abolition of slavery there and sent a plan for its gradual extermination to the "Independent Chronicle" of Nov. 14, 1776, which is very severe on slaveholders and paints the deathbed of one of them.[2]

In the Constitutional Convention[3] of 1787 we have full expression of the views of Roger Sherman and Oliver Ellsworth, two of Connecticut's three delegates. The former said "that the abolition of slavery seemed to be going on in the United States and that the good sense of the several States would probably by degrees complete it."[4] He regarded the slave trade as iniquitous; but, the point of representation having been settled after much difficulty and deliberation,[5] he did not think himself bound to make opposition." He objected, however, to the tax on imported slaves, as implying that slaves were property, and that the tax imposed was too small to prevent importation.[6] He thought that, "as the States were now possessed of the right to import slaves, as the public good did not require it to be taken

[1] Trumbull's "Memorial History of Hartford Co.," II., p. 192.
[2] Moore, "Notes on Slavery in Mass.," p. 177.
[3] Connecticut voted for Jefferson's ordinance of 1784.
[4] Livermore, "Historic Research," p. 51.
[5] Madison Papers, V., 391 (Elliot).
[6] Wilson, "Rise and Fall," p. 51.

from them, and as it was expedient to have as few objections as possible to the proposed scheme of government, it would be best to leave the matter as we find it."[1] He said, when Baldwin of Georgia, a man of Connecticut birth, stated his State would not confederate unless allowed to import, that it was better to let the Southern States import slaves[2] than to lose those States, if they made that a *sine qua non*. He thought it would be the duty of the General Government[2] to exercise the power of prohibiting importation, if it were given it. He preferred not to use the word slaves in the Constitution, and saw no[3] more propriety in the public seizing and surrendering a slave than a horse. Ellsworth said, "Let every State import what it pleases. The morality or wisdom of slavery are considerations belonging to the States. What enriches a part enriches the whole, and the States are the best judges of their particular interests. The old Confederation had not meddled with this point, and he did not see any greater necessity for bringing it into the policy of the new one." He had[4] "never owned a slave and could not judge of the effects of slavery on character." He said, however, that, if it was "to be considered in a moral light, we ought to go further and free those already in the country. As slaves also multiply so fast in Virginia and Maryland, it is cheaper to raise than import them, whilst in the sickly rice swamps, foreign supplies are necessary. If we go no further than is urged, we shall be unjust towards South Carolina and Georgia. Let us not intermeddle. As population increases, poor laborers will be so plenty as to render slaves useless. Provision is already made in Connecticut for abolishing it, and the abolition has already taken place in Massachusetts. As to the dangers of insurrections from foreign influence, that will become a motive to kind treatment of the slaves."[5]

---

[1] Livermore, p. 56.   [2] Livermore, p. 60.

[3] Elliot, V., pp. 457-461 and 471. Connecticut voted to extend the open period from 1800 to 1808.

[4] Livermore, p. 57.

[5] In 1787, Connecticut voted in the Constitutional Convention for the three-fifths compromise.

Mistaken in many respects as these men were, they undoubtedly represented the current opinion of their time.

We find a contrary opinion in the resolves of the Danbury Town Meeting on December 12, 1774, that, " It is with singular pleasure, we notice the second article of the Association, in which it is agreed to import no more Negro slaves, as we cannot but think it a palpable absurdity, so loudly to complain of attempts to enslave us, while we are actually enslaving others, and that we have great reason to apprehend the enslaving the *Africans* is one of the crying sins of our land, for which Heaven is now chastising us. We notice also with pleasure the late Act of our General Assembly, imposing a fine of £100 on any one, who shall import a Negro Slave into this Colony. We could also wish that something further might be done for the relief of such, as are now in a state of slavery in the Colony,[1] and such as may hereafter be born of parents in that unhappy condition."

STATE LEGISLATION ON SLAVERY.

The growth of free ideas went on apace, after the State became independent. In 1780, a bill for gradual emancipation passed the Upper House, was continued until the next session and then, apparently, set aside. It provided that no Indian or colored child, then living and under seven years of age, nor any born afterwards, should be held as a slave beyond the age of twenty-eight.[2] In 1784, however, the measure was passed and emancipation was begun. The Legislature enacted that, " Whereas sound public policy requires that the abolition of slavery should be effected, as soon as may be consistent with the rights of individuals and the public safety and welfare," no negro or mulatto, born after March 1, 1784, should be held as a slave after reaching the age of twenty-five.[3] This regard for the exist-

---

[1] Am. Arch., IV., I., pp. 1038.
[2] Jameson, " Essays in Const. Hist.," p. 296 (Brackett, " Status of the Slave, 1775-1789 ").
[3] Revision of 1808, Title CL., Ch. I., Sec. 13. Fowler, "Hist. Status," p. 85, shows that this really made slaves in the same con-

ing rights of property was shown by the gradual abolition of slavery in Connecticut,[1] the holding of slaves not being absolutely forbidden until 1848, when any one to be a slave must have been sixty-four years old.

In October, 1788, a bill was passed, forbidding any inhabitant of Connecticut to receive on his vessel " any inhabitants of Africa as slaves," under penalty of $1,667 for the use of the vessel and $167 additional for each slave carried.[2] Half of this fine was to go to the plaintiff and half to the State; but, by the act of October, 1798,[3] prosecutions must begin in three years. Furthermore, insurance on ships used in the slave trade, or on slaves carried, is to be void. We have seen the importation of slaves forbidden in this act: the exportation " of any free negro, Indian, or mulatto, or person entitled to freedom at twenty-five," inhabitants of Connecticut, was to be punished by a fine of $334 levied on any who should, as principal or accessory, " kidnap, decoy, or forcibly carry away " such persons from the State. "Any friend of the inhabitant " carried off may prosecute and receive " fit damages," and must give bond to use such rightly for " the injured inhabitant,"[4] or family. This prohibition was not to prevent persons removing from the State from taking their slaves with them, nor to prevent persons living in Connecticut from sending their slaves out of the State, on ordinary and necessary business. This sale of slaves out of the State was soon stopped, for, in May, 1792, the law was so changed that the taking a slave from the State, or assistance therein, was punishable with a

---

dition as apprentices, and claims the law was passed partly through economical reasons, as there were more laborers than employment.

[1] In October, 1788, owners must file certificate of birth of each slave within six months thereof, or pay $7 for each month's delay, half to complainant and half to poor of town. October, 1789, the latter half was to go to the State. Revision of 1808, Title CL., Ch. V., Sec. 5, and Ch. VI.

[2] Revision of 1808, Title CL., Ch. V., Sec. 1. Penalty changed to $170 and $1700 by Revision of 1821, Title 93, Sec. 7. Penalty was originally £1000. Root's Reports, I., xxxi.

[3] Revision of 1808, Title CI., Ch. III.

[4] Revision of 1808, Title CL., Ch. V., Secs. 3-4. Penalty changed to $350 in Revision of 1821, Sec. 6.

like fine of $334, half of which should go to the plaintiff and half to the State. Notes, bonds, or mortgages given in payment for slaves thus sold out of the State were to be void. The same exemptions as to persons removing from the State or sending their slaves out temporarily, were made as in the former law.[1]

At the same session of the Assembly, the age of the slave at manumission was limited to the period between twenty-five and forty-five years, and the certificate given at emancipation by the selectmen was ordered to be recorded in the Town Records.[2] This somewhat reactionary act, modifying the law of 1702, designed to regulate the giving of freedom, was followed in five years by one still further limiting the bounds of slavery; for in May, 1797, it was enacted that no negro or mulatto born after August, 1797, should be a slave, after reaching the age of twenty-one.[3]

Here the laws with regard to slavery remained without essential change for many years. Not until 1833 do we find another important act passed in regard to slavery, and then, under the influence of the outcry against Miss Prudence Crandall, the Legislature put on the statute-book the most shameful law we meet in our study.[4] It stated that, " whereas attempts have been made to establish literary institutions in this State, for the instruction of colored persons belonging to other States and countries, which would tend to the great increase of the colored population of the State and thereby to the injury of the people," any person establishing such a school without the consent in writing of the selectmen and civil authority of the town, should pay a fine of $100 to the State Treasurer for the first offense and double for each

---

[1] Revision of 1808, Title CL., Ch. VI., Secs. 1, 2, 3.

[2] Revision of 1808, Title CL., Ch. II. Free negroes could vote until the Constitution of 1818 restricted the suffrage to white males.

[3] Revision of 1808. Title CL., Ch. III.

[4] May 24, 1833. Act of 1833, Ch.   Sec. 1. Sec. 2 provided that a colored person not an inhabitant of Connecticut, residing in a town for education, might be removed as any other alien. Sec. 3 provided that the evidence of such colored person is both admissible and compulsory against the teacher.

succeeding one, the fines increasing in geometrical progression. The law was not destined to be a blot upon any of the States' codes, but was repealed in 1838 by the Legislature, under the leadership of Francis Gillette,[1] a young representative from Hartford, who was afterwards United States Senator. That same Legislature passed resolutions against the annexation of Texas, the slave trade in the District of Columbia, and in favor of the right of petition. Nay more, that same year was passed the "Act for the Fulfilment of the Obligations of this State imposed by the Constitution of the United States in regard to persons held to service or labor in one State and escaping into another, and to secure the right of trial by jury in the cases herein mentioned."[2] Prof. W. C. Fowler called this law a "nullification"[3] of the United States Act of 1793, which provided that the owner or his attorney could take the fugitive slave before any magistrate of the county, city, or town wherein the arrest might be made, and, on proof by oral testimony or affidavit, taken before and certified to by a magistrate of any State or Territory, the magistrate must give a certificate, which should be sufficient warrant for removing the slave from the State.

Let us see now how Connecticut fulfilled her obligations, in this early personal liberty law. Instead of following the provisions of the United States law, she enacted that the captured fugitive should be brought before the county or city court on a writ of *habeas corpus*, and no magistrate not having the power to issue that writ should give the claimant any warrant or certificate, under penalty of $500. When he arrived at court, the claimant must pay all fees in advance and must, "by affidavit, set forth minutely" the ground of

---

[1] Wilson, "Rise and Fall of the Slave Power," I., 372. The Legislature, however, by a vote of 165 to 33, rejected a constitutional amendment allowing negroes the suffrage. Niles' Reg., Vol. 54, p. 193. In 1842 the State again protested against the annexation of Texas. Niles' Reg., Vol. 62, p. 140.

[2] Revision of 1838, Title 97, Ch. II.

[3] Local Law in Mass. and Conn., p. 98.

his claim to the slave's services, the time of the slave's escape, and the place where the slave then was, or was believed to be. The judge was next to allow necessary time for further proof and, meantime, commit the fugitive to the custody of the sheriff. The questions of fact were to be tried by a jury, on which no one was to sit "who believes there is not, constitutionally or legally, a slave in the land," in this showing the early distrust of the Abolitionists. If the claimant does not prove the claim, he is liable to the payment of costs and damages; if he does prove it, he may take the slave from the State, but must, "without unnecessary delay," take him by the "direct route" to his home. In the same act, the law against transporting slaves from the State, save as above, is made universal and the penalty for its violation fixed at $500, to go to any one prosecuting. Any fugitive arrested, contrary to the act, may have a writ of *habeas corpus* sued out by his next friend; and, as an afterthought, at the very end, we read that nothing in this act shall extend to the United States Courts.

As the feeling grew more bitter, even this law was felt to be too much of a yielding in principle and, in 1844,[1] the Legislature decided that no Judge, Justice of the Peace, or other officer should issue a warrant "for the arrest or detention of any person escaping into this State, claimed to be fugitive from labor or service as a slave," or grant a certificate to the claimant. Such papers, if issued, are to be void, but, as before, the people soothed their consciences with the belief they were fulfilling their obligations, by saying "nothing herein shall interfere with United States officers."[2]

In 1847,[3] by a great majority, the State rejected a proposal

[1] Compilation of 1854, Title 51, Sec. 5. The preamble stated that "it has been decided by the Supreme Court of the United States since" 1838 "that both the duty and the power of legislation on that subject pertains exclusively to the National government."

[2] In 1845 the Legislature of Connecticut protested against the admission of Texas as a Slave State. Niles' Reg., Vol. 69, p. 246.

[3] The vote was, for. 5.353; against, 19.148. Over half the legal voters did not vote. Niles' Reg., Vol. 73, Nov. 6, 1847. Fowler, p. 152.

to allow colored men the ballot, but the next year[1] it decreed,
what was already almost accomplished by the action of
former laws, "that no person shall hereafter be held in
slavery in this State," that emancipated slaves must be supported by their masters,[2] and that no slave shall be brought
into Connecticut. Thus Connecticut became in law a Free
State, as she long had been in fact. When the fugitive slave
law of 1850 was passed, the rising tide of indignation swept
over Connecticut. Here and there some resisted the torrent and organized Union Saving Meetings, like the one
the famous Rev. N. W. Taylor addressed at New Haven,
deprecating agitation, counseling obedience, declaring that
he had not been able to discover that the article in the Constitution for the rendition of fugitives was "contrary to the
law of nature, to the law of nations, or the law of God," and
claiming that it was "lawful to deliver up fugitives for the
high, the great, the momentous interests of the Southern
States."[3] But the majority sympathized rather with Gov. H.
B. Harrison, when he introduced his "personal liberty bill"
in the Senate of 1854,[4] and "avowed his belief that it would
render the fugitive slave law inoperative in Connecticut."
The Hon. Henry C. Deming, in opposing the bill, said,
though it was "nicely drawn," he thought it conflicted in
spirit with the United States Constitution, as it undoubtedly
did, and that "it was not in equity and justice deserved by
our Southern brethren, if they behave pretty well." The
advocates of the bill used no such mild terms. The Hon.
John Boyd, late Secretary of State, said "desperate diseases
require desperate remedies." He had "some faith in the
homoeopathic remedy that like requires like," and, as he believed "the exigencies of the time" demanded it, he thanked
Mr. Harrison for introducing the bill. He added, "if Shy-

[1] Compilation of 1854, Title 51, Secs. 1 and 2. *Vide* Conn. Repts., II., 355.
[2] Remember all such must have been over sixty-four years of age.
[3] Wilson, "Rise and Fall of the Slave Power," II., 318.
[4] Fowler, "Local Law in Mass. and Conn.," pp. 98-99. It was introduced about June 25.

lock claims his pound of flesh, he must be careful not to take any of the blood." Judge Sanford saw in the bill "new and important principles, which he believed were entirely constitutional and would be so decided by the Supreme Court." Ex-Gov. Wm. S. Miner could not find a "single line, sentence, or word" unconstitutional in the bill. Judge Sanford spoke again and again, using such language as this: that he thought the South had driven this matter so fast that it had "driven us back to our reserved rights, if we had any." He would occupy the last inch the Constitution left them, come square up to the line, but not one step over. He would oppose the fugitive slave law by any means in his power within the limits of the Constitution. He said, with great clearness, dignity, and force, that the bill was constitutional, that the emergencies of the times demanded such a law; he portrayed the odious features of the fugitive slave law and said the slave-catcher was the most despicable of men. At the same time a bill was introduced, which, however, did not pass, prohibiting the use of any court-house, jail, or other public building for the trial or confinement of fugitive slaves. To this, Mr. Boyd proposed an amendment that a building used for such a purpose should "be rased to the foundation and remain a perpetual ruin." Even the excited Senate had good sense enough to vote this frantic proposition down.

The law as passed, entitled "An Act for the Defense of Liberty in this State," provided that "any person, who shall falsely and maliciously pretend that any free person is a slave, intending to remove him from Connecticut, shall pay a fine of $5000 and be imprisoned five years in the State Prison." In trials, two credible persons, or equivalent evidence, were required to prove the defendant a slave, and depositions were not to be received as evidence. Witnesses falsely representing free persons as slaves are to receive the punishment mentioned above, and, with the intention to satisfy their consciences that they were not violating United States law, the legislators added that any person hindering an officer from the arrest of a fugitive, or aiding an accused person to escape, was to be imprisoned one year in State's prison. The last section of the bill contained an interesting reminder of colonial customs, in providing that the act should not cover the case of apprentices.

Though slavery is still found as a title in the Revision[1] of 1866, the last act on the subject was passed in 1857, and with that the statutory history of slavery in Connecticut may well be ended. At that time it was enacted that " any person held to service as a slave in any other State or country," and not being a fugitive from another of the United States, " coming into this State, or being therein, shall forthwith become and be free."

CASES ADJUDICATED IN THE HIGHER COURTS WITH REFERENCE TO SLAVERY.

The question as to the manumission of slaves by service in the Continental Army with the master's consent, was decided in the case of *Jack Arabas* versus *Ivers*.[2] Ivers, the master, permitted Arabas to enlist in the army. He served through the war and was discharged at its end, when Ivers again claimed him. He fled to the eastward, was overtaken and brought back to New Haven, where he was put in the jail for safekeeping. He sued out a " habeas corpus " and the court granted it, " upon the ground that he was a free man, absolutely manumitted from his master by enlisting and serving in the army." It was a fine idea, that he who helped to free his country could not be a slave.

The only other case in the Connecticut reports as to manumission is *Geer* versus *Huntington*,[3] where the plaintiff claimed a negro as his slave by a bill of sale from his former mistress, while the defendant claimed that the mistress had told him he should be servant to no one but her and should be free at the age of twenty-five. As he had passed that

---

[1] Title LVIII., Secs. 1-6.   [2] Root's Reports, I., p. 92, 1784.
[3] Root's Reports, II., 364.

age before he left her service, the court held him to have been
freed, by a liberal interpretation of her pr mise.

The only case I have found tried in Connecticut in regard
to the Slave Trade, save the famous Amistad case, to be
treated later, is that of the *United States* versus *John Smith.*[1]
It was an action to recover double the value of Smith's
interest in over one hundred negro slaves, transported
in the brig Heroine, of which he was sole owner and
master, from Africa to Havana, and there sold, contrary to
the Act of Congress of May 10, 1800. The Heroine was
in Africa between Dec. 1, 1805 and April 1, 1806, and, arriving at Havana before June 1, Smith sold the slaves before
the end of that month for not less than $10,000, so action
was brought for $20,000. One of the crew was offered
as a witness by the government; but Smith's attorney objected to this testimony on the ground that it would incrimi-
nate the man and subject him to a fine of not over $2000 and
two years imprisonment, according to the above-mentioned
Act of Congress. The government said they had entered a
nolle prosequi in his case and it was too late to institute
another proceeding against him. The defense pleaded that
the witness had fled from justice and that in such case the
statute of limitations would not hold. Further, he might be
excused from testifying, as he was unwilling; but the judge
ruled that a witness could not plead his wrong-doing as a
defense and must testify. However, there was a verdict for
the defendant, as the judge charged the jury that the offense
was completed when the vessel arrived at Havana, not when
the slaves were sold, and the prosecution, though begun
within the prescribed period, two years, of the latter date,
was not within two years of the former.

The most frequent cause of negroes appearing in cases
before the Supreme Court was the law of settlement. When
negroes became infirm and were penniless, it was an important question who should support them, and from this several

---

[1] Day's Reports, IV., p. 121. U. S. Circuit Court, Hartford, Sept.,
1809. Fowler's "Hist. Status," pp. 16-18, has interesting facts on
slave trade in Conn.

cases arose. The first of these,[1] *Wilson et al.* vs. *Hinkley et al.*, in the Tolland County Court, was a case of an appeal from a judgment of a Justice of the Peace. In this court, Hinkley and others, selectmen of the town of Tolland, sued the selectmen of the town of Coventry for support of Amy Caesar and her children. This Amy, daughter of an Indian woman, was born in Tolland, and lived with a citizen of that town as servant till eighteen years of age. Then she was set at liberty and, after four years more in Tolland, married Timothy Caesar, also a child of an Indian woman and slave to a citizen of Mansfield, where they lived nine months. Thence they removed to Coventry, Timothy being granted permission to do so by his master. There they lived eighteen months, since which time Amy and her children had apparently lived in Tolland. Tolland's claim for reimbursement was resisted by Coventry, which said the former masters of Amy and Timothy should support them. The court decided that Timothy, "being born of a free woman, a native of the land, was not a slave," applying apparently the old civil law maxim. "Nor" was he "a servant bound for time, nor an apprentice under age, nor under disability to gain settlement by commorancy"; therefore, by residence in Coventry over a year he had gained settlement for himself and wife, and, as she was never a "slave or servant bought for time," Coventry must pay the expense of her support.

The next case was also one in which the same town of Tolland was interested; *Ebenezer Kingsbury* vs. *Tolland.*[2] Joseph Kingsbury, of Norwich, bought two native Africans, Cuff and Phyllis, as "servants for life," and gave them to his wife. She died, December, 1773, freeing them. In 1776, with the consent of Ebenezer Kingsbury, their former mistress's sole executor, they removed to Tolland and, after living there nine years, came to want and were supported by the town. The town brought suit against Kingsbury and won in the County Court; but in the Court of Appeals lost its case, on the technicality that he was sued personally and not

---

as executor. The court, however, in an *obiter dictum,* intimated the personal representatives and next of kin were liable,
if sued as such, for the support of freed slaves, if there were
sufficient assets.

A third case was *Bolton* vs. *Haddam,*[1] by which was determined that a slave was domiciled with his master and, if manumitted in any way, continued an inhabitant of the same town
as before, unless he became legally settled elsewhere.

Twenty years now pass before we find another such case;
then, November, 1817, was decided the case of *Windsor* vs.
Hartford.[2] This rather important case regarded the residence of a negress, Fanny Libbet, and her two illegitimate
children. Fanny, herself illegitimate, was born in Hartford
in 1785 and, at the age of three, was given by her master to
his son in Wethersfield. There she lived until twenty-five
years of age, when her term of service by law expired. Her
mother had been sold to a citizen of Windsor in 1795 and
was emancipated by him in 1801. Fanny went to her mother
as soon as she could, and there her two children were born.
Windsor supported them for a while and then sued Hartford,
on the ground that Fanny, born after March 1, 1784, was
never a slave and so took her settlement from her birthplace,
Hartford. The court so decided, stating that " she is to be
considered as a free person and never was a slave," an important interpretation of the act of 1784. Her residence in
Wethersfield was that of an apprentice, and she had never
gained settlement in Windsor. As she never had been a
slave, her former master was not liable to her support.

Soon after was tried the case of the *Town of Columbia* vs.
Williams et alium. A citizen of Groton had left a slave,
Adam, who had, after his master's decease, removed to
Columbia and there became a town charge. The town sued
the heirs of Williams, and they claimed that the suit was
improperly brought, that Groton ought have been sued, as
Adam had a settlement with his master there, which town

---

[1] Root's Reports, II., p. 517. February, 1797. Tolland County.
[2] Conn. Reports, II., p. 355.
[3] Conn. Reports, III., 467, October 28, 1820.

could then have recovered from them. As it was admitted that Adam had never been manumitted, the court sustained the claims of the defendants, and the town, on this point, lost its case and a new trial was ordered, which seems never to have come off.

Flora,[1] slave of Elisha Pitkin, gave rise to two cases. *Pitkin et al.* vs. *Pitkin et al.*, the first, was brought by the executors of Elisha Pitkin against certain of his heirs. He executed a deed of gift of all his real estate to the plaintiffs and defendants in 1816, but kept it in his possession until his death, three years later. When he died, he bequeathed his[2] remaining property by testament to the plaintiffs and certain of the defendants, to be equally divided among them, they being enjoined to take care of Flora and bear the expense equally, or to have the executors reserve sufficient estate for her support. The executors claimed they paid "large sums" for her support, supposing there was sufficient estate; but, at final settlement, found not enough was left outside of the real estate conveyed by deed. This they ask the court to order sold, sufficiently to provide for Flora's support. The defendants demurred, and their demurrer being sustained, the plaintiffs carry the case to the higher court. The plaintiffs contended that, "where there is service for life there must be support for life," and, therefore, the support of the slave was a charge upon the estate, that Mr. Pitkin's intention was to have her supported, that it was the duty of the executors to support her, and they were consequently not volunteers and had a superior equity to that of the defendants, and that the court should decide the case according to its equities. The defendants said Mr. Pitkin did not charge Flora's support on the real estate, that the executors were volunteers, having nothing to do with the real estate, and that, if the land should be liable, it should be so decided in a probate, not in a chancery court. The court decided in favor of the defendants,

---

[1] Conn. Reports, VII., p. 315, June, 1829, and VIII., 392, June, 1831.

[2] Probably not all, though of this I am not absolutely sure.

on this last contention, and on the ground that it could not foresee what sums migh† be needed for her support, and hence could not determine on the quantity of land to be sold.

Having lost their case, the executors seem to have given up trying to support Flora and to have endeavored to throw the expense on the town of East Hartford, which sued them in 1831, alleging that it had supported Flora three years. The defendants demurred that the selectmen were not obliged to support her, and as volunteers they cannot recover, for " the duty of support rests on the master alone," and he is only liable to the town for the support of emancipated slaves. " Slavery is not founded in reason and justice, like the relations of husband and wife." Thirdly, as the supplies were not furnished in Elisha Pitkin's lifetime, the defendants should be sued as owners, not executors. The prosecution, on the other hand, asserted that the relation of master and slave is recognized by statute law; during the continuance of this relation the master is liable for support of slave, which slave if unemancipated remains part of the estate; that a needy slave must be relieved by the town in which is his settlement, for which relief recovery is to be had at law. Judge Daggett, in his majority opinion, confined himself to the obligation of the selectmen for her support. He said the only cases where the town would have to support a slave were when both master and slave were paupers, or a slave emancipated in accordance with the act of 1792 should become such. In this suit neither was the fact, and the town was a volunteer and could no more recover than if it had supported a wife or child of a man of means. Chief Justice Hosmer agreed with this reasoning, from which Judge Peters dissented, though he agreed with the decision. He said, " The relation of master and servant, or qualified slavery, has existed in Connecticut from time immemorial and has been tolerated (not sanctioned) by the legislature. But absolute slavery, where the master has unlimited power over the life of the slave, has never been permitted in this State." He continued, Flora at Mr. Pitkin's death, not being specially devised, vested as a chattel in the executors. "They alone could sell her; they became her masters and she their slave, and they alone were to maintain her." He thought, however, she ought to be maintained by the town as a vagrant, when the town could recover by implied promise; basing his decision for the defendants, on the technicality that, "when an executor covenants or promises, he binds himself personally and not the heirs or estate of the testator, therefore they should not have been sued as executors, but as persons."

Judge Williams filed a dissenting opinion, in which Judge Bissell concurred. He placed the chief importance on the implied promise, stating, "that slavery has existed in this State cannot be denied, and a few solitary cases still exist, to attest to the melancholy truth...The man who had a right to all the time and services and even offspring of his unhappy slave, must, of course, be bound to maintain him." Executors are liable for debts arising after death of the testator, "where the demand arises from an obligation existing upon the testator in his life." Such an obligation was the support of this slave, which, as personal property, vested in the executors. He thought that it was not necessary to sue them personally, that the *onus probandi* rested on them, that there were no assets. The town was not a volunteer, for "the woman must be relieved by the town where she was, or starve." He quoted a statute providing that "all poor and impotent persons," without estate or relatives, "shall be provided for and supported by the town." The town cannot wait to hunt up the persons legally liable, before rendering aid. "The owner of the slave is primarily liable, and it is only his neglect of duty which makes the defendants liable at all, and it is admitted that, in consequence of that neglect, the defendants would be responsible to any *individual* who supplied the necessities of the slave," and the judge then said he saw no reason why the town also should not recover. His opinion, leaving the interpretation of the statutes and basing itself on abstract considerations, stated that, "by the principles of natural justice they are bound to refund, and I

am not satisfied that any technical rule of law can be interposed to prevent it."

The opinions in this case seemed important enough to
devote some space to it. The next case[1] we note is that of
Colchester vs. *Lyme*, for support of Jenny. She had belonged to a citizen of Lyme until fifty-six years of age, when
she was emancipated and went to live in Colchester. Coming to want, the town sued her old residence for her support,
claiming that, as she was over forty-five when emancipated,
the liability of her master to support her continued, and,
" while the liability of the master to support the slave remains,
the incapacity of the slave to acquire a new settlement remains also." This the defense denied, and the court decided
in their favor. The opinion stated: " If she had been white,
or never a slave, she would have had a settlement in Colchester. Does the fact she was once a slave alter matters?
There was nothing in the statute (of 1777) which in the least
impaired the right of the master to give entire freedom to his
slave at any time." The want of a certificate only continued
the master's liability to support the slave. " By relinquish-
ing all claims to service and obedience," he " effectually
emancipated her, and thus she became *sui juris* and entitled
to all the rights and privileges of other free citizens of the
State, among which the right of acquiring a new place
of settlement was the most important....The town where
the emancipated slave belongs or has a settlement, is the
town empowered by statute to recover from the master or
his heirs,...and if Colchester is such a town, then Colchester only can recover from the former master or his
representatives."[2]

The last case of the kind is *New Haven* vs. *Huntington*,
decided as late as 1852, in which it was adjudged that the
settlement of a free woman in Connecticut is not superseded
by marriage with a slave of another State, nor by his subsequent emancipation, unless the laws of the other State (which

---

[1] Conn. Reports, XIII., p. 274, July, 1839.
[2] *Guilford* vs. *Oxford*, Conn. Reports, IX., 321, is a suit for the
support of an illegitimate free mulatto.

in this case was New York) so provide, and her settlement is communicated both to legitimate and illegitimate children born in Connecticut after the marriage.[1]

Considerable attention has been given to these cases, as they illustrate important principles of the laws of the State and show how the judges interpreted those laws.

Miss Prudence Crandall and her School.

In the autumn of 1831,[2] Miss Crandall, a Quakeress, residing in the southern part of Canterbury, opened a girls' school in that town. She had taught at Plainfield successfully, and moved to Canterbury, at the request of some prominent citizens, buying a house on the Green. Her school was a success from the outset, until she received as pupil a colored girl, Sarah Harris, about seventeen years of age, the daughter of a respectable man who owned a small farm near the centre. The girl was a member of the village church, and had been at the district school, in the same class as some of Miss Crandall's pupils. She now wished "to get a little more learning—enough to teach colored children." Previous to this admission to the school, Miss Crandall had employed as a servant a "nice colored girl," Marcia, who was afterward married to Charles Harris, the brother of Sarah. Young Harris took Garrison's "Liberator" and loaned it to Marcia, who used frequently to show the paper to Miss Crandall. "Having been taught from early childhood the sin of slavery," as she wrote in 1869, "my sympathies were greatly aroused," and so Miss Crandall agreed to receive Sarah Harris as a day scholar. "By this act," she continued, in the same letter, "I gave great offense. The wife of an Episcopalian clergyman, who lived in the village, told me that, if I continued that colored girl in my school, it

---

[1] Conn. Reports, XXII.

[2] The chief authorities are Larned's "Hist. Windham Co.," Vol. II., Book IX., Chap. III., pp. 491 sq.; S. J. May, "Recollections of the Anti-slavery Conflict," pp. 47-71, which Wilson, "Rise and Fall," I., pp. 240-245, and Williams, "Hist. Negro Race," II., pp. 149-156, almost entirely followed; Crandall vs. Conn., Conn. Reports.

could not be sustained. I replied to her '*that it might sink, then, for I should not turn her out.*' I very soon found that some of my school would not return, if the colored girl was retained. Under the circumstances, I made up my mind that, if it were possible, I would teach colored girls exclusively." Now, though Miss Crandall was undoubtedly shamefully treated by the people of the town, they nevertheless had just ground of complaint from the course she pursued. Because some of her patrons were offended at the entrance of one colored girl into her school, she determined to give up teaching white girls entirely, and to bring a number of colored children into the most aristocratic part of the town, while the people who had received her most kindly and had consented to act as visitors to her school were not regarded. She consulted leading Abolitionists in New York and Boston, but no one in the town, whose interests were most immediately concerned in the opening of such a school. Some irritation might therefore have been expected, but the conduct of the townspeople went beyond all bounds and was thoroughly disgraceful. Miss Crandall's conduct, on the other hand, apart from her initial lack of consideration for the judgment of those around her, was consistent, courageous, and praiseworthy.

When she announced her purpose to open a school for " young ladies and little misses of color," dismay seized all. A committee of four of the chief men of the village visited her to remonstrate with her, and, on her proving obdurate, a town meeting was called for March 9, 1833, to meet in the Congregational Meeting-house. Miss Crandall had not shown a conciliating spirit. When Esquire Frost had labored to convince her of the impropriety of her step " in a most kind and affecting manner," and " hinted at danger from these leveling opinions " and from intermarriage of whites and blacks, Miss Crandall at once replied, " Moses had a black wife." She asked Rev. Samuel J. May, pastor of the Unitarian Church in Brooklyn, George W. Benson, the President, and Arnold Buffum, Agent of the New England

Anti-Slavery Society, to present her cause at the town meeting. Judge Rufus Adams offered the following resolutions: "Whereas, it hath been publicly announced that a school is to be opened in this town on the first Monday of April next, using the language of the advertisement, 'for young ladies and little misses of color,' or in other words for the people of color, the obvious tendency of which would be to collect, within the town of Canterbury, large numbers of persons from other States, whose characters and habits might be various and unknown to us, thereby rendering insecure the persons, property, and reputations of our citizens. Under such circumstances, our silence might be construed into an approbation of the project. Thereupon:

"Resolved, that the locality of a school for the people of color, at any place within the limits of this town, for the admission of persons of foreign jurisdiction, meets with our unqualified disapprobation, and it is to be understood that the inhabitants of Canterbury protest against it in the most earnest manner.

"Resolved, that a committee be now appointed, to be composed of the civil authority and selectmen, who shall make known to the person contemplating the establishment of said school, the sentiments and objections entertained by this meeting, in reference to said school, pointing out to her the injurious effects and incalculable evils resulting from such an establishment within this town, and persuade her to abandon the project."

The Hon. Andrew T. Judson, a Democratic politician, later Congressman and United States District Judge, who resided next to Miss Crandall, and who had been horrified at the prospect of having a school of negro girls as his neighbor, addressed the meeting "in a tone of bitter and relentless hostility" to Miss Crandall. After him, Rev. Mr. May and Mr. Buffum presented a letter from Miss Crandall to the Moderator, asking that they might be heard in her behalf. Judson and others at once interposed and prevented their speaking. They had intended to propose that, if the town

would repay Miss Crandall the cost of her house and give
her time to remove, she would open her school in some more
retired part of the town or vicinity. Doubtless this would
not have been satisfactory to the people, but that does not
excuse the lack of courtesy on the part of the people in
refusing to hear what Miss Crandall's agents had to propose.
The resolutions were passed, but nothing deterred the fear-
less woman. She opened her school with from ten to twenty
girls as pupils.[1] This still more enraged the townspeople,
and, at a second town meeting, it was resolved: " That the
establishment or rendezvous, falsely denominated a school,
was designed by its projectors, as the *theatre*, as the place to
promulgate their disgusting doctrines of amalgamation and
their pernicious sentiments of subverting the Union. Their
pupils were to have been congregated here from *all quarters*,
under the false pretense of *educating them;* but really to
SCATTER FIREBRANDS, *arrows, and death* among brethren of
our own blood." A committee of ten was appointed to draw
up and circulate a petition to the General Assembly, " deprecating the evil consequences of bringing from other States
and other towns, people of color for any purpose, and more
especially for the purpose of disseminating the principles and
doctrines opposed to the benevolent colonizing system."
Other towns were asked to prefer " petitions for the same
laudable object." The people had completely lost their
heads and were mad with rage and fear. As a result of this
petition, the shameful act of May 24, 1833, before referred to,
was passed.

The conduct of the people of Canterbury was even more
indefensible than their words. They hunted up an obsolete
vagrant law, providing that the selectmen might warn any
non-inhabitant of the State to depart, demanding $1.67 for
each week they should thereafter stay, and, if the fine were
not paid, or the person were still in the town after ten days,
he should be whipped on the bare body, with not over ten

[1] Pupils came from Philadelphia, New York, Providence, and
Boston, says May.

stripes. An endeavor was made to put this law in force against Miss Crandall's pupils, and one of them, Ann Eliza Hammond, a girl of seventeen, from Providence, was arrested. Rev. Mr. May and other residents of Brooklyn gave bonds for $10,000, so the attempt was given up.

The lawless treatment of the school and scholars was worse than the legal one. The stage-driver refused to carry the pupils to the school, the neighbors refused to give Miss Crandall a pail of water, though they knew their sons had filled her well with stable refuse the night before. Boys followed the school with horns and hootings on the streets, and stones and rotten eggs were thrown at Miss Crandall's windows. A systematic policy of boycotting and intimidation was carried out. The village stores were closed against the school. Men went to Miss Crandall's father, a mild and peaceable Quaker living in the southern part of the town, and told him, "when lawyers, courts and jurors are leagued against you, it will be easy to raise a mob and tear down your house." He was terrified and wished his daughter to yield, but she boldly refused. He petitioned the Legislature against the passage of the act of May 24, 1833, but in vain. The sentiment of men from other towns was that they would not want a negro school on their common.

After the passage of the act, two leading citizens told him "your daughter will be taken up the same way as for stealing a horse or for burglary. Her property will not be taken, but she will be put in jail, not having the liberty of the yard. There is no mercy to be shown about it."

A few days later, Messrs. May and George W. Benson visited Miss Crandall, to advise with her as to the fine and imprisonment provided by the act as penalty for teaching colored children not residing in the State. As Wilson puts it, the result of their conference was a determination to leave her in the hands "of those with whom the hideous act originated."

On June 27, 1833, Miss Crandall was arrested, brought before a Justice of the Peace and committed for trial before

the County Court in August.   Mr. May and her friends were
told that she was in the sheriff's hands and would be put in
jail unless bonds were given.   They resolved not to do so,
but to force the framers of the statute to give bonds themselves or commit her to.jail.   The sheriff and jailer saw this
would be a disgrace and lingered; but her friends were firm,
and Miss Crandall spent the night in a cell which had last
been occupied by a condemned murderer.   The next morning bonds were given, by whom it does not appear; but the
fact of her incarceration caused a revulsion of popular feeling in her favor.   Mr. Arthur Tappan wrote at once to Mr.
May, indorsing his conduct, authorizing him to spare no
reasonable cost in defense at his expense and to employ the
ablest counsel.

The Hon. Wm. W. Ellsworth, Calvin Goddard, and Henry
Strong were retained and prepared to argue that the laws
were unconstitutional.   Mr. Tappan took such interest in the
case that he left his business to have a personal interview
with Miss Crandall and Mr. May.   To the latter he said,
"The cause of the whole oppressed race of our country is to
be much affected by the decision of this question.   You are
almost helpless without the press.   You must issue a paper,
publish it largely, send it to all persons whom you know in
the country and State, and to all the principal newspapers of
the country.   Many will subscribe for it and contribute
largely to its support, and I will pay whatever it may cost."
Mr. May took the advice and started the "Unionist," with
Charles C. Burleigh, of Plainfield, as editor.

On August 23, the case of *The State* versus *Crandall* was
tried at Brooklyn, before Judge Joseph Eaton; Messrs. A. T.
Judson, Jonathan Welch, Esq., and J. Bulkley appearing as
counsel for the State.   Mr. Judson denied that negroes were
citizens in States where they were not enfranchised, and
asked why men should be educated who could not be freemen.   The defense claimed that the law conflicted with the
clause of the United States Constitution allowing to citizens
of one State equal rights in others.   The judge charged

the jury that the law was constitutional, but the jury disagreed, standing seven for conviction and five for acquittal.

The prosecution did not wait for a new trial in December, but went before the Connecticut Superior Court. Judge Daggett presided over the October Session. According to Mr. May, he was known to be an advocate of the new law, and in the course of an elaborate opinion said, " it would be a perversion of the terms and the well known rule of construction to say that slaves, free-blacks, or Indians were *citizens* within the meaning of the Constitution." The jury gave a verdict against Miss Crandall and her counsel appealed to the Court of Errors. It heard the case on July 22,[1] 1834, and reversed the previous decision, on the ground of "insufficiency of information," and that there was no allegation that the school was set up without a license, and so left the constitutional question unsettled.

Meantime the school had been continued, W. H. Burleigh and his sister and Miss Crandall's sister Almira assisting in the work.[2] They even had at times a sort of exhibition of the pupils' progress. The opposition to the school in Canterbury did not diminish; the trustees of the Congregational church refused to let Miss Crandall and her pupils worship there. The Friends Meeting at Black Hill and the Baptist church at Packerville, both a few miles off, received them, but were almost the only ones to show kindness. Even the physicians of the place refused to attend Miss Crandall's household. After the opponents failed in the courts, they resorted more than before to violent means. Early in September an attempt was made to burn her house, and her enemies went so far as to arrest a colored man she had employed to do some work for her, and to claim she had the fire started to excite sympathy. A still more dastardly attack was made on the building on September 9, by a body of men, who at night broke all the windows and doors with

---

[1] A. T. Judson and C. F. Cleaveland for State, W. W. Ellsworth and Calvin Goddard for Miss Crandall.

[2] Larned, II., p. 499.

clubs and crowbars. The house was left nearly uninhabit-
able. Miss Crandall's friends all advised her to give up the
school, and she did so, sending the twenty girls then compos-
ing it to their homes. Mr. May said when he gave the
advice to yield, the words blistered his lips and his bosom
glowed with indignation. " I felt ashamed of Connecticut,"
he wrote in his Memoirs, "ashamed of my State, ashamed of
my country, ashamed of my color."

Miss Crandall was soon after married to Mr. Calvin
Philleo and left Canterbury. The town, feeling obliged to
justify its conduct, spread upon its records the following
resolve: " That the Government of the United States, the
nation with all its institutions, of right belong to the white
men, who now possess them,... that our appeal to the
Legislature of our own State, in a case of such peculiar
mischief, was not only due to ourselves, but to the obligations devolving upon us under the Constitution. To have
been silent would have been participating in the wrongs
intended.... We rejoice that the appeal was not in vain."

Here ends the wretched story. But its results were far-
reaching. As Larned, the historian of Windham County, well
writes, if Miss Crandall did not succeed in educating negro
girls, she did in altering the opinions of that part of Connecticut, which became the strongest anti-slavery part of the
State.

NANCY JACKSON VS. BULLOCH.

This celebrated case, interpreting the acts of 1774 and 1784
and practically ending slavery in Connecticut, deserves
especial notice. In this case, the Supreme Court of the State,
by a bare majority, decided that the statutes just mentioned
" were designed to terminate slavery in Connecticut and that
they are sufficient for that purpose. The act of 1774 aimed a
blow at the increase of slaves, that of 1784 struck at the
existence of slavery. The former was intended to weaken
the system; the latter to destroy it. The former lopped off a
limb from the trunk; the latter struck a deadly blow at the

root, and ever since it has withered and decayed, and, with
the exception of here and there a dying limb, slavery has
disappeared from our State and will in a short time be known
only in our history, unless indeed it is to revive and flourish,
by the construction we shall now give to the statutes. To us
it appears as if there was nothing in the intent of the Legislature, or in the words of the act, which requires such a construction."[1]

The facts of the case were as follows: J. S. Bulloch, a
citizen of Georgia, owned a slave, Nancy Jackson, born in
Georgia in 1813. In June, 1835, he came to Connecticut and
settled at Hartford, to live there temporarily while his children
were being educated.

Since that time Nancy had been residing with Bulloch's
family in Hartford, while he had only spent the summer in
Connecticut, returning to Georgia for the winter. Nancy,
through her next friend, brought an action for unjust confinement against Bulloch, and, a writ of Habeas Corpus being
sued out, the case was heard in June, 1837. Chief Justice
Williams, in giving the opinion of the Court, went over the
whole law of slavery, and this makes the decision more valuable. He took the broad ground " that every human being
has a right to liberty, as well as to life and property, and to
enjoy the fruit of his own labor; that slavery is contrary to
the principles of natural right and to the great law of love;
that it is founded on injustice and fraud and can be supported
only by the provisions of positive law, are positions which it
is not necessary to prove." The defendant admitted that
slavery was local and must be governed by State law, and
that neither the fugitive slave clause nor any other clause
of the United States Constitution applies to this case; therefore he can have no higher claims than an inhabitant of a
foreign State. " It cannot be denied that in this State we
have not been entirely free from the evil of slavery....A
small remnant still remains to remind us of the fact....
How or when it was introduced into this State we are not

---

[1] Conn. Reports, XII., p. 38.

informed....It probably crept in silently, until it became
sanctioned by custom or usage." He went on to state that
if it depended entirely on that fact, it might be enquired
whether the custom was "reasonable," but for a century
slavery has been somewhat recognized by statute and thus has
received the implied sanction of the Legislature. He then
takes up the claims of the plaintiff's counsel that the slaves
are freed by the first article of the Bill of Rights, which states
that all men are equal in rights "when they form a social
compact." This, says the Judge, does not apply, as slaves
would not be parties to a social compact, and the article is not
as broad as the famous Massachusetts one. Another article
of the Bill of Rights states, "the people shall be secure in
their persons, houses, papers, and possessions from unreasonable searches and seizures"; but the usage of "people" in
the United States Constitution proved, according to the
court, that the word here need not include slaves. A third
article in the Bill of Rights provided that "no person shall be
arrested, detained, or punished, except in cases clearly warranted by law." But was this detention warranted by the
law? This is to be answered by examination of the statutes;
that of 1774 prohibited the importation of slaves into Connecticut, that of 1784 provided that all born "in the State"
after March 1 of that year should be free at the age of twenty-
five. This last law, Swift thought,[1] "has laid the foundation
for the gradual abolition of slavery; for, as the children of
slaves are born free, being servants only until twenty-five
years of age, the consequence is that as soon as the slaves
now in being shall have become extinct, slavery will cease,
as the importation of slaves in future is prohibited...As
slavery is gradually diminishing and will in a short time
be extinguished, there being but few slaves in the State, it
will be unnecessary, in this place, to make any remarks upon
a subject that has so long engrossed the attention of the
humane and benevolent part of mankind in the present age."
These words are quoted approvingly and the statement is

[1] Swift's System, I., 220.

425]   *History of Slavery in Connecticut.*   55

made that, unless there is some defect in the acts, there has been no real slavery in Connecticut since 1784. The acts were passed, not to interfere with vested rights, but to prevent the increase of evils which would result from the competition of slave labor " with the labor of poor whites, tending to reduce the price of their work and prevent their employment, and to bring the free laborer, in some measure, into the ranks with slaves." The Court decided that, though the law of 1774 did not prevent a master transporting a slave through the State, it did prevent him from keeping her there, and that a slave may be " left," " although the owner does not intend to reside permanently himself, or to suffer such slave permanently to remain here." On the construction of this word " left," and on the *post-nati* argument from the act of 1784, the Court declared Nancy free. As to the words " born within this State," in the act of 1784, the Court held " within this State " surplusage, stating, as a reason, that the Legislature could not legislate for any other State. At any rate it is certain that foreigners could claim no more rights than natives, and as natives can only hold persons as slaves under twenty-five years of age, citizens of other States could do no more.

The dissenting judges laid stress on the words " in this State " in the act of 1784, and claimed that " left," in the act of 1774, meant to desert, abandon, withdraw, or depart from, that mere length of stay does not matter, as long as the *animus revertendi* remains. They state, however, they are glad their interpretation does not consign the woman to slavery; though they " maintain that the State of Connecticut, from time immemorial, has been, and to a certain extent now is, a slave-holding State."

This case showed clearly that the judiciary of the State would lean to the side of freedom whenever possible, and virtually made Connecticut a free State by its liberal construction of the laws, though the formal removal of the State from the slaveholding column was not to take place for some ten years more.

THE NEGROES ON THE "AMISTAD."

In August, 1839,[1] the people of Connecticut, New York
and Rhode Island were excited by tidings of a suspicious
craft, thought to be a pirate. It was a long, low, black
schooner, manned by negroes, and orders were issued to the
United States steamer Fulton and several revenue cutters to
chase her. On August 26, 1839, the United States brig
Washington was sounding off Culloden Point, lying between
Gardner's and Montauk Points. While there, a vessel was
noticed lying off the shore and a boat passing between her
and the shore, where a number of persons were with carts and
horses. Lieut. Gedney, commanding the Washington, sent
a boat to investigate, and when the vessel was boarded she
proved to be manned by negroes, of whom about twenty
were on board, together with two white men, who came forward and claimed protection.[2] The story was soon told.
The vessel was a slaver, the Amistad, which had brought
African slaves kidnapped in April, from Lemboko, in the
Mendi country, near Liberia. Jose Ruiz bought forty-nine
of them and Pedro Montes took four more. These they
re-embarked on the Amistad at Havana on June 27, 1839,
and sailed for Guanajah, Porto Principe. It will be remembered that the slave trade was prohibited by Spain and the
Africans so introduced ought still to be free. The trade was,
however, carried on surreptitiously to a large extent, and
those thus taken to Cuba were called " Bozals," in distinction from the " Ladrinos,"[3] or native slaves. The ship's

---

[1] This account is chiefly drawn from Wilson, "Rise and Fall of
the Slave Power," Vol. I., pp. 456-466; J. Q. Adams' Diary; Niles'
Register; Williams, "Hist. of Negro Race," II., p. 93; Barber,
Jno. W., "A History of the Amistad Captives...with Biographical Sketches of each of the surviving Africans, also an account of
the trials had on their case, etc.," New Haven, 1840; S. E. Baldwin, "The Captives of the Amistad," N. H. Col. Hist. Papers, IV.,
pp. 397-404.
[2] Niles' Reg.. Vol. 57. pp. 1. 28. 29.
[3] A false translation of this word in a public document caused
great trouble. Niles' Reg., Vol. 59, p. 301.

papers falsely referred to them as "ladrinos," legal slaves. The captain of the ship was Ramon Ferrers, and the crew seems to have consisted of two men and a cook, besides a negro cabin-boy. On the fifth night out from Havana the slaves rose, under the leadership of Joseph Cinquez or Cingue, attacked and slew the captain and cook with knives such as were used to cut sugar-cane, and, according to one story, slew the two men in the crew. The cabin-boy, Antonio, however, said in court that the men lowered a small boat and escaped. Ruiz and Montes were bound and kept alive to navigate the ship. The negroes tried to return to Africa and had the vessel steered eastward by the sun during the day, while by night the white men steered to the northwest, hoping to fall in with a man-of-war or to reach some country. After boxing for four days in Bahamas Channel, they steered for St. Andrew Island, near New Providence; thence to Green Key, where the blacks laid in a supply of water; thence for New Providence, where the negroes would not suffer the vessel to enter port, but anchored off the coast every night. The whites were treated with some severity, and with the constant fear of death staring them in the face, their lot must have been most unenviable. Montes, too, was suffering from two wounds in the head and arm. The ship was three days off Long Island, to the eastward of New Providence, and then two months on the ocean, during which time they were boarded several times by vessels, once by an American schooner from Kingston, which remained alongside for twenty-four hours and traded with the negroes, finding they had plenty of money. This was the Spaniards' story, to which they added that they were always sent below in such cases. Our admiration for Cinquez rises when we consider that, for this long period, he managed to continue his ascendancy over his comrades, especially considering how difficult were the circumstances of the case. On August 20, near New York harbor, a pilot-boat met the Amistad and furnished the negroes apples, and when, shortly after, a second one met them, they suspected the whites had taken them to a

strange land and refused to let the pilot board her, while they
exhibited such anger towards the Spaniards that they feared
for their lives more than ever. On the 24th, off Montauk
Light, the Spaniards tried to run the vessel aground, but
failed, and the tide drifted it on, until they anchored where
they were found. After anchoring, about twenty of the
negroes went on shore for water and three of them bought
dogs from some of the inhabitants. The news quickly
spread. Capt. Green, who came up, according to his report,
induced the negroes to promise to give him the ship. They
desired him to take them to Sierra Leone. Just then
appeared Lieut. Gedney and took possession of the vessel and
of the negroes. Before Cinquez would suffer himself to be
taken he leapt overboard and loosed from his waist into the
water 300 doubloons which he had taken from the captain.
The Africans taken were forty-four in number,[1] the rest having died. Of this number, three were girls, the rest men.
Cinquez, the leader, was described as about twenty-five or
twenty-six years of age, five feet eight inches in height, erect
in figure, well built, and very active. His countenance was
unusually intelligent; he possessed uncommon decision and
coolness, and a composure indicative of much courage. Lieut.
Gedney took the Amistad with all on board to New London,
where a judicial investigation was held on August 29, on
board the Washington, before the United States District
Judge A. T. Judson, whom we have already seen in the Crandall trouble. As a result of this examination the Africans
were taken to the New Haven jail on Sept. 1, and on the 14th
were removed to Hartford, save one left behind on account of
sickness. The case now became very complicated. Ruiz and
Montes claimed the Africans as their slaves and preferred
charges of murder against them. The Africans claimed freedom and, through their friends, preferred charges of assault
and battery and of false imprisonment against Ruiz and

---

[1] Niles' Reg., Vol. 57, p. 48 and 50. They were shown in Hartford
at 12½ cents admission. Wild stories were spread that one of them
was a cannibal.

Montes. Lieut. Gedney claimed salvage on vessel, cargo and slaves. Capt. Green and the Long Islanders had a counter claim for the same. The owners of the cargo in Havana claimed it, and the Spanish minister, " forgetful of his country's laws," demanded not only that it, but also that the blacks be given up under the treaty of 1795, that the negroes might be tried in Cuba, and maintained that if they should be tried, convicted and executed in Connecticut, the effect would not be as good as if done in Cuba. The District Attorney, Holabird, claimed that the Africans should be held subject to the President's orders, to be taken back to Africa, according to the Act of 1819, and that, as the Government of Spain had claimed them, they should be kept until the pleasure of the United States be known. Holabird was thoroughly subservient to the slavery interest and wrote to the Secretary of State asking if there were not treaty stipulations which would authorize " our government " to deliver them up to Spain, and if so, " whether it would be done before our court sits," as he did not wish them tried there. The Secretary of State knew there was no such treaty, and if there were, as Wilson well says, the President could not supersede criminal warrants, but he instructed the District Attorney " to take care that no proceedings of your Circuit Court, or any other judicial tribunal, place the vessel, cargo, or slaves ('a gratuitous assumption,' remarks Wilson) beyond the control of the Federal Executive." While the demands of Calderon, the Spanish minister, were supported by the pro-slavery press, the anti-slavery men in New York City appointed a committee, composed of S. S. Jocelyn, Joshua Leavitt, and Lewis Tappan, to solicit funds, employ counsel, and see that the interests of the Africans were carefully cared for. As a result, Seth P. Staples and Theodore Sedgwick, Jr., of New York, were employed as counsel and wrote to President Van Buren denying that these Africans were slaves, contending that, in rising against the whites, they only obeyed the dictates of self-defense, and praying that their case should not be decided " in the recesses of the Cabinet, where these unfriended men can have no counsel and can produce no proof; but in the halls of Justice, with the safeguards she throws around the unfriended and oppressed." The letter was turned over to Felix Grundy, the Attorney General, a violent opponent of emancipation, and one who favored surrender to Spain. He replied he could see no "legal principle upon which the government would be justified in going into an investigation for the purpose of ascertaining the facts set forth in the papers clearing the vessel from one Spanish port to another" as evidence as to whether the negroes were slaves or not. He thought, as the Africans were charged with violation of Spain's laws, they should be surrendered; so that, if guilty, "they might not escape punishment," and that, to fulfil treaty obligations, the President should issue an order, directing the marshal to deliver the vessel and cargo to such persons as Calderon should designate. This Van Buren could not do, as there was no extradition treaty with Spain, which fact Grundy ought to have known. On Sept. 17th, the United States Circuit Court met in Hartford, Judge Thompson presiding, and on the 18th a writ of Habeas Corpus was applied for by the two lawyers mentioned and Roger S. Baldwin of New Haven, in behalf of the three girls, who were only detained as witnesses. On the 21st instant, the same writ was applied for in behalf of the rest of the Africans. Judge Thompson overruled the claim of Lieut. Gedney and Capt. Green for salvage, but refused to grant habeas corpus to any, though ample security were offered, on the ground that the case would first come regularly before the District Court, and the District Court having jurisdiction is bound to provide necessaries for the Africans, until their status is determined. Mr. Staples claimed the case should be tried in New York; but the judge decided that, as the ship was taken on the high seas, *i. e.*, beyond low water-mark, the suit should be tried where the vessel was first brought to land. He also decided the Africans should not be held for murder on the high seas.[1] On Oct. 19th, the District Court met, heard testimony, and

---

[1] Full text of decision in Niles' Reg., Vol. 57, pp. 73-75.

adjourned to meet in New Haven, Jan. 7th, 1840.[1]   On Nov. 26th, 1839, De Argaiz, the new Spanish minister, wrote to the Secretary of State, denying the right of the United States courts to take cognizance of the case, and complained that through their delay, public vengeance had not been satisfied, for Spain " does not demand the delivery of slaves but of assassins." From this high moral tone, he descended in another letter to ask that, on the release of the negroes by the court, the President should order the transportation of the negroes to Cuba in a government vessel. The assurance of this request was not resented by the President. On the contrary, he ordered such a vessel to be ready to take the negroes, if released, to Cuba and deliver them to the Captain General of the island. This vessel, the Grampus, was stationed off New Haven, three days after the court assembled, ostensibly to give the negroes " opportunity to prove their freedom." Before the court even assembled, Lieuts. Gedney and Meade of the Washington were ordered to be ready to go to Cuba with the negroes at the United States' expense, " for the purpose of affording their testimony in any proceedings that may be ordered by the authorities of Cuba in the matter." This shameful pre-judgment of the case and eager desire to be subservient to the slavery interest is most disgraceful to Van Buren's administration. On Jan. 7th, 1840, the District Court met, and the counsel for the Africans offered such conclusive testimony that the negroes were native Africans and not Spanish subjects, that Judge Judson said the point was clearly proved. Gedney[2] claimed one-third of the vessel and cargo as salvage, which was given him by the Court; but his claim for salvage on the negroes was refused by the Court, as the negroes could not be sold, there being no law to permit this to be done. Green said he did not wish salvage on flesh, but, if the negroes were slaves, he wanted his share.

---

[1] Full text of proceedings in Niles' Reg., Vol. 57, pp. 222, 223.

[2] The Spanish owners unsuccessfully tried to prevent his getting salvage, on the ground that, as a United States officer, what he did was in the line of his duty and should have no pay.

The Court speedily dismissed his claim and decided that only Antonio, the cabin-boy, should be given up to Spain, and that the rest should be transported to Africa. This decision was made by a strong Democrat and a man in nowise friendly to negroes, as was shown in the Canterbury affair, and is so the more noteworthy.[1] The District Attorney, by order of the Secretary of State, appealed the case and, in his zeal, sent a messenger to Washington to have a clerical mistake in the President's warrant corrected, that the negroes might be held. In returning the warrant, Mr. Forsyth, the Secretary of State, wrote, " I have to state, by direction of the President, that if the decision of the court is such as is anticipated, the order of the President is to be carried into execution, unless an appeal shall actually have been interposed. You are not to take it for granted that it will be interposed." That is, if the counsel for the Africans did not at once appeal, these were to be hurried on the Grampus and taken to Cuba. On the very day[2] the court assembled, Van Buren sent directions to the Marshal for this purpose, and so " flagitious and barefaced was deemed this order," says Wilson, that some of Van Buren's friends said later that it was issued without his knowledge, by his " sanguine and not over-scrupulous Secretary." Justice Thompson affirmed the decision of the District Court *pro forma*, and left the whole matter to be decided by the United States Supreme Court on an appeal. The committee appointed to care for the Africans now prepared for the last appeal, without stint of time or money, and to the four[3] lawyers already employed added John Quincy Adams, with " his great learning and forensic ability, his commanding position and well-earned reputation." As early as Sept. 23d, 1839, we read in the diary of the " old man eloquent," " Mr. Francis Jackson brought me a letter from Mr. Ellis Gray Loring, requesting my opinion upon the knotty questions involved in the case of the Spanish ship

[1] Niles' Reg., Vol. 57, pp. 336, 352, 384.
[2] April 29, 1840, at New Haven. Niles' Reg., Vol. 58, p. 160.
[3] Mr. Kimberley made the fourth.

Amistad.... I desired Mr. J. to say that I felt some deli-
cacy about answering his letter, until Judge Thompson's
opinion shall be published and until the final decision of the
Government in the whole case." Meantime he asked Jackson to look up the records. Soon after, on Oct. 1st, we read,[1]
" that which now absorbs a great part of my time and all my
good feelings is the case of fifty-three African negroes, taken
at sea off Montauk Point by Lieut. Gedney."[2] He gives a
summary of the case up to that date and, on the next day,
having thrown himself into the case with all his accustomed
zeal and energy, he writes that he has examined all the
authorities. " Here is an enormous consumption of time,
only to perplex myself with a multitude of questions upon
which I cannot yet make up opinions, for which I am willing
to be responsible."[3] We hear no more of the case for some
time. On Feb. 10th, 1840, he offered a resolution calling
upon the President[4] for papers concerning the Amistad and,
on May 25th, offered a resolution denouncing the detention
and imprisonment of the Africans, which was read but not
received.[5] His interest in the case continued, and on Oct.
27th, Ellis Gray Loring and Lewis Tappan called on this
dauntless advocate of the right of petition and entreated him[6]
to act as assistant counsel for the Africans at the January
term of the Supreme Court. He writes: " I endeavored to
excuse myself upon the plea of my age and inefficiency, of
the excessive burden of my duties.....But they urged me
so much and represented the case of those unfortunate men
as so critical, it being a case of life and death, that I yielded
and told them that, if by the blessing of God my health and
strength should permit, I would argue the case before the
Supreme Court, and I implore the mercy of Almighty God
so to control my temper, to enlighten my soul, and to give
me utterance, that I may prove myself in every respect equal
to the task."[7]

[1] Diary, X., 132.   [2] Diary, X., 133.   [3] Diary, X., 135.
[4] Diary, X., 215. Niles' Reg., Vol. 58, p. 59.
[5] Diary, X., 296.   [6] Diary, X., 358.
[7] Diary, X., 360. Niles' Reg., Vol. 57, pp. 99, 105, 176.

A month later, Nov. 17th, he visited Gov. Baldwin in New Haven and saw the prisoners, thirty-six of whom were confined in one chamber, in size about 30 by 20 feet. All but one of the men seemed under thirty. Three of them tried to read to him from the New Testament, and one wrote a tolerable hand. The chiefs, Cinquez and Grabow, had remarkable countenances, he thought. The people of New Haven, and especially the students in the Yale Divinity School, did not neglect the temporal or spiritual interests of the captives; they fed and clothed them, studied their language, taught them to read and write, and instructed them in the truths of Christianity.

During the following months' Mr. Adams busily prepared for the case, being assisted by Mr. Stephen Fox, the British minister. On Feb. 22d, the Amistad case came up before the august tribunal. On that day, Attorney-General Henry D. Gilpin spoke for the government and Gov. Baldwin for the captives, in a "sound and eloquent, but exceedingly mild and moderate argument,"[2] which he continued on the next day.

On the 24th, John Quincy Adams rose[3] to speak before an audience that filled, but did not crowd, the court-room, and in which he remarked there were not many ladies. He wrote in his diary: "I had been deeply distressed and agitated till the moment when I rose, and then my spirit did not sink within me. With grateful heart for aid from above, though in humiliation for the weakness incident to the limits of my powers, I spoke for four hours and a half...The structure of my argument...is perfectly simple and comprehensive...admitting the steady and undeviating pursuit of one fundamental principle." Against him "an immense array of power—the Executive Administration, instigated by the minister of a foreign nation, has been brought to bear in

---

[1] Diary, X., 396, 399, 401. Niles' Reg., Vol. 57, p. 417, Vol. 58, p. 3. Calhoun animadverts on British interference on March 13, 1840. Niles' Reg., Vol. 58, p. 140.

[2] Diary, X., 429.   [3] Diary, X., 431.

this case on the side of injustice....I did not, I could not
answer public expectation; but I have not yet utterly failed.
God speed me to the end." On the 25th, he spoke for four
and a half hours more, and on March 1st, the Court having
meantime been in adjournment on account of the sudden
death of Mr. Justice Barbour, he spoke four hours more and
finished his argument. On the next day Mr. Gilpin closed
the case for the United States. Mr. Adams, in his argument,
sternly condemned the National Government from the President down.[1] He maintained that these Africans were torn
from home and shipped against the laws of the United States
and the laws of nations, that their passage on the Amistad
was in law and fact a continuance of the original voyage, and
that sixteen of the number had perished through the cruelty
of Ruiz and Montes, on whose souls the ghosts of these slain
must sit heavy through the closing hours of life. He anim-
adverted severely on the conduct of the Secretary of State,
saying that he ought instantly to have answered the Spanish
minister that his demands were inadmissible and that the
President had no power to do what was requested. He
should have said that he could not deliver up the ship to the
owner, for he was dead; that the question depended upon the
courts; that a declaration to the President that the courts had
no power to try the case involved an offensive demand, and
that the delivering the negroes by the President and sending
them beyond the seas for trial was making the President " a
constable, a catchpole." The Secretary of State had not
asserted the rights of the nation against these extraordinary
demands. "He has degraded the country in the face of the
civilized world, not only by allowing these demands to
remain unanswered, but by proceeding, I am obliged to say,
throughout the whole transaction, as if the Executive were
earnestly desirous to comply with every one of these
demands." He said the Spanish minister persisted in his
requests because "he was not told instantly, without the
delay of an hour, that this government could never admit

---

[1] Diary, X., 435.

such claims, and would be offended if they were repeated, or any portion of them. Yet all these claims, monstrous, absurd, and inadmissible as they are, have been urged and repeated for eighteen months on our government, and an American Secretary of State evades answering them—evades it to such an extent that the Spanish minister reproaches him for not answering his arguments." In his scathing and relentless manner he next proceeded to attack Grundy's order, mentioned previously, and asking why it was not acted upon, he cried out, "Why did not the President send an order at once to the marshal to seize these men and ship them beyond the seas, or deliver them to the Spanish minister? I am ashamed—I am ashamed of my country, that such an opinion should have been delivered by any public officer, especially by the legal counsellor of the Executive. I am ashamed to stand up before the nations of the earth with such an opinion recorded before us as official, and still more, adopted by a Cabinet which did not dare to do the deed." Such is a brief outline of his forcible address.

A week later, March 9, Justice Story gave the opinion of the court[1] that the Africans were kidnapped and unlawfully transported to Cuba, purchased by Ruiz and Montes with knowledge of the fact that they were free, and did not become pirates and robbers in taking the Amistad and trying to regain their country; that there was nothing in the treaty with Spain which justified a surrender, and that the United States had to respect the Africans' rights as much as those of the Spaniards. "Our opinion is that the decree of the Circuit Court affirming that of the District Court ought to be affirmed, except so far as it directs the negroes to be delivered to the President to be transported to Africa, in pursuance of the Act of the 3d of March, 1819, and as to this it ought to be reversed, and that the said negroes be declared to be free and be dismissed from the custody of the court and go with-

---

[1] Text of decision in Niles' Reg., Vol. 60, p. 40 ff., *vide* Vol. 60, p. 32. The influence of Great Britain was continuously thrown on the side of freedom. Niles' Reg., Vol. 59, p. 402.

out day." The battle was won. John Quincy Adams[1] wrote
to Lewis Tappan, " The captives are free. The part of the
decree of the District Court which placed them at the disposal of the President of the United States to be sent to
Africa, is removed. They are to be discharged from the
custody of the marshal, free."

A week later,[2] on March 17, Mr. Adams asked Webster,
the new Secretary of State, for a public ship to take the
Africans home, as the court had taken from them " the vessel
found in their possession...and her cargo, their lawful
prize of war." Webster, Adams writes in his diary, appeared
startled at the idea that the Amistad and her cargo were the
property of the Africans, but afterwards said he saw no
objection to furnish them with a passage in a public ship and
would speak of it to the Secretary of the Navy. He, however, finally refused to grant the request.[3]

Lewis Tappan had been largely instrumental in their
release. He left his business and traveled for weeks in their
behalf, counseling with friends, getting money, and making
arrangements to send them to Africa. He exhibited them
throughout the North for an admission fee to raise money for
their passage. After their release,[4] they were sent to Farmington, Connecticut, for instruction, and many of them learned
to speak English and became Christians. Religious people
throughout the country became interested in them, and when
they went back to Africa on November 25, 1841, five missionaries went with the thirty-five that survived.[5] They
landed at Sierra Leone on January 15, 1842, whence the

---

[1] Adams wrote on March 17, 1841, strenuously opposing many of
the incidental positions taken by the lower courts. Text in full in
Niles' Reg., Vol. 60, p. 116.

[2] Diary, X., 446. The vessel was sold at New London in October,
1840. The cargo was also sold, the whole bringing about $6000.
Niles' Reg., Vol. 59, pp. 144, 318, 347.

[3] Niles' Reg., Vol. 62, p. 144.

[4] Diary, X., 450. Niles' Reg., Vol. 60, p. 64; Vol. 62, pp. 17, 128,
311.

[5] Niles' Reg., Vol. 62, pp. 96, 224.

British Government assisted them home, and from this band of negroes in the Amistad sprung the Mendi Mission.[1]

In 1844, C. J. Ingersoll,[2] Chairman of the Committee of Foreign Affairs of the House of Representatives, reported a bill to pay $70,000 to the pretended owners of the Africans; but the burning words of Giddings and Adams secured the passage of a motion to lay on the table and prevented that national disgrace. As late as 1847, however, Polk, in his message, recommended an appropriation to the Spanish Government to be distributed among the claimants.[3]

Of the fifty-three Africans on the Amistad when it left Cuba, nine died on the way, eight at New Haven, and one at Farmington, while Cinque and thirty-four others lived to return home.[4]

GROWTH OF THE ANTI-SLAVERY SPIRIT.

The coming of the Revolution caused men to question the rightfulness of holding one's fellow-man in bondage, and the article in the *Norwich Packet* and the resolutions of the Danbury town meeting, already quoted, clearly show this. The feeling spread. In 1778, the Wethersfield town records show a slave, Prince, manumitted, on his master's "being convinced[5] of the injustice of the general practice of the country in holding negro slaves, during life, without their consent."

Many other such instances are doubtless hidden away in the manuscripts of the Town Clerks' offices, but the only other one I have come across is that of Abijah Holbrook,

---

[1] On February 27, 1843, President Tyler recommended Congress, by a special message, to refund the salvage on the Amistad to the Spanish Government. Niles' Reg., Vol. 64, p. 66.

[2] Adams issued an address to his constituents on this subject concerning this. The text is in Niles' Reg., Vol. 68, p. 85.

[3] Niles' Reg., Vol. 73, Dec. 11, 1847.

[4] Niles' Reg., Vol. 60, pp. 206, 208, 400. The cabin-boy Antonio was to have been returned to Cuba, but escaped. Niles' Reg., Vol. 60, p. 96.

[5] Mag. of Am. Hist., XXI.. 422.

who came from Massachusetts to Torrington in 1787, and in 1798 freed his slave, "then about 28 years old" and "desirous of being free,...being influenced by motives of humanity and benevolence, believing that all mankind by nature are entitled to equal liberty and freedom." His negroes, he said, "have served me with faithfulness and fidelity, and they being now in the prime and vigor of life, and appear to be well qualified, as to understanding and economy, to maintain and support themselves by their own industry, and they manifesting a great desire to be delivered from slavery and bondage,"[1] he grants their desire. Before that, however, an organized anti-slavery sentiment had arisen. In February, 1789, the Rhode Island[2] Anti-Slavery Society was founded, with Jonathan Edwards the younger, pastor of a New Haven church, as one of the members. In Connecticut there were less than 3000 slaves, yet "the strong pro-slavery feeling and conservative interest which obtained there opened a wide and important field for an Abolition Society." So, in 1790, the Connecticut Anti-Slavery Society[3] was formed, with President Ezra Stiles, of Yale College, as its president, and Simeon Baldwin as its secretary.

The Society speedily showed great activity. On January 7, 1791, it issued a petition[4] to Congress, which was referred to a special committee and never more heard of.

In the petition,[5] the Society, though "lately established," claims it has "become generally extensive through the State, and we fully believe embraces on this subject the sentiments of a large majority of the citizens. From a sober conviction of the unrighteousness of slavery, your petitioners have long beheld with grief a considerable number of our fellow-men

---

[1] Orcutt's "Hist. of Torrington," p. 212.
[2] Wilson, "Rise and Fall," I., p. 26.
[3] Poole, "Anti-Slavery Opinions before 1800," p. 50.
[4] Presented to Congress, Dec. 8, 1791. Wilson, "Rise and Fall," I., p. 67.
[5] Found in "Memorials presented to Congress by Different Societies instituted for promoting the Abolition of Slavery." Phila., 1792, pp. 7-11.

doomed to perpetual bondage, in a country which boasts of her freedom... The whole system of African slavery is unjust in its nature, impolitic in its principles, and in its consequences ruinous to the industry and enterprise of the citizens of these States." They pray that Congress should, by constitutional means, " prevent, as much as possible, the horrors of the slave-trade,... prohibit the citizens of the United States from carrying on the trade,... prohibit foreigners from fitting out vessels... in the United States for transporting persons from Africa,... and alleviate the sufferings of those who are now in slavery, and check the further progress of this inhuman commerce."

The same year[1] in which this temperate appeal was written, Jonathan Edwards, Jr., speaking before the Connecticut Society, said, " Every man who cannot show that his negro hath by his voluntary conduct forfeited his liberty, is obliged immediately to manumit him." " To hold a man in a state of slavery who has a right to his liberty, is to be every day guilty of robbing him of his liberty, or of man-stealing, and is a greater sin in the sight of God than concubinage or fornication." In these trenchant words, as Wilson truly remarks,[2] " was clearly promulgated the duty of immediate emancipation, as distinctly as it has ever been enunciated... before or since."

Though not so extreme as this, when a proposition for a duty on slaves was before the Congress of the United States, at about the same time, Roger Sherman objected to this being included in the general import bill, saying,[3] " He could not reconcile himself to the insertion of human beings as a subject of import, among goods, wares, and merchandise." On this same subject, some years later, Roger Griswold spoke

---

[1] " Injustice and Impolicy of the Slave Trade and of the Slavery of the Africans, illustrated in a sermon before the Connecticut Society for the promotion of freedom and for the relief of persons unlawfully holden in Bondage, at their annual meeting." By Jonathan Edwards, D. D., New Haven, Sept. 15, 1791.

[2] Wilson, " Rise and Fall," I., 27.

[3] Wilson, "Rise and Fall," I., p. 56.

against laying a tax on imported slaves,[1] though he was opposed to the slave-trade, lest it should seem the United States raised money from commerce in slaves. The mass of the citizens of Connecticut at this time were evidently abolitionists of a moderate type, believing, as did the Fathers of the Republic, that emancipation would come gradually. Meantime the movement towards liberty was growing, and when the Anti-Slavery Societies became strong enough to hold their first Convention at Philadelphia, on January 1, 1794, the Connecticut Society was represented by Uriah Tracy. On the 8th of May of the same year,[2] the day of the inauguration of the Governor, the Society was entertained by an address at the North (now Centre) Meeting House, delivered by Theodore Dwight, its secretary. His address was published, and it was probably from having seen or heard of it that Bishop Gregoire mentioned Dwight in the list of fifteen to whom he dedicated his "Literature of Negroes." In this list, it may be remarked, were the names of two other Connecticut men: Joel Barlow and Col. Humphreys.

At the time of Dwight's address, there were Committees of Correspondence at Hartford,[3] and in New London, Windham and Tolland Counties. When the second Anti-Slavery Convention met at Philadelphia in 1795, Connecticut was represented by Jonathan Edwards, Uriah Tracy, and Zephaniah Swift. The first of these was made chairman of the committee on business, and prepared an address to South Carolina,[4] appealing for " a numerous class of men, existing among

---

[1] In 1804. Wilson, " Rise and Fall," I., p. 87.

[2] Poole, "Anti-Slavery Opinions before 1800," pp. 50, 80. " Oration Spoken before the Conn. Society for the Promotion of Freedom and the Relief of Persons unlawfully Held in Bondage, Convened at Hartford on the 8th Day of May, 1794, by Theodore Dwight." Hartford, 1794, pp. 24, 8vo. At that time Chauncey Goodrich was vice-president and Ezekiel Williams assistant secretary.

[3] At Hartford the Committee consisted of Dr. Lemuel Hopkins, Theodore Dwight, Thomas Y. Seymour, and Ezekiel Williams, Jr. Trumbull's " Memorial Hist. of Hartford Co.," Vol. I.

[4] Poole, "Anti-Slavery Opinions," pp. 28, 77.

you, deprived of their natural rights and forcibly held in bondage." He called on the State to improve their condition and to educate them, and stated that by the slave-trade, of necessity, "the minds of our citizens are debased and their hearts hardened, by contemplating these people only through the medium of avarice or prejudice."

The early anti-slavery feeling,[1] however, gradually died away in Connecticut, as elsewhere, and was succeeded by the colonization idea, as advanced by the American Colonization Society, of which Dr. Leonard Bacon wrote, "It is not a missionary society, nor a society for the suppression of the slave-trade, nor a society for the improvement of the blacks, nor a society for the abolition of slavery; it is simply a society for the establishment of a colony on the coast of Africa." In the same line of thought, the New Haven *Religious Intelligencer* condemned measures calculated to bind the colored people to this country, by seeking to raise them to a level with the whites, whether by founding colleges or in any other way, "because it would divert attention and counteract and thwart the whole plan of colonization." It was this same spirit that aroused the opposition to Miss Crandall, and which opposed the attempt of a convention of free colored people in Philadelphia in 1831 to establish a collegiate school on the manual labor plan at New Haven. The idea of this convention was to raise $20,000 for this school, of which they stated $1000 was already offered, provided the rest should be subscribed. The reasons for their selecting New Haven were these: the site of the town was healthy and beautiful; the inhabitants friendly, pious, generous, and humane; the laws of Connecticut salutary and protected all without regard to complexion; the boarding there was cheap and the provisions good; the situation was as central as any that could be obtained with the same advantages; the extensive West India trade of New Haven might induce many wealthy colored inhabitants of the West Indies to send their

---

[1] Wilson, "Rise and Fall," I., p. 215.

sons there for an education; and lastly, the literary and scientific character of New Haven renders it a desirable place to locate their college.[1]

The plan was not looked upon with any pleasure in New Haven, and " created the most profound excitement and called forth the most determined resistance." The Mayor called a public meeting " to take into consideration a scheme said to be in progress for the establishment in this city of a college for the education of colored youth." At the meeting held September 8, 1831, resolutions were passed " that we will resist the establishment of the proposed college in this place by every lawful means," and, in the preamble, the citizens expressed their conviction that immediate emancipation and the founding of colleges for colored persons were unwarrantable and dangerous interference with the internal concerns of the State, which ought to be discouraged. To these sentiments only one man, the Rev. Simeon S. Jocelyn, entered a protest. This opposition of the residents of New Haven rendered any attempt to carry out the convention's scheme futile. The party of the *status quo ante* was triumphant throughout the State; but, as often when the hour is the darkest, the daylight was at hand.

However, there had never been lack of men to protest against human slavery, and the halls of Congress had often heard bold sentiments from Connecticut men. In November, 1797, when the Pennsylvania Quakers complained to Congress that slaves emancipated by Friends in North Carolina had again been made slaves, Allen of Connecticut said he trusted the petition would not be rejected, as that would be disrespectful to a society revered by every man who sets value on virtue. In December, 1799, when the Southerners were raging on account of a petition from the negroes of Philadelphia for gradual emancipation, Edmond of Connecticut said they were acting with " inattention that passion alone could dictate." In the session of 1806-7, when South-

---

[1] Williams, " Negro Race," II., pp. 63, 64. Fowler, " Hist. Status." p. 151.

erners sneered at the North's opposition to the slave-trade,
Moseley of Connecticut said if any of his section were convicted of being in the slave trade, his constituents would thank
the South for hanging them.[1]   In January, 1818, when a bill
to enforce the fugitive slave law was under debate, Williams
of Connecticut opposed a clause permitting freemen to be
dragged to another part of the country, saying, " In attempting to guard the rights of property to one class of citizens, it
was unjust that the rights of another class should be put in
jeopardy."

In 1833, however, the influence of those in favor of immediate abolition of slavery began to be felt in Connecticut, contending with the pro-slavery and colonization influences.   In
that year, the New Haven Anti-Slavery Society was founded,
being one of the first societies[2] based on the principle of immediate, unconditional abolition.   It sent its greetings to the old
Pennsylvania Abolition Society, and received from it a cordial
response.   Among the leading spirits of the Connecticut
Society were two clergymen,[3] Samuel J. May and Simeon S.
Jocelyn, both of whom were prominent at the organization of
the American Anti-Slavery Society in December, 1833.

The feeling of the learned and powerful city of New Haven
was further shown in the public meeting called by the Mayor
and Council of the city to consider the report and resolutions
of Charleston, S. C., held August 10, 1835, and sent to each
incorporated city and town in the United States.   Charleston's resolves were concerning " societies and individuals who
have circulated incendiary publications through some of the
Southern States," and were violently against anti-slavery publications.   Henry S. Edwards acted as president of the New
Haven meeting, and Noah Webster and David Daggett as
vice-presidents.   It passed resolutions condemning abolitionist publications, denouncing their being sent by mail,

---

[1] Wilson, "Rise and Fall," I., pp. 73, 77, 82, 96.
[2] Wilson, "Rise and Fall," I., p. 25.
[3] May was Vice-President.   Wilson, " Rise and Fall," I., 250 and
260.

quoting a report of a committee of Congress in 1790 that that body " have no authority to interfere in the emancipation of slaves, or in the treatment of them in the different States, it remaining with the several States alone to provide any regulations therein which humane and true policy may require." To this utterance of non-interference, they coupled another quotation from a letter of Oliver Wolcott, Sr., to his son of the same name. " I wish that Congress would prefer the white people of this country to the black. After they have taken care of the former, they may amuse themselves with the other people."[1]

Hartford held a similar meeting on Sept. 26, 1835, and, with Isaac Toucey as president and Elisha Phelps and Joseph Platt as vice-presidents, affirmed that " certain persons in the Middle and Eastern States have formed associations for the avowed purpose of effecting the abolition of slavery in the other States, and in pursuance of said design, have established a press from which they issued several newspapers and periodicals devoted to the aforesaid objects and filled with the most inflammatory matter, whereby the confederacy is endangered."

In that same year a negro woman,[2] who had fled from her master and lived in Hartford as a servant for several years, met a nephew of her former master on the streets of the city. He spoke kindly to her and told her his family had ceased to count her as their property, and that he had only friendly feelings for her. He continued that he had some clothing for her at the hotel where he was stopping, which he asked her to

---

[1]Another resolution favored colonization in Africa. Fowler, " Local Law," pp. 96, 97. Full text in Niles' Reg., Vol. 49, p. 73. R. S. Baldwin opposed these resolutions. On the same page in Niles' Reg. is a letter copied from the Middletown *Advocate*, and written by Rev. Wilbur Fisk, first President of Wesleyan University, stating that though he wished " freedom to the slave," he would sign no petitions for abolition of slavery, as " the ultra-abolitionists, by their imprudent movements and ill-timed and ill-managed system of agitation have, as I think, removed all hope of success in any measure of this kind at the present time."
[2]Trumbull's " Hartford County," I., 609.

go with him and get. She incautiously went to his room on the third floor, when he locked the door to hold her prisoner. She rushed to the front window and leapt out, and, falling on an awning, escaped alive. Mr. Elisha Colt, in whose family she served, raised a purse and bought her, that he might set her free.

Another fugitive slave in Hartford was Rev. James Pennington, D.D., who, escaping when a boy, was educated abroad at Heidelberg. He became pastor of the Talcott St. Church in Hartford, and being fearful of capture after the passage of the fugitive slave law of 1850, induced Gen. Joseph R. Hawley, then a young lawyer in the office of John Hooker, Esq., to visit his former owner and buy him for Mr. Hooker. Mr. Hooker held the deed for a day, to enjoy the sensation of owning a doctor of divinity, and then emancipated him.

In 1836[1] the Connecticut Society, urged on by the Crandall case, started the *Christian Freeman* at Hartford, with Wm. H. Burleigh as editor. In 1845, that paper was merged in the *Charter Oak*, whose office was mobbed by a Democratic mob during the Mexican War, on account of the outspoken character of its sentiments. The *Charter Oak* was merged in the *Republican* in later years, that in the *Evening Press*, and that in the well known *Hartford Courant.*[2]

Under the stimulus of the zeal of the leaders of this new movement, violent discussion and debate sprang up throughout the State.[3] Amos A. Phelps, a brilliant and able speaker, a native of Farmington, took the matter up in that town, and the church in the town was nearly rent in twain from the violence of the parties.[4] What nearly happened in Farmington came to pass in Guilford, where the pastor

---

[1] The increased interest in the subject is shown by the number of pamphlets issued upon slavery in Connecticut about this time.

[2] Trumbull's " Hartford County," I., p. 609.

[3] Niles' Reg., Vol. 56, p. 410, has a long letter from Roger M. Sherman, dated June 26, 1838, written to the National Anti-Slavery Society, in which, in dignified language, he states his opposition both to slavery and the methods of the abolitionists.

[4] Trumbull's " Hartford County," II., p. 192.

changed from the advocacy of colonization to that of abolition, and caused such a bitter dissension that, though he
eventually resigned and left the town, his followers, who constituted a minority in the old church, left and established another one, which remains separate to this day.   In that town
the use of the church was refused the local Anti-Slavery
Society for its meetings, and in Norwich, which, on Oct. 14,
1800, had directed its selectmen to instruct the town's representatives "to use their influence in obtaining a resolve...
prohibiting the migration of negroes...from other States
into this State," now the inhabitants in town meeting
"Resolved that, as it is the duty of every good citizen to dis-
countenance seditious or incendiary doctrines of every sort,
we do deny entirely the use of the Town Hall, or of any other
building belonging to the town, for any purpose connected
in any way with the abolition of slavery."[1]

Miss Abbey Kelley,[2] a Quakeress, who spoke against
slavery, was denounced from the pulpits in Litchfield County
as "that woman Jezebel, who calleth herself a prophetess to
teach and seduce my servants"; but she and others gathered
so many adherents that in January, 1837, a meeting was held
at Wolcottville to organize an anti-slavery society.   The
gathering had to be in a barn, as churches and other public
places were closed.   Even there a mob broke up the meeting,
which adjourned to Torrington Church, where it continued
two days.   The Litchfield County Sociey[3] so formed soon
began holding monthly meetings in barns, sheds, and groves,
and propagating its tenets by lectures, tracts, etc.

---

[1] Caulkins, "Norwich," p. 568.

[2] Orcutt's "Torrington," pp. 212, 218. For the opposition an
early anti-slavery advocate received in Washington, Litchfield
County, see "The Master of the Gunnery," a memorial volume to
F. W. Gunn.

[3] Roger S. Mills of New Hartford was made president, Erastus
Lyman of Goshen vice-president, with Gen. Daniel B. Brinsmade
of Washington, Gen. Uriel Tuttle of Torringford, and Jonathan
Coe of Winsted. Rev. R. M. Chipman of Harwinton was made
secretary, and Dr. E. D. Hudson of Torringford treasurer. Torrington was the birthplace of John Brown of Ossawattomie and
Harper's Ferry fame.

From 1840 onward, the progress of anti-slavery sentiments in Connecticut was gradual.[1]   In 1840 she cast 174 votes for Birney; in 1844 she gave him 1943; in 1848 Van Buren received 5005; in 1852 Hale obtained 3160.   Then under the influence of the Kansas-Nebraska Bill the State rapidly moved towards abolitionism.   In 1854 the Anti-Nebraska candidate for Governor polled 19,465 votes; in 1856 Fremont carried the State and received 42,715 votes, and Connecticut was placed in the ranks of the Republican States for many years.

Social Condition of Slaves.

The slave showed the usual imitation of his white masters. We read of negro balls, negro governors, and negro training days.   In religious affairs they, for the most part, were of the Congregational faith; few became Baptists or Methodists, as at the South.   The annual election of a negro Governor[2] was a great event, and one, as far as I know, unique to Connecticut.   It occurred as recently as 1820, and came off generally on the Saturday after election day.   It was participated in by all the negroes in the capital, and not only a governor, but also minor officers were chosen.   They borrowed their masters' horses and trappings and had a grand parade after the election.   " Provisions, decorations, fruits, and liquors were liberally " given them.   " Great electioneering prevailed, parties often ran high, stump harangues were made, and a vast deal of ceremony expended in counting the votes, proclaiming the result, and inducting the candidate into office, the whole too often terminating in a drunken frolic, if not a free fight," says one writer.   Scaeva, in his " Sketches of Hartford in the Olden Time," adds other

---

[1] On Dec. 26, 1843, J. Q. Adams notes in his Diary that he presented a petition from Connecticut for the abolition of slavery and the slave trade in the District of Columbia.   Diary, XI., 461.   In 1845 the Abolition or Liberty nominated full State and Congressional tickets.   Niles' Reg., Vol. 68, p. 23.   1841 is the earliest year in which I find an Abolition State ticket.   Niles, Reg., Vol. 62, p. 80.

[2] Caulkins, " Norwich," pp. 330.   Stiles, " Windsor," I., 490.

touches. The negroes, " of course, made their election to a
large extent deputatively, as all could not be present, but
uniformly yielded to it their assent.... The person they
selected for the office was usually one of much note among
themselves, of imposing presence, strength, firmness, and
volubility, who was quick to decide, ready to command, and
able to flog. If he was inclined to be arbitrary, belonged to a
master of distinction, and was ready to pay freely for diver-
sions—these were circumstances in his favor. Still it was
necessary he should be an honest negro, and be, or appear to
be, wise above his fellows." What his powers were was
probably not well defined, but he most likely " settled all grave
disputes in the last resort, questioned conduct, and imposed
penalties and punishments sometimes for vice and misconduct." Such an officer is a remarkable instance of the
negro's power of mimicry. In his election parade " a troop
of blacks, sometimes one hundred in number, marching
sometimes two and two on foot, sometimes mounted in true
military style and dress on horseback, escorted him through
the streets with drums beating, colors flying, and fifes, fiddles,
clarionets, and every ' sonorous metal ' that could be found,
' uttering martial sound.' After marching to their content,
they would retire to some large room, which they would
engage for the purpose of refreshments and deliberation."

In Norwich,[1] it would seem there was a special Governor
for the negroes; for the graveyard contains a stone: " In
memory of Boston Trowtrow, Governor of the African tribe
in this Town, who died 1772." After him ruled Sam Hunt-
ingdon, slave of the Governor of the same name, and he is
described as, " after his election, riding through the Town on
one of his master's horses, adorned with painted gear, his
aids on each side, *à la militaire,* himself puffing and swelling
with pomposity, sitting bolt upright and moving with a slow
majestic pace, as if the universe was looking on. When he
mounted or dismounted his aids flew to his assistance, hold-

---

[1] Caulkins, " Norwich," p. 330. *Vide* Fowler, " Hist. Status," p.
81.

ing his bridle, putting his feet into the stirrup, and bowing to the ground before him. The Great Mogul in a triumphal procession never assumed an air of more perfect self-import-ance than the negro Governor."

Of negro trainings, Stiles in his "Ancient Windsor" tells amusing tales, and doubtless such occurred in many other towns where there were sufficient blacks.

The Connecticut negroes, when freed, often left the State, and we have record that, when Massachusetts passed an act on March 26, 1788, that "Africans, not subjects of Morocco or citizens of one of the United States, are to be sent out of the State," there were found nine negroes and twelve mulat-toes from Connecticut, though apparently not citizens of that State, as they were ordered to leave Massachusetts by a given day.[1] We hear but little of fugitive slaves. Occasionally we come across advertisements in the old Connecticut papers for runaways, but these are but few and disappear as the years pass by.[2] Generally slaves were "most tenderly cared for" in the families of their masters until death, and were sold but seldom.[3] Emancipations, beginning to be common just before the Revolution, increased more as time went on, and we frequently find applications on record to the select-men to free the masters from responsibility in case of eman-cipating slaves.

It is said that at Torrington, when three men, joint owners of a female slave, in her old age hired her out to be cared for by a colored man, some indignation was raised.

When emancipated, it is noticeable that the negroes, with their gregarious tendencies, left the country places and con-gregated in the larger towns.[4] For example, in Suffield, where slaves were found as early as 1672, when Harry and Roco, Major Pynchon's negroes, helped build the first saw-

---

[1] Moore, "Notes on Slavery in Mass.," pp. 232-235.
[2] *Vide* Mag. of Am. Hist., XV., 614.
[3] Mag. of Am. Hist., XV., 614. N. H. Gazette, 1787.
[4] Mag. of Am. Hist., XXI., 422. Caulkins, "Norwich," p. 330. Trumbull's "Hartford County," II., p. 199.

mill, and where before 1740 there were but few slaves, mostly
owned by magistrates, parsons, and tavern-keepers, the number of negroes was twenty-four in 1756; thirty-seven in 1774;
fifty-three in 1782; twenty-eight in 1790; four in 1800. The
last of these was manumitted in 1812, and after a few years
none were left in the town. They had been a social, happy
race, some of whom had married there, and all of whom had
been well cared for by their masters, but when freed they all
drifted away to the cities, where they could have the society
of others of their race. In the cities, special effort was made
for the spiritual welfare of the negroes. In 1815[2] the Second
Church of Norwich, under the leadership of Chas. F. Har-
rington, began a Sunday School for blacks, and later the Yale
students in New Haven took up the same work in the Temple
Street and Dixwell Avenue Schools, the latter of which is
still maintained.

In general, Connecticut has little to be ashamed of in her
treatment of the negroes. She treated them kindly as slaves
and freed them gradually, thus avoiding any violent convulsion. Though opposed to abolitionism and interference with
slavery in another State, until the aggressive character of the
slaveholding power was clearly manifested, she then swung
into line with the rest of the Northern States to do away with
it from the soil of the whole country.

There is a steady and progressive development of the conduct of the State towards slavery. Beginning with a survival
of the idea that captives in war were slaves, as shown in the
conduct towards the Pequods, Connecticut acquiesced thoroughly in the principles of slavery through all the Colonial
period. Her treatment of the slaves was almost always kind
and generous. A master, in true patriarchal style, regarded
them as in truth a part of his family.[3] With the coming of the

---

[1] Trumbull's " Hartford County," II., p. 406. Fowler, " Hist.
Status," p. 149, says in Durham in 1774 there were 44 negroes, in
1868 only 3.

[2] Caulkins, " Norwich," p. 556. Fowler, " Hist. Status," p. 150,
speaks of eight negro churches in the State in 1873.

[3] Fowler, " Hist. Status," pp. 81-83, gives many interesting instances of this.

Revolution and the struggle of the Colonists for freedom, a feeling arose that it was not just to hold other men in bondage, and as a result, importation of slaves was forbidden in 1774. Negroes were allowed to fight side by side with the whites, and gradual emancipation was begun in 1784. The claims of the masters were, however, respected by saving their right to those they then held as slaves, and though manumission was encouraged, the law put wise restrictions on the cruelty which would employ a man's best years in labor for another and leave him to be supported by public alms at last.

The case of Miss Prudence Crandall and of the Amistad proved effective reinforcements to the arguments of the Abolitionists, and the case of Jackson versus Bulloch showed that the courts were inclined towards the support of liberal interpretations of the anti-slavery laws. So when the formal abolition of slavery came in 1848, it found few to be affected by its provisions. The movement against slavery went on. From abolishing slavery within its borders, the State went on to forbid the seizure of a slave on its soil, and then gladly joined with the other Northern States in the great struggle which ended in the destruction of slavery throughout the United States.[1]

---

[1] In 1865, the question of negro suffrage was submitted to the voters and decided adversely by a vote of 27,217 to 33,489. In May, 1869, the legislature, by a party vote, adopted the Fifteenth Amendment to the United States Constitution. The vote in the Senate stood 12 to 5, in the House 126 to 104. Fowler. p. 266.

APPENDIX.

In addition to the works quoted in the body of the monograph, the following may be mentioned as a part of the bibliography of this subject:

Bacon, Leonard. "Slavery discussed in Occasional Essays from 1833 to 1846." New York, 1846.

Beecher, Catharine E. "An Essay on Slavery and Abolitionism." Philadelphia, 1837.

Bowne, Rev. George. "Picture of Slavery in the United States." Middletown, 1834.

Dickinson, James T. "Sermon delivered in the Second Congregational Church, Norwich, July 4, 1834, at the Request of the Anti-Slavery Society of Norwich and Vicinity." Norwich, 1834.

Fisk, Wilbur. "Substance of an Address delivered before the Middletown Colonization Society at the Annual Meeting, July 4, 1835." Middletown, 1835.

Porter, Jacob, translator. "The Well-spent Sou, or Bibles for the Poor Negro." New Haven, 1830.

Stuart, Charles. "The West India Question, reprinted from the English Quarterly Magazine and Review of April, 1832." New Haven, 1833.

Tyler, E. R. "Slaveholding a Malum in Se or Incurably Sinful." (2 editions.) Hartford, 1839.

"Fruits of Colonization—the Canterbury Persecution." 1833.

May, Samuel J. "The Right of Colored People to Education vindicated—Letters to Andrew T. Judson, Esq., and others in Canterbury, relative to Miss Crandall and her School for Colored Females." 1833.

Van Buren, Martin. Message, 1840 (Amistad).

Baldwin, Roger S., and *Adams, John Q.* "Arguments before the United States Supreme Court in the Case of the African, Cinquez or Jinque."

SLAVES AND FREE NEGROES IN CONNECTICUT.

	Slaves.		*Free Negroes.*
1680,	30, (Answers to Board of Trade),		...
1715,	1,500, (Niles' Register, vol. 68, p. 310),		...
1730,	700, (Answers to Board of Trade),		...
1756,	3,634, (Fowler, " Hist. Status," p. 150),		...
1762,	4,590, (Stiles MSS.),		...
1774,	6,562, (Fowler, " Hist. Status," p. 150),		...
1782,	6,281, " " "		...
1790,	2,759, (U. S. Census),		2,801
1800,	951, "		5,330
1810,	310, "		6,453
1820,	97, "		7,844
1830,	25, "		8,047
1840,	17, "		8,105
1850,	... "		7,693
1860,	... "		8,627
1870,	... "		9,668
1880,	... "		11,547
1890,	... "		12,302

N. B.   Negroes on the Amistad not counted in 1840.

SLAVERY IN MISSOURI
1804-1865

SERIES XXXII

NO. 2

JOHNS HOPKINS UNIVERSITY STUDIES

IN

HISTORICAL AND POLITICAL SCIENCE

Under the Direction of the

Departments of History, Political Economy, and
Political Science

SLAVERY IN MISSOURI
1804-1865

BY

HARRISON ANTHONY TREXLER, Ph.B.
Assistant Professor of Economic History, University of Montana

BALTIMORE
THE JOHNS HOPKINS PRESS
1914

TABLE OF CONTENTS

PREFACE

The subject of this study was suggested to the writer several years ago by Professor Jonas Viles of the University of Missouri. Later it was again taken up and expanded when the author entered the Seminary in American History at the Johns Hopkins University. The writer is under great obligations to Professor J. M. Vincent for his advice throughout the preparation of the study, especially for the idea of emphasizing the economic side of Missouri slavery. Dr. R. V. D. Magoffin facilitated the work of collecting material both by his own efforts and by pointing out efficient methods of research. Although this study was practically completed before the election of Professor J. H. Latané to the chair of American History at the Johns Hopkins University, he has critically examined the entire work and made many suggestions which were gladly received.

To Mr. William Clark Breckenridge of St. Louis the writer owes much of the best that the study may afford. Mr. Breckenridge not only pointed out many valuable lines of work, but submitted for use his large private collection of manuscripts, newspaper files, and pamphlets. He also introduced the author to many collections of materials and made possible interviews with many antebellum citizens of St. Louis and Missouri. The writer is also indebted to Miss Mae Symonds of the Mercantile Library of St. Louis, Mr. Gaillard Hunt of the Library of Congress, Messrs. F. A. Sampson and F. C. Shoemaker of the State Historical Society of Missouri, Dean Walter Williams and Professor Jonas Viles of the University of Missouri, and to Judge Walter B. Douglas of the Missouri Historical Society for his cooperation and aid in finding materials in St. Louis.

In addition the writer wishes to express his thanks to Mr. K. Roberts Greenfield of the Historical Department of the

Johns Hopkins University for his aid in correcting manuscript.   Above all he wishes to acknowledge the faithful and
untiring assistance of his wife in collecting and organizing
the materials of this study.

H. A. T.

SLAVERY IN MISSOURI, 1804-1865

CHAPTER I

MISSOURI SLAVERY AS AN ECONOMIC SYSTEM

When Louisiana was purchased in 1803, there were between two and three thousand slaves within the present
limits of Missouri, of which only the eastern and southern
portions were then settled.[1] By 1860 the State contained
114,931 slaves and 3572 free negroes.[2] Natural increase
was one cause for this increase in the number of slaves, and
importations from other slave States represented the other.
The relative number of negroes gained from these two
sources cannot be learned with any accuracy. The number
of slaves born within the State is not given in the Federal
census returns. In 1860 of the 1,063,489 whites of Missouri
160,541 were foreign born, and 475,246 were natives of the
State. Of the remainder, 273,808 were born south of
Mason and Dixon's line, and 153,894 in the free States and
Territories.[3] It may fairly be assumed that these slave-
state immigrants brought most of the slaves imported. Of
these southern settlers 99,814 were from Kentucky, 73,594
from Tennessee, 53,957 from Virginia, and 20,259 from
North Carolina. It would perhaps be incorrect to assume
that the slaves brought to Missouri were in exact proportion to the whites from the several Southern States, yet one
may assert with a fair measure of safety that the imported
blacks came from the four slave States named and from

---

[1] In 1810 there were 17,227 whites, 3011 slaves, and 607 free blacks
in Missouri Territory (Eighth Federal Census, Population, p. 601).
For a summary of the various census returns of the Missouri country before the cession of Louisiana see J. Viles, " Population and
Extent of Settlement in Missouri before 1804," in Missouri Historical Review, vol. v, no. 4, pp. 189-213.
[2] Eighth Federal Census, Population, pp. 275, 281-282.
[3] Ibid., p. 301.

the other slave States in some rough proportion to the whites from those States.[4]

To some counties immigration came in waves. In the thirties Carolinians settled in Pike County with their slaves; later others came from Virginia and Kentucky.[5] A large body of Union sympathizers from eastern Tennessee took up land in Greene County; Kentuckians and Virginians also settled on the rich soil of this county.[6] Other counties experienced similar movements. By no means all of the settlers who came from slave States brought negroes or favored slavery, but, as will be learned in another chapter, hundreds of immigrants, especially those coming from Kentucky, Tennessee, and Virginia, brought negroes, and some of them considerable bodies of slaves.[7]

The birth-rate was perhaps about the same as it is among the negroes of the State today, but because of the property interest of the master the death-rate may have been lower. For the year ending June 1, 1850, the slave births in Missouri numbered 2699, while the deaths amounted to 1293.[8] If these figures are correct, the births were double the death toll. It would be unsafe, however, to generalize from these limited data.

The growth of the different classes of the population of Missouri was as follows:—[9]

Year	Whites	Free Colored	Slaves¶
1810	17,227	607	3,011
1820	54,903	376	9,797
1830	115,364	569	25,091
1840	322,295	1478	57,891
1850	592,004	2618	87,422
1860	1,063,489	3572	114,931

[4] Six thousand and fifteen whites came to Missouri from Maryland, 4395 from Arkansas, 3913 from South Carolina, 3473 from Alabama, 3324 from Mississippi, and so on (ibid.).
[5] Statement of Ex-Lieutenant Governor R. A. Campbell of Bowling Green.
[6] Statement of Mr. Dorsey D. Berry of Springfield.
[7] See below, pp. 102–103.
[8] Seventh Federal Census, p. 665.
[9] The figures for 1810 are from the Eighth Federal Census, Population, p. 601. The other returns are from the Fourth Census, p. 40; Fifth Census, pp. 38, 40–41; Sixth Census, p. 418; Seventh Census, p. 655; Eighth Census, Population, pp. 275–283.

It appears from these figures that the slaves increased in number but at a decreasing ratio to the whites. Between 1810 and 1820 the slave increase was 239.48 per cent, in the next decade 145.46 per cent, in the next 132.11, in the next—1840 to 1850—50.1 per cent, while between 1850 and 1860 the increase was only about 33 per cent.[10] We must not conclude that slavery was declining because the increase was less decade by decade while that of the whites was continually greater. It must be remembered that the land of greatest fertility was naturally occupied first, and as a result there was less and less room for expansion. The back counties were not so rich and were more difficult to reach. By 1840 Texas and other new regions were beginning to divert settlers from Missouri. However, non-slaveholding whites continued to fill the towns and the rougher land which was less adapted to slave labor. Agriculture was the great source of slave profit. The artisan class was white, and the filling up of the country rather increased than decreased their possibilities in developing manufactures. Had slave labor in Missouri been as profitable as was German labor in Illinois, the occupation of the best soils would have limited its growth in time. Increase in population means more intensive agriculture. Slave labor, being largely unintelligent and lacking initiative, is better suited to extensive farming.

The fact that the increase of the slave population of Missouri was limited by the supply of new lands was first noticed in the old Mississippi River settlements. The old French counties along the Mississippi from St. Louis south—Jefferson, St. Genevieve, Cape Girardeau, and so forth—contained 11,647 slaves in 1850 and but 11,528 in 1860.[11] Another decrease is found in the counties along the Missouri from its mouth to the boundaries of Callaway and Cole—St. Louis, St. Charles, Franklin, Warren, Montgomery,

---

[10] Seventh Federal Census, p. 665.
[11] For these and the following figures see the Seventh Federal Census, pp. 654–655, and the Eighth Federal Census, Population, pp. 280–283.

Gasconade, and Osage—which in this decade fell from 11,-732 to 11,597 slaves. Increases are found in the counties lying on the Mississippi from the mouth of the Missouri to the Iowa line,—St. Charles, Lincoln, Ralls, Pike, Marion, Lewis, and Clark. In 1850 these counties contained 13,171 slaves and in 1860 there were 15,618. The slaves in the counties along the Iowa border increased from 897 in 1850 to 1009 in 1860.

To find the real location of the slave increase of the State we must turn to the west. The large and excessively rich Missouri River counties from Callaway and Cole to the Kansas line—Boone, Howard, Chariton, Cooper, Saline, Lafayette, Ray, Clay, Jackson, and Manitou—contained 34,135 slaves in 1850 and 45,530 ten years later.[12] The whole series of counties along the Kansas border from Iowa to Arkansas—Atchison, Buchanan, Platte, Jackson, Cass, Jasper, and the rest—had but 20,805 bondmen in 1850, while in 1860 they contained 29,577.

For two reasons these western counties increased in slave population faster than the eastern. In the first place, the land of the western counties was better, and hemp culture made slave labor profitable. A soil map of Missouri shows that the rich loam along the Missouri River surpassed any other land in the State. Here the slaves increased both in value and in price as in no other section. The eastern region was earlier settled, and as a consequence fewer and fewer slave-owners came from the South to locate there, while to the west settlers were still coming in large numbers when the Civil War opened.

The distribution of the slaves, as well as of the free population of Missouri, was controlled by the same conditions. The French and Spanish located along the Mississippi both because the land was fertile and because the river offered the

12 Some of these counties are counted twice where they are located at corners, or where two series of counties meet. In 1860 the counties ranked as follows in slave population: Lafayette, Howard, Boone, Saline, Callaway, St. Louis, Pike, Jackson, Clay. All of these counties save Pike are on the Missouri River.

only means of communication with the outer world.   As the
Anglo-Saxons invaded the Territory after the American occupation, they went up the Missouri to the Osage, then to the
Bonne Femme, and then on west.   Settlements thus followed the great streams and their tributaries.   In general
the slave-master also followed the streams, this fact being
due to the coincidence that the river counties were not only
more accessible than the back counties, the products from
them being therefore more readily marketed, but were also
more productive.   It may be said, then, that the slaveholder followed the river because the railroad and the highway were not yet opening the back country.   He remained
in these river counties because they contained lands of un-
surpassed fertility.

In Missouri as in the other border States the slave was put
to general farm work rather than to the producing of a
staple crop.   The great plantation of the Mississippi and
Louisiana type with its white overseer and gangs of driven
blacks was comparatively uncommon in the State.   Very
few masters had a hundred slaves, not many had half that
number.   There were some farmers, however, who employed a considerable body of negroes.

The number of slaves held is most difficult to find with
any accuracy.   Personal information from contemporaries
conflicts with the census reports and the county tax returns.
For example, an old boat's clerk, Mr. Hunter Ben Jenkins
of St. Louis, who spent much time in the great Missouri
River slave counties, claims that the largest slaveholder of
the State was Jabez F. Smith of Jackson County, who
owned 165 negroes.   In contrast with this statement the
Jackson County tax book of 1860 credits Jabez F. Smith
with but 42 slaves.[13]   Therefore, Smith either dodged his

---

[13] MS. Tax Book, Jackson County, 1860, pp. 151–152. The Eighth
Federal Census (Population, p. 280) gives the Jackson County slave
population at 3440 as against the 3316 listed in the tax book of that
year. But this small difference does not account for the discrepancy
of four to one in the reported numbers of Smith's slaves. Mr.
James Peacock of Independence, who was an acquaintance of

taxes enormously or had fewer slaves by far than his neighbors thought.

From the local returns gathered for the Federal census
it is found that there were some fairly large slaveholders
for a country of diversified agriculture which, as compared
with the plantations further south, was a community of small
farms. These figures should be more complete than the
tax returns, as they were not collected for purposes of
taxation. These census reports for 1850 show that in
Cooper County John H. Ragland was the leading slave-
owner, being credited with 70 negroes, including infants and
the aged. He lived on a farm of 1072 acres, 500 of which
were under cultivation. Of these 70 slaves 29 were over
fifteen years of age. His land was worked by 34 horses,
mules, and oxen. His produce in hand was large,—4000
bushels of wheat, the same amount of corn, 400 bushels of
oats, and 7000 pounds of tobacco. He had 140 swine and
24 head of cattle besides his oxen.[14]

The second largest Cooper County slaveholder was Henry
E. Moore, who had 32 negroes, of whom 23 were over
fifteen years of age. He possessed 250 acres of improved
and 150 acres of unimproved land, 57 work animals, 5000
bushels of corn, 400 of oats, 200 swine, and 32 cattle.[15]
These represent the more affluent Missouri farmers who
were not engaged in producing a staple crop. An example
of a less favored farmer is Joseph Byler, who owned 11
slaves, only 4 of whom were over fifteen years of age—2
men and 2 women. Byler owned 100 acres of improved

Smith's, told the present writer that "Smith had many more than
forty-two slaves." Mr. Peacock suggested that the infants and aged
negroes were often not listed by the assessor, but 123 of Smith's 165
slaves could hardly have been infants and very old people. In the
tax books old and young are alike given, as is the case with Smith's.
In the earlier tax returns young negroes were not included. In the
St. Charles County tax book of 1815 only slaves above ten years of
age are listed, while in the Franklin County tax list of 1823 only
those over three years were given. But if the assessor did omit the
infants and the aged, he but eliminated those who were not effective
producers, and with such a class there is little concern here.
[14] MS. Census Enumeration, Cooper County, 1850, Schedule no. 2.
[15] Ibid.

and 140 acres of unimproved land, 14 work animals, 32 head
of cattle, 80 sheep, 50 swine, 1000 bushels of corn, and 200
each of wheat and oats.[16]   These examples give an idea of
the external economic conditions of the slave society in a
rich river county.

If the old French Mississippi River county of St. Genevieve in eastern Missouri is examined, some large holders
are found there.   In 1860 John Coffman was the chief
slave-owner, having 78 negroes living in fourteen cabins.
Joseph Coffman, the second largest holder, had 32, and the
third, Hiram Blaclege, possessed 27 slaves who were domiciled in eight cabins.[17]   Although the tax levies discount
slave property, nevertheless in many cases they are the only
means of obtaining information.   If the tax lists omit the
slave children and the wornout blacks, they but fail to include those who did not labor and who had little economic
significance save as a burden to the owner.   The probate
records would be an exact source of knowledge as to the
size of slave holdings, but as only those who died in slavery
days had their slaves listed in such records, an examination
must be made of the assessors' returns.[18]

In Boone County the heirs of R. King were assessed in
1860 with 57 slaves,[19] and W. C. Robinett with 50.[20]   In the
adjoining county of Howard William Swinney paid taxes
on 86 slaves valued at $44,800 and on 1369 acres of land.[21]
J. C. Carter of Pike County was assessed in 1859 with
43 slaves,[22] and Andrew Ashbaugh with 37.[23]   In 1856
Dugan Frouts of Buchanan County was listed as having 28

[16] MS. Census Enumeration, Cooper County, 1850, Schedule no. 2.
[17] MS. Census Enumeration, St. Genevieve County, 1860, Schedule no. 2.
[18] Thomas A. Smith of Saline County left in 1844 a large estate
in which were included 77 negroes (MS. Probate Records, Saline
County, Box no. 248, Inventory and Appraisement, filed November
11, 1844).
[19] The heirs of R. King (MS. Tax Book, Boone County, 1860,
p. 18).
[20] This was William C. Robinett (ibid., p. 118).
[21] MS. Tax Book, Howard County, 1856.   George Cason was
second with 52 negroes, and John R. White third with 46 (ibid.).
[22] MS. Tax Book, Pike County, 1859, p. 48.
[23] Ibid., p. 1.

negroes and 320 acres of land,[24] and J. C. Ingram as having
26 slaves and 160 acres.[25] The Clay County tax books
could not be found entire. However, figures for 1858 are
obtainable for the southwestern portion of the county, the
section just across the Missouri from Kansas City. Here
on the rich riverbottom John Daugherty was assessed with
33 negroes and 2420 acres of land,[26] and Michael Arthur
with 30 slaves and 1880½ acres.[27]

In southeast Missouri the records show that in Cape
Girardeau County the largest holders were assessed with 40
slaves in 1856.[28] In the southwest portion of the State, in
the rich county of Greene, Daniel D. Berry was taxed on
37 negroes worth $13,300, 23 horses and mules, and 4320
acres of land worth $33,760, and John Lair and Solomon C.
Neville on 24 slaves each, the former's valued at $16,200
and the latter's at $10,000.[29] In the northern counties of
Daviess and Macon the holdings were smaller. In 1854
Alfred Ray of Macon County was taxed on 31 slaves, and
the second largest holder, James W. Medley, on 13,[30] while
in Daviess County Milton N. Moore, the chief owner of
slaves, was assessed with but 16.[31]

The Reverend Frederick Starr ("Lynceus") says that
there were some plantations along the Missouri River having
from 150 to 400 slaves. From the above figures it appears
that a Missouri plantation with as many as 400 slaves must
have been extremely rare.[32] In fact, the average slave-
master had many less than the great holders mentioned in
the preceding paragraphs. For instance, in Cooper County
in 1850 of the 636 slaveholders 173 had but 1 negro each,

[24] MS. Tax Book, Buchanan County, 1856, p. 59.
[25] Ibid., p. 85.
[26] MS. Tax Book, Clay County, 1858, p. 17.
[27] Ibid., p. 2.
[28] MS. Tax Book, Cape Girardeau County, 1856. These were T.
H. and Lucy Walker.
[29] MS. Tax Book, Greene County, 1858. By 1860 Berry's slaves
on the tax book numbered 42 (MS. Tax Book, Greene County,
1860).
[30] MS. Assessors' List, Macon County, 1854, pp. 86, 63.
[31] MS. Tax Book, Daviess County, 1857, p. 29.
[32] Letters to the People in the Present Crisis [1853], Letter no.
I, p. 9.

and 102 possessed but 2. The average for the whole county
was 4.67 slaves to the master.[33] Just across the Missouri
in Boone County the average was almost the same—4.83 per
owner in 1860.[34] Journeying on west up the Missouri to
Jackson County a similar condition is met. Here in 1860
the average was 4.5 slaves to the master.[35] To the north of
Jackson in Buchanan County the average was considerably
less—3.6 in 1856,[36] which was a little higher than the average
sixteen years previously in the same county, when it
was 3.2.[37]

In looking eastward to the prosperous Mississippi River
county of Pike the average is found to be slightly less. In
this county in 1859 there were listed on the tax book 3733
slaves owned by 908 masters, or 4.18 negroes to the master.[38]
To the north of Pike in the extreme northeastern corner of
the State is Clark County. The 129 masters of this county
averaged 3.14 slaves each in 1860.[39] In the old French
county of St. Genevieve the average holding in 1860 was
5.16 negroes.[40]

---

[33] MS. Census Enumeration, Cooper County, 1850, Schedule no. 2.
The Reverend Mr. Starr, who in 1853 endeavored to prove that
slavery was declining in Missouri, divided the number of farms in
the State, as given by the Federal census of 1850, and found the
number of slaves per farm (Letter no. 1, pp. 9 10). But as even a
small truck farm, which naturally could not support slave hands,
was included in the government report, his results seem purpose-
less. It appears much more to the point to find the average of those
who really had slaves than to find how many each farmer would
have in case of an equal division—a condition impossible on its face.
Hinton R. Helper stated that there were 19,185 slaveholders in Missouri in 1850 (The Impending Crisis, p. 146). From the averages
given above in this study the 114,931 slaves of the State were owned
by about 24,000 masters. This is merely a rough estimate.
[34] MS. Tax Book, Boone County, 1860, gives 4354 slaves and 902
owners.
[35] MS. Tax Book, Jackson County, 1860: 3316 slaves and 736
owners.
[36] MS. Tax Book, Buchanan County, 1856: 1534 slaves and 425
owners.
[37] MS. Tax Book, Buchanan County, 1840: 177 slaves and 55
owners.
[38] MS. Tax Book, Pike County, 1859: 3733 slaves and 908 owners.
[39] History of Lewis, Clark, Knox and Scotland Counties (St.
Louis and Chicago, 1889), p. 305: 405 slaves and 129 owners.
[40] MS. Census Enumeration, St. Genevieve County, 1860, Schedule
no. 2: 615 slaves and 119 owners.

Many of these masters actually held only one or two negroes each. In 1860 Jackson township, St. Genevieve County, contained 32 slaves owned by 10 persons. Of these 10 owners there were three who had but one slave, 2 had 2 negroes, 2 owned 3, 2 had 6, and another 7.[41] In this year there were 497 masters paying taxes on 1383 slaves in St. Louis city. Of these owners 217 were taxed on 1 negro each and 104 on 2 negroes. In other words, 321 of the 497 slaveholders of the city returned less than 3 negroes.[42] In Greene County in 1858 there were 567 slaves in the district about Springfield. These were owned by 108 persons, of whom 38 held 1 slave each and 31 held 2, 69 of the 108 masters having less than 3 slaves.[43] A similar situation is found in the newer county of Audrain in the earlier period, where in 1837 there were 26 masters and 68 taxable slaves. Of these 26 owners 13 were assessed with 1 slave and 8 with 2 each.[44]

From the figures given it appears that Missouri was a State of small slaveholdings. How these slaves were employed will next claim our attention.

The single slave held by so many persons was usually a cook or a personal servant, or perhaps a "boy" for all-round work. Often a slave man and his wife were owned. The probate records are filled with the appraisements of estates holding one or two slaves.[45] Captain Joseph A. Wilson of

---

[41] MS. Census Enumeration, St. Genevieve County, 1860, Schedule no. 2.

[42] MS. Tax Book, St. Louis City, 1860, six vols. It is interesting to learn that among these St. Louis slaveholders of 1860 were Frank Blair, who was taxed on 1 negro (ibid., Book A to B, p. 115); Senator Trusten Polk, on 2 (ibid., Book P to S, p. 44); Mrs. U. S. Grant, on 3 (ibid., Book G to K, p. 59), and the St. Louis University, which held 6 taxable slaves (ibid., Book P to S, p. 220).

[43] MS. Tax Book, Greene County, 1858. At this time Greene County was much larger than at present.

[44] MS. Tax Book, Audrain County, 1837. This return lacks the taxpayers whose initials were A and B, but this would not necessarily change the proportion. James E. Fenton was taxed on 17 of the 68 slaves then on the list.

[45] An interesting example of this holding of a single servant is found in the appraisement of the estate of Louise Ann Pippin, whose personal property was composed of six trunks containing clothing

Lexington declared that every decent Missouri family had at least one slave, and usually from two to four, as house servants. So many of the antebellum settlers of the State being from the border and Southern States, the idea of white servants was not congenial, even had there been a supply of them. Many slaves, as in other southern communities, were nurses and acted as maids to the female members of the family. " Slavery in western Missouri," wrote a contemporary, " was like slavery in northern Kentucky—much more a domestic than a commercial institution. Family servants constituted the bulk of ownership, and few families owned more than one family of blacks. The social habits were those of the farm and not of the plantation. The white owner, with his sons, labored in the same fields with the negroes both old and young. The mistress guided the industries in the house in both colors."[46]

The fifteen hundred slaves of St. Louis seem to have been quite largely employed as domestics, though as the city grew the German and the Irish immigrant assumed this work. When Anthony Trollope visited St. Louis in 1862, the Civil War and the coming of the alien had nearly driven the household slave from the city.[47] The further discussion of the slave as a domestic is not necessary, as this function of the negro is a commonplace.

The slave was early put to work at clearing the land, much of which was timbered. Advertisements for such negroes are to be found in the papers of the early period.[48]

---

appraised at $75, and " 1 negro Boy Philbert aged 18 Years," valued at $550 (MS. Probate Records, St. Louis, Estate no. 2653, filed August 14, 1849).

[46] J. G. Haskell, " The Passing of Slavery in Western Missouri," in Transactions of the Kansas State Historical Society, vol. vii, p. 31.

[47] North America, p. 381. He writes: " Slaves are not generally employed in St. Louis for domestic service . . . St. Louis has none of the aspects of a slave city." When Maximilian, Prince of Wied, visited St. Louis in 1832–34, he found that " the greater part of the workmen in the port, and all the servants of St. Louis, are negroes . . . who in the State of Missouri are all slaves" (" Travels in the Interior of North America," in R. G. Thwaites, Early Western Travels, vol. xxii, p. 216).

[48] " Wanted, To hire . . . an industrious negro man who is a good hand at choping with an axe" (Missouri Herald [Jackson], Septem-

The rivers were the great highways for both passenger and freight traffic till the forties and fifties brought the railroads, and they quite largely retained the freight traffic till after slavery days. The boating business being very lucrative, the hire of surplus slave labor for cabin and deck work was very common. As early as 1816 Pierre Chouteau bought a slave who was "a working hand on a keel boat."[49] A traveller descending the Mississippi in 1858 stated that the crew and stokers on the boats were all slaves.[50] A Kansas immigrant who ascended the Missouri in 1857 observed that the deck hands were colored,[51] while another contemporary states that the Missouri River boats usually had a cabin crew of about twenty, "generally colored."[52]

This use of blacks on the rivers caused race feeling. An old boatman says that there were not enough free negroes, and consequently slaves were used as cabin crews. Therefore the custom developed that whites would not permit negroes to touch the freight. This division of the races seems evident from the following advertisement of 1854: "Wanted to hire by the Year, Ten negro boys, from 15 to 20 years of age—suitable for cabin boys. Also fifteen negro men for firemen, on a steamboat. Smith and Watkins."[53] According to an old boatman, these colored river

---

ber 4, 1819). In the Missouri Intelligencer and Boone's Lick Advertiser (Franklin) of November 25, 1823, is read, "A Negro Woman, Healthy and Masculine, who can turn out 100 rails per day. May be hired."

[49] Lagrange v. Chouteau, 2 Mo., 19.

[50] C. Mackay, Life and Liberty in America, p. 151.

[51] A. D. Richardson, Beyond the Mississippi River, p. 285. In the St. Joseph Commercial Cycle of May 11, 1855, there is found an expense account of a steamer running between St. Louis and St. Joseph. In this table are listed twelve "boys" at $25 each per month. As this term was applied to negro men and as the above accounts state that the cabin crews were generally colored, it seems probable that negroes were here meant. "Uncle" John Dill of Cape Girardeau claims that good river hands brought as high as $45 per month, as a trusted boat hand was considered very valuable. He stated that he knew of masters who gave their negroes a silver watch or a bill after a cruise on the river.

[52] G. B. Merrick, Old Times on the Upper Mississippi [1854–1863], p. 64.

[53] Republican (St. Louis), February 7, 1854. There is found the

hands received from twenty to thirty dollars a month and keep.[54] The employment of free blacks and slaves on the river caused a strong protest on the part of a St. Louis editor in 1841. He asserted that the practice enabled abolitionists to communicate with the slaves of the State, and made them discontented. He spoke of the crews as " the profligate reckless band of slaves and free negroes . . . habitually employed as stewards, firemen, and crews on our steamboats."[55]

A considerable number of slaves seem to have been worked in the Missouri and Illinois lead mines.[56] In 1719 Renault brought a few to work the Fort Chartres and later the Missouri lead deposits. Some were seen working at Potosi as miners by Schoolcraft in 1819.[57] Later travellers, however, do not mention slaves working the mines of that region. Missouri slaves hired to work the saline deposits of the Illinois country provoked much litigation and a careful interpretation of the Ordinance of 1787.[58]

The slave also did general work about town and city as the negroes do today.[59] The chief interest here, however,

following advertisement in the Daily Missourian (St. Louis) of May 7, 1845: "For hire—a woman chambermaid in the city or on the river . . . I. B. Burbbayge."
  [54] Mr. Hunter B. Jenkins of St. Louis.
  [55] Daily Evening Gazette (St. Louis), August 18, 1841.
  [56] American State Papers, Public Lands, vol. iv, p. 800.
  [57] H. R. Schoolcraft, A View of the Lead Mines of Missouri, pp. 15, 40.
  [58] See below, pp. 216–217.
  [59] Schoolcraft also states that "there are a considerable number [of slaves] at present [1819] nearly every good plantation, and many mines being wrought by them." He also states that many slaves served as blacksmiths and carpenters. "It has led to a state of society which is calculated to require their assistance" (pp. 40, 176). Slaves were also used as draymen, according to a traffic regulating ordinance of St. Louis of June 13, 1835, sec. 12 (Missouri Argus [St. Louis], June 19, 1835). This use of slaves caused some trouble (Mayor, etc., of St. Louis v. Hempstead, 4 Mo., 242). Slaves were also licensed as hucksters, hawkers, and so on (St. Louis Ordinances, 1836, p. 145). In the Jeffersonian Republican (Jefferson City) of January 16, 1835, there is the notice of an escaped slave who had worked in "Massey's Iron Works" near Jefferson City. The tobacco firm of Spear and Swinney of Fayette employed slaves. They were assessed with 34 negroes in 1856 (MS. Tax Book, Howard County, 1856).

lies in the agricultural slave. Whether or not free labor could have been obtained to work the fields of Missouri is a question about which contemporaries still living are not agreed. From their statements it is evident that the supply of free labor varied in the different parts of the State,[60] but the fact remains that slave labor really did the larger part of the work of the State.

Missouri was a State with a great variety of topography and soils, and a number of products were raised in great abundance.[61] The majority of Missouri bondmen were employed as general field hands. Statements of men who lived in various parts of the State convey the idea that the plantation with its overseer, "task system," and great negro gangs was not common. Except in hemp culture, where the task system prevailed, the Missouri rural negro is to be considered a general farm hand as he is today. A prominent Kansan who viewed slavery as it existed in western

[60] Among some two dozen contemporaries living in the great slave counties opinion as to the availability of free labor was varied. Most of those questioned claimed that free white labor was scarce. Colonel D. C. Allen of Liberty said that abolition agitation kept white labor from the State. Colonel R. B. C. Wilson of Platte City stated that there was no free labor in Platte County. Captain J. A. Wilson of Lexington declared that free black labor was considered a menace, and that white labor was scarce in Lafayette County. Colonel James A. Gordon of Marshall said that free labor was usually obtainable in Saline County. "Uncle" Henry Napper, who was a slave in the same county, remembers that his master hired some free labor at harvest and other heavy seasons. "Lynceus" (Reverend Frederick Starr), who endeavored to prove that slavery was dying in the State, declared (1853) that the price of slaves was high because there was so little white labor (Letter no. i, p. 6). James Aull of Lexington, who was a prominent trader of western Missouri, wrote to a correspondent in Philadelphia on June 15, 1835: "We are the owners of slaves, in this State as well as in other slave holding states you must either have slaves for servants or yourself and family do your own work" (to Siter, Price and Company. In the collection of Messrs. E. U. Hopkins and J. Chamberlain of Lexington).

[61] For the year ending June, 1850, Missouri produced 2,981,652 bu. of wheat; 44,268 bu. rye; 36,214,537 bu. corn; 5,278,079 bu. oats; 17,113,784 lbs. tobacco; 1,627,164 lbs. wool; 939,006 bu. Irish and 335,505 bu. sweet potatoes; 23,641 bu. buckwheat; 116,925 tons hay; 15,968 tons hemp; 527,160 lbs. flax, and so forth. The State also contained 225,319 horses; 41,667 asses and mules; 230,169 milch cows; 112,168 oxen; 449,173 other cattle; 762,511 sheep; 1,702,625 swine (Seventh Federal Census, p. lxxxii).

Missouri states that the slave was an all-round laborer, there being no classification of "domestic servants" and "field hands."[62]

The severity of the slave's labor will be treated in a later chapter of this study, but the nature of his work, especially in the hemp country, deserves attention in this connection. Hemp was the great Missouri staple, although its culture was mostly restricted to the Missouri River counties. Other products were raised in greater abundance, but in some regions hemp was the chief crop. "From the first settlement of the county," wrote a citizen of Platte County, "hemp was the staple product. We became wealthy by its culture. No soil on earth, whether timber or prairie, is better adapted to hemp than Platte County. . . . But no machinery ever invented superseded the hand-break in cleaning it. . . . Negroes were, therefore, in demand, and stout men sold readily for $1,200 to $1,400."[63] As a hemp State Missouri was second only to Kentucky, and the quality of her hemp was said by J. C. Breckinridge to be even superior to that of his own State.[64] American hemp passed through many vicissitudes because of the tariff, and often met the competition of better hemp from Russia. The market

[62] Haskell, p. 31.
[63] W. M. Paxton, Annals of Platte County, p. 37. In 1854 Judge Leonard of Buchanan County raised 1426 lbs. per acre on a ten-acre field. It was a virgin crop, however (St. Joseph Commercial Cycle, May 18, 1855).
[64] B. Moore, A Study of the Past, the Present, and the Possibilities of the Hemp Industry in Kentucky, p. 60, quoting from a letter of Breckinridge's of January 10, 1854, to C. J. Sanders. In 1860 the great Missouri hemp counties were: Saline 3920 tons; Lafayette 3547 tons; Platte 1783 tons; Pike 1608 tons; Buchanan 1479 tons; the whole State 19,267 tons. Some of this was water-rotted, but most of it was dew-rotted. Gentry County produced 600 tons of water-rotted hemp but no dew-rotted (Eighth Federal Census, Agriculture, pp. 90–94). In 1850 Missouri was credited with 4 "hemp dressers," 48 ropemakers, and 191 rope-making establishments, each turning out over $500 worth of material a year (Seventh Federal Census, Statistics, p. 674). In 1850 the great hemp counties were: Platte 4345 tons; Lafayette 2462 tons; Buchanan 1894 tons; Saline 1559 tons; Clay 1274 tons; the whole State 15,968 tons, of which 60 tons were water-rotted (ibid., pp. 679–680).

finally dropped about 1870 when the South substituted iron hoops for hemp rope in baling cotton.[65]

The healthy western Missouri negro must have been a profitable investment as a hemp cutter and breaker if the slave was a paying investment anywhere. " I can remember how twenty or thirty negroes would work in line cutting hemp with sickles. It was then left to rot till January. Then it was broken and the pith removed by means of a heavy crusher which the slave swung up and down. He often received the lash if not breaking his one hundred pounds. I have seen a long line of wagons loaded with hemp extending from the river nearly to the court house." Thus a citizen of Lexington describes the hemp culture in Lafayette County.[66]   " The farmers of Missouri seldom

[65] Thomas S. Forman of Louisville wrote in 1844: " The price of hemp, bagging and bale rope has declined almost in ratio of their increased production; thus in 1835 with a crop of 7,000 or 8,000 tons in all the western States, it was $10.00 to $12.00 per hundred weight. . . . Since then, under the stimulating influence of the tariff of 1842, the products are four or five times the amount they were in 1835, and the price is $3.00 per hundred weight. . . . These prices do not remunerate the grower or manufacturer" (Moore, Hemp Culture in Kentucky, pp. 53–54). The poorer American dew-rotted hemp had to compete with the superior Russian water-rotted, which was said to exceed the former by at least ten or fifteen pounds per hundred weight (ibid., p. 55). The loss of the cotton crop during the Civil War injured the demand for hemp bagging and rope. " Formerly, when bagging and rope were worth more per pound than cotton, they were considered one of the expenses of cotton shipping; now that cotton was twenty-five cents a pound, the bagging and rope were only six or seven cents a pound, rope and bagging were not spared, since they weighed in with the cotton bale. It was for the sake of the spinner rather than the cotton grower, that iron ties were substituted for hemp rope during the years around 1870. The inability of Kentucky to supply bagging enough created competition of jute bagging, which, during the early seventies, almost completely disabled hemp bagging " (ibid., pp. 62–63).

[66] Statement of Captain Joseph A. Wilson. In 1855 one S. A. Clemens of St. Louis invented a hempbreaker which was propelled by steam or by horsepower. The hemp stocks could be used for fuel. It was said to have a capacity of breaking a ton in ten hours, and if the hemp was very fine, a ton and a half. Three men could run it (St. Joseph Commercial Cycle, May 18, 1855). W. B. Napton states that " John Lock Hardeman, about 1850 . . . invented a hemp breaking machine, which lessened the labor to a considerable extent, and about the year 1854 an attachment had been added to the McCormick reaper by which hemp was cut by machinery also " (Past and Present in Saline County, p. 132). Mr. Napton claims to write from

stack hemp," runs a letter of the slavery regime. "They suffer it to receive enough rain, after cutting, to color it. It is then taken up and shocked without binding. About the middle of October it is spread out to rot. Our winters are so dry that the hemp must receive several rains before it is shocked."[67]

It was the task of the slave to break one hundred pounds of hemp a day, receiving one cent per pound for all broken in excess of that amount. Many slaves broke from a hundred and seventy-five to two hundred, some as many as three hundred pounds a day. The work seems to have been heavy, but the possibility of making a dollar or more a day made it popular with the ambitious slaves.[68] Hemp became the staple in western Missouri to such an extent that, according to the statement of an old negro, his master could find no market for his wheat.[69] Hemp was even

personal experience. On the other hand, Mr. Paxton asserts that no machine that was ever invented superseded the handbreaking of hemp by the slave. The work was so very arduous that after the War the freed negro would not engage in it (p. 37).

[67] Paxton, p. 81, quoting a letter of unknown date from an unknown person.

[68] Mr. Dean D. Duggins of Marshall stated that their old Jim could break 300 pounds a day at one dollar per hundred over the task, and that Jim had quite a sum of money when the War opened. "Uncle" Henry Napper of Marshall, a wiry little negro, formerly owned by Mr. Duggins's family, said that he could not break over 175 pounds, but that many broke 200, and some 300 pounds. "Uncle" Eph Sanders of Platte City claims that he could break 200 pounds. Captain J. A. Wilson of Lexington stated that many slaves made a dollar a day and were paid in silver at Christmas, the negroes keeping accounts on notched sticks and the owner or overseer in his books. Mr. Hunter B. Jenkins knew slaves in Lafayette County who made from seventy-five cents to a dollar a day breaking hemp. "Uncle" Peter Clay of Liberty said that he broke 165 pounds in a day, and that he would as soon break hemp as do any other hard work, while Henry Napper said that it was very hard labor. Dr. John Doy says that while he was a prisoner in the Platte City jail a young negro owned by one William Rywaters, living near Camden Point, told him that "both men and women had a task given them, the latter to break one hundred pounds of hemp a day and the former still more, and received a lash for every pound they fell short" (J. Doy, Narrative of John Doy of Lawrence, Kansas, p. 60). But Doy had both a political and a private grudge against slaveowners, and consequently gathered all the hard tales about them he could find.

[69] Statement of Henry Napper of Marshall.

used as a medium of commerce in some cases, like tobacco in old Virginia.[70]

The other staple crops of Missouri were tobacco and cotton. The culture of the latter was restricted to the southern part of the State. Tobacco was raised to a greater or less degree throughout the eastern and central regions. As today, many farmers raised tobacco, not as a staple, but as they did corn or wheat.[71] " In the tobacco regions of the State," says a prominent citizen of Pike County, " there was no task system for the slaves. They were expected, and in many instances required, to do a reasonable day's work."[72]

The slave seems to have been a very slight factor in the cotton culture of the State. The cotton counties ranked as follows in 1860: Stoddard, Shannon, Dunklin, Dallas, Jasper, and Barry.[73] Their slave population was very small,—Stoddard 189, Shannon 6, Dunklin 152, Dallas 88, Jasper 317, and Barry 217.[74] Contemporaries remember few or no slaves in the cotton fields and no task system. As in the tobacco culture, the few slaves employed worked as general field hands.[75] Outside of the hemp fields the task system was seldom practiced in the State. A negress who was a slave in Madison and St. Francis Counties claims that

[70] The following notice is found in the Weston Platte Argus of December 19, 1856: "All persons indepted to us . . . are hereby requested to come forward and settle, with Cash, Hemp or give approved security . . . Belt, Coleman & Co."
[71] In 1860 Missouri ranked seventh in tobacco culture, producing 25,086,196 lbs. The great tobacco counties were: Chariton 4,356,024 lbs.; Howard 2,871,584 lbs.; Randolph 1,918,715 lbs.; Callaway 1,433,374 lbs.; Macon 1,396,673 lbs.; Lincoln 1,356,105 lbs.; Monroe 1,325,386 lbs.; Pike 1,194,715 lbs. (Eighth Federal Census, Agriculture, pp. xliv, 88–94).
[72] Statement of Ex-Lieutenant-Governor R. A. Campbell of Bowling Green.
[73] Missouri was credited with no tobacco in 1850. In 1860 the State raised 44,188 bales of 400 lbs. each. Stoddard County produced 19,100 bales, Shannon 10,877, Dunklin 7000, Dallas 1200, Jasper 972, and Barry 500 (Eighth Federal Census, Agriculture, pp. 90–94).
[74] Eighth Federal Census, Population, p. 280.
[75] Several old settlers of the cotton counties were questioned, but all denied that a task system existed in the cotton fields or that any number of slaves were employed in them.

she had to weave four yards a day and fill the quills. The spinning of eight "cuts" (one hundred and fifty threads to the "cut") was a day's work. Often she wove or spun till dark after working all day in the fields. She worked neither Saturday afternoons nor Sundays.[76]

The Missouri law forbade a master to work his slaves on Sunday, except in regular housework or labor for charity. Field work was thus forbidden on Sunday. The penalty for the master was one dollar for each negro so employed.[77] This law was enforced in some instances at least, as on February 28, 1853, the Boone County circuit court fined R. R. Rollins five dollars "for working slaves on Sunday."[78]

As there were few great plantations in the State, the systematic but brutal overseer—that grewsome evil genius of so many slave tales—was not often seen in Missouri. Widows who needed a farm manager at times employed an overseer, and some tobacco and hemp farmers had white managers. Usually a trusted slave, called a "driver," or one of the sons laid out the work for the slaves, so that the hired white overseer managing great gangs of negroes was not a characteristic Missouri figure. Contemporaries are nearly unanimous on this point.[79]

---

[76] Mrs. Anice (or Alice) Washington of St. Louis.
[77] Law of July 4, 1825 (Revised Laws, 1825, vol. i, p. 310, sec. 90).
[78] MS. Records, Boone County Circuit Court, Book F, p. 190.
[79] Ex-Lieutenant-Governor R. A. Campbell of Pike County stated that some widows and a few tobacco farmers of the county had overseers, but that general farming was the rule in most of the county. Mr. J. H. Sallee of Mexico, formerly of Marion County, remembers no overseers or task system in that county. Mr. John W. Beatty of Mexico said that the overseer and the task system were seldom seen in Audrain County, Robert St. Clair having the only overseer he remembers. Mr. Robert B. Price of Columbia stated that there were no overseers in the southern sense in Boone or neighboring counties. Mr. George Carson remembers a few over- seers in Howard and adjacent counties. Captain J. A. Wilson of Lexington said that there were a few overseers in Lafayette County, some farmers with over twenty negroes hiring one, but that usually a son or a negro "driver" managed the hands. The latter was often more severe than a white overseer. Colonel D. C. Allen of Liberty said that there were some white overseers in Clay County. Mr. E. W. Strode of Independence stated that he knew of very few

Without the overseer and the horror of drudgery in pestilent rice and sugar swamps, the despair of the slave could not have been so great as in the far South. As the negroes of Missouri today work about the town or the farm, so they must have labored in slavery days, except that more of them worked than now and the hours of labor were longer. The great slave counties of antebellum days are the great negro counties of today, save where urban attractions have caused the negroes to flock to the cities.

Many slave-owners naturally had more of such labor than they could utilize. Negroes inherited by professional men and other townsmen often had little work except as household servants. The excess hands were therefore hired to those needing their services.[80] These slave-masters retained their slaves either because they thought the investment was paying, or in order to preserve the family dignity, which was largely based on slave property. Widows were unable to alienate their slaves if there were other heirs, and consequently hired them out as a means of income. The slaves of orphans and of estates in probate were annually hired

---

overseers in Jackson County, as a negro foreman usually managed the slaves. Mr. George F. Shaw of Independence, formerly of Franklin County, said that there were few overseers in the latter county, as general farming was the rule. Mr. Dorsey D. Berry and Mr. Martin J. Hubble of Springfield stated that the overseer was not seen in Greene County.

Overseers were at times advertised for, as may be learned from the Daily Missourian of November 16, 1845: "Wanted—an overseer with a wife to go on a farm. . . . I. B. Burbbayge." The Seventh Federal Census states that there were 64 "overseers" in Missouri in 1850 (p. 674). In 1860 there were 256 of them in the State (Eighth Federal Census, Population, p. 303). This term seems to have been applied to the familiar negro overseer, as of the 37,830 in the United States 32,458 were accredited to the slave States (ibid., pp. 670–671). On the other hand, Pennsylvania is given 1241 of these "overseers" (ibid., p. 440), and Massachusetts 1098 (ibid., p. 228). From this it appears that the term in some cases must have been applied to ordinary foremen or managers.

[80] One Alexander Stuart offered to hire out nineteen slaves, which were doubtless excess hands as he at the same time advertised for an overseer, and so could hardly have been giving up farming (The Missourian [St. Charles], December 31, 1821).

out by the court, bond being necessary " for the amount
of hire."[81]

As the State developed, the hire of the slave advanced in
price approximately in proportion to the increasing value of
slave property. Excepting in the earlier part of this
period,[82] negroes seem to have been hired almost entirely by
the year, without reference to the busy planting and harvest
seasons or to the slack months when their possession must
have been a burden. Some were even hired for terms of
years.[83] This well illustrates the weakness of the entire
slavery system. In addition to the cash paid by the hirer,
he also furnished the slave with medical attention, food, and
a customary amount of clothing. An old slave claims that
the hired slave of western Missouri usually received two
pairs of trousers, two shirts, and a hat the first summer, a

---

[81] Law of January 23, 1829 (Session Laws of Missouri, 1828, ch. i,
sec. 1). The slaves of estates in probate or of minor orphans were
to be hired to the highest bidder once each year at the court house
door where the administrator or guardian resided, unless the court
otherwise directed. The former was to give twenty days' notice of
such hiring of slaves at the court house and at two other places in
the county. No private hiring of slaves belonging to such estates
or such minors was allowed, the penalty being five hundred dollars.
An example of one of these published notices is found in the Farmers' and Mechanics' Advocate (St. Louis) of February 20, 1834:
" By order of the Court there will be hired to the highest bidder, for
the term of one year, at the court house door in the City of St.
Louis, on the first day of March next, Two Negro Men, belonging
to the estate of William C. Fugate, deceased. Bond and approved
security will be required for the payment of the hire and rede-
livery of said negroes. Isaac J. Price, Admr." But slaves were privately hired as the law provided. The probate court of Saline
County on February 5, 1860, "ordered that McDowell, Poage and
Maupin as administrators of the Estate of Samuel M. McDowell,
deceased, hire publically or privately the slaves belonging to said
Estate" (MS. Probate Records, Saline County, Book G [1859-66],
p. 111).

[82] The following advertisements show that in the early days slaves
were at times hired by the month: " Wanted, To hire, by the month
an industrious negro man" (Missouri Herald, September 4, 1819);
"A NEGRO WOMAN . . . may be hired at $6 per month" (Mis-
souri Intelligencer, November 25, 1823). R. H. Williams, en route
from Virginia to Kansas in 1855, hired his three slaves in St. Louis
by the week (With the Border Ruffians, p. 64).

[83] The following advertisement is found in the St. Louis Enquirer
of May 24, 1820: " FOR SALE, Four negroes for the term of four
years each, from the 1st of August next. . . . Also two others for
2 years each. . . . W. Brown."

coat and a pair of trousers in the winter, and two pairs of
trousers the second summer.[84]

The yearly hiring price of the slave was of course dependent on the nature of the work and on the character,
sex, age, and individual strength of the negro.[85] The rate
steadily increased till the Civil War. A number of figures
were obtained by the author from old Missouri masters and
slaves which are very similar to those obtained from the
county records and other sources.[86] The market rate for

[84] " Uncle " Peter Clay of Liberty. He adds that the slave was
clever enough to go to his new employer in his worst rags in order
to get the full quota of clothing.

[85] The hirer often demanded good references as to the slave.
This form of advertisement is frequently found: "WANTED TO
HIRE, A healthy, sober, and industrious Negro Woman . . . one
that can be well recommended" (Jeffersonian Republican, May 28,
1836).

[86] Mr. Hunter B. Jenkins of St. Louis, formerly of Lexington,
said: " Many slaves received from $15 to $20 per month and board
and clothing as farm hands, and from $20 to $30 as roustabouts on
the river." Major G. W. Lankford of Marshall stated that most
slaves hired for from $150 to $250 as hemp hands, many bringing
$200. " Good livery-stable hands brought from $200 to $250," said
Captain J. A. Wilson of Lexington. " Mechanics received more. I
knew a good carpenter whose master received $250 for his hire."
Peter Clay of Liberty stated that his master hired him out as a
general field hand at $175 per year. " Aunt " Melinda Sanders of
Platte City said: " I was hired out by my mistress, a widow woman,
for one dollar a week and had to keep house for a family of seven.
I was fed very badly." Professor Peter H. Clark, formerly of the
Colored High School of St. Louis, said he knew of slaves who paid
their masters several hundred dollars for the master's share of the
yearly hire. General Haskell of Kansas says that he knew a trusty
negro who returned to his Missouri master with $150 in gold as the
latter's share of his earnings, and that this was an " exceptional but
not an isolated case " (p. 32). The Reverend William G. Eliot in
an article of unknown date wrote that in St. Louis "prime male
house servants received $150 per year and females $75 per year and
in the country slave labor appeared equally unprofitable, $100 on an
average being received by the owner for the hire of his best field
hands," while free labor could be had for $10 per month and no
clothing (C. C. Eliot, William Greenleaf Eliot, p. 142). In the History of Lewis, Clark, Knox, and Scotland Counties it is stated that
in northeast Missouri a good man hired for about $250 a year with
specified clothes, food, and so on. "In case of sickness his owner
usually took care of him and paid the doctor's bills " (p. 630). In
many cases, however, the hirer paid the bills in case the slave was
sick, unless the illness was more or less permanent. Mr. William
M. Paxton, the historian of Platte County, now in his ninety-sixth
year (1913), was interviewed by the author at his home in Platte

slave hire is difficult to discover for a certain period because
of the individual differences in the negroes. However, two
papers found in the probate records of St. Louis show the
ratio between the hiring price and the value in the year
1838.[87] The slaves were all men but one. Their ages,
value, and annual hire were as follows:—

Name	Age	Value	Year's Hire
Solomon	22	$800	$119
Antoine	25	800	96
John	23	600	90
Bill	16	600	87
Henry	35	300	47
Edd	12	350	45
Frank	14	350	45
Lucy	10	300	15

For the closing years of the slavery period when negroes
were considered gilt-edged property there are the following
comparisons of the value and the hiring price in the rich
river county of Boone. In 1858 a body of slaves were
valued and hired as follows by the probate court of that
county:—[88]

Name	Value	Year's Hire
Men—Charles	$1200	$194.00
Jack	1200	190.00
Sam	1100	176.00
Stephen	1200	150.00
Bob	1000	132.50
Joe	1000	120.00
Fil	800	105.00
Elijah	800	101.00
Ben	600	22.00
Women—Palma	$ 900	$ 83.00
Lizzy	300	52.00
Ann, and child	500	46.00
Amy, and child	1000	41.00

City on August 1, 1912. In describing the hemp culture he stated
that he remembered that $200 was frequently paid as the annual hire
of a good hemp-breaking negro.

[87] These figures are taken from papers of the Estate of Thomas
Withington. The ages and values are given in the Bill of Appraisement, filed June 14, 1838, p. 12. The hiring price is found in the Bill
of Sale, pp. 14–15 (MS. Probate Records, St. Louis, Estate no. 1374).

[88] MS. Probate Records, Boone County, Inventories, Appraisements, and Sales, Book B, pp. 87–89. Appraisement filed December
30, and Sale Bill December 31, 1858.

Name	Value	Year's Hire
Mary, and child	1100	35.00
Nancy	500	18.00
Alsey	550	16.00
Milly	500	10.00
Lucy, and Servis, her husband.	10	.50

From the above figures it will be seen that in the case of the men the rate was between one seventh and one eighth of the valuation, or about fourteen per cent. The hire of the women averaged only about one sixteenth of the value. This difference was caused largely by the fact that in three cases the children were taken with the mothers; these, unless they were fairly large, would be an expense to the hirer and would demand some of the mother's time. Roughly, the hiring price was in proportion to the valuation. Fourteen per cent hardly seems an excessive rate for a developing country famous for its fertility when we consider that the owner must subtract taxes, wear and tear, risk of escape, and permanent injury if received through no fault of the hirer. He had also to figure on the deterioration in value and the approaching old age of the slave, whom he must support when past working.[89]

In Saline County a slave named Cooper was hired for $231 in 1857, the following year for $200, and again in 1859 for $190.[90] Cooper was a valuable negro and Saline a rich county.[91] For the above three years Cooper's hire

---

[89] The owner's risk by disease is well illustrated by the following letter: "Sister . . . desires me to say that Dr. Johnson was to see the Negro Woman Elinzra & pronounces her not worth a Cent as she is deformed & diseased in several ways & thinks it will in all probability terminate in Consumption" (MS. J. L. Talbot to S. P. Sublette, dated St. Louis, October 1, 1854, Sublette Papers). The present writer looked into the question of the insurance of slave property. Several of the oldest insurance men of St. Louis remembered nothing of the kind. Mr. Martin J. Hubble of Springfield, who well remembers slavery days and who has long been in the insurance business, said, "No, slaves were never insured." But the contract quoted on page 221 of this study implies that it might have been done at times.

[90] Estate of Jas. D. Garnett, MS. Probate Records, Saline County, Inventories, Appraisements, and Sales, Book 1, p. 606, filed April 5, 1860.

[91] Major G. W. Lankford of Marshall stated that Cooper was a valuable negro.

averaged $207, or $17.25 per month. In comparison with this figure, it is found that in the adjoining river county of Cooper the average monthly wage of a white farm hand with board was $10 in 1849–50,[92] and in St. Genevieve the average was $12 a month in 1859–60.[93] Even admitting that the above-named slave lived in a very wealthy county, his hire seems liberal, especially so when it is remembered that in addition he was fed, clothed, and given medical attention. Except for the ever-threatening danger of escape, the western Missouri slaveholder must have had a good investment in the ownership of a slave like Cooper from his fifteenth to his fiftieth year, yet the cost of his raising must have been heavy. The risk of absconding, injury, and future decrepitude of a slave were stalking menaces which the easy-going slaveholder could not escape but apparently did not always consider.

The hiring price of female slaves has been referred to in the preceding pages. It was considerably less than that of the men because their labor was less productive. The loss of time resulting from the birth and rearing of children was also an item which was not overlooked. The German traveller, Graf Adelbert Baudissin, claims that in the early fifties a negress was worth from $500 to $700 and was hired for from $40 to $60.[94] In some cases a high price was paid for a negress who was competent. Just before the Civil War a former citizen of Franklin County hired a negress as cook and housekeeper for $150.[95]

---

[92] MS. Census Enumeration, Cooper County, 1850, Schedule no. 6.
[93] MS. Census Enumeration, St. Genevieve County, 1860, Schedule no. 6.
[94] Der Anziedler in Missouri Staat, p. 56. His book was published in 1854. A woman was hired in 1834 for $42 (Blanton v. Knox, 3 Mo., 241), and one in 1839 for $40 (MS. Probate Records, St. Louis, Estate of John W. Reel, Estate no. 1359, paper filed March 11, 1840). As late as August, 1863, a negress was hired in Lafayette County for $40 (MS. Probate Records, Lafayette County, Estate of Jas. H. Crooks, Inventories, Book D, filed August 3, 1863). From the context it appears that in case the slave escaped during the turmoil of the War the time was to be deducted.
[95] Mr. George F. Shaw of Independence, formerly of Franklin County.

A contract for slave hire was protected on both sides by the law. If a slave was hired for a year and died within that time, the hirer was bound for payment only to the time of the slave's death.[96] If the hirer caused the slave's death by his cruelty, he was responsible to the owner for the value of the negro and was subject to criminal prosecution as well.[97] Should a slave, hired without the owner's consent, be killed while so employed, though by no act of the employer, the latter was responsible.[98] It was held as early as 1827 that "the law is that if the . . . covenanter disable himself by his own act [in injuring a hired slave] to perform his covenant . . . this shall not excuse his own performance " to pay for the hire of the slave.[99] The sickness of a hired slave might cause trouble. One case was found in which the hirer attempted to return the negro to the owner before the contract had expired.[100]

The hirer was bound to take reasonable care that the slave did not escape. He was honestly to endeavor to recapture a fugitive whom he had hired.[101] Because of the precarious position of Missouri's slave property the owner took considerable risk in hiring his negro as a hand on a Mississippi River boat.[102] Concerning such a case the supreme court in 1847 instructed a jury as follows: " The jury is authorized

[96] Dudgeon v. Teas, 9 Mo., 867. A statement of this case as it appeared before the Warren County circuit court can be found in the Jefferson Inquirer (Jefferson City) of October 2, 1845. The supreme court confirmed the lower decision.

[97] Adams v. Childers, 10 Mo., 778.

[98] Garneau v. Herthel, 15 Mo., 191.

[99] Mann v. Trabue, 1 Mo., 508.

[100] On April 4, 1853, Theodore La Beaume wrote Solomon J. Sublette: " Your boy George that I hired last January at the Courthouse, I believe has strong Symptoms of Consumption and if not taken from hard work will not last long. . . . So says the Doctor, as long as he is exposed. I am willing to give him up, and I think that it will be to your advantage as well as his to have him under your immediate charge " (MS. Sublette Papers).

[101] Elliott v. Robb, 6 Mo., 323. This opinion was also followed in Perkins v. Reeds, Admr., 8 Mo., 33, and in Beardslee et al. v. Perry et al., 14 Mo., 88. In case a slave committed a crime while in the service of the hirer "the owner and not the temporary master of the slave . . . is the proper person to pay the costs of conviction" (Reed v. Circuit Court of Howard County, 6 Mo., 44).

[102] Merrick, p. 64.

to consider the peculiar circumstances of the country, the vicinity of the city of St. Louis . . . and Missouri to free States, the difficulties of retaining negroes in slavery, the age, character, sagacity, color and general appearance of the negro. . . . Where a slave is hired as a boathand, we must presume that the owner is fully aware, that every facility for escape is afforded by the very nature of the service. . . . Does the owner expect, that in case his slave escapes, whilst the boat is . . . putting off freight . . . the captain and crew will relinquish the boat, or abandon the trip for the purpose of hunting up the slave?"[103]

There were apparently many careless masters and numerous wandering slaves in the State at times, despite the laws passed to prevent the practice mentioned above. The Code of 1804 provided that an owner should be fined thirty dollars for allowing his slave to go about as a free man and hire himself out. If a negro was permitted to so hire his own time, he could be sold by the sheriff at the next term of court, after being advertised at the court-house for twenty days.[104] The Code of 1835 fined an owner from twenty to one hundred dollars for hiring a slave to another slave or suffering him to go at large and hire himself out.[105]

Cases occurred where persons were fined for violating this law. In 1860 one R. Schooling was fined twenty dollars in Boone County for "hiring a slave his time."[106] The following entry appears in the circuit court records of St. Louis for 1832: "Sam a Negro Man Slave who is in the custody of the sheriff on charge of having hired himself out contrary to the statute in such cases made and provided, being now brought before the court . . . it is ordered by the court that therefore said slave Sam be discharged from custody on the charge aforesaid and that the court do further order that Smith the person in whose service he

---

[103] Perry and Van Houten v. Beardsley and Wife, 10 Mo., 568.
[104] Territorial Laws of Missouri, vol. i, ch. 3, secs. 18, 19.
[105] Revised Laws, 1835, p. 581, art. i, sec. 7; reenacted February 15, 1841 (Session Laws, 1840, p. 146, sec. 1).
[106] The State v. R. Schooling, MS. Records, Boone County Circuit Court, Book H, p. 169.

now is do pay the costs of this proceeding and those incurred in consequence of his arrest and imprisonment."[107]

From an early date this law seems to have been hard to enforce. The press and the public continually complained of its non-enforcement to the detriment of the negro and the danger of the community.[108]   A St. Louis editorial of 1824, after quoting the law, explains the real or supposed seriousness of this custom as follows: " The reasons for this enactment are obvious: and the reasons resulting from the neglect to enforce it are already severely felt. Slaves hiring their own time of their masters, as is the case in numerous instances, take upon themselves at once the airs of freemen and often resort to very illicit modes to meet their monthly payments. . . . They become unsteady and vicious, and corrupt their associates, and perhaps at length resort to theft as an easier mode of paying their masters. This practice, is in fact, one principal source of the irregularity and crimes of slaves in this place."[109]

At a mass-meeting of St. Louis citizens, held October 31, 1835, there were drawn up a series of resolutions which show the magnitude of the problem as contemporaries viewed it. " Resolved, That no slave should be suffered to live or dwell in this city or county at any place other than the same lot or parcel of ground on which his owner . . . shall reside. . . . Resolved, That this meeting view the practice of slaveholders hiring their slaves their time, one of the greatest evils that can be inflicted on a community in a slave State." The committee on abolition was given power to see that the practice was stopped.[110]   A Columbia

---

[107] MS. Records, St. Louis Circuit Court, vol. 6, p. 301.

[108] Governor Dunklin in his message to the General Assembly of November 8, 1834, said: " I lay before you a presentation of a grand jury in the County of St. Louis. So much of it as relates to free negroes; . . . and slaves hiring their time of their owners, is entitled to your consideration " (Senate Journal [Journals of the General Assembly of Missouri, House and Senate Journals], 8th Ass., 1st Sess., p. 20). Perhaps this advice resulted in the above provisions in the Code of 1835.

[109] Republican, July 19, 1824.

[110] Daily Evening Herald and Commercial Advertiser (St. Louis), November 3, 1835, resolutions no. 10, 18, 19.

editor in 1856 complained that the law covering this point was "frequently violated." Its enforcement was demanded.[111]

It is quite evident that the Missouri slave-master indulged his bondman in many ways. It would have been a hardship to the negro to have hired him at a distance from his family. The hirer often allowed him to return to his owner's plantation at night, but if working at some distance the slave was able to return home only over Sunday.[112] A traveller states that a slave was often given a horse on which to visit his family and in some cases his prospective wife.[113] These favors could but have made the lot of the slave easier and his contentment and faithfulness more assured.

No question concerning slavery is more difficult to handle than the value of slave property. The selling price of individual negroes and of lots of them can be found in the county records and in the newspapers, but to generalize on these figures for any one period or to compare values in different periods would be most misleading. For example, if a male slave twenty years of age sold for $500 in 1820 and another of the same age sold for $1400 in 1860, little is learned. The first negro may have been less healthy, less tractable, and less intelligent than the other. There fore the difference of $900 could not represent the general rise in prices or the increased value of slave labor. To illustrate this point concretely, two slaves were sold in Ray County in 1854; both were twenty-six years of age, yet one brought $1295 and the other $670.[114] This shows how unsafe it is to compare specific sales.

On the other hand, by comparing the prices brought by bodies of negroes about the same age and in the same

[111] Weekly Missouri State Journal (Columbia), February 7, 1856. The charter of Carondelet of 1851 empowered the city council "to impose fines, penalties and forfeitures on the owners and masters of slaves suffered to go at large or to act or deal as free persons" (pamphlet, art. v, sec. 21).
[112] Statement of Mr. Hunter B. Jenkins of St. Louis.
[113] Baudissin, p. 56.
[114] Notice of the sale of the slaves of the estate of Thomas Reeves (Richmond Weekly Mirror, January 5, 1855).

locality an approximately sound conclusion is reached. In
general it can be said that there was a gradual rise in slave
values up to the Civil War. It was exceptional indeed when
a negro brought over $500 before 1830.[115] A prime male
servant from eighteen to thirty-five years of age was in
this early period worth from $450 to $500, and a woman
about a fourth less.[116] When Auguste Chouteau's negroes
were appraised in 1829, the eleven men among them who
were between the ages of sixteen and thirty-five averaged
$486.35 each, the highest being valued at $500 and the
lowest at $300. The eleven women between the ages of
sixteen and thirty-nine averaged $316.35, the highest valua-
tion being $350 and the lowest $130.[117]

From the third decade of the century on there is an increase in value. Men brought considerably more by the late
thirties. In 1838 prime hands were bringing from $600 to

---

[115] The following representative examples of slave values of the
territorial period are found in the St. Louis probate records. In the
will of the Widow Quénel of March, 1805, four slaves are listed
and valued as follows: two women at 376 and 641 "piastres" respectively; Sophie, aged 13, at 900 piastres, Alexander, aged 5, at
300, and a cow at 10 piastres. If the latter was a normal animal,
some idea may be had of the comparative value of the negroes (MS.
Probate Records, Estate no. 7). Joseph Robidoux's estate was probated in August, 1810. His slaves were listed as follows: Felecite
with child at breast, 300 piastres, her daughter 8 years old, 150, a
girl of 6, 125, and "Une autre petite Negrette" 100 (ibid., Estate
no. 59). In 1817 the following values were attached to slaves in
Cape Girardeau County: two men, $900, woman and two children,
$800, woman and child, $550, woman, $350, and five men, $2700 (MS.
Probate Records, Cape Girardeau County, Appraisement of the Estate of Elijah Betty, filed June 2, 1817, Estate no. 628). H. R.
Schoolcraft, writing in 1820 or 1821, stated that a good slave sold
for $600 in Missouri (Travels in the Central Portion of the Missis-
sippi Valley, p. 232).
[116] In 1830 the following values were given in St. Louis: Charles,
aged 32, $450; Anthony, aged 30, $400; Antrim, aged 24, $450; Allen,
aged 24, $500 (Estate of John C. Sullivan, MS. Probate Records, St.
Louis, Estate no. 882, Appraisement filed October 9, 1830). The
appraisement values correspond very closely with the amounts received at the sales; in some cases slaves sold for more than the
appraisal value and in others for less. In Pike County in 1835
a negress aged 22 years and her three children aged 4 years, 3 years,
and 3 months respectively, sold for $650 (MS. receipt of sale, dated
May 2, 1835, Dougherty Papers).
[117] MS. Copy of Appraisement, dated May 11, 1829, in the Missouri Historical Society.

$900 in St. Louis.[118]   Up to 1840 female slaves were worth from $300 to $350 when men were bringing from $500 to $600.   Children from two to five years of age were sold for from $100 to $200.   In St. Louis, Thomas Withington's slave children were appraised as follows in 1838: Frank, aged 14, $350; Lucy, aged 10, $300; Sophia, aged 5, $200; Charlotte, aged 3, $100; Harriet and Jane, aged 2, $75 and $100 respectively.[119]   In the same year W. H. Ashley's women and children were valued as follows: Berril (boy), aged 12, $350; Celia, aged 9, $250; Lucy, aged 9, $250; Catherine, aged 7, $200; and Betsy, aged 30, and her infant son, $500.[120]   The above are representative prices for the forties.   At Marshall, Thomas Smith's women and children were valued as follows in 1844: Harriet, aged 32, $300; Patsy, aged 22, $350; Wilson, aged 8, $200; Lizzy, aged 3, $125; Betty, aged 2, $150; Emiline, aged 1, $75, and Leah, aged ten months, $75.[121]

The golden age of slave values is the fifties.   The prime male slave of Missouri in 1860 was worth about $1300 and the negresses about $1000.   The fabled $2000 negro is found more often in story than in record.   "Uncle" Eph Sanders of Platte City, still a very intelligent and powerful negro, claims that his master refused $2000 for him in 1859 when he was twenty-three.[122]   Contemporaries, however, place the normal limit at about $1500.   Mr. Paxton says that stout hemp-breaking negroes "sold readily for from $1200

---

[118] The estate of Thomas Withington received $800 each for two men, aged 22 and 25, and $600 each for one 23 and one 16 (MS. Probate Records, St. Louis, Estate no. 1374, Bill of Sale dated June 14, 1838).   This same year a man of 21 brought $650, and one 35 sold for $900 (ibid., Estate of W. H. Ashley, Estate no. 1377, Inventory and Appraisement, filed June 20, 1838).   In 1844 in Saline County good hands sold at about the same figures.   Thomas A. Smith's blacks were valued as follows: $500 each for three men, $550 each for two others, and one for $600 (MS. Probate Records, Saline County, Box no. 248, Inventory and Appraisement filed November 11, 1844).
[119] MS. Probate Records, St. Louis, Estate no. 1374.
[120] Ibid., no. 1377.
[121] MS. Probate Records, Saline County, Box no. 248.
[122] Mr. Hunter B. Jenkins of St. Louis claims that in the late fifties a good sound black brought from $1500 to $2000.

to $1400" in the heyday of Platte County hemp culture.[123]
Dr. John Doy asserts that one sold in Weston in the late
fifties for $1800.[124]

Although the above figures may be exceptional, there is
plenty of evidence that negroes were very valuable in these
years. In 1854 the slaves of Thomas Reeves were sold in
Richmond for fine prices. The ages and prices of these
negroes were as follows:—[125]

Sex	Age	Value
Man	23	$1440
Man	26	1295
Man	23	1245
Man	40	1115
Man	31	911
Man	33	904
Man	26	670
Man	58	115
Boy	13	851
Boy	14	825
Boy	11	795
Boy	13	775
Woman	49	510
Girl	12	942

---

[123] P. 37. G. B. Merrick says that while he was on the Mississippi
as a boatman in the late fifties, a male slave sold for from $800 to
$1500 (p. 64). At the Lexington Pro-Slavery Convention of 1855
President James Shannon of the State University declared that the
average Missouri slave was worth $600, and that field hands " will
now readily sell for $1,200 " (Proceedings of the Convention, p. 7).
[124] P. 59.
[125] Richmond Weekly Mirror, January 5, 1855. One thousand to
$1200 seems to have been the common figure for good men in the
late fifties. In 1858 in Boone County four men were valued at $1200
each, one at $1100, and another at $1000. Two women were rated
at $900 each (MS. Probate Records, Boone County, Inventories,
Appraisements, and Sales, Book B, pp. 87–88, filed December 30,
1858). The following year in Greene County two men were valued
at $1100 each (MS. Probate Records, Greene County, Inventories and
Appraisements, Book A, p. 31, Estate of Jonathan Carthel, filed
August 4, 1859). In 1860 in the same county a man was rated at
$1200 (ibid., p. 160, Estate of Jacob Rodenkamer, filed May 18, 1860).
The same year a woman was sold for $1190, and two men for $1150
and $1260 respectively (ibid., p. 202, Estate of James Boaldin, Sale
Bill not dated). In Henry County in 1860 a man aged 29 was valued
at $1250, a girl of 12 at $1000, one of 15 at the same figure, a girl
of 9 and two boys of 7 at $800 each. A boy 5 years old was valued
at $600 (MS. Probate Records, Henry County, Inventories, Appraise-
ments, and Sales, p. 126, Estate of A. Embry, filed September 26,
1860).

In the same issue of the Richmond Weekly Mirror which published the above items there is an account of the disposal of the negroes of Charity Creason, which were sold on January 1, 1855. They brought the following prices: a man aged 23, $1439; another aged 38, $1031; a woman aged 26 and her 18-months child, $1102.50; a girl of 3, $400, and a woman of 59, $1.

During the middle and late fifties all classes of negroes were priced high. In 1856 a lot of children was sold as follows: a boy of nine for $550, one of seven for $500, and another of five for $300.[126] A Saline County inventory of 1859 shows what good prices negroes in general were commanding in the closing years of the slavery regime:—[127]

Name	Age	Value
Henry	17	$1300
Daniel	36	1200
George	13	950
Stephen	8	650
Addison	8	550
Thomas	5	440
Ellen	20	1300
Mary, 21, and child of 14 mos.		1250
Susan	15	1150
Eliza	17	1050
Francis	10	800
Minerva	12	800
Marie, 35, and son, 18 mos.		775
Delia	46	500
Marie	7	625
Julia	4	400
a girl	6 mos.	50

Top prices are found in Boone County, where in 1860

126 Estate of Benjamin Moberly (MS. Probate Records, Saline County, Appraisements, and Sales, 1855–61, vol. i, pp. 118–119, filed January 26, 1856). At Hannibal on April 15, 1855, a girl of 9 sold for $450, and a boy of 4 for $321 (Weekly Pilot [St. Louis], April 21, 1855).

127 Estate of H. Eustace (MS. Probate Records, Saline County, Appraisements, and Sales, 1855–61, vol. i, pp. 602–603, filed April 4, 1859). In this same year two men (age not given) were appraised in Saline County at $1300 each, and another at $1100. A mother and child were together valued at $1100 (ibid., Estate of Samuel M. McDonald, Box no. 169, Inventory filed November 20, 1859). In these records there are many similar valuations.

George W. Gordon's blacks received the following valuations:—[128]

Name	Age	Value
Lou	25	$1500
Horace	30	1500
Charles	34	1600
Roger	36	1500

It appears from the foregoing pages that the highest official value placed upon a negro man was $1600, and upon a woman $1300. A difficulty in finding the exact price of slave women is that the small children are often included with them.

When the Civil War opened and escapes became more numerous, the values of slave property began to decline. Compared with the above figures there is the following appraisement of the estate of Lawson Calvin of Saline County, filed July 11, 1861, after the War had engulfed the State in a torrent of strife:—[129]

Name	Age	Value
Lewis	18	$800
George	12	600
Narcissa	16	600
Lewis	47	500
Henry	7	300
Mag	40	275

Nevertheless, it is surprising to note how slave values persisted during the Civil War. The prices kept fairly high, as the probate records of Lafayette, Missouri's greatest slave county, bear witness. Two men were actually appraised at $1100 and $800 respectively, and a woman at $1000, in November, 1861.[180] In January, 1862, one woman was in-

[128] MS. Probate Records, Boone County, Inventories, Appraisements, and Sales, Book B, p. 287, filed December 25, 1860). In 1859 William W. Hudson's negro named Beverley, aged 29, was valued at $1500, three other men at $1200 each, and four men at $1000 each (ibid., p. 170, filed September 12, 1859).
[129] MS. Probate Records, Saline County, Inventories, and Appraisements, 1855–61, vol. i, p. 677. The appraisement of the estate of Elizabeth Huff of July 7, 1861, bears similar testimony to the effect of the War on slave property (ibid.).
[180] The Estate of Colonel John Brown, Appraisement filed November 18, 1861 (MS. Probate Records, Lafayette County, Inventories, Appraisements, and Sales, vol. ii, p. 24).

ventoried at $650 and another at $550, and a boy of seventeen at $650, while one of eleven was rated at $500.[131] By
the last of July, 1863, the price had further decreased, but
although Gettysburg had been fought and Missouri was
overrun by bushwhackers, values did not fall as much as
one conversant with conditions in the border States might
expect. In the above month two women aged twenty-three
and sixteen were appraised at $300 each, and a boy of eigh-
teen at $400.[132] Slave property was not merely appraised
this late. On June 3, 1863, the negroes of Samuel F. Taylor
of Lafayette County were actually sold as follows: Amanda,
$380; Milky (girl), $370; Jack, $305; Georgetta, $300;
William, $250; Eunis, $200; and Sam, $200.[133] There was
an appraisal of an estate in Lafayette County made on
October 2, 1863, but the slaves were not assigned value.[134]
Over a month later, on November 5, 1863, negroes were still
appraised, but this is the last official valuation of slave
property in Lafayette County records. On that date a
"boy" named Charles was appraised at $300 and a girl of
fourteen at $200.[135]

The total value of slave property is of course very difficult to estimate. Contemporaries were far from agreeing
on this point. For instance, in 1854 John Hogan of the
Republican, in an article which was intended to boom St.
Louis and Missouri, placed the average value at $300.[136]
In contrast with this low estimate, the "Address to the
People of the United States," prepared by a committee of
the Lexington Pro-Slavery Convention of 1855, valued the
50,000 slaves of western Missouri at $25,000,000, or $500

[131] Estate of John D. Bailey, Inventory filed January 2, 1862 (ibid.,
p. 18).
[132] Estate of Randell Latamer, Appraisement filed July (?), 1863
(ibid., p. 261).
[133] Estate of Samuel F. Taylor, Bill of Sale filed June 6, 1863
(MS. Probate Records, Lafayette County, Inventories and Sale Bills,
Book D, p. 69). Several slaves appraised in the early part of this
year are found in these records. The values show a gradual decline.
[134] Estate of Western Woollard (MS. Probate Records, Lafayette
County, Inventories, Appraisements, and Sales, vol. ii, p. 267).
[135] Estate of F. U. Talliferro (ibid., p. 262).
[136] Thoughts about the City of St. Louis . . . pamphlet, p. 65.

each.[137]   Governor Jackson in his inaugural address of January 3, 1861, estimated the 114,931 slaves of the State to be worth $100,000,000.[138] Of course the governor was speaking in general terms, but his average would be nearly $700 a slave.

The above figures are in excess of those given by the county assessors of the period. Tax values are usually considered lower than market values. The Jackson County tax average for 1860 was $438.05 per slave,[139] and that of Boone County $372.30.[140] The average in Pike County in 1859 was $434.78.[141] In 1856 in Buchanan County it was $450.92,[142] and that of the 170 slaves of its county seat, St. Joseph, was $434.70.[143] Evidently the assessors of the various counties had no uniform standard in rating negroes, but despite the fact that the figures vary they show at least that slave property was increasing in price. In 1828 the 239 slaves of Lafayette County were taxed at an average of $249.68.[144] This is at least a third less than the average rate in the counties above mentioned in the years around 1860. At the same time, in comparing these values the decreasing purchasing power of money should be taken into consideration.

A very bitter experience which the slave might at any time be forced to undergo was his removal to a strange region far from his wife or children or old associations.

---

[137] Proceedings of the Convention, p. 3, or in the Weekly Missouri Sentinel (Columbia), October 5, 1855. This address was signed by W. B. Napton, Governor Sterling Price, and others.
[138] Pamphlet, p. 7.
[139] MS. Tax Book, Jackson County, 1860: 3316 slaves, tax value $1,452,591.
[140] MS. Tax Book, Boone County, 1860: 4354 slaves, tax value $1,721,000.
[141] MS. Tax Book, Pike County, 1859: 3733 slaves, tax value $1,623,085.
[142] MS. Tax Book, Buchanan County, 1856: 1534 slaves, tax value $691,825.
[143] M. H. Nash, city registrar, valued the 170 slaves of the town at $73,900 (St. Joseph Commercial Cycle, September 7, 1855).
[144] The History of Lafayette County (St. Louis, 1881), p. 306. The total valuation was $59,665, as copied by the author of the above work from the tax book.

This disruption of the negro family was entirely dependant upon the humanity of the individual owner. The sale of the slave to be taken south was known in Missouri as in the other border States, but the Missourians deny that it was ever practised save where financial reverses, an excess of hands, or a chronic spirit of viciousness or of absconding on the part of the slave made it necessary.[145]   Whether to mollify the new antislavery party which developed during the Compromise struggle, or whether through pure conviction, the constitution of 1820 provided that the legislature might pass laws to prohibit the introduction of slaves into the State as "an article of commerce."[146]   The provision was not taken seriously, and the General Assembly never acted upon the suggestion.

The slave-trader is generally pictured as the brutal, conscienceless, evil genius of the slavery system, detested even by those with whom he dealt. In Missouri he held no very enviable position.   "Slavetraders and whiskey-sellers were equally hated by many," wrote one antislavery clergyman of St. Louis,[147] while another maintained that "large fortunes were made by the trade; and some of those who made them were held as fit associates for the best men on 'change'."[148] Dr. John Doy, the Kansas abolitionist, who had a personal grievance against the Missouri slaveholder, claimed that General Dorris, whom he described as a brutal dealer, was highly respected and "belonged to the aristocracy of Platte county."[149]   Some of the slaveholders who were interviewed

---

[145] "I never heard of any Missourian who consciously raised slaves for the southern market. I feel sure it was never done," said Ex-Lieutenant-Governor R. A. Campbell of Bowling Green. Mr. Robert B. Price of Columbia denied that slaves were consciously bred for the southern market. Mr. J. W. Beatty of Mexico stated that there was a general feeling that the sale of negroes south was not right. Letters from old residents and slaveholders in all parts of the State deny that in Missouri, at least, slave breeding was ever engaged in as the antislavery people so often charged. The better classes at any rate frowned upon the practice.

[146] Art. iii, sec. 26.

[147] G. Anderson, The Story of a Border City During the Civil War, p. 171.

[148] W. G. Eliot, The Story of Archer Alexander, p. 100.

[149] P. 59.

declared that the slave-trader and the saloon-keeper were tolerated as necessary evils, but that they were personally loathed and socially ostracised. Others, however, stated that it was a question of the individual trader, some being liked and some disliked.[150]

If the slave-trader was a hard man and detested, he at least had the satisfaction of knowing that the wisest and gentlest of men would be hated by many if plying his trade. The very nature of the business made it contemptible. If the Missouri system was as patriarchal and the tie between master and man as close as one is led to believe they were, the dealer who higgled and bargained even for the most unruly servant must have been disliked. This feeling would naturally be enhanced if financial reverses compelled the sale of family slaves.[151]

---

[150] Captain J. A. Wilson of Lexington declared that slave-traders were considered worse than saloon-keepers, many of them about Lafayette County being gamblers. Mr. R. B. Price of Columbia stated that they were considered a questionable class in Boone County. Messrs. J. H. Sallee and J. W. Beatty of Mexico said that like any other class of people some were respected and some were detested. James Aull of Lexington, a prominent merchant and slaveholder, wrote in 1835: "A traffic in slaves we never could consent to embark in. No hope of gain could induce us to do it . . . we entirely and forever abandon the least share in the purchase of Negroes for Sale again" (MS. Aull to Siter, Price and Company of Philadelphia, June 15, Aull Papers).

[151] Many dealers were undoubtedly brutal men. An escaped Missouri slave later wrote that he was once hired to a dealer named Walker who collected Missouri slaves for the Gulf markets. This Walker forced a beautiful mulatto slave into concubinage, and years after sold her and his four children by her into slavery before marrying a white woman (W. B. Brown, Narrative of William B. Brown, A Fugitive Slave, p. 47). Once while on a negro buying expedition Walker was annoyed by the continual wailing of an infant in the gang. He seized it from the mother and ran into a wayside house with the child hanging by one leg. Despite the shrieks of the mother he gave it to a woman who thankfully received it. The gang then marched on to St. Louis (ibid., p. 49). John Doy says that while a prisoner in Platte City he met many brutal dealers. He thus describes a slave gang: "At midnight Gen. Dorris, his son and assistants came to the jail and ordered the slaves to get ready to leave. As it was quite cold a pair of sox were drawn over the fists and wrists of the men, in place of mittens, they were then hand cuffed together in pairs and driven into the street, where they were formed in marching order behind the wagons containing the women and children—some of the former tied with rope when considered unruly" (p. 64).

In addition to the vicious, the runaway, and the slave of
the financially depressed owner, there was a surplus from the
natural increase, and consequently a considerable amount of
business in the local exchange of negroes existed.   Besides
this there was the itinerant buyer for the southern markets.
The smaller towns seem to have been regularly visited, while
the larger centers had permanent dealers.   There were two
such in Lexington in 1861, but they are said to have had
difficulty in getting sufficiently large gangs to make the business pay.[152]   There was at least one permanent firm of
dealers in St. Joseph in 1856.[153]   John Doy asserts that
while he was imprisoned in St. Joseph many negroes were
shipped from there to Bernard Lynch, Corbin Thompson,
and other large St. Louis buyers.[154]   Columbia and Marshall
were regularly visited, and Platte City had quite a thriving
trade.[155]   John R. White of Howard County was a wealthy
planter of good repute who dealt in slaves.   He lived on a
farm of 1053 acres and was taxed with 46 negroes in
1856.[156]   The slave-trader, like the stock dealer, undoubtedly
plied his trade wherever he could obtain his commodity.

---

[152] Captain J. A. Wilson has a map of Lexington executed by
Joseph C. Jennings in 1861. It also contains a business directory in
which are given two slave-traders, A. Alexander at the City Hotel,
and R. J. White at the Laurel Hotel. The latter, Captain Wilson
remembers, had a three-story building which he used as a slave pen,
but found it difficult to collect many negroes.

[153] Wright and Carter, who were "located permanently at the
Empire on Second Street" (St. Joseph Commercial Cycle, August
15, 1856).

[154] P. 98.

[155] Mr. R. B. Price remembers that dealers came regularly to Columbia. "Uncle" Henry Napper said that buyers came regularly
to Marshall and picked up unruly slaves and those of hard-up masters. John Doy wrote: "During our imprisonment [in Platte City
in the late fifties] numbers of slaves were lodged in the jail by
different traders, who were making up gangs to take or send to the
south. Every slave when brought in, was ordered to strip naked,
and was minutely examined for marks, which with the condition of
the teeth and other details, were carefully noted by the trader in his
memorandum-book. Many facts connected with these examinations
were too disgusting to mention" (p. 59). J. G. Haskell states that
unless unruly the slave had little danger of being sold to a distant
market; "the oldest inhabitant remembers no such thing as a market
auction block in western Missouri" (p. 31).

[156] MS. Tax Book, Howard County, 1856. Mr. George Carson of
Fayette gave the above description of White's character.

St. Louis became a considerable center for shipping gangs down the Mississippi. One Reuben Bartlett openly advertised for negroes for the "Memphis and Louisiana Markets."[157] St. Louis was "fast becoming a slave market," wrote the Reverend W. G. Eliot, an antislavery clergyman, "and the supply was increasing with the demand. Often have I seen gangs of negroes handcuffed together, two and two, going through the open street like dumb cattle, on the way to the steamboat for the South. Large fortunes were made by the trade."[158] "I had to prepare the old slaves for the market," stated William Brown, a slave who worked for a trader on a boat from St. Louis south on the Mississippi; "I was ordered to have the old men's whiskers shaved off, and the grey hairs plucked out where they were not too numerous, in which case he [the trader] had a preparation of blacking to color it, and with a blacking brush we put it on. . . . These slaves were then taught how old they were . . . after going through the blacking process they looked fifteen years younger."[159] In one issue of the Republican three firms, perhaps to imply great prosperity or to outdo one another, advertised for five hundred, one thousand, and twenty-five hundred slaves respectively.[160]

The St. Louis Directory of 1859 lists two "Slave Dealers" among the classified businesses. These were Bernard M. Lynch, 100 Locust Street, and Corbin Thompson, 3 South Sixth Street.[161] The former may be taken as a

157 Republican, April 23, 1852.
158 W. G. Eliot, p. 100.
159 P. 43. Brown claims that "Missouri, though a comparatively new state is [1847] very much engaged in raising slaves to supply the southern market" (p. 81). On the other hand, the antislavery clergyman, Frederick Starr, said in 1853: "It is true that our papers are defiled by the advertisements of slave-traders, but they are few. Our Court-house witnesses the sale [of slaves] . . . and yet, this is emphatically a free city . . . most of the sales are for debt, or to close estates in accordance with the statute law" (Letter no. i, p. 8).
160 Issue of January 7, 1854.
161 Published by L. and A. Carr, p. 131. In the directory of 1859, published by R. V. Kennedy and Company, this same list appears, but Lynch's address is given as 109 Locust Street (p. 615). In a letter to S. P. Sublette of January 19, 1853, Lynch gave his address as 104 Locust Street (MS. Sublette Papers).

type of the great Missouri slave-dealer, who had his corre-
spondents in the outlying parts of the State. His historic
slave-pen in St. Louis was afterward used as a military
prison.[162] Like other dealers, Lynch advertised his business
in the newspapers, and posted in his office the rates and the
conditions under which he handled negroes. This latter
broadside placard read as follows:—[163]

"RULES

No charge less than one Dollar
All Negroes entrusted to my care for sale or otherwise
must be at the Risk of the Owners,—
A charge of 37½ cents will be made per Day for board of
negroes & 2½ per cent on all Sales of Slaves,—
My usual care will be taken to avoid escape, or, accidents,
but will not be made Responsible should they occur,—
I only promise to give the same protection to other negroes
that I do to my own, I bar all pretexts to want of diligence,
These must be the acknowledged terms of all Negroes found
in my care, as they will not be received on any other—
As these Rules will be placed in my Office, so ' That all can
see that will see.' The pretence of ignorance shall not be a
plea.

1st January 1858   B. M. LYNCH
                                          No. 100 Locust St."

Lynch could not have been the terror-inspiring ogre that
the slave-dealer is usually pictured to be. On two different
occasions slaves ran for refuge to his door.[104] Statistics of
his business are also uncertain, for he was evidently clever
enough to empty his " pen " on tax assessment day. In 1852

---

[162] An account of this building can be found in the Encyclopedia
of Missouri History, vol. iii, p. 1333. There was also a slave-pen
at Broadway and Clark Streets (J. L. Foy, " Slavery and Emancipation in Missouri," in ibid., vol. iv, p. 2079). Another was located
at Fifth and Myrtle Streets (Anderson, p. 184). Lucy Delaney
states that her mother was sold at an " auction-room on Main
Street" (From the Darkness Cometh the Light, p. 22). Father D.
S. Phelan of St. Louis remembers seeing slaves sold at the block on
the northeast corner of Fifth and Elm Streets.
[163] Photo-facsimile copy in the Missouri Historical Society.
[164] On December 16, 1852, Lynch wrote Solomon P. Sublette,
" Your negro woman Sarah came to the gate for admittance, she is
here and will be held subject to your order, Very Respectfully B. M.
Lynch " (MS. Sublette Papers). On January 19, 1853, Lynch wrote
Sublette, " Your Negro woman with child rang about 4 oclock this
morning for admittance and will be retained subject to your order "
(ibid.).

Lynch was taxed on three slaves,[165] on the same number in 1857,[166] and on four in 1860.[167]

The slave-dealer had his own difficulties, and was perhaps a little prone to "horse-swapping" methods. His commodity at times fell back upon his hands. "I received your letter yesterday," runs a note from John S. Bishop to S. P. Sublette in 1854, "in reference to the negro Girl I sold you. I will be on my way South by the last of October . . . and will take the negro and pay you the money—Or if you should see my Bro. G. B. Bishop . . . he perhaps will pay you the money, and request him if he does to leave the girl at Mullhalls at the Stock Yards."[168]   In February, 1855, Bishop again wrote Sublette: "I received yours of Feb 8 & was rather surprised . . . times is hard & money scares. I would of taken her as I was going South but do not want her now in hard times as Negroes have fallen. I bought her above here & Paid $600 for her as a Sound Negro & a very good one & will have My recorse where I bought her so you will know how to pro sede according to law."[169]

In some respects the slave-trade was unique. In the earlier days of the State the negro was frequently used as a medium of exchange in the purchase of land.[170]   Some dealers bought both horses and slaves.[171]   Others handled

---

[165] MS. Tax Book, St. Louis City, 1852, Second District, p. 117.

[166] MS. Tax Book, St. Louis City, 1857, vol. ii, p. 96.

[167] MS. Tax Book, St. Louis City, 1860, Book L to O, p. 74.

[168] MS., dated Mexico, Missouri, September 26, 1854, Sublette Papers.

[169] MS., dated February 14, 1855, Sublette Papers. A guarantee of soundness for a slave sale reads as follows: "Franklin, County, Mo. March 1st, 1856. Received of Mr. Solomon P. Sublette Eight hundred and fifty dollars in full payment for a Negro Girl Eliza, aged seventeen years, the above described Negro girl I warrant sound in body and mind a Slave for life & free from all claims. . . . W. G. Nally" (ibid.).

[170] In the Farmers' and Mechanics' Advocate (St. Louis) of November 21, 1833, is an example of this. Such advertisements are common.

[171] Advertisement of George Buchanan in the Republican of March 19, 1849.

negroes, real estate, and loans.[172]   In some cases slaves
were taken on trial.[173]   Some dealers sold negroes on commission, boarding them till sold at the owner's risk and at
his expense.[174]

Many sorrows were undoubtedly borne by bereaved slave
families and much misery was suffered by negroes at the
hands of traders, but the master at times endeavored to
make his departing bondman comfortable.   In the Republican of January 7, 1854, may be read the following:
" For Sale; A good negro man, 32 years old, and not to be
taken from the city."   In the same issue a dealer offered
to find homes for negroes within the city or the State if
requested.   These provisions were either to prevent the
separation of slave families or to insure the master that his
negro would not be sold south.

The official negro auction block of St. Louis was the
eastern door of the court-house.[175]   Some of these sales,
especially when negresses were on the block, may have been
accompanied by obscene jibes and comment.   The fre-
quency of this is denied by contemporaries.   " I have often,"
said a citizen of Lexington, " heard the auctioneer cry, ' A
good sound wench, sixteen years old, good to cook, bake,
iron, and work.   Warranted a slave for life.'   Crowds
would flock to the court house to see the sight.   I never
heard or saw any indecency on such an occasion."[176]
William Brown stated that it was not uncommon in St.

---

[172] " I. B. Burbbayge, General Agent, and proprietor of the old
established Real Estate, Negro, Slave, Money Agency and Intelligence Office, Third Street between Chestnut and Market streets "
(Daily Missourian, May 1, 1845).

[173] This advertisement is found in the Richmond Weekly Mirror
of October 20, 1854: " Negro Woman for Sale. . . . She can be taken
on trial if preferred."

[174] See the advertisements of Blakey and McAfee (Republican,
March 6, 1849) ; of B. M. Lynch (Daily Union [St. Louis], February 6, 1849) ; of R. Bartlett (Republican, January 7, 1854), and
that of Wright and Carter (St. Joseph Commercial Cycle of August
15, 1856).

[175] Most of the notices of official slave sales state that the bidding
would take place at the east door of the court house.   Slaves were
also sold at the north door (see this study, ch. vi, note 5).

[176] Captain J. A. Wilson.

Louis to hear a negress on the block thus described: "How much is offered for this woman? She is a good cook, good washer, a good obedient servant. She has got religion!"[177] Nevertheless, the slave traffic at its best was perhaps the worst feature of the system. Unruly slaves were continually threatened with being "sold south" as a means of encouraging industry or of enforcing discipline. Families were actually separated and obedient slaves often sold into a life of misery "down the river," either because of callousness on the part of the owner or because financial straits demanded it.[178] Many sad incidents occurred at the block. Children were at times wrung from their parents. Professor Peter H. Clark of St. Louis remembers a house on the southwest corner of Morgan and Garrison Streets in which lived a woman who bought up infants from the mothers' arms at the slave-markets of St. Louis and raised them for profit.

On the other hand, a little good was inadvertently done by some dealers. The story of the finding of Wharton Blanton's slave-pen near Wright City, Warren County, is most interesting. Certain mounds in that vicinity, some two score in number, were supposed to mark the resting-place of the members of some ill-fated Spanish expedition, or of an Indian tribe. Investigation was started and the mounds were opened, but the bodies encountered were found to be those of negroes. Eventually it was learned that one

---

[177] P. 83.

[178] Lucy Delaney states that she was continually threatened with being sold south. Her father was sent south despite the will of his late master. Lucy herself escaped this fate by hiding with friends in St. Louis (pp. 14, 22). Undoubtedly the sale of slaves was discouraged by the better classes. The following letter is dated St Joseph, November 26, 1850: "I must Know tell you what I have done with Kitty, I found her two expensive and I sold here for one hundred and fifty dollars which money started me House Keeping it was through necesity I sold here" (MS. Wm. S. Hereford to S. P. Sublette, Sublette Papers). The separation of families was also decried. "I have a Negro Woman in St. Louis," runs a letter of November 1, 1848; "she should remain [in St. Louis] if she prefers it—She may have a child or children, if so, dispose of the whole family to the same person" (MS. Captain G. Morris to W. F. Darby, Darby Papers).

Blanton had bought up diseased negroes about St. Louis and taken them to Warren County for recuperation. Those who died on his hands were buried in this mysterious cemetery.[179]

The incidental and often exceptional results of the system were juicy morsels for the antislavery agitators. The public too often generalized on these exceptions, which were perhaps only too numerous, but were not the normal conditions of slavery in Missouri.

Missouri as a slave State differed from others in many respects. As it is today, the State was then a vast region of unlimited resources both in minerals and soils. It was not homogeneous, but displayed a great variety of interests, of products, and of industries. As a slave State it was a region of small farms, small slave holdings, and relatively few slaves. All these conditions make it most difficult to reach a conclusion as to the profit or loss of the slavery system.[180] It must always be borne in mind that some farmers are good managers and can get a profit from almost any soil with almost any kind of labor, while others fail under the greatest advantages. The statement of a slaveholder pro or con must always be considered in connection with the personal equation.

When the question is asked, "Was slave labor a paying proposition in Missouri?" one of three things may be in mind: Was slave labor in Missouri as good an investment as it was in Texas, Georgia, or some other slave State? Was slavery in Missouri as profitable as white labor in Ohio Iowa, or some other free State? Would free labor have

[179] This information was obtained by Mr. T. C. Wilson of Columbia, Missouri, who was one of the excavators of this cemetery. His knowledge of the traffic of Blanton was gained from old residents of the neighborhood. He also learned a great deal from Mr. Emil Pollien of Warrenton, Missouri, the present possessor of this property. According to Mr. Pollien's papers the land came into the possession of the Blanton family in 1829.

[180] When this study was begun the author hoped to arrive at a satisfactory conclusion as to the profitableness of slave labor in the State. The results have been disappointing.

brought greater returns to the Missouri farmer than did slave labor?

The first question is simply a comparison of slave labor under different conditions. It may well be doubted whether this could ever be answered. If the second is meant, it must be said that to come to any adequate conclusion the account books of hundreds of farmers of Iowa or Ohio ought to be compared with those of farmers of Missouri to find their profits and losses. There would have to be taken into consideration the differences in land values, interest rates, market prices, labor rates, cost of raising slaves and of clothing them, losses by escape, accident, and deterioration, and a mass of other facts. To begin with, few if any farmers ever kept such accounts, hence it is not difficult to see that the question is insolvable, or at least that any conclusion would be unconvincing to both friend and foe of the slavery system.

Likewise, if the questioner has in mind the comparative profits of slave and white labor on the same soil, the data are equally unresponsive. As already stated in another part of this chapter, white labor was not to be had in some counties and was scarce in all. To say that the farmer of Lafayette or Pike County was a poor manager in employing slave labor is unreasonable. Through tradition, through habit, through necessity, he used slave labor.

A large number of old slaveholders were asked the question, "Do you think that slavery paid in Missouri?" Four fifths of them replied in the negative. They were then asked a second: "*At the time* did Missouri slaveowners think that free labor would have been better for the State?" A large majority answered that some perhaps thought slavery was an economic burden, but that most of them were well satisfied with conditions as they were. After the Civil War the advantages of free labor were realized, but not in slavery days.

A prominent Missouri historian declared that "relatively, slavery declined in Missouri from 1830 onward to emancipation."[181] As was seen in the early pages of this chapter, the whites increased much faster than the slaves in the State as a whole, but this is not valid proof that slavery was actually declining or that it did not pay. Enormous sections of the State were unfit for slave labor. These districts invited the westward moving settlers, because the land was cheap and because white labor shunned the slave portions of the State. Because the whites increased faster in the State as a whole is not proof that slave labor did not remunerate the farmer of Saline or of Marion County.

Little information of value is gained from the local literature of the time. Most of it is political and therefore written for a purpose. The proslavery element denied emphatically that slavery was anything but a blessing, whether viewed from a financial, a social, or a religious point of view. "The slave population of the State of Missouri has grown rapidly in the last ten years," exclaimed Senator Green in the United States Senate in 1858, "and it is retained because it is profitable."[182] Even Frank Blair, Missouri's most forcible antislavery agitator, declared in 1855 that the staples of the State, hemp and tobacco, could "only be cultivated by slave labor."[183] On the other hand, there were a number of prominent Missourians who never ceased to decry slavery as a curse. They held the system responsible for keeping free labor away from the State, for hampering the commerce and industry of St. Louis, and, in fact, for preventing Missouri from realizing her possibilities.[184]

[181] C. M. Harvey, "Missouri," in Atlantic Monthly, vol. lxxxiv, p. 63.
[182] Speech in reply to Preston King, May 18, 1858 (Congressional Globe, 35th Cong., 1st Sess., part iii, p. 2207).
[183] Speech at a joint session of the General Assembly, January, 1855, pamphlet, p. 4. Blair emphasized this point. In its "Address to the people of the United States" the Lexington Pro-Slavery Convention of 1855 declared that in the great slave counties of western Missouri agriculture was prospering. Slavery was held to be the cause of this prosperity (Proceedings of the Convention, pp. 3-4).
[184] The Reverend Frederick Starr in 1853 showed how the whites were outgrowing the blacks, and how the alien was battering down the slavery system. He used the phrase of the time, "One German

The whole question of the profit and loss of slave labor and the relative prosperity of the slave and the free States is academic.   Hinton R. Helper and his opponents in their day thrashed over the question from beginning to end, and based their conflicting conclusions on the same census figures.   No matter what contemporaries or present-day authorities conclude, the problem is not one to be mathematically settled.   The amount of data is so enormous and at the same time so incomplete and so contradictory that one is not justified in drawing conclusions.

knocks out three slaves and one Irishman two" (Letter no. i, entitled, " Slavery in Missouri," p. 6).   " The feeling is becoming painful, throughout the State, that slavery is retarding its growth, . . . making men supercilious, the women dolls, and the children imbeciles" (ibid., p. 17).   See B. Gratz Brown's speech in the Missouri House of Representatives, February 12, 1857.   He shows how slavery was being swamped in the State by the white immigrants.   The Reverend Galusha Anderson, who was pastor of a Baptist church in St. Louis during the late fifties and the sixties, declared that proslavery sentiment prevailed.   " Those who cherished it [proslavery belief] were often intense and bitter, and controlled the entire city. But on the other hand the leading business men of the city were quietly, conservatively, yet positively, opposed to slavery . . . [considering it] a drag upon the commercial interests of the city" (p. 9).

CHAPTER II

The Slave Before the Law

Slavery, both of the negro and of the Indian, had existed in the Louisiana country from the earliest days. Upon the cession of the province to the United States slave property was presumably guaranteed by the Treaty of 1803.[1] The binding force of the clause protecting property at once caused much discussion in the Missouri region and later in Congress during the debate on the Compromise of 1820. Immediately upon the annexation of Louisiana the upper or St. Louis portion, called the "District of Louisiana," was placed under the government of the Indiana Territory.[2] This action caused rather a strong outburst of feeling in the St. Louis region. In January, 1805, "Representatives elected by the Freemen" of the District of Louisiana protested against this assignment for several

[1] Territorial Laws, vol. i, ch. 2, sec. 3. This section reads as follows: "The inhabitants of the ceded territory will be incorporated into the Union of the states and admitted, as soon as possible . . . and during this time they will be upheld and protected in the enjoyment of their liberty, property, and religion they profess."

[2] Law of March 26, 1804 (United States Statutes at Large, vol. ii, p. 287, sec. 12). Whether or not this statute guaranteed the inhabitants in the possession of their slaves is a question. Section thirteen reads: "The laws in force in the said district of Louisiana, at the commencement of this act, and not inconsistent with any of the provisions thereof, shall continue in force until altered, modified or repealed by the governor and judges of Indiana territory, as aforesaid." The powers of the latter seem quite large. The law of March 3, 1805, which made the Missouri country a separate territory, required that the laws must be consistent with the "constitution and laws of the United States" (ibid., p. 331, sec. 3). Section nine of this statute reads: "And be it further enacted, That the laws and regulations, in force in the said district, at the commencement of this act and not inconsistent with the provisions thereof, shall continue in force, until altered, modified, or repealed by the legislature." This seems to give much latitude to the legislature, and ultimately of course to Congress and the President, who controlled the Territory.

reasons, one of the chief of which was that they feared for their slaves, because such property was proscribed in the Indiana Territory. They were apprehensive lest this connection with Indiana should "create the presumption of a disposition in Congress to abolish at a future day slavery altogether in the District of Louisiana." This they declared would be an infringement of the French treaty.[3]

In October, 1804, the Indiana judges formulated for the new district an extensive slave code which would have answered for a much larger slave society,[4] there being but 3011 slaves in the Missouri Territory as late as 1810.[5] This code did not state who were slaves, but did fix the status of those to be considered colored, as "every person other than a negro whose grandfather or grandmother any one is, or shall have been a negro ... and every such person who shall have one-fourth or more of negro blood, shall in a like manner be deemed a mulatto."[6] Neither this code nor any subsequent Missouri legislation distinguishes between the life bondman or slave and the limited bondman or servant, as was done in several of the States. However, there were some bond servants, either black or white, in the State as late as 1832, in which year there were thirty-seven "bound to service for a term of years."[7]

The constitution of 1820 guaranteed slave property, as no slaves were to be emancipated "without the consent of

---

[3] Remonstrance and Petition of the Representatives elected by the Freemen of the Territory of Louisiana, dated January 4, 1805, pp. 11–12. Among other things the petition requested "that Congress would acknowledge the principle of our being entitled in virtue of the treaty, to the free possession of our slaves, and to the right of importing slaves into the District, under such restrictions as to Congress in their wisdom appear necessary" (ibid., p. 22).

[4] Territorial Laws, vol. i, ch. 3.

[5] Eighth Federal Census, Population, p. 601. Governor Delassus gave the slave population of the twelve districts which comprise eastern Missouri as 883 in 1799, and the free blacks 197 (American State Papers, Miscellaneous, vol. i, p. 383).

[6] Territorial Laws, vol. i, ch. 3, sec. 6. Reenacted in Revised Laws, 1825, vol. ii, p. 600, sec. 1.

[7] Senate Journal, 7th Ass., 1st Sess., pp. 60–61, 124. There were 64 of this class in the State according to the state census of 1824 (Senate Journal, 3d Ass., 1st Sess., p. 41).

their owners, or without paying them, before such emancipation," and as any " *bona fide* emigrants to this state, or
actual settlers therein," were to be secure in such property
" so long as any persons of the same description are allowed
to be held as slaves by the laws of this state."[8]   But the
lack of any positive municipal law enslaving the negro must
have caused some misunderstanding.   In the case of Charlotte v. Chouteau, which was argued three times before the
Missouri supreme court to settle the status of a negress
whose mother was born in Canada, the court each time declared that no positive law was necessary.   In the final
hearing in 1857 it was held that " slavery now exists in
Louisiana, Missouri, and Florida without any act of legislation introducing it, and none was necessary, for being in
existence under the sanction at least of France and Spain
in 1803 . . . it was continued, and was not dependent on any
positive law for its recognition."[9]

The Missouri slave law, like that of Kentucky, is usually
said to have been taken largely from the Virginia statutes.
This statement seems to be fairly well founded if the early
Missouri laws are compared with those of Virginia.   The
Code of 1804 bears many close resemblances, in some cases
having the identical wording of the Virginia statutes.[10]   In

[8] In Revised Laws, 1825, vol. i, p. 15, art. iii, sec. 26.   This section
is nearly identical with the Kentucky constitutions of 1792 and 1799
(B. P. Poore, Federal and State Constitutions, vol. i, p. 647, art.
ix; p. 657, art. vii).
[9] 25 Mo., 465.   In Chouteau v. Pierre it was held that "the system
being recognized in fact, it devolved upon the plaintiff, he being a
negro, to show the law forbidding it" (9 Mo., 3).   In Charlotte v.
Chouteau it was stated that the existence of slavery in fact was presumptive evidence of its legality (11 Mo., 193).   The next time this
case was tried it was held that African slavery was recognized as
legal in the Spanish, French, and British colonies, though no law
could be found reducing that race to bondage (21 Mo., 590).
[10] For Virginia statutes with which to compare the Missouri Code
of 1804 see: Statute of 1723 (Hening's Statutes of Virginia, vol.
iv, p. 126, secs. 8–14) ; Statute, 1832 (ibid., p. 327) ; Statutes, 1748
(ibid., vol. v, p. 432; p. 548, sec. 4; p. 558; vol. vi, p. 105, secs, 2, 3,
13–16) ; Statute, 1753 (ibid., p. 356, secs. 4, 9, 28) ; Statute, 1765 (ibid.,
vol. viii, p. 135, sec. 1) ; Statute, 1769 (ibid., p. 359, secs. 1, 3–8) ;
Statute, 1772 (ibid., p. 522, sec. 1) ; Statute, 1776 (ibid., vol. ix, p.
186) ; Statute, 1782 (ibid., vol. xi, p. 39, secs. 1–3) ; Statute, 1785
(ibid., vol. xii, p. 145, secs. 22, 23) ; Statute, 1788 (ibid., p. 531, sec. 2).

addition to this internal evidence is the fact that Governor Harrison and one of the three Indiana judges were natives of the Old Dominion, while another judge came from Kentucky.[11] As later Missouri slave law was based largely on this code, being reenacted in some cases verbatim up to the Civil War, the legal status of the Missouri slave in many aspects can be traced to the original home of so many of the antebellum Missourians. This similarity of the two legal systems, as far as slave law is concerned, will in the more striking instances be compared in the notes.

The Code of 1804 made the slave personal property, and each revision of the laws followed this precedent.[12] The widow's dower in slaves and the division of estates holding negroes were the subjects of much technical legislation.[13]

---

[11] The Indiana judges in 1804 were Henry Vanderburgh, born in Troy, New York, John Griffin, born in Virginia, and Thomas Terry Davis. The latter came to Indiana from Kentucky where he had served as a member of Congress; the place of his birth could not be found ("The Executive Journal of the Indiana Territory," edited by W. W. Wooley, D. W. How, and J. P. Dunn, in Publications of the Indiana Historical Society, vol. iii, no. 3, p. 91). D. W. How says that the Indiana slave law of 1803, which was almost identical with the Missouri Code of 1804, was adapted from that of Virginia. He declares that the Indiana law as a whole was from the following sources: seven laws from Virginia, three from Kentucky, two from Virginia and Kentucky, one from Virginia and Pennsylvania, one from New York, Pennsylvania, and Virginia, and two from Pennsylvania ("The Laws and Courts of the Northwest and Indiana Territories," in ibid., vol. ii, no. 1, pp. 20–22).

[12] Territorial Laws, vol. i, ch. 3, sec. 27. Revised Laws, 1835, p. 581, art. iii, sec. 1. The slave was not always considered ordinary personal property, but assumed the nature of real estate in certain cases, as in a law of January 11, 1860, which provided that "when slaves or real estate shall be taken in execution . . . it shall be his [the sheriff's] duty to expose the same for sale at the court house door" (Session Laws, Adjourned Session, 1859, p. 63, sec. 1).

[13] Until the widow's dower was assigned the court was to grant her an income from realty rents and slave hire "in proportion to her interest in the slaves and real estate" (Revised Laws, 1835, p. 40, art. vi, sec. 12). The widow was very often bequeathed the slaves "during her natural life." A number of such wills can be found in the MS. Probate Records of Saline County (Will Record Book, No. A, 1837–1860). If the husband had no children by his last wife, "in lieu of dower [she could] elect to take in addition to her real estate, the slaves and other personal property" which came to her through this marriage (Revised Laws, 1835, p. 227, sec. 3; see also provision concerning dower in slaves in Session Laws, 1836, p. 60).

In case of an inability to divide an estate "the court may order the sale of slaves, or other personal property."[14]   The court often exercised this power.   Descriptions of the distribution of negroes belonging to an estate, showing how some of the heirs gave or took cash to equalize the division in case the slaves varied in value, can be found in the probate records of the various counties.[15]

Slaves could be seized in execution on a lien under certain conditions.[16]   Whenever sold in such distraint the negroes were to be advertised by hand bills or by publication in a newspaper twenty days before the sale.[17]   A law of 1835 provided that " if the perishable goods [of the deceased] be not sufficient to pay the debts, the executor . . . [shall dispose] of the slaves last until the debts and legacies are all paid."[18]   Examples of the sale bills of slaves sold in execution are numerous in the probate records.[19]

---

[14] Revised Laws, 1835, p. 40, art. vi, sec. 4.   The Code of 1804 made this same provision (Territorial Laws, vol. i, ch. 3, sec. 30).

[15] For an instance of such a division of slaves see the example given in The History of Henry and St. Clair Counties (St. Louis, 1883), p. 130.   The probate court of St. Louis in 1844 appointed appraisers who divided the slaves between the children of Antoine Chenie.   This arrangement did not satisfy them, and so on March 21 of that year they filed a petition stating that "an equal division of the said slaves cannot be made . . . without great prejudice to said petitioners and praying the Court to order the sale of the said slaves and cause the money to be distributed according to the several rights of said petitioners" (MS. Probate Records of St. Louis, Estate No. 1731).   The circuit court records of the several counties are quite rich in petitions for the division of groups of slaves.

[16] Revised Statutes, 1855, vol. i, p. 669.   This law also placed slaves on an equality with other personal property.

[17] Session Laws, 1859, p. 93, sec. 1.   This law was to apply specifically to the judicial circuit of Cape Girardeau County.

[18] Revised Laws, 1835, p. 40, art. vi, ch. 2, sec. 32.

[19] " In the St. Louis Circuit Court, April Term 1845.   This bill of sale made this twenty seventh day of September . . . by John W. Reel . . . and Henry M. Shreeve of the second part . . . for and in consideration of Seven hundred & fifty Dollars . . . a Negro man named William about thirty years of age and a slave for life" (MS. Probate Records, St. Louis, November, 1859, Estate of John W. Reel, Bill of Sale filed June 17, 1845).   For an example of an advertising bill of a slave sold in execution we read in the Western Monitor (Fayette), July 4, 1829: " PUBLIC SALE of a valuable Negro Man On the first day of the July term of Howard County Circuit Court to be holden at Fayette on the first monday in July next, I will sell at public sale to the highest bidder for cash in hand, a likely

While in probate the slaves of an estate were to be hired to the highest bidder, "unless the court order otherwise."[20] This form of property caused more trouble than most others because of the peculiar risks. One widow complained that a slave on whose labor she depended was very prone to abscond for months at a time. She obtained permission to sell this negro and purchase another, but this one also became a source of great trouble.[21] The Code of 1804 forbade a widow to leave the State with slaves in whom other heirs had a claim.[22] This provision was reenacted in 1831,[23] and apparently was rigorously enforced.[24]

Slaves do not always appear to have been considered as mere chattels. An old ordinance of the city of St. Charles required the whites and the slaves in common to turn out

negro man belonging to the estate of Thomas Crews deceased in order to raise funds to pay off the debts due by said estate. David D. Crews, Exec'r T. Crews dec'd."

[20] Revised Laws, 1835, p. 40, art. ii, sec. 41. A guardian could also sell slaves and loan the proceeds of the sale (Local and Private Acts, 1855, p. 402). An administrator could sell the slaves, the proceeds going to the widow for life (ibid., p. 448).

[21] MS. Probate Records, St. Louis, No. 2068, Estate of Beverley Allen. Papers filed June 23, 1848, and March 20, 1850. The danger and peculiarity of slave property is shown in the provisions by which slave title passed. Slaves were transferred (1) by will only under the set form, (2) by "deed in writing, to be proved by not less than two witnesses, or acknowledged by donor, and recorded in the county where one of the parties lives, within six months after the date of such deed" (Revised Laws, 1835, p. 581, art. iii, sec. 2). This article was not placed in the later revisions. Slaves seemingly took on the character of real estate in this provision.

[22] Territorial Laws, vol. i, ch. 3, secs. 28, 29. A Virginia statute of 1785 forbade a widow to remove slaves from the State unless the heirs in reversion gave their consent (Hening, vol. xii, p. 145, secs. 22, 23).

[23] Session Laws, 1830, ch. 70. Somewhat modified in Revised Laws, 1835, p. 384, secs. 30, 33.

[24] In 1841 one Adolphus Bryant, accompanied by William Kio, took two slaves from St. Louis to New Orleans. These negroes were the temporary property of Bryant's wife, her first husband's children having an interest in them after her death. These heirs had Bryant and Kio arrested for slave-stealing. The captain and clerk of the steamer Meteor were forced to give bail, but Bryant and Kio could not furnish bond and were consequently jailed (Daily Evening Gazette, August 13, 1841).

and work the streets of the town under a penalty.[25]   As a slave could not vote this could not have been a poll tax.   It was therefore really a double tax on slave property, as the master also paid a property tax on his negroes.

Ownerships in slaves were often held by free colored persons.   Sometimes these were owned as bona-fide property, but usually merely in the interim between the date when the free negro purchased the freedom of the slave and the date of the latter's liberation.   The following item appears in the St. Louis circuit court records for March 16, 1837: "Thomas Keller a free man of colour, comes into court and acknowledges a deed of Emancipation in favor of his negro slave named Ester, a woman aged thirty-nine years."[26]   Many such entries appear in the circuit court records of the various counties.   In David v. Evans the state supreme court by a decision of 2 to 1 held that a free negro could legally hold slaves.[27]   Thus it can readily be seen that slave ownership was unique.   It was declared by the law to be personal estate, but both the law and circumstances made so many exceptions that it became a form of property peculiar to itself.

A slave could hold no property in his own right.   In 1830 it was held that the mere fact that a negro was keeping a "barber's shop and selling articles in that shop is such evidence of freedom as ought to have gone to the jury."[28]   This assertion implies that a property right gave the presumption of a free status.   Other decisions bear out this impression.

---

[25] Ordinance of April 28, 1821, "Concerning the Streets of St. Charles." Section three reads: "All able bodied persons of the age of 16 to 50 years, are required to work on the streets to which they may be assigned and on failing . . . each person shall forfeit and pay $2.00 each day, if a man of full age, if a minor by his parents or guardian, and if a slave by his master, overseer or employer" (printed in the Missourian of May 2, 1821).

[26] MS. Records St. Louis Circuit Court, vol. 8, p. 194. For further examples of this practice see ibid., p. 240, ibid., vol. 6, p. 421, and also a paper dated December 3, 1855, in the MS. Darby Papers.

[27] 18 Mo., 249. See also Machan (negro) v. Julia Logan (negress), 4 Mo., 361.

[28] The State v. Henry, 2 Mo., 177.

The local Dred Scott decision of 1852 possibly influenced the court in its later renderings and general sentiment regarding most phases of slave rights.[29]   In reversing a lower decision relative to the purchase of goods by a slave for his master, the state supreme court held in 1857 that " our system of slavery resembles that of the Romans rather than the villanage of the ancient common law. . . . Under the former law, slaves were ' things ' and not ' persons '; they were not the subjects of civil rights, and of course were incapable of owning property or of contracting legal obligations."[30]   This being the case, the slave had no legal right even to the clothes on his back.   Hence he could make no valid contract, nor could he either sue or be sued.

The court applied this principle rigidly in 1860.   In that year a case was tried in which the owner had sold a slave after entering into a contract to manumit him on the payment of a specific sum.   The slave held a receipt from the master for most of the stated amount.   After denying the slave any right to sue in the courts of the State, the court held that " the incapacities of his condition . . . suggest, at the threshold of the inquiry, insuperable obstacles to the specific enforcement of an executory contract between the master and himself . . . even where there might be a complete fulfillment on the part of the slave."[31]   Thus at the very close of the slavery regime the doctrine was again enunciated that the slave had absolutely no property rights independent of his owner.

It has been seen that a slave had a legal right to no property whatever, although he naturally held temporarily the furniture and utensils necessary for carrying on his small household in the slave quarters.   As laws against the commercial dealings of slaves date from the earliest slave code in old Louisiana and are continuously reenunciated from then till 1860, the conclusion must be reached that this was a serious problem.   The Missouri laws are unfortu-

[29] Scott (a man of color) v. Emerson, 15 Mo., 570.
[30] Douglas v. Richie, 24 Mo., 177.
[31] Redmond (colored) v. Murray et al., 30 Mo., 570.

nately not often prefixed by preambles, whether elaborate
or only brief, hence the reasons for the law are left largely
to speculation. For petty crimes of this nature the slave
was simply haled before a justice of the peace, and consequently there are no records by which one may judge of
the real gravity of the situation. It might well have been
feared that the slave, by buying or selling without permission, would dispose of his owner's goods. But there
was also, as in the case of the slave hiring himself out without his master's consent, the danger that he might grow
independent and unruly in disposition.

The Black Code of 1724 forbade buying or selling without
a written permission from the master, and fixed a fine of
fifteen hundred livres upon any one so dealing with a slave
without permission. When the owner gave his negro such
permission, he was responsible for the commercial acts of
the slave.[32] The police regulations of Governor Carondelet
of 1795, under penalty of twenty-five lashes, prohibited a
slave from selling without his master's consent even the
products of the waste land given him for his own use.[33]
The Code of 1804 fined a dealer four times the value of the
consideration involved, with costs, while the informer of
such a transaction received twenty dollars. A free negro
for the same offense was given thirty stripes " well laid on "
in default of the payment of this fine.[34] This section seems

---

[32] B. F. French, Historical Collections of Louisiana, vol. iii, p. 89,
secs. 15, 23.

[33] American State Papers, Miscellaneous, vol. i, p. 380. The Laws
of Las Seite Partidas bound the master to all commercial acts of the
slave if the former commissioned the slave to "exercise any trade
or commerce" (vol. i, p. 485). It is not known what binding force
these semiclerical laws had in the Louisiana colonial courts. The
translators of these laws claim that they had the force of law as
late as 1820 (translator's note, vol. i, p. 1). In 1745 Governor Pierre
Regant De Vandreuil drew up a police regulation in which a white
person for illegally dealing with a slave was to be placed in the
pillory for the first offense and sent to the galleys for the second
(C. Gayarré, History of Louisiana, vol. ii, app., p. 361, art. xvii).
The severity of the penalty implies that the problem was somewhat
grave.

[34] Territorial Laws, vol. i. ch. 3, sec. 11. The master was also
liable for the transactions of his slave (ibid., sec. 18).

to have been taken almost word for word from Virginia
statutes of 1753 and 1785, the only difference being that the
information fee was to be five pounds instead of twenty
dollars.[35] The Missouri legislature reenacted this law
verbatim in 1822,[36] 1823, 1835, 1845, and 1855.[37] Many of
the Missouri statutes sprang from this superimposed code of
the Indiana judges of 1804, and continued in operation with
little or no change till slavery disappeared in the State.

The charter of Carondelet of 1851 empowered the city
council "to impose fines, penalties and forfeitures on the
owners and masters of slaves suffered to go at large or to
act or deal as free persons."[38] Other particular communities seem also to have experienced grave apprehensions from
this cause, as is indicated by a statute passed in 1861 which
forbade any owner in Macon County to permit his slave to
sell refreshments or do huckstering of any kind unless under
the direction of himself or an overseer. The penalty was
from fifteen to twenty dollars, which was to go to the county
school fund. Such cases were to be taken before a justice
of the peace.[39]

The slave early caused apprehension by both vending and
imbibing liquor. In 1811 an ordinance was passed in St.
Louis fining an offender ten dollars for selling a negro any
"spiritous or ardent liquor" without his master's consent.
If a person found a slave in a state of intoxication in the

---

[35] Hening, vol. vi, p. 356, sec. 9; ibid., vol. xii, p. 182, sec. 6. A
statute of 1769 fined a master £10 for allowing his slave to go at
large and trade as a free man because of numerous thefts thereby
committed (ibid., vol. viii, p. 360, sec. 8).

[36] Territorial Laws, vol. i, p. 399, sec. 1.

[37] Law of March 1, 1823 (Laws of Missouri, 1825, vol. ii, p. 746,
sec. 1). If the consideration was over ninety dollars, the case could
be carried to the circuit court. Reenacted in Revised Laws, 1835, p.
581, art. i, sec. 37; Revised Statutes, 1845, ch. 167, art. i, sec. 31;
Revised Statutes, 1855, ch. 150, art. i, sec. 31.

[38] Art. v, sec. 21. This section also refers to careless owners who
permitted their slaves to hire themselves out without due formality.
It was a pressing problem in Missouri (see above, pp. 35-37). It was
decided in 1853 that "hiring a slave to maul rails without the consent of his master is not a dealing with the slave," manual labor not
being considered "dealing" under the law (State v. Henke, 19
Mo., 225).

[39] Session Laws, 1860, p. 417, secs. 1, 2.

streets or other public place, he was to give the offender ten
lashes. The master or mistress of such slave was to be
fined five dollars for neglecting to punish him.[40] A law of
1833 forbade a store, tavern, or grog-shop keeper to permit
slaves or free negroes to assemble on his premises without
the owner's assent, under a penalty of from five to fifty
dollars.[41] The Act of 1835 Regulating Inns and Taverns
fined the keepers of such places from ten to fifty dollars for
"bartering in liquors" with slaves, free blacks, or apprentices without the consent in writing of their masters.[42] The
Grocers' Regulation Act of the same year fined such a
person for this offence from fifteen to fifty dollars and
costs and revoked his license.[43] Cases on record indicate
that these provisions were at times enforced. In 1853
James Hill was fined twenty-five dollars by the Boone
County circuit court for selling liquor to slaves,[44] and in
1859 Henry Hains was similarly punished.[45]

The slave as well as the white and the free black engaged
in illicit liquor dealing. The Revision of 1835 placed a fine
of three hundred dollars upon the master who allowed his
slave to sell or deliver any spiritous or vinous liquors to
any other slave without the consent of the latter's owner,
and the offending slave was to receive not more than
twenty-five stripes after a summary trial before a justice of
the peace. He was to be released only after the master had

---

[40] An Ordinance concerning Slaves in the Town of St. Louis,
February 5, 1811 (MS. Record Book of the Trustees of St. Louis,
pp. 23-25, secs. 1, 3). That the slave often drank to excess is learned
from the following advertisements: "Runaway this morning, my
negro man David. He is a black man . . . stout made, fond of
whiskey, getting drunk whenever he can procure it" (Missouri Gazette [St. Louis], March 9, 1820, advertisement of Nathan Benton).
"Ranaway from the farm of General Rector . . . my servant John,
a very bright freckled mulatto . . . he is remarkably fond of
whiskey" (ibid., July 5, 1820).
[41] Session Laws, 1832, ch. 41, secs. 1, 2.
[42] Revised Laws, 1835, p. 315, sec. 22. Reenacted, Revised Statutes, 1845, ch. 83, sec. 22.
[43] Revised Statutes, 1845, p. 291, sec. 7. It was necessary to prove
that the grocer was actually licensed when the liquor was sold to
slaves (Fraser v. The State, 6 Mo., 195).
[44] MS. Circuit Court Records, Boone County, Book F, p. 190.
[45] Ibid., Book H, pp. 82, 173, 282.

paid the costs and had given a bond of two hundred dollars
for his negro's good behavior for one year. The slave could
be sold if not removed from jail by the second day of the
following session of the county court.[46] The Revision of
1845 fixed the maximum punishment of a slave selling liquor
at thirty-nine lashes, and his owner was to pay all costs.[47]
In addition to this penalty the Revision of 1855 fined the
owner from twenty to one hundred dollars.[48]

It was held in 1850 that if a person sold liquor to a slave
without the master's consent and the negro was made drunk
and died, the vendor of the liquor was liable for legal
damages, even though a clerk sold the liquor without the
proprietor's knowledge.[49] Despite the number of statutes
on this subject, the press does not reflect a serious condition of drunkenness among the slaves. Lack of money on
the part of the negro as well as fear on the side of the merchant prevented the problem from assuming alarming proportions.

Although the Missouri slave was without any property
rights, he was not a mere thing. He was not absolutely at
the mercy of his master. The constitution of 1820 required
the legislature to pass laws " to oblige the owners of slaves
to treat them with humanity, and to abstain from all in-
juries to them extending to life or limb." The slave was
also to be given a jury trial, and, if convicted of a capital
offence, was to receive the same punishment as a white
person for a like offence, " and no other," and he was to be
assigned counsel for his defence.[50] The definite principle

---

[46] Revised Laws, 1835, p. 591, art. i, secs. 17–22.

[47] Revised Statutes, 1845, ch. 72, secs. 7, 25.

[48] Revised Statutes, 1855, ch. 57, secs. 17, 19, 23.

[49] Skinner et al. v. Hughes, 13 Mo., 440.

[50] Art. iii, secs. 26, 27. " No other state constitution gave so much
protection to the rights of the slave as this one" (F. C. Shoemaker,
The First Constitution of Missouri, p. 55). These sections are nearly
identical with the Kentucky constitutions of 1792 and 1799 (Poore,
p. 647, art. ix; p. 657, art. vii). In the territorial period two cases are
recorded in the MS. Records of the St. Louis general court or court
of record, wherein it appears that the slave had fair treatment in
court. In United States v. Le Blond (vol. ii, pp. 86, 96) the latter
was fined $500 and costs and imprisoned for two months for killing

was declared that "any person who shall maliciously deprive of life or dismember any slave, shall suffer such punishment as would be inflicted for a like offence if it were committed on a free white person."[51] For striking his master a law of 1825 condemned an unruly slave to punishment after conviction before a justice, but gave the master no permission to punish him.[52] Furthermore, several decisions were at various times rendered by the supreme court of Missouri which show that it was disposed to protect the slave against the arbitrary will of his master. In Nash v. Prinne it is incidentally stated that "the justice of the country shall be satisfied," and that the slayer of a bondman was first to be criminally prosecuted before civil damages could be allowed.[53] In other words, the court declared that in the maiming of a slave the public was outraged to a greater extent than the owner was injured financially. Justice was not to be sacrificed for the personal gain of the master. In 1846 a person sought escape from prosecution for injuring a slave on the plea of an improper indictment, but the court in this instance declared that "it made no difference whether the slave belonged to the defendant or to a third person. . . . It could answer no useful purpose whatever, unless to designate with greater certainty the person of the injured slave."[54] Thus a white man was not allowed to escape justice on a technicality, even though his victim was a bondman.

---

his slave. Le Blond's provocation is not stated. In 1820 one Prinne was found not guilty on a charge of murdering his slave, Walter, by confining him "in a dungeon or cell dangerous to his health" (ibid., pp. 226, 230, 234, 236). The Missouri Gazette of September 4, 1818, gave accounts of two negroes then being tried for murder before the local court, one being defended by two and the other by three counsel. The above provision is very similar in nature to a Virginia statute of 1772 which provided that slaves suffering death for burglary were not to be refused benefit of clergy "unless the said breaking, in the case of a freeman would be burglary" (Hening, vol. viii, p. 522, sec. 1).

[51] Art. iii, sec. 28. A case was decided under this section twenty years later (Fanny v. The State, 6 Mo., 122).

[52] Revised Laws, 1825, vol. i, p. 309, sec. 84.

[53] 1 Mo., 125.

[54] Grove v. The State, 10 Mo., 233.

The right of any other white than the master to mistreat a slave was emphatically denied, one decision holding that " such offences stand on the same ground as when white persons cruelly use each other."[55]   The whole subject of the treatment of the slave will be considered in the following chapter.   Whatever the practice of individuals may have been, the wording of the statutes and of the court decisions is certainly humane and praiseworthy.

In most of the States there was a stiffening up of the criminal laws following insurrections or severe antislavery agitation, but the Missouri slave code of 1835 was reenacted almost verbatim in 1845 and again in 1855.   More stringent patrolling regulations were enacted and there was an increasing bitterness toward outside interference or the free airing of antislavery views at home, but of a growing hostility toward the negro or fear of trouble there is little reflection in law or decision.   Even the newspapers, despite their occasional rancorous political vituperation, evince a spirit of justice to the black bondman, even if not toward the white opponent in politics.   Some of the most lofty opinions regarding the duty of the whites toward the slave and his right to seek freedom under the laws are to be found in the period between the Compromise of 1850 and the Civil War. Even the obvious danger of the Kansas struggle, instead of reacting on the slave, seems to have been focussed on the white abolitionist and the Bentonites.   More severe control of movement and stricter inspection of slave meetings and assemblies are evident, but of change in the personal treatment of the bondman, either in law or practice, little can be seen other than what would naturally follow a growing system needing more orderly control.

At the same time the Dred Scott dictum as enunciated by the Missouri supreme court in 1852 shows that in principle the State was ready to change her policy the better to protect the system.   The Missourians who favored slavery desired not to depress their blacks, but rather to extend slave terri-

[55] The State v. Peters, 28 Mo., 241.

tory in order to safeguard their colored property. Thus as late as 1860, when her own slaves numbered scarcely one eighth of her total population, Missouri was made the battering-ram to fight against the abolition influence in Kansas.

The criminal legislation affecting the slave falls according to penalties under three heads: capital offences; mutilation; whipping.

The Code of 1804 provided the death penalty without benefit of clergy "if any negro or other slave shall at any time consult, advise or conspire to rebel or make insurrection or shall plot or conspire the murder of any person or persons whatever."[56]   The same punishment was to be inflicted for administering poison or "any medicine whatever" unless there was no evil intent and no actual harm resulted.[57] Thus the slave was responsible for both the intent and the result of his act, while with the white the old common-law idea of the intent alone was considered in a criminal charge.

When these provisions are compared with the general criminal law of 1808, it is found that if the slave was cruelly used the white man was no less severely handled. Under that statute any individual, black or white, was to suffer castration for rape, thirty-nine lashes for burglary, disfranchisement and an hour in the pillory for perjury, forty-nine lashes on the bare back "well laid on" for stealing and branding horses and cattle, and death for stealing or enslaving a negro whom he knew to be free.[58]

---

[56] Territorial Laws, vol. i, ch. 3, sec. 14. This provision is identical with a Virginia statute of 1748 (Hening, vol. vi, p. 105, sec. 2).

[57] Hening, vol. vi, p. 105, secs. 15, 16. In 1825 a law likewise made it a death penalty for a slave to prepare, exhibit, or administer any medicine whatever, but if such medicine was found to be harmless and no evil intent was evident, he was to receive stripes at the discretion of the court (Revised Laws, 1825, vol. i, p. 312, sec. 98). In 1843 an act was passed fining any person a maximum of fifty dollars for selling poisoned drugs to any slave without the written consent of the owner (Session Laws, 1842, p. 102, secs. 1, 2). In 1818 a slave was tried on a poison charge in St. Louis (MS. Records of St. Louis Court of Records, vol. ii, pp. 180, 184).

[58] Territorial Laws, vol. i, p. 210, secs. 8, 11, 16, 18, 21, 22, 39, 45. That some of these provisions were literally carried out is learned from the Missouri Intelligencer of April 24, 1824, wherein is an

The law of 1804 as to conspiracy was virtually reenacted in 1825, but the punishment was limited to thirty-nine stripes if the slave simply conspired without committing the " overt act," unless he " unwittingly " entered the conspiracy and voluntarily confessed with " genuine repentance " before being accused of the crime. In the latter case he might be pardoned, but the second offence was to be punishable by death in any case.[59] As already stated, the constitution of 1820 limited the punishment of a slave for a capital offence to the same degree of punishment that would be inflicted upon a white person for the same crime.[60] There seems to have been no slave insurrection of any magnitude in Missouri, but the commission of a number of crimes punishable by death is recorded, the accounts often not specifying whether they were committed by slaves or by free colored persons.[61]

advertisement for one William Job, a horse thief, who had broken out of the Cooper County jail. He could be recognized as he " has lately been whipped for the said crime, and his back in all probability is not yet entirely healed." Cases of selling free blacks into slavery seem to have been rare. On January 27, 1835, one Jacob Gregg was " granted relief " for expenses in taking Palsa Rouse and Sarah Scritchfield, " arrested for having sold a free person as a slave" (Senate Journal, 8th Ass., 1st Sess., p. 208).
[59] Revised Laws, 1825, vol. i, p. 312, secs. 96, 97.
[60] Art. iii, sec. 27.
[61] In December, 1835, Israel B. Grant of Callaway County, a member of the legislature, was murdered, his throat being cut. "We have been informed that this horrid deed has been traced to one of his own slaves," reads the account in the Jeffersonian Republican of January 9, 1836. In 1836 a sheriff submitted a bill for fees in holding a slave charged with murder (Senate Journal, 9th Ass., 1st Sess., p. 127). In 1841 four negroes (status not given) were hanged for murder and incendiarism (R. Edwards and M. Hopewell, Edwards's Great West and her Commercial Metropolis, p. 372). In April, 1847, a slave named Eli was lynched in Franklin County for murdering a white woman (History of Franklin, Jefferson, Washington, Crawford and Gasconade Counties, p. 283). In Lincoln County a slave named Gibbs was burned for murdering his master during a brawl when both were drunk. The date of this affair is not given (History of Lincoln County [Chicago, 1888], pp. 365–368). In 1850 a white man named McClintock and a slave woman were hanged by a Clay County mob for murdering a white woman. Being a slave, her testimony could not be accepted against her white confederate, and so both were lynched (History of Clay and Platte Counties [St. Louis, 1885], pp. 158–159). Several attacks were made in the year 1855 by slaves on their masters and mistresses (ibid., pp. 158–159). Two slaves were tried for murder in 1852 (Weekly Missouri Sen-

That his bondage was no absolute deterrent in preventing criminal assault by the negro can be seen by a survey of the slavery period in Missouri. The general criminal law of 1808 punished rape, whether committed by a white or a black, by castration.[62] In 1825 another criminal law likewise made mutilation the punishment of any one who assaulted a girl under ten years of age, but a slave who assaulted any white woman, no matter what her age might be, was to suffer castration.[63] Although both whites and blacks were to be thus punished, no record of a white being so used has been noted, but several instances of negroes treated in this manner are on record.[64]

---

tinel, August 10, 1853). On July 12, 1854, a slave woman poisoned the Kent family of Warren County. The victims recovered (Republican, August 1, 1854). In August, 1854, W. T. Cochran of Trenton was stabbed by a slave (Richmond Weekly Mirror, August 11, 1854). A negress killed Robert Newson near Fulton on June 23, 1855 (Missouri Statesman [Columbia], July 6, 1855). In 1857 in Boone County a slave named Pete was given twenty-five lashes for a murderous attack. Charles Simmons, his owner, was ordered to pay the costs of the prosecution (MS. Circuit Court Records, Boone County, Book G, p. 281, Book H, pp. 226, 246). In 1859 a slave named Jack Anderson murdered his master, Seneca Diggs, in Howard County, and escaped to Canada (Session Laws, 1860, p. 534).

[62] Territorial Laws, vol. i, p. 210, sec. 8.

[63] Revised Laws, 1825, vol. i, p. 312, secs. 10, 11, 99.

[64] In 1844 a slave was sentenced to be castrated for a rape (Nathan, a slave, v. The State, 8 Mo., 631). In 1853 two negroes (status not given) were so sentenced (The State v. Anderson, 19 Mo., 241). The Republican of April 30, 1838, records that a negro (status not given) was thrown overboard from a river boat and drowned for an assault. Several negroes murdered Dr. Fisk and child of Jasper County in July, 1852. His wife was raped and killed and the house was burned (Weekly Missouri Sentinel, August 4, 1852). In 1853 a negro was taken from jail and hanged for an assault (ibid., August 25, 1853). At Boonville in September, 1853, a negro was caught "and beat almost to death" for an attempted rape (ibid., September 1, 1853). In the same year at Springfield two negroes were burned and one was hanged for an assault (A. D. Richardson, "Free Missouri," in Atlantic Monthly, vol. xxi, pp. 363, 492). In 1859 a slave was dismissed for some reason by the Greene County circuit court after having been indicted for rape by a special session of the grand jury (MS. Records, Book Djr., pp. 487–488, 501). In The State v. Anderson it was held that the character of the white girl or that of her parents was not relevant, as it was simply a question of the assailant being a negro and the victim a white female (19 Mo., 241). In many cases the accounts do not state whether the negro in question was free or a slave, but as the slaves of the State outnumbered the free blacks thirty to one the presumption is strong that they were slaves.

The slave was not to be fined or imprisoned,[65] save at his master's request.[66] He was therefore punished physically in cases where a white man would be fined or incarcerated. In some instances the maximum and minimum number of lashes are given while in others the matter was left to the "discretion" of the court. All whippings, whether received by whites or blacks, were to be given in public "and well and truly laid on such offenders' bare backs, and that without favor or affection."[67] In theory at least the law made no distinction between the white and the black offender in the early days. Punishment by stripes being the only form of punishment for the slave besides

---

[65] Revised Laws, 1825, vol. i, p. 312, sec. 99. Females other than slaves could not be whipped (ibid., sec. 101).

[66] Local police regulations made exceptions to this provision. In St. Louis slaves were imprisoned unless the owner paid fines imposed for various offences (St. Louis Ordinances, 1836, p. 89, sec. 2; p. 25, sec. 5). An early ordinance of St. Louis fined a master one dollar a year if his slave kept a dog within the city limits (Ordinance of February 25, 1811, MS. Record Book of the Trustees of St. Louis, p. 42, sec. 3). An ordinance of St. Charles fined an owner ten dollars if his negro littered the streets of the town (Ordinance of the Board of Trustees of St. Charles, April 28, 1821, in the Missourian of May 2, 1821). Another ordinance of St. Charles fined the master the same amount if the slave injured the woods on the village common (ibid., April 13, 1822, in the Missourian of April 18, 1822).

[67] Revised Laws, 1825, vol. i, p. 312, sec. 30. But all whippings were not performed in public. Thomas Shackelford states that when he was a boy one of their slaves was unjustly condemned to be whipped. The family were indignant, but the neighbors demanded that the negro be punished. The sheriff took the slave into a shed and bound him to a post. The crowd waited till they heard the lash applied and the negro yell with pain. After the crowd had disappeared the sheriff brought the slave out to young Shackelford, who was told to keep the matter secret as the sheriff had only lashed the post and had made the negro scream that the crowd might be mollified ("Early Recollections of Missouri," in Missouri Historical Society Collections, vol. ii, no. 2, p. 9). When the old sheriff's house was destroyed at Lexington, Captain J. A. Wilson secured the slave whip which had been the official Lafayette County flagellum. It is composed of a wooden handle attached to a flat piece of rubber strap about eighteen inches long, an inch and a half wide, and a quarter of an inch thick. It has the appearance of having been cut from rubber belting, being reenforced with fibre as is rubber hose. It would cause a very painful blow without leaving a scar. If scarred the negro would be less valuable, as a prospective buyer would consider him vicious or liable to absconding if bearing the marks of punishment (see below, p. 96).

hanging and mutilation, it was thus more or less definitely limited to prevent either a too severe or a too lenient sentence.

Resistance to the owner or overseer was considered the gravest offence after the two treated above.[68]   The Code of 1804 fixed the maximum at thirty lashes for lifting a hand against any person not a negro or mulatto unless " wantonly assaulted."[69]   The general criminal law of 1825 empowered the master to incarcerate his slave in the public jail, at his own expense, if the slave resisted his " lawful demands " or refused to obey him, " and if any slave shall, contrary to his bounden duty, presume to strike or assault his or her master . . . such slave, on conviction before a justice of the peace, shall be whipped not exceeding thirty-nine stripes."[70]

Although no insurrections of any importance were ever even threatened in Missouri, there was a continual reenactment of the early legislation to prevent seditious speeches and riotous meetings.   The Missouri slaveholder, being surrounded on three sides by free territory where abolitionism was more or less active, and knowing that the great rivers of the State offered a ready means of escape for the slave, feared the loss of his property rather than personal danger. Hence the amount of legislation and litigation concerning the fugitive.   The Missourians retained the laws which the Indiana judges had given them in 1804 relative to slave insurrections.   These laws were later reenacted so as to be in harmony with those of the other slave States, which were continually threatened with servile outbreaks.   The subject of slave assemblages will be treated in Chapter VI of this study.

The evidence that might be offered by the slave was a

---

[68] The terms " master," " mistress," " owner," and " overseer " are used interchangeably in this paper.   The law provided that these terms were to be considered synonymous before the courts (Revised Statutes, 1835, vol. i, p. 581, sec. 39).

[69] Territorial Laws, vol. i, ch. 3, sec. 12.   A Kentucky law of 1798 provided that a slave be sentenced by a justice of the peace to thirty lashes for striking any person not a negro (J. C. Hurd, The Law of Freedom and Bondage, vol. ii, p. 14).

[70] Revised Laws, 1825, vol. i, p. 309, sec. 84.

point which caused considerable legislation. In the first section of the Code of 1804 it was provided that "no negro or mulatto shall be a witness except in pleas of the United States against negroes or mulattoes or in civil pleas where negroes alone shall be parties."[71] Practice gave rise to some exceptions, and a number of decisions later modified this provision in some details; but the principle was never deserted. Slaves were allowed to testify against whites in some instances. When the Illinois abolitionists, Burr, Work, and Thompson, were placed on trial at Palmyra in 1841, their counsel sought in vain to exclude the testimony of the slaves whom they had sought to liberate. This testimony was given through the masters of these slaves, which the narrator implies was the custom.[72]

In cases where suit was brought for damages in selling an unsound slave the latter's declaration of "a symptom or appearance of disease, is competent evidence to prove that the slave was at the time diseased."[73] In Hawkins v. The State it was held that "on the trial of an indictment against a white person, the State may give in evidence a conversation between the accused and a negro in relation to the offense charged, when the conversation on the part of the negro is merely given in evidence as an indictment, and in illustration of what was said by a white person, and not by the negro."[74] This case seems very close to the line of allowing a negro to testify against a white, the technical distinction being between an indictment before a grand jury and a trial.

---

[71] Territorial Laws, vol. i, ch. 3, sec. 1. A Virginia law of 1732 forbade a negro, mulatto, or Indian to give evidence except in cases involving one of his own race (Hening, vol. iv, p. 327). When giving evidence against one of their own race negroes took the oath and testified as whites. The following entry appears in the St. Louis Coroners' Inquest Record for 1836: "Spencer a colored man after being duly sworn on his oath said that on Wednesday . . . he saw a colored boy belonging to I. A. Fletcher throw a brick bat and strike the above named William on the head . . . 12th day of April, 1836, John Andrews, Coroner" (MS. Record of Coroners' Inquests, City of St. Louis, 1822–1839, not paged).

[72] R. I. Holcombe, History of Marion County, Missouri, p. 239.

[73] Marr v. Hill & Hayes, 10 Mo., 320. Also, Wadlow v. Perrymans, Admr., 27 Mo., 279.

[74] 7 Mo., 190.

The court in 1855 took a very peculiar view of the law in accepting a slave's evidence against himself which rendered his master liable to damages. In this instance the action was brought against the owner for a larceny committed by his slave. The latter's declaration as to the whereabouts of stolen goods, in connection with the fact that the goods were actually found in the place mentioned, was held by the supreme court to be admissible as evidence.[75] Thus it appears to be a point of fact rather than testimony. Had the stolen property not been found, the court seems to imply that the negro's evidence would not have been accepted. Whatever may have been the means by which slave evidence was admitted, it is certain that it was occasionally accepted and at the expense of the master or other whites.

By the Missouri practice the slave was also protected from cruelty in forcing evidence from him. In one case where a slave testified against himself it was held that a confession extorted by pain was not to be admitted as evidence.[76] Here the court declared plainly that " it is settled that confessions induced by the flattery of hope or terror of punishment, are not admissible as evidence."[77]

In the early period procedure in slave indictments for misdemeanors was similar to that of the whites. Later the

---

[75] Fackler v. Chapman, 20 Mo., 249.

[76] Hector v. The State, 2 Mo., 135.

[77] Hawkins v. The State, 7 Mo., 190. It is interesting to note that the division of the whole Methodist Church largely revolved about the point of admitting negro evidence in a church trial in Missouri. In 1840 the Reverend Silas Comfort appealed to the General Conference of the Methodist Church from a decision of the Missouri Conference which had adjudged him guilty of mal-administration in admitting the testimony of colored members against a white. On May 17 the General Conference of 1840 rejected a resolution confirming the Missouri decision. The following day Mr. I. W. Few of Georgia introduced the following resolution, which was adopted by a vote of 74 to 46: " Resolved, That it is inexpedient and injustifiable for any preacher among us to permit colored persons to give testimony against white persons in any state where they are denied that privilege in trials at law." Bad feeling resulted, and by the next general conference the church was ripe for a division. The question of the right of bishops and preachers to hold slaves was the rock upon which the church split (J. M. Buckley, History of Methodism in the United States, vol. ii, p. 12).

practice was modified. A law of 1825 required that a bondman should be taken before the circuit court for serious
offences.[78] Six years later the justice court was given
jurisdiction over thefts amounting to less than twenty
dollars. If the master so requested, the offending slave
was to be given a jury trial. The punishment for either a
misdemeanor or a theft could be fixed by the justice, the
maximum penalty being thirty-nine lashes.[79] The justice
court was the tribunal to which the slave was haled for
most of his offences. In many respects the procedure re-
sembled that of the old English market court of " Pied
poudre." As the justice of the peace was not required to
keep permanent records, it is not possible to gain a very
close view of the procedure or of negro punishment. The
county circuit court records contain many accounts of slaves
tried for the more serious crimes.

The owner was responsible for the depredations committed by his negro as for injury done by his other live
stock. The liability of the master was the cause of considerable legislation and was continually brought before the
courts. A law of 1824 made the owner, or the employer in
case the slave was hired out at the time of the trespass,
responsible for his injury to trees, crops, and other forms of
property.[80] In 1830 a statute limited this liability to the
value of the offending slave.[81]

The slave naturally differed from other forms of property
in the point of the responsibility of the owner in that, being
human, he had his abettors and his colleagues in crime, both

[78] Revised Laws, 1825, vol. ii, p. 790.

[79] Session Laws, 1830, p. 35. In 1853 the supreme court of Missouri held that this statute did not provide for an appeal in cases
of petit larceny (The State v. Joe, 19 Mo., 223).

[80] Revised Laws, 1825, vol. ii, p. 781, sec. 4. The owner was also
responsible if his slave fired the prairie or forest with his knowledge
(ibid., p. 798, sec. 4). These provisions were both reenacted in
Revised Laws, 1835, p. 612, sec. 5; p. 624, sec. 4.

[81] Session Laws, 1830, p. 35. In 1859 a law was passed making a
person hiring a slave from a party not a resident of the State responsible for any trespass, felony, or misdemeanor committed by such
slave (Session Laws, 1858, p. 90, sec. 2).

white and black. In reversing a lower decision in 1855 it was held that if the slaves of several persons united in committing larceny, the owner of one of the negroes so offending would be liable for the damages committed by all.[82]

Although the old Spanish practice held to the contrary,[83] the supreme court declared in 1837 that a master was not liable if his slave killed the negro of another. The court here held that the law did not provide for injury to that form of property by a slave,[84] but this does not mean that the slave was mere property. That the slave was punished for injuring another slave, although the master was relieved of pecuniary responsibility, is learned from an issue of the Liberty Tribune of 1848: " The black man of Mr. J. D. Ewing of this county [Clay], charged with the murder of Mr. Robert Thompson's black man, had his trial on Monday last and was sentenced to receive 39 lashes and transported out of the State."[85]

The Indian slave occupied an entirely different position from that of the negro. Although feared as a race, the Indians were socially never under the ban as were the Africans. Conscious and legal as well as clandestine sexual relations existed in the Mississippi Valley, especially where the French settled. The French " voyageurs " mingled with the natives and produced a mixed race, but as slaves they seem to have come under the regular servile law. " Indian slaves," says Scharf, "it is obvious were treated and regarded as negro slaves were, with the difference, however, that more Indians than negroes were manumitted. Many of the en-

---

[82] Fackler v. Chapman, 20 Mo., 249. In 1857 a master was held not to be responsible if his slave fired a stable and thereby injured a horse belonging to a third party not the owner of the stable (Stratton v. Harriman, 24 Mo., 324). This opinion reaffirmed the decision of the lower court, and it was again reaffirmed in Armstrong v. Marmaduke, 31 Mo., 327.

[83] For the responsibility of the master for injury done by his slave to that of another during the Spanish regime see F. L. Billon, Annals of St. Louis, vol. i, pp. 58–60.

[84] Jennings v. Kavanaugh, 5 Mo., 36.

[85] Quoted from an October issue of 1848 in the History of Clay and Platte Counties, p. 140. The date of issue is not given.

slaved women were probably the concubines of their masters, and were set free, because they had borne them children."[86]

The enslavement of Indians had nearly disappeared in the Eastern States before the cession of Louisiana, although the practice still existed in a modified form.[87] In the Mississippi Valley there was also a continuous opposition to the bondage of the Indian, but the custom could not easily be prevented in such an extensive region so far from the home government. Intertribal wars led to the sale of captives rather than to their execution, and the natural thirst of the Indian for liquor and his weakness for gaming placed before the whites a most lucrative traffic which they could not always forego.

As early as 1720 Bienville forbade the enslavement of the natives along the Missouri and the Arkansas rivers who had been taken in war by the "voyageurs" upon pain of the forfeiture of their goods.[88] In 1769 Governor O'Reilley also forbade the practice, but nevertheless it continued.[89] As late as 1828 it was declared by the Missouri supreme

---

[86] J. T. Scharf, History of Saint Louis City and County, vol. i, p. 304. On December 26, 1774, St. Ange de Bellerive bequeathed three Indian slaves, a mother and two children, to his niece, Madame Belestre; the mother was to be freed at the death of Madame Belestre and the children when twenty years of age (MS. St. Louis Archives, vol. iii, p. 289).

[87] J. C. Ballagh, A History of Slavery in Virginia, p. 50. The practice was prohibited by implication in 1691 and in 1777. There were vestiges of it, however, as late as 1806.

[88] "La Compagnie ayant appris que les voyageurs, qui vont traiter sur les rivières du Missouri et des Akansas, taschent de semer la division entre les nations sauvages et de les porter à se faire la guerre pour se procurer des esclaves qu'ils achettent, ce qui non seulement est contraire aux ordonnances du Roy, mais encore très préjudiciable au bien du commerce de la Compagnie et aux establissemens qu'elle s'est proposé de faire audit pays, elle a ordonné et ordonne par la présente au sieur de Bourmont, commandant . . . de faire arrester, confisquer les marchandises des voyageurs qui viendront traiter dans l'estendue de son commandement, sans prendre sa permission et sans luy declarer les nations avec lesquelles ils ont dessein de commercer.—Mande la compagnie au sieur Lemoyne de Bienville, commandant général de la colonie." October 25, 1720 (quoted by P. Margry, Découvertes et Établissements Des Français Dans L'ouest et dans Le Sud de L'Amérique Septentrionale, vol. vi, p. 316).

[89] American State Papers, Miscellaneous, vol. i, p. 380.

court that " Indians taken captive in war, prior to 1769, by
the French, and held or sold as slaves, in the province of
Louisiana, while the same was held by the French [are]
. . . lawful slaves, and if females, their descendants likewise."[90] Six years later the same court repassed on this
case. Two of the three judges decided that the holding of
Indians as slaves was not lawful in Louisiana under either
France or Spain.[91] Thus Indian slavery passed away in
Missouri. It was already practically extinct, as little or no
mention of it is made after the American occupation.

[90] Marguerite v. Chouteau, 2 Mo., 59.
[91] Marguerite v. Chouteau, 3 Mo., 375. Judge Wash dissented.
An historical discussion of Indian servitude can be found in this
decision.

CHAPTER III

The Social Status of the Slave

In discussing the social relations of the slave it is difficult to escape being commonplace. Many points in the everyday experience of the negro have been incidentally touched in the preceding pages of this study. The ordinary life of the slave was very similar to that of the negro of today in so far as it was affected by temperament and inclination, hence it will be the endeavor of this chapter to deal simply with the more vital points of slave existence, mentioning only a few of the numerous items gathered on the different phases of the subject.

A question which caused much concern both to the slaveholder and to his antislavery critic was the education of the slave and of the free negro. After the different servile insurrections many of the eastern slave States enforced more rigidly old laws or passed new ones forbidding the teaching of the slaves. This was done largely to prevent the negroes from reading the abolition literature then being sent South.[1] Missouri, however, was less subject to social than to political or financial hysteria. Never having a slave population equal to more than a fifth of the total, being far from the insurrections to the east and south, and each master averaging so few negroes, Missouri seems not to have been affected by the movements which concerned so many of

[1] Commenting on the North Carolina law of 1830 which prohibited the teaching of the slaves to read and write, J. S. Bassett says: " This law was no doubt intended to meet the danger from the circulation of incendiary literature; yet it is no less true that it bore directly on the slave's religious life. It cut him off from the reading of the Bible—a point most insisted on by the agitators of the North. . . . The only argument made for this law was that if a slave could read he could soon become acquainted with his rights " ("Slavery in the State of North Carolina," in J. H. U. Studies, series xvii, p. 365).

the slave States. She did not change her law in common
with them, although much of it was originally copied from
Kentucky and Virginia.

When the Missouri country passed into the hands of the
United States, education among the old French settlers was
at a very low point, and undoubtedly the condition of their
slaves was worse. As late as 1820, long before a law had
been passed to prevent the teaching of negroes, a slave who
could read was something of a novelty. A fugitive is thus
described in a paper of that year: "Ranaway . . . a negro
man named Peter. . . . He pretends to be religious and can
read a little."[2] Apparently his ability to read was calculated
to attract attention.

An apprenticeship law of 1825 relieved the master from
the duty of teaching negro and mulatto apprentices reading,
writing, or arithmetic, but " if such apprentice or servant be
a free negro or mulatto he or she shall be allowed, at the
expiration of his or her term of service, a sum of money in
lieu of his education to be assessed by the probate court."[3]
This provision seemingly had no reference to masters who
desired to teach their slaves. In May, 1836, the faculty of
Marion College forbade their students to instruct "any
slave to read without the consent of his owner being first
given in writing."[4] From this statement it is learned that
the teaching of slaves must have been practiced by some
masters at least.

Either to conform to the law and practice in the Southern
States or because of interference on the part of abolitionists,
a statute was passed in 1847 which provided that " no person
shall keep or teach any school for the instruction of any
negroes or mulattoes, in reading or writing in this State "

---

[2] St. Louis Enquirer, June 14, 1820.
[3] Session Laws, 1825, p. 133, sec. 5.
[4] Fourth Annual Report (1837) of American Anti-Slavery Society,
p. 81. The Reverend J. M. Peck wrote from St. Charles in October,
1825: "I am happy to find among the slave holders in Missouri a
growing disposition to have the blacks educated, and to patronize
Sunday Schools for the purpose" (R. Babcock, Memoir of John
Mason Peck, p. 210).

under a penalty of five hundred dollars or not more than six months' imprisonment or both.[5] This statute was broken by indulgent masters and their families. " Many of us," says a prominent citizen of Lafayette County, " taught our niggers to read despite the law, but many of them refused to learn."[6] A colored educator of St. Louis asserts that Catholic sisters in that city often taught illegitimate colored girls, while free colored women, under the guise of holding sewing classes, taught negro children to read. Sometimes slave children slipped into these classes. Such a school was carried on by a Mrs. Keckley (colored) of St. Louis.[7]

As will be seen later, rigorous laws, increasing in severity in proportion to the activity of free-state neighbors in assisting slaves to escape, were passed to prevent negro assemblages, whether religious or social.[8] Nevertheless the patriarchal Missouri system fostered the religious instruction of the slave. The antebellum frontiersman was very religious and very orthodox, and the newspapers, the public speeches, and even the journals of the General Assembly abound in expressions of deep fervor. It was not a busy industrial society, and outside of St. Louis and a few other sections the liberal alien was as yet hardly known. The northern clergy with their developing unitarianism were abhorred. The master and the mistress and even the children considered themselves personally responsible for the spiritual welfare of the slave. In the rural sections the bondman usually attended his master's church.[9] " In the old Liberty Baptist church the servants occupied the northeast corner. After the whites had partaken of the Communion the cup was passed to the slaves," says a con-

---

[5] Session Laws, 1846, p. 103, secs. 1, 5.
[6] Captain Joseph A. Wilson.
[7] Statement of Professor Peter H. Clark.
[8] Pages 179–181.
[9] " Uncle " Peter Clay of Liberty stated that he went to the Baptist Church because his master did, but that after the War he joined the Methodist Church " because the Nothen Methdists stood foh freedom from slavery an freedom from sin."

temporary.[10] Very often the negroes were placed in the gallery. William Brown, a fugitive Missouri slave, declares that the slaves were instructed in religion at the owner's expense as a means of making them faithful to their masters and content in their state of servitude. He admits, however, that the owner really had a pious desire to give his negroes Christian training.[11] The restriction on negro preachers will be treated later.[12]

The statistics given of the various churches include the free colored along with the slaves, and hence are of little value in obtaining an idea of slave membership. In St. Louis, where there was a large free negro population, both classes seem to have attended the same churches, one colored minister, the Reverend Richard Anderson, having a flock of one thousand, " fully half of whom were free."[13] The other half must necessarily have been slaves. The St. Louis Directory of 1842 mentions two colored churches, each having a pastor.[14] Another negro church, organized in 1858, had seventy-five members.[15] That slaves, whether Protestant or Catholic, were often very devout is indicated by numerous touching accounts.[16]

[10] Statement of Colonel D. C. Allen of Liberty. "Uncle" Eph Sanders of Platte City said that the slaves had a corner in the Baptist Church in that town and partook of the Sacrament after the whites and from the same cup.

[11] Pp. 36, 83. A traveller passing through Independence in 1852 heard a negro preacher say in a sermon, " It is the will of God that the blacks are to be slaves . . . we must bear our fate." This writer heard that the blacks believed that bad negroes became monkeys in the next world, while the good ones became white and grew wings (J. Froebel, Seven Years Travel in Central America . . . and the Far West of the United States, p. 220).

[12] Page 180.

[13] Anderson, p. 12.

[14] These were the Reverend John Anderson, Methodist, Green and Seventh Streets, and the Reverend J. Berry Meachum, Baptist, South Fifth Street (p. vi).

[15] Scharf, vol. ii, p. 1697.

[16] The Reverend Timothy Flint, a Presbyterian missionary, states that in September, 1816, he celebrated Communion at St. Charles. On that occasion a " black servant of a Catholic Frenchman," running in, fell on his knees and partook of the Sacrament with passionate devotion (Recollections of the Last Ten Years in the Valley of the Mississippi, p. 112).

The relations 'between the old French inhabitants of Missouri and their slaves were very close. The Catholic church was the special guardian of the bondman. It was very common for the white mistress to stand as sponsor for the black babe at its baptism, or for the slave mother to act as godmother to the master's child.[17] The following entry may be read in the records of the St. Louis Cathedral: "On the thirtieth October 1836, I baptized William Henry, six weeks old, and John, six years old, both slaves belonging to Mr. H. O'Neil, born of Mary, likewise Slave belonging to Mr. H. O'Neil, Sponsors were Henry Guibord and Mary O'Neil. Jos. A. Lutz."[18]

The Catholic church considered slavery as a part of the patriarchal life of the old French settlements. The growth of the country, however, soon commercialized the system, the French families becoming as prone to slave-dealing as were the newcomers. One has but to examine the probate records of the older counties to realize this fact. The Catholic clergy themselves often held slaves whom they did not govern very strictly. Some of the religious orders inherited negroes,[19] and in 1860 St. Louis University paid taxes on six slaves.[20]

---

[17] Father D. S. Phelan of St. Louis said that he officiated at such baptisms. "The relations between the master's family and the slaves were close," he said. "I have seen the black and the white child in the same cradle, the mistress and the slave mother taking turns rocking them."

[18] MS. Records, St. Louis Cathedral, Baptisms 1835–1844, p. 37. Scharf counted 945 negro baptisms in Roman Catholic parishes in St. Louis up to 1818 (vol. i, p. 171). The present author, in company with Father Schiller of the Roman Catholic Cathedral, found several entries in the records similar to the above.

[19] Father Phelan stated that he once owned a couple of slaves but never knew what became of them. He remembers that the Lazarus Priests and other orders were at times bequeathed negroes.

[20] MS. Tax Book, St. Louis, 1860, Book P to S, p. 220. Bishops Rosati and Kenrick were taxed with no slaves, according to the St. Louis tax books covering the years 1842–60. The old Cathedral choir of the thirties and forties, led by Judge Wilson Primm, contained among others "Augustine, a mulatto slave of Bishop Dubourg, a fine tenor" (W. C. Breckenridge, "Biographical Sketch of Judge Wilson Primm," in Missouri Historical Society Collections, vol. iv, no. 2, p. 153).

The marriage relation of the slaves was necessarily lax, as the right of the owner to separate the parties was a corollary of his property right. This was the subject of very bitter criticism by antislavery people, as most of the churches admitted that the removal of either party sundered the marriage bond. A Unitarian minister of St. Louis wrote indignantly that "the sham service which the law scorned to recognize was rendered by the ministers of the gospel of Christ."[21] He also states that a religious ceremony was "according to slavery usage in well regulated Christian families."[22] William Brown, a Missouri refugee, says that the slaves were married, usually with a ceremony, when the owner ordered, but that the parties were separated at his will. He declares that he never heard of a slave being tried for bigamy.[23] Scharf claims that the official registration of a slave marriage was almost unknown in St. Louis.[24]

On the other hand, the Catholic church regularly married slaves and held the tie to be as sacred as any other marriage. The following entry appears in the Cathedral records: "On the twenty-fourth of December, Eighteen Hundred and twenty-eight the undersigned Parish priest at St. Louis received the mutual consent at Mariage between Silvester slave of Mr. Bosseron born in St. Louis and Nora Helen slave of Mr. Hough born in the city of Washington and gave them the nuptial benediction in the presence of the undersigned witnesses. Wm. Sautnier." Then follow the

---

21 W. G. Eliot, app., p. i.
22 Ibid., p. 40.
23 P. 88.
24 Vol. i, p. 305, note. In the Republican of February 16, 1854, there is the complaint of a free negress that her husband had taken another wife. "As the subject of the second marriage is a slave, and some fears being entertained that he might take her out of the state to the injury of the master, the City Marshall sent some police officers in search of him and had him arrested." Financial loss rather than moral delinquency seems to have been the burden of interest in this matter.

crosses which represent the signatures of Silvester, Nora Helen, and four other slaves and one free negro.[25]

Several old slaves were questioned 'regarding the subject of marriage, and their statements show differences in practice.   One said that he and his wife liked one another, and as they both belonged to the same master they "took up" or "simply lived together," and that this arrangement was the custom and nothing was said.[26]   A negro of Saline County who was a child in slavery days stated that his parents belonged to different persons, and, by the consent of both, were married by the squire.   The children went to the mother's master.   After the War they were again married in conformity with the new state constitution.[27] Doubtless the experience of many slave families was similar to this last.

The slave marriage was never recognized by the law, consequently a statute was passed in 1865 requiring a legal marriage of all slaves in the State under a penalty.[28]   An illustration of the legal position of the old slave marriage is best gained from a reading of the case of Johnson v. Johnson, which was handed down by the state supreme court in 1870.   Here it was held that the old slave marriages were simply moral agreements and had no legal force whatever.[29]

---

[25] MS. Records, St. Louis Cathedral, Register of Marriages 1828–1839, p. 10.   Father Phelan stated that Catholics never sold their slaves and thus escaped the predicament of severing a Church marriage.   The probate records, however, belie his statement.   The Chouteaus, Chenies, and other Catholic families bought and sold many slaves.

[26] "Uncle" Henry Napper of Marshall.

[27] John Austin of Marshall.

[28] This law reads: "In all cases where persons of color, heretofore held as slaves in the State of Missouri, have cohabited together as husband and wife, it shall be the duty of persons thus cohabiting to appear before a justice of the peace of the township where they reside, or before any other officer authorized to solemnize marriages, and it shall be the duty of such officer to join in marriage the persons thus applying, and to keep a record of the same."   The children previously born to such parties were thereby legitimatized. A fee of fifty cents was received by the recorder and sent to the one who performed the ceremony.   Those refusing to be thus married were to be criminally prosecuted (Statutes, 1865, ch. 113, secs. 12–16).

[29] "In this State marriage is considered a civil contract," said

Crime was existent among the negroes in the slavery period, although it is often asserted that the black man has degenerated since his emancipation and a mass of revolting crimes is cited in evidence. If more crimes are committed today than in slavery days, it must be remembered that there are three negroes in the South today to one in 1860, and that a massing of population in towns undoubtedly increases crime. It was to the financial advantage of the master to shield his slave and smother his crimes, while today the race problem and race feeling encourage an airing of the failings of the blacks.

While at times the misbehavior of the slave and the free negro worked the populace into mob violence, such action was of a local and temporary nature.[30]   Neither the legisla-

---

the court, "to which the consent of the parties capable in law of contracting is essential. In none of the States where slavery lately existed did the municipal law recognize the marriage rites between slaves. . . . They were responsible for their crimes, but unconditional submission to the will of the master was enjoined upon them. By common consent and universal usage existing among them, they were permitted to select their husbands and wives, and were generally married by preachers of their own race, though sometimes by white ministers. They were known and recognized as husband and wife by their masters and in the community in which they lived; but whatever moral force there may have been in such connections, it is evident there was nothing binding or obligatory in the laws. . . . The slave, in entering into marriage, did a moral act; and though not binding in law it was no violation of any legal duty. If, after emancipation, there was no confirmation by cohabitation or otherwise, it is obvious that there would be no grounds for holding the marriage as subsisting or binding. . . . That in his earlier days he was previously married can make no difference. His first marriage in his then state of servitude had no legal existence; he was at liberty to repudiate it at pleasure; and by his continuing to live with respondent and acknowledge her as his lawful wife after he had obtained his civil rights, he disaffirms his first marriage and ratifies the second" (45 Mo., 598). "Uncle" Henry Napper of Marshall stated that he knew many negroes who took advantage of the interpretation of the new statute to leave the neighborhood and marry a young wife.

[30] In 1837 the governor "unconditionally" pardoned a slave woman who had been condemned for murder. His action caused no popular criticism (House Journal [Journals of the General Assembly of Missouri, House and Senate Journals], 9th Ass., 1st sess., p. 319). But when in 1854 a slave, condemned by the supreme court for raping a white girl, was pardoned, the Republican of February 7 stated editorially: "We are at a loss to determine upon what grounds the Executive thought proper to exercise his clemency . . . it was

tion nor the court decisions seem to have been influenced by any crimes on the part of the slaves. Of the two negro cases which caused the most feeling, one, the McIntosh affair of 1836, concerned a free negro, and the other, that of "Jack" Anderson, was a murder committed by a slave who had resided for some time in Canada.[81] Consequently there was no such feeling toward the slave as there was throughout the period toward the free negro. The Missourian, though irritated by political interference with his property and bitter against those who sought to carry off his blacks, had a rough good humor, and apparently exercised a spirit of fairness toward his bondmen.

The old slave masters without exception declare that the system was patriarchal in Missouri and that the bond between the owner and the owned was very close. The small number of slaves held by the vast majority of the masters was one reason for this condition. When the young Virginian or Kentuckian and his negroes emigrated to far-off Missouri, they suffered in common the pangs of parting, and together went to develop the virgin soil amid common dangers and common hardships. Thus there undoubtedly grew up an attachment that the older communities had long since outgrown.

For the territorial period there is evidence that the rela-

---

an outrage of the most flagrant character, and deserved the severest punishment." Even this criticism of the court seems very calm considering the color of the offender.

[81] Francis McIntosh, a powerful negro, stabbed two officers who were escorting him to prison. He was burned by a St. Louis mob. A full account of this event is given in J. F. Darby, Personal Recollections of Men and Events in St. Louis, pp. 237–242. See also below, p. 117. Anderson had escaped to Canada. While on a visit to Missouri to remove his family he was apprehended by Seneca Diggs of Howard County, whom he shot (September 24, 1859). This episode caused much excitement. His extradition was still pending when the Civil War opened, as he had again fled to Canada. On March 27, 1861, certain citizens of Howard County were petitioning for money advanced by them to prosecute Anderson (Session Laws, 1860, p. 534). There is also a short account of this episode in W. H. Siebert, The Underground Railroad from Slavery to Freedom, p. 352. This affair is discussed, and also the action of the Canadian authorities and courts, in the Twenty-Eighth Annual Report of the American Anti-Slavery Society (1861), pp. 167–170.

tion between the races was friendly. Judge J. C. B. Lucas of St. Louis, a man who certainly had no love for the slavery system and who in 1820 advocated its restriction, admitted this fact. " I confess," he wrote, " that I do not entertain very serious apprehension of slaves as domestics . . . they are usually treated with a degree of humanity, and not infrequently of paternal affection. The opportunities they have to observe the conduct of the master's family, to attend public worship, and the satisfaction they receive from enjoying in a reasonable degree the comforts of life, generally induces them to respect the rights of others and be harmless."[32]

This condition of fellowship between master and man, made possible by deep respect on the part of the slave, continued on to the Civil War in many rural communities. " The Missouri slave holders," said Mr. Robert B. Price of Columbia, " were not such through choice. They inherited their negroes and felt duty bound to keep them." Colonel J. L. Robards of Hannibal stated that his father left him a number of slaves to whom he was fondly attached and whom he considered as a family trust. Mr. E. W. Strode of Independence claims that the negro was closely united to the master's family. Mr. Strode stated that his grandfather required in his will that the slaves be kept in the family, and that they were so held till the Civil War. " The children of the master," said Mr. Strode, " played and fought with the slave children with due respect, there being no need for race distinction."

The slave not only worshipped at his master's church and partook of the same sacraments as his master, but was ministered to by the same pastor and attended by the family physician.[33] In the quaint little cemetery south of Colum-

---

[32] Letter in the Missouri Gazette of April 12, 1820.

[33] Although as property the slave was naturally well protected, yet the following item shows how really sincere the master generally was in the care of his slaves. This news item appeared in the Missouri Intelligencer in 1835: " We with pleasure announce for the benefit of the public, that on Wednesday last, Dr. William Jewell of this Town [Fayette], successfully performed the great operation of

bia, where lie William Jewell and Charles H. Hardin, rest also the family servants. The latter are buried together side by side under small marble markers in the further side of the lot. Nothing can give a better impression of the strong tie between the slave and his master. This presents an idea of the system in its ideal state and under men who both intellectually and politically made life brighter in Missouri. " My mother," said Mr. R. B. Price, " labored incessantly to clothe and nurse our slaves—with no thought of any ulterior motive." Thus there is presented a picture of the system in the hands of the responsible and the conscientious, but economic pressure, human depravity, and greed too often made the picture morbid and disgusting. Herein lay the weakness of the system. The comparatively unlimited power of the master might be used for the blessing of the slave, or for his misery.

A general view of the condition of the Missouri slave can be gained from the recollections of one of the most eminent antislavery statesmen of the period, General George R. Smith of Sedalia. " The negroes," he wrote, " had Saturday ' evenings' as the afternoons were called, in which to do work for themselves; and what they made during this time they could sell and so get a little money. For money, however, they had little need, as they had no opportunities for higher life. . . . The masters were usually humane and there was often real affection between master and slave— very often great kindliness. There were merciful services from each to the other: there was laughter, song, and happiness in the negro quarters. . . . The old negroes had their comfortable quarters, where each family would sit by their own great sparkling log fires. . . . They sang their plantation songs, grew hilarious over their corn shuckings and did the bidding of their gracious master. Their doctor's

---

Lithotomy, or cutting for stone in the bladder. . . . The individual operated upon by the Doctor was a little yellow boy, about eight years of age, the property of Archibald W. Turner, Esq." (quoted in the Jeffersonian Republican of May 2, 1835, from an unknown issue of the Intelligencer).

bills were paid; their clothing bought, or woven by themselves in their cabins, and made by their mistress; their sick
nursed; and their dead laid away,—all without thought
from themselves."[34]   " I was but a lad in slavery days," says
Mr. Dean D. Duggins of Marshall, " but my recollections of
the institution are most pleasant.   I can remember how in
the evening at husking time the negroes would come singing
up the creek.   They would work till ten o'clock amidst
singing and pleasantry and after a hot supper and hard cider
would depart for their cabins.   The servants were very
careful of the language used before the white children and
would reprove and even punish the master's children."[35]
" How well I remember those happy days!" wrote Lucy
A. Delaney.   " Slavery had no horror then for me, as I
played about the place, with the same joyful freedom as the
little white children.   With mother, father, and sister, a
pleasant home and surroundings, what happier child than
I!"[36]

The life of the slave was often made happy by privileges
which a negro can appreciate as can no one else.   Colonel
R. B. C. Wilson of Platte City says that the happiest hours
of his life were on Saturday afternoons in the slavery days
when he and the negroes and dogs went tramping through
the woods for game.   The slaves had their dances under

---

[34] S. B. Harding, Life of George R. Smith, pp. 50–51.   As General
Smith spent his life in Kentucky and Missouri, it may be inferred
that he here refers to slave life in these States.

[35] Major G. W. Lankford of Marshall stated that the old servants
often made the master's children behave.   Captain Joseph A. Wilson
of Lexington tells the following story: " One day my brother, a
slave girl, and myself were playing with sticks which represented
river boats.   We had seen the boats run past the landing and then
turn about and land at the dock prow foremost.   But the slave girl
insisted on running her boat in backwards.   My mother, who was in
an adjoining room, soon heard the slave girl give a great howl,
screaming that Henry had slapped her.   ' Henry, why did you strike
that child,' said mother.   ' Well, she is always landing stern first,'
protested Henry.   This anecdote shows how paternal the system
was in our part of the state."

[36] P. 13.   Later Lucy Delaney had less humane masters and mistresses.   Her book, few copies of which are now extant, gives a
good picture of slave life in St. Louis, despite her hostile attitude
toward the system.

regulations and with officers present. The circus was also open, occasionally at least, to the slaves, who with the children went in for half price.[87]

The treatment of the negro was seen from various angles by contemporaries. One general statement was that " the slaves were universally well treated, being considered almost as one of the other's family . . . and in all things enjoyed life about as much as their masters."[88] Frank Blair, who worked for emancipation and colonization throughout his career, said in a speech at Boston in 1859 that the Missouri slaveholder was kind to his negro.[89] Blair was certainly not a man to trim for political purposes by praising slave-owners, especially in Boston. Gottfried Duden, who visited Missouri in 1824–27, declared that the slave in the grain-producing States was well off—as well or better situated than the day laborer of Germany.[40] Another German, Prince Maximilian of Wied, who travelled about the State in 1832–34, remarked that " though modern travellers represent in very favorable colors the situation of this oppressed race, the slaves are no better off here than in other countries. Everywhere they are a demoralized race, little to be depended upon. . . . We were witnesses of deplorable punishments of these people. One of our neighbors at St. Louis, for instance, flogged one of his slaves in the public

<hr>

[87] The following advertisement is found in the St. Joseph Commercial Cycle of June 29 and July 6, 1855: " E. T. and J. Mabies' Grand Combined Menagerie. . . . Admission 50 cents: children and servants 25 cts." The word " servant" was applied through the South to the negro slave in polite language. In the law, however, as in formal language, the word " slave " was used.

[88] H. C. Levens and U. M. Drake, A History of Cooper County, Missouri, p. 120. A secondary authority gives a similar picture of the happiness and the close relation of the races in the territorial period. He even goes so far as to declare that " they [the master and his slave] counseled together for the promotion of their mutual interests: the slave expressed his opinion . . . as freely as his mistress or master; nor did he often wait to be solicited." No authority for this statement is given (D. R. McAnally, A History of Methodism in Missouri, vol. i, pp. 146–147).

[89] F. P. Blair, Jr., The Destiny of the Races of this Continent, p. 25.

[40] Bereicht ueber eine Reise nach den Westlichen Staaten Nordamerika's, p. 146.

streets, with untiring arm. Sometimes he stopped a moment to rest, and then began anew."[41]

The physical punishment of the slave was the joint of antislavery attack, and was undoubtedly an often abused necessity on the part of the owner. "We treated our slaves with all humanity possible considering that discipline had to be maintained," said Colonel D. C. Allen of Liberty. It has always been argued that corporal suasion alone could influence a creature as primitive as the slave. The law forbade unnecessary cruelty to slaves and public sentiment opposed it. The Reverend William G. Eliot, though having very decided antislavery views, stated that "the treatment of slaves in Missouri was perhaps exceptionally humane. All cruelty or 'unnecessary' severity was frowned upon by the whole community. The general feeling was against it."[42] Another antislavery clergyman, the Reverend Galusha Anderson, said that the St. Louis slaves were mostly well treated, but that he knew of several notorious cases of bad treatment.[43] Those who had no sympathy with the system easily found much that was revolting.[44] Reports coming from such sources make no mention of the benefits which partly counterbalanced the evils.

Exact knowledge of the treatment of the slave is difficult to reach. A wide difference of opinion is found even among

---

[41] "Travels in the Interior of America," in R. G. Thwaites, Early Western Travels, vol. xxii, p. 216.

[42] W. G. Eliot, p. 39. He mentions several cases of very cruel treatment that he observed (ibid., pp. 39, 91–94, 101–103).

[43] P. 170.

[44] Brown, pp. 28–38. He dwells upon several very disgusting instances which he witnessed as a Missouri slave. Dr. John Doy gives several tales of cruelty which he both saw and heard while a prisoner at Platte City and St. Joseph (pp. 61–62, 94–99, 102–103). The American Anti-Slavery Society tract, "American Slavery as It Is (1839)," is rich in revolting tales, and contains several accounts of events which it claims took place in Missouri (pp. 71, 88–89, 127, 158). A Virginia slaveholder on his way to Kansas, where he later joined a company of Southern Rangers, stopped in Missouri for a few weeks. He prevented a mule dealer named Watson from beating his negro with a chain. "If he had not been checked when he was so mad, he might have killed the poor darkey, and nothing would have been thought of it" (Williams, p. 69).

contemporaries living in the same locality. Colonel D. C. Allen of Liberty asserted that he had never witnessed any instances of bad treatment, while " Uncle " Eph Sanders, an old Platte County slave, stated that for every kind master there were two brutes who drove their negroes as they did their mules. " But my own master," said " Uncle " Eph, " was very good. The slaves were treated about like his own family. He allowed no one to mistreat us and hated the hard masters of the neighborhood." As it would be impossible to reduce the matter to mathematical exactitude, we must be content to generalize from the particular instances given.[45]

Self-interest naturally prevented treatment that was severe enough to affect the slave physically, except in the case of an owner blind to all sense of his own advantage. Captain J. A. Wilson of Lexington, a man of clear insight and one who saw the evils as well as the good in the system, says: " There was not much public whipping. It was an event which attracted a crowd and was thought worthy of comment. It made the slave resentful, if he was innocent, and but hardened him if he was guilty. If a slave bore the scars of the lash his sale would be difficult. In Lafayette county ill treatment of the slave was condemned. William Ish killed one of his slaves with a chisel for not working to suit him. The public sentiment was bitter against him. He spent a fortune to escape the penitentiary." J. B. Tinsley of Audrain County threatened to prosecute the patrol for whipping one of his slaves.[46] A slave was once whipped by the patrol as he was returning at night from the livery stable in Lexington where he was hired. The hirer sued the patrol, as the negro was on legitimate business.[47] From

---

[45] Anice Washington of St. Louis said: " Some slaves were very bad and they deserved to be whipped. My master once struck me when I was a girl and I have the scar on my wrist yet. I refused to go and get the cows when he ordered. I was owned by two masters. One treated me much better than the other, but he was better off."
[46] Statement of Mr. J. W. Beatty of Mexico.
[47] " Uncle " Peter Clay of Liberty.

what could be learned the slaves, while by no means considered as equals or comrades, were very jealously guarded by their masters. Missouri was so surrounded by free territory that it was necessary to keep the negro in as good humor as possible.

The punishment of the slave for indolence, sedition, and other forms of misconduct was largely left to the master. The State punished the negro for crime, but could hardly be expected to enforce the master's personal demands upon him. However, in some cases the public took an interest in the matter. An ordinance of Jefferson City permitted owners having "refractory" slaves to require an officer to give them "reasonable punishment." The constable or other official so whipping the slave was to receive for his services fifty cents, which was collectable as were his other fees.[48]

The amount of labor required of the slave has already been considered.[49] Some were undoubtedly cruelly worked. William Brown, a slave who lived on a tobacco and hemp plantation "thirty or forty miles above St. Charles on the Missouri River," says that the slaves were given ten stripes with a loaded whip if not in the fields at four-thirty in the morning, and that their wounds were washed with salt water or rum.[50] This may be a true account, but it was exceptional. However, other cases of long hours have been found. Anice Washington stated that while a slave in Madison County she went to the fields at four, and after supper spun or knit till dark. "We had dinner at noon of meat and bread with greens or other vegetables in summer, and bread and milk for supper. While in St. Francis county I did not have enough to eat." "I had a good master," said a Saline County slave, "and had plenty to eat. We had three meals a day—bacon, cabbage, potatoes,

---

[48] Mandatory Ordinance relative to the City Police, and to Prevent and Restrain the Meeting of Slaves, of June 16, 1836, sec. 5 (Jeffersonian Republican, June 25, 1836).

[49] Above, pages 26–27.

[50] Pp. 14, 20–24.

turnips, beans, and some times molasses, coffee, and sugar.
We also had milk and some times butter. We got a little
whiskey at harvest. We were in the field before sun-up
but were not worked severely. One of the neighboring
farmers had a lot of slaves and he was a hard man. He
shoved 'em through. We had another neighbor who un-
mercifully whipped his slaves if they shirked."[51] A Platte
County slave declared that he had a good master and had
plenty to eat and wear. "We were given liquor in harvest
and had no Saturday afternoon nor Sunday work. Christmas week was also a holiday. But all slaves were not
treated so well. I have seen mothers go to the field and
leave their babies with an old negress. They could go to
them three times during the day."[52] This negro's wife
stated that she was once hired out by her mistress, and often
had only sour rice and the leavings of biscuits to eat.
"Uncle" Peter Clay of Liberty said that he was well
enough fed and was given whiskey at harvest, corn shuck-
ing, and Christmas time.

Although bitterly opposed to slavery, the abolitionist,
George Thompson, in order to prove that the negro was
capable of making his own way, stated that while a prisoner
in the Palmyra jail in 1841 he saw slaves who were certainly anything but oppressed. "The slaves here, on the
Sabbaths, dress like gentlemen. They get their clothes by
extra work, done on the Sabbaths and in the night, and yet
they can't take care of themselves. Shame on those who
hide under this leaf."[53] The War brought no immediate
relief to many of the slaves, as the reports of the Western
Sanitary Commission show. "At one time an order was

---

[51] Henry Napper of Marshall. Thomas Summers of Cape Girardeau lived near Jackson in slavery days. "I was never exposed
in such weather nor worked so hard while a slave as since I have
been free," he said, "but I would rather be free and eat flies than
be a slave on plenty." His mistress made the clothes of the slaves
and they were well fed. He remembered few slaves being cruelly
used in the county.
[52] Eph Sanders of Platte City.
[53] P. 42.

issued forbidding their payment [for excavating, teaming, and other camp work] on the ground that their master would have a claim against the Government for their services. All the while they were compelled to do most of the hard work of the place [St. Louis] and press gangs were sent out to take them in the streets. . . . Sometimes they were shot down and murdered with impunity. They were often driven with their families into 'Camp Ethiopia' with only cast off army tents to shield them. At one time an order was issued driving them out of the Union lines and into the hands of their old masters."[54]

So much has been written on the life of the slave, and so much of this has been argumentative, that little more than a brief sketch of the everyday life of the slave has been attempted here.

[54] Rev. J. G. Forman, The Western Sanitary Commission (1864), pp. 111-112.

CHAPTER IV

The Slavery Issue in Politics and in the Churches

The motives behind the fight for statehood in Missouri during the years 1819–21 have been discussed by several writers.[1] The opinion of the majority of authorities on this subject is that the sentiment of Missouri in 1819 shifted from the old Jeffersonian dislike of slavery, or at least from a cold support of the system, to an avowed proslavery position. This change of attitude is said to have been caused by the attack of the northern representatives in Congress on Missouri's efforts to secure statehood, this northern opposition being based on avowed hostility to slavery extension. This is the orthodox view, and it is held by those who declare that the South at heart had no great solicitude for slavery till northern interference pricked her pride. At first glance this appears plausible, but a closer inspection of the materials relating to the period shows this opinion to be both superficial and unreasonable.

The people of Missouri were in favor of slavery from the earliest days of its existence as a Territory. Even before Missouri became a Territory her citizens had what appears to have been more than a mere nominal attachment to "the peculiar institution." On January 4, 1805, the settlers about

---

[1] F. H. Hodder, "Side Lights on the Missouri Compromises," in American Historical Association Reports, 1909, pp. 151–161; L. Carr, Missouri: A Bone of Contention, ch. vi, vii; F. C. Shoemaker, The First Constitution of Missouri. The author of the present study treated this point briefly in his "Slavery in Missouri Territory," in Missouri Historical Review, vol. iii, no. 3, pp. 196–197. Governor Amos Stoddard in discussing slavery in Louisiana refers rather to the system as he viewed it on the lower Mississippi. Speaking of the slave States as a whole he says: "Their feelings, and even their prejudices, are entitled to respect; and a system of emancipation cannot be contrived with too much caution" (Sketches Historical and Descriptive of Louisiana, p. 342).

St. Louis protested warmly at being joined to the Indiana Territory under the title of "The District of Louisiana." Their pride was touched and their grievances were many, but of all their complaints the fear for their slave property seems to have been one of the most weighty. Their memorial to Congress reads as follows: "Slaves cannot exist in the Indiana Territory, and slavery prevails in Louisiana, and here your petitioners must beg leave to observe to your honorable Houses, that they conceive their property of every description has been warranted to them by the treaty between the United States and the French Republic. . . . Is not the silence of Congress with respect to slavery in the District of Louisiana, and the placing of this district under the government of a territory where slavery is proscribed, calculated to alarm the people with respect to that kind of property, and to create the presumption of a disposition in Congress, to abolish at some future day slavery altogether in the District of Louisiana?" Again they claimed that the treaty warranted "the free possession of our slaves, and the right of importing slaves into the District of Louisiana, under such restrictions as to Congress in their Wisdom will appear necessary."[2]

This last statement at least was no mere attempt to conserve existing property, but was an open desire to import blacks. The full force of the slavery issue, however, did not develop till the struggle for statehood opened. Petitions to this end are said to have been signed by citizens of Missouri Territory as early as 1817.[3] Apparently no mention of slavery was made in them. On January 8, 1818, the

---

[2] Representation and petition of the representatives elected by the Freemen of the territory of Louisiana. 4th January, 1805. Pp. 11-12, 22. This original printed petition is in the Library of Congress. The text of the petition can also be found in American State Papers, Miscellaneous, vol. i, pp. 400-405. One petition was signed September 29, and another September 30, 1804, at St. Louis (ibid.).

[3] L. Houck mentions one which was circulated in 1817 and was presented in 1818 (History of Missouri, vol. iii, pp. 243-245). Scharf quotes the Missouri Gazette of October 11, 1817, as stating that a memorial praying for statehood was being circulated (vol. i, p. 561, note).

speaker of the House of Representatives " presented a petition from sundry inhabitants of the Territory of Missouri
praying that the said Territory may be admitted into the
Union; on an equal footing with the original States."[4]
John Scott, the territorial delegate, presented several similarly described papers on February 2 and March 16, 1818.[5]
There is in the Library of Congress a printed petition signed
by sixty-eight Missourians. It is not dated and makes no
mention of slavery, though it deals extensively with territorial needs and abuses.[6]

That the Missouri of 1820 really had considerable slave
property to fight for is evident. Between 1810 and 1820 the
slave population of the Territory had grown from 3011 to
10,222.[7] That this gain was not simply the natural increase
of the negroes of the old French settlers is learned from
many sources. An item in the Missouri Gazette of October
26, 1816, says that " a stranger to witness the scene would
imagine that Virginia, Kentucky, Tennessee, and the Carolinas had made an agreement to introduce us as soon as
possible to the bosom of the American family. Every ferry
on the river is daily occupied in passing families, carriages,
wagons, [and] negroes." The same paper on June 9, 1819,
gives the following report from St. Charles: " Never has
such an influx of people . . . been so considerable, . . . flow-
ing through our town with their maid servants and men
servants . . . the throng of hogs and cattle, the whiteheaded
children, and curlyheaded Africans." Another item in the
same issue states that " 170 emigrants were at the Portage
des Sioux at one time last week." The papers for nearly
every week from the above date are filled with similar statements. That the newcomers were of the kind to make

[4] Annals of Congress, 15th Cong., 1st Sess., vol. i, p. 591.
[5] Ibid., vol. ii, pp. 839, 1391. Alphonso Wetmore mentions a Missouri petition of 1818, but says nothing as to any slavery clauses
being in it (Gazetteer of the State of Missouri, p. 212).
[6] This petition is in the Manuscripts Division. At least one signature has been removed and with it the lower right-hand corner,
which perhaps also contained the date. It was printed by S. Hall
of St. Louis.
[7] Federal Census, Statistical View, 1790–1830, p. 27.

Missouri a slave State there is no trouble in discovering.
The St. Louis Enquirer of November 19, 1819, informs us
that a citizen of St. Charles counted for nine or ten weeks
an average of one hundred and twenty settlers' vehicles per
week, with an average of eighteen persons per vehicle.
"They came," it continues, "almost exclusively from the
States south of the Potomac and the Ohio bringing slaves
and large herds of cattle." The Gazette of January 26,
1820, states that "our population is daily becoming more
heterogenious [sic] . . . scarcely a Yankee has moved into
the country this year. At the same time Virginians, Carolinians, Tennesseeans, and Kentuckians are moving in great
force." The St. Louis Enquirer of November 10, 1819,
claims that in October of that year two hundred and
seventy-one four-wheeled and fifty-five two-wheeled vehicles
passed "Mrs. Griffith's in the point of the Missouri," bound
for Boone's Lick, and speculates that from ten to fifteen
thousand people would settle in Missouri during the autumn.
Timothy Flint, a New England clergyman, counted a hundred persons passing through St. Charles in one day. " I
have seen . . . nine wagons, harnessed with from four to six
horses. We may allow one hundred cattle . . . and from
three or four to twenty slaves to each wagon. The slaves
seem fond of their masters."[8]

This change in the character of the population is reflected
in the personnel of the constitutional convention of 1820.
According to one partisan paper there was not "a single
confessed restrictionist elected."[9] At Mine à Burton the

[8] P. 201.
[9] St. Louis Enquirer, May 10, 1820. Benjamin Emmons of St.
Charles is rumored to have been the only antislavery man in the
convention. Vermont and New York are both said to have been
his native State. If Emmons was marked as the only emancipationist in the convention, it is strange that he had the confidence of
his fellow members to such an extent as he did. He was actually
placed on the most important committee, considering the slavery
agitation of the time,—the legislative committee, which drafted the
slavery sections of the new constitution (ibid., June 14, 1820). Emmons was later elected to the state Senate, and at a St. Charles
mass-meeting of December 19, 1821, he was made chairman (The
Missourian, January 24, 1822). Emmons was a tavern keeper, and
his advertisement may be seen in the above issue.

"Manumission Men" were beaten by 1147 to 61 votes,[10] at St. Louis by about 3 to 1,[11] and in Cape Girardeau County by 4 to 3.[12] It therefore appears that this influx of new-comers had brought into the Territory many who had financial or hereditary reasons for favoring slavery. A letter of Judge J. B. C. Lucas of St. Louis, written October 27, 1820, confirms the fact that slavery was the basis, at least to a considerable extent, of the local struggle against restriction. "I was a candidate," wrote Judge Lucas, "for the state convention. I did not succeed because being re-quested to declare my sentiments on the subject of slavery, I expressed an opinion that it would be proper to limit the importation of slaves to five years or a short period from the date of the Constitution . . . the ardent friends of slavery, in all its extent and attributes, charged me, or suspected me to be hostile to the principles altogether, and contended that I dare not go the whole length of my opinion, knowing it to be unpopular. In fact I was called an eman-cipator and this is the worst name that can be given in the state of Missouri."[13] Judge Lucas also stated that as he was known to oppose the Spanish land claims these claim-ants, in order to procure his defeat—in which object they succeeded—spread the report that he opposed slavery.[14] If such an issue was raised to defeat a candidate, St. Louis at least must have been strongly proslavery in sentiment in 1820, but it was not the "Lawyer Junto" of that city alone which had this feeling, as will be seen later. It seems hardly possible that the hardheaded frontiersmen with their ten thousand slaves would thunder at Congress for two years on an abstract question of constitutional equality.[15]

[10] St. Louis Enquirer, May 10, 1820.
[11] Missouri Gazette, May 20, 1820.
[12] St. Louis Enquirer, May 31, 1820.
[13] Lucas to Robert Moore (J. B. C. Lucas, Jr., comp., Letters of Hon. J. B. C. Lucas, from 1815 to 1836, pp. 28–29).
[14] Lucas to William Lowndes, November 26, 1821 (ibid., p. 158); Lucas to Rufus King, November 16, 1821 (ibid., p. 148).
[15] This view is somewhat stronger than that expressed in my former study of this period (see note 1 of this chapter). Professor Hodder is of the contrary opinion. He states regarding the sweep-

The immigration of southern settlers during the late territorial period changed the social complexion of Missouri. To this fact can be traced the real cause of the anxiety of the people to be admitted as a slave State.   This lay at the heart of the outcry against the attempt of Congress to force conditions on the new commonwealth.   The merits of the slavery question were soon obscured, and the excitement veered over into the constitutional field.[16]   Slavery was theoretically condemned, and at the same time the right to import negroes was asserted.   At least a denial of the right of Congress to prevent the introduction of slaves became the cry of the proslavery party.   "No Congressional Restriction!" was the shibboleth of the day.   "I regret as much as any person," declaimed John Scott, the territorial delegate in 1819, "the existence of Slavery in the United States.   I think it wrong in itself, nor on principle would I be understood as advocating it; but I trust I shall always be an advocate of the people's rights to decide on this question . . . for themselves. . . . I consider it not only un-

ing victory of the proslavery party in the constitutional convention election of 1820 that "the result seems to have been due not so much to any very strong sentiment in favor of slavery as to a fierce resentment bred by the Congressional attempt at dictation" (p. 155). Professor Woodburn agrees with this view. "It does not appear," he writes, "that any of those who argued for the free admission of Missouri ventured to defend the institution of slavery. . . . The defence for Missouri rested almost altogether on the constitutional phases of the question.   They touched the evils of slavery only in minor and incidental ways" ("The Historical Significance of the Missouri Compromise," in American Historical Association Reports, 1893, p. 284).   On the other hand, Frank Blair went so far as to say, "The effort [to restrict slavery] was defeated by the interposition of 10,000 slaves in Missouri, and the threat to dissolve the Union, unless permitted to constitute it a slave state" (The Destiny of the Races of this Continent, p. 7).

[16] This purely constitutional nature of the struggle is denied by a correspondent signing his name "X." He denies the charge that the slavery restrictionists favored congressional tyranny.   "It is a notorious fact," he continues, "that many, if not all of the individuals who are opposed to slavery, were equally opposed to the interference of Congress on the subject."   He also says that "every individual, who happened to believe slavery an evil, and its further introduction into Missouri prejudicial, have been indiscriminately abused" (Missouri Gazette, May 31, 1820).

friendly to the slaves themselves to confine them to the South, but wholly incompetent on Congress to interfere."[17]

In this same strain Henry Carroll, on presenting a resolution from Howard County against congressional interference, said: "There are none within my view, none it might be said in Boone's Lick country . . . who would not lend efficient co-operation to achieve all the good within their compass, and wipe from the fair cheek the foul stain which soils it . . . [but] a rejection of slavery cannot fail to shut out of our country those disposed to migrate hither from the southern states, under a repugnance to separate from the labor useful to them."[18]   On September 11, 1819, the Baptist Association in session at Mount Pleasant Meeting House in Howard County adopted a petition to Congress in which these words are found: "Although with Washington and Jefferson . . . we regret the existence of slavery at all . . . and look forward to a time when a happy emancipation can be effected, consistent with the principles of . . . Justice . . . the constitution does not admit slaves to be freemen; it does admit them to be property . . . we have all the means necessary for a state government, and believe that the question of slavery is one which belongs exclusively to the people to decide on."[19]

The efforts of Congress to dictate the slave policy of Missouri raised a veritable tidal wave of antagonism in the Territory. On April 28, 1819, citizens of Montgomery County vigorously criticized Congress.[20]   Resolutions followed to the same effect in Franklin County on July 5,[21] in Washington County on the 29th,[22] and in New Madrid County soon after.[23]   In some cases the theory of limiting importations of negroes into the new State was advocated, but any tampering with the slaves already in the Territory

---

[17] Missouri Intelligencer, July 16, 1819.
[18] Ibid., July 9, 1819.
[19] St. Louis Enquirer, October 20, 1819.
[20] Missouri Herald, August 20, 1819.
[21] Missouri Intelligencer, July 9, 1819.
[22] Missouri Herald, August 4, 1819.
[23] Ibid., August 20, 1819.

was condemned.   Such a declaration was made at a meeting
at Herculaneum in Jefferson County in April, 1819,[24] and
the grand jury of the county followed the example in July.[25]
On April 11, 1819, nearly a hundred citizens of St. Louis
met and condemned any further importations of slaves into
the State, but decried any interference with the local system
as it existed.[26]

Official bodies joined in the protest against Federal
tyranny.   The grand jurors of St. Louis on April 5, 1819,
declared that "they believe that all the slave-holding states
are virtually menaced and threatened with eventual destruction [if slavery is prohibited in Missouri]."[27]   The
grand jurors of Montgomery County in July said, " They
view the restriction attempted to be imposed on the people
of Missouri Territory in the formation of a State Constitution as unlawful, unconstitutional, and oppressive."[28]   The
Washington County grand jury put themselves similarly on
record during the same month.[29]   The editorials, the correspondence, and the general material of the press during
these months bear witness to the interest which Missouri
took in the slavery question.

If the mere naked words and phrases of the multitude of
indignant resolutions and declarations of the period be accepted as the expression of honest opinion, we should be
forced to the conclusion that the majority of the inhabitants
of the Territory in 1820 thought less of slave labor than of
constitutional rights.   Nevertheless, the present writer and
at least one other student of the period are forced by both
internal and external evidence to the belief that the declara-

[24] Missouri Gazette, April 26, 1819.   At this meeting at Herculaneum a three-column argument against slavery in the abstract was
drawn up.   It was argued that a restriction of importations would
ultimately wipe out the system.   " This perhaps will be the only time
that you will ever have in your power to oppose the Horrible system
with effect," concludes this statement.
[25] Missouri Herald, September 10, 1819.
[26] Missouri Gazette, April 12, 1819.
[27] Ibid., May 12, 1819.
[28] Missouri Herald, September 4, 1819.
[29] Ibid., August 20, 1819.

108 SLAVERY IN MISSOURI, 1804–1865 [290

tions of the press and of the various individuals and political
bodies should not be taken on faith as being the real sentiments of the day.[30] No great liberties need be taken in
interpreting the phraseology of the documents of these years
to arrive at this view. The real solicitude of the "anti-
restriction" men for slavery creeps out here and there with
bald frankness.

On April 5, 1819, the "Grand Jury of the Northern Circuit of the Territory of Missouri," meeting at St. Louis,
declared that congressional restriction of slavery was "an
unconstitutional and unwarrantable usurpation of power
over our unalienable rights and privileges as a free people.
. . . Although we deprecate anything like an idea of disunion
which next to our personal liberty and security of property
is our dearest right . . . we feel it our duty to take a manly
and dignified stand for our rights and privileges."[31] It appears that these jurors, at least, struck at the root of the
whole matter when they advanced "personal liberty and
security of property" as alone being dearer than the Union.
Another illustration of this point appears in the account of
the celebration at St. Louis on March 30, 1820, to com-
memorate the enabling act which Congress had just passed,
admitting Missouri with slavery. Among other features of
this celebration was one "representing a slave in great
spirits, rejoicing at the permission granted by Congress to
bring slaves into so fine a country as Missouri."[32] This

[30] When the author of this study and Mr. Floyd C. Shoemaker
compared conclusions, it was found that they were identical on this
point. We had arrived at them independently. He had judged
from internal evidence in studying the convention in detail and the
constitution which resulted from its work. My own conclusions
were largely gained from external evidence, a study of the make-up
of the population, previous and subsequent expressions and events,
and also by reflecting back the whole later slavery struggle in Missouri upon this period when not only Missouri but the entire South
was finding its bearings on the slavery question. Mr. Shoemaker's
study, an enlargement of his early study of the Constitution of
Missouri of 1820, will soon appear in print.
[31] MS., signed by John McKnight, foreman, and the other jurors,
and by Archibald Gamble, clerk, Dalton Collection.
[32] Missouri Gazette, April 5, 1820.

affair does not look like the celebration of a victory over a point of constitutional law.

The real strength of an immediate emancipation party during these years is not difficult to measure. Joseph Charless of the Missouri Gazette, who led the forces of those who opposed the introduction of slaves, stated editorially that he had spoken personally with all the convention candidates on his slate—Lucas, Bobb, Pettibone, and so forth. He said: "I am apprised of the sentiments of all those candidates who were favorable to the restriction of slavery. . . . They are decidedly opposed to any interference with the slaves now in the territory."[33] Judge Lucas, in a long statement in the Gazette of April 12, 1820, denied that he was an immediate emancipationist, but said that he did favor the limitation of the period allowed for the importation of negroes lest the State be filled with thieving slaves and with overgrown slaveholding "nabobs" who would corrupt the democratic institutions of Missouri. He also argued that slaves would cause white labor to shun the State, and so argued for restriction.

Of all the convention candidates whose cards appear in the four papers examined which cover the campaign period not one advocated any interference whatever with the slave property of the Territory.[34] Many were for the restriction of future importations, but none favored any meddling with the slaves already on the soil. Most of them condemned slavery in the abstract, but at the same time came out boldly for temporary importations. Pierre Chouteau, Jr., who is a fair example of these, declared that should he be elected

---

[33] Missouri Gazette, April 12, 1820. Charless wrote this in answer to "A Farmer" who disclaimed any desire to see more slaves imported, but opposed emancipating those then in the Territory. The candidates of the various factions were listed in the Gazette of April 3, 1820, and other issues.

[34] The Missouri Gazette supported the "Restrictionists" and the St. Louis Enquirer the "Anti-Restrictionists." The Missouri Herald of Jackson, Cape Girardeau County, and the Missouri Intelligencer of Howard County—then in the extreme western part of the Territory—advocated no restriction also. The first issue of the Missourian, published at St. Charles, that could be found is dated subsequent to the election.

to the convention, "any attempt to prevent the introduction of slaves . . . will meet my warmest opposition."[35]

Not only in St. Louis was there strong proslavery feeling. James Evans, running for election in Cape Girardeau County, advertised as follows: "I frankly declare that I am in favor of the future introduction of slaves into the new State."[36] Thomas Mosly of the same county was for no "constitutional restriction on the subject whatever."[37] Several others advocated the same policy. A lone restrictionist came out in Cape Girardeau County. George H. Scripps declared that increased slave importations would keep free labor from the State, and would result in race amalgamation.[38]

In Lincoln County John Lindsay stated that "as to slavery, I shall be in favor of it."[39] Abner Vansant of Jefferson County did not deny that slavery affected morals and had other bad features, but considered that "perhaps it would be politic to permit the future introduction of them [slaves] for a short time."[40] Indeed several candidates, as, for example, Robert Simpson, were not strongly proslavery in feeling, but thought it expedient to "allow a reasonable time for those owning slaves and who may become interested in our soil, to emigrate to the state."[41] Rufus Pettibone also favored no restriction for a number of years "for the sake of encouraging emigration."[42] This economic motive was doubtless an important factor in arousing opinion against restriction. The broad prairies were there to be developed, and slave labor was to be the means of accomplishing the task.

[35] Missouri Gazette, April 19, 1820. For the St. Louis candidates see the issues of April 5, 12, 19, 1820.
[36] Missouri Herald, April 8, 1820.
[37] Ibid.
[38] Ibid., April 22, 1820.
[39] Missouri Gazette, April 12, 1820. Two candidates, Robert Simpson and John Robb, fearing lest Missouri later deal in slaves as an article of commerce, favored restriction in the period of importations (ibid., April 19).
[40] Ibid., April 26.
[41] Ibid., April 5.
[42] Ibid, April 12.

From the constitutional convention itself one may gain a clear-cut view of the sentiment of the period. The procedure of this assembly, together with the origin and development of the slavery clauses, has been minutely examined and analyzed by others, and the subject need not enter into the present discussion.[43] The slavery sections of the constitution will be set forth in the various chapters of this study according to their subject matter. In general it may be said that the document laid no restriction upon bonafide importations of slaves, and only by the consent of the master could they be emancipated.[44] Benton's claim to the authorship of the clause preventing emancipation without the owner's consent and without reembursing him was not made by him until years after the convention had assembled. He repeatedly maintained that he secured the insertion of this provision, but his claim is backed by his own word alone.[45] The constitution apparently satisfied the pro-slavery element.[46] The question seemed legally settled,

[43] Shoemaker, pp. 49–51. The original published Journal of the convention is now very rare, but a photo-facsimile was printed in 1905.

[44] Art. iii, sec. 26, paragraphs 1, 2.

[45] "I was myself the instigator of that prohibition, and the cause of it being put into the constitution—though not a member of the convention—being equally opposed to slavery agitation and slavery extension" (Thirty Years' View, vol. i, pp. 8–9). Benton was exasperated when Frank Blair and Gratz Brown became active supporters of emancipation in the legislature. "They know perfectly well," he said, "that I introduced the clause against Emancipation into the Constitution of the state, with a view to keep this slavery agitation out of politics, and that my whole life has been opposed to their present course" (Republican, July 26, 1858). Benton wrote Gale and Seaton on February 29, 1856, that he was "most instrumental in getting that clause put in for the express purpose of keeping slavery agitation out of the State" (quoted in the St. Joseph Commercial Cycle, March 28, 1856).

[46] The St. Louis Enquirer was well pleased with the constitution, even calling it "immortal" on one occasion (issue of September 1, 1821). The Gazette, on the other hand, had no praise for the slavery sections (issue of July 21, 1820). "A Planter" sent to the Missourian of August 26, 1820, the following note of satisfaction as to the work of the convention: "What better security can slave holders have that their rights will be secured, and their habits respected in Missouri, than the provisions of the constitution. . . . I hear nobody advocating emancipation: all my neighbors say the question is set-

although the free-negro clause was to keep Missouri and the whole country roused for another year.

After the Compromise of 1820 Missouri sat down to enjoy the fruits of her effort, her legally secure black labor. The first decade of her statehood was one of development. With her great and pugnacious senator, Thomas Hart Benton, she was becoming influential in the land. In these years there occurred an episode which was so spontaneous and romantic and so long kept secret that but for the high authority who vouches for it one might well consider the whole story comparable to Jefferson's shimmering salt mountain and other airy legends of Mississippi Valley lore. This is the emancipation conspiracy of 1828 which was years after revealed by the Whig leader, Mr. John Wilson of Fayette. He, with Senators Benton, Barton, and other prominent statesmen of both parties, "representing every district of the State," met in secret to plan a movement for gradual emancipation. Candidates were to be canvassed, and both parties were to get memorials signed to be presented to the legislature. At this juncture appeared the widespread newspaper canard representing that Arthur Tappan of New York "had entertained at his private table some negro men and that, in fact, these negroes rode out in his private carriage with his Daughters." This report raised a storm of indignation in the State, and the scheme of the emancipationists was abandoned. Mr. Wilson claims that "but for that story of the conduct of the great original fanatic on this subject we should have carried, under the leadership of Barton and Benton, our project and begun the future emancipation of the colored race that would long since have been followed by Kentucky, Maryland, Virginia ... our purpose after we got such a law safely placed on the Statute Book, was to have followed it up by a provision requiring the masters of those who should be born to be

---

tled fairly, and they have no wish to renew it. . . . The worst sort of restrictionists are the men that wish to tie the people, neck and heels, to prevent them from injuring themselves."

free to teach them to read and write.   This shows you how little a thing turns the destiny of nations."[47]

Assuming that the meeting took place, its first peculiarity is the really naïve confidence of the participants that but for the Tappan story " we should have carried, under the leadership of Barton and Benton, our project."   The furor which convulsed Missouri during the Compromise debate would seem to have been sufficient to appal any one who might be minded to tamper anew with the slavery question.   It hardly seems possible that Benton, who systematically smothered the slavery issue, should have pushed such a program, but the apparently permanent calm which followed the Compromise and the material prosperity of the State during these years may have warranted a venture at wiping out an institution which Benton considered a potential cause of bitter agitation and political unrest.

Again, one can scarcely believe that sentiment in Missouri had materially changed between 1821 and 1828 when it is considered that she more than doubled her slave population between 1820 and 1830.[48]   It might be answered that Benton was clever enough to feel the public pulse, and that if he entered into any such project there must have been appearances to justify his hopes of success.   But Benton was not an infallible reader of the signs of the times.   It is known how he mistook popular sentiment when he made his disastrous "Appeal" to the voters of his party twenty years later.   Another fact which appears to make the success of any such emancipation scheme doubtful in 1828 is that in

---

[47] MS. Wilson to Thomas Shackelford, January 13, 1866, in the possession of the Missouri Historical Society. In his Illustrated History of Missouri (pp. 221–223) Switzler quoted this letter but took several liberties with the text which later writers have copied. From the text of the letter Wilson did not remember whether the meeting was held in 1827 or 1828. Meigs in his Life of Benton does not mention this episode. He even thinks Benton was the "devoted friend of Missouri" who published a long article in the St. Louis Enquirer of April 26, 1820, which advocated slavery in the State (p. 119).

[48] The Federal census of 1820 gave Missouri 10,222 slaves, and that of 1830, 25,091 (Federal Census, Statistical View, 1790–1830, p. 27).

January of the next year the Missouri General Assembly passed a resolution declaring it to be unconstitutional for Congress to vote money for the American Colonization Society.[49]

There was some antislavery sentiment in the State prior to the Garrisonian movement. As early as 1819 one Humphrey Smith was indicted by the Howard County grand jury for inciting slaves to revolt.[50] In 1820 certain ministers of the Methodist body were accused of preaching sedition to slaves. This was denied by one A. McAlister of St. Charles County, who declared that he had talked to them and had heard most of them preach. The " Methodist Church," he continued, " would no sooner countenance such conduct than they would any other gross immorality."[51]

There must have been some effective antislavery feeling in the General Assembly in these early years. On December 30, 1832, Lane submitted the following resolution to the House: " Resolved. . . . That the following amendment to the Constitution of this State be proposed. . . . That so much of the twenty sixth section of the third article of the Constitution, as declares that the General Assembly shall have no power to prevent BONA FIDE emigrants to this State . . . from bringing [their slaves] from any of the United States . . . shall be and is hereby repealed."[52] This amendment got as far as a second reading, but does not reappear in the journal. It must have had some supporters to have gone even as far as that. During the year 1835 there was a demand for a state convention to meet and settle various needs, among others to bring about emancipation.

An insight into the views of this precise period can be gained from a prominent citizen who had much at stake and great opportunities for observation. James Aull of Lexing-

---

[49] Session Laws, 1828, p. 89. These resolutions passed January 23, 1829.

[50] St. Louis Enquirer, October 20, 1819.

[51] Missouri Gazette, May 24, 1820. McAlister's letter is dated May 5.

[52] House Journal, 7th Ass., 1st Sess., p. 126.

ton was a trader of considerable prominence throughout western Missouri. He had mercantile establishments at Lexington, Independence, Liberty, and Richmond. In answer to an antislavery Quaker firm, Siter, Price, and Company of Philadelphia, who refused to have business relations with any firm dealing in negroes, Aull wrote on June 15, 1835: "We are the owners of Slaves, . . . [but] it would gratify me exceedingly to have all our negroes removed from among us, it would be of immense advantage to the State, but to free them and suffer them to remain with us I for one would never consent to. I once lived in a town where about 1/10 of the whole population was free Negroes and a worse population I have never seen." Aull then discusses the emancipation movement of the time as follows: " At our August elections it will be proposed to our people the propriety of calling a convention, if the convention meet one of the most important subjects to be brought before it will be the gradual abolition of slavery. I have no doubt that we will have a convention and I have as little doubt that such steps will be taken as will free all our slaves in a limited number of years. Many of our Slave holders are the warm advocates of this doctrine but I have not conversed with a man who would consent to let them remain amongst us after they are free."[53]

From this letter it appears that from an early date one of the fundamental problems of emancipation was prominent,— the free negro. The slaveholder had before him not only the fear of losing, in case of legal emancipation, the only labor then available, but also the spectre of a great body of free blacks as his neighbors, who he felt would be both an economic and a social burden.

Although no convention met, despite the prediction of Mr. Aull, there seems to have been a somewhat widespread idea that gradual emancipation could be effected by this

---

[53] In the collection of Messrs. E. U. Hopkins and J. Chamberlain of Lexington.

means.[54] The Missouri Argus states that several articles favoring gradual emancipation had appeared in various papers, although no sheet had definitely declared for it. Some papers opposed the meeting of any convention lest the slavery subject should be discussed. The Missouri Argus stated editorially that " the slave-holders cannot be frightened, as they know that they have the power in their own hands. They never will consent to turn their slaves loose among us. Some system of disposing of the blacks would have to be devised. . . . Such a question should be discussed at a time when the public-mind is entirely serene and peaceful."[55]   Again, the Argus stated in the same issue that a discussion of slavery would tend to check southern immigration to the State and would cause restlessness and insubordination on the part of the slaves. " We are conversant with men in every section of the State, and fully believe that the proposition to abolish slavery at this time would be voted down by a majority of four or five to one. So exceedingly unpopular and illy received is it, that no candidate dare avow himself its advocate." Whether the Argus was wholly correct or not may be questioned, but the fact that the convention was never held makes it probable that the editor had well analyzed the situation.

At this period there seems to have been little race feeling. The Daily Evening Herald of St. Louis of June 9, 1835, in commenting on the burning of two Alabama negroes for murdering two white children, said: " We have no such punishment known to our laws, and it argues an evil state of public mind that can permit this punishment of feudal tyranny to be inflicted upon men, in defiance of the law, because they are black." Another statement which illustrates the broad feeling of the time and the strength of the emancipation party of the State is found in the following

---

[54] The Daily Evening Herald and Commercial Advertiser of June 9, 1835, quotes an issue of the National Intelligencer of unknown date as follows: " Several of the leading Missouri papers are advocating the gradual emancipation of the slaves of the State."
[55] Issue of May 22, 1835. The abolition agitation was exciting the country.

editorial: "Is it not wonderful that the citizens of free States
will not allow the doctrines of Abolition and negro equality
to be lectured upon but at the risk of pelting with eggs,
when here in Missouri we calmly allow a political party to
subserve party ends, to attempt to break up the very founda-
tions, the whole slave interests in Missouri?"[56] Such sympathy for the negro seems to have been the calm and judicial
feeling in the State on the eve of a period in which anti-
negro sentiment was as bitter and as violent in its demon-
strations as any the State ever witnessed.

On April 28, 1836, the mulatto, Francis McIntosh, was
burned by a St. Louis mob for stabbing an officer.[57] A
young New England editor, the Reverend Elijah P. Lovejoy, of the Observer, already disliked for his anti-Catholic,
antimob, and antislavery sentiments, severely criticized the
mob and the judge who upheld their action.[58] By the fall
of 1835 the agitation created by Lovejoy was at least strong
enough to cause apprehension on the part of his friends.
On October 5 of this year a letter was sent to the Observer
by several prominent citizens, among whom was Hamilton
R. Gamble, later the Union governor and the champion of
gradual emancipation. These men suggested that "the

[56] Missouri Argus [St. Louis], May 22, 1835.
[57] There are several contemporary accounts of this episode. The
mayor of St. Louis at the time was J. F. Darby. He mentions the
affair in his Personal Recollections (pp. 237-242). Perhaps the
fullest account, although a biased one, is found in the Quarterly
Anti-Slavery Magazine for July, 1836 (vol. i, pp. 400-409). This
narrative claims that some of the St. Louis aldermen even aided in
McIntosh's death (p. 403). Accounts can also be found in the
Fourth Annual Report of the American Anti-Slavery Society (pp.
78-79), and in Niles' Register (vol. l, p. 234). The Missouri press
of the months of May and June contains scattered fragments of
news on the subject. Judge L. E. Lawless's statement of his action
is found in the Missouri Argus of July 1, 1836. He here calls Lovejoy a "sanctimonious enthusiast."
[58] The career of Lovejoy is well discussed by N. D. Harris, History of Negro Slavery in Illinois and of the Slavery Agitation in
that State, ch. vi, vii. His account, although antislavery in tone, is
based on newspapers and other local sources. Some of Lovejoy's
papers can be found in the Memoir by his brothers and in Thomas
Dimmock's Address at the Church of the Unity, St. Louis, March
14, 1888. A very eulogistic account of Lovejoy can be found in E.
Beecher, Narrative of the Riots at Alton.

present temper of the times require a change in the manner
of conducting that print [The Observer] in relation to the
subject of domestic slavery.   The public mind is greatly
excited, and owing to the unjustifiable interference of our
Northern brethren in our social relations, the community
are, perhaps, not in a situation to endure sound doctrine on
this subject . . . we hope that the concurring opinion of so
many persons having the interest of your paper and of
religion both at heart, may induce you to distrust your own
judgment, and so far change the character of the OB-
SERVER as to pass over in silence everything connected
with the subject of slavery."[59]

Lovejoy, however, would not be silenced.   His criticism
of Judge Lawless and the McIntosh mob brought a storm of
indignation, and he prepared to move up the Mississippi to
Alton, Illinois, after a mob had pillaged his office.   It is said
that Lovejoy's criticism of the Catholics, and of Judge Lawless as such, added to his attacks on mob rule and slavery,
caused this affair,[60] and the slavery issue is therefore not
to be considered as the only cause of the feeling which compelled his flight.   To follow Lovejoy's career to his violent
death would be of no immediate pertinence in this con-

[59] Quoted by Dimmock, p. 7.   Whatever may have been Lovejoy's early conservatism in his antislavery crusade, he became fanatical later on.   After removing to Alton, he wrote to the editor of
the Maine Christian Mirror as follows: " I have seen the ' Recorder
and the Chronicle' with column after column reasoning coldly about
sin and slavery in the abstract, when the living and awful reality
was before them and about them; disputing about . . . the precise
amount of guilt to . . . be attached to this or that slave-holder as
coolly and with as much indifference, as if no manacled slaves stood
before them with uplifted hands . . . beseeching them to knock off
their galling, soul-corroding chains . . . how long, oh! how long
shall these beloved, but mistaken brethren continue to abuse their
influence . . . and retard the salvation of the slave?"   This plea is
certainly strong, and in the temper in which the State was in these
years any such sentiments would hardly be endured (quoted in the
Fourth Annual Report of the American Anti-Slavery Society, pp.
81–82, note).

[60] See Judge Lawless's statement in the Missouri Argus of July
1, 1836.

nection.[61]   His retirement to Alton has been considered to
mark the close of an epoch in Missouri history.   This period
is said to have been characterized by a somewhat general
demand for gradual emancipation.   That there was such a
movement is evident, but it seems improbable that those who
favored the issue were numerous enough to have been successful at any time.

Lovejoy's expulsion from St. Louis was looked upon as
justifiable by most of his local contemporaries.   " As I remember," wrote the Reverend W. G. Eliot, " very few
persons, even among the best citizens, expressed either regret or condemnation."[62]   The Bulletin of St. Louis expressed the sentiment of a considerable number when it
stated editorially that " we have read, with feelings of profound contempt and disgust a paragraph in the Alton
Observer . . . in which . . . Elijah P. Lovejoy, the fanatic
editor . . . spits his venom at the Judge [Lawless]. . . .
We in common with every honest man consider this 'Reverend' libeler to have disgraced . . . the town which has the
misfortune to have him for an inhabitant. . . . The epithet
of ' infamous' which this fanatic bestows upon Judge Lawless, is properly applied to himself alone.   Such vile language sufficiently explains his expulsion from this city."[63]

The reformer's efforts apparently did little to better the
lot of the Missouri slave.   Unfortunately he made his plea
just when the Garrisonian movement was agitating both the
country and Congress.   Lovejoy's program was naturally
considered a part of the general abolition movement, so that
the people were prejudiced against him when he began his
preaching.

---

[61] Lovejoy was killed by a mob at Alton on the night of November 7, 1837.   Mayor John M. Krum of Alton made an official statement of the affair which can be found in Niles' Register, vol. liii,
pp. 196–197.

[62] W. G. Eliot, p. 111.

[63] In quoting the above from an unknown issue of the Bulletin
the editor of the Missouri Argus remarks, " We . . . need hardly
add that we fully coincide with the Editor of the Bulletin " (issue
of December 9, 1836).

The same year that the anti-abolition feeling drove Lovejoy from St. Louis an episode growing out of the slavery situation convulsed Marion County. Dr. David Nelson, president of Marion College, who was a Southerner and a former slaveholder, read at a religious meeting a paper presented to him by Colonel John Muldrow " proposing to subscribe $10,000 himself and asked others to subscribe, to indemnify masters for their slaves when government should think proper to abolish slavery in that way." This led to a personal encounter between Muldrow and a certain extreme pro-slavery citizen named John Bosley, in which Bosley was severely injured. The people were highly incensed, and the college president was forced to flee the State.[64] Muldrow was tried at St. Charles and was acquitted, Edward Bates acting as his counsel.[65] It is interesting to note that his proposition was in harmony with the twenty-sixth section of the third article of the constitution of 1820 which provides that slaves were not to be emancipated " without the consent of their masters, or without paying them." The incident indicates that this clause had become unpopular, at least in Marion County.

Two other men, Williams and Garrett, were ordered from Marion County the same year for receiving literature from the American Colonization Society. The feeling became so warm that upon Dr. Nelson's return to attend his sick son a public meeting was called at Palmyra, May 21, 1836, and it was resolved " That we approve the recent conduct of a portion of our citizens towards Messrs. Garrett and Williams

---

[64] Among the contemporary accounts of this turmoil, which convulsed Marion County in 1836, is the rather biased but full one sent by a correspondent of the New York Journal of Commerce, which was quoted in the Fourth Annual Report of the American Anti-Slavery Society, pp. 78–81, note. This same narrative is also found in the Quarterly Anti-Slavery Magazine for July, 1837 (vol. ii, pp. 395–397). R. I. Holcombe outlines the story (pp. 203–207). He gained his information from old newspaper files and the statements of contemporaries. His account agrees with the above in most particulars.

[65] Bosley soon recovered, and the excitement " blew off " within a month, according to the anonymous writer of a letter dated Palmyra, June 8 (printed in the Missouri Argus of July 29, 1836).

(two avowed advocates and missionaries of abolition) who came among us to instruct our slaves to rebellion by the use of incendiary pamphlets . . . eminently calculated to weaken the obligations of their obedience."[66]   The faculty of Marion College were suspected because of Dr. Nelson's course.   Conscious of the public temper, they exhibited a resolution passed by them the day before this meeting, in which it was resolved " That the faculty of Marion College utterly disapprove, as unchristian and illegal the circulation of all books, pamphlets, and papers, calculated to render the slave population of the State discontented."   They had taken even such definite action as to forbid the students to talk sedition to slaves, circulate any antislavery literature, hold any antislavery meetings or discuss slavery matters before the public, or instruct slaves without the consent of their masters.[67]

The feeling exhibited in the events just recounted persisted in Marion County for years.   In July, 1841, the Illinois abolitionists, George Thompson, James Burr, and Alanson Work, were betrayed near Palmyra by slaves whom they attempted to entice into Canada.[68]   After a stormy imprisonment and trial they were sentenced to the penitentiary for twelve years, but were pardoned before their terms expired.[69]   This event caused the formation of a vigilance

---

[66] Fourth Annual Report of the American Anti-Slavery Society, p. 80.

[67] Ibid., p. 81.

[68] Republican, July 23, 1841, quoting from the Missouri Courier of unknown date. See also the Daily Evening Gazette of July 26, 1841. The Gazette claims that these abolitionists attended the " Mission Institute near Quincy." Holcombe says that the citizens raised $20.62½ for the slaves who betrayed Thompson and his colleagues (p. 239). An account of the affair can also be found in Thompson, passim.

[69] A Palmyra correspondent of the Republican declared that this trial caused " Great Excitement " in that city. The defence argued that they simply " attempted " to entice the slaves, used no force, and had no idea of profit in mind. This it was claimed did not come within the statute. The attempt to escape on a technicality inflamed the citizens. "Our informant," continues the report, "states that it was the general understanding that they could not be indicted: and if it should so turn out, there would probably be worse fare for the prisoners than if they went to the penitentiary" (Republican, September 11, 1841).

committee in each township of the county to examine strangers who could not well explain their business, and suspected persons were expelled from the county and were also threatened with a penalty of fifty lashes should they return.[70]   Some doubtful sympathy seems to have been felt for Thompson and his companions by certain Missourians. The Daily Evening Gazette lamented that Missouri had no "Lunatic Asylum," as "the poor, deluded creatures" were victims of "monomania—a case not where the morals are stained, but where the mind is disordered."[71]   At the same time anti-abolition feeling in Marion County continued.   On March 8, 1843, citizens set fire to the institute of the Quincy abolitionist, Dr. Eels.   They were not prosecuted.[72]

While these events were occurring in eastern Missouri, the western portion of the State was in an uproar over the "Mormon War."   The extent of the slavery element in the Mormon troubles is debated, but the citizens of western Missouri were convinced that their slave property was endangered by the sectaries, whether the Mormons deserved the imputation or not.   On July 20, 1833, a large meeting of "Gentiles" was held at Independence.   It is said that nearly five hundred were present.   A manifesto was published by this meeting, a portion of which is as follows: "More than a year since, it was ascertained that they [the Mormons] had been tampering with our slaves, and endeavoring to rouse dissension and raise seditions among them. . . . In a late number of the STAR published at Independence by the leaders of the sect, there is an article inviting free negroes and mulattoes from other states to become Mormons, and remove and settle among us.   This exhibits them in still more odious colors . . . [this] would corrupt our blacks, and instigate them to bloodshed."[73]

[70] Holcombe, p. 263.
[71] Issue of September 16, 1841.
[72] Holcombe, p. 266.
[73] Quoted by W. A. Linn, The Story of the Mormons, p. 171. Another portion of this manifesto reads: "Elevated as they [the Mormons] mostly are but little above the condition of our blacks either in regard to property or education, they have become a subject

Other meetings were called to take action against the
Mormons. In the summer of 1838 citizens of Carroll
County condemned " Mormons, abolitionists, and other disorderly persons."[74] This implies that the slavery issue in
some cases entered into the " Mormon War." On the other
hand, citizens of Ray County, meeting about the same time,
passed seven resolutions against Mormon shortcomings, but
did not mention slavery among these.[75] The Mormons
asserted that nothing but the bitter prejudice of the Missouri
" Gentiles " and their greed for the well-improved Mormon
farms was the motive underlying the trouble. Etzenhouser,
writing with a strong pro-Mormon bias, quotes General
Doniphan as denying that the slavery question " had anything to do with it [the Mormon War]."[76]

The position of the Mormons on the slavery issue is said
to have shifted at different periods.[77] Be that as it may, the

of much anxiety on that part, serious and well grounded complaints
having been already made of their corrupting influence on our
slaves" (quoted by Elder R. Etzenhouser, From Palmyra, New
York, 1830, to Independence, Missouri, 1894, p. 328).

[74] Southern Advocate (Jackson), September 1, 1838. The date of
this meeting is not given.

[75] Southern Advocate, September 8, 1838. The date of this meeting is not given. The editor did not seem to be aware of the slavery
issue entering into the Mormon troubles. "What is the precise
nature of the offence of this deluded people," he said, "and in what
particular they are troublesome neighbors, we are uninformed"
(ibid., September 1). This paper was published in Cape Girardeau
County, far from the seat of the Mormon difficulties.

[76] Etzenhouser quotes from the Kansas City Journal (date not
given): "Question: 'Do you think, Colonel, that the slavery question had anything to do with the difficulties with the Mormons?'
Colonel Doniphan, 'No, I don't think that matter had anything to do
with it. The Mormons, it is true, were northern and eastern people,
and " free soilers," but they did not interfere with the negroes and
we did not care whether they owned slaves or not'" (p. 304).

[77] The Utah Mormons took a novel stand—a sort of compulsory
neutrality—on the slavery question. About 1850 the official organ of
the Church declared: "We feel it our duty to define our position in
relation to slavery. . . . There is no law in Utah to authorize
slavery, neither any to prohibit it. If a slave is disposed to leave
his master, no power exists here either legal or moral, that will prevent him. But if a slave chooses to remain with his master, none are
allowed to interfere between the master and the slave. . . . When
a man in the Southern States embraces our faith, and is the owner
of slaves, the Church says to him: If your slaves wish to remain

consideration here is of the effect of the negro question on the Missourians of the day. Whether real or alleged, activity relative to slavery on the part of the Mormons was used by the western Missouri people during the thirties as a campaign slogan, and the issue must therefore have been vital and important. That the Missourians thought the Saints were negro thieves seems certain. When Burr, Work, and Thompson attempted to entice slaves from Marion County in 1841, the people thought at once that they were Mormons.[78] As late as 1855 a St. Joseph editor, in quoting Brigham Young's denial that the Mormons had ever stolen slaves, remarked: "We think that the latter day saints are not so bad after all."[79] Evidently Young's statement was a surprise.

In another quarter at this period a movement less violent but of enormous consequences to the slave interests of the State was developing. This was the Platte Purchase, which added six very rich counties to the slave power. Benton and Linn pushed the measure in the Senate, the former always taking great pride in its accomplishment, both because of the magnitude of the undertaking and because of

with you, put them not away; but if they choose to leave you, or are not satisfied to remain with you, it is for you to sell them, or to let them go free, as your own conscience may direct you. The Church on this point assumes the responsibility to direct. The laws of the land recognize slavery; we do not wish to oppose the laws of the country" (The Frontier Guardian [date not given], quoted in the Eleventh Annual Report [1851] of the American and Foreign Anti-Slavery Society, pp. 94–95).

[78] Republican, July 23, 1841, quoting from an issue of the Missouri Courier (Palmyra): "On Tuesday morning of the present week our town was thrown into considerable excitement by the arrest of three white men (supposed to be disciples of the Mormon Prophet Jo. Smith) who were caught in the act of decoying from their rightful owners several slaves of the neighborhood." The issue of the Courier is not given.

[79] St. Joseph Commercial Cycle, May 18, 1855. "Formerly the rumor was," said Young, "that they [the Mormons] were going to tamper with the slaves . . . we never had thought of such a thing. . . . The blacks should be used like servants, and not like brutes, but they must serve." The Cycle gives no reference for this statement of Brigham Young.

its importance to Missouri.[80]   In his message of November
22, 1836, Governor Boggs stated that the General Assembly
had memorialized Congress on the subject, and that Congress had agreed to grant the request when the Territory
should be secured from the Indians.[81]

That the State was anxious to obtain the rich river
bottoms of this region cannot be doubted. It does not seem
likely that this was a preconcerted grab for more slave territory as von Holst asserts,[82] and as Horace Greeley apparently believed. The latter says that the bill passed " so
quietly as hardly to attract attention."[83] Either the North

---

[80] " This was a measure of great moment to Missouri. . . . The
difficulties were three-fold: 1. To make still larger a State which
was already one of the largest in the Union. 2. To remove Indians
from a possession which had just been assigned to them in perpetuity. 3. To alter the Missouri Compromise line in relation to
slave Territory, and thereby convert free soil into slave soil. . . .
And all these difficulties to be overcome at a time when Congress
was inflamed with angry debates upon abolition petitions. . . . The
first step was to procure a bill for the alteration of the compromise
line and the extension of the boundary: it . . . passed the Senate
without material opposition. It went to the House of Representatives; and found there no serious opposition to its passage. . . .
The author of this view was part and parcel of all that transaction—
remembers well the anxiety of the State to obtain the extension—her
joy at obtaining it the gratitude which all felt to the Northern
members without whose aid it could not have been done" (Benton,
Thirty Years' View, vol. i, pp. 626–627). Switzler claims that the
idea originated at a militia muster at Dale's farm, three miles from
Liberty, in the summer of 1835, and that the originator was General
Andrew S. Hughes. " At this meeting," he says, " and in public
addresses, he proposed the acquisition of the Platte country; and the
measure met with such emphatic approval that the meeting proceeded at once by the appointment of a committee to organize an
effort to accomplish it." Among others the committee was composed of D. R. Atchison and A. W. Doniphan. Missouri had, however, agitated the annexation for several years prior to 1835.

[81] House Journal, 9th Ass., 1st sess., p. 36. The bill granting the
cession and providing for the Indian treaties necessary for its con-
summation was signed by the President June 7, 1836. The treaties
were secured, and were proclaimed February 15, 1837.

[82] H. Von Holst, Constitutional and Political History of the
United States, vol. ii, pp. 144–145. " The matter was disposed of
quietly and quickly. . . . The legislative coach of the United States
moved at a rapid rate when the slavery interest held the whip "
(ibid.).

[83] A History of the Struggle for Slavery Extension or Restriction
in the United States, pp. 30–31. Greeley says that the bill " floated
through both Houses without encountering the perils of a division."

wished to win the favor of Benton and his constituents, or, as Carr says of the act, " It did not and could not add to the voting strength of the South in the Senate."[84] Whether or not this accession contravened the Missouri Compromise has no direct bearing on the discussion of the local slavery system, and consequently will not be considered here.

During the late thirties and early forties the slavery question began to affect the religious bodies of the country. In Missouri the change did not fail to manifest itself,[85] but the scope of this study will limit the discussion to a few of the denominations in which the struggle occurred. The Methodist Church labored heavily in this storm. As early as 1820 little patience was manifested toward those who instigated negroes to discontent or preached to them anything that might cause sedition.[86] In 1835 the Missouri Annual Conference, while praising the Colonization Society, at the same time condemned the " Abolition Society " and its agents, declaring the latter to be " mischievous in character,

---

[84] P. 186.

[85] During the earlier period the feeling against the colored race was far from inhuman in Missouri. Judge R. C. Ewing states that as late as 1836 he heard a mulatto preacher, the Reverend Nicholas Cooper, speak from the same pulpit with the prominent Cumberland Presbyterian ministers in the Bethel Church at the Boone County Synod. Cooper had been a slave (History and Memoirs of the Cumberland Presbyterian Church, in Missouri, p. 18). The Baptists of Illinois and Missouri had in the territorial days an organization called the " Friends of Humanity." When " Father " John Clark visited Boone's Lick in 1820, he found some families belonging to this society. This organization is said not to have opposed slavery in all its forms, but to have sought gradually to bring about emancipation ("An Old Pioneer" [pseudonym], Father John Clark, pp. 256–257). This society allowed the holding of slaves by certain persons: (1) young owners who intended to emancipate their negroes when older; (2) those who purchased slaves in ignorance and would let the church decide on the date of emancipation; (3) women who were legally unable to emancipate; (4) those holding old, feebleminded, or otherwise incapacitated slaves. Another authority says that Clark came to St. Louis a Methodist in 1798, but that he and one Talbot immersed one another and became " The Baptized Church of Christ, Friends of Humanity." They had strong antislavery feeling, Clark even refusing his salary if it came from slaveholders (W. B. Sprague, Annals of the American Pulpit, vol. vi, pp. 492–493). Some deny that Father Clark was a real Baptist.

[86] Letter of A. McAlister in the Missouri Gazette of May 24, 1820.

and not calculated to better the situation of the people of color of the United States."[87]

The Missouri feud stirred up a general and bitter discussion elsewhere, and, indeed, was the immediate cause of the slavery issue being injected into debates of the church. The question was transmitted to wider circles by the appeal of the Reverend Silas Comfort in 1840 from the Missouri to the General Conference of that year. The Missouri Conference had adjudged him guilty of maladministration in admitting the testimony of colored members against a white member in a church trial. On May 17, after a protracted debate, the General Conference reversed the decision of the Missouri Conference. Much bitterness was aroused, and when the next General Conference met at New York in 1844, the sectional break was imminent. Despite the protests of the southern members, Bishop Andrew was suspended for indirectly holding slaves through his wife.[88] In the following spring the Southern Methodist Church was formed at Louisville.

The Missouri Conference of 1844, held after the session of the General Conference, remained firm in its position on slavery. "We are compelled to pronounce the proceeding

[87] Resolutions of the conference in the Daily Evening Herald of October 1, 1835. D. R. McAnally discusses the early Methodist Church in the State at some length. Without giving any authority, he speaks of the close relation between the races in the missionary period of the territorial and early statehood days. He declares that the negroes often led in the singing and in the testimony meetings (vol. i, pp. 147–148).

[88] Debates in the General Conference of the Methodist Episcopal Church During its Session at New York, May 3 to June 10, 1844. George Peck, editor, pp. 190–191. Bishop Soule was very influential in this conference. He does not appear as a radical. While Bishop Andrew's case was before the conference, he declared (May 9) that there could be no compromise if the Northern Methodists held slavery to be a "moral evil" (ibid., pp. 166–172). On May 31 he and Bishops Hedding, Waugh, and Morris petitioned the conference to drop the matter till the next conference and thus permit time to heal the trouble (ibid., pp. 184–185). On June 1 Bishop Andrew was suspended by a nearly sectional vote, the result being 111 to 69. All the Missouri delegates voted in the negative (ibid., pp. 190–191). However, when the Reverend Francis A. Harding was suspended for a similar offence, one of the Missouri members voted against him (ibid., p. 240).

of the late General conference against Bishop Andrew extra-judicial and oppressive," said one of the resolutions of the committee of nine who reported on October 4, 1844.[89] But the conference does not seem to have been very bitter against the Northern Methodists at this time. It even condemned some of the southern agitators for their " violent proceedings." The resolutions of the conference contain the following worthy clause: " We do most cordially invite to our pulpits and firesides all our bishops and brethren who, in the event of a division, shall belong to the northern Methodist Church."[90] The members of the conference deeply regretted " the prospect of separation," and declared that they most sincerely " pray that some effectual means, not inconsistent with the interests and honor of all concerned, may be suggested and devised by which so great a calamity may be averted." Nevertheless, they approved the call of the Southern Methodist Convention to be held at Louisville the following May, and requested the individual churches to state their position regarding a separation from the Northern Methodists.[91]

The Annual Conference assembled at Columbia on October 1, 1845, under the presidency of Bishop Soule. The Southern Church had already been formed, and a great deal of interest and heat was manifest in the debates on the action to be taken by Missouri. By a vote of 86 to 14 the conference decided to separate, and a new organization was thereupon effected.[92] Some ministers refused to accede,

[89] Report of the Missouri Conference on Division (Committee of Nine), resolution no. 2. This can be found in the official Southern Methodist source, History of the Organization of the Methodist Episcopal Church, South, Comprehending all of the Official Proceedings, pp. 124–127. It can also be found in the official Northern Methodist account by the Reverend Charles Elliott, entitled, History of the Great Secession in the Methodist Episcopal Church, p. 1065.

[90] Report of the Committee of Nine, resolution no. 9.

[91] Ibid., nos. 3, 4.

[92] Jefferson Inquirer of October 16, 1845, quoting the Missouri Statesman of October 10. " The debate was a protracted one," according to the official account in the Missouri Statesman. The members who were dissatisfied with the action of the conference were given

and an active antislavery minority continued to flourish in the State.[93] It was ambitious, and was so tenacious of purpose that it was accused of courting martyrdom. These so-called "Northern Methodists" came out openly against slavery, and their propaganda caused intense bitterness until, in the fifties, hostility to the ministers of this organization became implacable. In Fabius township, Marion County, a public meeting on February 18, 1854, protested against these persons, and demanded that they refrain from preaching in the county.[94] On October 11, 1855, resolutions were passed by citizens of Jackson County requesting the Northern Methodists not to hold their conferences in the county,[95] and public meetings in Andrew, Cass, and other counties uttered condemnations.[96]

The Northern Methodists, however, would not be silenced or driven from the field. At times they denied that they preached abolition doctrines. At their quarterly conference at Hannibal in 1854 they declared that the opposition to them was "a base persecution. . . . That, while we regard

leave to join the northern body if they wished, and were dismissed "without blame" as to their moral position. Each member arose in the conference and stated his individual position on the issue (ibid.). The Northern Methodist account claims that the St. Louis churches were especially opposed to a division of the church. When the author of this statement visited the city in October, 1846, he considered that a majority of the members were still in the old church, the northern body comprising two English churches with 200 members, two German churches with 284 communicants, and two colored churches with 180 members (Elliott, History of the Great Secession in the Methodist Episcopal Church, p. 593).

[93] One of the dissenting ministers, Lorenzo Waugh, states that his charge at Hermon Mission was unanimously opposed to separation. Immediately after the New York General Conference of 1844, the Missouri Conference met at St. Louis. Waugh says that there was "some excitement," and that a number wished a new church. At the Columbia Conference he claims that "most of the older preachers" were determined to "go South," and that those who opposed them were unfairly restricted in debate (A Candid Statement of the Course Pursued by the Preachers of the Methodist Episcopal Church South in Trying to Establish Their New Organisation in Missouri, pp. 7–8).

[94] Elliott, A History of the Methodist Episcopal Church in the South West, pp. 39–42.

[95] Ibid., pp. 68–69.

[96] W. Leftwich, Martyrdom in Missouri, vol. i, pp. 102–104.

the system of slavery as a great moral, social, and political
evil, we do most heartily protest against any attempt, directly
or indirectly, at producing insubordination among slaves;
we do heartily condemn . . . the underground railroad operation, and all other systems of negro stealing."⁹⁷ At a
Warrensburg meeting in May, 1855, they protested that " the
constitution and the laws guaranteeing to us the right to
worship God according to the dictates of conscience we
regard as sacred, and the course pursued at meetings held
in our own and sister counties in proscribing ministers of
the Gospel of certain denominations, is tyrannical, arbitrary,
illegal and unjust."⁹⁸

The struggle soon degenerated into a hatred which long
outlasted slavery days. Northern Methodist ministers were
expelled. Benjamin Holland was killed at Rochester in
Andrew County in 1856,⁹⁹ and Morris and Allen were driven
from Platte County.¹⁰⁰ " The whole course of this
Northern Methodist Church since the separation, has been
faithless and dishonorable," declared an editorial of 1855.
" They are sending preachers into this State against an
express agreement and plighted faith. . . . They send them
. . . not for the purpose of propagating the Christian faith

---

⁹⁷ Elliott, A History of the Methodist Episcopal Church in the
South West, p. 42. The proslavery party refused to believe that the
Northern Methodists were not abolitionists. The following letter
from a Rhode Island Methodist to the Hannibal Courier appeared
in the Richmond Weekly Mirror of September 8, 1854: " You are
right in charging our Missionaries in Missouri with laboring for the
overthrow of slavery; or else we are deceived at the East. According to the published report we have forty-one charges or circuits
in Missouri, and only two self-supporting. We have been told again
and again at the east, that it is for our highest interest as abolitionists to keep these missionaries there to operate against slavery."
⁹⁸ The History of Clay and Platte Counties, p. 174.
⁹⁹ R. R. Witten, Pioneer Methodism in Missouri, pp. 17–18.
¹⁰⁰ History of Clay and Platte Counties, p. 644. W. M. Paxton
mentions the treatment accorded Morris (p. 198). In April, 1855,
a proslavery meeting was held in Parkville to protest against abolitionism. One of the resolutions adopted reads as follows: " Resolved, That we will suffer no person belonging to the Northern
Methodist Church to preach in Platte county after date, under penalty of tar and feathers for the first offence, and a hemp rope for
the second " (Missouri Statesman, April 27, 1855).

. . . but to overthrow slavery."[101]   When the press was declaring itself in this manner we cannot wonder that the populace detested the name.

In 1857 the Northern Methodists petitioned the legislature for a charter to found a university. A bill was introduced in the House on November 4 to grant such a charter.[102] After being amended, it was tabled on November 12 by a vote of 95 to 16.[103] This action of the General Assembly called forth at the Annual Conference at Hannibal the following year this protest: "While we are aware that our anti-slavery sentiments were well known, we knew our peaceable and law-abiding character was equally well known. . . . Could we with reason have anticipated that a hundred ministers, and ten thousand members of our church, and a population of fifty thousand . . . would be denied a charter because their views of the peculiar institution did not correspond with those of a majority of the Legislature? "[104]

The slavery question gave rise to many peculiar situations. Men found their positions perplexed by conflicting elements of religion, politics, and social status. The stand of the Reverend Nathan Scarritt well illustrates this point. His biographer says: "The division of his Church [the Methodist] left him connected with the Southern branch, where he has ever since remained, because, although opposed to slavery, he agreed with the Church South in her views of the relations of the Church to slavery as a civil institution."[105] Such confusion of interests makes it very unsafe to attribute absolute party alignment to the slavery issue.

[101] Weekly Pilot (St. Louis), March 10, 1855. A similar editorial also appears in the issue of March 17.
[102] House Journal, 19th Ass., Adj. Sess., p. 110.
[103] Ibid., p. 169. Twelve members were absent or sick. On March 10, 1860, the House of Representatives refused its hall to a Northern Methodist preacher (Missouri Statesman, March 16, 1860).
[104] Minutes of the Eleventh Session of the Missouri Annual Conference of the Methodist Episcopal Church, meeting at Hannibal May 6 to 10, 1858, pp. 17–18.
[105] C. R. Barns, ed., The Commonwealth of Missouri, Biographical section, p. 770.

Dr. Scarritt, for instance, was a Whig, a Southern Methodist, in theory but not in practice opposed to slavery, and a strong Union supporter in 1860.[106]

The Presbyterian Church also divided on the slavery issue, but much later than the Methodist. " The whole New School Church," wrote an influential clergyman who was a witness of the events of the period, " was known to be opposed to slavery, and continued discussion was had at every meeting of the General Assembly until 1857, when such decisive action was taken as led to a separation from the General Assembly of all the synods in slaveholding states. In the Old School there was but little discussion on the subject, and the generally understood public sentiment of Missouri was that nothing was to be said against the institution, and consequently, so far as Missouri was concerned there was a constant tendency on the part of those of the New School, who wished for quiet, to leave that body and enter the Old." The New School was embarrassed by its connection with the American Home Missionary Society, for this organization would not commission a slaveholder or aid a church which contained slaveholding members. "Out of this struggle the New School Synod came out a very small band."[107]

The Congregational Church was known in the State as an abolitionist body, and was regarded with little favor in Missouri as a whole, although it was fairly strong in St. Louis.[108] In 1847 the Reverend Truman M. Post was called

---

[106] Barus, p. 770. Dr. Scarritt pleaded for the Union in 1860.

[107] Reverend T. Hill, Historical Outlines of the Presbyterian Church in Missouri, A Discourse delivered at Springfield, Mo., Oct. 13, 1871. Pp. 27–28. Hill states that the Missouri Home Missionary Society permitted slaveholders to represent them, but that the American Home Missionary Society demanded that even this society conform to its regulations. This resulted in the formation of the Home Missionary Committee, "which entered upon its work with immediate success" (ibid.).

[108] A good idea of this feeling toward the Congregational Church can be gained by reading the "Ten Letters on the Subject of Slavery" (1855), by the Reverend N. L. Rice of the Second Presbyterian Church of St. Louis; note especially p. 24. He argued that all agitation of the slavery issue should be suppressed.

to the Third Presbyterian Church of St. Louis. This organization became the First Congregational Church, and was very antislavery in feeling. Dr. Post, because of his slavery views, looked upon the call with some misgivings, whereupon two of the leading members, Dr. Reuben Knox and Mr. Moses Forbes, wrote him advising his acceptance. Dr. Knox even alleged that the few slaveholding members were "mostly as anti-slavery as you or I, and long to see the curse removed."[109]   Even before foreign immigration came to St. Louis in such large numbers there was apparently a strong antislavery body in the city which had migrated thither from the Northern and the border States.[110]

---

[109] Reuben Knox to Post, February 15, 1847. "You may perhaps be of the number," he wrote, "who suppose we are not allowed to speak for ourselves and hardly think our own thoughts in the slave state and among slaveholders, but you need not fear. Though we have three or four families who own slaves, they are mostly as anti-slavery as you or I, and long to see the curse removed" (T. A. Post, Truman M. Post, p. 151). The same day Moses Forbes wrote Dr. Post: "You are looked upon as opposed to the system and as feeling it your duty to preach upon the subject as upon the other great moral and political evils and sins, and that for the wealth of the Indies you would not consent to be muzzled. At the same time you are not viewed as being so exclusive as to suppose there are no Christians who own slaves, or so unwise as not to use good judgment and sound discretion as to times and seasons, ways and means of treating the subject and removing the evil" (ibid., pp. 151-152).

[110] A portion of the St. Louis press from the middle forties on was antislavery. It was apparently not until the fifties that the distinction between the abolitionists and the mere antislavery sympathizers was denied. The Kansas struggle largely caused this revulsion of feeling against any one not pronounced in his proslavery views.

CHAPTER V

SENATOR BENTON AND SLAVERY

Returning to the field of politics, it may be observed that the state legislature took little official notice of the Garrisonian program till the congressional debates raging about the abolition petitions and the use of the mails to scatter antislavery literature had stirred the whole land. On February 1, 1837, a law was passed which subjected to fine and imprisonment "any person [who] shall publish, circulate, or utter by writing, speaking, or printing any facts, arguments, reasoning, or opinions, tending directly to excite any slave or slaves, or other person of color, to rebellion, sedition, . . . or murder, with intent to excite such slave or slaves." The punishment for the first offence was to be a fine of one thousand dollars and imprisonment for not more than two years, for the second offence imprisonment for not more than twenty years, and for the third, imprisonment for life.[1] Although several individuals were punished for attempts to run slaves over the borders, there is a dearth of records dealing with prosecutions under the statute of 1837, but what the law failed to accomplish popular feeling effected, and several persons were forced to flee the State for airing their antislavery views.[2]

An idea of the feeling of insecurity caused by the abolition crusade can be gained from the fact that the above law passed the House of Representatives by a vote which was unanimous—61 to 0.[3] George Thompson states that while he and his companions were prisoners at Palmyra in 1841,

---

[1] Session Laws, 1836, p. 3.
[2] See above, pp. 118, 120.
[3] House Journal, 9th Ass., 1st Sess., p. 383. This law passed the House on January 28, 1837, and the Senate on December 23, 1836 (Senate Journal, 9th Ass., 1st Sess., p. 147). The vote in the Senate is not given.

their counsel informed them that it was a violation of the
Missouri law to read even the Declaration of Independence
or the Bible to a slave.[4] On February 12, 1839, the Assembly passed resolutions protesting against the efforts of
the North to interfere with "the domestic policy of the
several states." Each slave State would be forced to "look
out for means adequate to its own protection, poise itself
upon its reserved rights, and prepare for defending its
domestic institutions from wanton invasion, whether from
foreign or domestic enemies, peaceably if they can, forcibly
if they must."[5] On February 2, 1841, the Assembly in
joint session voted an address of thanks to President Van
Buren for his "manly and candid course on the subject of
abolitionism." For some unknown reason the vote was
close—47 to 43, ten members being absent.[6] Two weeks
after this vote of thanks the legislature passed a series of
resolutions condemning Governor Seward of New York for
having demanded a jury trial before consenting to the rendition of fugitive slaves. The Assembly declared that such
a jury "frequently would be Abolitionists," and character-

---

[4] P. 60.

[5] Session Laws, 1838, p. 337. These resolutions read as follows:
(1) As the Constitution does not deprive States of power to regulate domestic slavery, it is a reserved right. (2) Interference by
citizens of non-slaveholding States "is in direct contravention of
the constitution of the United States . . . derogatory from the dignity of the slaveholding states, grossly insulting to their sovereignty
and ultimately tending to destroy the union, peace and happiness of
these confederated states." (3) They approved the course of the
southern representatives in Congress. (4) They viewed "the active
agents [abolitionists] in this country in their nefarious schemes to
subvert the fundamental principles of this government" as destructive
of our "domestic peace and reign of equal law." (5) The slave
States had "no other safe alternative left them but to adopt some
efficient policy by which their domestic institutions may be protected
and their peace, happiness, and prosperity restored." (6) Copies
were to be sent to each governor and member of Congress.

[6] House Journal, 11th Ass., 1st Sess., pp. 342-343. In his reply to
Goode on February 2, 1855, J. S. Rollins said that the Democrats
voted unanimously for this Address (ibid., p. 14). Most of the
Whigs must therefore have opposed the measure, undoubtedly rather
through enmity to Van Buren and Van Buren politics than through
any love for abolitionists.

ized Seward's action as "frivolous and wholly unworthy of a statesman."[7]

Some conception of the grip with which the State was held by slavery can be gained from the action of the constitutional convention which assembled at Jefferson City in November, 1845. A reporter at the convention wrote as follows on November 24: "Mr. Ward presented a petition from one solitary individual, on the subject of the abolition of slavery. He remarked that he arose to perform a delicate duty—present a petition on the subject of abolition, containing 27 reasons. Every person who knew him, was aware of his opposition to abolitionism in every shape. He wanted to get rid of the petition, and therefore he moved to lay it on the table." Mr. Ewing then moved that it be not received. The vote was unanimously in favor of this motion—64 to 0. "Mr. Hunter called for ayes and noes that the world might know the sentiment of this body on the subject of abolitionism."[8] The subjects of abolition or of emancipation did not again appear before the convention. The actual provisions of the constitution of 1845 relating to the negro deserve some further consideration.

Although this constitution was defeated, its failure was due to causes other than the slavery sections, which were identical with those of the constitution of 1820. The changes were leveled at the free negro rather than at the slave. For example, to article iii, section 26, paragraph i, was added a clause compelling the removal of newly emancipated negroes from the State. The same clause was also

[7] Session Laws, 1840, pp. 236–237.
[8] Jefferson Inquirer, November 26, 1845. See also the Journal of the Constitutional Convention of 1845, p. 38. Two members were absent when the above vote was taken. The proceedings of the convention are briefly given in the above Journal. The full debates can be found in the Jefferson Inquirer of November 19, 22, 26, 29, December 3, 6, 10, 12, 15, 19, 23, 31, 1845, January 5, 9, 1846. The constitution can be found in the Journal and in the Jefferson Inquirer of January 21, 1846. This constitution was defeated by "about 9000 votes" in a poll of "about 60,000" (Switzler, p. 259).

added to paragraph iv of the same section.[9] This evident
satisfaction of the convention with the old provisions implies that the public may have been similarly minded. The
vote on the various paragraphs cannot be learned as they
were not passed on singly.

Reviewing the discussion thus far as a whole, and bringing it to a point, it is evident that from the later territorial
days Missouri was largely inhabited by a citizenship which
came from slaveholding communities. Arriving in Missouri
already acclimated to the economic and social atmosphere
of a slave society, and themselves possessing considerable
slave property, it can hardly be conceived that these people
would immediately turn their backs on the traditions which
they so dearly loved and renounce a system which not only
involved a great amount of capital, but was the only source
of labor then available.

This early period of Missouri slavery sentiment and its
influence upon politics and religion conveniently closes with
the opening of the Mexican War. It is marked by western
good humor and fair play toward the negro, if not always
toward the political opponent. One event after another set
the populace in a furor. Emancipationists and even a few
abolitionists there were in the State throughout these years,
and the Colonization Society was fairly well supported.[10]
But agitation for emancipation was more common among
individuals than in political parties, and that general emancipation could have taken place before 1861 does not seem
probable to the present writer.

The annexation of Texas early engaged the attention of
the State. On November 18, 1844, Governor Marmaduke
in his last message to the legislature made a plea for annexation. He argued that many Missourians had settled in

[9] Journal of the Convention, app., p. 43. The vote on article iii
is given in ibid., pp. 241-242. It is interesting to note that the old
trouble-making clause forbidding free negroes to enter the State
was placed in this constitution (art. iv, sec. 2, par. i), but with the
condition that it was not to "conflict with the laws of the United
States" (ibid.).
[10] See ch. vii of this study.

Texas,[11] that its markets were valuable, and that if the
United States did not act it might either become a prey to
the English or to the savages. In this message there is no
reference to slavery.[12] Two days later the new governor,
Edwards, sent his message to the Assembly, but it took no
notice whatever of the Texas question.[13] The thoughts of
the State, however, were on the new republic, for on November 26, 1844, Ellis introduced in the Senate joint resolutions relative to annexation.[14] These strongly favored that
action, approved Senator Atchison's vote on the Texan
treaty in the Federal Senate, opposed a division of Texas
into free and slave States, and declared that the decision of
the question of slavery should be left to the citizens of
Texas.[15] Resolutions appeared in the House on November
29, December 9, and December 12, also favoring annexation.[16] After various amendments and substitutes had been
proposed, Gamble, on December 12, offered ten resolutions
which condemned the Texan treaty as " an intrigue for the
Presidency," provided that the boundary of Texas should
not exceed in extent the largest State in the Union, and
declared that Benton's vote against the treaty " was in strict
conformity with the sovereign will of Missouri."[17] After
a protracted debate these resolutions were rejected on December 18 by a vote of 63 to 27, ten members not being
present.[18] These resolutions were so conglomerate that this
vote cannot be taken as a gauge of sentiment against Benton.

[11] " During the last two weeks, a vast number of families have
passed through this place for Texas. . . . They are principally from
. . . this State and Illinois " (Jefferson Inquirer, November 6, 1845).
A party of from fifty to a hundred was solicited in St. Louis in 1840
to settle on a tract of land near Nacogdoches (Daily Pennant [St.
Louis], November 3, 1840).
[12] House Journal, 13th Ass., 1st Sess., pp. 18–19.
[13] Ibid., pp. 27–37.
[14] Ibid., p. 56. The vote on these resolutions in the Senate varied
from 26 to 6 on the second and third ballots to 18 to 14 on the sixth.
There were eight in all (ibid., pp. 100–102).
[15] House Journal, 13th Ass., 1st Sess., pp. 108–111. The above
Senate Resolutions are given in full on these pages.
[16] House Journal, 13th Ass., 1st Sess., pp. 70, 108–111, 120–122.
[17] Ibid., pp. 120–122.
[18] Ibid., p. 136.

On the same day that Gamble's resolutions failed the original Senate resolutions relative to annexation passed by a margin of 55 to 25, nineteen members being absent.[19]

In this Texas agitation the legislature was following rather than leading the State. On June 8, 1844, the Democracy of St. Louis city and county passed resolutions demanding the "reoccupation of Oregon and the reannexation of Texas at the earliest practicable period." "We pledge ourselves," they boasted, "not to be behind the foremost in the contest . . . until the stars and stripes shall wave in triumph over the Union with Texas included."[20] It will soon be seen that their jingoism was not mere froth. Not only Democrats but Whigs as well were most enthusiastic in the cause of Texas from this time till the close of the Mexican War.

The demand of Missouri, and in fact of the whole Southwest, for Texas was probably due in greater degree to native love of expansion for its own sake than to any desire for new slave territory. The poverty of the exhausted soil and the need of fresh acres might have influenced portions of the old South, but Missouri was in 1844 still in the exploitative stage, and the economic pressure could not have been severe. This western democracy was indignant at outside, and especially at northern, dictation. Annexation made a good campaign issue, even for home use. There is indication that it was employed for this purpose in the resolutions of a meeting in favor of the annexation of Texas held in Greene County in April, 1845. The declaration runs: "Resolved, That we look upon the re-annexation of Texas to the United States as a measure calculated to reunite the democratic party of this State."[21]

The later course of the Texan question and the war in which it culminated appealed with particular force to the

---

[19] House journal, 13th Ass., 1st Sess., p. 140. This vote has been analyzed by H. Tupes, The Influence of Slavery upon Missouri Politics, pp. 21–25. The Whigs and nine Democrats voted in the negative.

[20] Western Pioneer (Liberty), June 21, 1844. This newspaper strongly advocated annexation.

[21] Jefferson Inquirer, April 17, 1845.

Missourians.   Switzler mentions the enthusiasm with which
the State raised troops for this conflict.[22]   Irrespective of
party affiliation, the flower of Missouri enlisted.   Such
prominent Whigs as A. W. Doniphan were among the
leaders of the State in this war.   Missouri furnished 6733
of the 71,309 volunteers who enlisted during the Mexican
War.   Only two States, Louisiana and Texas, furnished
more, and they were much closer to the seat of war than
was Missouri.[23]   In 1840 the white population of Missouri
was but one forty-fifth of that of the whole country, nevertheless that State furnished one eleventh of the nation's
volunteers in the Mexican War.[24]

The Wilmot Proviso was most distasteful to the Democratic party of Missouri.   Benton disliked the act because it
stirred up the slavery issue.   The proslavery wing of the
party was indignant because the bill sought to restrict the
system in the Territories.   The General Assembly on February 15, 1847, passed instructions to the Missouri senators
in Washington to vote according to the spirit of the Missouri
Compromise, which of course was considered as at variance
with the Wilmot Proviso.[25]   Popular sentiment, however,
seems to have viewed the proviso with less fear than did the
legislature.   On January 8, 1848, a meeting of St. Louis

[22] Pp. 260–263.   Switzler speaks from personal observation.
[23] Adjutant General's Report of April 5, 1848 (Executive Documents, 30th Cong., 1st Sess., vol. viii, pp. 45, 76, Doc. no. 62).
Louisiana furnished 7728 volunteers, Texas 7313, Georgia 2047, Kentucky 4800, Virginia 1303, Illinois 5973, Ohio 5530, New York 2665,
Massachusetts 1047, and so on (ibid., pp. 28–49).   For the enthusiasm
of the South and the West for the Mexican War see W. E. Dodd,
"The West and the War with Mexico," in Journal of the Illinois
State Historical Society, vol. v, no. 2, p. 162.
[24] The white population of the United States in 1840 was 14,581,453,
and that of Missouri 323,888 (Sixth Federal Census, Population,
pp. 476, 418).
[25] "Be it enacted: 1. That the peace, permanency and welfare of
our National Union depend upon the strict adherence to the letter
and spirit" of the Compromise of 1820. 2. "That our Senators in
the Congress of the United States are hereby instructed and our
Representatives requested, to vote in accordance with the provisions
and spirit of the said . . . act, in all questions which may come
before them in relation to the organization of new Territories or
States" (Session Laws, 1846, pp. 367–368).   These resolutions were
considered a victory for Benton and his faction.

Democrats was held in the court house rotunda. Trusten Polk and Frank Blair were among those present. Judge Mullanphy offered the following special resolution: "Resolved, That the declaration of the Congress of the United States 'that war existed by act of Mexico' 'IS TRUE.'" Regarding the proviso this meeting made a declaration which was evidently so worded as to save Benton, whose attitude upon the question had caused much criticism in the State. The fifth of the thirteen resolutions read as follows: "Resolved, That as we are now approaching a period when the struggle for the control of the Government is again to be contested by the Federalists, we think it time to give over disputes in Congress; upon such abstractions as the Wilmot Proviso . . . we think this [absurd Proviso] has lived long enough, and time sufficient has elapsed to enable every man to perceive the folly of it."[26]

A bitter struggle, however, developed over the proviso. Some in the State even favored disunion, if a prominent contemporary, Colonel W. F. Switzler, interpreted the period correctly.[27] This intense feeling is reflected in a

---

[26] The Address, Resolutions, and Proceedings of the Democracy of St. Louis, in the Rotunda of the Court House, January 8, 1848, pp. 6-8. Attached to the account of this meeting are comments from the Daily Union of January 10. One of these reads as follows: "The Wilmot proviso is properly stigmatized by the St. Louis Democracy as an act of folly—a miserable stalking horse, on which a few small politicians have mounted. . . . The true doctrine on the Slavery question, is:—The Federal Government must keep hands off—leave it to be controlled by the people in the several States and Territories, as a local matter" (ibid., p. 8). Regarding local opinion relative to the justice of the Mexican War, this strong statement is made: "Here [in St. Louis] no Democrat hesitates for a moment, to declare that the war in which we are now engaged, was forced upon us by Mexico. . . . Indeed, that feeling extends beyond the Democratic ranks; and many of the most intelligent and patriotic Whigs openly avow their detestation of Clay, Webster, and Corwin's sentiments" (ibid., p. 7).

[27] "It was quite natural," says Switzler, "that a large portion of the people of Missouri without regard to party distinctions, should share these convictions with varying degrees of intensity. Some, it is true, were so wedded to the institution of slavery that rather than abandon it in Missouri even through the process of gradual emancipation or submit to an act of Congress prohibiting it in the territories they seemed willing to abandon, and even to adopt measures to disrupt, the National Union itself" (pp. 264-265). Some idea of

letter written by F. P. Blair, Sr., in January, 1849: "Frank [F. P. Blair, Jr.] writes me from St. Louis that his legislature will instruct him against the Wilmot Proviso—in which case Frank insists he ought to resign or . . . make an appeal to the people of Missouri."[28] This declaration was made about the same day that the so-called "Jackson" Resolutions against Benton were introduced into the Missouri Senate (January 1), and brought to pass the "Appeal" of that senator from his legislative instructions to the people of the State.

The protracted debate and intense excitement growing out of the pertinacity of the Wilmot Proviso brought Benton's political record squarely before the people on the eve of his sixth attempt to represent Missouri in the United States Senate. Since the events leading up to and concerning Benton's defeat have been treated by several authorities,[29] it will be the province of this study to take up the various political struggles only in so far as they are affected by the slavery issue. Some writers maintain that slavery in itself was the cause of Benton's fall, while others would have it that those of the rising generation who had political ambitions, jealous of his dictatorship, and grieved by their exclusion from public affairs, had most to do with overturning

the feeling of the radical element in Missouri can be gained from a resumé of Senator Atchison's speech against the proviso in the Federal Senate as it is given in the Jefferson Inquirer of June 22, 1850. In the same year a Clay County meeting bitterly condemned both abolitionists and disunionists, and also declared that they regarded the "Wilmot Proviso and all kindred measures with the most perfect abhorrence" (quoted in the History of Clay and Platte Counties, pp. 155–156). The date of this meeting is not given.

[28] MS. F. P. Blair, Sr., to Van Buren, January 6, A. L. S. [Autograph Letter Signed], Van Buren Papers, vol. lvi.

[29] The best account is that of P. O. Ray, The Repeal of the Missouri Compromise, Its Origin and Authorship, ch. i. Ray, however, used no manuscript sources, and the questionable thesis that Atchison originated the repeal engages most of his attention. The subject is also treated by W. M. Meigs, The Life of Thomas Hart Benton, ch. xxi. Meigs's materials were also limited. In his Thirty Years' View Benton makes no comments on his retirement from the Senate. Switzler does not give much light on the subject. Neither does Roosevelt or Rogers in his biography of Benton. The press of the period is too bitterly partisan to be of great assistance.

his power. The arguments of this chapter will go to show
that both of these elements enter into the fight. The slavery
question seems to have been the real vital force behind
the struggle, although the personal equation of Benton's im-
periousness cannot be overlooked.

It was said that of all his colleagues in the Senate Dr.
Linn alone was treated with consideration by Benton. The
man who dared to look Andrew Jackson in the eyes and
who would as soon meet his opponents with pistols as with
eloquence was not the man to brook criticism from local
politicians. His arrogance is said to have been supreme.
" In 1828," declared Lewis V. Bogy, " Col. Benton sent a
series of instructions addressed to Spencer Pettus, then
Secretary of State, in his own hand writing, and told the
Legislature that they were not to cross a T or dot an I,
but they must be passed as sent."[30]   Benton's friend, the
editor of the Jefferson Enquirer, lamented that his enemies
had seized " upon his traits of character, and upon what
they call his vanity, egotism, and self conceit," and admitted
that he was not "infallible" on these points.[31]   The Whigs
had had little use for Benton for a generation.   One Whig
editor warned his party not to aid the Benton wing of the
Democrats.   " Benton," he wrote, " has ruled this state, for
thirty years with a despotism rarely equalled, in any
country."[32]

From 1820 to 1844 Benton's control was hardly questioned. His hold on his party, despite the fact that he took
little interest in Missouri politics, was undoubtedly due to
the pride which his constituents felt in a statesman whose
national prominence shed such lustre on a new and western
State. The old settlers worshipped a Missourian who was

---

[30] Speech of Colonel Lewis V. Bogy, the Democratic nominee for
Congress. . . . Delivered at the Rotunda [of the Court House] May
27, 1852, pamphlet, p. 11. President Polk in his Diary for March 29,
1847, speaks of Benton's " domineering disposition and utter im-
patience of contradiction or difference of opinion" (The Diary of
James K. Polk During His Presidency, vol. ii, p. 445).
[31] Issue of January 18, 1851.
[32] Weekly Missouri Sentinel, August 28, 1852.

the equal of Clay and Webster in debate and who feared
not to castigate Calhoun for his nullification program, but
with the debate on the Texan Treaty of 1844 and the
Wilmot Proviso a radical proslavery wing of the Democratic party developed which realized that its first task was
to unseat Benton. The situation is very hard to analyze
because of the bitterness on both sides. Benton's enemies
covered whatever personal animus and rivalry they might
have borne him with the cloak of the slavery issue. To
extricate the slavery needle from the haystack of political
furor which buried Missouri from 1849 to 1852 is most
difficult. That Benton's whole slavery vote and policy were
contrary to those of a large portion of his own party in
Missouri is certain. To what extent this fact was used by
his enemies both within the State and without deserves some
attention.

Benton's position on the various great political struggles
revolving about the slavery issue was quite consistent. He
opposed the Texan Treaty of 1844 which all knew meant
war with Mexico. "Atlantic politicians," he said on June
10, 1844, "hot in pursuit of Texas, may have no sympathy
for this Mexican trade, but I have! and it is my policy to
reconcile the two objects—acquisition of Texas and the
preservation of the Mexican trade—and, therefore, to
eschew unjust war with Mexico as not only wicked but
foolish. . . . I am for treating her with respect, and obtaining her consent fairly and honorably . . . to the annexation
of Texas."[33] Benton opposed the war with Mexico up to
its declaration.[34] "Col. Benton called . . . and I gave him
a copy of the message 'declaring war on Mexico,'" wrote
President Polk in his diary for May 11, 1846. "I found
he did not approve it in all its parts. He was willing to vote

---

[33] T. H. Benton, Abridgment of the Debates of Congress, vol. xv,
p. 145.

[34] Polk, who loved the Texan Treaty much and Benton little, says
that the latter was sorry for his opposition to the treaty. "Col.
Benton feels he has lost cast[e] with Democracy on the Texan
question, and feels sore and dissatisfied with his position" (Diary
for March 4, 1846, vol. i, p. 265).

men and money for defence of our territory, but was not prepared to make aggressive war on Mexico. . . . I inferred too, from his conversation that he did not think the territory of the United States extended west of the Nueces River."[35] After war had been declared, however, Benton became quite enthusiastic.   He advised Polk that a general-in-chief should be appointed, "a man of talents and resources as well as a military man," and modestly intimated to the President that "if such an officer was created by Congress, he would be willing to accept the command himself."   Polk continues: "He [Benton] alluded to what was apparent to every one, that the Whigs were endeavoring to turn this war to party account. . . . I [Benton] have returned. . . to Washington to render you any aid in my power."[36]   Benton received an appointment but without the plenary powers which he desired. Congress was unwilling to create the office of lieutenant-general, to which Polk intended to appoint Benton.   Polk did, however, appoint him major-general and his appointment was confirmed by the Senate, but Benton refused to accept unless he was placed in supreme command and also given full diplomatic powers.   Polk concluded that he had no right to put him over the four major-generals already in the field.

Benton played the patriot and supported the war when it actually took place, but he was never reconciled to either the justice or the expediency of the enterprise, and repeatedly accused Calhoun of causing it.[37]   From the day he opposed the Texan Treaty his enemies gave him no peace. "There is cogent logic," ran an editorial of June, 1844, "as well as a severe rebuke in the . . . letter of the 'Hero of New Orleans' [Jackson's letter of February, 1843, favoring annexation, which was published in 1844] that must have been gall and wormwood to Benton.   Jackson has fixed the

---

[35] Diary, vol. i, p. 390.
[36] Ibid., for November 10, 1846, vol. ii, pp. 227–228.
[37] See Benton's speech in the Senate, February 24, 1847 (Congressional Globe, 29th Cong., 2d Sess., pp. 497–498) ; also his Jefferson City Speech of May 26, 1849 (see note 44 of this chapter).

stigma on Benton's recreant brow—let it rest there forever."[38] Other papers and individuals as well were disgusted with Benton's stand on the whole Texan question.[39]

The Compromise of 1850 was generally popular with the
Missouri Democracy. Benton, however, opposed most of
its provisions. He decried compromise on principle.
"Clay is destroying the Union with his humbug compromises," he wrote Clayton in December, 1850.[40] Among
the provisions of the Compromise of 1850 which he disliked
was that which dealt with slavery in the District of Columbia. He maintained that Congress had the power to
abolish slavery in the District, "but," he said, "I am one of
those who believe that it ought not to be touched while
slavery exists in the States from which the District was
ceded."[41]

Benton was also against "mixing up the question of
admitting California with all the questions which slavery
agitation has produced in the United States. . . . I asked
for California a separate consideration."[42] He argued that
slavery was already abolished in the territories acquired
from Mexico. He then read the Mexican Decree of
Emancipation of 1829 and the article of the Mexican constitution of 1843 which forbade slavery in all the Mexican
territories. "The practical application which I make of this
exposition of law is," he continued, "that the proviso

[38] Western Pioneer, June 21, 1844. The Pioneer likewise spoke
of Benton's Texas position as giving him the nature of a "self-
executioner" (ibid.).
[39] A mass-meeting held at St. Genevieve on January 8, 1845, passed
resolutions favoring "the principles of the Tyler Treaty." They
praised Atchison's and condemned Benton's vote on the treaty,
claiming that the latter "did not cast the vote of Missouri" on that
occasion. "We approve the vote of our State Senator, Hon. C.
Detchemendy, against the reelection of Col. Benton" (Missouri
Reporter [St. Louis], January 18, 1845). This sheet spoke of Benton's Texan position as "treason," and condemned him for not
obeying his instructions on annexation (ibid., January 4, 1845).
[40] MS. Benton to John M. Clayton, December 8, 1850, A. L. S.,
Clayton Papers, vol. viii, p. 1803.
[41] Congressional Globe, 31st Cong., 1st Sess., pt. i, p. 712. Speech
of April 11, 1850.
[42] Ibid., p. 656. Speech of April 8, 1850.

[Wilmot's] of which we have heard so much is of no force whatever—unnecessary from any point of view—and of no more effect, if passed, than a blank piece of paper pasted on the statute book." He declared that positive law alone could introduce slavery into California and New Mexico.[43] Distasteful as this whole argument, with its conclusion, must have been to many of his constituents, Benton continued to preach it, and even elaborated it in his Jefferson City speech of May 26, 1849.[44]

As to a fugitive slave law, Benton urged an " efficient and satisfactory" act, but " it must be as a separate and independent measure." He believed that the seduction of slaves was " the only point . . . at which any of the non-slave-holding States, as States, have given just cause of complaint to the slave-holding States."[45]

When the movement for the acquisition of the 54:40 line and the demand for " all of Oregon" appeared, Benton was likewise in opposition while the Missourians clamored for the Columbia River country.[46] In his speech at Jefferson City, mentioned above, Benton said that his position on the slavery question had been consistent. " In my vote on the Oregon bill," he declared, " in which I opposed the introduction of slavery there—and, again in my letter to the people of Oregon . . . I declared myself to be no propagandist of slavery." He did not stop here, but openly decried the system: " My personal sentiments, then, are against the institution of slavery, and against its intro-

---

[43] Ibid., pp. 430–432. Speech of February 27, 1850.

[44] Speech Delivered by the Hon. Thomas H. Benton at Jefferson, the Capital of Missouri on the 26th of May, 1849, pamphlet, pp. 11–12. This speech can also be found in Niles' Register, vol. lxxv, pp. 390–392, 397–399.

[45] Congressional Globe, 31st Cong., 1st Sess., pt. i, p. 657.

[46] Resolutions favoring the " reoccupation" of Oregon were common throughout the State. On January 8, 1846, a great mass-meeting was held at Jefferson City where the state constitutional convention was then in session. Many of the convention delegates were present. Governor Marmaduke acted as chairman and J. S. Green as secretary. Resolutions demanding all of Oregon and endorsing the Monroe Doctrine were passed. President Polk was congratulated on the success of his Texas policy (Jefferson Inquirer, January 14, 1846).

duction into places in which it does not now exist. If there was no slavery in Missouri today, I should oppose its coming in . . . as there is none in New Mexico and California I am against sending it to those territories."[47]

Regarding the question of slavery in, and the power of Congress over, the Territories, Benton gave out what must have been unpalatable doctrine to his Jefferson City hearers. "It is absurd," he said, "to deny to Congress the power to legislate as it pleases upon the subject of slavery in the territories. . . . Congress has power to prohibit, or to admit slavery, and no one else. . . . Congress has the constitutional power to abolish slavery in [the] territories."[48]

Benton was no sentimental antislavery enthusiast. He had considerable slave property himself. "I was born to the inheritance of slaves," he said, "and have never been without them. I bought some but only at their own entreaty. . . . I have sold some, but only for misconduct. I had two taken from me by the Abolitionists, and never inquired after them; and liberated a third who would not go with them. . . . I have slaves in Kentucky. . . . I have slaves in Washington City—perhaps the only member of Congress who has any there."[49]

Benton's whole attitude toward slavery was open to the world, and must have been anything but satisfactory to an influential portion of his party. There is, therefore, a reasonable basis for supposing that the opposition to him might well have been based, not immediately perhaps, but certainly ultimately, on the slavery issue. Of course this was by no means the only motive that caused his defeat. The personal and political bitterness was deep-seated, but Benton himself always thought that it was the disunion faction headed by Calhoun which brought about his downfall.

To the southern radicals, with their doctrine of nullification and their hatred for his stalwart defence of the Union,

[47] Jefferson City Speech, p. 17.
[48] Ibid., p. 11.
[49] Ibid., p. 17.

Benton laid the charge of seeking his ruin by undermining him at home. From the day when he and Jackson "were made friends together" the rift between the Jacksonian Unionists and the Calhoun "Nullifiers" was never closed. In the open Senate on March 2, 1847, Benton formally charged Calhoun with conspiring to consummate his defeat.[50] His speeches of the following years are burdened with the most abusive denunciations of Calhoun and the latter's famous Resolutions of 1847, the prototype of the so-called "Missouri" or "Jackson" Resolutions to which attention will be called later.[51] Benton so hated and abominated Calhoun that he severely criticized President Shannon of the State University for placing Calhoun's newly published works in the University library.[52] Calhoun, on his part, denied any complicity in the imaginary conspiracies to unseat Benton. "He [Benton] seems to think," wrote the former, "I stand in his way, and that I am ever engaged in some scheme to put him down. I, on the contrary, have never for a moment thought of raising him to the level of a competitor, or rival; nor considered it of any importance to me whether he should be put down or not."[53]

There is some evidence, however, that Calhoun and other extreme southern leaders were at least corresponding with Benton's enemies at home who had his defeat as their chief political goal. Judge W. C. Price of Springfield, who claims to have been Benton's arch-opponent in Missouri, states that he opened the fight against Benton in 1844. The judge, according to his own story, was in constant communication with Calhoun, Davis, Benjamin, and other extremists of the South. He declared that it was in 1844, at a time when Benton refused to aid in the repeal of the Missouri Com-

[50] Congressional Globe, 29th Cong., 2d Sess., p. 563.

[51] See the whole of the Jefferson City Speech, and that delivered at Fayette on September 1, 1849, which may be found in the Jefferson Inquirer of October 6, 1849.

[52] Letter of Shannon of July 26, 1852, in the Missouri Weekly Sentinel of August 12, 1852.

[53] John C. Calhoun to the People of the Southern States, Or Reply to Benton, pamphlet, p. 1.

promise in order to save Missouri from a free-soil neighbor
to the west, that he declared war on the latter and worked
incessantly to undermine him.[54]   These reminiscences need
not be taken too seriously.   Benton's stand on the Texan
Treaty had already given him bitter enemies,[55] and even
earlier than this there was an active faction against him in
his own party in the State.   So perhaps Judge Price over-
estimated his own importance in claiming to be the
"original" anti-Benton man.

There was in fact a distinct anti-Benton movement within
the Democratic ranks of Missouri before the Texan Treaty
came up.   On July 5, 1843, one V. Ellis, a St. Louis Whig,
wrote to George R. Smith relative to the appointment of
certain Indian agencies, that "Benton's days are numbered.
V. Buren has no chance for the nomination . . . it shall
not be my fault if things do not work right.   Select Democrats in all cases, & such as are opposed to Benton."[56]   In
March, 1844, Charles D. Drake sent out printed instructions
for the Whigs in the approaching presidential election.
The Whigs were to launch an aggressive campaign, and, by
dividing the Democrats, win.   "Is there, or can there be
created, such a division," said a portion of this suggestive
query, "as would enable the Whigs by their votes to elect
an anti-Benton man, . . . or if no anti-Benton man can be
found, one who will go with us on these measures?"[57]

Nevertheless, the stand of Benton on the Texas question
can be considered as the real cause of the organized opposition.   "Ever since 1844, when Mr. Benton commenced
opposing the Democratic party and its great measure . . .
the annexation of Texas," said a published letter of 1857,
"his followers have never doubted his position."[58]   On

[54] Statement made by Price to W. F. Connelley and quoted by
Ray, pp. 248–249.
[55] See the Western Pioneer of June 21, 1844, quoted above.
[56] MS. Smith Papers.
[57] Printed letter in the Smith Papers.   Dated March 19, 1844, and
circulated by Drake as "Cor. Sec. St. Louis Clay Club."
[58] Printed letter of William Palm to C. C. Zeigler of the state
legislature.   Dated St. Louis, January 25, 1857.   This same idea is

October 1, 1844, Benton was severely criticized at Hannibal by one Davis, who answered him from the platform, and declared that " he was dissatisfied, and others were dissatisfied . . . with the Colonel's [Benton's] position on the subject of Texas."⁵⁹

There is very substantial ground for presuming that Benton's enemies took advantage of his position on the slavery question in general and used it as a lever. Senator Atchison implied as much in a speech at Platte City on September 26, 1849. He said: " I have been and am now making war on him [Benton], Free Soilism, Abolitionism, and all similar isms . . . and if he is not driven from the United States Senate, it will be no fault of mine."⁶⁰ The observations of Montgomery Blair, a shrewd man of affairs, leave the impression that the slavery issue was by no means the sole root of Benton's trouble. " I have no doubt," he wrote Martin Van Buren from St. Louis early in 1849, just after the passage of the " Jackson " Resolutions, " but that we can sustain Col. Benton . . . his enemies are in the ascendant now in this State & it requires something potent to physic them with. Fortunately for him, I think, they have taken the Slavery chute, imagining that the safe channel, while the course of his old associates and his own

given in the official anti-Benton campaign pamphlet of 1856, entitled, A Statement of Facts and a Few Suggestions in Review of Political Action in Missouri, p. 6.

⁵⁹ The Mill Boy (St. Louis), October 12, 1844. This was a St. Louis Whig organ. The account of the above meeting is as follows: On October 1 Benton spoke to a large audience at Hannibal, after which " Mr. Jamison, of Callaway, followed. . . . Mr. Jamison remarked that if there were any persons present who were not satisfied with Col. Benton's course on the Texan question . . . the Colonel would be pleased to give further explanation. . . . Thereupon, Mr. Davis took the stand, and announced that he was dissatisfied, and other Democrats were dissatisfied . . . with the Colonel's position upon the subject of Texas, and especially with reference to the subject of instructions by the legislature." Benton replied " that he did not desire instructions, and would not hold his seat when he believed he was not acting in conformity with the views of his party."

⁶⁰ Republican, October 6, 1849.

vote on the Oregon bill would they think effectually destroy him."[61]

As above quoted, Montgomery Blair is casually stating to a personal friend that Benton's enemies had chosen the "Slavery chute" as the most convenient exit by which to discharge him, evidently believing that Benton's slavery policy was not the real cause of the attack upon him. Even one of Benton's opponents, W. C. Price, acknowledged that it was not only because of their honest displeasure with his stand against slavery, but as much because of their jealousy of his dominance, that the enemies of Benton sought his downfall.[62] Benton himself thought that the slavery issue was a mere subterfuge to place him in a bad position. Calhounism and secession appeared to him as the sole inspiration of his enemies. "The slavery question," he wrote Clayton in 1855, "is a cover for the real motives which, with the politicians, [is] ambition—with the masses, [is] a belief that the Union works to the disadvantage of the South."[63]

The means used to force Benton to declare himself was the passage of the so-called "Jackson" Resolutions of 1849.[64] Frank Blair and his St. Louis Bentonites openly charged the anti-Benton faction with this intent. "His [Benton's] friends will see at once," was the statement by Blair, "that those most busy in Missouri, in denouncing the proviso, are none others than Benton's old enemies, and although many of them are northern men, and must therefore be disinclined to the extension of slavery . . . it is

---

[61] MS. Van Buren Papers, dated St. Louis, March 12, vol. lvi, pp. 13161–13162.

[62] Statement of Price, quoted by Ray, pp. 248–249.

[63] MS. Benton to Clayton, July 21, 1855, Clayton Papers, vol. xi, pp. 2107–2108.

[64] Regarding this point the Jefferson Inquirer stated editorially on August 20, 1853, that "the Jackson nullification resolutions were gotten up for this purpose [getting rid of Benton] and every Democrat who would not join in the crusade against Missouri's beloved statesman, was denounced as a free soil traitor." "The object of the anti-Benton proceedings, as we infer from the St. Louis Republican," comments Niles' Register, "[is] to cut off Col. Benton from, or commit the [democracy] against any appeal or justification which he may have to make for his course in the Senate on the Wilmot Proviso " (vol. lxxv, p. 288).

enough . . . that Benton voted for the proviso for Oregon, and denounced the attempt . . . to carry slavery to the Pacific shore."[65]

The "Jackson" or "Jackson-Napton" Resolutions have been discussed by almost every writer on Missouri history, hence elaborate consideration of the text of them would be out of place in a study merely of the slavery issue. Their origin, however, deserves attention. By chance Claiborne F. Jackson has often been given credit for these resolutions, but Judge William B. Napton of Saline County, an old enemy of Benton, deserves the honor of originating them. The copy of a letter dated August 8, 1849, from Sterling Price to Benton conclusively proves that Napton was the author, although at the time he seems to have denied it. In this letter Sterling Price asserted that Napton drew them up during the winter of 1848–49 and told him (Price) that he expected that either Carty Wells or Claiborne F. Jackson would introduce them in the legislature.[66]

On January 1, 1849, the resolutions were introduced in the Senate by none other than Carty Wells of Marion

---

[65] F. P. Blair, Jr., and thirty-seven others, "Address to the Democracy of Missouri," pamphlet, p. 14. Date 1850(?).

[66] This letter was published by Benton in the Weekly Republican (St. Louis) of May 25, 1852. It is as follows:—

"VAL VERDE, Aug. 8, 1849.

HON. THOS. H. BENTON:

"*Dear Sir;* having very recently seen a communication from Judge W. B. Napton, replying to your charge, touching the points of issue between you, in which he evidently conveys the idea that he was not the author of the Missouri Resolutions, I feel constrained to offer my testimony; and thereby comply with the promise made when I last saw you. The facts are these;

"During my visit to Jefferson City, last winter, Judge Napton invited me into his room and showed me a set of resolutions which he informed me had been prepared by himself, and which I believe are the same which passed the Missouri Legislature. I will merely add that another gentleman of high respectability and credit was also invited to hear them, and that he too had prepared a set of resolutions, which were laid aside and Judge Napton's accepted. I conceive it unnecessary to give his name . . . and I am sure he stands ready to corroborate, by his testimony my statement. In connection with my visit to Judge Napton's room he informed me that his resolutions would be presented by either Carty Wells or Claiborne F. Jackson. I remain, with regard, your obedient servant,
STERLING PRICE."

County.[67] They were referred to the committee on Federal relations, and on January 15 were reported by its chairman, Claiborne F. Jackson.[68] This caused Jackson's name to be associated with them. Parallel resolutions were introduced in the House of Representatives on January 5.[69] Amendments, substitutes, and counter-resolutions were offered by the Whigs, who opposed the measure in both houses. On March 6 Jones proposed that Benton be commended for his "long and brilliant career in the Senate," whereupon Wilkerson offered an amendment approving of Senator Atchison's political record "generally, and particularly his course in reference to the subject of slavery."[70] On January 26 the resolutions[71] as a whole passed the Senate by a

[67] Senate Journal, 15th Ass., 1st Sess., p. 64.
[68] Ibid., p. 111.
[69] House Journal, 15th Ass., 1st Sess., p. 82.
[70] Ibid., pp. 490–491.
[71] These resolutions are as follows:—
"Resolved, by the General Assembly of the state of Missouri,
"1st. That the Federal Constitution was the result of a Compromise between the conflicting interests of the states which formed it, and in no part of that instrument is to be found any delegation of power to Congress to legislate on the subject of slavery, excepting some special provisions having in view the prospective abolition of the African slave trade and for the recovery of fugitive slaves. Any attempt therefore on the part of Congress to legislate on the subject so as to affect the institution of slavery in the States, in the District of Columbia, or in the Territories, is, to say the least, a violation of the principle upon which that instrument was founded.
"2d. That the territories acquired by the blood and treasure of the whole nation ought to be governed for the common benefit of the citizens of all the states; and any organization of the territorial governments excluding the citizens of any part of the Union from removing to such territories with their property would be an exercise of power by Congress inconsistent with the spirit upon which our federal compact was based, insulting to the sovereignty and dignity of the States thus affected, calculated to alienate one portion of the Union from another, and tending ultimately to disunion.
"3d. That this General Assembly regard the conduct of the Northern States on the subject of slavery as releasing the slaveholding States from all further adherence to the basis of compromise fixed on by the act of Congress of the 6th of March, 1820, even if such act ever did impose any obligation upon the slaveholding States, and authorizes them to insist on their rights under the Constitution; but, for the sake of harmony and the preservation of our Federal Union, they will still sanction the application of the principle of the Missouri Compromise to the recent territorial acquisitions, if by such concession future aggression upon the equal rights of the States

vote of 23 to 6, four members not being present.[72] They passed the House on March 6 by a vote of 53 to 27, thirteen members being absent and sick.[73] Of these twenty-seven voting nay, Switzler, who was a Whig member, says that all but four were Whigs, and that seventeen members, all Whigs but two, voted " from first to last " against the resolutions.[74]

Benton refused to stand by the instructions which the resolves embodied, and made his celebrated " Appeal " to the voters of the State.[75] On May 26 he delivered his

may be arrested and the spirit of antislavery fanaticism be extinguished.

" 4th. The right to prohibit slavery in any territory belongs exclusively to the people thereof, and can only be exercised by them in forming their constitution for a State government, or in their sovereign capacity as an independent State.

" 5th. That in the event of the passage of any act conflicting with the principles herein expressed, Missouri will be found in hearty co-operation with the slaveholding States in such measures as may be deemed necessary for our mutual protection against the encroachments of Northern fanaticism.

" 6th. That our Senators in Congress be instructed, and our Representatives be requested, to act in conformity with the foregoing resolutions."

These resolutions may be found in Session Laws, 1848, p. 667; and in the Congressional Globe, 31st Cong., 1st Sess., pp. 97–98. They can also be found in almost any history of Missouri or biography of Benton.

[72] Senate Journal, 15th Ass., 1st Sess., p. 176. The vote on the individual resolutions was: first, 24 to 6, 3 absent; second, 25 to 5, 3 absent; third, 23 to 7, 3 absent; fourth, 23 to 6, 4 absent; fifth, 23 to 6, 4 absent; sixth, 23 to 6, 4 absent.

[73] House Journal, 15th Ass., 1st Sess., pp. 479–483. The vote on the individual resolutions was: first, 59 to 25, 9 absent; second, 63 to 21, 9 absent; third, 56 to 27, 9 absent; fourth, 62 to 29, 11 absent; fifth, 53 to 29, 12 absent; sixth, 54 to 27, 12 absent.

[74] See Switzler, pp. 267–268. Switzler himself was one of these. The committee of the House on Federal relations failed to agree; the proslavery minority report which was neutralized by an expression of loyalty to the Union was defeated the day before this vote, March 5, by a vote of 62 to 20 (ibid., p. 267). This report can be found in House Journal, 15th Ass., 1st Sess., app., pp. 219–222.

[75] His formal "Appeal" was dated St. Louis, May 9, 1849. It is given among other places in Niles' Register, vol. lxxv, p. 332. Benton's enemies claim that he was far from consistent on the question of legislative instruction. L. V. Bogy asserted that Benton had once written a Missouri friend that "the Legislature had a right to instruct, and the Senator was in duty bound to obey the resolutions, or resign" (Bogy's Speech of May 27, 1852, at St. Louis, p. 11). Benton was very sensitive on the whole question, and sharply criti-

famous "Calhounic" at Jefferson City. He accused the South Carolinian of undermining him in Missouri, castigated his local enemies, and gave an exposition of his own views regarding slavery.[76] When Benton made his "Appeal," not only he but as astute a politician as Montgomery Blair thought that he would be successful. "I have no doubt," wrote Blair, "but that we can sustain Col. Benton in the doctrines here ascribed to him. . . . I think now that they [Benton's enemies] have no longer the fostering care of Mr. Polk at Washington if Col. Benton will carry out his determination to visit the whole state [he will be able to] annihilate them with the questions which only need to be explained to be as strong with the people as the Bank question was. It must be confessed however that the work remains to be done, but I am strong in the faith that it will be accomplished."[77] Two months later Blair was still sanguine, though he could not overlook the obstacles with which the old warrior's way was beset. He wrote Van Buren: "I still think he will succeed although he has great difficulties to contend against," the greatest of these difficulties being his absence from and loss of touch with local politics; in fact he had not "been in the State or made a political speech out of it for two years."[78] Just after his Jefferson City speech Benton was full of cheer, and wrote to F. P.

---

cized President Shannon in 1852 for permitting a student at the last commencement to deliver an oration on The Right of Appeal. Shannon, however, denied that Benton's name had been mentioned in the speech (Weekly Missouri Sentinel, July 30, 1852).

[76] Printed in pamphlet form, as well as in the press, from which quotations have already been given in this chapter.

[77] MS. Montgomery Blair to Van Buren, dated St. Louis, March 12, 1849, A. L. S., Van Buren Papers, vol. lvi, pp. 13161–13162.

[78] MS. ibid to ibid., May 12, 1849, A. L. S., Van Buren Papers, vol. lvi, pp. 13180–13182. Blair emphasizes this last point relative to Benton's loss of contact with the local situation: "The greatest of his difficulties has heretofore been that his feelings were so engrossed in another quarter as almost entirely to withdraw his attention from politics, & if he is defeated it will be mainly owing to that cause. For during the time when his enemies have possessed the general and State Governments & have been using incessant efforts against him, he has written but one private political letter and that containing but a few lines & he has not been in the State or made a political speech out of it for two years."

Blair, Sr., " that he was never better received by his constituents."[79] In December even the hopeful Blairs were anxiously fearing a coalition of Whigs and anti-Bentonites,[80] but as late as November, 1850, Benton wrote from Missouri that he was " victorious there." The two younger Blairs, however, were fearing that the " best that can happen will be no election."[81] Although Benton was defeated and a Whig took the seat he had so honored for thirty years, he was far from politically dead, as he himself viewed the situation. The fierce torrent which swirled about his " Appeal " was to convulse Missouri and split his party beyond repair.

It is not the aim of this paper to follow Benton's campaign during 1849–50, but it is of importance to learn something of the influence of his " Appeal " in moulding later politics. In his Jefferson City speech he admitted that he had " no idea that the mass of the members who voted for the resolutions in the last General Assembly, had any idea that they were Calhoun's, or considered the dissolution of the Union which they announced, as a thing in actual contemplation. But they are not the less injurious on that account. They are the act of the General Assembly, and stand for the act of the State, and bind it to the car of Mr. Calhoun."[82] Nevertheless, in his speech at Fayette on September 1, 1849, he took a different view. " The whole conception, concoction, and passage of the resolutions," he said, " was done upon conspiracy, perfected by fraud. It was a plot to get

[79] MS. F. P. Blair, Sr., to Van Buren, June 10, 1840, A. L. S., Van Buren Papers, vol. lvi, pp. 13193–13194. On August 8 F. P. Blair, Sr., wrote Van Buren that " Benton plays his part like a great Bear surrounded by a yelping pack of whelps. He slaps one down on this side—another on that—and grips a third with his teeth—then tosses him with his snout " (A. L. S., ibid., pp. 13216–13218).

[80] MS. F. P. Blair, Sr., to Van Buren, December 3–4, 1849, A. L. S., Van Buren Papers, vol. lvii, pp. 13250–13251; also see ibid. to ibid., August 1, 1850, A. L. S., ibid., pp. 13352–13353.

[81] MS. ibid. to ibid., November 12, 1850, A. L. S., Van Buren Papers, vol. lvii, p. 13376.

[82] Jefferson City Speech, p. 9.

me out of the Senate and out of the way of the disunion plotters."[83]

During this campaign Benton was at once so extravagantly lauded and so scorchingly condemned that it is very hard to discern the real motives of the contestants. "We have already noticed the difficulty," said an editorial in the Missouri Republican of September 10, 1849, "which attends our purpose to give a faithful history of the quarrels between Benton and his enemies in this State." A fair idea of the furor which swept over the State can be gained from the following account of a meeting held in St. Louis, February 12, 1849. "The meeting was organized amid much confusion," and a committee was appointed to draft resolutions. The committee reported a series of resolutions declaring for the power of Congress over the Territories, denouncing the late Washington convention of southern men as a "Hartford Convention," and praising Benton for seeing the imminent danger which was threatening the Union. Amid confusion Mr. Hoyt offered the late ("Jackson") resolutions of the legislature. These were laid on the table by "a large majority." After this the Benton resolutions were carried.[84] Throughout the State, resolves were drafted favoring Benton and condemning him. Letters attacking him and letters taking his part and prints of speeches pro and con crowd the press of the years 1849-53. The editorial comments are at times so vitriolic as to appear amusing to those living in an age when personalities are not so important in politics.[85]

---

[83] Jefferson Inquirer, October 6, 1849. At this meeting he was not well received, but at other points he evidently was. "Col. Benton was here in Boonville making speeches in the vicinity," reads a letter of June, 1849, "and creating great excitement and confusion in the democratic ranks. I heard him yesterday at the Choteau Springs—his speech was very well rec[eive]d" (MS. Freeman Wing to Mrs. E. Ashley, June 24, A. L. S., J. J. Crittenden Papers).

[84] Niles' Register, vol. lxxv, pp. 239–240.

[85] At a Platte County meeting in July, 1849, among other resolutions passed was one calling upon Benton to obey his legislative instructions or else resign (Republican, July 16, 1849, quoting the Weston Platte Argus of unknown date). It was openly charged that Benton was in alliance with the abolitionists (letter dated St. Genevieve, September 30, 1849, in ibid., October 3). Such accusa-

The swirl of excitement engulfed even the Whigs themselves. "And the Whigs," wrote a contemporary, "were to
some extent divided into Benton and Anti-Benton Whigs,
designations which attached to the one segment or the other
according to the intensity of its pro-slavery or anti-slavery
sentiments."[86]   One gets a good deal of light on the position
of the Whigs in this contest from the reply of James S.
Rollins to Goode, a St. Louis Whig.

Mr. Goode: "Though there was nothing in the resolutions ["Jackson"] in which he did not heartily concur, yet
he deemed their introduction at the time was inexpedient."

Mr. Rollins: "Every Whig in the General Assembly
except the gentleman from Scott, (Mr. Darnes) voted
against those resolutions when they were introduced. Their
action was endorsed by every Whig newspaper in the State.
Every Whig of prominence and distinction in Missouri
sustained the action of their Representatives in this hall.
Including our distinguished candidate for the Senate (Col.
Doniphan)."

Mr. Darnes said that the Whigs had approved his vote
(above) and that "at public meetings of Whigs held shortly
after the resolutions were passed in support of the Jackson
resolutions and of his action in that hall."

---

tions were common. Atchison so criticized him September 26, 1849
(ibid., October 6, 1849). Adam Klippel of St. Joseph wrote S. P.
Chase, September 14, 1849, that "nine out of 22 democratic papers
in the State, it appears, are out against Benton, and are unbounded
in villifying him" (Chase Correspondence, in American Historical
Association Reports, 1902, vol. ii, pp. 471-472). During the session of
1850-51 resolutions were introduced into the House condemning
Benton for not obeying his instructions (House Journal, 16th Ass.,
1st Sess., app., p. 240). So bitter became the struggle that Frank
Blair of the Republican and L. Pickering of the Daily Union almost
came together with bowie knives on January 28, while the resolutions were still before the legislature (Daily Union, February 3,
1849). On March 5, they met on the corner of Olive and Second
Streets and jabbed at one another with their umbrellas. Pickering
received an injury to one of his eyes (ibid., March 6). The trouble
had started by Pickering's declaring that Blair's statement calling
Benton a true Democrat was "twaddle at least, and only shows the
littleness of the writer" (ibid., February 3).

[86] Switzler, p. 273. Colonel Switzler was in the legislature when
the "Jackson" Resolutions were passed. As an editor he keenly
observed the situation.

Mr. Rollins: "But on that particular occasion I was with Col. Benton. The Whig party of Missouri was with Col. Benton upon that question, and against the anti-Benton wing of the Democratic party. I condemned the Jackson resolutions because they sprung a baleful agitation upon the State, and also because they embodied nullification and tended to disunion . . . the Whigs were united almost to a man on this question."[87]

The effects of Benton's "Appeal" were most important. The Democratic party was so riven by hatred and bitterness that the cleavage between slavery and antislavery became more and more distinct. Benton's failure of reelection in 1851 but aroused him and his friends to carry the war to the last extremity. To "put down Benton" was easier than to eradicate the force and pertinacity of his followers. Henceforward the anti-Bentonites became the active proslavery organization, although by no means a secession party.

For years the Democratic party was in a precarious condition. The Napton Resolutions were the rocks on which the party was shattered. Yet despite dangers at the hands of the jubilant Whigs, one wing of the Democrats, led by Frank Blair, risked party success to repeal them. The Claiborne F. Jackson faction held solid for no retraction. The legislative session of 1852–53 was disrupted by the "irrepressible" resolutions and by the three-cornered fight for the speakership between Bentonites, anti-Bentonites, and Whigs. The power of Congress over slavery in the Territories also embittered the partisans, "the animus of the discussion foreshadowing to many the terrible catastrophe in which our national troubles culminated in 1861."[88]

---

[87] Jas. S. Rollins, Speech in Joint Session of the Legislature, Feb. 2, 1855, in reply to Mr. Goode of St. Louis, pamphlet, p. 17. Also given in the Missouri Statesman, March 16, 1855.

[88] Switzler, pp. 275–277. Switzler was in the legislature off and on during this period. Some idea of this bitterness within the party can be gained from the Speech of L. V. Bogy of May 27, 1852. "Col. Benton appealed from those resolutions, and since that time the party has been divided. . . . This division spread throughout the length and breadth of the State, and a feeling of hostility—a deadly feud, sprung up between the two wings of the party" (p. 6).

The Democratic party longed for peace but found it not. On December 22, 1851, the Democracy of Oregon County passed resolutions declaring that, whereas the divisions in the party had given the Whigs a senator and three congressmen, " unless these unhappy divisions are amicably adjusted . . . the Whigs will have both the executive and the legislature of the State."[89] A Platte County gathering of January 8, 1852, begged for a healing of the schism.[90] For weeks the press was full of accounts of similar pleas. But as much as they loved peace and harmony they loved principle more. The Democrats of Ray,[91] Osage, Cooper, Boone, Lafayette, Randolph, Monroe,[92] and other counties determined " to lay aside personal animosities and petty bickerings," but at the same time declared plainly that the instruction of senators and even of representatives was " a vital principle of republicanism."

The Democratic state convention met at Jefferson City on April 5, and the party seemed again united.[93] Candidates were nominated, and a solid front was arrayed to meet the Whigs. Colonel Lewis V. Bogy was nominated to represent St. Louis in Congress. Even the St. Louis Democracy on April 24, under the leadership of Frank Blair, B. Gratz Brown, and Trusten Polk, swore to support the ticket.[94] But the pipe of peace was rudely knocked from the lips of the sanguine politicians. Benton announced his independent candidacy for Congress. The whole conflict now reopened.

---

[89] Jefferson Inquirer, January 31, 1852.
[90] Ibid. In July, 1854, the anti-Benton candidate for the state Senate for Clay and Platte Counties begged his Bentonite rival to come to an agreement so that one could withdraw, lest the Whigs should win (Republican, July 25, 1854).
[91] Jefferson Inquirer, January 31, 1852.
[92] Ibid., February 14, 1852.
[93] This convention was by no means harmonious. One delegate, Dr. Lowry, thus expressed himself: " He said he was an anti-Benton man all over, and he expected to stand on the Jefferson platform, that he came to the Convention for the purpose of fraternizing, etc." (Weekly Missouri Sentinel, April 8, 1852).
[94] Quoted by Bogy in his Speech of May 27 from the Daily Union of unknown date (pp. 14–15).

The Bentonites struck at the Napton Resolutions.[95]   On February 1, 1853, Frank Blair in a long speech moved the repeal of the resolutions, declaring they "did not express the sentiments of the people of this State."[96]   A week later Claiborne F. Jackson reviewed Benton's whole career as an antislavery statesman.[97]   On the 15th the rescinding resolution was tabled by a vote of 72 to 49.[98]   The resolutions therefore remained, and along with them the ill-feeling.

The Whigs loved not the Napton Resolutions, but they loved still less Democratic peace and harmony.   "We always opposed making these questions [Napton Resolutions] a test of orthodoxy in the whig ranks," declared the Hannibal Journal.   "Besides, if the whigs were to repeal these resolutions, the only bone of contention would be taken from the democratic ranks, and the cohesive power of public plunder would bring their disjointed ranks together, and then the Whigs might bid adieu to all hope of ever getting power in this State."[99]   Other Whig papers agreed with the Journal, while some favored the repeal of the resolutions.[100]

With his election to Congress in 1852 Benton opened his agitation for the " Central National Highway to the Pacific." But even this popular issue could not save him.   In 1854 he was defeated for reelection to Congress, and two years later failed in his efforts to become governor.   Benton was a

---

[95] For an account of this action of Benton as told by his opponents see their pamphlet entitled A Statement of Facts and a Few Suggestions in Review of Political Action, pp. 8–9.

[96] Jefferson Inquirer, March 5, 1853.

[97] Ibid., February 12, 19, 1853.   For a review of Benton's slavery record also see the printed letter of James S. Green to Messrs. Farish, Minor, Roberts, and Burks, December 10, 1849.

[98] Jefferson Inquirer, February 19; or in House Journal, 17th Ass., Extra Sess., p. 519.   Nine members were absent and sick.   On February 25, 1857, the fifth resolution was rescinded by a vote of 20 to 7 in the Senate, eight members either being absent or not voting (Senate Journal, 19th Ass., 1st Sess., p. 340).

[99] Quoted from an unknown issue of the Journal by the Weekly Missouri Sentinel of August 28, 1852.

[100] The Sentinel cautioned the Whigs to "keep hands off," and criticized the Boonville Observer and the Missouri Statesman for favoring repeal (May 16, 1852).

fighter and never knew when he was beaten. His Jacksonian Unionism was out of date. His revenge, however, was
sweet, for David R. Atchison, his inveterate enemy, was as
politically dead as himself,—so dead that, as Frank Blair
said, "We have ceased to look ät the spot where he went
down."[101] Against Benton's protests the Missouri Compromise was repealed, but his enemies merely digged their
own pit, for Kansas was soon filled with abolitionists. So
passes Thomas Hart Benton from the field of Missouri
politics, of which for thirty years he had been the master.
With him passed the Democrats who believed in the Union
at any price. Following Benton came the most passionate
period of Missouri history.[102]

The Whigs were the conservative force in Missouri
politics, but the Kansas convulsion loosened many of them
from their ancient moorings. On the slavery issue that
party, like Benton, largely favored moderation. They
prided themselves on their sound financial tenets. Agitation they naturally shunned. "Resolved, That we are
equally opposed to the abolitionists of the North, and the
Nullifiers of the South, as enemies of the Union, and will
hold no political communion with either," said the Daviess
County Whig convention declaration of 1852.[103] Fifty of
the sixty Whig members of the legislature met on Christmas
day, 1854, and, after condemning those who opposed the
Kansas-Nebraska Bill and those who sought to defeat the
purpose of the Fugitive Slave Law, declared unanimously
that they would support no candidates tarred with the free
soil or the abolition stick.[104]

James S. Rollins was the intellectual leader of the Whigs
for years. His statement of the orthodox Whig position on
slavery is as follows: "I will reiterate what I consider to
be the correct doctrine upon the subject of slavery," he said
to a joint session of the legislature in 1855; "Congress . . .

---

[101] Speech delivered by Blair in St. Louis, date not given (St.
Joseph Commercial Cycle, March 23, 1855).
[102] See ch. vi of this study.
[103] Convention held at Gallatin, April 12, 1852 (Republican, April 24).
[104] Richmond Weekly Mirror, January 5, 1855.

has the power to legislate in the territories. . . . But if Congress has the power, as I believe it has, to legislate upon the slavery in the territories, justice, honor and expediency forbid its exercise. . . . Upon the question of slavery, I think, I may safely say, that the great Whig party of Missouri, is sound and conservative, ready to resist illegal Northern aggression and abolitionism on the one hand, and to suppress Southern fanaticism and nullification on the other. Above all things the people want repose upon this question. The safety of their property, the integrity of the Union, and the permanency of the Government itself, cries aloud against further agitation! Let it cease!" Mr. Rollins then read a resolution which had been previously drawn up for a Boone County meeting, and "which," he said, "I believe embodies on this question the Whig sentiments of this State." This document is as follows: "Resolved, That although the people of this State have always been willing to abide by the Missouri Compromise, yet believing the best and only method of settling the slavery question is to submit it to the judgment of the people; we approve of the establishment of the territories of Kansas and Nebraska with the power of the people who settle in those territories to regulate the subject of slavery within their limits according to their own pleasure."[105]

The Whigs as a party never admitted that slavery was anything but a personal matter. They would not allow their party to become an instrument for or against it. "There is a Whig ticket for the City of St. Louis," caustically remarked an antislavery German editor, "upon which appear the proud names of slave-raising millionaires, and millionaire slave-raisers, and at the head of them is Luther M. Kennett."[106]

---

[105] Speech in Reply to Goode, February 2, 1855, pp. 14, 16.
[106] Anzeiger des Westens of July 7, 1854, quoted by the Republican of July 8. The position of the Whigs on the slavery issue has been analyzed by Tupes (pp. 17–18). His thesis as a whole is somewhat too statistical, as the analysis of the vote on certain measures has been too strictly interpreted as measuring public as well as personal sentiment. He takes little account of the complexity of conflicting issues entering into each measure.

The American party of Missouri, composed largely of old-time Whigs, was also far from favorable to the antislavery program. At a Boone County meeting held on February 4, 1856, resolutions were adopted condemning congressional interference with slavery in the Territories, advocating the enforcement of the Fugitive Slave Law, and pleading for a cessation of slavery agitation.[107]

A great force in Missouri politics, especially during the fifties, was the German element of St. Louis. Detesting slavery and slaveholders on the one hand, and hating still more what they thought slavery stood for—disunion—they became active antislavery agitators. The old southern portion of the State was both shocked and outraged by these uncouth iconoclasts, many of whom had little respect for a slaveholding aristocracy, Calhoun politics, or the Puritan Sabbath.[108] Boernstein of the Anzeiger des Westens was exceptionally obnoxious to the proslavery people. "The tremendous majority of the citizens of our State are tired of the improper influence of the Slavocratic interest. They are not willing any longer to be tyrannized by a few thousand slaveholders," declared the Anzeiger in 1854.[109] The

---

[107] W. F. Switzler's Scrapbook, 1856-57, p. 31. Switzler himself submitted these resolutions. "The American party has therefore nowhere spoken its views on the subject of Emancipation," he said at a joint session of the legislature on January 25, 1857 (Missouri Statesman, April 10, 1857).

[108] On January 14, 1857, Akers of Missouri complained in Congress that the board of aldermen of St. Louis, "consisting in part" of Germans, had voted to repeal the Sabbath laws (Congressional Globe, 34th Cong., 3d Sess., app., p. 151). But practical politics demanded that the slaveholder be not too squeamish when votes were needed from the contemptible "Dutch." In his message of December 29, 1858, Governor Stewart endeavored to wean the Teuton away from the new Republican party by honeyed words. Slavery, and in fact all labor systems, he said, were the result of climatic conditions and of experience. The governor declared that he had no apprehension from foreigners. He hinted that the North was endeavoring to make labor a slave to capital as had been done in England (Senate Journal, 20th Ass., 1st Sess., pp. 33-36).

[109] Anzeiger, July 21, 1854, quoted by the Republican of July 24, 1854. "We must oppose the extension of slavery over the Territories," continued the editor. "Slavery is a perfect pestilence to the State of Missouri. No one denies it, but . . . the establishment of slave States on our western borders will make the abolition of

Germans do not seem to have advocated an unqualified abolition program. "We are for the abolition of slavery in Missouri, but only constitutionally and in a manner to pay due respect to the just claims of the citizens of the State," explained the Anzeiger.[110] "On the subject of slavery, being an institution recognized by the laws of the country," stated the Volksblatt in 1856, "although we would favor a plan for gradual emancipation, we are against any forcible and unconstitutional interference for its abolition. And, therefore we are decidedly opposed to the Abolition party."[111]

The Germans even held slaves in some cases. In 1860 nineteen Germans of St. Louis paid taxes on forty out of the thirteen hundred and eighty-three slaves taxed in the city. Of these German slavemasters O. C. Schauenburg led with six negroes, C. W. Gauss was second with five, and George Heise and J. R. Lienberger were taxed on three each.[112] When the South seceded, the Germans, with hardly an exception, supported the Union. Of the 10,730 Federal

slavery in our own State still more difficult, if not entirely impossible. We are for the abolition of slavery in Missouri, but only constitutionally . . . we demand of the Northern States that they constitutionally fight the South for every foot of land that has not yet been conquered for slavery!"

[110] Anzeiger, July 21, 1854, quoted by the Republican of July 24, 1854.

[111] Volksblatt of unknown date quoted by the Weekly Pilot of April 26, 1856.

[112] These Germans and the number of slaves on which they paid taxes in 1860 were as follows: Richard K. Bechtel, 1 slave (MS. Tax Book, St. Louis City, 1860, Book A to B, p. 81); Edward Benkendorp, 1 slave (ibid., p. 87); C. B. Fallenstein, 1 slave (ibid., Bk. C to F, p. 207); George Heise, 4 slaves (ibid., Bk. G to K, p. 122); C. W. Gauss, 5 slaves (ibid., p. 18); Jacob Iseler, 2 slaves (ibid., p. 149); Charles Hoeser, 2 slaves (ibid., p. 248); John Knipperberg, 1 slave (ibid., p. 238); J. R. Lienberger, 4 slaves (ibid., Bk. L to O, p. 41); Louis I. Mantz, 1 slave (ibid., p. 42); Samuel Myerson, 2 slaves (ibid., p. 197); Robert Ober, 2 slaves (ibid., p. 218); George Schaffner, 2 slaves (ibid., Bk. P to S, p. 139); O. C. Schauenburg, 6 slaves (ibid., p. 141); N. J. Strautman, 2 slaves (ibid., p. 253); R. C. Weinck, 1 slave (ibid., Bk. T to Z, p. 84); Thomas H. Weit, 1 slave (ibid., p. 122); Z. F. Wetzel, 1 slave (ibid., p. 125), and A. Weisman, 1 slave (ibid., p. 137). Naturally it is difficult to distinguish between German immigrants and Pennsylvania German settlers. But if the latter held slaves it would also be a matter of interest.

volunteers raised in St. Louis in 1861 four fifths, according to the state adjutant general's report of that year, were Germans.[113] One German writer boasts that his countrymen who did not support the Union could be counted on his fingers.[114]

Throughout the slavery period the subject of emancipation was unceasingly preached by an ever active minority, while, on the other hand, a mighty effort was made to keep the agitation out of politics. "Our own representative, the Hon. Willard P. Hall, is a slave holder both in theory & practice," wrote Adam Klippel of St. Joseph to Salmon P. Chase in 1849, "and although his constituents, by a large majority, are non-slaveholding, yet he never dares to speak a word in favor of freedom."[115] "We do not apprehend much trouble from the slavery question," said a St. Louis editor the same year, "for . . . the great majority of our citizens look upon the subject as we do: that it is more dangerous for the politicians than for the people at large."[116] On the other hand, the St. Louis newspaper, the Organ, in this same year claimed that there was a widespread desire for emancipation in the State and that "not a single paper in Missouri, out of St. Louis, condemns or disapproves the agitation of the question."[117] From the evidence touched upon in foregoing pages it is clear that this editor did not know the rural press of the State. The conservative old paper, the Republican, ever counseled caution and deprecated agitation.

---

[113] Adjutant General's Report, 1861, p. 6.
[114] W. Kaufman, Die Deutschen im amerikanischen Burgerkriege, p. 194. Another German says that of the 85,400 Federal volunteers raised in Missouri the Germans furnished 30,899 (A. B. Faust, The German Element in the United States, vol. i, p. 523). E. D. Kargau states that the first four Union regiments of the State were composed entirely of Germans ("Missouri's German Immigration," in Missouri Historical Society Collections, vol. ii, no. 1, p. 33). On this point see also J. F. Hume, The Abolitionists, p. 182, and W. G. Bek, The German Settlement Society of Philadelphia, and Its Colony, Hermann, Missouri, pp. 124-126.
[115] Chase Correspondence, p. 473.
[116] Daily Union, February 17, 1849.
[117] Quoted from an issue of the Organ of unknown date by Niles' Register, vol. lxxvi, p. 259.

In spite of all caution, the activity of the great anti-slavery leaders, Frank Blair, B. Gratz Brown, Boernstein, and George R. Smith, continually brought the disagreeable spectre before the people. Evidently Gratz Brown's electorate in St. Louis favored his views. " I sent you a few days since a copy of my remarks upon the Emancipation resolutions," he wrote George R. Smith in 1857. " It was a startling speech to the House in some respects, and took the opposition members by surprise. In St. Louis I hear it raised quite a furor. . . . It was framed principally as you will see from reading it to suit my own meridian, but I am sanguine enough to hope that it will not be without good effect even in other counties of Missouri."[118]

The extent of emancipation sentiment during the last years of the slavery regime in Missouri cannot be measured either in its volume or in its intensity. The opinion is often advanced that the State was ready for emancipation at any time between 1804 and 1860, but that the attitude of the antislavery faction caused justifiable resentment on the part of the slaveholders. " Let it be understood," said a pro-slavery contemporary many years later, " that Missourians did not so much oppose the emancipation of their slaves as they did the means used to accomplish it. For thousands of slave holders believed that the abolition of slavery would be a blessing both to the slave and to the master, if it could be done in a lawful and peaceable way. . . . For ten years before the war it was a foregone conclusion with intelligent classes that slavery would be abolished in Missouri, and a system of free labor adopted that would be more successful in developing the resources of the State."[119] It is doubtful if this writer would have made the above statement in slavery days. Such musings were common after slavery was dead and the success of free labor realized in Missouri. The mass of slave-owners were well satisfied with their property, and bitterly resented any hint that emancipation

---

[118] MS. Brown to Smith, dated Jefferson City, March 3, 1857, Smith Papers.
[119] Leftwich, vol. i, pp. 96–97.

was either advisable or possible, especially if the negroes were to remain in the State after being liberated.

The proslavery leaders at the time denied that slavery was a burden either economically or socially. The Address of the Lexington Pro-Slavery Convention to the People of the United States, drawn up by Sterling Price, Judge W. B. Napton, and others, mentioned the fact that the idea was prevalent " that Missouri contained but a small slave population, and that the permanence of this institution here was threatened by the existence of at least a respectable minority of her citizens . . . we think it proper to state, that the idea above alluded to is unfounded; and that no respectable party can be found in this State, outside of St. Louis, prepared to embark in any such schemes. In that city . . . it will not seem surprising that its wild and heterogeneous population should furnish a foothold for the wildest and most visionary projects."[120]

One of the great slavery advocates of the State in the late fifties was Senator Green. In the United States Senate on May 18, 1858, he said: " It has been my privilege to live there [in Missouri] nearly twenty years, to mix freely with the people of all classes. . . . I know it [sentiment in Missouri] to be exactly the reverse of what he [Senator King] represents it. . . . The public common sentiment of the people of the State is for peace, for law, . . . and to abide by our institutions as they are, . . . I undertake to say that the sentiment to which the Senator alludes in the State of Missouri is exceptionally small."[121] " Emancipation! a new word in our political discussions; a new theme in this State for the contemplation of the people," exclaimed W. F. Switzler in a joint session of the legislature in 1857.[122] The following year Switzler repeated his statement, and claimed that not fifteen thousand voters could be found in the State who favored emancipation.[128]

---

[120] Proceedings of the Convention, p. 4.
[121] Congressional Globe, 35th Cong., 1st Sess., part 3, p. 2207.
[122] Speech of January 25 (Missouri Statesman, April 10, 1857).
[128] Ibid., July 30, 1858.

Although the active emancipation party in Missouri in the late fifties was comparatively small, it was menacing. The General Assembly felt called upon to denounce the movement. On February 10, 1857, Carr introduced the following resolution in the Senate: "Be it therefore Resolved, That the emancipation of all the slaves held as property in this State, would not only be unpracticable, but any movement having such an end in view, would be inexpedient, impolitic, unwise, and unjust, and should, in the opinion of the General Assembly be discountenanced by the people of the State." This declaration passed the Senate by a vote of 25 to 4, seven members being absent or not voting.[124] It passed the House by a majority of 107 to 12, thirteen members being absent or not voting.[125]

A general spirit of intolerance toward agitators was manifested during the last decade of the slavery regime in Missouri. The State University was in a condition of unrest for years. President James Shannon, who had served as a minister of the Christian Church and as president of a denominational college in Kentucky, was accused of preaching sectarianism and proslavery politics in the classroom. On December 22, 1852, a committee was appointed by the Senate, and on January 25, 1853, one was named by the House, to examine the university.[126] A report was made on February 24, signed by five of the faculty and many students, declaring that the charges were false.[127]

Early in 1856 a student of Bethany College named Barns lectured on "Liberty." A reporter stated that Barns was offensive to the proslavery people, and fled after receiving threatening letters. The reporter, however, declared that

---

[124] Senate Journal, 19th Ass., 1st Sess., pp. 213–214.
[125] House Journal, 19th Ass., 1st Sess., p. 303. The resolutions passed the House February 13.
[126] Senate Journal, 17th Ass., 1st Sess., p. 107; House Journal, 17th Ass., 1st Sess., p. 381.
[127] House Journal, 17th Ass., 1st Sess., app., pp. 349–365. There was also a minority report. One student declared that President Shannon disagreed with a text-book which condemned slavery and referred the students to his own Philosophy of Slavery. This student, however, admitted that the president was fair-minded and argued as he did purely for the sake of argument (ibid., p. 364).

Barns was not badly used, but craved martyrdom.[128] One Ross, a temperance lecturer, in 1855 created "quite a row" in Howard, Boone, and Cooper Counties by his antislavery utterances, but there was no proof that he was an abolitionist. His relatives were told to watch him lest he get into trouble.[129] In April, 1855, at Chillicothe, a Christian minister, the Reverend David White, was ordered to leave the county as his sermons were "strongly tinctured with Abolition sentiments." A vigilance committee was appointed to carry out the decrees of the protesting citizens.[130]

Even some of the most ardent emancipationists of the Civil War period, the "Charcoalers" of 1863, were far from being abolitionists at this time. General George R. Smith, who with Charles D. Drake led the unconditional emancipationists later, resented bitterly being styled an abolitionist in 1856. "I have never either published or charged you privately with being an abolitionist," indignantly wrote Silas H. Woodson to Smith on July 1, 1856; "I am mortified and astonished that you should become so evidently disaffected toward me on the strength of rumor."[131]

One fact which should always be kept in mind is that secession and slavery bore no close relation to one another in Missouri. Out of a total poll of 166,518 in 1860, Breckinridge received but 31,317 votes, while Lincoln received but 17,028.[132] A year later, however, the Camp Jackson affair considerably changed sentiment in favor of the South. It is very unsafe to gauge sentiment by count of votes, especially at a presidential election, yet to realize the conservative nature of the Missourians when it came to a clear division one has but to glance at the combined vote of the radicals, Breckinridge and Lincoln, in comparison with the 117,173 votes received by Douglas and Bell, or to turn back to 1857

---

[128] St. Joseph Commercial Cycle, February 22, 1856.
[129] Ibid., November 2, 1855. In July, 1851, Mr. Wyman of St. Louis was widely praised for refusing to rent his hall to an abolition lecturer (Daily Intelligencer [St. Louis], July 7, 1851).
[130] Missouri Statesman, April 27, 1855. The public meeting referred to was held on April 8.
[131] MS. dated Independence, Smith Papers.
[132] Switzler, p. 297.

when Stewart defeated Rollins by only 334 votes for governor in a State which was considered strongly Democratic.[133] The slaveholding Missourian of the fifties valued his property, and he longed for peace. If national issues—the tariff, the currency, internal improvements—were temporarily submerged, the slaveholder turned to a candidate who would secure the integrity of existing conditions. Slavery may have been the ultimate but it certainly was not the immediate cause of the Civil War as far as Missouri was concerned.

---

[133] Switzler, p. 271. It is not within the scope of this study to deal with party politics, as the slavery issue was a small factor in influencing struggles between Whig and Democrat. James S. Rollins had been a staunch Whig. His son, Mr. Curtis B. Rollins, gave the present writer a description of his father. He worshipped the doctrines of the Whig party. His friends claim, and some Democrats have admitted, that Rollins was really elected in 1857, although he was defeated by nearly fifteen thousand votes in 1848 (ibid., p. 255). Despite the wild excitement of the Kansas troubles, Rollins's efforts to calm the storm may have driven many proslavery voters to him for security. "Rollins is sweeping everything before him in this part of the State," gleefully wrote Silas Woodson to George R. Smith from Independence in July, 1857. "His position, and past personal history upon the slavery issue, though highly conservative was altogether acceptable to the most of the ultra pro-slavery men of our party [Whig], and I believe he will not lose five old time Whigs in our County" (MS. dated July 26, Smith Papers). Mr. George Carson of Fayette says that Rollins was the most polished orator he ever heard. He was not only eloquent but was brilliant. Mr. Carson remembers hearing Benton when he delivered his famous speech at Central College, Fayette, in 1849. He declared that Benton spoke very slowly and deliberately. He was not eloquent, but was a convincing speaker.

CHAPTER VI

MISSOURI AND KANSAS

To understand the great movements which excited Missouri and agitated the entire country on more than one occasion—the Compromise of 1820, the Kansas-Nebraska Act and the resulting struggle in Kansas, and the Dred Scott Case—one must get a picture of the State which gave them birth. The exposed position of Missouri—"a slave-holding peninsula jutting up into a sea of free-soil"—was primarily the cause of her continued unrest. This peninsula, unnaturally formed for political reasons to reconcile irreconcilable sections, was exposed still more by the two great rivers. The Missouri, coming out of free territory, flowed past free Kansas for a hundred miles and then swerved off through the heart of Missouri's great slave counties. The Mississippi for hundreds of miles alone separated Missouri from an ever-watchful abolitionist minority in Illinois. The great interstate shipping along the Mississippi offered a chance of freedom to any plucky black who might be hired as a boat hand or stowed away by a sympathetic or a venal crew till a free port was reached. The Underground Railroad was busy on three borders of the State. The spectre of a "horde of negro-stealing Abolitionists" permanently settled in Kansas with the avowed purpose of strangling the "peculiar institution" was both irritating and economically appalling to the hardheaded, self-made frontiersman, who resented any interference with his God-given institution. Slave-stealing was abhorrent to his idea of fair play and sacrilegious in the light of his interpretation of the Constitution. Despite present-day claims to the contrary, the newspapers, the journals of the General Assembly, and contemporary correspondence prove that Missouri was from its very inception in a state of unrest and feverish apprehension which subsequent events seem to have justified.

Throughout the slavery period most of the Missouri law dealing with the absconding black was concerned with the recovery of the fugitive. The Code of 1804 fined any person five dollars and costs for harboring a runaway negro.[1] In 1817 a form of procedure for seizing a fugitive was passed. He was to be taken first before a justice of the peace. The sheriff was then to serve notice on the owner. If the latter refused to pay the summons fee, the justice might "issue execution as in ordinary cases." For the benefit of non-resident owners the names of escaped slaves were to be published for ninety days in a territorial paper. The master was to pay costs before receiving his property. If the slave was not claimed within ninety days, he was to be sold to the highest bidder for "ready money." After deducting the jail fees and five dollars for apprehending the negro, the residue was to be deposited in the treasury to satisfy the future claims of the master.[2] The punishment of the slave for absconding seems to have been left entirely to the owner.

A law of 1823 gave any person the right to apprehend a slave and place him in the "common gaol" of the county,[3] unless the owner or employer of the fugitive resided in the county, in which case the negro could be directly delivered to the claimant. Any slave found twenty miles from home without a pass was to be deemed a fugitive. On suspicion of an escaped slave lurking about the county a justice was to direct the sheriff or the constable to lodge him in prison. The negro, after being advertised for twelve months, was to be sold, and if the claimant did not appear within five years

---

[1] Territorial Laws, vol. i, ch. 3, sec. 9.

[2] Ibid., ch. 187, secs. 1, 2.

[3] On January 23, 1865, a committee was appointed by the House to investigate the rumor that the state penitentiary was being used for the safekeeping of slaves (House Journal, 22d Ass., 1st Sess., p. 143). On February 28, 1848, Mrs. Francis A. Sublette paid jail fees to the amount of $6.75 for the keeping of her negro named London for twenty-four days, at the rate of twenty-five cents per day, and a fee of seventy-five cents for the turnkey (MS. Sublette Papers).

the money was to go to the State University. The master
must prove his property by witnesses, and, in addition to any
reward which may have been offered, must pay the apprehending fee of ten cents a mile for the distance traversed in
returning the slave. If after seizing a negro the justice was
satisfied that he was not a fugitive, he could be discharged
by habeas corpus proceedings. In cases where a negro died
in jail or was discharged from custody the State was to pay
these fees.[4] The provisions of the Revised Code of 1835
were very similar to the above, but were more precise as to
the method of claiming the slave.[5] This law, with some
modifications, remained as the working statute till slavery
disappeared in the State. It was reenacted in 1845, again
ten years later, and finally again in 1861, at a time when the
escapes of slaves were increasingly numerous.[6]

---

[4] Revised Laws, 1825, vol. ii, p. 747, secs. 1-10.

[5] Revised Laws, 1835, p. 589, art. iv, sec. 12. The claimant was to
prove that he had lost a slave and that the negro in question was the
same, and he had to give bond to indemnify the sheriff for his
services, and give a certificate of proof and security under seal of
court. Examples of the sheriffs' notices of the sale of fugitives are
numerous in the newspapers of the period. The following is an
illustration: "NOTICE OF A RUNAWAY SLAVE. There was
committed to the common jail of St. Louis County . . . as a runaway slave, a negro who says . . . that he belongs to Milton Cooper
of Ashland in the State of Arkansas. Said negro is about thirty
one years of age. . . . The owner of the above slave is hereby required to make application for him . . . and pay all charges incurred
. . . otherwise I will, on Tuesday, the 25th day of January next . . .
at the north door of the Court House . . . sell the said negro . . .
to the highest bidder for cash, pursuant to the statute in such cases
made and provided. John M. Wiener, Sheriff of St. Louis Co."
(Jefferson Inquirer, November 27, 1852).

[6] Revised Statutes, 1845, ch. 167, art. iii; Revised Statutes, 1855,
ch. 150, art. iii; Session Laws, 1860, p. 90. A law of 1835 gave the
method by which an out-of-state slaveholder could recover his property. Such a claimant was to secure a warrant from some "justice
or justice of the peace" requiring the sheriff to present the fugitive
to some court or magistrate. "The proof to entitle any person to
such warrants shall be by affidavit, setting forth, particularly and
minutely, the ground of such claim." After the court had heard the
testimony he could return the negro to jail if further testimony was
thought necessary. If the negro in question was not a fugitive, the
one causing his arrest was to pay him $100 and pay all costs (Revised
Laws, 1835, p. 286). A law of 1845 granted the sheriff a fee of $100
for taking a fugitive without the State if he was over twenty years
of age, if under twenty half that amount, in addition to the reward.

Toward slave-stealing the law was very severe, whether the deed was perpetrated through sentiment or for profit. In the Code of 1804 either the selling of free negroes into slavery or the stealing of slaves was punished by death without benefit of clergy.[7] In 1843 it was declared grand larceny to " decoy or carry any slave " from the State, whether done as a theft or to free the negro. The offender was to suffer five years' imprisonment, whether the attempt succeeded or failed.[8] This statute was reenacted in 1845 and again in 1861.[9] That this provision was enforced is learned from the inspectors of the penitentiary, who in 1854 reported that there were seven inmates in that institution for the " attempt to decoy slaves."[10] In 1858 there were six,[11] and in 1860 ten such prisoners.[12] Seemingly none of these efforts had succeeded, as all are reported as being " attempts," nor is it possible to tell whether the convicts were abolitionists or

---

The fee was to be $25 and the reward if the slave was taken within the State. After a slave had been advertised for three months he was to be sold and the residue kept for the claimant, after the sheriff's claims had been settled (Revised Statutes, 1845, ch. 168, secs. 1–6, reenacted in Session Laws, 1860, p. 90). For apprehending a slave within his own county the sheriff was to receive $5, or $10 if in an adjoining county over twenty miles from the home of the fugitive (Revised Statutes, 1845, ch. 169, sec. 1). The question of the legal recipient of the reward must have been a subject of some dispute. In Daugherty v. Tracy the state supreme court held that " a person who actually apprehends the slave, makes the affidavit and has the slave committed to jail, is to be deemed the taker of the slave." If a private person called in an officer to take up a slave, the latter was entitled to the reward if he committed the slave (11 Mo., 62).

[7] Territorial Laws, vol. i, ch. 3, secs. 21, 22. A law of 1825 reduced the punishment for enslaving a free person or for decoying such out of the State to a maximum of thirty lashes and imprisonment for ten years, unless the kidnapped negro was meanwhile returned, in which case the punishment was to be a fine of one thousand dollars and costs (Revised Laws, 1825, vol. i, p. 283, sec. 13).

[8] Session Laws, 1842, p. 133, secs. 1, 2, 3.

[9] Revised Statutes, 1845, ch. 168, sec. 7. The same punishment was given a white or a free negro for forging a pass so that a slave could escape (ibid., secs. 7, 9).

[10] Senate Journal, 17th Ass., 1st Sess., app., p. 223.

[11] Senate Journal, 20th Ass., 1st Sess., app., p. 138.

[12] House Journal, 21st Ass., 1st Sess., app., p. 314. In 1846 there was one such prisoner (House Journal, 14th Ass., 1st Sess., app., p. 54). In 1856 there were two such inmates (Senate Journal, 18th Ass., 1st Sess., p. 284).

mere thieves. Two very famous cases of slave abduction
were that of Burr, Work, and Thompson in Marion County
in 1841,[13] and that of "old" John Doy of Kansas at St.
Joseph and Platte City in the late fifties.[14]

Missouri's great rivers had early caused both legislation
and litigation. The Code of 1804 forbade the master of a
vessel to carry a slave from the "district" of Louisiana
without permission.[15] The Codes of 1825, 1835, 1845, and
1855, which were based on a law of 1822, fined a ferryman
the full value of the slave and costs for taking him across the
Mississippi without a special permit, and a shipmaster for
the same offense was fined one hundred and fifty dollars, to
be recovered by the owner by action for debt. He might be
further subject to common-law action.[16] A statute of 1841
made any "master, commander or owner of any boat or
other vessel" liable for the value of the slave "without
prejudice to the right of such owner to his action at common
law," for carrying any slave from one point to another
within the State without permission.[17]

This statute was the result of a feeling that abolitionists
and free blacks were using the shipping as a means of systematically running off Missouri slaves. A contemporary
editorial illustrates the dangers and fears of the time and

[13] Thompson, passim. In August, 1841, these three Illinois abolitionists came over from Quincy to take certain slaves to Canada.
The slaves betrayed them, and they were sent to the penitentiary
after an exciting trial. The term was to be twelve years, but was
later reduced. An account of this episode can also be found in the
Bulletin (St. Louis), September 13, 1841. See also pp. 121-122, above.

[14] Doy, passim. Doy was caught in Kansas by a crowd of Missourians in an attempt to take to Canada some negroes of Lawrence,
who feared kidnapping. The Missourians claimed that these were
fugitives and not free blacks. Doy was imprisoned for several
months, but was finally taken from the St. Joseph jail by a band of
antislavery Kansans. His account, like Thompson's, is bitter, but
gives a good idea of the struggles of the period.

[15] Territorial Laws, vol. i, ch. 3, secs. 35, 36.

[16] Revised Laws, 1825, vol. ii, p. 747; Revised Laws, 1835, p. 581,
art. i, sec. 36; renewed in Revised Statutes, 1845, ch. 167, art. i, sec.
28; also in Revised Statutes, 1855, ch. 150, art. i, secs. 28, 29.

[17] Session Laws, 1840, p. 146. A law of 1823 had fined a ferryman
the value of the slave, in addition to the damages and costs, for carrying him over the Mississippi (Revised Laws, 1825, vol. ii, p. 747,
sec. 2).

12

the price which St. Louis paid for her great and boasted
river commerce. "Recent events demonstrate the fact that
the employment of free negroes, mulattoes, and free slaves
who hire their own time, on board of steamboats on the
western waters, is a cause of serious loss and danger to the
slave states and slave owners. . . . These have the opportunity of constant communication with slaves of Missouri,
Kentucky and the other southern States, and have also very
frequent communication with the free negroes and abolitionists of Illinois, Indiana, Ohio, and Pennsylvania. This communication renders the slaves restless and induces them to
run away, and furnishes them a means of escape. . . . The
negro hands on board the steamboats can frequently conceal
runaway negroes . . . without the consent of the captain . . .
their association with the slaves is not a cause of suspicion
and discovery, as a similar association between white emissaries and slaves would certainly be."[18]

The coming of the railroad furnished a new means of
escape for slaves. Captain J. A. Wilson of Lexington claims
that the people of western Missouri were apprehensive lest
the Pacific Railroad, for which Benton and his constituents
had fought for years, should run their slaves to Kansas.
The old boat law with some changes was applied to railways
in 1855. The offenders were liable for double the value of
the escaped slave and for common-law action as well.[19] A
number of negroes evidently escaped by rail. In 1857 the
people of Franklin County complained of their slaves escaping by this means.[20] The trouble must have continued, for
on March 1, 1860, a resolution was introduced into the
House of Representatives that the General Assembly should
"vote for no bill knowingly granting state aid to railroads
whose Board of Directors is composed of a majority of
Black Republicans." The resolution was tabled by a vote
of 82 to 17, and may simply have been a general thrust at

18 Daily Evening Gazette, August 18, 1841.
19 Session Laws, 1854, p. 169. Repealed February 6, 1864 (Session
Laws, 1863, p. 41).
20 House Journal, 18th Ass., 1st Sess., p. 233 (February 7).

antislavery activity.[21] Apparently fewer slaves used the
railroads as a means of escape than the river shipping, as the
newspapers of the day do not contain many notices of such
absconding, while the press and court records note many
escapes by boat.

Assemblies of slaves, both public and private, were more
or less carefully regulated. The Code of 1804 brought pressure to bear on both the slave and the master. If the slave
left his master's "tenements" without leave, he could be
punished with stripes at the discretion of a justice of the
peace. If he entered another's plantation, that planter could
give him ten stripes. If a free colored person or a slave
carried a gun, powder, shot, or a club, the justice could punish him with a maximum of thirty stripes, but if living on
the frontier the latter could give him permission to carry
such weapons. All "riots, routs, unlawful assemblies and
seditious speeches" were to be punished at the discretion of
the justice.[22] For allowing more than five slaves to gather on
his plantation at one time a fine of one dollar per slave was
to be levied against the offending planter, and for permitting
a slave, without the owner's permission, to remain on his
plantation for more than four hours he was to be fined three
dollars.[23] This did not prevent slaves from assembling at a
public mill "with leave" except at night or on Sunday.
They could also go to church by written consent.[24] Passes,

---

[21] House Journal, 20th Ass., Called Sess., p. 31. Absent and not
voting, 32.

[22] Territorial Laws, vol. i, ch. 3, sec. 7. This provision is found
word for word in a Virginia statute of 1785 (Hening, vol. xii, p.
182, sec. 4).

[23] An ordinance of St. Louis of February 5, 1811, punished a slave
with ten lashes for attending such an assembly, and the master
was to be fined five dollars if the slave was not punished. A free
negro or white person was to receive twenty lashes and a fine of
ten dollars for attending without the owner's permission (Ordinance
of February 5, 1811, MS. Record Book of the Trustees of St. Louis,
pp. 23–25, secs. 4, 5, 6).

[24] Territorial Laws, vol. i, ch. 3, secs. 3, 4, 5, 7, 8. These sections
are very similar to an old Virginia statute of 1723 which provided
a penalty of five shillings per slave if a master allowed more than
five slaves, other than his own, to meet on his property. Slaves
could meet at church or a public mill. If living on the frontier
slaves could carry weapons, if so licensed by a justice of the peace
(Hening, vol. iv, p. 126, secs. 8, 9, 14).

however, were somewhat liberally granted, and were not always necessary.[25] The revisions of 1835, 1845, and 1855 accepted these provisions of 1804 in most cases verbatim, and in addition fined any white person ten dollars and any free negro ten dollars and ten lashes for joining in any slave meeting. The sheriffs, constables, justices, and other officials were to suppress these assemblies and to bring offenders to justice under penalty for neglect of duty.[26]

Manifestly intended to prevent loafing and intemperance as well as the usual dangers connected with slave assemblages, a law was passed in 1833 fining a store- or tavern-keeper from five to fifty dollars for allowing slaves or free negroes to assemble at any time on his premises, especially on Sundays, unless sent on business by their owners.[27] In 1847 every religious assembly of negroes or mulattoes was required, if the preacher was a negro, to have some official present " in order to prevent all seditious speeches and disorderly and unlawful conduct of every kind."[28] In September, 1854, two slaves were convicted in Platte County, fined one dollar each and costs, and ordered committed till this was paid, for " preaching the gospel to their fellows, with no officer present, on Atchison Hill."[29] It is probable that abolition emissaries and a temptation to abscond were feared more than conspiracies to revolt. Unless watched, the

---

[25] General George R. Smith of Sedalia wrote: " It is melancholy to remember . . . that Uncle Toby, Uncle Jack, and other gray-haired men and women . . . were compelled to have written permissions to leave home and would come even to me, a little child, when the older members of the family were busy, to give them a written pass to go to town" (Harding, p. 49). Anice Washington of St. Louis, who was a slave in Madison and St. Francis Counties, said that a pass was demanded by her owners only when the negroes went to a dance. They could go to the church, which was two miles off, on Sundays without one.
[26] Revised Laws, 1835, p. 581, art. i, secs. 26–33. Section 32 is not in the Revision of 1845 (vol. ii, ch. 167, art. i), otherwise it is identical. The revision of 1855 (vol. ii, ch. 110, art. i) is the same as that of 1845.
[27] Session Laws, 1832, ch. 41, secs. 1, 2.
[28] Session Laws, 1846, p. 103, secs. 2, 3.
[29] Paxton, p. 187.

preacher, particularly if a negro, might give his audience views of liberty and worldly ambition.[30]

The punishment of the slave for leaving his owner's plantation and for actually running away seems to have been left largely with the master. The slave was to be punished "with stripes" for leaving his master's "tenements" without a pass, and the one on whose property he was found was to give him ten lashes.[31] The Revision of 1835 increased this summary punishment to twenty lashes, and any person who found a slave off his master's property could take such slave before a justice, who was to punish him at his discretion. Any slave who concealed a fugitive was to be punished with not more than thirty-nine stripes by a justice of the peace.[32] The law of 1825 establishing patrols ordered these officers to punish any slave found off his master's plantation by ten lashes, or by not more than thirty-nine after conviction by a justice.[33] The revised statutes of ten years later reduced this punishment by the justice to twenty stripes, and this number remained till slavery was abolished.[34]

The city of St. Louis had its special slave problems because of its numerous free negroes and dissolute whites, natural to a great port with a large alien population. Its enormous shipping interests likewise affected slave conditions. An ordinance of 1835 punished a slave with from five to fifteen lashes for being at a religious or other meeting without permission later than nine at night from October to March, or ten o'clock the other six months of the year. If the master paid two dollars and the costs, the punishment could be remitted.[35] This provision was modified somewhat by one passed later in the same year which prohibited a slave

---

[30] See above, p. 85, note 11, for an example of a slave sermon.

[31] Territorial Laws, vol. i, ch. 3, secs. 2, 3. This same punishment was accorded by a Virginia statute of 1723 (Hening, vol. iv, p. 126, sec. 13).

[32] Revised Laws, 1835, p. 581, art. i, secs. 23, 24, 25.

[33] Revised Laws, 1825, vol. ii, p. 614.

[34] Revised Laws, 1835, ch. 129, sec. 5.

[35] Ordinance of May 11, 1835, sec. 3 (Ordinances of St. Louis, 1836, p. 125). This ordinance is also printed in the Missouri Argus of June 5, 1835.

from being in the streets of the city from ten p. m. to four
a. m. during the summer months, or from nine p. m. to five
a. m. in winter, " under any pretense whatever unless such
slave have a written pass . . . of that day's date." The
master of a slave was to be fined five dollars for the first,
ten dollars for the second, and twenty dollars for subsequent
offenses, and the slave could be imprisoned till this fine was
paid.[36] This ordinance was reenacted March 16, 1843, with
very little alteration, and remained without change till the
Civil War.[37]

An ordinance of 1850 gave the mayor power to issue general passes to free negroes of good character and to grant
them permission to hold religious or social assemblages after
eleven p. m. The city guard was to watch all assemblies
when so commanded by the mayor. Whites were fined from
twenty to fifty dollars for being present at unlawful meetings. Offending slaves were to be sent to the workhouse on
default of the payment of the fine by their owners. Any
person fraudulently issuing a pass was to be fined from
twenty to one hundred dollars.[38] The enforcement of these
ordinances was not always satisfactory. " A large meeting "
of St. Louis citizens on October 22, 1846, resolved among
other things " That the City Council be requested to pass an
ordinance, prohibiting all assemblages and passing of negroes
after dark."[39]

In 1825 the General Assembly passed an act establishing
patrols. The patrol was to visit the negro quarters and
assemblages with power to arrest any suspicious blacks who
might be wandering about without passes and to inflict not
more than ten lashes. If the patrol took any such negroes
before a justice of the peace, they could be punished with a

[36] Ordinance of December 22, 1835 (Ordinances of St. Louis, 1836,
p. 89, secs. 1, 2).
[37] Ordinances of 1843, p. 522; Ordinances of 1846, p. 229; Ordinances of 1850, pp. 297–299; Revised Ordinances, 1856, pp. 564–566;
Ordinances of 1861, pp. 522–524.
[38] Ordinance of March 29, 1850 (Revised Ordinances, 1853, no.
2377, secs. 2, 3, 4, 6, 7, 8, 9).
[39] Scrapbook of James S. Thomas, vol. i, p. 26.

maximum of thirty-nine stripes.[40]   The county patrols were established in 1837.   The act gave the county court power to appoint township patrols to serve for one year.   The stripes to be given by a justice were reduced to a maximum of twenty.   This law was reenacted in 1845, and again in 1855.[41]   Cities had their own systems of slave regulation. As early as 1811 a patrol was established in St. Louis to arrest stray negroes and prevent fires in slave cabins after dark.[42]   Jefferson City in 1836 passed an ordinance which was very similar to the county patrol act.[43]   The same year a supplementary ordinance was published which compelled all citizens, under a penalty, to aid the patrol if called upon.[44]

The courts seem to have been rigid in interpreting the laws covering slave escapes.   Steamboats as well as ferryboats and other small craft were held to be under the statute.[45]   It was not necessary to prove that the captain of the boat knew that the negro he carried was a slave.[46]   The owner of the steamboat was liable for the value of the negro if the latter was carried off by the carelessness of the captain in permitting the slave to ship.[47]   Later still it was held that the

[40] Revised Laws, 1825, vol. ii, p. 614.

[41] Session Laws, 1836, p. 81; Revised Statutes, 1845, ch. 129; Revised Statutes, 1855, ch. 121. The captain of the patrol could be fined if derelict in his duty. The members of the patrol were to serve a minimum of twelve hours a month, and were not to receive over twenty-five cents an hour. In 1860 a special act was passed providing a patrol to search for firearms in the possession of the slaves of Cooper County (Session Laws, 1859, p. 471). Captain J. A. Wilson of Lexington said that patrol duty was irksome, and as a consequence the better classes often left the duty to a class that was brutal. "Uncle" Peter Clay of Liberty claims that the young slaves took great delight in docking the tails of the horses of the patrol and tripping them at night by means of ropes stretched across the roads.

[42] Ordinance of February 9, 1811 (MS. Record Book of the Trustees of St. Louis, pp. 26-27). Stray slaves on the streets after nine o'clock were to receive ten lashes, and the owner was to be fined five dollars if they were not punished. In 1818 this was increased to fifteen lashes (ibid.).

[43] Ordinance of January 21, 1836 (Jeffersonian Republican, January 23).

[44] Mandatory Ordinance, of June 16, 1836, in Jeffersonian Republican, June 25.

[45] Russell v. Taylor, 4 Mo., 550.

[46] Eaton v. Vaughan, 9 Mo., 743.

[47] Susan Price v. Thornton et al., 10 Mo., 135.

owner was responsible even when the captain did not know that the slave was on board, unless the captain used proper care to guard against such an occurrence—"that degree of care . . . that prudent men would take in conducting their own affairs."[48] The shipowner was held responsible not only for the carelessness of his agent, the captain,[49] but also for that of the boat's clerk if the latter took money for the slave's passage, which fact was considered sufficient proof of trespass.[50]

The strictness with which the courts applied the law is illustrated by a case from the Buchanan circuit court, as reported in a newspaper of 1855: "Dr. Fox's slave—a negro girl—was decoyed on board the Aubrey [at St. Joseph] by the watchman of the boat in the night time without the knowledge or consent of the commander or any of his subordinates. . . . No moral delinquency is attributed to any officer of the Aubrey, except the watchman and he had been very promptly discharged. The girl was found on board between this city and Boonville, and as soon as discovered was immediately secured and afterwards placed in jail at that place, by Mr. Glime (chief clerk) who also from that place sent telegraphic dispatches to Dr. Fox, and the agents of the boat . . . by which means the slave was promptly restored to her owner. . . . This case . . . has been completely and amicably settled; the defendant having paid to the plaintiff the sum of $450, and the plaintiff having given a full release of all claims against the boat."[51] This shows that the risk of escape, undoubtedly increased by the proximity of St. Joseph to the then turbulent Kansas, had affected the courts to such an extent that heavy damages were paid in a case where it was acknowledged that "no moral delinquency" existed, and where the defendants had done everything to right the matter, including the immediate return of the slave.

---

[48] Withers v. Steamboat El Paso, 24 Mo., 204.
[49] Susan Price v. Thornton et al., 10 Mo., 135.
[50] Calvert v. Rider and Allen, 20 Mo., 146.
[51] T. H. Fox v. Steamer F. X. Aubrey (St. Joseph Commercial Cycle, September 7, 1855).

Perhaps Missouri suffered, especially during the fifties, from loss of slave property as did no other border State. The Underground Railroad ran into the State from three sides, and its service appears to have been efficient. "The Underground Railroads," declared Trusten Polk in the United States Senate in 1861, " start mostly from these [the border] states. Hundreds of dollars are lost annually. And no state loses more than my own. Kentucky it is estimated, loses annually as much as $200,000. The other border states no doubt in the same ratio. Missouri much more."[52]   As early as 1847 the legislature memorialized Congress for a better treaty of rendition, " as the citizens of this State are annually subjected to heavy losses of property, by the escape of their slaves, who pass through the State of Illinois, and finally find a secure place of refuge in Canada."[53]   In 1846 a mass-meeting of St. Louis citizens was held in the court house " to devise ways and means to protect their slave property in this city and county."[54]   " When," mourns a Boone County editor in 1853, " will the abominable system of man-stealing, practiced by a portion of our northern people, find their operations checkmated and discountenanced by that professedly Christian and law-abiding people?"[55]

The loss of negroes by escape became unbearable as a result of the filling of Kansas by antislavery settlers, and the subject deserves attention at this point. The question of the real motive or motives behind the settlement of Kansas and the struggle which resulted has been a fruitful subject of debate. Many writers, especially those with antislavery leanings, have maintained that the whole affair from the conception of the repeal of the Missouri Compromise to the

---

[52] Congressional Globe, 36th Cong., 2d Sess., p. 356. In the introductory pages of the Federal census of 1860 there is the unsubstantiated statement that " the greatest increase of escapes appears to have occurred in Mississippi, Missouri, and Virginia" (Population, p. xv).

[53] Session Laws, 1846, p. 360. St. Genevieve County in 1845 petitioned the legislature for relief from the escape of her slaves through Illinois (House Journal, 13th Ass., 1st Sess., p. 332).

[54] James S. Thomas Scrapbook, vol. i, p. 26.

[55] Weekly Missouri Sentinel, April 28, 1853.

admission of Kansas as a State was an organized effort of
the slave States to expand their territory.[56]   Slaveholding
Missourians, however, have always asserted that from the
standpoint of Missouri proslavery people it was purely a
defensive movement to conserve existing slave property and
an existing slave society.   The present writer has come to
the conclusion that as far as Missouri was concerned this
latter argument is in the main correct, no matter what territorial ambitions to spread may have moved the South as a
whole.   While it cannot be denied that many Missourians
had the desire to enlarge the slave power, yet one thing is
certain, that outside of the Missouri counties near or immediately bordering on the Kansas line—Jackson, Platte, Clay,
Ray, Holt, Buchanan, and so on,—sentiment for action was
sluggish, and only fiery stump oratory and a wild plea from
the radical press, both Democratic and Whig, aroused the
populace to activity.   As will be seen in the sequel, very few
permanent settlers ever went from Missouri to Kansas with
their slaves, and this is the chief argument against the contention that Missourians were engaged in a general offensive
movement toward Kansas in order to spread slave territory.

No matter how greatly many Missourians may have
craved the rich prairies of Kansas as a field of exploitation
for their black labor, it appears that their first thought was
to defend what they already possessed.   An observing man
like W. F. Switzler dwells upon this point, but makes no
mention of any idea of expansion.[57]   " When Missourians
have seen her citizens robbed of their property," wrote J.

[56] As an example see J. W. Burgess, The Middle Period, ch. xix.
The Kansans have always taken pride in their instrumentality in
driving slavery from Missouri, or at least in making the system
most precarious there.   But General J. G. Haskell admits that
western Missouri looked upon an antislavery settlement of Kansas
with indifference till the South pushed her to action, the slaveholder regarding an inhabited Kansas as merely a new market for
his crops, which were largely raised by slave labor (pp. 32–37).

[57] " Apprehensive that Kansas would become a free State, many
of our citizens especially on the Kansas border became seriously
alarmed for the safety of their slaves, and in the excitement of
the conflict were induced without authority of law, to cross over
into Kansas with arms and with ballots to coerce the new State
into the Union with a pro-slavery constitution " (p. 282).

Locke Hardeman of Saline County in June, 1855, " and
members insulted and imprisoned for merely appealing to
the laws of the land that proposes to guarantee the rights of
property. . . . What shall Missourians do? . . . If Kansas be
settled by Abolitionists, can Missouri remain a slave State?
If Missouri goes by the board what will become of Kentucky? Maryland? Virginia?"⁵⁸ Senator David R. Atchison
as early as 1853 saw the real danger clearly. " Will you sit
here at home," he said in a speech at Weston, " and permit
the nigger thieves, the cattle, the vermin of the North to
come into Nebraska . . . run off with your negroes and
depreciate the value of your slaves. . . . But we will repeal
the Compromise. I would sooner see the whole of Nebraska
in the bottom of hell than see it a Free State."⁵⁹

⁵⁸ MS. Hardeman to George R. Smith, June 10, 1855, Smith Papers. Judge William C. Price of Springfield claimed the honor of
originating the demand for the repeal of the Missouri Compromise.
" He claimed," says W. E. Connelley, " that he pressed this idea on
the South, saying that Missouri could not remain slave with Iowa
free on the North, Illinois free on the east, and a free state on the
west. In short, Missouri had to accomplish the Repeal or become
a free State. That was what Judge Price preached for twenty
years before the War " (Statement of Price to Mr. Connelley, quoted
by Ray, p. 247). On December 28, 1854, Mothersead of Gentry
County introduced a resolution into the House declaring it to be
the duty of " the State and her citizens to use all means consistent
with the Constitution . . . to prevent if possible that beautiful country [Kansas] from becoming an asylum for abolitionists and free
soilers, to harass and destroy our peace and safety " (House Journal,
18th Ass., 1st Sess., pp. 35-36). In his address at the Lexington
Convention of 1855, President James Shannon of the State University read a series of thirteen resolutions by Dr. Lee, the eighth of
which reads as follows: " Resolved, That the whole state is iden-
tified in interest and sympathy with the citizens on our Western
border, and we will co-operate with them in all proper measures to
prevent the foul demon of Abolition from planting a colony of
negro-thieves on our frontier to harass our citizens and steal their
property " (Proceedings, p. 29). " Already many of our slaves
have been carried off and as self preservation is the first law of nature, it certainly cannot be objected to, if Missourians should adopt
the most summary method to secure themselves against this avalanche of abolitionists on our frontier " (editorial in Richmond
Weekly Mirror, January 26, 1855).
⁵⁹ Quoted by J. N. Holloway, History of Kansas, p. 97. This
quotation in slightly different form is given in the Weston Platte
Argus of December 26, 1856. But the editor claims that Atchison
made no such statement and that the Reverend Frederick Starr lied
in claiming that he stood immediately in front of Atchison and

Undoubtedly Atchison made this passionate plea to arouse feeling, but the very fact that emotion could be aroused by harping on this string makes it appear evident that the fear for property was stronger than the wish to expand slave territory. The first was a less abstract and less distant proposition. The antislavery forces of Missouri realized the whole situation. Kansas as a free State meant eventually a free Missouri. "So soon as Kansas will have constituted herself a free state," confidently boasted the Anzeiger des Westens in 1858, " slavery must fall in Missouri."[60]

It is not the purpose of this study to follow all of the struggles that Missouri experienced in her antebellum days, but simply to attempt to explain the motives of those actions which are related to the slavery issue. Others have sketched the development of the general agitation for the repeal of the Missouri Compromise, and its immediate effect upon Kansas.[61] Here will be considered only the movement within the State, which practically begins on January 2, 1849, when the state Senate passed a resolution declaring that the Missouri Compromise of 1820 was unconstitutional and void, and holding " Squatter Sovereignty" to be an axiom. " Whether the slave, or the free States," said this statement, " are willing to abide by said act, as a compromise, or not, is a matter of perfect indifference to the people of the territories. Their right to self-government is wholly independent of all such compromises."[62] This idea is in harmony with the Napton Resolutions, which were before the legislature at the same time. An anti-Benton wing of the Democratic party consistently hammered away on this theme. Even Atchison was taken unawares, and seems to have lost courage. In his Fayette speech late in 1853 he refused to vote for the organization of the Nebraska Territory till the Com-

heard him deliver the speech. Frank Blair on March 1, 1856, quotes Atchison himself as having made this statement (A Statement of Facts and a Few Suggestions in Review of Political Action, p. 75).
[60] Issue of April 10, quoted by the Republican of April 20, 1858.
[61] Ray, ch. iii; Hodder, Genesis of the Kansas-Nebraska Act, pp. 69–86.
[62] Daily Union, January 6, 1849.

promise of 1820 should be repealed.[63] Benton's plea for the organization of the Kansas country as a necessity for developing his " Central National Highway from the Mississippi to the Pacific " was most warmly advocated by his supporters, the Missouri Democrat and the Jefferson Inquirer.[64] On January 9, 1854, Frank Blair, Gratz Brown, and others declared at a meeting of St. Louis Democrats that they regarded " all who oppose it [the immediate organization of Nebraska Territory] upon whatever pretext, as hostile to the best interest of this State."[65]

Whatever may have been the sincerity of the sparring between Benton and Atchison, it is evident that many Missourians emphatically demanded the opening of Kansas. Was this an economic desire for the spread of hemp culture by Missouri slavemasters, or was it to forestall the possible free-state emigration? Both of these elements entered into the situation. Ray gives a number of contemporary quotations to prove that the desire of Missourians for the rich Kansas hemp lands was the cause of the whole movement.[66] Besides the statements noted by Ray several others could be men-

---

[63] Jefferson Inquirer, December 17, 1853. Ray has well described Atchison's position during this period and also Benton's " Central National Highway " (ch. iii). But Ray insistently keeps before the reader his untenable thesis that Atchison was the real author of the movement and of the Kansas-Nebraska Bill. If Atchison was the father of the bill, his neighbors either did not know it or jealously denied him the honor. The St. Joseph Commercial Cycle, a Whig sheet, on September 28, 1855, sneered at the editor of the Weston Platte Argus for giving Atchison the honor.

[64] No attempt will be made in this study to outline this issue. Benton's nine-column letter on the subject can be found in the St. Louis Inquirer of April 2, 1853. The Missouri Democrat (St. Louis) in its issues of the early winter of 1852–53 had advocated the movement.

[65] Republican, June 21, 1854, as quoted by Atchison in his letter " To the People of Missouri."

[66] Pp. 81–83, 169–171, 250, etc. Ray was visibly impressed by Colonel John A. Parker's statement that the primary object which induced the initiation of the measure to repeal the Missouri Compromise " was to secure the reelection of Mr. Atchison to the Senate. The means to be employed was to repeal the Compromise in order that the people of Missouri might carry their slaves to Kansas and there raise hemp " (" The Secret History of the Kansas-Nebraska Bill," in National Quarterly Review, July, 1880 [no. lxxxi], pp. 105–118).

tioned, but they are so few that it seems evident that the hemp issue was a minor one.[67] The Parkville Industrial Luminary and the St. Joseph Commercial Cycle preached hemp lands and Kansas with a vim, but otherwise there was little advocacy of such a program. These prints apparently were more deeply engaged in rousing the Missourians to settle the Territory than in giving them disinterested advice.

The Kansas-Nebraska Bill, which repealed the Missouri Compromise and opened Kansas to slavery under the "Squatter Sovereignty" policy, was enthusiastically supported by the anti-Benton Democrats and many of the Whigs of the State. All of the Missourians in Congress save

[67] The following appeared in the Weekly Missouri Sentinel of October 6, 1853: "The Industrial Luminary expresses the opinion that many of those who have been waiting for the favorable action of Congress . . . in relation to Nebraska will wait no longer but will go over and make their settlements before 'cold weather sets in.'" The Howard County Banner of October 6, 1853, stated editorially: "Is any one so bigoted and blind enough to suppose that this broad expanse of fertile territory in the very heart of our country; and in the only road from ocean to ocean, left to savages and buffalo, and to remain a desert; one must be very . . . little acquainted with American character and enterprise [to have such an idea]. . . . The people will not await the slow motion of Congress" (quoted by the Missouri Sentinel of October 13). In arousing Missouri to colonize Kansas to save it from the abolitionists the St. Joseph Commercial Cycle pleaded on March 30, 1855, as follows: "What could commerce do without cotton, hemp, indigo, tobacco, rice and naval stores? All these are products of slave labor, and one of the articles, hemp, will be the main staple of Kansas." Frank Blair, fearing that the rich soil of Kansas would invite Missouri slave-owners, endeavored to frighten them by raising the phantom of competition. He said at a joint session of the legislature in January, 1855: "A large proportion of the soil of Kansas is adapted to the cultivation of the staples produced in Missouri, and which can only be cultivated by slave labor. The whole extent of the Kansas river is adapted to the cultivation of hemp. All of Kansas along the Missouri river . . . is likewise well suited to produce hemp and tobacco. . . . It is but natural to suppose, therefore, that many of the people of Missouri will sell out and move to these new, cheap, and fertile lands. . . . It will be no advantage to our State . . . to raise up a rival in the production of a staple in which, from the superior freshness and cheapness of her soil, she will very soon be able to undersell Missouri" (On the Subject of Senatorial Election, pamphlet, pp. 4–5). Immediately after the opening of Kansas to settlement the "Union Emigrant Society" was organized in Washington. Blair was elected vice-president. Eli Thayer's Massachusetts Aid Society seems to have caused more ill-feeling in Missouri, however (Republican, July 3, 1854).

Benton voted for the measure.[68]   The Whigs of Boone
County declared in March, 1854, that they approved "of the
establishment of the Territories of Kansas and Nebraska,
with power in the people who may settle in those Territories
to regulate the subject of slavery within their own limits
according to their own pleasure."[69]   "Resolved that the
Whigs of Marion County are in favor of the immediate
organization of the Nebraska Territory," said another statement, "and that we indorse and are in favor of the bill now
pending."[70]   Similar resolutions were passed by the fourth
Congregational Whig convention meeting at Plattsburg, July
8, 1854.[71] Fifty of the sixty Whigs in the legislature met on
Christmas day, 1854, and unanimously decreed that they
would support only such candidates as acquiesced in the
Kansas-Nebraska Bill.[72]   The party as a whole seems to
have been a unit on this question.

The anti-Benton Democrats were especially hostile toward
the Compromise of 1820. "There is no power given Congress to say that slavery shall exist on one side of a line of
latitude and shall not on the other," read Governor Sterling
Price's message of December 25, 1854, "and hence in my
opinion, that clause of the Missouri act was a nullity."[73]
The press of the period was burdened with Democratic resolutions favoring the repeal. In St. Louis a meeting of second
ward Democrats declared on June 3, 1854, that they "con-
gratulate the country on the cheering fact that the Kansas-
Nebraska Bill is now the law of the land."[74]   Democratic
expressions similar to the above are numerous. On the other
hand, the Benton Democrats—Frank Blair, B. Gratz
Brown, and others—were implacable enemies of the repeal.

[68] On this point see the comments of the Republican of June 22,
1854.
[69] Ibid., March 16, 1854.
[70] Ibid.
[71] Missouri Statesman, July 17, 1854.
[72] Richmond Weekly Mirror, January 5, 1855. The St. Joseph
Commercial Cycle, a Whig organ, on September 28, 1855, complimented Stephen A. Douglas for being the author of the repeal of
that "odious measure," the Missouri Compromise.
[73] House Journal, 18th Ass., 1st Sess., p. 31.
[74] Republican, June 5. 1854.

Benton was most vociferous in condemning the attack on
the Missouri Compromise, which he always considered a
sacred compact. However, in 1855, the year following the
repeal, his supporters claimed that he deserted this position
and betrayed them as a bid for Missouri favor.[75] Whether
this is true or not, it but proves the popularity of the repeal
in the State.

When Kansas was once open to settlement, its future
status as a slave or a free State depending on whether pro-
slavery or antislavery votes were in the majority when the
constitution was adopted, events took place with great rapid-
ity. In the late summer of 1853 colonists had arrived from
Iowa, Minnesota, and Missouri, although lands were not yet
" subject to lawful settlement."[76] Some proslavery people
at first looked upon efforts to make Kansas a free State as
harmless. " Doubtless many more will be sent out to Kansas
by these Societies of the North with a view of making Kansas a free State. . . . But we do not at present believe they
will be able to accomplish it," the St. Joseph Gazette said.[77]
The correspondent of the Republican wrote his sheet from
Leavenworth, Kansas Territory, on December 17, 1854, that
" notwithstanding the Aid Societies have poured in hordes
of her paupers for the purpose of Abolitionizing Kansas,
they either become initiated in our institutions, or leave as
soon as they arrive. Now, if the South does her duty, and
especially Missouri, the Northern hope of Abolitionizing
Kansas, will be a phantom hope."[78]

---

[75] " Benton has I think kicked over the pail of milk he produced
for his friends by his vote to sustain the Missouri Compromise.
He has made another speech acquiescing in the fraud [the repeal
of the Compromise], evidently looking to Missouri prospects. He
loses by it all prospects of the Presidency through the northern vote
but stands better in Missouri" (MS. F. P. Blair, Sr., to Martin
Van Buren, February 9, 1855, A. L. S., dated Silver Spring, Maryland. Van Buren Papers, not bound).

[76] Weekly Missouri Sentinel, September 29, 1853, quoting the
Parkville Luminary of unknown date.

[77] Date of issue not stated, quoted by the Republican of August
24, 1854.

[78] Republican, December 30, 1854. Other proslavery people were
also sanguine. " Kansas must of necessity be a slave state, as the
slavery interest has now in possession nearly all the timber of the
territory" (letter in Missouri Statesman, June 8, 1855).

Missouri was soon called upon by the radical press and by
"Atchison, Stringfellow & Co." to do her "duty." Jackson, Platte, Clinton, and other western counties by resolution
and by organization condemned the settlement of Kansas by
northern immigrants, and advocated proslavery action.[79]
On July 29, 1854, a large meeting was addressed at Weston
by Atchison. B. F. and J. H. Stringfellow, and George
Galloway were present. Here the "Platte County Self Defensive Association" was formed. By resolution it was
determined that the settlers sent out by the Emigrant Aid
Society were to be turned back. The Defensive Association
was to hold public meetings, urge the settlement of Kansas
by proslavery men, and guard the territorial elections against
frauds. The Kansas League, a subsidiary institution composed chiefly of the same persons, was formed to carry out
the decrees of the association. It worked in secret, was
bound by an oath, held meetings in the night, suppressed
antislavery newspapers, and silenced Northern Methodist
ministers.[80] The anti-Atchison forces answered by calling
the Law and Order meeting at Weston on September 1.
Their declaration was signed by one hundred and thirty-three
citizens. They declared their loyalty to the General Government and their opposition to "violence and menace."[81]

The slave interests of the State were now thoroughly
aroused. On December 28, 1854, Mothersead of Gentry

[79] See the Republican of July 13, 1854. On June 6, 1853, Atchison
had harangued at Weston and on June 11 at Platte City (Republican, June 22, 1853). At Parkville on August 8 he also aroused
his hearers as to free-soil invasions of Kansas (ibid., August 31).
[80] Paxton, p. 184. Their badge was a skein of bleached silky
hemp. Over five hundred signed the association agreement. Anti-
slavery merchants and sympathizers were boycotted (The History
of Clay and Platte Counties, p. 635). Under the auspices of the association B. F. Stringfellow wrote a series of essays which attempted
to prove that slavery as found in the United States was a "bless:ng."
From the Federal census reports of 1850 he sought to prove that
there was less blindness, deafness, insanity, and idiocy among slaves
than among whites or free blacks (St. Joseph Commercial Cycle,
February 2, 1855). The whole series was published in this paper in
the issues from February 2 to March 9, 1855. The title is, "Negro
Slavery No Evil or The North and the South."
[81] Paxton, pp. 185–186; History of Clay and Platte Counties, p. 535.

County submitted five resolutions to the House of Representatives which declared that " the law organizing the Territories of Kansas and Nebraska maintains the equality of the States, and the justice of the Constitution, and therefore demands our decided approval," and " That the State of Missouri as a slave State, and from local position, is deeply interested in the character of the Government that is instituted in Kansas Territory, and that it is the duty of the State and her citizens, to use all means, consistent with the Constitution . . . to prevent, if possible, that beautiful country becoming an asylum for abolitionists and free-soilers, to harass and destroy our peace and safety."[82]   Appeals were now made by the proslavery party for emigrants. " You can without exertion send 500 of your young men who will vote in favor of your institution," pleaded Atchison at Platte City on November 6, 1854. " Should each county in the state of Missouri only do its duty the question will be decided quietly and peaceably at the ballot box."[83]   The press now loudly called for volunteer voters for Kansas. " Will Kansas be a free or a slave State?" queried the Liberty Tribune in the autumn of 1854, and continued: " Citizens of Missouri you must ACT . . . you must go to Kansas; nothing else will do . . . you must go to Kansas NOW, for an election is soon to take place for a Delegate to Congress and the Territorial Legislature, and it is all important that the Abolitionists should be defeated in the first election, for by the Territorial law their Legislature can exclude slavery . . . you must nip the thing in the bud."[84]   " The hour for action in Kansas is at hand," was the clarion cry of a St. Joseph Whig editor in March, 1855, " and we call every free voter to the polls! to the polls!! to the polls!!! . . . Let the minion of . . . his Aid Society stand back until he has redeemed the birthright he ignominiously sold, by a service of hard labor in tilling

---

[82] House Journal, 18th Ass., 1st Sess., p. 35, secs. 3, 4. On February 25, 1855, these were referred to the committee on Federal relations (ibid., p. 175). They could not be traced farther.

[83] Quoted by Switzler, p. 492.

[84] Quoted by the Richmond Weekly Mirror of November 7, 1854. Date of Tribune not given.

the soil of Kansas."[85]   The Richmond Weekly Mirror was
comforted by the fact that " Missouri and the entire South
are awake to a sense of their danger," and it bade God-speed
to the departing voters.   It advised the emigrants, however,
to settle in Kansas and thereby become legal voters.[86]   In
Ray County six local meetings were held in February, 1855,
and a call was made for voters to go to Kansas for the
March election.[87]   The practice at local county meetings was
to elect delegates who would go to Kansas to vote.   Yet for
some the movement was too slow.   The young bloods were
dissatisfied with the efforts of their elders.   On March 17 a
body of the State University students assembled under the
lead of Adjunct-Professor B. S. Head.   They criticized the
apathy of the Kansas meeting held the same day in Columbia, and passed the following declaration: " Be it resolved
That we the youth of the South having within our bosoms
a spark left of that patriotic spirit that fired the minds . . . .
of our Revolutionary sires . . . do hereby express our condemnation of the course . . . pursued by those whose age and
mature judgment should have prompted them to set a nobler
example to the rising generation."   They passed a resolution
to send a delegate voter to Kansas.[88]

At the time the Missourians made no denial of voting in
Kansas and leaving that territory immediately afterward.
They claimed that they were simply counteracting the deceit-
ful and illegal action of the Emigrant Aid Society.   In May
the St. Joseph Commercial Cycle resented Governor Reeder's
statement that the Missourians had carried the Kansas elec-

---

85 St. Joseph Commercial Cycle, March 30, 1855.
86 Issue of March 24, 1855.
87 Richmond Weekly Mirror, February 16, 1855.   An idea of the
intense feeling engendered at this time can be gained from the following editorial: " On yesterday a train of about forty abolition
vagabonds and negro stealers passed through our town enrout for
Kansas Territory.   May the devil get them before they arrive at
their journey's end.   We understand they came off the steamer
Golden State, now lying at Brunswick" (ibid., March 3).   The
Mirror was a Whig organ.
88 Missouri Statesman, March 30, 1855.   One Boone County citizen
was so disgusted with the impudence of the students that he wrote
a stinging letter in which he berated Professor Head and his
" gosling " students (ibid.).

tion by " fraud, violence, and corruption." " We hurl back upon the head of this debased wretch, the vile slander which none but he . . . would proclaim to the world." That any fraud or violence was committed was flatly denied. " The people of Missouri were present at many of the precincts . . . to see that quiet and order might prevail."[89] The Liberty Tribune declared that Missourians voted in Kansas, " but only those who considered Kansas their home, and who were staying temporarily in Missouri, in order to shelter their families."[90] Colonel D. C. Allen of Liberty stated that the Missourians went to Kansas feeling that they were justified, as the South considered that the North had broken a tacit agreement in engulfing Kansas after being given Nebraska. " There can be no doubt of there being secret organizations to secure votes in Kansas," he said. A Lexington editor in May, 1855, declared that the able-bodied males of that place had all gone to Kansas with a sense of deep sacrifice to the cause of the South.[91]

Endeavors were also made to colonize Kansas with slave-holders as the only permanent means of securing victory. The St. Joseph Commercial Cycle on October 12, 1855, agitated " a tax of one or two per cent, on all . . . real and personal property for the purpose of colonizing one thousand proslavery men in Kansas."[92] Silas Woodson and others issued a call for a meeting to consider an organization for

---

[89] Issue of May 25, 1855. As a Whig sheet the Cycle was in a peculiar position. It condemned Kansas abolitionists on the one hand and, on the other, their arch enemy Atchison as being a " Demagogue" and a " disunionist" (issue of July 13, 1855). It will be remembered that the Cycle was proslavery Whig and Atchison a proslavery Democrat.

[90] Quoted by the Republican of April 26, 1855, from the Tribune of unknown date.

[91] Republican, May 24, quoting from the Lexington Express of unknown date. It was claimed that Lafayette County spent $100,000 on the Kansas invasions (Harvey, p. 125). " On the Kickapoo ferryboat, the following notice appears: ' Some illy-disposed persons have tried to injure my ferry by stating that I refused to carry persons last fall to the election. This is false. It would be difficult to find one more sound on the goose than I am. John Elles'." (Paxton, p. 198).

[92] For advocating this policy the Daily Intelligencer flayed the editor of the Cycle on October 20 (Cycle of November 2).

this purpose,[93] and on December 31, 1855, the "Proslavery Aid Society" of Buchanan County was formed. Shares were to be sold as stock at twenty-five dollars each. Biennial meetings were to be held at the St. Joseph city hall. A vote was to be given for each share of stock, and a paid agent was to remain in Kansas. "All of the means of this society shall be faithfully applied to the purchasing of lands, and in furthering the interests of the proslavery party in Kansas Territory."[94] For very good reasons this society was a failure, and later efforts to colonize Kansas fared no better. When on March 17, 1855, it was proposed to send settlers from Boone County to Kansas it was found that "no one was heard of who desired to go to Kansas to live."[95] In some cases, however, success was partially realized. "Many citizens from Platte go over to Kansas," is read in an entry in the Annals of Platte County for September, 1854, "and locate claims and then return. Some were in earnest, and became actual settlers."[96] An attempt to raise money in Ray County at a meeting held on March 5, 1855, brought little result.[97] Benton contemptuously belittled the whole proslavery program to settle Kansas or vote there. "But a very small part of Missouri, and that in Atchison's neighborhood [Platte County] had anything to do with it," he wrote to J. M. Clayton in July, 1855.[98]

While the advance proslavery party were planning the invasion of Kansas with ballot and musket,[99] a tidal wave of

---

[93] St. Joseph Commercial Cycle, December 28, 1855.
[94] Ibid., January 11, 1856. Articles of Incorporation.
[95] Missouri Statesman, March 30, 1855.
[96] P. 188.
[97] Richmond Weekly Mirror, March 10.
[98] MS. dated Washington, July 29, A. L. S., Clayton Papers, vol. xi, p. 2108.
[99] Considering the class of Missourians who agitated the Kansas invasion it does not seem possible that the "Border Ruffians" were the blear-eyed, maudlin, bloodthirsty brutes they are often pictured to have been. Excited they were with a fanatical crusading spirit, but low-lived sots they could not have been as a class. Neither were John Brown, Jim Lane, "Old Doctor" Doy, and their satellites the coarse-grained blacklegs of literature. They committed crimes as do all men laboring under a self-righteous enthusiasm. Many criminals naturally followed both camps, but the rank and file of both "armies" seem to have conscientiously followed an ideal.

political hysteria swept over western Missouri. " The abolition excitement has been running so high at Weston," wrote
a correspondent from Westport on August 1, 1854, "that the
authorities have ordered all free gentlemen of color to leave
the town."[100] " Proslavery harangues provoked the people
to frenzy and outrage. Those living east and north of Platte
City became almost insane," reads an entry in the Annals of
Platte County for April, 1855.[101] On April 14 a meeting
was held at Parkville to threaten Northern Methodists. G.
S. Park and W. J. Patterson of the Luminary were threatened with a plunge into the Missouri if they reappeared in
the village, "and if they go to Kansas to reside, we pledge
our honor as men, to follow and hang them whenever we
can take them." The press was then dumped into the
river.[102] " Atchison, Stringfellow & Co. have worked up
quite a portion of Platte County to a fever-heat excitement,"
says the account of a conservative slaveholder, "and they
appear ready for almost any rash act; but that feeling does
not extend above that county. Buchanan, Andrew, Holt,
etc., are quite calm and conservative in feeling and action.
Some effort was made in Buchanan to raise steam, but it
proved an entire failure."[103] On May 17, 1855, William
Phillips, a Leavenworth abolitionist, was brought to Weston

[100] From a proslavery correspondent in the Republican of August
4, 1854.
[101] P. 198.
[102] Missouri Statesman, April 27, 1855. See also Paxton, p. 198.
This action was indorsed by meetings in Platte County and at Liberty (ibid., pp. 198–200). The statement of Park which caused the
trouble can be found in the Missouri Statesman of June 1, 1855.
[103] Letter dated May 10, from "One of the largest slaveholders
in Andrew county" (Missouri Statesman, June 8, 1855). The Bentonites and the Whigs, though many of the latter were radically pro-
slavery, incessantly accused Atchison of arousing feeling to insure
his reelection to the Federal Senate. His Whig competitor at the
time was A. W. Doniphan. Early in July, 1855, a proslavery meeting
was held in Platte County. Atchison's party pushed through the
following resolution: " That in the selection of persons for office,
State, Federal, or county, we will hereafter disregard all questions
which have heretofore divided us as Whigs and Democrats." As
the Whigs were in the majority at this meeting, one of them immediately moved that Doniphan be supported for the Senate. The
Atchison party then withdrew its conciliatory resolution (letter in
ibid., July 13, 1855).

where he was tarred and feathered, had half of his head shaved, was ridden on a rail, and was finally sold at auction by a negro. It was claimed, however, that the citizens of Weston did not participate in this affair.[104]

By the summer of 1855 the furor had become pretty general in western and central Missouri. The anti-Bentonites and radical Whigs advocated strenuous action, while Bentonites, with some exceptions, and conservative Whigs preached law and order.[105] A letter of May 24 from James S. Rollins to George R. Smith well describes the conditions in Boone and neighboring counties. " I endorse your position throughout, and commend you, for having the courage to take it, unless the conservative men of the Country stand firm, and resist the spirit of reckless unprincipled fanaticism, which a few dangerous demagogues are exciting, there is positively no predicting what is to become of our institutions. . . . The demagogues are doing all in their power to get up excitement in this locality,—thus far they have not succeeded—they renew their efforts on the 2nd of June when a public meeting is called in this place. The principal instigators here, are . . . old McBride and . . . Shannon the Irishman, at the head of the college. . . . Let me tell you that no man is doing more to corrupt the public mind of Missouri, on these exciting questions than the aforesaid Shannon . . . the excitement is confined chiefly to Platte, Clay & Jackson. . . . We should not hesitate to make the issue which Atchison and his Mobocrats have tendered and if the law abiding conservative portion of Missouri, those indeed, the real slave owners, most deeply interested in this question, are overpowered, it will only be that much worse for the country . . . let us act."[106]

---

[104] Republican, May 25, 1855, quoting from an issue of the Weston Platte Argus of unknown date. Another abolitionist, J. W. B. Kelly, was condemned by a Clay County public meeting in August, 1855, and as they had no tar he was asked to leave, which he did (Missouri Statesman, August 20, 1855).
[105] The Commercial Cycle of St. Joseph and the Weekly Mirror of Richmond were strongly proslavery Whig papers, while the Fulton Telegraph, Boonville Observer, and Hannibal Messenger were conservative Whig sheets.
[106] MS. Smith Papers. The underlining of clauses for the sake of emphasis as made by the writer has been omitted, as it is the rule rather than the exception.

˙The meeting of June 2, referred to in the above letter, well portrays the spirit of the extremist element. Radical Democrats and Whigs for the time buried the hatchet. Three of each party were appointed to draft resolutions which were reported to the Assembly by W. F. Switzler, who had gone temporarily into the jingo camp. Slavery was declared to be a legal institution, abolitionism was excoriated, " Squatter Sovereignty " and the Kansas-Nebraska Act were endorsed, and the agitation of the slavery issue in or out of Congress was condemned. The Union was declared to be the " palladium of our liberties," and Governor Reeder of Kansas was censured and with him the antislavery element in Kansas. Dr. Lee, one of the above committee of six, then offered a series of resolutions which declared that " odious measure," the Missouri Compromise, to be unconstitutional, and stated that " while we deprecate the necessity, we cannot too highly appreciate the patriotism of those Missourians who so freely gave their time and money for the purpose, in the recent election in Kansas of neutralizing said abolition efforts."[107]

Meanwhile there was a demand for a state proslavery convention. The St. Louis Intelligencer on June 6 advocated such an assemblage, and prayed that every delegate be a slave owner, as " we never yet knew a mob composed of slaveholders."[108] On June 21 a " Committee of Four " sent out a call from Lexington " To the Members of the General Assembly of the State, and all true friends of the South and the Union."[109]

As a result the convention met at Lexington, July 12 to 14, 1855.[110] The " Irishman " James Shannon, president of

[107] Switzler's Scrapbook for Years 1844-55, p. 229. Also in Missouri Statesman of June 8, 1855.
[108] Quoted by the Missouri Statesman of June 15.
[109] Ibid., June 29. Delegates to the convention were chosen at local county meetings. For example, on July 4 the proslavery party of Audrain County assembled in the court house at Mexico, selected representatives, and passed resolutions (Dollar Missouri Journal, July 19). But there were no Audrain County delegates listed in the official roster of the convention.
[110] The work of the convention can be found in the official published Proceedings and Resolutions. This pamphlet contains President

the State University, delivered on July 13 a fanatical tirade on abolitionism in general and on the antislavery forces of Missouri and Kansas in particular. His effort so pleased the leaders of the movement—Judge W. B. Napton, Sterling Price, and others—that it was ordered to be printed with the proceedings.[111]

Great enthusiasm marked the progress of the convention. Twenty-five counties were represented on the opening day. Later two delegates arrived from St. Louis, bringing the number up to 226 from 26 counties.[112]   Of these delegates one writer found that 150 were from counties which had gone Whig in the previous election, 18 were from anti-Benton counties, 15 from Benton counties, and the other 41 were from counties which were Whig and anti-Benton.[113] This analysis, however, is most misleading. Naturally it was the radical proslavery element alone in any county which met to elect the delegates, and the majority party in the county did not necessarily have any control in the selection. That many Whigs joined the Kansas invasions and helped to fan the flame at home is certain.[114]   On the other hand, the law and order forces were led by the great Whigs— Rollins, Smith, Doniphan, and others. In 1855 Whig and Democrat differed fundamentally on the tariff, the currency, and kindred subjects, but differences on the slavery

---

Shannon's address, the Address of the Convention to the People of the United States, and the Proceedings and Resolutions. The proceedings can also be found in the Missouri Statesman of July 20, the Missouri Weekly Sentinel of July 20, the Weekly Pilot of July 21, the Dollar Missouri Journal of July 19, and in most of the other Missouri papers.

[111] Proceedings, pp. 6-31. The opposition criticized Shannon as being "unprofessional" and "anti-ministerial" in his public activity (Missouri Statesman, October 20, 25, 1855). President Shannon was a minister in the Christian (Disciples) Church.

[112] Proceedings, pp. 19-21.

[113] Tupes, p. 61. He did not include the two delegates from St. Louis.

[114] "I will not talk about the Kansas troubles," said Mr. Martin J. Hubble of Springfield. "I did not favor the agitation. Many Whigs did, however." "Party made no difference in the Kansas struggle," stated Colonel D. C. Allen of Liberty. "James H. Moss and Hiram A. Bledsoe of Lafayette county were prominent Whigs who led in the invasions."

question were largely a matter of personal opinion, not a party issue.

Judge W. B. Napton seems to have been the leading spirit in the convention. He introduced a series of resolutions covering the whole subject of slavery in the abstract and in its concrete application to Kansas. A committee of five was appointed to draw up an address to the people of the United States "setting forth the history of this Kansas excitement."[115] In this paper the danger to western Missouri slave property, and indeed to the slavery system throughout the country, was enlarged upon. Emigrant aid societies were condemned, the presence of a widespread desire for emancipation in Missouri was denied, and the entire political situation as it related to slavery was elaborately discussed.[116]

The resolutions of the Lexington convention did not carry with them the pacification of the whirlwind in Missouri. As northern settlers continued to pour into Kansas, political convulsions in Missouri increased. Nearly a year after the convention R. C. Ewing wrote George R. Smith from Lexington: "I find . . . the Slavery question . . . all absorbing. . . . Your reported opinion in relation to Kansas is doing you a deal of damage in Saline, Lafayette, & Jackson. . . . You had as well try to oppose an avalanche as the influence of this Kansas excitement."[117] Armed invasions of Kansas by Atchison and his henchmen ensued, but in this connection we are interested only in the effect of the settlement of Kansas on the escape of the Missouri slave.

After the struggle had resulted in a victory for the anti-slavery forces, the golden age of slave absconding opened.

---

[115] Proceedings, pp. 22–24. Torbert of Cooper County advocated retaliatory measures against the products and manufactures of Massachusetts and other States which had opposed the Fugitive Slave Law. This resolution was adopted (ibid., p. 25). Knownslar of Lafayette County introduced a resolution to make more "effective laws, suppressing within said States [slave States] the circulation of abolition or freesoil publications, and the promulgation of freesoil or abolition opinions." This resolution was also adopted (ibid., p. 27).

[116] Besides being printed with the Proceedings, the Address can be found in the Weekly Pilot of October 5 and in the Missouri Statesman of October 19.

[117] MS. dated June 19, 1856, Smith Papers.

Escapes apparently increased each year till the Civil War caused a general exodus of slave property from the State. The enterprising abolition fraternity of Kansas—Brown, Lane, Doy, and the rest—seemingly made it their religious duty to reduce the sins of the Missouri slaveholder by relieving him of all the slave property possible. The problem became so grave that in 1857 the General Assembly by joint resolution instructed the Missouri representatives in Congress to demand of the Federal government the securing of their property as guaranteed by the Constitution, and in particular protested against the action of certain citizens of Chicago who had aided fugitives to escape and had hindered and mistreated Missouri citizens in search of their slaves.[118] In this same year two members of the legislature independently introduced amendments to the patrolling laws, which, although not adopted, received such strong support that they were printed in the appendix of the House Journal. These bills provided that special patrols should be created in the counties on the Illinois, Iowa, and Kansas borders, to be supported by a special tax levied on the slave property of the State. These patrols were to watch free negroes and examine all ferries and other river craft. Any boat not licensed was to be cut loose, and if it was not chained and locked the owner was to be fined one thousand dollars.[119] This shows the nature and the constancy of the danger to which the slaveholder's property was subjected.

The Underground Railroad was now running very smoothly. Neighboring States reveled in Missouri's misery. Galesburg, Illinois, and Grinnell, Iowa, were con-

[118] House Journal, 18th Ass., 1st Sess., p. 296, and app., p. 313, February 14, 1857. An account of this Chicago episode is found in the Weekly Pilot of May 26, 1855. At times Illinois seems to have done her duty in enforcing the Fugitive Slave Law. "Last week, two negro men supposed to be slaves, who had escaped from a steamboat whilst ice bound in the river . . . were arrested in the town of Benton, Illinois. As the citizens had no means of detaining them, not having sufficient evidence that they were slaves, they were lodged in jail under a charge of petit larceny. This charge, however, would not justify a long detention" (Republican, January 18, 1852).
[119] House Journal, 18th Ass., Adj. Sess., app., pp. 276-278.

sidered havens for the fugitive.[120]   Philo Carpenter of Chicago is said to have helped two hundred Missouri slaves to Canada.[121]   The route of the western Missouri division of the Underground was by Kansas, circling Leavenworth, Atchison, Lecompton, and other proslavery settlements, and thence by way of Tabor, Iowa, to Canada. John E. Stewart and Dr. John Doy are said to have shipped a hundred slaves, averaging in value $1000, for the recovery of each of which a reward of $200 was offered. John Brown was rumored to have carried off sixty-eight.[122]

To many Missouri slaveholders the seriousness of the problem must have been overwhelming. " It [slave abduction] threatens to subvert the institution in this State," said an editorial of 1855, " and unless effectually checked will certainly do so. There is no doubt that ten slaves are now stolen from Missouri to every one that was spirited off before the Douglas bill."[123]   As a result of this unrest many

[120] Siebert, pp. 97–98.

[121] Ibid., p. 147.

[122] Anonymous, " The Underground Rail Road in Kansas " (Kansas City Star, July 2, 1905). As Lecompton lay between Lawrence and Topeka, both the Mound City and the Lawrence routes made for Holton and then for Nebraska City and Tabor (ibid.). According to another writer, many are said to have escaped by way of Tabor, but no figures or particulars are given (A. A. Minick, " The Underground Railway in Nebraska," Collections of the Nebraska State Historical Society, ser. ii, vol. ii, p. 70). Ten or twelve disappeared from Platte County during 1854–55 (History of Clay and Platte Counties, p. 632). Four slaves escaped from Platte County in June, 1855, through the aid of three whites (Missouri Statesman, June 29, 1855, quoting from the Parkville Democrat of June 16). The legends which were woven about the slave raids from Kansas were often most fantastically colored. For instance, James Redpath states that after Brown's famous raid the slave population of Bates and Vernon Counties was reduced from five hundred to " not over fifty slaves " from being sold south and from escapes (Public Life of Captain John Brown, p. 221). As a matter of fact, these two counties together had 471 slaves in 1856 (State Census, 1856, Senate Journal, 19th Ass., 1st Sess., fly-leaf in the appendix), while in 1860, after Brown's raid, there were more than before the raid, 535 being accredited to these counties in the Federal census of 1860 (Population, p. 208). The depositions of several border county slave-owners who lost property through Kansas forays can be found in House Journal, 20th Ass., 1st Sess., app., pp. 79–80.

[123] Quoted by Siebert, p. 194, from the Independent of January 18, 1855, which in turn quotes from an issue of the Daily Intelligencer of unknown date.

owners seem to have moved their negroes to safer regions. General Haskell of Kansas states that while going down the Missouri in December, 1858, there was a continuous stream of slaves driven on board his boat. By the time he reached Jefferson City there were three hundred and fifty bondmen aboard.[124] This account is confirmed by a similar report in a St. Joseph paper of 1860. "Within ten days no less than one hundred slaves were sold in this district, and shipped South. Owners are panic struck, and are glad to sell at any price." An "excellent house-keeper" sold for $900 for whom $1200 had been offered the year before.[125]

Not all slaveholders considered western Missouri as unsafe for slave property, as did the above. An army officer in 1857 wrote from St. Louis to George R. Smith of Pettis County that he had ten negroes at Fort Leavenworth whom he feared the abolitionists might run off. "I wish to purchase a tract of land for cultivation," he wrote, "to put my negroes on. . . . I am offered fine tracts near Jefferson City and Boonville. I am advised by some of my friends to make a location in Mississippi. . . . I will visit your county if your answer to my questions seem to warrant it."[126] A man as well informed as an army officer would not debate between Missouri and Mississippi when several thousand dollars' worth of slaves were concerned if he thought the State was as unsafe a place for slave property as many believed it. At the same time, newspaper accounts of escapes are numerous during the years from 1850 to 1860.[127] As in the other

---

[124] P. 37. The Reverend Frederick Starr claimed that escapes were so numerous in 1853 that the planters of river counties were moving to Texas (Letter no. i, p. 16).

[125] Quoted in the Twenty-Eighth Annual Report (1861) of the American Anti-Slavery Society, p. 141, from the St. Joseph Democrat of unknown date.

[126] MS. Lackfield Maclin to Smith, June 25, 1857, Smith Papers.

[127] "We have noticed with regret, that for more than a year the negroes have been running away from the eastern part of this [Lafayette] county, and the western part of Saline, while in the other parts of this county and adjoining counties very few attempt to escape. Is there no cause for this? Is there not some branch of the underground railroad leading from the neighborhood of Dover and Waverley?" (Richmond Weekly Mirror, September 15, 1854).

border States, the advertisement, with a cut of the flying negro with his earthly goods in a bandana swinging from a stick over his shoulder, is seen in almost every issue of nearly every paper.

The opening of the Civil War at once released thousands of negroes. As it continued many of the slaves of western Missouri ran for Kansas. "$200,000 of colored wealth walked off in the night to the bleeding shores of our neighboring state and 'turned up' there as citizens," said a contemporary.[128] An entry in the Annals of Platte County for February 1, 1865, states that the Missouri was frozen over and that many slaves had crossed to Kansas and enlisted in the Federal army, and another item for April 1 declares that slaves were daily escaping, being enticed away by Union soldiers.[129] The Federal census of 1860 gave Missouri 114,931 slaves.[130] Of these but 73,811 were in the State in 1863.[131] Many had enlisted in the Federal army, and many had fled to free territory. So many Missouri slaves took active part in the War that even the emancipationists were alarmed. In the "Charcoal" Convention of September, 1863, the radical emancipation party expressed their indignation. McCoy of Caldwell County offered among other resolutions the following: "Whereas, The slaves heretofore held in bondage in Missouri are rapidly escaping into surrounding States, and entering the army there, being credited to those states and as circumstances necessitate the draft for filling up the decimated regiments of our own State. . . .

Six slaves were discovered storing arms in Marion County preparatory to trying the "Underground" in 1855 (Weekly Pilot, April 28, 1855). Eight hundred dollars reward was offered for four slaves who escaped from C. Cox and R. Middleton of St. Joseph on September 22, 1855. "It is believed that said slaves are aiming to go to Iowa and thence to Chicago," runs this advertisement (St. Joseph Commercial Cycle, September 28, 1855).

[128] William Kauscher of Oregon, Missouri, in a speech delivered by him at that place on July 4, 1876, entitled, "Holt County During the War" (Wm. Hyde Scrapbook, volume on "Early St. Louis and Missouri").
[129] Pp. 325, 327.
[130] Eighth Federal Census, Population, p. 280.
[131] Report of the State Auditor of Missouri for 1865, p. 39.

We respectfully demand of General Schofield, permission to
recruit colored men belonging to disloyal men of this State
. . . to be accredited on the quota of Missouri troops."[132]

From what has been said it is clear that the escape of the
slave was a problem in Missouri throughout the whole
slavery period. It may have been that in many instances the
press and political agitators sought to arouse popular fear by
holding up the spectre of a vast negro migration, representing millions of capital and the only obtainable labor, moving
across the sluggish Missouri in the skiffs of the Massachusetts abolitionists, with "Beecher's Bible" in hand and
with Underground ticket in pocket, or by predicting a general exodus over the level boundaries of Jackson and Cass
Counties, guided by dark, bearded satellites of John Brown
or Jim Lane. Events proved that the slavery system, especially in western Missouri, was in danger, and in the fifties
the hard-headed Missourian needed no lurid tales to arouse
his fears and stir his resentment.

---

[132] Journal, Missouri State Radical Convention, 1863, p. 10.

CHAPTER VII

Manumission, Colonization, and Emancipation

The power of the master to manumit his slave was recognized from colonial days.[1] Although Missouri was in the throes of slavery agitation many times, and although the free negro was as little favored there as elsewhere, yet the privilege of granting freedom under a set legal form was never denied, despite the fact that attempts were made to abridge it.[2] Nevertheless the power to manumit a slave appears to have been considered a privilege rather than a right, as its exercise was thought dangerous to society. On one occasion the state supreme court declared that "that power [manumission] could only be exercised by the consent of the sovereignty . . . the whole community being alike interested."[3]

The effect of Christian baptism upon the status of the slave had been settled by the older slave States long before the Missouri country came under the dominion of the United

---

[1] The words "emancipation" and "manumission" were used synonymously in the laws, but as the former has assumed a political significance, meaning the freeing of the whole race, the latter term, having a strict legal and personal relation, will be used in this portion of the chapter.

[2] On January 7, 1833, the Senate rejected an amendment to limit "every act of emancipation" to a period of six months. All slaves manumitted contrary to this act were to become the property of the county at the end of six months. This amendment was rejected by a vote of 10 to 5 (Senate Journal, 7th Ass., 1st Sess., pp. 152–153). On January 14 the Senate passed a "rider" providing that the former masters of slaves thereafter freed should be "responsible and reliable for the conduct of the person or persons emancipated" as long as the latter resided in the State. It passed the Senate by a vote of 10 to 7 (ibid., p. 172), but in the House was rejected along with the bill to which it was attached by a vote of 25 to 20 (House Journal, 7th Ass., 1st Sess., p. 214).

[3] Rennick v. Chloe, 7 Mo., 197. In Charlotte v. Chouteau it was stated that it was not the policy of the slaveholding States to "favor" the liberation of the slave (11 Mo., 193).

States.[4] Emancipation was not a consequence of this religious rite, hence the subject needed no discussion in Missouri.
Emancipation by testament was possible, and the Code of
1804 gave the form of procedure by which a slave could be
liberated by will or other instrument in writing. When this
was under seal of the district court of the Territory and was
attested by two witnesses, the document made the slaves as
free " as if they had been particularly named and freed by
this act." To prevent fraud the freedman could be seized to
satisfy his owner's debts contracted before his liberation.
To prevent the free negro becoming a burden to society the
slave manumitted must be " sound in mind and body," not
over forty years of age or under twenty-one if a male, or
eighteen if a female. The late owner's property could be
attached if his former slave was incapable of self-support.
Should an executor neglect to obtain the necessary papers
for the one manumitted he was liable to a thirty-dollar fine.
A negro without the papers proving his freedom was to be
held by a justice until they could be obtained. If he could
not pay his taxes, he was to be hired out.[5]

The constitution of 1820 gave the legislature power to
pass laws permitting the freeing of the slave but " saving

---

[4] This subject is discussed in Ballagh, p. 119; and in J. R. Brackett,
" The Negro in Maryland " in J. H. U. Studies, extra volume vi,
pp. 28-29.

[5] Territorial Laws, vol. i, ch. 3, secs. 23, 24, 25. The papers proving the slave's freedom, which the various codes provided that he
must receive, were often very jealously carried about by him. The
following is a specimen of one of these: " Know all men by these
presents that I James Johnson of the County of Gasconade in the
State of Missouri for divers good considerations me unto moving
and inducing have emancipated set free and discharged from slavery
my negro girl named Parthenia aged about twenty six years to be
and remain from this time a free woman discharged from bondage.
St. Louis October 15th, 1853." The witnesses were M. S. Carré
and United States Senator Trusten Polk. It was also signed by
the manumittor in the St. Louis circuit court. This paper is in the
collection of Mr. W. C. Breckenridge of St. Louis. It is numbered
504. Mr. Breckenridge also has a deed of manumission dated as
late as August 27, 1864. It was granted by Russell H. Westcott to
Indy Hines. Dr. John Doy, the Kansas abolitionist, claimed that he
knew of several cases in which free negroes had their papers destroyed and were then sold into bondage (pp. 61, 93-95).

the rights of creditors."⁶   The later slave codes followed
the form of 1804 in substance, adding that " such emancipation shall have the effect to discharge the slave from the performance of any contract entered into during servitude, and
shall make such slave as fully and perfectly free, as if such
slave had been born free."⁷   Of course this would not give
the freedman the legal status of the white but simply that of
the despised free negro who could not be educated,⁸ who
had no standing in court save when a negro was on trial,⁹
and who was usually treated with indignity.¹⁰

In 1836 the law was somewhat loosely interpreted, it being
held that " when any person owns a slave, and is desirous
to set him free... the same can be done by a deed or instrument in writing . .·. acknowledged before a justice of the
peace . . . without any reference whatever to that part of the
act which requires a deed under seal to be attested by two
witnesses," as the latter was needed only when immediate
emancipation was in view.¹¹   Some years later it was stated
that the mere promise of the late owner was not sufficient,
but that the legal document was necessary,¹² while in 1856 it
was held that a will regularly drawn, though not probated,
was a valid act of manumission even if inefficacious as a

⁶ Art. iii, sec. 26.
⁷ Revised Laws, 1835, p. 581, art. ii, sec. 2; Revised Statutes, 1845,
ch. 167, art. ii, sec. 2; Revised Statutes, 1855, ch. 150, art. ii, sec. 2.
These laws were all repealed February 15, 1864 (Session Laws, 1863,
p. 108, sec. 1).   The above statutes were evidently influenced by a
Virginia law as old as 1782 which required a deed of manumission
to be signed by two witnesses in the county court, and further providing that the negroes " shall thereupon be entirely and fully discharged from the performance of any contract entered into during
servitude, and enjoy as full freedom as if they had been particularly
named and freed by this act " (Hening, vol. xi, p. 39, sec. 1).
⁸ See above, p. 83.
⁹ See above, p. 76.
¹⁰ All religious and other assemblies of free negroes were under
surveillance (see above, p. 180).   The admission of free blacks to the
State was forbidden at various times (Constitution, 1820, art. iii,
sec. 26; Revised Laws, 1825, vol. ii, p. 600, sec. 4).   In how many of
the States the free negro was a complete citizen under the law is
still a question.
¹¹ Paca v. Dutton, 4 Mo., 371.
¹² Robert v. Melung, 9 Mo., 171.

will.[13]   In the very rigid case of Redmond v. Murry et al., wherein a slave held his master's receipt for most of his purchase price, it was plainly enunciated that this contract of manumission, being "a mere intention or promise by the master, not consummated in the manner pointed out by law, however solemn such promise may have been made, can confer no power or capacity on the slave to have it enforced."[14]

By 1863 the Civil War had so changed the fortunes of the slave power that in a decision of that year Judge Bay declared that an act or will providing freedom might be presumed from such acts of the master as afforded a sufficient ground for the presumption.[15]

This form of manumission took effect either immediately, or at the death of the owner, or within a stated period. In one instance a negress was to be hired out for a term of four years after the master's death, and a child she bore within that time was sold to pay certain debts and expenses of the estate.[16] Another negress was to serve for ten years and then be free. A child she bore within those years was also held to be a slave.[17]

Although not encouraging manumission, Missouri seems to have given the slave ample opportunity to sue for freedom. As early as 1807 the territorial government passed quite a comprehensive procedure permitting "any person held in slavery to petition the general court of common pleas, praying that such person may be permitted to sue as a poor person." Under this legal fiction a slave could have full opportunity to fight for his freedom. The court was to assign counsel for the petitioner, allow him reasonable liberty to attend his counsel, and see that he was not subjected to any severity by his owner for bringing the suit. If the court feared a violation of this provision, the slave could be taken by habeas corpus and hired out, the earnings of such hire to go to the party winning the suit. The jury was to be in-

---

[13] Schropshire v. London et al., 23 Mo., 393.
[14] 30 Mo., 570.
[15] Louis et al. v. Hart Adm'r, 33 Mo., 535.
[16] Erwin v. Henry, 5 Mo., 470.
[17] Lee v. Sprague, 14 Mo., 476.

structed that the " weight of evidence lies with the petitioner
[the slave]," and jurors were to have regard not only to the
written evidence of the claim to freedom, but also to such
other proofs either at law or equity as the very right and
justice of the case might require. Either party might appeal the case to the general court.[18] In practice as well as
in the word of the law the court was liberal toward the
suing slave. Instances can be found in which the court
ordered that the slave be protected while the case was pending and be given freedom to communicate with his attorney.[19]

An act very similar to the above was passed in 1824. It
provided that " such actions shall be conducted in other respects in the same manner as the like actions in other
cases."[20] A law still more liberal was passed in 1835 which,
being reenacted in the later revisions, became the working
statute about which a multitude of cases were argued down
to the time of the Civil War. The circuit courts were substituted for the old territorial district court as the body before which the manumissions were recorded.[21]

---

[18] Territorial Laws, vol. i, ch. 35, secs. 1–4. In the MS. Records
of the St. Louis General Court are several cases arising under this
law: Matilda v. Van Ribber (vol. ii, p. 144) ; Layburn v. Rice (ibid.,
p. 164) ; and Whinney v. Phoebe Rewitt (ibid., p. 172). The habeas
corpus clause of this law must have caused some dissatisfaction, as
in the Revision of 1855 it was stated that " no negro or mulatto
held as a slave within this State or lawfully arrested as a fugitive
from service from another State . . . shall be discharged . . . under
. . . this act [habeas corpus]" (vol. i, ch. 73, art. iii, sec. 8).

[19] The following entry is found in the MS. Records of the St.
Louis Circuit Court for July 24, 1832: "Stephen W. Ferguson presents
the petition of Susan a girl of color praying that she may be permitted to institute suit against Lemon Parker for establishing her
right to freedom and that she may be permitted to sue as a poor
person, therefore the court permitted the said Susan and assigned
the said Stephen W. Ferguson Esq., as her counsel and it is ordered
by the court that said Lemon Parker permit the said petitioner to
have reasonable liberty of attending her counsel and the court
when the occasion may require it, that the said petitioner shall not
be taken or removed out of the jurisdiction of the court, or be
subject to any severity of treatment on account of her said application for freedom " (vol. vi, pp. 337–338).

[20] Revised Laws, 1825, vol. i, p. 404. In Gordon v. Duncan a negro
was given the value of his services during the pending of the suit
(3 Mo., 272).

[21] Revised Statutes, 1835, p. 284. It was also here provided that
the judge could grant the deed of manumission during the vacation

The classical Missouri suit for freedom is of course the case of Dred Scott, the story of which has been often told.[22] An account which well shows the struggle experienced by some negroes in suing for their liberty is that of Lucy Delaney. The story is undoubtedly told with bias. She states that her mother and three other colored children were kidnapped from Illinois and taken to Missouri, where they were sold into slavery. Later Lucy's mother married a slave of Major Taylor Berry of Franklin County. Before entering a fatal duel the latter "arranged his affairs and made his will, leaving his negroes to his wife during her life time and at her death they were to be free." Nevertheless Lucy's father was sold south. Her mother later brought suit and gained her own freedom. On September 8, 1842, the mother started proceedings to obtain Lucy's freedom from her old master's daughter. The court required this lady's husband to give bond for two thousand dollars as a guarantee that he would not remove Lucy from the State while the case was pending. The guarantor then had her placed in jail, lest, as he said, "her mother or some of her crew might run her off, just to make me pay the two thousand dollars; and I would like to see her lawyer or any other man in jail that would take up a . . . nigger case like that." Lucy was kept in jail for seventeen months. As the mother when suing for her own freedom had not mentioned her children, the defence endeavored to prove that they were not hers. At this point Edward Bates took up the matter,

of the court and that the slave could be hired out if the defendant (master) refused to enter into a recognizance, and the plaintiff was denied the right to recover damages for false imprisonment in case his enslavement was held to be illegal (ibid., secs. 1, 2, 8, 14). This law was reenacted in the Revision of 1845 (ch. 70). A section was added giving the sheriff power to collect the slave's earnings, in case he was hired out by the court pending the suit, and invest them at from three to six per cent. In this shape the law was reenacted in the Revision of 1855 (ch. 69).

[22] The best account of this negro is that of F. T. Hill, " Decisive Battles of the Law: Dred Scott v. Sanford," in Harper's Monthly Magazine, vol. cxv, p. 244. The various legal treatises covering the case will be found in note 40 of this chapter.

and after much difficulty obtained the girl's freedom.[23] This was perhaps an exceptional case, but it shows what the negro might be forced to undergo, even when he appealed to the courts.

As was learned above, the burden of proof lay with the plaintiff, who was further at a disadvantage in that "color raised the presumption of slavery."[24] The court, however, declared that the legislature in framing the law endeavored to put fairly the question of freedom between the parties.[25] Just before the Civil War the court held further that "if a negro sues for his freedom he must make out his case by proof like any other plaintiff, but the law does not couple the right to sue with ungenerous conditions; and he may prove such facts as are pertinent to the issue, and may invoke such presumption as the law derives from particular facts."[26] It was held that the claimant of a slave could not enter court "and disprove the matter [in the petition], and thereby prevent the institution of a suit," as this would result in "every object of the law" being defeated. It would also be equivalent to a master's bringing suit against his slave, a procedure which could not be allowed without statutory provision.[27] The plaintiff had to sue in person, another not being competent to do it for him, since he was a slave "as long as he acquiesced in his condition."[28] On the other hand, the slave had the common-law privilege of having excluded as testimony any admission he might ever have made that he was rightfully a slave.[29] Property in slaves did not lapse through the statute of limitations. A master might permit an infant to remain with its free

[23] Pp. 2–11, 24–35.
[24] See also Susan v. Hight, 1 Mo., 82, and Rennick v. Chloe, 7 Mo., 197.
[25] Susan v. Hight, 1 Mo., 82.
[26] Charlotte v. Chouteau, 25 Mo., 465.
[27] Catiche v. Circuit Court of St. Louis County, 1 Mo., 432.
[28] Calvert v. Steamboat "Timolene," 15 Mo., 595.
[29] Vincent v. Duncan, 2 Mo., 174.

mother, and when grown up it might even work and return its wages to the mother, but it continued to be a slave.[30]

A great deal of litigation arose relative to the Ordinance of 1787. Settlers moving from the eastward to Missouri often took up land in Illinois as they passed through the State, then at some later time moved on to Missouri with their slaves. From this situation there resulted a long series of cases culminating in the Dred Scott case of 1852. As there was no Missouri law to apply to this class of cases, the court interpreted the ordinance as it appeared to intend and as the Illinois court construed it. Governor St. Clair wrote President Washington, June 11, 1794, that "the anti-slavery clause of this Ordinance did not go to the emancipation of the slaves they [the people of the Territory] were in possession of and had obtained under the laws by which they had formerly been governed, but was intended simply to prevent the introduction of others. In this construction I hope the intentions of Congress have not been misunderstood, and the apprehensions of the people were quieted by it."[31]   The Illinois constitution of 1818 allowed indentures of negroes for terms of years, permitting those bound under previous laws to be held till their terms had expired. The children subsequently born to these were to be free at twenty-one if males and at eighteen if females.[32]   The courts of Illinois

---

[30] David v. Evans, 18 Mo., 249. The origin of a suit for freedom seemingly annulled a contract of sale of slaves. The administrator of the estate of Therese C. Chouteau obtained the following order of court in 1843: "Pierre Rose having commenced a suit for freedom was not offered for sale,—that Charlotte, [and] Victorine . . . were sold to Kenneth Mackenzie, and Antoine to Henry Chouteau, but after the sale and before payment was made . . . said Charlotte instituted a suit to establish her right to freedom and that of her children . . . and in consequence the said Mackenzie and Chouteau refuse to pay the sums bid by them for the slaves aforesaid, whereupon the court . . . order that the said Administrator do cause defense to be made against the claims set up by the said Pierre Rose and Charlotte" (MS. Probate Records, St. Louis, Estate no. 1745, paper filed September 11, 1843).

[31] Wm. M. Smith, ed., The St. Clair Papers. The Life and Public Services of Arthur St. Clair, vol. ii, p. 176.

[32] Poore, vol. i, p. 445, art. vi, secs. 2, 3.

for years permitted long-term indentures which were virtual slavery.[33]

The Missouri interpretation of the Ordinance of 1787 was in principle consistent until overturned by the Dred Scott opinion. In 1827 a negro child who had been born in Illinois after 1787 was declared to be free.[34] The following year it was held that the ordinance was " intended as a fundamental law, for those who may choose to live under it, rather than as a penal statute to be construed by the letter against those who may wish to pass their slaves through the country." A permanent residence was therefore held to work emancipation, as the court further declared that " any sort of residence contrived or permitted by the legal owner . . . in order to defeat or avoid the ordinance, and thereby introduce slavery de facto, would doubtless entitle a slave to freedom."[35] The court perhaps based this rendering on the constitution of Illinois of 1818 which read: " No person bound to labor in any other State shall be hired to labor in this State, except within the tract reserved for the saltworks near Shawneetoun; nor even at that place for a longer period than one year at any one time; nor shall it be allowed after the year 1825. Any violation of this article shall effect the emancipation of such person from his obligation to service."[36] In 1830 a case was decided which definitely laid down the principle that a slave might be hired out in Illinois for at least two years without working his freedom, but that if the owner intended to reside in Illinois and so resided with his slaves they would

---

[33] Harris, pp. 7–14. The interpretation of the Illinois courts is treated by Harris in ch. viii. He found instances in which negroes bound themselves to service for thirty-five, forty-nine, and even ninety-nine years. They were often made to believe that they were really slaves under the law.

[34] Merry v. Tiffin and Menard, 1 Mo., 520. If slaves were brought from Canada and were not lawfully held as slaves there, they could not be so held in Missouri (Charlotte v. Chouteau, 21 Mo., 590).

[35] La Grange v. Chouteau, 2 Mo., 19. But it was also here held that if an owner resided in Illinois and chose to employ his slave on a Missouri boat which touched at Illinois ports, he was in no way seeking to engraft slavery on that State.

[36] Art. vi, sec. 2.

become free.[37]   These decisions were used as precedents,
and this idea of the Ordinance of 1787 was held until overturned in 1852.[38] (A case very similar to that of Dr. Emerson and his man Dred Scott was already on record.   An
army officer named Walker in 1836 actually forfeited his
slave by virtue of the ordinance by taking her as a servant
into the Northwest Territory for a number of years.[39]

Consequently, when the Dred Scott case was taken to the
Missouri supreme court on a writ of error from the St.
Louis district court, the whole mass of preceding decisions
was swept away.   The court held that "the voluntary removal of a slave by his master to a State, Territory, or
country in which slavery is prohibited, with a view to reside
there, does not entitle the slave to sue for his freedom, in
the courts of this State."[40]   After 1852 this principle was
followed to the letter.[41]

---

[37] Vincent v. Duncan, 2 Mo., 174. But in Ralph v. Duncan it was
held that a master by permitting his slave to hire himself out in
Illinois offended against the ordinance as much as though taking
the slave there himself (3 Mo., 139).

[38] In Theodeste v. Chouteau it was decided that the ordinance did
not impair any rights then existing, and that negroes born and held
as slaves before its passage were not entitled to freedom under it
(2 Mo., 116). In Ralph v. Duncan the court limited the force of
the ordinance to the time when Congress admitted Illinois as a State
(3 Mo., 139). In Chouteau v. Pierre the ordinance was held not to
be in force until the western posts were evacuated by the British
under the Treaty of 1794, in districts controlled by such posts (9
Mo., 3). J. P. Dunn outlines several of these Missouri slave cases
(Indiana: A Redemption from Slavery, ch. vi). In some of these
cases the court was somewhat exacting of the slave-owner. In one
instance it was declared that if he intended leaving Illinois but hired
out his slave for "a day or two" for pay, the slave was entitled to
freedom (Julia v. McKenney, 3 Mo., 193). In Nat v. Ruddle a
slave was declared to be free if he was taken by his master to work
in Illinois, but if he ran away from Missouri to his master in Illinois
or went to visit him there and was allowed by him to work, he
would not be free (3 Mo., 282). On this point see also Whinney v.
Whitesides, 1 Mo., 334, Milly v. Smith, 2 Mo., 32, and Wilson v.
Melvin, 4 Mo., 592.

[39] Rachel v. Walker, 4 Mo., 350.

[40] Scott (a man of color) v. Emerson, 15 Mo., 576. The lower
decision was reversed. Judge Ryland concurred with Judge Scott
in the opinion, Judge Gamble dissented. For a history of the case
see the Federal decision in Howard, vol. xix, p. 393. The local situation is briefly discussed by F. T. Hill, p. 244. The legal phase of
the subject is treated from different angles by E. W. R. Ewing, The

This view of the court aroused immediate indignation. Missouri had been liberal toward the slave seeking release from unlawful bondage. Senator Benton always took great pride in this fact, and claimed that negroes preferred to be tried in Missouri and Kentucky rather than in the free States north of the Ohio.[42]   Senator Breese of Illinois admitted in 1848 that " in all his observation and experience . . . he had discovered that the courts of the slave States had been much more liberal in their adjudications upon the question of slavery than the free States. The courts of one of them (Illinois) has uniformly decided cases against the right of freedom claimed by persons held in bondage under a modified form of servitude recognized by its old constitution.   In precisely similar cases the courts of Kentucky and Missouri . . . decided in favor of the rights of freedom."[43]

The abandonment of this liberal policy was clearly recognized at the time. The Missouri chief justice in his minority opinion said, " I regard the question as conclusively settled by repeated adjudications of this court."[44]   In 1856 Justices Curtis and McLean of the Federal Supreme Court enlarged upon this complete reversal of precedent by the Missouri court in their individual opinions.[45]   The majority of the Missouri court admitted that precedent was against them, but claimed that a higher law demanded that abolition be

Legal and Historical Status of the Dred Scott Case, and by T. H. Benton, Historical and Legal Examination of the Dred Scott Case. Both of these are bitterly partisan.

[41] For example, see Sylvia v. Kirby, 17 Mo., 434.

[42] Benton, Historical and Legal Examination of the Dred Scott Case, pp. 44–45, note.

[43] Benton, Abridgement of the Debates of Congress, vol. xvi, p. 226. Breese delivered this speech on July 24, 1848.

[44] 15 Mo., 576. Chief Justice Gamble continued: " I would not feel myself any more at liberty to overthrow them [former decisions], than I would any other series of decisions by which the law of any other question was settled. There is with me nothing in the law relating to slavery which distinguishes it from the law on any other subject."

[45] Justice Curtis's opinion may be found in Dred Scott v. Sandford (Lawyers' Co-operative edition, Supreme Court Reports, vol. xv, pp. 767–795) ; and Justice McLean's (ibid., pp. 752–767). The subject of the reversal of precedent by the Missouri court is treated in the Thirteenth Annual Report of the American Anti-Slavery Society, p. 39 (report for 1853).

rebuked and the institution of slavery in the State be conserved. "Cases of this sort are not strangers in our courts," reads their opinion. "Persons have been frequently here adjudged to be entitled to their freedom, on the ground that their masters held them in slavery in Territories or States in which that institution is prohibited . . . on the ground it would seem, that it was the duty of the courts of this State to carry into effect the constitution and laws of other States and Territories regardless of the rights, the policy, or the institutions of the people of this State . . . times are not as they were when the former decisions on the subject were made. Since then, not only individuals but States have been possessed with a dark and fell spirit in relation to slavery, whose gratification is sought in the pursuit of measures whose inevitable consequence must be the overthrow and destruction of our government. Under such circumstances, it does not behove the State of Missouri to show the least countenance to any measures which might gratify this spirit."[46]

To this open acknowledgment of the influence of the political heat of the time on the decision there is the following answer from Chief Justice Gamble: "There is nothing with me in the law relating to slavery which distinguishes it from the law on any other subject, or allows any more accommodation to the temporary public excitements which are gathered about it."[47] The Missouri court decided the Dred Scott case in 1852. Benton had fought for and lost his reelection to the United States Senate in 1849–51. Party feeling was extremely bitter, and the slavery issue divided Democrats and Whigs alike. The court recognized this "dark and fell spirit in relation to slavery." To such political forces one must look for the inspiration of the then novel decision in Scott against Emerson.

Two motives entered into the act of liberating a slave,—financial consideration, and sentiment. In many cases pure sentiment was the moving force. Often it was mere barter

---

[46] Scott (a man of color) v. Emerson, 15 Mo., 576.
[47] Ibid.

in which the slave or his friends or relatives bought his freedom. This resulted in many free negroes temporarily owning slaves—parents their children, a husband his wife— between the time of purchase and the date of manumission.[48] In many cases the elements of sentiment and cash both entered,[49] while the force of sentiment alone undoubtedly moved other emancipators.[50] Colored mistresses are known to have been freed by their owners, a familiar case being that of J. Clamorgan who in 1809 manumitted two such negresses who were mothers of his children.[51] Many slaves were freed by will. Some of these were required to reimburse the heirs of the estate for their loss by such manumission, while a few were allowed to pay for their freedom in installments.[52]

---

[48] For examples of the holding of slaves by free negroes, see p. 63 above.

[49] The following is an illustration: "Know all men by these presents that I William Howard . . . do, for and in consideration of her former good qualities, correct deportment and faithful services to me, together with the further consideration of Tu Hundred Dollars to me in hand paid . . ." set free the slave under consideration. Granted in the St. Louis Circuit Court, December 16, 1843. In the possession of W. C. Breckenridge. Paper no. 208.

[50] As is the case today, the negro was attached to his old home and master. Some freed slaves preferred to remain with the erstwhile owner. The following proves this point: "Said Slaves thus manumitted . . . are so to remain without hindrance or molestation, and that at the date of my death, are to work and labor for themselves, and not to look to my estate for support. . . . That said slaves have been well and truly provided whilst in servitude, and that in consideration of my affection for them I will provide for them meat and drink and suitable wearing apparel. And that Said Slaves thus emancipated must look in future to themselves for support. . . . But whilst they remain with me, they must be subject to my control and direction" (MS. Deed of Henry Dearing, dated December 17, 1855, St. Louis Court House Papers, Missouri Historical Society).

[51] MS. Records of St. Louis, vol. B, pp. 368–372, under date of September 12.

[52] "Whereas Beverley Allen deceased by his will, directed that his slave Joe should be emancipated upon his paying Five Hundred Dollars and the said Joe not being able to pay that sum at one time We are willing to allow a specified time for the payment in installments." Joe was to pay $50 when the papers were given him and the same amount on January 1, 1847, and each four months thereafter till the total was paid. "And if the undersigned Penelope Allen should also receive from the hire of the said Joe or he should otherwise pay to her the sum of Ten dollars per month until

Accounts are on record of most heroic and pathetic sacrifices on the part of relatives to liberate slaves. That of George Kibby of St. Louis and his wife Susan is very instructive. In 1853 Kibby entered into a contract with Henry C. Hart and his wife Elizabeth L. Hart to purchase their negress named Susan, whom he wished to marry. The price was to be eight hundred dollars. The contract is devoid of all sentiment and is as coolly commercial as though merchandise was the subject under consideration. Kibby had but two hundred dollars to pay down. He was to pay the remainder in three yearly installments, and upon the fulfilment of the contract Susan was to receive her freedom. In the meantime Kibby was to take possession of Susan under the following conditions: "Provided however said Kibby shall furnish such security as may be required by the proper authorities, to such bond as may be required for completing such emancipation, so as to absolve . . . Hart and wife from all liability for the future support and maintainance of said Susan and her increase. This obligation to be null and void on the part of said Hart and wife, if said Kibby shall fail for the period of one month, after the same shall become due and payable, to pay to said Hart and wife said sums of money as hereinbefore specified, or the annual thereon, and in the event of such failure, all of the sum or sums of money whether principal or interest, which may have been paid by the said Kibby shall be forfeited, and said Kibby shall restore to said Hart and wife said negro girl Susan and such child or children as she may then have, such payments being hereby set off against the hire of said Susan, who is this day delivered into the possession of said Kibby. And said Kibby hereby binds himself to pay said sums of money as hereinbefore specified, and is not to be absolved therefrom on the death of said Susan, or any other contingency or plea whatever. He also binds himself to keep at his own expense a satisfactory policy of insurance on the life of said

the said sum " was paid, he was to receive his freedom (MS. Probate Records of St. Louis, Estate no. 2068, paper filed September 18, 1846).

Susan, for the portion of her price remaining unpaid, payable to T. J. Brent trustee for Mrs. E. L. Hart, and that said Susan shall be kept and remain in this County, until the full and complete execution of this contract."

Attached to the back of this contract are the receipts for the installments. The first reads thus: "Received of George Kibby one mule of the value of sixty five dollars on within contract Feb. 1st, 1854, H. C. Hart." The fifth and last payment was made on December 3, 1855—two years lacking six days following the date of the contract. Accompanying the contract is the deed of manumission of Susan, likewise dated December 3.[53] Thus Kibby fulfilled his bargain in less than the time allowed him.

Cases can be found where slaves directly purchased their own freedom. One deed reads as follows: "For and in consideration of the sum of five hundred dollars, I have this day bargained and confirmed my right title interest and claim in and to a certain Negro Slave named Jackson . . . the said Sale being made unto Jackson himself with the intent . . . that the said slave shall henceforth be a free man."[54] As to the nature of the transaction, most deeds of manumission were mere quit-claim contracts, while others seem to have been a guarantee of the grantor. The following was evidently such: "I Benjamin J. Vancourt . . . for a good and valuable consideration have emancipated . . . My Slave Dolly Maria . . . She . . . being entitled as against me and my heirs, . . . and against all persons whomsoever claiming by through or under me to all the rights privileges & immunities belonging to Free persons of color."[55] This

---

[53] MS. original in the St. Louis Court House Papers at the Missouri Historical Society.

[54] MS. deed signed by James W. Scott, November 27, 1854 (in ibid.). One free negro of St. Louis, Jerry Duncan, was quite fortunate in emancipating his family. After buying the freedom of his wife and child, he purchased a home in the city. Later the police found his house filled with stolen goods. His family was then thought to have been purchased by dishonest means (Daily Evening Gazette, July 29, 1841).

[55] Filed November 20, 1846, no. 292. In the collection of Mr. W. C. Breckenridge.

provision, however, may have been a mere precaution to
prevent the heirs from causing the slave in question future
trouble.

At times the General Assembly by special act manumitted
negroes. Two slaves were thus freed by the legislature in
February, 1843, one in Jefferson and the other in Callaway
County. In both cases the bill was " read the first time, rule
suspended, read the second time, considered as engrossed,
read the third time and passed." There seems to have been
no opposition to these acts. "Sundry citizens of Callaway
county " even petitioned in the one case in favor of the
negroes under consideration.[56]

The actual number of slaves passing over into the class of
free negroes can be learned with accuracy in so far as the
circuit court records are complete, as all deeds of manumission were granted by these courts.[57] The census returns
give little aid in calculating totals, as the free negroes are
not always listed in the returns. The free black also went
from one county to another, and so the increase per county
is difficult to find. The two motives leading to manumission
—sentiment and money—are so inextricably merged that it
is doubtful whether the conclusions drawn from such figures
would throw much light on the sentiment of the State relative to the subject of emancipation.

The number of slaves given their freedom from year to
year was not great except in St. Louis. For the ten years
between January 1, 1851, and January 1, 1861, but a single
slave was freed in the Howard County circuit court.[58] In

[56] Senate Journal, 12th Ass., 1st Sess., p. 344; House Journal, 12th
Ass., 1st Sess., p. 253.
[57] " Any person may emancipate his or her slave, by last will, or
any other instrument in writing under hand and seal attested by two
witnesses, and approved in the circuit court of the County, where
he or she resides, or acknowledged by the party in the same court "
(Revised Statutes, 1835, p. 581, art. ii, sec. 1). The later revisions
follow this form.
[58] MS. Circuit Court Records, Howard County, Book 11, p. 174.
In examining these records the present writer in some cases covered
a series of years and in other cases took years widely separated in
order that a fair impression might be gained. The volumes were
carefully gone over, indexes and digests not being relied upon. The

the adjoining county of Boone but eight were liberated in these same ten years,[59] while to the southwest in Henry County only two were manumitted.[60] In the prosperous southwest Missouri county of Greene not a single slave was given freedom in the circuit court in the sixteen years preceding the Civil War—1845 to 1861.[61] The old Mississippi River county of Cape Girardeau in the southeastern part of the State witnessed no manumissions in the years 1837, 1844, 1850, and 1851; there were four in 1858, and none in 1859.[62]

In St. Louis County there was an entirely different situation. From the early days slaves were steadily and increasingly liberated. In 1830 four were manumitted, in 1831 three, in 1832 twelve, and in 1833 three.[63] Even in the years 1836 and 1837, while Congress was being thrown into a furor by abolition activity, twenty-eight were liberated.[64] In the year 1855, while the Kansas-Nebraska Bill and the settlement of Kansas were forcing the State into a fever of excitement, no less than forty-nine slaves received their freedom before the circuit court at St. Louis. Thirty-nine persons manumitted these forty-nine negroes.[65] In 1858 forty-nine slaves were liberated by nineteen different owners.[66]

Evidently many free blacks moved from county to county or else the natural increase of the free negro was large. Al-

---

volumes covering the earlier period in Howard County were also examined. The same result was found. For the years 1835–37 no manumissions were recorded (ibid., Books 5, 6).

[59] MS. Circuit Court Records, Boone County, Book E, pp. 451, 479–480, 510; Book F, pp. 195, 429; Book G, p. 92; Book H, pp. 66, 98.

[60] MS. Circuit Court Records, Henry County, Book B, pp. 49, 99.

[61] MS. Circuit Court Records, Greene County, Books C, Dsr, Djr, E.

[62] MS. Circuit Court Records, Cape Girardeau County, Book J, p. 79.

[63] MS. Circuit Court Records, St. Louis, vol. 6, pp. 4, 101, 156, 197, 221, 276, 316, 317, 323, 340, 351, 338, 393, 492.

[64] Ibid., vol. 8, pp. 7, 13, 36, 46, 52, 96, 99, 109, 128, 130, 139, 144–145, 189, 194, 195–196, 218, 220, 240, 276, 272, 367, 421.

[65] MS. Duplicate Papers in the Missouri Historical Society received from the Clerk of the St. Louis Circuit Court.

[66] MS. Circuit Court Records, St. Louis, vol. 27, pp. 6, 179; vol. 28, pp. 198, 231, 232, 249, 279.

though but eight were freed in Boone County between 1851 and 1861, the free negroes there increased from 13 in 1850 to 69 in 1860, and Howard County, while manumitting but a single slave in these ten years, increased her free colored population from 40 to 71. No slaves were liberated in Greene County between 1845 and 1861, nevertheless the free blacks of the county increased from 7 in 1850 to 12 in 1860. The gain of St. Louis County, however, was consistent with her numerous liberations, increasing from 1470 in 1850 to 2139 in 1860.[67]

The census returns, both state and Federal, contain so many omissions, especially in the free negro column, that little can be gained from comparisons of the relative growth of the slaves and the free blacks. Moreover, the state census returns do not harmonize with the Federal. For Missouri as a whole the relative gains of the three classes, whites, slaves, and free colored, are as follows according to the Federal census returns:—[68]

	1820	1830	1840	1850	1860
Whites	54,903	115,364	322,295	592,004	1,063,489
Slaves	9,797	25,091	57,891	87,422	114,931
Free Negroes	376	569	1,478	2,618	3,572

From the above figures it appears that the free negroes and the slaves continued at about the same ratio, while both were outstripped by the whites. Law and sentiment kept the number of free blacks from being swelled from without, but slave accessions were not restricted. Would the free negro class tend naturally to increase as fast as the slaves? To answer this question a detailed study of the life of the free colored as well as of that of the slave would be necessary, and even if such a study should be made, it would be denied by many that the birthrate of the despised free negro was governed by any economic law.

---

[67] Seventh Federal Census, pp. 654–655; Eighth Federal Census, Population, p. 275.
[68] Fourth Federal Census, p. 40; Fifth Federal Census, pp. 38, 40–41; Sixth Federal Census, p. 418; Seventh Federal Census, p. 655; Eighth Federal Census, Population, pp. 275–283.

The various portions of the State differed in sentiment as in interest. Outside of St. Louis County the slaves increased faster than the free negroes. St. Louis was a city of one hundred and sixty thousand inhabitants in 1860, of whom sixty per cent were foreign born.[69] The rural sections of the State looked askance at the liberal, antislavery, commercial spirit of the metropolis. The business interests of the city blamed slavery for keeping free labor from the State. The German element was strongly nationalistic and antislavery in feeling. As a consequence St. Louis County differed from the State as a whole. The Federal census reports for the county are as follows:—[70]

	1820	1840	1850	1860
Whites	8,253	30,036	99,097	182,597
Slaves	1,810	4,631	5,967	3,825
Free Negroes	225	706	1,470	2,139

The city of St. Louis contained more free negroes than slaves. In 1860 its population was divided as follows:—[71]

Whites	157,476
Slaves	1,542
Free Negroes	1,755

The increase of the free colored population was more rapid than that of the slaves. The cause of this lies not only in the fact that the people of St. Louis perhaps favored the freeing of the blacks more than did the State at large, but also in the fact that the great commerce of the city and its growing industry offered greater opportunities for labor than did the

---

[69] Eighth Federal Census, Population, p. xxxi. The population was 160,773. Of these, 96,086 were foreign born—50,510 of them Germans, 29,926 Irish, and 5513 English.

[70] See note 68. Scharf states that of the 1259 free blacks in the city of St. Louis in 1851 over one half, or 684, were in the city "in violation of the law" or without a license (vol. ii, p. 1020). Scharf's figures are far below those of the Federal census. He gives a number of manumissions in vol. i, p. 305, note. Free negro licenses were granted by the county courts. The MS. County Court Records of St. Louis contain many such records of licenses. In the year 1835 one hundred and forty-two were licensed (vol. i, pp. 455–459, 461–462, 463–464).

[71] Eighth Federal Census, Population, p. 297.

interior of the State. The negro when released from his bonds has tended to drift cityward, and such must have been the case with the free negro before the Civil War. In addition the antislavery views of so many of the people of the city might naturally attract the free black to a congenial environment.

From the foregoing pages it is evident that the freeing of the slave was tolerated but not welcomed in Missouri. The law provided that it should be done only at the risk of the owner, and the free negroes were looked upon with distrust. This contempt for and fear of the free black was the chief reason for the limited number of manumissions in all of the Southern States.

It is not the purpose of this study to discuss the free negro except where such a treatment affects the slavery system, yet the movement to colonize the free blacks is closely related to the slave in that the fear and dislike of the free colored population often prevented the manumitting of the bond-man. Colonization in Africa by American negroes was a definite program favored by the slaveholders of the South and the philanthropists of the North as a means of ridding the country of free negroes. The organized movement had hearty support from the second decade of the nineteenth century till long after the Civil War. James Madison and Henry Clay were early presidents of the national society. It was recognized as a slaveholders' movement.

The Missouri society was late in its origin and never developed to great proportions. Even Arkansas seems to have supported the movement with greater ardor than did her neighbor to the north. Missouri contained few free colored persons, and the economic burden of slaveholding, if such a burden there was, seems not to have been generally felt at the time. The first colonization society of the State was the "Auxilliary Society of St. Louis," which was founded about 1827. In this year William Carr Lane was president, James H. Peck, Governor Cole of Illinois, George Thompkins,

and William S. Carr vice-presidents, T. Spalding and D.
Hough secretaries, and Aaron Phule treasurer.[72]   In 1832
this was as yet the only society in the State, and it still had
the same officers.[73]   The legislature gave the movement at
least indirect support in resolutions passed in 1829 which
declared unconstitutional the action of Congress in appro-
priating funds for the use of the national society.[74]

The churches pushed the work, and the St. Louis society
often met under the auspices of the Methodists.[75]   Indeed,
the Missouri Conference of that body in 1835 put itself on
record as being enthusiastic over the subject of colonization:
"Resolved, That we highly approve of the Colonization
enterprise as conducted by the American Colonization Society; we will use our influence and reasonable endeavors
to promote its interests, and we recommend its claims to the
people among whom we may be appointed to labor."[76]   Other
churches were also interested.   In 1846 " Reverend W. Pat-
ton's church " of Fayette sent $7.50 to the national society,[77]
while two years before the Reverend A. Bullard had enclosed
$66 to aid a colonist.[78]   The Unitarian church of St. Louis
raised $150 for the society at a meeting in 1849.[79]

[72] Tenth Annual Report (1827) of the American Society for Colonizing The Free People of Color of the United States, app., p. 79.
This is the first notice the present writer found of the society in
Missouri.   Scharf claims that the St. Louis society was founded in
March, 1825, in the Methodist Church, and permanently organized
in 1828 (vol. ii, p. 1757).   But the above reference proves that it
was officially recognized at least a year before this latter date.
[73] Fifteenth Report, American Colonization Society, p. 63.
[74] Session Laws, 1828, p. 89.
[75] " I will attend to paying up the Sum you direct for the Colonization Society," wrote the Reverend Joseph Edmundson to a fellow
pastor in 1831.   " It meets on next Monday night in the Methodist
church " (Edmundson to Rev. J. R. Greene, May 18, in M. Greene,
Life and Writings of Reverend Jesse R. Greene, pp. 70–71).
[76] Resolutions of the Methodist Episcopal Annual Conference,
1835 (Daily Evening Herald, October 1, 1835).
[77] The African Repository and Colonial Journal, June, 1846 (vol.
xxii, p. 199).
[78] Ibid., September, 1844 (vol. xx, p. 288).
[79] C. C. Eliot, p. 139.   There is found in Scharf the statement that
the Young Men's Colonization Society met in the Unitarian Church
of St. Louis on January 11, 1848, its pastor, Dr. Eliot, being president (vol. ii, p. 1757).

The Missouri State Colonization Society was organized in 1839 with Beverley Allen as president.[80]   This association evidently prospered, for in 1845 its "Agent," the Reverend Robert S. Finley, sent $50 to the organ of the national society, the Repository.[81]   It even advocated the raising of $1000 in the State with which to cooperate with the Illinois society in sending a packet twice a year to Liberia.[82]   During that decade there were numerous signs of active interest. Public meetings were held, and colonial literature was sent to the clergymen of the State,[83] but whatever may have been the activity of the society the number of negroes sent from Missouri to Liberia was not great.   Up to 1851 only 21 blacks had been sent to Africa from the State out of a total of 6116 sent from the United States.[84]   Within the next five years Missouri sent 62 more.[85]

An illustration of the manner in which a local society was formed and the real motives behind the movement can be gained from the contemporary account of the genesis of the Cole County society.   On November 17, 1845, a gathering was addressed in the Jefferson City Methodist church by the state colonization agent, the Reverend R. S. Finley. Officers were elected, and the society adjourned to meet in the Capitol on the following evening.[86]   The state constitutional convention was in session at Jefferson City at the time, and many of its members were present at this second meeting.   Colonel James Young of Callaway County was made

---

[80] Scharf, vol. ii. p. 1757.

[81] African Repository, April, 1845 (vol. xxi, p. 256).

[82] R. S. Finley, "Circular Appealing for Aid for Colonizing Free Negroes in Liberia," in Journal of the Illinois State Historical Society, vol. iii, p. 95.

[83] Twenty-Ninth Annual Report of the American Colonization Society, p. 10.   In 1851 the society was active.   It had organized a movement to memorialize the legislature on the subject of colonization (Thirty-Fourth Report, p. 17).

[84] Thirty-Fourth Annual Report of the American Colonization Society, p. 84.   Kentucky had sent 225 and Tennessee 177 in these years (ibid.).

[85] Fortieth Annual Report of the American Colonization Society, p. 16.   During the year 1856 the Missouri society had remitted $313.48 to the treasurer of the national society (ibid., p. 21).

[86] Jefferson Inquirer, November 19, 1845.

chairman and General Aaron Finch of Dade County secretary. Colonel Young offered a resolution in favor of the society and its work, and recommended the movement to the people of the State. This resolution was " unanimously adopted." General Finch then made a speech in which he lauded the society. He urged that the work of colonizing Africa with these negroes should be vigorously pushed, as it was the only means of removing from the State the free blacks, who were an " injury to our country " and constantly " corrupt our slaves."⁸⁷ From the above account it is evident that it was the slaveholders and not the abolitionists who led the movement. At the same time many radical antislavery agitators such as Frank Blair likewise advocated the colonization program, yet the movement was entirely distinct from the organized antislavery agitation.

The policy of supporting the colonization program was apparently popular in the closing days of the slavery regime. The cautious and prominent Presbyterian clergyman, the Reverend N. L. Rice of the Second church of St. Louis, who dreaded both northern and southern agitators, wrote a series of public letters to the General Assembly of his church in 1855 in which he declared that colonization alone could save the country from northern abolitionism and southern radicalism.⁸⁸ When on January 1, 1852, Captain Andrew Harper of St. Charles turned his twenty-four slaves over to the society upon the condition " that they be immediately Colonized to Liberia," the conservative old St. Louis Republican declared it a " noble New Year's gift." " How can the affluent hope to dispense their wealth better than in generously aiding in this effort to let the bondman go free?"⁸⁹

⁸⁷ Jefferson Inquirer, November 22.
⁸⁸ Ten Letters on the Subject of Slavery to the General Assembly of the Presbyterian Church, pamphlet, p. 6. In 1850 the Reverend James A. Lyon of the Westminster Presbyterian Church of St. Louis advocated that the legislature grant the state society $2000 with which to plant a " Missouri Colony in Liberia." The state society, he claimed, was " efficient and well organized " (An Address on the Missionary Aspect of African Colonization, pamphlet, pp. 20–21).
⁸⁹ Republican, January 1, 1852. These negroes all reached Liberia

Even the political heat engendered by the Kansas struggle and the war between the Benton and anti-Benton forces seems to have had little effect on the popularity of colonization. On January 14, 1858, Frank Blair delivered in Congress an able speech in favor of a resolution introduced by himself which provided that territory be acquired in Central or South America on which to plant a colony of free negroes of the United States.[90] Senator Green of Missouri, a strong proslavery man, in a speech of May 18 on this measure expressed his own favorable attitude toward colonization, but resented Senator King's statement that Blair as a Missourian was the logical person to push the measure. He declared that only "a few individuals" in the State favored emancipation.[91] This illustrates how easily the colonization movement might be confused with the active antislavery program. In 1860 among the ninety-seven vice-presidents of the national society were Edward Bates and John F. Darby of St. Louis,[92] showing that the project had able and influential supporters in Missouri in the closing days of the slavery period.

It will be the aim of the following paragraphs to depart entirely from the military and political affairs which engulfed Missouri from 1861 to 1865 and to outline the development of the movement toward emancipation.

When Governor Jackson was driven from Jefferson City and the " Rebel " legislature moved to Neosho, Hamilton R.

save two, who were beguiled by "free negroes and abolitionists" to stop by the wayside while en route through Pennsylvania (ibid., May 13, 1852). In 1844 the administrator of the estate of Thomas Lindsay of St. Charles sent the national society $600 "toward the support of eighteen persons left by him to be sent to that colony" (African Repository, July, 1844 [vol. xx, p. 223]). In the case of a negro who was freed by will on condition that he be sent to Liberia by the Colonization Society it was held that his manumission was valid only if he had the means as well as the "willingness" to go (Milton [colored] v. McHenry, 31 Mo., 175).

[90] Congressional Globe, 35th Cong., 1st Sess., pt. i, pp. 293–298.
[91] Congressional Globe, 35th Cong., 1st Sess., pt. iii, p. 2208.
[92] Forty-Third Annual Report of the American Colonization Society, p. 3.

Gamble, a lifelong Whig and antislavery man, was made governor. His party was conservative, and hoped by gentle means to placate those who had believed in the " Union with slavery." Opposed to this party were the " Radicals " or "Charcoalers," headed by Charles D. Drake and General George R. Smith. These latter preached immediate emancipation, and accused the governor and his friends of having lurking proslavery sentiments.[93]

When the state convention met in March, 1861, to decide the relation of Missouri to the Union, Uriel Wright declared that emancipation meant the destruction of the agricultural interests of the South.[94] The majority of the committee on Federal relations were otherwise minded, and they maintained that the interests of Missouri would suffer from the policy of free trade as advocated by the South. They condemned secession, and thought that the North could never be at peace with the South as a separate nation, as the question of fugitive slaves would force a free North to police her territories for a slave South.[95] The convention was loyal to the Union, but could not be said to be at all in favor of materially affecting the slavery system.

In August, 1861, General Frémont, in command of the Union forces of the State, by proclamation declared the property of all rebels to be forfeited, and emancipated their slaves. But President Lincoln on New Year's day, 1862, modified this provision so that it applied only to those who had taken up arms against the United States or had aided her enemies.[96]

---

[93] " Governor Gamble was then [August, 1861] a . . . pro-Slavery man . . . he believed the people of Missouri to be pro-slavery people " (C. D. Drake, Union and Anti-Slavery Speeches, Delivered During the Rebellion, p. 348). In December General Halleck and Governor Gamble reprimanded Thomas C. Fletcher for saying that " having arms in our hands we never intended to lay them down while slavery existed " (Harding, p. 338).
[94] Journal and Proceedings of the Missouri State Convention, held at Jefferson City and St. Louis February 28 to March 22, 1861, p. 35.
[95] Ibid., p. 35. The committee reported March 9.
[96] Paxton, p. 317. See also Switzler on this point (pp. 391–392). Switzler says that Frémont with his own hand liberated two slaves of Colonel Thomas L. Snead on September 12, 1861 (p. 391).

When the state convention reassembled in June, 1862, emancipation was immediately agitated. Breckenridge for the committee on the constitution introduced a series of resolutions which provided for the abolition of the slavery clauses of the state constitution; for the liberation of all slaves born in the State on and after the first of January, 1865, when such should reach the age of twenty-five years; for indemnifying the masters of slaves for their losses, and for requiring the reporting of slave births within six months under a penalty of the confiscation of the slave. No slaves were to be imported. The proposal of the President to aid the State in reimbursing her slaveholders was favorably considered. These resolutions were tabled by a vote of 52 to 19.[97] On June 13 Governor Gamble submitted to the convention the offer of President Lincoln of the recent congressional provision proposing to pay Missouri slave-owners in case of gradual emancipation. The governor, however, feared that the measure " would produce excitement dangerous to the State," and hinted that in such a contingency the President would not consider the " action disrespectful " if the offer were rejected. The proposition was thereupon tabled and ordered printed.[98] Hitchcock then moved that the offer of the President be considered, that he be advised of the danger its acceptance might cause, and that he be duly thanked. A committee of five was appointed for this purpose.[99]

The convention was not composed entirely of kindred spirits. Hall immediately moved a counter-resolution declaring that " the people in choosing the Convention, never intended or imagined that body would undertake any social revolution wholly unconnected with the relations between the State and the General Government." This resolution

---

[97] Journal, Appendix, and Proceedings of the Missouri State Convention, held at Jefferson City, June 2 to 14, 1862, p. 19.
[98] Ibid., p. 37.
[99] Ibid., p. 40. This resolution reads: " Resolved, That . . . a majority of this Convention have not felt authorized at this time to take action with respect to the delicate and grave questions of private right and public policy presented by said resolution."

was rejected by a vote of 35 to 30.[100] Birch then moved
that the President's offer be "respectfully declined." This
was rejected by a vote of 38 to 22, whereupon Breckenridge
moved to submit the communication of the governor, along
with the motion of Hitchcock, to the President. This
motion passed by a vote of 37 to 23.[101] It is evident from
the action of this convention and from a survey of the vote
on the various motions that the time was not yet ripe for
radical interference with the slavery system.[102]

By 1863 a large portion of the Union element, which party
then controlled the situation in the State, was in favor of
emancipation. Some wished immediate and some gradual
emancipation. Charles D. Drake said to the convention
which he and his followers called in 1863 that in the summer
of 1861 "a large majority—perhaps seven-eights—of them
[the people of Missouri] then were proslavery people." But
during the two years which followed, he claimed that the
"sentiments of the people of Missouri in regard to the
institution of slavery underwent a radical change." He
added that Lincoln's offer of cooperation in reimbursing the
slaveholders was largely responsible for this transition.[103]
This change in feeling regarding emancipation is also
vouched for by the Reverend J. W. Massie of England, who
was sent to the United States in 1863 by a band of four
thousand French and English clergymen. "I was as free
to utter my antislavery sentiments in Missouri as I had been

[100] Journal of the Missouri State Convention, 1862, pp. 45–46.
[101] Ibid., p. 46.
[102] For an idea of Governor Gamble's views of the emancipation
situation at this time see his message to the General Assembly of
December 30, 1862 (Senate Journal, 22d Ass., 1st Sess., pp. 13–15).
"The General Emancipation Society of Missouri" was formed in
April of this year (Constitution and By Laws of the General Emancipation Society of Missouri, adopted at St. Louis April 8, 1862).
"I think," wrote Anthony Trollope in January, 1862, "there is every
reason to believe that slavery will die out in Missouri. The institution is not popular with the people generally and as white labor
becomes more abundant—and before the war it was becoming more
abundant and profitable—men recognize the fact that the white man's
labor is more profitable" (p. 380).
[103] Speech at Jefferson City, September 1, 1863 (Drake, pp.
348–349).

in Connecticut. The Reverend H. Cox at whose church I spoke [Methodist] affirmed that such an address would not have passed without a mob, and the probable destruction of the place, only the year before."[104]

When the legislature met for the regular session of 1862–63, Governor Gamble submitted his message, which dealt largely with the negro situation.[105] On January 21 concurrent resolutions were introduced in the House declaring that $25,000,000 would be necessary to carry emancipation into effect in the State and requesting that amount of Congress for the purpose. This was amended by various members to read a greater and again to read a less amount. Zerely moved that Missouri had no wish that the slaves when emancipated should remain in the State. He was declared out of order. On the following day the original motion passed by a vote of 70 to 34, nineteen members being absent for one cause or another.[106] In the Senate this resolution appeared on January 26, was likewise amended, and finally passed the next day, the vote being 26 to 2, four members not being present.[107] But as the slaves could not be liberated without paying their owners, the constitution of 1820 so providing, the legislature felt its power to be limited, and therefore the governor on April 15 called the convention to reassemble on June 15.[108]

---

[104] America: The Origin of her Present Conflict, p. 255. An observing contemporary who was prominent in politics during these years makes the following observation as to the changing effect of the War on political parties: "During the preceding election [1863] little or nothing remained of previously existing national political parties. The mad torrents of civil war had swept them all away. New issues and new combinations, with new objects arose. . . . It was during the judicial canvass of 1863 that the nuclei of the present political parties of the State were formed; one as the 'Conservative' and the other as the 'Radical'; and now known as the 'Democrat' and 'Republican.' All the ante-bellum issues had gone down in the bloody vortex of fratricidal war. Elements hitherto antagonistic, now coalesced on the living issues of an all-absorbing present" (Switzler, p. 446).
[105] Senate Journal, 22d Ass., 1st Sess., pp. 13–15.
[106] House Journal, 22d Ass., 1st Sess., pp. 129–141.
[107] Senate Journal, 22d Ass., 1st Sess., pp. 115–140.
[108] In his message calling the convention of 1863 Governor Gamble stated the position of the legislature on the subject, and also the

The convention met as called. On the following day Smith introduced an ordinance for the "emancipation of slaves."[109] On June 23 Gamble resigned as governor in order to retain his position in the convention as chairman of the committee on emancipation. At the request of the convention he consented to continue as governor till the election of the following November.[110] He then submitted an ordinance repealing the slavery sections of the constitution; abolishing slavery after July 4, 1876; liberating all slaves thereafter brought into the State not then belonging to citizens of Missouri; freeing any slaves who had been taken into one of the seceding States after such had passed the Ordinance of Secession, and declaring that the legislature had no power to emancipate slaves without the consent of the owners.[111] A number of amendments were proposed reducing the period of servitude. These were rejected.[112] Drake moved that all slaves over forty years of age remain as apprentices for the remainder of their lives and those under twelve till they were twenty-three, and that all others be free on July 4, 1874.[113] Broadhead amended Drake's proposition to read July 4, 1870, instead of 1874, and moved that these "apprentices" should not be sold without the State or to non-residents after 1870. In this form the ordinance passed by a vote of 55 to 30.[114] On July 1, 1863, with some slight changes it was adopted as a whole, the vote being 51 to 30, seven members not being present. The governor approved the ordinance the same day.[115]

needs of the State and what the convention was expected to accomplish (Journal, Appendix, and Proceedings of the Missouri State Convention, held at Jefferson City, June 15 to July 1, 1863, pp. 1-5).
[109] Ibid., p. 12.
[110] Ibid., pp. 24-25. Governor Gamble died in January, 1864.
[111] Journal of the Missouri State Convention, 1863, Appendix, p. 13.
[112] Ibid., Journal, pp. 28-29. Gravelley moved that the masters be given $300 per slave in case of emancipation. This amendment was tabled (ibid., p. 29).
[113] Ibid., p. 36.
[114] Ibid., p. 38.
[115] Ibid., pp. 47-48. The ordinance can be found in the Journal of the Convention (p. 3). It reads as follows: "Be it ordained by the people of the State of Missouri in convention Assembled: Sec-

In those stormy days events took place in rapid succession and issues developed readily. The halfway measures of the convention in framing the ordinance displeased the "Radicals." Quantrell's raid on Lawrence in the late summer, the ill success of the state guard in maintaining order, and the occasional success of Confederate sympathizers aroused Drake and his followers.[116] They met in convention at Jefferson City on September 1. Seventy-two counties were represented, St. Louis sending one hundred and six delegates, most of whom were Germans. On the

tion 1, The 1st and 2nd clauses of the 26th section of the constitution are hereby abrogated. Sec. 2. That slavery and involuntary servitude, except for the punishment of crime, shall cease to exist in Missouri on the 4th day of July, 1870 and all slaves within the State at that day are hereby declared to be free; Provided, however, That all persons emancipated by this ordinance shall remain under the controll and be subject to the authority of their late owners or their legal representatives, as servants, during the following period; towit: Those over forty years for and during their lives; Those under twelve years of age until they arrive at the age of twenty-three years, and those of all other ages until the 4th of July, 1870. The persons or their legal representatives, who, up to the moment of the emancipation were the owners of slaves thus freed, shall, during the period for which the services of such freed men are reserved to them, have the same authority and control over said freed men for the purpose of receiving possession and service of the same, that are now held absolutely by the master in respect to his slave. Provided, however, That after the said 4th day of July, 1870, no person so held to service shall be sold to a non resident of or removed from the State of Missouri by authority of his late owner or his legal representatives. Section 3. That all slaves hereafter brought into this State and not now belonging to citizens of this State, shall thereupon be free. Section 4, All slaves removed by consent of their owners to any seceded state after the passage by such state of an act or ordinance of secession and hereafter brought into this State by their owners shall thereupon be free. Section 5, The General Assembly shall have no power to pass laws to emancipate slaves without the consent of their owners. Section 6, After the passage of this ordinance no slave in this State shall be subject to State, county, or municipal taxes."

[116] On November 21, 1862, Surgeon John E. Bruere and Ferdinand Hess, Adjutant, Missouri State Militia, swore that Colonel Guitar, in command of the Union troops at Fulton, allowed twelve slaves working as army teamsters to be seized by their late masters (House Journal, 22d Ass., Adjourned Sess., App., pp. 73–74). Complaints were made that the "rebels" were becoming active and insulting. The political events of these years have been best described by Samuel B. Harding in his Life of George R. Smith, and in his "Missouri Party Struggles in the Civil War Period," in American Historical Association Reports, 1900, vol. i, pp. 85–103.

opening day Drake addressed the convention. He condemned Governor Gamble for seeking to betray the will of
the people by opposing immediate emancipation.[117] This
"Radical" or "Charcoal" convention at once showed the
purpose of its meeting. On the opening day Lightner
offered a resolution declaring "That Missouri requires and
demands as indemnity for past and security for the future
the extinction of slavery, and the disfranchisement of
rebels." This resolution was referred to a committee.[118]
A committee of one from each county was appointed to go
to Washington and interview the President on the subject
of immediate emancipation.[119] The Germans of the State
were thanked for their "undivided support and defense of
the Government and the Constitution." "Without a dissenting voice" the convention declared "that we demand a
policy of immediate emancipation in Missouri because it is
necessary not only to the financial success of the State and
the prosecution of its internal improvements, but especially
because it is essential to the security of the lives of our
citizens."[120]

During the year 1864 emancipation was loudly advocated
throughout the State. B. Gratz Brown of the Missouri
Democrat was especially active both in and out of the legislature.[121] On February 15 the restrictions on legal manu-

---

[117] Drake, pp. 348–357.
[118] Missouri State Radical Emancipation Convention, held at Jefferson City September 1 to 3, 1863, p. 20.
[119] Drake, p. 26. This mission was a failure, as a contemporary
tells us. "The writer was once a member of a delegation of Missouri Charcoals that went to Washington to see the President," says
J. F. Hume. "An hour was set for the interview, and we were
promptly at the door of the President's chamber, when we were kept
waiting for a considerable time. As the door opened, but before
we could enter, out stepped a little old man who tripped away very
lightly for one of his years. That little old man was Francis P.
Blair, Sr., and we knew that we had been forestalled. The President received us politely and patiently listened to what we had to
say, but our mission was fruitless" (p. 162).
[120] Missouri State Radical Emancipation Convention, 1863, pp.
27, 39–40.
[121] See his speech in the State Senate of March 8, 1864, printed in
pamphlet form.

mission were removed by the General Assembly.[122] But slavery still existed in the State, despite the hopeless condition of the Confederacy and the abolition of the system in several of the Southern States through the Emancipation Proclamation.[123] " Slavery is not extinct. It dies slowly," says an item in the Annals of Platte County for May, 1864.[124]

On January 6, 1865, the state convention reassembled at St. Louis. On January 9 Owens moved an ordinance repealing the slavery clauses of the constitution and the ordinance passed by the convention the year before. Slavery was to be abolished entirely. On January 11 this ordinance passed by a vote of 60 to 4.[125] The members voting in the negative were Switzler of Boone, Morton of Clay, Harris of Callaway, and Gilbert of Platte. Charles D. Drake was the warhorse of the convention.[126] After pushing through his ordinance, he secured the passage of a provision forbidding any apprenticeship of the negro, save where the laws would later affect individuals.[127] On April 8 the new constitution passed by a vote of 38 to 13, thirteen members not being

---

[122] Session Laws, 1863, p. 108.

[123] For examples of the vitality of slave property in the State see above, pp. 42–43.

[124] P. 362.

[125] Journal and Appendix of the Missouri State Convention, held at St. Louis January 6 to April 10, 1865, pp. 13, 26. Two members were absent. This ordinance reads: " Be it Enacted by the People of Missouri in convention assembled, That hereafter, in this state, there shall be neither slavery nor involuntary servitude except in punishment of crimes, whereof the party shall have been duly convicted; and all persons held to service or labor as slaves are hereby declared free" (ibid., Journal, p. 281). A MS. copy written on parchment, perhaps the original, is in the Missouri Historical Society. On the back in red ink is the following: " Ordinance of Emancipation, Filed May 14th 1865, Francis Rodman, Secretary of State."

[126] Switzler, who was a dissenting member of the convention, wrote: " Charles D. Drake was the Ajax Telamon of the Convention, and left upon the Convention the impress of his spirit and ability. Owing to this fact the body was known as the 'Drake Convention' the Constitution as the 'Drake Constitution,' and the disfranchising portion of it as the 'Draconian Code'" (p. 453, note).

[127] Missouri State Convention, 1865, Journal, p. 27. The vote on this provision was 57 to 3, four members not being present.

present.[128]   By its provisions slavery was forbidden and the educational and civil position of the negro was fixed.

While the convention was in session, the legislature was acting upon the Thirteenth Amendment of the Federal Constitution.   A concurrent resolution which ratified the above amendment was passed by the House on February 9 by a vote of 85 to 8, thirty-nine members not being present.[129] On February 6 it passed the Senate, the vote being 25 to 2, five members not being present.[130]   Governor Fletcher signed the measure on the 10th.[131]

Thus Missouri voluntarily abolished slavery by convention a month before the General Assembly ratified the Thirteenth Amendment.   The slaveholders of the State were never reimbursed for their losses, but by 1865 there could have been few actual slaves in Missouri.   The State has always been proud of its voluntary action in freeing the remnant of its black population.

---

[128] Missouri State Convention, 1865, Appendix, p. 255.
[129] House Journal, 23d Ass., 1st Sess., p. 300.
[130] Senate Journal, 23d Ass., 1st Sess., p. 250.
[131] Ibid., p. 303.   The amendment is given in Session Laws, 1864, p. 134.

BIBLIOGRAPHY

The following titles have been referred to in the preceding pages of this study:—

MANUSCRIPT SOURCES

A. OFFICIAL.
1. Circuit Court Records, Boone County, years 1851–61, Books D, E, F, G, H.
2. Circuit Court Records, Cape Girardeau County, years 1837, 1844, 1850, 1851, 1858, 1859, Books D, F, G, H, J, K.
3. Circuit Court Records, Greene County, years 1845–60, Books C, Dsr, Djr, E.
4. Circuit Court Records, Henry County, years 1851–61, Books B, C.
5. Circuit Court Records, Howard County, years 1835–37, 1851–61, vols. 5, 6, 10, 11, 12.
6. Records of the St. Louis Supreme Court of Record, or General Court (Territorial Court), 1812–20, 2 vols. In the Supreme Court Library at Jefferson City.
7. Circuit Court Records, St. Louis County, years 1830–33, 1836–37, 1855, 1858, vols. 6, 8, 27, 28.
8. Manumission Papers from the Circuit Court of St. Louis County, years 1853–56. In the Missouri Historical Society.
9. Probate Records, Boone County, Inventories, Appraisements, and Sales, Book B, 1854–61.
10. Probate Records, Cape Girardeau County, Files, years 1816–25.
11. Probate Records, Greene County, Inventories and Appraisements, Book A, 1857–65.
12. Probate Records, Henry County, Appraisements, Inventories, and Sales, 1854–66.
13. Probate Records, Lafayette County, Inventories, Sale Bills, etc., Books A, B, C, D, 1855–65.
14. Probate Records, St. Louis County, Files, 1805–65.
15. Probate Records, Saline County, Will Record, Book A, 1837–60. Inventories, Appraisements, and Sales, Book 1, 1855–61; ibid., 1861, Book 2. Files, 1840–55. Records, Book G, 1859–66.
16. Census Enumeration, Cooper County, 1850, Slave Enumeration, Schedule no. 2; Social Statistics, Schedule no. 6. E. E. Buckner, Ass't Marshal (United States).
17. Census Enumeration, St. Genevieve County, 1860, Slave Enumeration, Schedule no. 2; Social Statistics, Schedule no. 6. F. I. Ziegler, Ass't Marshal, J. Moreau, Ass't Marshal.
18. Tax Returns, Audrain County, 1837. Incomplete.

242   SLAVERY IN MISSOURI, 1804–1865   [424

19. Tax Book, Boone County, 1860.
20. Assessor's Returns, Buchanan County, 1840, 1843, 1846, 1856.
21. Tax Book, Cape Girardeau County, 1855, 1856, 1857.
22. Tax Book, Clay County, 1858. Incomplete.
23. Personal Assessment List, Daviess County, 1867.
24. Tax List, Franklin County, 1823.
25. Tax Book, Greene County, 1858, 1860.
26. Tax Book, Jackson County, 1860.
27. Assessor's Book, Henry County, 1845.
28. Tax Book, Howard County, 1856.
29. Assessor's List, Macon County, 1854.
30. Tax Book, Pike County, 1854, 1859.
31. Tax List, St. Charles County, 1815.
32. Tax Book, or Assessment Book, St. Louis, 1829.
33. Tax Book, St. Louis, 1842; 1843; 1845; 1848; 1850, 2 vols.;
    1852, 2 vols.; 1857, 4 vols.; 1860, 6 vols.
34. Records of the County Court of St. Louis, 11 vols., 1824–
    61. At the St. Louis City Hall.
35. Records of the City of St. Louis, Vol. B, 1805–10. City Hall.
36. Record Book of the Trustees of the City of St. Louis, 1811–
    23. City Hall.
37. Record of Coroners' Inquests, City of St. Louis, 1822–39.
    City Hall.

B. UNOFFICIAL RECORDS AND PRIVATE PAPERS.
    1. Records of the Old Cathedral Church of St. Louis, Record
       of Baptisms, 1835–44. At the old Cathedral.
    2. Records of the Old Cathedral Church of St. Louis, Registre
       des Mariages ouverte en 1828 Clos 1839. At the old
       Cathedral.
    3. James Aull Papers, in the Collection of Messrs. E. U. Hop-
       kins and John Chamberlain, of Lexington, Missouri.
    4. The William Clark Breckenridge Collection of Manumission
       and other papers. In possession of Mr. William Clark
       Breckenridge of St. Louis.
    5. The John M. Clayton Papers. Contain Papers of the Blairs,
       Benton, etc. In the Library of Congress.
    6. The J. J. Crittenden Papers. Papers by various members of
       the Crittenden family. Many relating to Missouri. In the
       Library of Congress.
    7. The Dalton Collection. Various miscellaneous papers. In
       the Missouri Historical Society.
    8. The John F. Darby Collection, 1835–65. Papers of various
       members of the Darby family. In the Missouri Historical
       Society.
    9. The Dougherty Collection. Papers of John Dougherty and
       other members of the Dougherty family. In the Missouri
       Historical Society.
    10. The Van Buren Papers. Papers of Martin Van Buren, con-
        taining letters from Benton, the Blairs, etc. In the Library
        of Congress.
    11. The George R. Smith Papers. Valuable on local Whig and
        slavery matters. Contain letters from James S. Rollins,
        Silas H. Woodson, and other Whig leaders. The most

valuable collection of local political material found in the
State. In the Missouri Historical Society.
12. The Sublette Papers. Papers of Solomon J. Sublette and
other members of the Sublette family. In the Missouri
Historical Society.

OFFICIAL PUBLICATIONS

A. FEDERAL PUBLICATIONS.
1. Poore, Benjamin Perley. The Federal and State Constitutions. 2 vols. Washington, 1877.
2. Statutes at Large of the United States, vols. i, ii.
3. American State Papers: Miscellaneous, vol. i; Public Lands, vol. iv.
4. Adjutant General's Report of April 5, 1848, R. Jones, Adjutant General, W. L. Marcy, Secretary of War. In Executive Documents, 30th Cong., 1st Sess., vol. viii, Doc. no. 62.
5. Statistical View of the Population of the United States, 1790–1830. Washington, 1835.
6. Fourth Census of the United States. Washington, 1821.
7. Fifth Census of the United States. Washington, 1832.
8. Sixth Census of the United States. Washington, 1841.
9. Seventh Census of the United States. Washington, 1853.
10. Eighth Census of the United States. Volumes on Population and Agriculture. Washington, 1864.
11. Twelfth Census of the United States. Population, vol. i. Washington, 1901.

B. STATE PUBLICATIONS.
1. Journals of the General Assembly of Missouri, House and Senate Journals, 1820–65. 45 vols.
No complete collections.
2. Laws of the Territory of Missouri. 2 vols. Jefferson City, 1842.
3. Session Laws of Missouri, 1820–65. 22 vols.
4. Laws of a Public and General Nature of the State of Missouri, 1803–36. 2 vols. Jefferson City, 1842.
5. Laws of the State of Missouri, Revised and Digested, 1825. 2 vols. St. Louis, 1825.
6. Revised Statutes of 1835. St. Louis, 1840.
7. Revised Statutes of 1845. 2 vols. St. Louis, 1845.
8. Revised Statutes of 1855, compiled by C. H. Hardin. 2 vols. Jefferson City, 1856.
9. Reports of the Supreme Court of the State of Missouri, 1820–70. 35 vols.
10. Report of the Auditor of Public Accounts of the State of Missouri to the 23rd General Assembly. Jefferson City, 1865.
11. Journal of the Missouri State Convention, 1820. Photofacsimile reprint of State Law Book Co., 1905, from the original printed by I. N. Henry and Co., St. Louis, 1820.
12. Journal of the Constitutional Convention of Missouri, held at Jefferson City November 17, 1845, to January 14, 1846. Jefferson City, 1846.

13. Journal and Proceedings of the Missouri State Convention, held at Jefferson City and St. Louis February 28 to March 22, 1861. St. Louis, 1861.
14. Journal, Appendix, and Proceedings of the Missouri State Convention, held at Jefferson City June 2 to 14, 1862. St. Louis, 1862.
15. Journal, Appendix, and Proceedings of the Missouri State Convention, held at Jefferson City June 15 to July 1, 1863. St. Louis, 1863.
16. Journal and Appendix of the Missouri State Convention, held at St. Louis January 6 to April 10, 1865. St. Louis, 1865.
17. Adjutant General's Report, 1861. St. Louis: Leo Knapp and Co., 1862.

MISCELLANEOUS COLLECTIONS OF SOURCES

1. French, B. F. Historical Collections of Louisiana. 5 vols. New York, 1846–53.
2. Margry, Pierre. Découvertes et Etablissements Des Français Dans L'ouest et dans Le Sud de L'Amerique Septentrionale (1614–1754). 6 vols. Paris, 1887.
3. Paxton, William M. Annals of Platte County, Missouri. Kansas City, 1897.
4. The St. Louis Directory of 1859. St. Louis: L. and A. Carr. 1858.
5. The St. Louis Directory of 1859. St. Louis: R. V. Kennedy. 1859.
6. The St. Louis Revised Ordinances for the years 1836, 1843, 1846, 1850, 1853, 1856, 1861.
7. Charter of the City of Carondelet, Approved March 1, 1851. St. Louis: Missouri Republican. 1851.

CONTEMPORARY ADDRESSES, PAMPHLETS, ETC.

1. Benton, Thomas H. Speech Delivered at Jefferson, The Capitol of Missouri on the 26th. of May, 1849. Extra Evening Post, 1849 (St. Louis?).
2. ——. Historical and Legal Examination of That Part of the Decision of the Supreme Court of the United States . . . which Declares the Unconstitutionality of the Missouri Compromise Act, And the Self-Extension of the Constitution to the Territories, Carrying Slavery Along with it. New York, 1857.
3. Blair, Francis P., Jr. On the Subject of the Senatorial Election (Speech in Reply to Carr), at the Joint Session of the General Assembly of Missouri, Jan.?, 1855. Publisher not given.
4. ——. On the Acquisition of Territory in Central and South America to be Colonized with Free Blacks, and held as A Dependency By the United States. House of Representatives, Jan. 14, 1858. Congressional Globe, 35th Cong., 1st Sess., part i, pp. 290–296, or in pamphlet form by Buell and Blanchard, Washington, 1858, 24 pp.

5. ——. The Destiny of the Races of This Continent. An Address delivered before the Mercantile Library Association of Boston, Massachusetts, On the 26ᵗʰ of January, 1859. Washington: Buell and Blanchard. 1859.
6. Bogy, Colonel Lewis V. Speech of Colonel Lewis V. Bogy, the Democratic Nominee for Congress in the First District. Delivered at the Rotunda [of the Court House], May 27, 1852. Saint Louis: St. Louis Times Office. 1852.
7. Calhoun, J. C. To the People of the Southern States (Reply to Benton). Written in 1849. Publishers not given.
8. Greeley, Horace. A History of the Struggle for Slavery Extension or Restriction in the United States. New York, 1856.
9. Green, James S. Letter to Messrs. John S. Farish, John W. Minor, Thomas Roberts, Wesley Burks, and other Citizens of Schuyler Co. Missouri, dated Washington, Dec. 10, 1849. 16 pp. Publisher not given.
10. Hogan, John. Thoughts about the City of St. Louis, her Commerce and Manufactures, railroads, etc. St. Louis: Republican Office. 1854.
11. Jackson, Governor Claiborne F. Inaugural Address of, to the General Assembly of the State of Missouri, January 3, 1861. Jefferson City, 1861.
12. Lyon, Reverend James A. An Address on The Missionary Aspect of African Colonization. St. Louis: T. W. Ustick. 1850. 21 pp.
13. Palm, William. Letter to C. C. Zeigler of the Legislature, dated January 25, 1857. 4 pp. Publisher not given.
14. Rice, Reverend N. L. Ten Letters on the Subject of Slavery. St. Louis, 1855.
15. Rollins, James S. Speech in the Joint Session of the Legislature Feb. 2, 1855, in reply to Goode of St. Louis. Jefferson City: Lusk's Press, 1855.
16. Shannon, President James. Address delivered before the Pro-Slavery Convention . . . in Lexington, July 13, 1855. Published with the Proceedings of the Convention.
17. Starr, Reverend Frederick ("Lynceus"). Letters for the People, on the Present Crisis . . . No. 1, Slavery in Missouri. [New York, 1853.]
18. Stringfellow, Benjamin F. Negro Slavery No Evil or The North and the South. Published in the St. Joseph Commercial Cycle, February 2 to March 23, 1855.
19. Waugh, Reverend Lorenzo. A Candid Statement of the Course Pursued by the Preachers of the Methodist Episcopal Church South in Trying to Establish Their New Organization in Missouri. Cincinnati: J. A. and U. P. James, 1848. 72 pp.

REPORTS AND PUBLICATIONS OF CONVENTIONS, CONFERENCES, AND SOCIETIES

1. Representation and petition of the representatives elected by the Freemen of the territory of Louisiana 4th January, 1805. Referred to Messrs. Eppes, Lucas, Clagett, Huger,

‌

Eustis, Fowler, and Bryan. Washington City: Printed by William Duane & Son. 1805. 30 pp.

2. Proceedings and Resolutions of the Pro-Slavery Convention, held at Lexington July 13 to 15, 1855. St. Louis: Republican Office, 1855.
   Contains also President James Shannon's Address and the Address to the People of the United States.

3. Missouri State Radical Emancipation Convention, held at Jefferson City September 1 to 2, 1863. Missouri Democrat's Special Report, St. Louis, 1863.

4. Tenth Annual Report of the American and Foreign Anti-Slavery Society (1850). New York, by the Society, Wm. Harned, Agent, 1850. Eleventh Report, ibid.; Thirteenth Annual Report, ibid., L. J. Bates, Agent, 1853.

5. Reports of the American Anti-Slavery Society, 1837–61. Published in New York by the Society.

6. Reports of the American Society for the Colonization of the Free People of Color of the United States, 1818–65. Published in New York by the Society.

7. Finley, Reverend Robert S. Circular Appealing for Aid for Colonizing Free Negroes in Liberia [1845]. In the Journal of the Illinois Historical Society, vol. iii, pp. 93–95.

8. Forman, Reverend J. G. The Western Sanitary Commission. St. Louis, 1864.

9. Constitution and By Laws of the General Emancipation Society of Missouri. St. Louis: Democrat Book and Job Office. 1862.

10. Debates in the General Conference of the Methodist Episcopal Church, During its Session in New York, May 3 to June 10, 1844, Geo. Peck, editor. New York, 1844.

11. History and Organization of the Methodist Episcopal Church, South; comprehending all the Official Proceedings of the General Conference; The Southern Annual Conferences and the General Convention. Nashville: Wm. Cameron for the Louisville Convention of the Methodist Episcopal Church South. 1845.

12. Elliott, Reverend Charles. History of the Great Secession from the Methodist Episcopal Church. Official Northern account provided by the Northern Conference of 1848. New York: The Methodist Book Concern. 1855.

13. Minutes of the Eleventh Session of the Missouri Annual Conference of the Methodist Episcopal Church, held at Hannibal May 6 to 10, 1858. St. Louis: R. P. Studley. 1858.

14. Address to the Democracy of Missouri. [St. Louis? 1850?] Signed by F. P. Blair and thirty-seven others. Distributed at 87 Second St. Publisher not given. 14 pp. In Library of Congress.

15. The Address, Resolutions and Proceedings of the Democracy of St. Louis in the Rotunda of the Court House, January 8, 1848. St. Louis: Union Office, 1848.

16. A Statement of Facts and A Few Suggestions in Review of Political Action in Missouri Demonstrating The Right of Admission To the Democratic National Convention. 1856. Publisher not given.

NEWSPAPERS

The following local newspapers have been referred to in this
study. The place of publication, date, and present location of the
files are as follows:—

Columbia
  1. The Missouri Statesman, 1852–58. State Historical Society.
  2. The Weekly Missouri Sentinel, 1853–54. Library of Congress.
  3. The Dollar Missouri Journal, 1856. Library of Congress.
  4. The Weekly Missouri State Journal, 1856. Library of Congress.

Fayette
  5. The Western Monitor, 1829. Library of Congress.

Franklin
  6. The Missouri Intelligencer and Boone's Lick Advertiser, 1819–30. State Historical Society.

Jackson
  7. Missouri Herald, 1819–21. Library of Congress.
  8. Southern Advocate, 1838. Library of Congress.

Jefferson City
  9. Jeffersonian Republican, 1831–40. Library of Congress.
  10. Jefferson Inquirer, 1845–57. Library of Congress.
  11. Jefferson Examiner, 1855–57. Library of Congress.

Kansas City
  12. Kansas City Star, 1904. State Historical Society.

Liberty
  13. Western Pioneer, 1844. Library of Congress.

Richmond
  14. Richmond Weekly Mirror, 1853–58. State Historical Society.

St. Charles
  15. The Missourian, 1820–22. Library of Congress.

St. Joseph
  16. The St. Joseph Commercial Cycle, 1855–56. Library of Congress.

St. Louis
  17. The Gazette under its various titles, 1812–22. Republic Office at St. Louis.
  18. The St. Louis Enquirer, 1819–25. Library of Congress.
  19. The Daily Pennant, 1840. Library of Congress.
  20. The Weekly Pilot, 1855. Library of Congress.
  21. The Missouri Reporter, 1845. Library of Congress.
  22. The Daily Union, 1846–49. Library of Congress.
  23. The Daily Intelligencer, 1850–51. Library of Congress.
  24. The Daily Missourian, 1845. Library of Congress.
  25. The Republican, Daily, 1848–60. Library of Congress and St. Louis Mercantile Library.
  26. The Weekly Republican, 1852. Library of Congress.
  27. Daily Evening Herald and Commercial Advertiser, 1835. Mercantile Library.
  28. Daily Evening Gazette, 1841–42. Mercantile Library.
  29. The Mill Boy, 1844. Mercantile Library.
  30. The Bulletin, 1855. Mercantile Library.

31. The Missouri Democrat, Daily, 1854–60.   Mercantile Library.
32. The Missouri Argus, 1835–39.   Library of Congress.
33. The Farmers' and Mechanics' Advocate, 1833.   W. C. Breckenridge Collection.

Weston

34. The Weston Platte Argus, 1856.   Library of Congress.
35. The William Hyde Scrapbooks of old Newspapers, Volume on "Early St. Louis and Missouri."   W. C. Breckenridge Collection.
36. The H. E. Robinson Scrapbook of old newspapers, Volume on "The Platte Purchase."   W. C. Breckenridge Collection.
37. The William F. Switzler Scrapbooks, 1844–60.   5 vols.   Volume 1856–57 on the American Party.   State Historical Society.
38. The James S. Thomas Scrapbook, from St. Louis Papers, vol. i (1833–59).   Mercantile Library.

OTHER PERIODICALS

1. The African Repository and Colonial Journal, 1820–40.   Johns Hopkins University Library.
2. Niles' Weekly Register, 1811–49.
3. Quarterly Anti-Slavery Magazine, 1836–37.   Johns Hopkins University Library.

CONTEMPORARY ACCOUNTS, MEMOIRS, AND TRAVELS

1. ANDERSON, REVEREND GALUSHA. The Story of a Border City During the Civil War. Boston, 1908.
2. ASHE, THOMAS. Travels in America, Performed in 1806. Newburyport, 1808.
3. BABCOCK, RUFUS. Memoir of John Mason Peck, D. D. Philadelphia, 1864.
4. BAUDISSIN, GRAF ADELBERT. Der Ansiedler im Missouri Staat. Iserlohn, 1864.
5. BEECHER, REVEREND EDWARD. Narrative of Riots at Alton. Alton, 1838.
6. Brackenridge, H. M. Recollections of Persons and Places in the West. 2nd ed. Philadelphia, 1868.
7. ——. Views of Louisiana. Baltimore, 1817.
8. BROWN, WILLIAM B. Narrative of William B. Brown a Fugitive Slave. Boston, 1847.
9. CHAPPELL, PHILIP E. "A History of the Missouri River." Transactions of the Kansas State Historical Society, vol. ix (1905–06), pp. 237–294.
10. CHASE, SAMUEL P. Diary and Correspondence. Report of the American Historical Association, 1902, vol. ii.
11. FATHER JOHN CLARK. A Memoir by "An Old Pioneer." New York, 1855.
12. DARBY, JOHN F. Personal Recollections of Men and Events in St. Louis. St. Louis, 1880.
13. DELANEY, LUCY A. From the Darkness Cometh the Light or Struggles for Freedom. St. Louis: J. T. Smith, 1892(?).
14. DIMMICK, REVEREND THOMAS. Lovejoy. An Address at the Church of the Unity at St. Louis, March 14, 1888.

15. Doy, Dr. John. The Narrative of John Doy, of Lawrence, Kansas. New York, 1860.
16. Drake, Charles D. Union and Anti-Slavery Speeches, Delivered During the Rebellion. Cincinnati, 1864.
17. Duden, Gottfried. Bericht über eine Reise nach den Westlichen Staaten Nordamerika's und einen mehrjährigen Aufenthalt am Missouri [1824-27]. Zweite Auflage. Bonn, 1834.
18. Edwards, Richard, and Hopewell, M. Edwards's Great West and her Commercial Metropolis. St. Louis, [1860].
19. Eliot, Charlotte C. William Greenleaf Eliot. Boston and New York, 1904.
20. Eliot, Reverend William G. The Story of Archer Alexander. Boston, 1885.
21. Etzenhouser, Elder R. From Palmyra, N. Y., 1830 to Independence, Mo., 1894. Independence, Mo., 1894.
22. Ewing, Judge R. C. History and Memoirs of the Cumberland Presbyterian Church in Missouri. Nashville, 1874.
23. Flint, Reverend Timothy. The History and Geography of the Mississippi Valley. Two vols. in 1. Cincinnati, 1832.
24. ——. Recollections of the Last Ten Years . . . in the Valley of the Mississippi. Boston, 1826.
25. Froebel, Julius. Seven Years' Travel in Central America . . . and the Far West of the United States. London, 1859.
26. Greene, Mary. Life and Writings of Reverend Jesse R. Greene. Lexington, Mo., 1852.
27. Haskell, General J. G. "The Passing of Slavery in Western Missouri." Transactions of the Kansas State Historical Society, vol. vii (1901-02), pp. 28-39.
28. Hill, Reverend Timothy. "The Early History of the Presbyterian Church in Missouri." American Presbyterian Quarterly Review, vol. x (1861-62), pp. 94-117.
29. ——. Historical Outlines of the Presbyterian Church in Missouri. A Discourse delivered at Springfield, Mo., October 13, 1871. Kansas City, 1871.
30. Hume, John F. The Abolitionists. New York and London, 1905.
31. Leftwich, Reverend William M. Martyrdom in Missouri. 2 vols. St. Louis, 1870.
32. Lucas, John B. C., Jr., Comp. Letters of Hon. J. B. C. Lucas from 1815 to 1836. St. Louis, 1905.
33. Mackay, Charles. Life and Liberty in America. New York, 1859.
34. Massie, J. W. America: The Origin of her Present Conflict. London, 1864.
35. Maximilian, Prince of Wied. "Travels in the Interior of North America, 1832-4." In R. G. Thwaites, Early Western Travels, vols. xxii, xxiii, xxiv.
36. Merrick, G. B. Old Times on the Upper Mississippi [1854-63]. Cleveland, 1909.
37. Napton, William B. Past and Present in Saline County, Missouri. Indianapolis and Chicago, 1910.
38. Parker, John A. "The Secret History of the Kansas-Nebraska Bill." National Quarterly Review, July, 1880 (no. lxxxi), pp. 105-118.

39. PITTMAN, CAPTAIN PHILIP. The Present State of the European Settlements on the Mississippi River. Original London edition of 1770, edited by F. H. Hodder. Cleveland, 1906.
40. POLK, JAMES K. The Diary of James K. Polk During His Presidency, 1845 to 1849. M. M. Quaife, editor. 4 vols. Chicago, 1910.
41. POST, T. A. Truman M. Post. Boston and Chicago, 1891(?).
42. The St. Clair Papers. The Life and Public Services of Arthur St. Clair. Wm. H. Smith, editor. 2 vols. Cincinnati, 1882.
43. SCHOOLCRAFT, HENRY R. Travels in the Central Portions of the Mississippi Valley. New York, 1825.
44. ——. A View of the Lead Mines of Missouri. New York, 1819.
45. SHACKELFORD, THOMAS. "Early Recollections of Missouri." Missouri Historical Society Collections, vol. ii, no. 2, pp. 1–20.
46. STODDARD, MAJOR AMOS. Sketches, Historical and Descriptive, of Louisiana. Philadelphia, Mathew Carey, 1812.
47. SWITZLER, WILLIAM F. Switzler's Illustrated History of Missouri. St. Louis, 1877.
    Much of his History was taken from his personal observations as a member of the legislature and as an editor.
48. THOMPSON, GEORGE. Prison Life and Reflections. Hartford, 1851.
49. TROLLOPE, ANTHONY. North America. 2 vols. New York, 1862.
50. WETMORE, ALPHONSO. Gazetteer of the State of Missouri. St. Louis, 1837.
51. WILLIAMS, R. H. With the Border Ruffians. New York, 1907.
52. WITTEN, REVEREND ROBERT R. Pioneer Methodism in Missouri. [Springfield?, Mo., 1906?.]

SECONDARY WORKS

1. BALLAGH, JAMES C. "A History of Slavery in Virginia." J. H. U. Studies, extra vol. xxiv.
2. BARNS, C. R. The Commonwealth of Missouri: A Centennial Record. St. Louis, 1877.
    W. F. Switzler's History of Missouri appears here in its first edition. The Biographical section of Barns's work has been referred to in this study.
3. BASSETT, JOHN S. "Slavery in the State of North Carolina." J. H. U. Studies, series xvii, nos. 7–8.
4. BEK, W. G. The German Settlement Society of Philadelphia and Its Colony, Hermann, Missouri. Philadelphia, 1907.
5. BRACKETT, JEFFREY R. "The Negro in Maryland." J. H. U. Studies, extra vol. vi.
6. BRECKENRIDGE, WILLIAM CLARK. "Biographical Sketch of Judge Wilson Primm." Missouri Historical Society Collections, vol. iv, no. 2, pp. 127–159.
7. BUCKLEY, J. M. History of Methodism in the United States. 2 vols. New York, 1898.
8. CARR, LUCIEN. Missouri, A Bone of Contention (American Commonwealth Series, vol. 11).
9. DAVIS, W. B., AND DURRIE, D. S. An Illustrated History of Missouri. St. Louis, 1876.
10. DODD, WILLIAM E. "The West and the War with Mexico." Journal of the Illinois State Historical Society, vol. v, no. 2, pp. 159–173.

11. DUNN, J. P. Indiana: A Redemption from Slavery (American Commonwealth Series, vol. 12).
12. ELLIOTT, REVEREND CHARLES. A History of the Methodist Episcopal Church in the South-West, 1844–1864. Cincinnati, 1868.
13. EWING, ELBERT W. R. Legal and Historical Status of the Dred Scott Decision. Washington, 1909.
14. FAUST, ALBERT B. The German Element in the United States. 2 vols. Boston and New York, 1909.
15. HARDING, SAMUEL B. Life of George R. Smith, Founder of Sedalia, Mo. Sedalia, 1904.
16. ——. "Missouri Party Struggles in the Civil War Period." Report of the American Historical Association, 1900, vol. i, pp. 85–103.
17. HARRIS, NORMAN D. History of Negro Slavery in Illinois and of the Slavery Agitation in That State. Chicago, 1906.
18. HARVEY, CHARLES M. "Missouri." Atlantic Monthly, vol. lxxxvi, pp. 63–73.
19. HELPER, HINTON R. The Impending Crisis of the South. New York, 1860.
20. HILL, FREDERICK T. "Decisive Battles of the Law: Dred Scott v. Sanford." Harper's Monthly Magazine, vol. cxv, pp. 244–253.
21. HODDER, F. H. "Genesis of the Kansas-Nebraska Act." Proceedings of the State Historical Society of Wisconsin, 1912, pp. 69–86.
22. HOLCOMB, R. I. History of Marion County, Missouri. St. Louis, 1884.
23. HOLLOWAY, J. N. History of Kansas from the First Exploration of the Mississippi Valley to its Admission into the Union. Lafayette, Ind., 1868.
24. VON HOLST, HERMANN. The Constitutional and Political History of the United States. 7 vols. Chicago, 1888.
25. HOUCK, LOUIS. A History of Missouri. 3 vols. Chicago, 1909.
26. HOWE, DANIEL WAIT. "The Laws and Courts of the Northwest and Indiana Territories." Publications of the Indiana Historical Society, vol. ii, no. 1.
27. HURD, J. C. The Law of Freedom and Bondage in the United States. 2 vols. Boston, 1858–62.
28. KARGAU, E. D. "Missouri's German Immigration." Missouri Historical Society Collections, vol. ii, no. 1, pp. 23–34.
29. KAUFMANN, WILHELM. Die Deutschen im amerikanischen Bürgerkriege. München und Berlin, 1911.
30. LEVENS, H. C., and DRAKE, N. M. A History of Cooper County, Missouri. St. Louis, 1876.
31. LINN, WILLIAM A. The Story of the Mormons. New York, 1902.
32. McANALLY, DAVID R. History of Methodism in Missouri, 1806–1881. 2 vols. St. Louis, 1881.
33. MEIGS, WILLIAM M. The Life of Thomas Hart Benton. Philadelphia, 1904.
34. MINICK, ALICE A. "The Underground Railway in Nebraska." Proceedings and Collections of the Nebraska State Historical Society, series ii, vol. 2, p. 70.
35. MOORE, BRENT. A Study of the Past, the Present, and the Possibilities of the Hemp Industry in Kentucky. Lexington, Ky., 1905.

36. RAY, PERLEY ORMOND. The Repeal of the Missouri Compromise, Its Origin and Authorship. Cleveland, 1909.
37. REDPATH, JAMES. The Public Life of Capt. John Brown. Boston, 1860.
38. RICHARDSON, A. D. Beyond the Mississippi. Hartford, 1867.
39. SCHARF, J. T. History of Saint Louis City and County. 2 vols. Philadelphia, 1883.
40. SHOEMAKER, FLOYD C. The First Constitution of Missouri, A Study of Its Origin. Typewritten copy, 1911.
41. SIEBERT, W. H. The Underground Rail Road from Slavery to Freedom. New York and London, 1898.
42. SPRAGUE, W. B. Annals of the American Pulpit. 9 vols. New York, 1850–1868.
43. TUPES, CAPTAIN HERSCHEL. The Influence of Slavery upon Missouri Politics. Typewritten copy, 1910.
44. VILES, JONAS. "Population and Extent of Settlement in Missouri before 1804." Missouri Historical Review, vol. v, no. 4, pp. 189–213.
45. WOODBURN, JAMES A. "The Historical Significance of the Missouri Compromise." Report of the American Historical Association, 1893, pp. 251–297.
46. ANONYMOUS. "The Underground Rail Road in Kansas." Kansas City Star, July 2, 1905.
47. The History of Lafayette County, Missouri. St. Louis, 1881.
48. The History of Clay and Platte Counties. St. Louis, 1885.
49. The History of Lewis, Clark, Knox, and Scotland Counties, Missouri. St. Louis and Chicago, 1887.

INDEX